Understanding Deep Learning

Understanding Deep Learning

Simon J.D. Prince

The MIT Press

Cambridge, Massachusetts

London, England

The MIT Press would like to thank the anonymous peer reviewers who provided comments on drafts of this book. The generous work of academic experts is essential for establishing the authority and quality of our publications. We acknowledge with gratitude the contributions of these otherwise uncredited readers.

This book was set in Latin Modern Roman by B. Jackowski and J. M. Nowacki (on behalf of TeX users groups). Printed and bound in the United States of America.

Fourth printing.

Library of Congress Cataloging-in-Publication Data is available.

ISBN: 978-0-262-04864-4

10 9 8 7 6 5 4

This book is dedicated to Blair, Calvert, Coppola, Ellison, Faulkner, Kerpatenko, Morris, Robinson, Sträussler, Wallace, Waymon, Wojnarowicz, and all the others whose work is even more important and interesting than deep learning.

Contents

Preface

The history of deep learning is unusual in science. The perseverance of a small cabal of scientists, working over twenty-five years in a seemingly unpromising area, has revolutionized a field and dramatically impacted society. Usually, when researchers investigate an esoteric and apparently impractical corner of science or engineering, it remains just that — esoteric and impractical. However, this was a notable exception. Despite widespread skepticism, the systematic efforts of Yoshua Bengio, Geoffrey Hinton, Yann LeCun, and others eventually paid off.

The title of this book is "Understanding Deep Learning" to distinguish it from volumes that cover coding and other practical aspects. This text is primarily about the *ideas* that underlie deep learning. The first part of the book introduces deep learning models and discusses how to train them, measure their performance, and improve this performance. The next part considers architectures that are specialized to images, text, and graph data. These chapters require only introductory linear algebra, calculus, and probability and should be accessible to any second-year undergraduate in a quantitative discipline. Subsequent parts of the book tackle generative models and reinforcement learning. These chapters require more knowledge of probability and calculus and target more advanced students.

The title is also partly a joke — *no-one* really understands deep learning at the time of writing. Modern deep networks learn piecewise linear functions with more regions than there are atoms in the universe and can be trained with fewer data examples than model parameters. It is neither obvious that we should be able to fit these functions reliably nor that they should generalize well to new data. The penultimate chapter addresses these and other aspects that are not yet fully understood. Regardless, deep learning will change the world for better or worse. The final chapter discusses AI ethics and concludes with an appeal for practitioners to consider the moral implications of their work.

Your time is precious, and I have striven to curate and present the material so you can understand it as efficiently as possible. The main body of each chapter comprises a succinct description of only the most essential ideas, together with accompanying illustrations. The appendices review all mathematical prerequisites, and there should be no need to refer to external material. For readers wishing to delve deeper, each chapter has associated problems, Python notebooks, and extensive background notes.

Writing a book is a lonely, grinding, multiple-year process and is only worthwhile if the volume is widely adopted. If you enjoy reading this or have suggestions for improving it, please contact me via the accompanying website. I would love to hear your thoughts, which will inform and motivate subsequent editions.

Acknowledgments

Writing this book would not have been possible without the generous help and advice of these individuals: Kathryn Hume, Kevin Murphy, Christopher Bishop, Peng Xu, Yann Dubois, Justin Domke, Chris Fletcher, Yanshuai Cao, Wendy Tay, Corey Toler-Franklin, Dmytro Mishkin, Guy McCusker, Daniel Worrall, Paul McIlroy, Roy Amoyal, Austin Anderson, Romero Barata de Morais, Gabriel Harrison, Peter Ball, Alf Muir, David Bryson, Vedika Parulkar, Patryk Lietzau, Jessica Nicholson, Alexa Huxley, Oisin Mac Aodha, Giuseppe Castiglione, Josh Akylbekov, Alex Gougoulaki, Joshua Omilabu, Alister Guenther, Joe Goodier, Logan Wade, Joshua Guenther, Kylan Tobin, Benedict Ellett, Jad Araj, Andrew Glennerster, Giorgos Sfikas, Diya Vibhakar, Sam Mansat-Bhattacharyya, Ben Ross, Ivor Simpson, Gaurang Aggarwal, Shakeel Sheikh, Jacob Horton, Felix Rammell, Sasha Luccioni, Akshil Patel, Alessandro Gentilini, Kevin Mercier, Krzysztof Lichocki, Chuck Krapf, Brian Ha, Chris Kang, Leonardo Viotti, Kai Li, Himan Abdollahpouri, Ari Pakman, Giuseppe Antonio Di Luna, Dan Oneață, Conrad Whiteley, Joseph Santarcangelo, Brad Shook, Gabriel Brostow, Lei He, Ali Satvaty, Romain Sabathé, Qiang Zhou, Prasanna Vigneswaran, Siqi Zheng, Stephan Grein, Jonas Klesen, Giovanni Stilo, Huang Bokai, Kevin McGuinness, Qiang Sun, Zakaria Lotfi, Yifei Lin, Sylvain Bouix, Alex Pitt, Stephane Chretien, Robin Liu, Bian Li, Adam Jones, Marcin Świerkot, Tommy Löfstedt, Eugen Hotaj, Fernando Flores-Mangas, Tony Polichroniadis, Pietro Monticone, Rohan Deepak Ajwani, Menashe Yarden Einy, Robert Gevorgyan, Thilo Stadelmann, Gui JieMiao, Botao Zhu, Mohamed Elabbas, Satya Krishna Gorti, James Elder, Helio Perroni Filho, Xiaochao Qu, Jaekang Shin, Joshua Evans, Robert Dobson, Shibo Wang, Edoardo Zorzi, Stanisław Jastrzębski, Pieris Kalligeros, Matt Hewitt, Zvika Haramaty, Ted Mavroidis, Nikolaj Kuntner, Amir Yorav, Masoud Mokhtari, Xavier Gabaix, Marco Garosi, Vincent Schönbach, Avishek Mondal, Victor S.C. Lui, Sumit Bhatia, Julian Asilis, Hengchao Chen, Siavash Khallaghi, Csaba Szepesvári, Mike Singer, Mykhailo Shvets, Abdalla Ibrahim, Stefan Hell, Ron Raphaeli, Diogo Tavares, Aristotelis Siozopoulos, Jianrui Wu, Jannik Münz, Penn Mackintosh, Shawn Hoareau, Qianang Zhou, Emma Li, Charlie Groves, Xiang Lingxiao, Trivikram Muralidharan, Rajat Binaykiya, Germán del Cacho Salvador, Alexey Bloudov, Paul Colognese, Bo Yang, Jani Monoses, Adenilson Arcanjo, Matan Golani, Emmanuel Onzon, Shenghui Yan, Kamesh Kompella, Julius Aka, Johannes Brunnemann, Varniethan Ketheeswaran, Alex Ostrovsky, Daniel Burbank, Gavrie Philipson, Roozbeh Ehsani, Len Spek, Christoph Brune, Mohammad Nosrati, Bian Li, Runqi Chen, Qifu Hu, Rasmi Elasmar, Ronaldo Butrus, Carles Mesado, Jeffrey Wolberg, Olivier Koch, Edoardo Lanari, Fanmin Shi, Neel Maniar, Maksym Taran, Falk Langhammer, Reinaldo Lepsch, Max Talberg, Vishal Jain, Christian Arnold, Charles Hill, Nikita Panin, Steven Dillmann, Suhas Mathur, Harris Abdul Majid, Guolong Lin, Charles Elkan, Benedict Kuester, Vladimir Ivanov, Mohammad-Hadi Sotoudeh, Daniel Enériz Orta, Ian Jeffrey, Kwok Chun, Yu Liu, Tom Vettenburg, Aravinda Perera, Daniel Gigliotti, Iftikhar Ramnandan, Adnan Siddiquei, Will Knottenbelt, Valerio Di Stefano, Srikant Jayaraman, and Goldie Srulovich.

I'm particularly grateful to Daniyar Turmukhambetov, Amedeo Buonanno, Andrea Panizza,

Mark Hudson, and Bernhard Pfahringer, who provided detailed comments on multiple chapters of the book. I'd like to especially thank Andrew Fitzgibbon, Konstantinos Derpanis, and Tyler Mills, who read the whole book and whose enthusiasm helped me complete this project. I'd also like to thank Neill Campbell and Özgür Şimşek, who hosted me at the University of Bath, where I taught a course based on this material for the first time. Finally, I'm extremely grateful to my editor Elizabeth Swayze for her frank advice throughout this process.

Chapter 12 (transformers) and chapter 17 (variational autoencoders) were first published as blogs for Borealis AI, and adapted versions are reproduced with permission of Royal Bank of Canada along with Borealis AI. I am grateful for their support in this endeavor. Chapter 16 (normalizing flows) is loosely based on the review article by Kobyzev et al. (2020), on which I was a co-author. I was very fortunate to be able to collaborate on Chapter 21 with Travis LaCroix from Dalhousie University, who was both easy and fun to work with, and who did the lion's share of the work.

Chapter 1

Introduction

Artificial intelligence, or *AI*, is concerned with building systems that simulate intelligent behavior. It encompasses a wide range of approaches, including those based on logic, search, and probabilistic reasoning. *Machine learning* is a subset of AI that learns to make decisions by fitting mathematical models to observed data. This area has seen explosive growth and is now (incorrectly) almost synonymous with the term AI.

A *deep neural network* is a type of machine learning model, and when it is fitted to data, this is referred to as *deep learning*. At the time of writing, deep networks are the most powerful and practical machine learning models and are often encountered in day-to-day life. It is commonplace to translate text from another language using a *natural language processing* algorithm, to search the internet for images of a particular object using a *computer vision* system, or to converse with a digital assistant via a *speech recognition* interface. All of these applications are powered by deep learning.

As the title suggests, this book aims to help a reader new to this field understand the principles behind deep learning. The book is neither terribly theoretical (there are no proofs) nor extremely practical (there is almost no code). The goal is to explain the underlying *ideas*; after consuming this volume, the reader will be able to apply deep learning to novel situations where there is no existing recipe for success.

Machine learning methods can coarsely be divided into three areas: supervised, unsupervised, and reinforcement learning. At the time of writing, the cutting-edge methods in all three areas rely on deep learning (figure 1.1). This introductory chapter describes these three areas at a high level, and this taxonomy is also loosely reflected in the book's organization. Whether we like it or not, deep learning is poised to change our world, and this change will not all be positive. Hence, this chapter also contains brief primer on AI ethics. We conclude with advice on how to make the most of this book.

1.1 Supervised learning

Supervised learning models define a mapping from input data to an output prediction. In the following sections, we discuss the inputs, the outputs, the model itself, and what is meant by "training" a model.

Figure 1.1 Machine learning is an area of artificial intelligence that fits mathematical models to observed data. It can coarsely be divided into supervised learning, unsupervised learning, and reinforcement learning. Deep neural networks contribute to each of these areas.

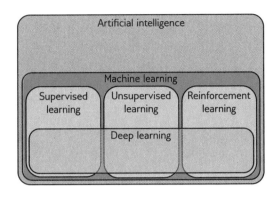

1.1.1   Regression and classification problems

Figure 1.2 depicts several regression and classification problems. In each case, there is a meaningful real-world input (a sentence, a sound file, an image, etc.), and this is encoded as a vector of numbers. This vector forms the model input. The model maps the input to an output vector which is then "translated" back to a meaningful real-world prediction. For now, we focus on the inputs and outputs and treat the model as a black box that ingests a vector of numbers and returns another vector of numbers.

The model in figure 1.2a predicts the price of a house based on input characteristics such as the square footage and the number of bedrooms. This is a *regression* problem because the model returns a continuous number (rather than a category assignment). In contrast, the model in figure 1.2b takes the chemical structure of a molecule as an input and predicts both the freezing and boiling points. This is a *multivariate regression* problem since it predicts more than one number.

The model in figure 1.2c receives a text string containing a restaurant review as input and predicts whether the review is positive or negative. This is a *binary classification* problem because the model attempts to assign the input to one of two categories. The output vector contains the probabilities that the input belongs to each category. Figures 1.2d and 1.2e depict *multiclass classification* problems. Here, the model assigns the input to one of $N > 2$ categories. In the first case, the input is an audio file, and the model predicts which genre of music it contains. In the second case, the input is an image, and the model predicts which object it contains. In each case, the model returns a vector of size N that contains the probabilities of the N categories.

1.1.2   Inputs

The input data in figure 1.2 varies widely. In the house pricing example, the input is a fixed-length vector containing values that characterize the property. This is an example of *tabular data* because it has no internal structure; if we change the order of the inputs and build a new model, then we expect the model prediction to remain the same.

Conversely, the input in the restaurant review example is a body of text. This may be of variable length depending on the number of words in the review, and here input

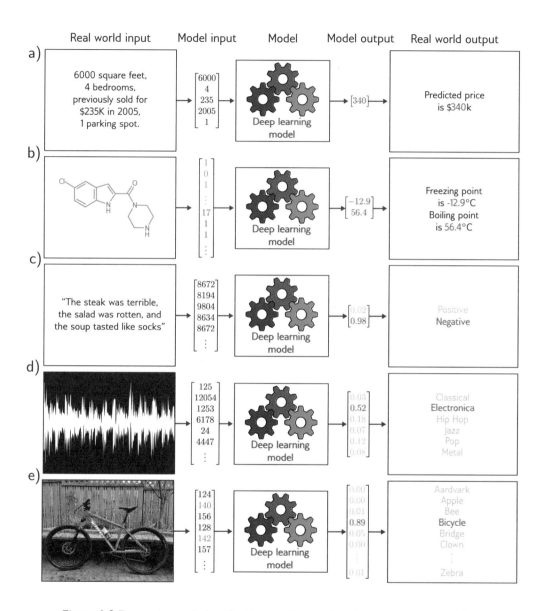

Figure 1.2 Regression and classification problems. a) This *regression* model takes a vector of numbers that characterize a property and predicts its price. b) This *multivariate regression* model takes the structure of a chemical molecule and predicts its freezing and boiling points. c) This *binary classification* model takes a restaurant review and classifies it as either positive or negative. d) This *multiclass classification* problem assigns a snippet of audio to one of N genres. e) A second multiclass classification problem in which the model classifies an image according to which of N possible objects it might contain.

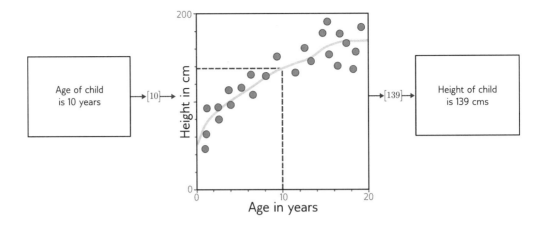

Figure 1.3 Machine learning model. The model represents a family of relationships that relate the input (age of child) to the output (height of child). The particular relationship is chosen using training data, which consists of input/output pairs (orange points). When we train the model, we search through the possible relationships for one that describes the data well. Here, the trained model is the cyan curve and can be used to compute the height for any age.

order is important; *my wife ate the chicken* is not the same as *the chicken ate my wife*. The text must be encoded into numerical form before passing it to the model. Here, we use a fixed vocabulary of size 10,000 and simply concatenate the word indices.

For the music classification example, the input vector might be of fixed size (perhaps a 10-second clip) but is very high-dimensional. Digital audio is usually sampled at 44.1 kHz and represented by 16-bit integers, so a ten-second clip consists of 441,000 integers. Clearly, supervised learning models will have to be able to process sizeable inputs. The input in the image classification example (which consists of the concatenated RGB values at every pixel) is also enormous. Moreover, its structure is naturally two-dimensional; two pixels above and below one another are closely related, even if they are not adjacent in the input vector.

Finally, consider the input for the model that predicts the freezing and boiling points of the molecule. A molecule may contain varying numbers of atoms that can be connected in different ways. In this case, the model must ingest both the geometric structure of the molecule and the constituent atoms to the model.

1.1.3   Machine learning models

Until now, we have treated the machine learning model as a black box that takes an input vector and returns an output vector. But what exactly is in this black box? Consider a model to predict the height of a child from their age (figure 1.3). The machine learning model is a mathematical equation that describes how the average height varies as a function of age (cyan curve in figure 1.3). When we run the age through this equation, it returns the height. For example, if the age is 10 years, then we predict that the height will be 139 cm.

More precisely, the model represents a family of equations mapping the input to the output (i.e., a family of different cyan curves). The particular equation (curve) is chosen using *training data* (examples of input/output pairs). In figure 1.3, these pairs are represented by the orange points, and we can see that the model (cyan line) describes these data reasonably. When we talk about *training* or *fitting* a model, we mean that we search through the family of possible equations (possible cyan curves) relating input to output to find the one that describes the training data most accurately.

It follows that the models in figure 1.2 require labeled input/output pairs for training. For example, the music classification model would require a large number of audio clips where a human expert had identified the genre of each. These input/output pairs take the role of a teacher or supervisor for the training process, and this gives rise to the term *supervised learning.*

1.1.4 Deep neural networks

This book concerns deep neural networks, which are a particularly useful type of machine learning model. They are equations that can represent an extremely broad family of relationships between input and output, and where it is particularly easy to search through this family to find the relationship that describes the training data.

Deep neural networks can process inputs that are very large, of variable length, and contain various kinds of internal structures. They can output single real numbers (regression), multiple numbers (multivariate regression), or probabilities over two or more classes (binary and multiclass classification, respectively). As we shall see in the next section, their outputs may also be very large, of variable length, and contain internal structure. It is probably hard to imagine equations with these properties, and the reader should endeavor to suspend disbelief for now.

1.1.5 Structured outputs

Figure 1.4a depicts a multivariate binary classification model for semantic segmentation. Here, every pixel of an input image is assigned a binary label that indicates whether it belongs to a cow or the background. Figure 1.4b shows a multivariate regression model where the input is an image of a street scene and the output is the depth at each pixel. In both cases, the output is high-dimensional and structured. However, this structure is closely tied to the input, and this can be exploited; if a pixel is labeled as "cow," then a neighbor with a similar RGB value probably has the same label.

Figures 1.4c–e depict three models where the output has a complex structure that is not so closely tied to the input. Figure 1.4c shows a model where the input is an audio file and the output is the transcribed words from that file. Figure 1.4d is a translation

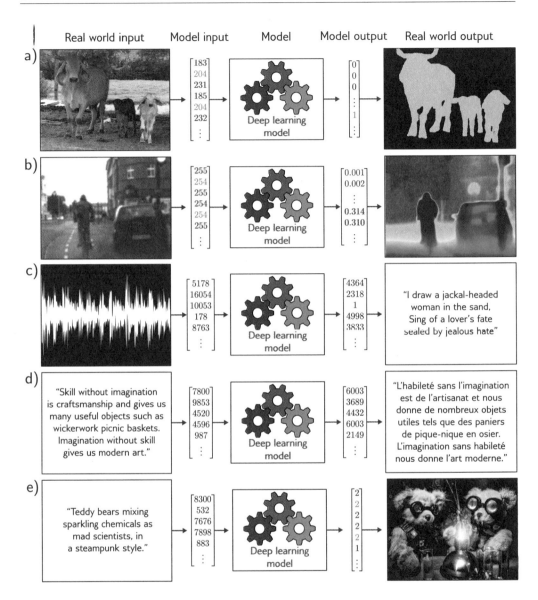

Figure 1.4 Supervised learning tasks with structured outputs. a) This semantic segmentation model maps an RGB image to a binary image indicating whether each pixel belongs to the background or a cow (adapted from Noh et al., 2015). b) This monocular depth estimation model maps an RGB image to an output image where each pixel represents the depth (adapted from Cordts et al., 2016). c) This audio transcription model maps an audio sample to a transcription of the spoken words in the audio. d) This translation model maps an English text string to its French translation. e) This image synthesis model maps a caption to an image (example from https://openai.com/dall-e-2/). In each case, the output has a complex internal structure or grammar. In some cases, many outputs are compatible with the input.

model in which the input is a body of text in English, and the output contains the French translation. Figure 1.4e depicts a very challenging task in which the input is descriptive text, and the model must produce an image that matches this description.

In principle, the latter three tasks can be tackled in the standard supervised learning framework, but they are more difficult for two reasons. First, the output may genuinely be ambiguous; there are multiple valid translations from an English sentence to a French one and multiple images that are compatible with any caption. Second, the output contains considerable structure; not all strings of words make valid English and French sentences, and not all collections of RGB values make plausible images. In addition to learning the mapping, we also have to respect the "grammar" of the output.

Fortunately, this "grammar" can be learned without the need for output labels. For example, we can learn how to form valid English sentences by learning the statistics of a large corpus of text data. This provides a connection with the next section of the book, which considers *unsupervised learning models*.

1.2 Unsupervised learning

Constructing a model from input data without corresponding output labels is termed *unsupervised learning*; the absence of output labels means there can be no "supervision." Rather than learning a mapping from input to output, the goal is to describe or understand the structure of the data. As was the case for supervised learning, the data may have very different characteristics; it may be discrete or continuous, low-dimensional or high-dimensional, and of constant or variable length.

1.2.1 Generative models

This book focuses on *generative unsupervised models*, which learn to synthesize new data examples that are statistically indistinguishable from the training data. Some generative models explicitly describe the probability distribution over the input data and here new examples are generated by sampling from this distribution. Others merely learn a mechanism to generate new examples without explicitly describing their distribution.

State-of-the-art generative models can synthesize examples that are extremely plausible but distinct from the training examples. They have been particularly successful at generating images (figure 1.5) and text (figure 1.6). They can also synthesize data under the constraint that some outputs are predetermined (termed *conditional generation*). Examples include image inpainting (figure 1.7) and text completion (figure 1.8). Indeed, modern generative models for text are so powerful that they can appear intelligent. Given a body of text followed by a question, the model can often "fill in" the missing answer by generating the most likely completion of the document. However, in reality, the model only knows about the statistics of language and does not understand the significance of its answers.

Figure 1.5 Generative models for images. Left: two images were generated from a model trained on pictures of cats. These are not real cats, but samples from a probability model. Right: two images generated from a model trained on images of buildings. Adapted from Karras et al. (2020b).

The moon had risen by the time I reached the edge of the forest, and the light that filtered through the trees was silver and cold. I shivered, though I was not cold, and quickened my pace. I had never been so far from the village before, and I was not sure what to expect. I had been walking for hours, and I was tired and hungry. I had left in such a hurry that I had not thought to pack any food, and I had not thought to bring a weapon. I was unarmed and alone in a strange place, and I did not know what I was doing.

I had been walking for so long that I had lost all sense of time, and I had no idea how far I had come. I only knew that I had to keep going. I had to find her. I was getting close. I could feel it. She was nearby, and she was in trouble. I had to find her and help her, before it was too late.

Figure 1.6 Short story synthesized from a generative model of text data. The model describes a probability distribution that assigns a probability to every output string. Sampling from the model creates strings that follow the statistics of the training data (here, short stories) but have never been seen before.

Figure 1.7 Inpainting. In the original image (left), the boy is obscured by metal cables. These undesirable regions (center) are removed and the generative model synthesizes a new image (right) under the constraint that the remaining pixels must stay the same. Adapted from Saharia et al. (2022a).

I was a little nervous before my first lecture at the University of Bath. It seemed like there were hundreds of students and they looked intimidating. I stepped up to the lectern and was about to speak when something bizarre happened.

Suddenly, the room was filled with a deafening noise, like a giant roar. It was so loud that I couldn't hear anything else and I had to cover my ears. I could see the students looking around, confused and frightened. Then, as quickly as it had started, the noise stopped and the room was silent again.

I stood there for a few moments, trying to make sense of what had just happened. Then I realized that the students were all staring at me, waiting for me to say something. I tried to think of something witty or clever to say, but my mind was blank. So I just said, "Well, that was strange.' and then I started my lecture.

Figure 1.8 Conditional text synthesis. Given an initial body of text (in black), generative models of text can continue the string plausibly by synthesizing the "missing" remaining part of the string. Generated by GPT3 (Brown et al., 2020).

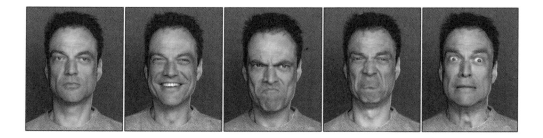

Figure 1.9 Variation of the human face. The human face contains roughly 42 muscles, so it's possible to describe most of the variation in images of the same person in the same lighting with just 42 numbers. In general, datasets of images, music, and text can be described by a relatively small number of underlying variables although it is typically more difficult to tie these to particular physical mechanisms. Images from Dynamic FACES database (Holland et al., 2019).

1.2.2 Latent variables

Some (but not all) generative models exploit the observation that data can be lower dimensional than the raw number of observed variables suggests. For example, the number of valid and meaningful English sentences is considerably smaller than the number of strings created by drawing words at random. Similarly, real-world images are a tiny subset of the images that can be created by drawing random RGB values for every pixel. This is because images are generated by physical processes (see figure 1.9).

This leads to the idea that we can describe each data example using a smaller number of underlying *latent variables*. Here, the role of deep learning is to describe the mapping between these latent variables and the data. The latent variables typically have a simple

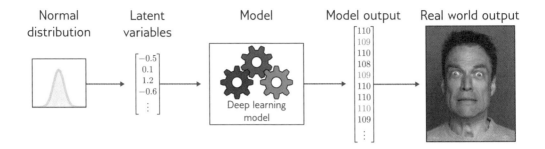

Figure 1.10 Latent variables. Many generative models use a deep learning model to describe the relationship between a low-dimensional "latent" variable and the observed high-dimensional data. The latent variables have a simple probability distribution by design. Hence, new examples can be generated by sampling from the simple distribution over the latent variables and then using the deep learning model to map the sample to the observed data space.

Figure 1.11 Image interpolation. In each row the left and right images are real and the three images in between represent a sequence of interpolations created by a generative model. The generative models that underpin these interpolations have learned that all images can be created by a set of underlying latent variables. By finding these variables for the two real images, interpolating their values, and then using these intermediate variables to create new images, we can generate intermediate results that are both visually plausible and mix the characteristics of the two original images. Top row adapted from Sauer et al. (2022). Bottom row adapted from Ramesh et al. (2022).

Figure 1.12 Multiple images generated from the caption "A teddy bear on a skateboard in Times Square." Generated by DALL·E-2 (Ramesh et al., 2022).

probability distribution by design. By sampling from this distribution and passing the result through the deep learning model, we can create new samples (figure 1.10).

These models lead to new methods for manipulating real data. For example, consider finding the latent variables that underpin two real examples. We can interpolate between these examples by interpolating between their latent representations and mapping the intermediate positions back into the data space (figure 1.11).

1.2.3 Connecting supervised and unsupervised learning

Generative models with latent variables can also benefit supervised learning models where the outputs have structure (figure 1.4). For example, consider learning to predict the images corresponding to a caption. Rather than directly map the text input to an image, we can learn a relation between latent variables that explain the text and the latent variables that explain the image.

This has three advantages. First, we may need fewer text/image pairs to learn this mapping now that the inputs and outputs are lower dimensional. Second, we are more likely to generate a plausible-looking image; any sensible values of the latent variables should produce something that looks like a plausible example. Third, if we introduce randomness to either the mapping between the two sets of latent variables or the mapping from the latent variables to the image, then we can generate multiple images that are all described well by the caption (figure 1.12).

1.3 Reinforcement learning

The final area of machine learning is reinforcement learning. This paradigm introduces the idea of an agent which lives in a world and can perform certain actions at each time step. The actions change the state of the system but not necessarily in a deterministic way. Taking an action can also produce rewards, and the goal of reinforcement learning is for the agent to learn to choose actions that lead to high rewards on average.

One complication is that the reward may occur some time after the action is taken, so associating a reward with an action is not straightforward. This is known as the *temporal credit assignment problem*. As the agent learns, it must trade off *exploration* and *exploitation* of what it already knows; perhaps the agent has already learned how to receive modest rewards; should it follow this strategy (exploit what it knows), or should it try different actions to see if it can improve (explore other opportunities)?

1.3.1 Two examples

Consider teaching a humanoid robot to locomote. The robot can perform a limited number of actions at a given time (moving various joints), and these change the state of the world (its pose). We might reward the robot for reaching checkpoints in an obstacle course. To reach each checkpoint, it must perform many actions, and it's unclear which ones contributed to the reward when it is received and which were irrelevant. This is an example of the temporal credit assignment problem.

A second example is learning to play chess. Again, the agent has a set of valid actions (chess moves) at any given time. However, these actions change the state of the system in a non-deterministic way; for any choice of action, the opposing player might respond with many different moves. Here, we might set up a reward structure based on capturing pieces or just have a single reward at the end of the game for winning. In the latter case, the temporal credit assignment problem is extreme; the system must learn which of the many moves it made were instrumental to success or failure.

The exploration-exploitation trade-off is also apparent in these two examples. The robot may have discovered that it can make progress by lying on its side and pushing with one leg. This strategy will move the robot and yields rewards, but much more slowly than the optimal solution: to balance on its legs and walk. So, it faces a choice between exploiting what it already knows (how to slide along the floor awkwardly) and exploring the space of actions (which might result in much faster locomotion). Similarly, in the chess example, the agent may learn a reasonable sequence of opening moves. Should it exploit this knowledge or explore different opening sequences?

It is perhaps not obvious how deep learning fits into the reinforcement learning framework. There are several possible approaches, but one technique is to use deep networks to build a mapping from the observed world state to an action. This is known as a *policy network*. In the robot example, the policy network would learn a mapping from its sensor measurements to joint movements. In the chess example, the network would learn a mapping from the current state of the board to the choice of move (figure 1.13).

1.4 Ethics

It would be irresponsible to write this book without discussing the ethical implications of artificial intelligence. This potent technology will change the world to at least the

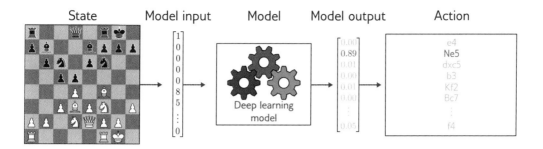

Figure 1.13 Policy networks for reinforcement learning. One way to incorporate deep neural networks into reinforcement learning is to use them to define a mapping from the state (here position on chessboard) to the actions (possible moves). This mapping is known as a *policy*.

same extent as electricity, the internal combustion engine, the transistor, or the internet. The potential benefits in healthcare, design, entertainment, transport, education, and almost every area of commerce are enormous. However, scientists and engineers are often unrealistically optimistic about the outcomes of their work, and the potential for harm is just as great. The following paragraphs highlight five concerns.

Bias and fairness: If we train a system to predict salary levels for individuals based on historical data, then this system will reproduce historical biases; for example, it will probably predict that women should be paid less than men. Several such cases have already become international news stories: an AI system for super-resolving face images made non-white people look more white; a system for generating images produced only pictures of men when asked to synthesize pictures of lawyers. Careless application of algorithmic decision-making using AI has the potential to entrench or aggravate existing biases. See Binns (2018) for further discussion.

Explainability: Deep learning systems make decisions, but we do not usually know exactly how or based on what information. They may contain billions of parameters, and there is no way we can understand how they work based on examination. This has led to the sub-field of explainable AI. One moderately successful area is producing local explanations; we cannot explain the entire system, but we can produce an interpretable description of why a particular decision was made. However, it remains unknown whether it is possible to build complex decision-making systems that are fully transparent to their users or even their creators. See Grennan et al. (2022) for further information.

Weaponizing AI: All significant technologies have been applied directly or indirectly toward war. Sadly, violent conflict seems to be an inevitable feature of human behavior. AI is arguably the most powerful technology ever built and will doubtless be deployed extensively in a military context. Indeed, this is already happening (Heikkilä, 2022).

Concentrating power: It is not from a benevolent interest in improving the lot of the human race that the world's most powerful companies are investing heavily in artificial intelligence. They know that these technologies will allow them to reap enormous profits. Like any advanced technology, deep learning is likely to concentrate power in the hands of the few organizations that control it. Automating jobs that are currently done by humans will change the economic environment and disproportionately affect the livelihoods of lower-paid workers with fewer skills. Optimists argue similar disruptions happened during the industrial revolution and resulted in shorter working hours. The truth is that we simply do not know what effects the large-scale adoption of AI will have on society (see David, 2015).

Existential risk: The major existential risks to the human race all result from technology. Climate change has been driven by industrialization. Nuclear weapons derive from the study of physics. Pandemics are more probable and spread faster because innovations in transport, agriculture, and construction have allowed a larger, denser, and more interconnected population. Artificial intelligence brings new existential risks. We should be very cautious about building systems that are more capable and extensible than human beings. In the most optimistic case, it will put vast power in the hands of the owners. In the most pessimistic case, we will be unable to control it or even understand its motives (see Tegmark, 2018).

This list is far from exhaustive. AI could also enable surveillance, disinformation, violations of privacy, fraud, and manipulation of financial markets, and the energy required to train AI systems contributes to climate change. Moreover, these concerns are not speculative; there are already many examples of ethically dubious applications of AI (consult Dao, 2021, for a partial list). In addition, the recent history of the internet has shown how new technology can cause harm in unexpected ways. The online community of the eighties and early nineties could hardly have predicted the proliferation of fake news, spam, online harassment, fraud, cyberbullying, incel culture, political manipulation, doxxing, online radicalization, and revenge porn.

Everyone studying or researching (or writing books about) AI should contemplate to what degree scientists are accountable for the uses of their technology. We should consider that capitalism primarily drives the development of AI and that legal advances and deployment for social good are likely to lag significantly behind. We should reflect on whether it's possible, as scientists and engineers, to control progress in this field and to reduce the potential for harm. We should consider what kind of organizations we are prepared to work for. How serious are they in their commitment to reducing the potential harms of AI? Are they simply "ethics-washing" to reduce reputational risk, or do they actually implement mechanisms to halt ethically suspect projects?

All readers are encouraged to investigate these issues further. The online course at https://ethics-of-ai.mooc.fi/ is a useful introductory resource. If you are a professor teaching from this book, you are encouraged to raise these issues with your students. If you are a student taking a course where this is not done, then lobby your professor to make this happen. If you are deploying or researching AI in a corporate environment, you are encouraged to scrutinize your employer's values and to help change them (or leave) if they are wanting.

1.5 Structure of book

The structure of the book follows the structure of this introduction. Chapters 2–9 walk through the supervised learning pipeline. We describe shallow and deep neural networks and discuss how to train them and measure and improve their performance. Chapters 10–13 describe common architectural variations of deep neural networks, including convolutional networks, residual connections, and transformers. These architectures are used across supervised, unsupervised, and reinforcement learning.

Chapters 14–18 tackle unsupervised learning using deep neural networks. We devote a chapter each to four modern deep generative models: generative adversarial networks, variational autoencoders, normalizing flows, and diffusion models. Chapter 19 is a brief introduction to deep reinforcement learning. This is a topic that easily justifies its own book, so the treatment is necessarily superficial. However, this treatment is intended to be a good starting point for readers unfamiliar with this area.

Despite the title of this book, some aspects of deep learning remain poorly understood. Chapter 20 poses some fundamental questions. Why are deep networks so easy to train? Why do they generalize so well? Why do they need so many parameters? Do they need to be deep? Along the way, we explore unexpected phenomena such as the structure of the loss function, double descent, grokking, and lottery tickets. The book concludes with chapter 21, which discusses ethics and deep learning.

1.6 Other books

This book is self-contained but is limited to coverage of deep learning. It is intended to be the spiritual successor to *Deep Learning* (Goodfellow et al., 2016) which is a fantastic resource but does not cover recent advances. For a broader look at machine learning, the most up-to-date and encyclopedic resource is *Probabilistic Machine Learning* (Murphy, 2022, 2023). However, *Pattern Recognition and Machine Learning* (Bishop, 2006) is still an excellent and relevant book.

If you enjoy this book, then my previous volume, *Computer Vision: Models, Learning, and Inference* (Prince, 2012), is still worth reading. Some parts have dated badly, but it contains a thorough introduction to probability, including Bayesian methods, and good introductory coverage of latent variable models, geometry for computer vision, Gaussian processes, and graphical models. It uses identical notation to this book and can be found online. A detailed treatment of graphical models can be found in *Probabilistic Graphical Models: Principles and Techniques* (Koller & Friedman, 2009), and Gaussian processes are covered by *Gaussian Processes for Machine Learning* (Williams & Rasmussen, 2006).

For background mathematics, consult *Mathematics for Machine Learning* (Deisenroth et al., 2020). For a more coding-oriented approach, consult *Dive into Deep Learning* (Zhang et al., 2023). The best overview for computer vision is Szeliski (2022), and there is also the impending book *Foundations of Computer Vision* (Torralba et al., 2024). A good starting point to learn about graph neural networks is *Graph Representation Learning* (Hamilton, 2020). The definitive work on reinforcement learning is *Reinforce-*

ment Learning: An Introduction (Sutton & Barto, 2018). A good initial resource is *Foundations of Deep Reinforcement Learning* (Graesser & Keng, 2019).

1.7 How to read this book

Most remaining chapters in this book contain a main body of text, a notes section, and a set of problems. The main body of the text is intended to be self-contained and can be read without recourse to the other parts of the chapter. As much as possible, background mathematics is incorporated into the main body of the text. However, for larger topics that would be a distraction to the main thread of the argument, the background material is appendicized, and a reference is provided in the margin. Most notation in this book is standard. However, some conventions are less widely used, and the reader is encouraged to consult appendix A before proceeding.

The main body of text includes many novel illustrations and visualizations of deep learning models and results. I've worked hard to provide new explanations of existing ideas rather than merely curate the work of others. Deep learning is a new field, and sometimes phenomena are poorly understood. I try to make it clear where this is the case and when my explanations should be treated with caution.

References are included in the main body of the chapter only where results are depicted. Instead, they can be found in the notes section at the end of the chapter. I do not generally respect historical precedent in the main text; if an ancestor of a current technique is no longer useful, then I will not mention it. However, the historical development of the field is described in the notes section, and hopefully, credit is fairly assigned. The notes are organized into paragraphs and provide pointers for further reading. They should help the reader orient themselves within the sub-area and understand how it relates to other parts of machine learning. The notes are less self-contained than the main text. Depending on your level of background knowledge and interest, you may find these sections more or less useful.

Each chapter has a number of associated problems. They are referenced in the margin of the main text at the point that they should be attempted. As George Pólya noted, "Mathematics, you see, is not a spectator sport." He was correct, and I highly recommend that you attempt the problems as you go. In some cases, they provide insights that will help you understand the main text. Problems for which the answers are provided on the associated website are indicated with an asterisk. Additionally, Python notebooks that will help you understand the ideas in this book are also available via the website, and these are also referenced in the margins of the text. Indeed, if you are feeling rusty, it might be worth working through the notebook on background mathematics right now.

Unfortunately, the pace of research in AI makes it inevitable that this book will be a constant work in progress. If there are parts you find hard to understand, notable omissions, or sections that seem extraneous, please get in touch via the associated website. Together, we can make the next edition better.

Appendix A
Notation

Notebook 1.1
Background
mathematics

Chapter 2

Supervised learning

A *supervised learning model* defines a mapping from one or more inputs to one or more outputs. For example, the input might be the age and mileage of a secondhand Toyota Prius, and the output might be the estimated value of the car in dollars.

The model is just a mathematical equation; when the inputs are passed through this equation, it computes the output, and this is termed *inference*. The model equation also contains *parameters*. Different parameter values change the outcome of the computation; the model equation describes a family of possible relationships between inputs and outputs, and the parameters specify the particular relationship.

When we *train* or *learn* a model, we find parameters that describe the true relationship between inputs and outputs. A learning algorithm takes a training set of input/output pairs and manipulates the parameters until the inputs predict their corresponding outputs as closely as possible. If the model works well for these training pairs, then we hope it will make good predictions for new inputs where the true output is unknown.

The goal of this chapter is to expand on these ideas. First, we describe this framework more formally and introduce some notation. Then we work through a simple example in which we use a straight line to describe the relationship between input and output. This linear model is both familiar and easy to visualize, but nevertheless illustrates all the main ideas of supervised learning.

2.1 Supervised learning overview

In supervised learning, we aim to build a model that takes an input $\mathbf{x}$ and outputs a prediction $\mathbf{y}$. For simplicity, we assume that both the input $\mathbf{x}$ and output $\mathbf{y}$ are vectors of a predetermined and fixed size and that the elements of each vector are always ordered in the same way; in the Prius example above, the input $\mathbf{x}$ would always contain the age of the car and then the mileage, in that order. This is termed *structured* or *tabular* data.

To make the prediction, we need a model $\mathbf{f}[\bullet]$ that takes input $\mathbf{x}$ and returns $\mathbf{y}$, so:

$$\mathbf{y} = \mathbf{f}[\mathbf{x}]. \tag{2.1}$$

When we compute the prediction $\mathbf{y}$ from the input $\mathbf{x}$, we call this *inference*.

The model is just a mathematical equation with a fixed form. It represents a family of different relations between the input and the output. The model also contains *parameters* $\boldsymbol{\phi}$. The choice of parameters determines the particular relation between input and output, so we should really write:

$$\mathbf{y} = \mathbf{f}[\mathbf{x}, \boldsymbol{\phi}]. \tag{2.2}$$

When we talk about *learning* or *training* a model, we mean that we attempt to find parameters $\boldsymbol{\phi}$ that make sensible output predictions from the input. We learn these parameters using a *training dataset* of I pairs of input and output examples $\{\mathbf{x}_i, \mathbf{y}_i\}$. We aim to select parameters that map each training input to its associated output as closely as possible. We quantify the degree of mismatch in this mapping with the *loss L*. This is a scalar value that summarizes how poorly the model predicts the training outputs from their corresponding inputs for parameters $\boldsymbol{\phi}$.

We can treat the loss as a function $L[\boldsymbol{\phi}]$ of these parameters. When we train the model, we are seeking parameters $\hat{\boldsymbol{\phi}}$ that minimize this *loss function*:[1]

$$\hat{\boldsymbol{\phi}} = \underset{\boldsymbol{\phi}}{\operatorname{argmin}} \left[L\left[\boldsymbol{\phi}\right] \right]. \tag{2.3}$$

If the loss is small after this minimization, we have found model parameters that accurately predict the training outputs $\mathbf{y}_i$ from the training inputs $\mathbf{x}_i$.

After training a model, we must now assess its performance; we run the model on separate *test data* to see how well it *generalizes* to examples that it didn't observe during training. If the performance is adequate, then we are ready to deploy the model.

2.2 Linear regression example

Let's now make these ideas concrete with a simple example. We consider a model $y = f[x, \boldsymbol{\phi}]$ that predicts a single output y from a single input x. Then we develop a loss function, and finally, we discuss model training.

2.2.1 1D linear regression model

A *1D linear regression model* describes the relationship between input x and output y as a straight line:

$$\begin{aligned} y &= f[x, \boldsymbol{\phi}] \\ &= \phi_0 + \phi_1 x. \end{aligned} \tag{2.4}$$

---

[1]More properly, the loss function also depends on the training data $\{\mathbf{x}_i, \mathbf{y}_i\}$, so we should write $L[\{\mathbf{x}_i, \mathbf{y}_i\}, \boldsymbol{\phi}]$, but this is rather cumbersome.

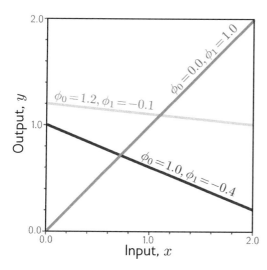

Figure 2.1 Linear regression model. For a given choice of parameters $\phi = [\phi_0, \phi_1]^T$, the model makes a prediction for the output (y-axis) based on the input (x-axis). Different choices for the y-intercept ϕ_0 and the slope ϕ_1 change these predictions (cyan, orange, and gray lines). The linear regression model (equation 2.4) defines a family of input/output relations (lines) and the parameters determine the member of the family (the particular line).

This model has two parameters $\phi = [\phi_0, \phi_1]^T$, where ϕ_0 is the y-intercept of the line and ϕ_1 is the slope. Different choices for the y-intercept and slope result in different relations between input and output (figure 2.1). Hence, equation 2.4 defines a family of possible input-output relations (all possible lines), and the choice of parameters determines the member of this family (the particular line).

2.2.2 Loss

For this model, the training dataset (figure 2.2a) consists of I input/output pairs $\{x_i, y_i\}$. Figures 2.2b–d show three lines defined by three sets of parameters. The green line in figure 2.2d describes the data more accurately than the other two since it is much closer to the data points. However, we need a principled approach for deciding which parameters ϕ are better than others. To this end, we assign a numerical value to each choice of parameters that quantifies the degree of mismatch between the model and the data. We term this value the *loss*; a lower loss means a better fit.

The mismatch is captured by the deviation between the model predictions $f[x_i, \phi]$ (height of the line at x_i) and the ground truth outputs y_i. These deviations are depicted as orange dashed lines in figures 2.2b–d. We quantify the total mismatch, *training error*, or *loss* as the sum of the squares of these deviations for all I training pairs:

$$
\begin{aligned}
L[\phi] &= \sum_{i=1}^{I} \left(f[x_i, \phi] - y_i\right)^2 \\
&= \sum_{i=1}^{I} \left(\phi_0 + \phi_1 x_i - y_i\right)^2.
\end{aligned}
\tag{2.5}
$$

Since the best parameters minimize this expression, we call this a *least-squares* loss. The squaring operation means that the direction of the deviation (i.e., whether the line is

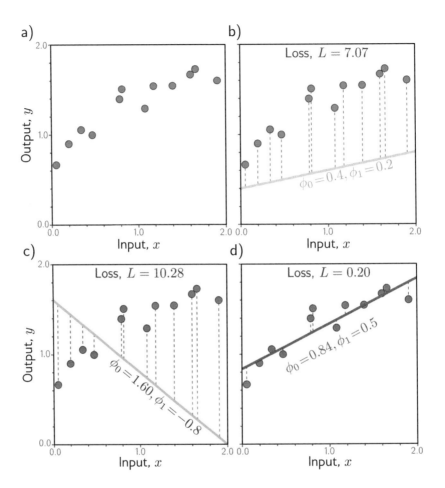

Figure 2.2 Linear regression training data, model, and loss. a) The training data (orange points) consist of $I = 12$ input/output pairs $\{x_i, y_i\}$. b–d) Each panel shows the linear regression model with different parameters. Depending on the choice of y-intercept and slope parameters $\boldsymbol{\phi} = [\phi_0, \phi_1]^T$, the model errors (orange dashed lines) may be larger or smaller. The loss L is the sum of the squares of these errors. The parameters that define the lines in panels (b) and (c) have large losses $L = 7.07$ and $L = 10.28$, respectively because the models fit badly. The loss $L = 0.20$ in panel (d) is smaller because the model fits well; in fact, this has the smallest loss of all possible lines, so these are the optimal parameters.

a)

b)

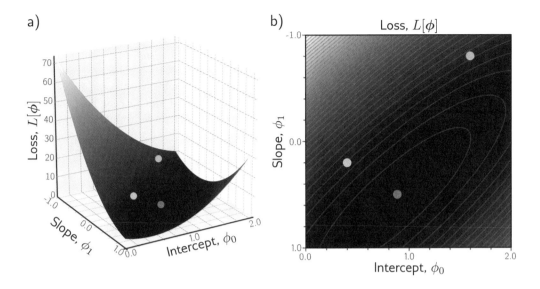

Figure 2.3 Loss function for linear regression model with the dataset in figure 2.2a.
a) Each combination of parameters $\phi = [\phi_0, \phi_1]^T$ has an associated loss. The resulting loss function $L[\phi]$ can be visualized as a surface. The three circles represent the lines from figure 2.2b–d. b) The loss can also be visualized as a heatmap, where brighter regions represent larger losses; here we are looking straight down at the surface in (a) from above and gray ellipses represent isocontours. The best fitting line (figure 2.2d) has the parameters with the smallest loss (green circle).

above or below the data) is unimportant. There are also theoretical reasons for this choice which we return to in chapter 5.

The loss L is a function of the parameters ϕ; it will be larger when the model fit is poor (figure 2.2b,c) and smaller when it is good (figure 2.2d). Considered in this light, we term $L[\phi]$ the *loss function* or *cost function*. The goal is to find the parameters $\hat{\phi}$ that minimize this quantity:

Notebook 2.1
Supervised
learning

$$
\begin{aligned}
\hat{\phi} &= \underset{\phi}{\operatorname{argmin}}\left[L[\phi]\right] \\
&= \underset{\phi}{\operatorname{argmin}}\left[\sum_{i=1}^{I}\left(\mathrm{f}[x_i, \phi] - y_i\right)^2\right] \\
&= \underset{\phi}{\operatorname{argmin}}\left[\sum_{i=1}^{I}\left(\phi_0 + \phi_1 x_i - y_i\right)^2\right].
\end{aligned}
\tag{2.6}
$$

There are only two parameters (the y-intercept ϕ_0 and slope ϕ_1), so we can calculate the loss for every combination of values and visualize the loss function as a surface (figure 2.3). The "best" parameters are at the minimum of this surface.

Problems 2.1–2.2

2.2.3 Training

The process of finding parameters that minimize the loss is termed *model fitting, training,* or *learning*. The basic method is to choose the initial parameters randomly and then improve them by "walking down" the loss function until we reach the bottom (figure 2.4). One way to do this is to measure the gradient of the surface at the current position and take a step in the direction that is most steeply downhill. Then we repeat this process until the gradient is flat and we can improve no further.[2]

2.2.4 Testing

Having trained the model, we want to know how it will perform in the real world. We do this by computing the loss on a separate set of *test data*. The degree to which the prediction accuracy *generalizes* to the test data depends in part on how representative and complete the training data is. However, it also depends on how expressive the model is. A simple model like a line might not be able to capture the true relationship between input and output. This is known as *underfitting*. Conversely, a very expressive model may describe statistical peculiarities of the training data that are atypical and lead to unusual predictions. This is known as *overfitting*.

2.3 Summary

A supervised learning model is a function $\mathbf{y} = \mathbf{f}[\mathbf{x}, \phi]$ that relates inputs $\mathbf{x}$ to outputs $\mathbf{y}$. The particular relationship is determined by parameters ϕ. To train the model, we define a loss function $L[\phi]$ over a training dataset $\{\mathbf{x}_i, \mathbf{y}_i\}$. This quantifies the mismatch between the model predictions $\mathbf{f}[\mathbf{x}_i, \phi]$ and observed outputs $\mathbf{y}_i$ as a function of the parameters ϕ. Then we search for the parameters that minimize the loss. We evaluate the model on a different set of test data to see how well it generalizes to new inputs.

Chapters 3–9 expand on these ideas. First, we tackle the model itself; 1D linear regression has the obvious drawback that it can only describe the relationship between the input and output as a straight line. Shallow neural networks (chapter 3) are only slightly more complex than linear regression but describe a much larger family of input/output relationships. Deep neural networks (chapter 4) are just as expressive but can describe complex functions with fewer parameters and work better in practice.

Chapter 5 investigates loss functions for different tasks and reveals the theoretical underpinnings of the least-squares loss. Chapters 6 and 7 discuss the training process. Chapter 8 discusses how to measure model performance. Chapter 9 considers *regularization* techniques, which aim to improve that performance.

---

[2]This iterative approach is not actually necessary for the linear regression model. Here, it's possible to find closed-form expressions for the parameters. However, this *gradient descent* approach works for more complex models where there is no closed-form solution and where there are too many parameters to evaluate the loss for every combination of values.

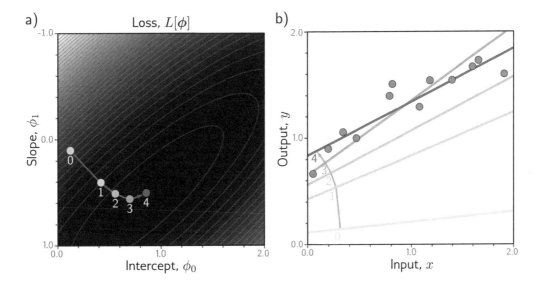

a) Loss, $L[\phi]$

b)

Figure 2.4 Linear regression training. The goal is to find the y-intercept and slope parameters that correspond to the smallest loss. a) Iterative training algorithms initialize the parameters randomly and then improve them by "walking downhill" until no further improvement can be made. Here, we start at position 0 and move a certain distance downhill (perpendicular to the contours) to position 1. Then we re-calculate the downhill direction and move to position 2. Eventually, we reach the minimum of the function (position 4). b) Each position 0–4 from panel (a) corresponds to a different y-intercept and slope and so represents a different line. As the loss decreases, the lines fit the data more closely.

Notes

Loss functions vs. cost functions: In much of machine learning and in this book, the terms loss function and cost function are used interchangeably. However, more properly, a loss function is the individual term associated with a data point (i.e., each of the squared terms on the right-hand side of equation 2.5), and the cost function is the overall quantity that is minimized (i.e., the entire right-hand side of equation 2.5). A cost function can contain additional terms that are not associated with individual data points (see section 9.1). More generally, an *objective function* is any function that is to be maximized or minimized.

Generative vs. discriminative models: The models $\mathbf{y} = \mathbf{f}[\mathbf{x}, \phi]$ in this chapter are *discriminative models*. These make an output prediction $\mathbf{y}$ from real-world measurements $\mathbf{x}$. Another approach is to build a *generative model* $\mathbf{x} = \mathbf{g}[\mathbf{y}, \phi]$, in which the real-world measurements $\mathbf{x}$ are computed as a function of the output $\mathbf{y}$.

Problem 2.3

The generative approach has the disadvantage that it doesn't directly predict $\mathbf{y}$. To perform inference, we must invert the generative equation as $\mathbf{y} = \mathbf{g}^{-1}[\mathbf{x}, \phi]$, and this may be difficult. However, generative models have the advantage that we can build in prior knowledge about how the data were created. For example, if we wanted to predict the 3D position and orientation $\mathbf{y}$

of a car in an image $\mathbf{x}$, then we could build knowledge about car shape, 3D geometry, and light transport into the function $\mathbf{x} = \mathbf{g}[\mathbf{y}, \boldsymbol{\phi}]$.

This seems like a good idea, but in fact, discriminative models dominate modern machine learning; the advantage gained from exploiting prior knowledge in generative models is usually trumped by learning very flexible discriminative models with large amounts of training data.

Problems

Problem 2.1 To walk "downhill" on the loss function (equation 2.5), we measure its gradient with respect to the parameters ϕ_0 and ϕ_1. Calculate expressions for the slopes $\partial L/\partial\phi_0$ and $\partial L/\partial\phi_1$.

Problem 2.2 Show that we can find the minimum of the loss function in closed form by setting the expression for the derivatives from problem 2.1 to zero and solving for ϕ_0 and ϕ_1. Note that this works for linear regression but not for more complex models; this is why we use iterative model fitting methods like gradient descent (figure 2.4).

Problem 2.3* Consider reformulating linear regression as a generative model, so we have $x = g[y, \boldsymbol{\phi}] = \phi_0 + \phi_1 y$. What is the new loss function? Find an expression for the inverse function $y = g^{-1}[x, \boldsymbol{\phi}]$ that we would use to perform inference. Will this model make the same predictions as the discriminative version for a given training dataset $\{x_i, y_i\}$? One way to establish this is to write code that fits a line to three data points using both methods and see if the result is the same.

Chapter 3

Shallow neural networks

Chapter 2 introduced supervised learning using 1D linear regression. However, this model can only describe the input/output relationship as a line. This chapter introduces shallow neural networks. These describe piecewise linear functions and are expressive enough to approximate arbitrarily complex relationships between multi-dimensional inputs and outputs.

3.1 Neural network example

Shallow neural networks are functions $\mathbf{y} = \mathbf{f}[\mathbf{x}, \boldsymbol{\phi}]$ with parameters $\boldsymbol{\phi}$ that map multivariate inputs $\mathbf{x}$ to multivariate outputs $\mathbf{y}$. We defer a full definition until section 3.4 and introduce the main ideas using an example network $\mathbf{f}[x, \boldsymbol{\phi}]$ that maps a scalar input x to a scalar output y and has ten parameters $\boldsymbol{\phi} = \{\phi_0, \phi_1, \phi_2, \phi_3, \theta_{10}, \theta_{11}, \theta_{20}, \theta_{21}, \theta_{30}, \theta_{31}\}$:

$$
\begin{aligned}
y &= \mathbf{f}[x, \boldsymbol{\phi}] \\
&= \phi_0 + \phi_1 \mathrm{a}[\theta_{10} + \theta_{11}x] + \phi_2 \mathrm{a}[\theta_{20} + \theta_{21}x] + \phi_3 \mathrm{a}[\theta_{30} + \theta_{31}x]. \quad (3.1)
\end{aligned}
$$

We can break down this calculation into three parts: first, we compute three linear functions of the input data ($\theta_{10} + \theta_{11}x$, $\theta_{20} + \theta_{21}x$, and $\theta_{30} + \theta_{31}x$). Second, we pass the three results through an *activation function* $\mathrm{a}[\bullet]$. Finally, we weight the three resulting activations with ϕ_1, ϕ_2, and ϕ_3, sum them, and add an offset ϕ_0.

To complete the description, we must define the activation function $\mathrm{a}[\bullet]$. There are many possibilities, but the most common choice is the *rectified linear unit* or *ReLU*:

$$
\mathrm{a}[z] = \mathrm{ReLU}[z] = \begin{cases} 0 & z < 0 \\ z & z \geq 0 \end{cases}. \quad (3.2)
$$

This returns the input when it is positive and zero otherwise (figure 3.1).

It is probably not obvious which family of input/output relations is represented by equation 3.1. Nonetheless, the ideas from the previous chapter are all applicable. Equation 3.1 represents a family of functions where the particular member of the family

Figure 3.1 Rectified linear unit (ReLU). This activation function returns zero if the input is less than zero and returns the input unchanged otherwise. In other words, it clips negative values to zero. Note that there are many other possible choices for the activation function (see figure 3.13), but the ReLU is the most commonly used and the easiest to understand.

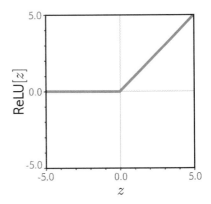

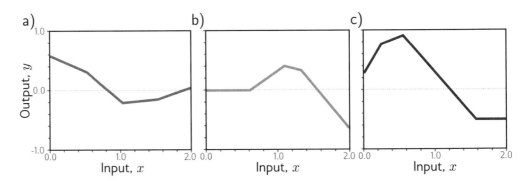

Figure 3.2 Family of functions defined by equation 3.1. a–c) Functions for three different choices of the ten parameters ϕ. In each case, the input/output relation is piecewise linear. However, the positions of the joints, the slopes of the linear regions between them, and the overall height vary.

depends on the ten parameters in ϕ. If we know these parameters, we can perform inference (predict y) by evaluating the equation for a given input x. Given a training dataset $\{x_i, y_i\}_{i=1}^{I}$, we can define a least squares loss function $L[\phi]$ and use this to measure how effectively the model describes this dataset for any given parameter values ϕ. To train the model, we search for the values $\hat{\phi}$ that minimize this loss.

3.1.1 Neural network intuition

In fact, equation 3.1 represents a family of continuous piecewise linear functions (figure 3.2) with up to four linear regions. We now break down equation 3.1 and show *why* it describes this family. To make this easier to understand, we split the function into two parts. First, we introduce the intermediate quantities:

$$h_1 = \text{a}[\theta_{10} + \theta_{11}x]$$
$$h_2 = \text{a}[\theta_{20} + \theta_{21}x]$$
$$h_3 = \text{a}[\theta_{30} + \theta_{31}x], \tag{3.3}$$

where we refer to h_1, h_2, and h_3 as *hidden units*. Second, we compute the output by combining these hidden units with a linear function:[1]

$$y = \phi_0 + \phi_1 h_1 + \phi_2 h_2 + \phi_3 h_3. \tag{3.4}$$

Figure 3.3 shows the flow of computation that creates the function in figure 3.2a. Each hidden unit contains a linear function $\theta_{\bullet 0} + \theta_{\bullet 1}x$ of the input, and that line is clipped by the ReLU function $a[\bullet]$ below zero. The positions where the three lines cross zero become the three "joints" in the final output. The three clipped lines are then weighted by ϕ_1, ϕ_2, and ϕ_3, respectively. Finally, the offset ϕ_0 is added, which controls the overall height of the final function.

Each linear region in figure 3.3j corresponds to a different *activation pattern* in the hidden units. When a unit is clipped, we refer to it as *inactive*, and when it is not clipped, we refer to it as *active*. For example, the shaded region receives contributions from h_1 and h_3 (which are active) but not from h_2 (which is inactive). The slope of each linear region is determined by (i) the original slopes $\theta_{\bullet 1}$ of the active inputs for this region and (ii) the weights $\phi_\bullet$ that were subsequently applied. For example, the slope in the shaded region (see problem 3.3) is $\theta_{11}\phi_1 + \theta_{31}\phi_3$, where the first term is the slope in panel (g) and the second term is the slope in panel (i).

Problems 3.1–3.8

Each hidden unit contributes one "joint" to the function, so with three hidden units, there can be four linear regions. However, only three of the slopes of these regions are independent; the fourth is either zero (if all the hidden units are inactive in this region) or is a sum of slopes from the other regions.

Notebook 3.1
Shallow networks I

Problem 3.9

3.1.2 Depicting neural networks

We have been discussing a neural network with one input, one output, and three hidden units. We visualize this network in figure 3.4a. The input is on the left, the hidden units are in the middle, and the output is on the right. Each connection represents one of the ten parameters. To simplify this representation, we do not typically draw the intercept parameters, so this network is usually depicted as in figure 3.4b.

---

[1] For the purposes of this book, a linear function has the form $z' = \phi_0 + \sum_i \phi_i z_i$. Any other type of function is nonlinear. For instance, the ReLU function (equation 3.2) and the example neural network that contains it (equation 3.1) are both nonlinear. See notes at end of chapter for further clarification.

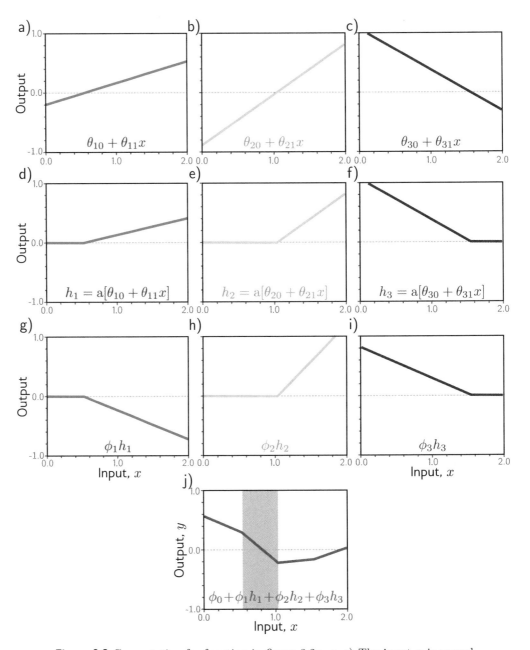

Figure 3.3 Computation for function in figure 3.2a. a–c) The input x is passed through three linear functions, each with a different y-intercept $\theta_{\bullet 0}$ and slope $\theta_{\bullet 1}$. d–f) Each line is passed through the ReLU activation function, which clips negative values to zero. g–i) The three clipped lines are then weighted (scaled) by ϕ_1, ϕ_2, and ϕ_3, respectively. j) Finally, the clipped and weighted functions are summed, and an offset ϕ_0 that controls the height is added. Each of the four linear regions corresponds to a different activation pattern in the hidden units. In the shaded region, h_2 is inactive (clipped), but h_1 and h_3 are both active.

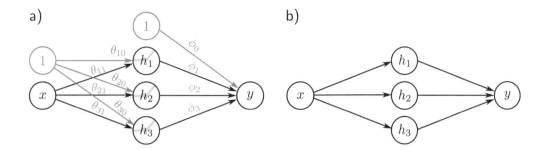

Figure 3.4 Depicting neural networks. a) The input x is on the left, the hidden units h_1, h_2, and h_3 in the center, and the output y on the right. Computation flows from left to right. The input is used to compute the hidden units, which are combined to create the output. Each of the ten arrows represents a parameter (intercepts in orange and slopes in black). Each parameter multiplies its source and adds the result to its target. For example, we multiply the parameter ϕ_1 by source h_1 and add it to y. We introduce additional nodes containing ones (orange circles) to incorporate the offsets into this scheme, so we multiply ϕ_0 by one (with no effect) and add it to y. ReLU functions are applied at the hidden units. b) More typically, the intercepts, ReLU functions, and parameter names are omitted; this simpler depiction represents the same network.

3.2 Universal approximation theorem

In the previous section, we introduced an example neural network with one input, one output, ReLU activation functions, and three hidden units. Let's now generalize this slightly and consider the case with D hidden units where the dth hidden unit is:

$$h_d = \text{a}[\theta_{d0} + \theta_{d1}x], \tag{3.5}$$

and these are combined linearly to create the output:

$$y = \phi_0 + \sum_{d=1}^{D} \phi_d h_d. \tag{3.6}$$

The number of hidden units in a shallow network is a measure of the *network capacity*. With ReLU activation functions, the output of a network with D hidden units has at most D joints and so is a piecewise linear function with at most $D+1$ linear regions. As we add more hidden units, the model can approximate more complex functions.

Indeed, with enough capacity (hidden units), a shallow network can describe any continuous 1D function defined on a compact subset of the real line to arbitrary precision. To see this, consider that every time we add a hidden unit, we add another linear region to the function. As these regions become more numerous, they represent smaller sections of the function, which are increasingly well approximated by a line (figure 3.5). The *universal approximation theorem* proves that for any continuous function, there exists a shallow network that can approximate this function to any specified precision.

Problem 3.10

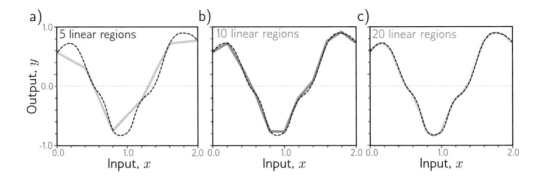

Figure 3.5 Approximation of a 1D function (dashed line) by a piecewise linear model. a–c) As the number of regions increases, the model becomes closer and closer to the continuous function. A neural network with a scalar input creates one extra linear region per hidden unit. The universal approximation theorem proves that, with enough hidden units, there exists a shallow neural network that can describe any given continuous function defined on a compact subset of $\mathbb{R}^{D_i}$ to arbitrary precision.

3.3 Multivariate inputs and outputs

In the above example, the network has a single scalar input x and a single scalar output y. However, the universal approximation theorem also holds for the more general case where the network maps multivariate inputs $\mathbf{x} = [x_1, x_2, \ldots, x_{D_i}]^T$ to multivariate output predictions $\mathbf{y} = [y_1, y_2, \ldots, y_{D_o}]^T$. We first explore how to extend the model to predict multivariate outputs. Then we consider multivariate inputs. Finally, in section 3.4, we present a general definition of a shallow neural network.

3.3.1 Visualizing multivariate outputs

To extend the network to multivariate outputs $\mathbf{y}$, we simply use a different linear function of the hidden units for each output. So, a network with a scalar input x, four hidden units h_1, h_2, h_3, and h_4, and a 2D multivariate output $\mathbf{y} = [y_1, y_2]^T$ would be defined as:

$$
\begin{aligned}
h_1 &= \text{a}[\theta_{10} + \theta_{11}x] \\
h_2 &= \text{a}[\theta_{20} + \theta_{21}x] \\
h_3 &= \text{a}[\theta_{30} + \theta_{31}x] \\
h_4 &= \text{a}[\theta_{40} + \theta_{41}x],
\end{aligned}
\tag{3.7}
$$

and

a)

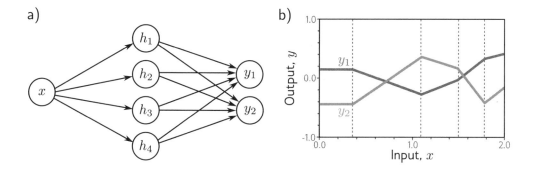

b)

Figure 3.6 Network with one input, four hidden units, and two outputs. a) Visualization of network structure. b) This network produces two piecewise linear functions, $y_1[x]$ and $y_2[x]$. The four "joints" of these functions (at vertical dotted lines) are constrained to be in the same places since they share the same hidden units, but the slopes and overall height may differ.

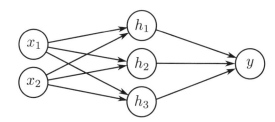

Figure 3.7 Visualization of neural network with 2D multivariate input $\mathbf{x} = [x_1, x_2]^T$ and scalar output y.

$$y_1 = \phi_{10} + \phi_{11}h_1 + \phi_{12}h_2 + \phi_{13}h_3 + \phi_{14}h_4$$
$$y_2 = \phi_{20} + \phi_{21}h_1 + \phi_{22}h_2 + \phi_{23}h_3 + \phi_{24}h_4. \tag{3.8}$$

The two outputs are two different linear functions of the hidden units.

As we saw in figure 3.3, the "joints" in the piecewise functions depend on where the initial linear functions $\theta_{\bullet 0} + \theta_{\bullet 1}x$ are clipped by the ReLU functions a[$\bullet$] at the hidden units. Since both outputs y_1 and y_2 are different linear functions of the same four hidden units, the four "joints" in each must be in the same places. However, the slopes of the linear regions and the overall vertical offset can differ (figure 3.6).

Problem 3.11

3.3.2   **Visualizing multivariate inputs**

To cope with multivariate inputs $\mathbf{x}$, we extend the linear relations between the input and the hidden units. So a network with two inputs $\mathbf{x} = [x_1, x_2]^T$ and a scalar output y (figure 3.7) might have three hidden units defined by:

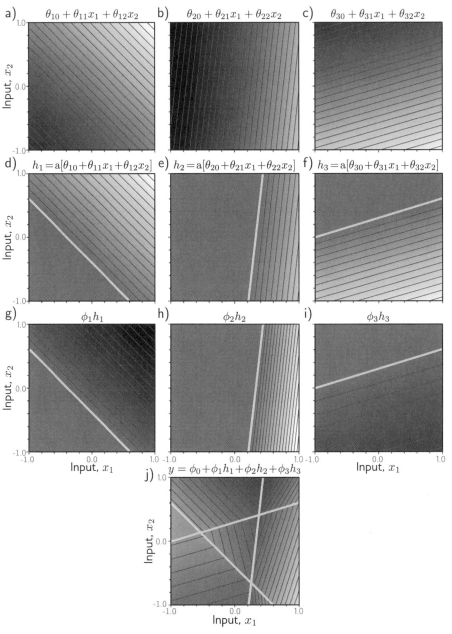

Figure 3.8 Processing in network with two inputs $\mathbf{x} = [x_1, x_2]^T$, three hidden units h_1, h_2, h_3, and one output y. a–c) The input to each hidden unit is a linear function of the two inputs, which corresponds to an oriented plane. Brightness indicates function output. For example, in panel (a), the brightness represents $\theta_{10} + \theta_{11}x_1 + \theta_{12}x_2$. Thin lines are contours. d–f) Each plane is clipped by the ReLU activation function (cyan lines are equivalent to "joints" in figures 3.3d–f). g-i) The clipped planes are then weighted, and j) summed together with an offset that determines the overall height of the surface. The result is a continuous surface made up of convex piecewise linear polygonal regions.

$$h_1 = \text{a}[\theta_{10} + \theta_{11}x_1 + \theta_{12}x_2]$$
$$h_2 = \text{a}[\theta_{20} + \theta_{21}x_1 + \theta_{22}x_2]$$
$$h_3 = \text{a}[\theta_{30} + \theta_{31}x_1 + \theta_{32}x_2], \tag{3.9}$$

where there is now one slope parameter for each input. The hidden units are combined to form the output in the usual way:

$$y = \phi_0 + \phi_1 h_1 + \phi_2 h_2 + \phi_3 h_3. \tag{3.10}$$

Figure 3.8 illustrates the processing of this network. Each hidden unit receives a linear combination of the two inputs, which forms an oriented plane in the 3D input/output space. The activation function clips the negative values of these planes to zero. The clipped planes are then recombined in a second linear function (equation 3.10) to create a continuous piecewise linear surface consisting of convex polygonal regions (figure 3.8j). Each region corresponds to a different activation pattern. For example, in the central triangular region, the first and third hidden units are active, and the second is inactive.

When there are more than two inputs to the model, it becomes difficult to visualize. However, the interpretation is similar. The output will be a continuous piecewise linear function of the input, where the linear regions are now convex polytopes in the multi-dimensional input space.

Note that as the input dimensions grow, the number of linear regions increases rapidly (figure 3.9). To get a feeling for how rapidly, consider that each hidden unit defines a hyperplane that delineates the part of space where this unit is active from the part where it is not (cyan lines in 3.8d–f). If we had the same number of hidden units as input dimensions D_i, we could align each hyperplane with one of the coordinate axes (figure 3.10). For two input dimensions, this would divide the space into four quadrants. For three dimensions, this would create eight octants, and for D_i dimensions, this would create 2^{D_i} orthants. Shallow neural networks usually have more hidden units than input dimensions, so they typically create more than 2^{D_i} linear regions.

Problems 3.12–3.13

Notebook 3.2
Shallow networks II

Appendix B.1.2
Convex region

Notebook 3.3
Shallow network
regions

3.4 Shallow neural networks: general case

We have described several example shallow networks to help develop intuition about how they work. We now define a general equation for a shallow neural network $\mathbf{y} = \mathbf{f}[\mathbf{x}, \boldsymbol{\phi}]$ that maps a multi-dimensional input $\mathbf{x} \in \mathbb{R}^{D_i}$ to a multi-dimensional output $\mathbf{y} \in \mathbb{R}^{D_o}$ using $\mathbf{h} \in \mathbb{R}^D$ hidden units. Each hidden unit is computed as:

$$h_d = \text{a}\left[\theta_{d0} + \sum_{i=1}^{D_i} \theta_{di} x_i\right], \tag{3.11}$$

and these are combined linearly to create the output:

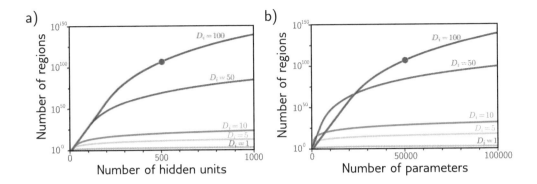

Figure 3.9 Linear regions vs. hidden units. a) Maximum possible regions as a function of the number of hidden units for five different input dimensions $D_i = \{1, 5, 10, 50, 100\}$. The number of regions increases rapidly in high dimensions; with $D = 500$ units and input size $D_i = 100$, there can be greater than 10^{107} regions (solid circle). b) The same data are plotted as a function of the number of parameters. The solid circle represents the same model as in panel (a) with $D = 500$ hidden units. This network has $51,001$ parameters and would be considered very small by modern standards.

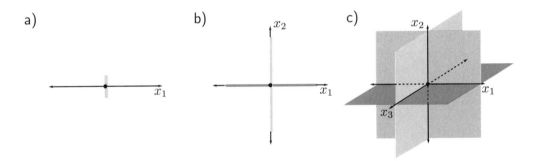

Figure 3.10 Number of linear regions vs. input dimensions. a) With a single input dimension, a model with one hidden unit creates one joint, which divides the axis into two linear regions. b) With two input dimensions, a model with two hidden units can divide the input space using two lines (here aligned with axes) to create four regions. c) With three input dimensions, a model with three hidden units can divide the input space using three planes (again aligned with axes) to create eight regions. Continuing this argument, it follows that a model with D_i input dimensions and D_i hidden units can divide the input space with D_i hyperplanes to create 2^{D_i} linear regions.

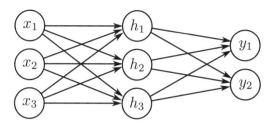

Problems 3.14–3.17

Notebook 3.4
Activation
functions

Figure 3.11 Visualization of neural network with three inputs and two outputs. This network has twenty parameters. There are fifteen slopes (indicated by arrows) and five offsets (not shown).

$$y_j = \phi_{j0} + \sum_{d=1}^{D} \phi_{jd}h_d, \tag{3.12}$$

where $a[\bullet]$ is a nonlinear activation function. The model has parameters $\phi = \{\theta_{\bullet\bullet}, \phi_{\bullet\bullet}\}$. Figure 3.11 shows an example with three inputs, three hidden units, and two outputs.

The activation function permits the model to describe nonlinear relations between input and the output, and as such, it must be nonlinear itself; with no activation function, or a linear activation function, the overall mapping from input to output would be restricted to be linear. Many different activation functions have been tried (see figure 3.13), but the most common choice is the ReLU (figure 3.1), which has the merit of being easily interpretable. With ReLU activations, the network divides the input space into convex polytopes defined by the intersections of hyperplanes computed by the "joints" in the ReLU functions. Each convex polytope contains a different linear function. The polytopes are the same for each output, but the linear functions they contain can differ.

3.5 Terminology

We conclude this chapter by introducing some terminology. Regrettably, neural networks have a lot of associated jargon. They are often referred to in terms of *layers*. The left of figure 3.12 is the *input layer*, the center is the *hidden layer*, and to the right is the *output layer*. We would say that the network in figure 3.12 has one hidden layer containing four hidden units. The hidden units themselves are sometimes referred to as *neurons*. When we pass data through the network, the values of the inputs to the hidden layer (i.e., before the ReLU functions are applied) are termed *pre-activations*. The values at the hidden layer (i.e., after the ReLU functions) are termed *activations*.

For historical reasons, any neural network with at least one hidden layer is also called a *multi-layer perceptron*, or *MLP* for short. Networks with one hidden layer (as described in this chapter) are sometimes referred to as *shallow neural networks*. Networks with multiple hidden layers (as described in the next chapter) are referred to as *deep neural networks*. Neural networks in which the connections form an acyclic graph (i.e., a graph with no loops, as in all the examples in this chapter) are referred to as *feed-forward networks*. If every element in one layer connects to every element in the next (as in all the examples in this chapter), the network is *fully connected*. These connections

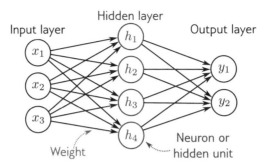

Figure 3.12 Terminology. A shallow network consists of an input layer, a hidden
layer, and an output layer. Each layer is connected to the next by forward connections (arrows). For this reason, these models are referred to as feed-forward
networks. When every variable in one layer connects to every variable in the
next, we call this a fully connected network. Each connection represents a slope
parameter in the underlying equation, and these parameters are termed weights.
The variables in the hidden layer are termed neurons or hidden units. The values
feeding into the hidden units are termed pre-activations, and the values at the
hidden units (i.e., after the ReLU function is applied) are termed activations.

represent slope parameters in the underlying equations and are referred to as *network
weights*. The offset parameters (not shown in figure 3.12) are called *biases*.

3.6 Summary

Shallow neural networks have one hidden layer. They (i) compute several linear functions
of the input, (ii) pass each result through an activation function, and then (iii) take a
linear combination of these activations to form the outputs. Shallow neural networks
make predictions $\mathbf{y}$ based on inputs $\mathbf{x}$ by dividing the input space into a continuous
surface of piecewise linear regions. With enough hidden units (neurons), shallow neural
networks can approximate any continuous function to arbitrary precision.

Chapter 4 discusses deep neural networks, which extend the models from this chapter
by adding more hidden layers. Chapters 5–7 describe how to train these models.

Notes

"Neural" networks: If the models in this chapter are just functions, why are they called
"neural networks"? The connection is, unfortunately, tenuous. Visualizations like figure 3.12
consist of nodes (inputs, hidden units, and outputs) that are densely connected to one another.
This bears a superficial similarity to neurons in the mammalian brain, which also have dense
connections. However, there is scant evidence that brain computation works in the same way
as neural networks, and it is unhelpful to think about biology going forward.

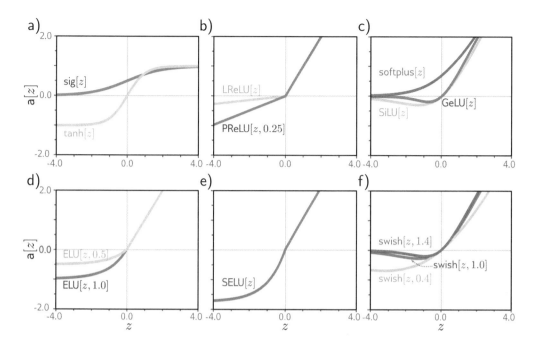

Figure 3.13 Activation functions. a) Logistic sigmoid and tanh functions. b) Leaky ReLU and parametric ReLU with parameter 0.25. c) SoftPlus, Gaussian error linear unit, and sigmoid linear unit. d) Exponential linear unit with parameters 0.5 and 1.0, e) Scaled exponential linear unit. f) Swish with parameters 0.4, 1.0, and 1.4.

History of neural networks: McCulloch & Pitts (1943) first came up with the notion of an artificial neuron that combined inputs to produce an output, but this model did not have a practical learning algorithm. Rosenblatt (1958) developed the *perceptron*, which linearly combined inputs and then thresholded them to make a yes/no decision. He also provided an algorithm to learn the weights from data. Minsky & Papert (1969) argued that the linear function was inadequate for general classification problems but that adding hidden layers with nonlinear activation functions (hence the term multi-layer perceptron) could allow the learning of more general input/output relations. However, they concluded that Rosenblatt's algorithm could not learn the parameters of such models. It was not until the 1980s that a practical algorithm (backpropagation, see chapter 7) was developed, and significant work on neural networks resumed. The history of neural networks is chronicled by Kurenkov (2020), Sejnowski (2018), and Schmidhuber (2022).

Activation functions: The ReLU function has been used as far back as Fukushima (1969). However, in the early days of neural networks, it was more common to use the logistic sigmoid or tanh activation functions (figure 3.13a). The ReLU was re-popularized by Jarrett et al. (2009), Nair & Hinton (2010), and Glorot et al. (2011) and is an important part of the success story of modern neural networks. It has the nice property that the derivative of the output with respect to the input is always one for inputs greater than zero. This contributes to the stability and efficiency of training (see chapter 7) and contrasts with the derivatives of sigmoid activation functions, which saturate (become close to zero) for large positive and large negative inputs.

However, the ReLU function has the disadvantage that its derivative is zero for negative inputs. If all the training examples produce negative inputs to a given ReLU function, then we cannot improve the parameters feeding into this ReLU during training. The gradient with respect to the incoming weights is locally flat, so we cannot "walk downhill." This is known as the *dying ReLU* problem. Many variations on the ReLU have been proposed to resolve this problem (figure 3.13b), including (i) the leaky ReLU (Maas et al., 2013), which also has a linear output for negative values with a smaller slope of 0.1, (ii) the parametric ReLU (He et al., 2015), which treats the slope of the negative portion as an unknown parameter, and (iii) the concatenated ReLU (Shang et al., 2016), which produces two outputs, one of which clips below zero (i.e., like a typical ReLU) and one of which clips above zero.

A variety of smooth functions have also been investigated (figure 3.13c–d), including the softplus function (Glorot et al., 2011), Gaussian error linear unit (Hendrycks & Gimpel, 2016), sigmoid linear unit (Hendrycks & Gimpel, 2016), and exponential linear unit (Clevert et al., 2015). Most of these are attempts to avoid the dying ReLU problem while limiting the gradient for negative values. Klambauer et al. (2017) introduced the scaled exponential linear unit (figure 3.13e), which is particularly interesting as it helps stabilize the variance of the activations when the input variance has a limited range (see section 7.5). Ramachandran et al. (2017) adopted an empirical approach to choosing an activation function. They searched the space of possible functions to find the one that performed best over a variety of supervised learning tasks. The optimal function was found to be $a[x] = x/(1 + \exp[-\beta x])$, where β is a learned parameter (figure 3.13f). They termed this function *Swish*. Interestingly, this was a rediscovery of activation functions previously proposed by Hendrycks & Gimpel (2016) and Elfwing et al. (2018). Howard et al. (2019) approximated Swish by the HardSwish function, which has a very similar shape but is faster to compute:

$$\text{HardSwish}[z] = \begin{cases} 0 & z < -3 \\ z(z+3)/6 & -3 \leq z \leq 3 \\ z & z > 3 \end{cases} . \tag{3.13}$$

There is no definitive answer as to which of these activations functions is empirically superior. However, the leaky ReLU, parameterized ReLU, and many of the continuous functions can be shown to provide minor performance gains over the ReLU in particular situations. We restrict attention to neural networks with the basic ReLU function for the rest of this book because it's easy to characterize the functions they create in terms of the number of linear regions.

Universal approximation theorem: The *width version* of this theorem states that there exists a network with one hidden layer containing a finite number of hidden units that can approximate any specified continuous function on a compact subset of $\mathbb{R}^n$ to arbitrary accuracy. This was proved by Cybenko (1989) for a class of sigmoid activations and was later shown to be true for a larger class of nonlinear activation functions (Hornik, 1991).

Number of linear regions: Consider a shallow network with $D_i \geq 2$-dimensional inputs and D hidden units. The number of linear regions is determined by the intersections of the D hyperplanes created by the "joints" in the ReLU functions (e.g., figure 3.8d–f). Each region is created by a different combination of the ReLU functions clipping or not clipping the input. The number of regions created by D hyperplanes in the $D_i \leq D$-dimensional input space was shown by Zaslavsky (1975) to be at most $\sum_{j=0}^{D_i} \binom{D}{j}$ (i.e., a sum of binomial coefficients). As a rule of thumb, shallow neural networks almost always have a larger number D of hidden units than input dimensions D_i and create between 2^{D_i} and 2^D linear regions.

Appendix B.2
Binomial
coefficient

Problem 3.18

Linear, affine, and nonlinear functions: Technically, a linear transformation f[•] is any function that obeys the principle of superposition, so $f[a+b] = f[a] + f[b]$. This definition implies that $f[2a] = 2f[a]$. The weighted sum $f[h_1, h_2, h_3] = \phi_1 h_1 + \phi_2 h_2 + \phi_3 h_3$ is linear, but once the offset (bias) is added so $f[h_1, h_2, h_3] = \phi_0 + \phi_1 h_1 + \phi_2 h_2 + \phi_3 h_3$, this is no longer true. To see this, consider that the output is doubled when we double the arguments of the former function. This is not the case for the latter function, which is more properly termed an *affine* function. However, it is common in machine learning to conflate these terms. We follow this convention in this book and refer to both as linear. All other functions we will encounter are nonlinear.

Problems

Problem 3.1 What kind of mapping from input to output would be created if the activation function in equation 3.1 was linear so that $a[z] = \psi_0 + \psi_1 z$? What kind of mapping would be created if the activation function was removed, so $a[z] = z$?

Problem 3.2 For each of the four linear regions in figure 3.3j, indicate which hidden units are inactive and which are active (i.e., which do and do not clip their inputs).

Problem 3.3* Derive expressions for the positions of the "joints" in function in figure 3.3j in terms of the ten parameters ϕ and the input x. Derive expressions for the slopes of the four linear regions.

Problem 3.4 Draw a version of figure 3.3 where the y-intercept and slope of the third hidden unit have changed as in figure 3.14c. Assume that the remaining parameters remain the same.

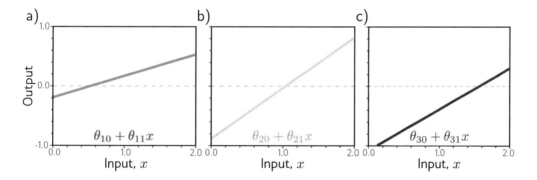

Figure 3.14 Processing in network with one input, three hidden units, and one output for problem 3.4. a–c) The input to each hidden unit is a linear function of the inputs. The first two are the same as in figure 3.3, but the last one differs.

Problem 3.5 Prove that the following property holds for $\alpha \in \mathbb{R}^+$:

$$\text{ReLU}[\alpha \cdot z] = \alpha \cdot \text{ReLU}[z]. \tag{3.14}$$

This is known as the *non-negative homogeneity* property of the ReLU function.

Problem 3.6 Following on from problem 3.5, what happens to the shallow network defined in equations 3.3 and 3.4 when we multiply the parameters θ_{10} and θ_{11} by a positive constant α and divide the slope ϕ_1 by the same parameter α? What happens if α is negative?

Problem 3.7 Consider fitting the model in equation 3.1 using a least squares loss function. Does this loss function have a unique minimum? i.e., is there a single "best" set of parameters?

Problem 3.8 Consider replacing the ReLU activation function with (i) the Heaviside step function heaviside[z], (ii) the hyperbolic tangent function tanh[z], and (iii) the rectangular function rect[z], where:

$$\text{heaviside}[z] = \begin{cases} 0 & z < 0 \\ 1 & z \geq 0 \end{cases} \qquad\qquad \text{rect}[z] = \begin{cases} 0 & z < 0 \\ 1 & 0 \leq z \leq 1 \,. \\ 0 & z > 1 \end{cases} \qquad (3.15)$$

Redraw a version of figure 3.3 for each of these functions. The original parameters were: $\phi = \{\phi_0, \phi_1, \phi_2, \phi_3, \theta_{10}, \theta_{11}, \theta_{20}, \theta_{21}, \theta_{30}, \theta_{31}\} = \{-0.23, -1.3, 1.3, 0.66, -0.2, 0.4, -0.9, 0.9, 1.1, -0.7\}$. Provide an informal description of the family of functions that can be created by neural networks with one input, three hidden units, and one output for each activation function.

Problem 3.9* Show that the third linear region in figure 3.3 has a slope that is the sum of the slopes of the first and fourth linear regions.

Problem 3.10 Consider a neural network with one input, one output, and three hidden units. The construction in figure 3.3 shows how this creates four linear regions. Under what circumstances could this network produce a function with fewer than four linear regions?

Problem 3.11* How many parameters does the model in figure 3.6 have?

Problem 3.12 How many parameters does the model in figure 3.7 have?

Problem 3.13 What is the activation pattern for each of the seven regions in figure 3.8? In other words, which hidden units are active (pass the input) and which are inactive (clip the input) for each region?

Problem 3.14 Write out the equations that define the network in figure 3.11. There should be three equations to compute the three hidden units from the inputs and two equations to compute the outputs from the hidden units.

Problem 3.15* What is the maximum possible number of 3D linear regions that can be created by the network in figure 3.11?

Problem 3.16 Write out the equations for a network with two inputs, four hidden units, and three outputs. Draw this model in the style of figure 3.11.

Problem 3.17* Equations 3.11 and 3.12 define a general neural network with D_i inputs, one hidden layer containing D hidden units, and D_o outputs. Find an expression for the number of parameters in the model in terms of D_i, D, and D_o.

Problem 3.18* Show that the maximum number of regions created by a shallow network with $D_i = 2$-dimensional input, $D_o = 1$-dimensional output, and $D = 3$ hidden units is seven, as in figure 3.8j. Use the result of Zaslavsky (1975) that the maximum number of regions created by partitioning a D_i-dimensional space with D hyperplanes is $\sum_{j=0}^{D_i} \binom{D}{j}$. What is the maximum number of regions if we add two more hidden units to this model, so $D = 5$?

Chapter 4

Deep neural networks

The last chapter described shallow neural networks, which have a single hidden layer. This chapter introduces deep neural networks, which have more than one hidden layer. With ReLU activation functions, both shallow and deep networks describe piecewise linear mappings from input to output.

As the number of hidden units increases, shallow neural networks improve their descriptive power. Indeed, with enough hidden units, shallow networks can describe arbitrarily complex functions in high dimensions. However, it turns out that for some functions, the required number of hidden units is impractically large. Deep networks can produce many more linear regions than shallow networks for a given number of parameters. Hence, from a practical standpoint, they can be used to describe a broader family of functions.

4.1 Composing neural networks

To gain insight into the behavior of deep neural networks, we first consider composing two shallow networks so the output of the first becomes the input of the second. Consider two shallow networks with three hidden units each (figure 4.1a). The first network takes an input x and returns output y and is defined by:

$$
\begin{aligned}
h_1 &= \text{a}[\theta_{10} + \theta_{11}x] \\
h_2 &= \text{a}[\theta_{20} + \theta_{21}x] \\
h_3 &= \text{a}[\theta_{30} + \theta_{31}x],
\end{aligned}
\tag{4.1}
$$

and

$$
y = \phi_0 + \phi_1 h_1 + \phi_2 h_2 + \phi_3 h_3.
\tag{4.2}
$$

The second network takes y as input and returns y' and is defined by:

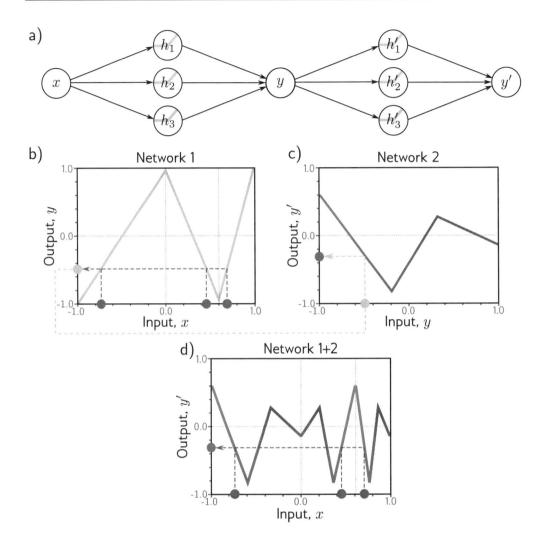

Figure 4.1 Composing two single-layer networks with three hidden units each. a) The output y of the first network constitutes the input to the second network. b) The first network maps inputs $x \in [-1, 1]$ to outputs $y \in [-1, 1]$ using a function comprising three linear regions that are chosen so that they alternate the sign of their slope (fourth linear region is outside range of graph). Multiple inputs x (gray circles) now map to the same output y (cyan circle). c) The second network defines a function comprising three linear regions that takes y and returns y' (i.e., the cyan circle is mapped to the brown circle). d) The combined effect of these two functions when composed is that (i) three different inputs x are mapped to any given value of y by the first network and (ii) are processed in the same way by the second network; the result is that the function defined by the second network in panel (c) is duplicated three times, variously flipped and rescaled according to the slope of the regions of panel (b).

$$
\begin{aligned}
h_1' &= \mathrm{a}[\theta_{10}' + \theta_{11}'y] \\
h_2' &= \mathrm{a}[\theta_{20}' + \theta_{21}'y] \\
h_3' &= \mathrm{a}[\theta_{30}' + \theta_{31}'y],
\end{aligned}
\tag{4.3}
$$

and

$$
y' = \phi_0' + \phi_1'h_1' + \phi_2'h_2' + \phi_3'h_3'.
\tag{4.4}
$$

With ReLU activations, this model also describes a family of piecewise linear functions. However, the number of linear regions is potentially greater than for a shallow network with six hidden units. To see this, consider choosing the first network to produce three alternating regions of positive and negative slope (figure 4.1b). This means that three different ranges of x are mapped to the same output range $y \in [-1, 1]$, and the subsequent mapping from this range of y to y' is applied three times. The overall effect is that the function defined by the second network is duplicated three times to create nine linear regions. The same principle applies in higher dimensions (figure 4.2).

Problem 4.1

Notebook 4.1
Composing
networks

A different way to think about composing networks is that the first network "folds" the input space x back onto itself so that multiple inputs generate the same output. Then the second network applies a function, which is replicated at all points that were folded on top of one another (figure 4.3).

4.2 From composing networks to deep networks

The previous section showed that we could create complex functions by passing the output of one shallow neural network into a second network. We now show that this is a special case of a deep network with two hidden layers.

The output of the first network ($y = \phi_0 + \phi_1h_1 + \phi_2h_2 + \phi_3h_3$) is a linear combination of the activations at the hidden units. The first operations of the second network (equation 4.3 in which we calculate $\theta_{10}' + \theta_{11}'y$, $\theta_{20}' + \theta_{21}'y$, and $\theta_{30}' + \theta_{31}'y$) are linear in the output of the first network. Applying one linear function to another yields another linear function. Substituting the expression for y into equation 4.3 gives:

$$
\begin{aligned}
h_1' &= \mathrm{a}[\theta_{10}' + \theta_{11}'y] &= \mathrm{a}[\theta_{10}' + \theta_{11}'\phi_0 + \theta_{11}'\phi_1h_1 + \theta_{11}'\phi_2h_2 + \theta_{11}'\phi_3h_3] \\
h_2' &= \mathrm{a}[\theta_{20}' + \theta_{21}'y] &= \mathrm{a}[\theta_{20}' + \theta_{21}'\phi_0 + \theta_{21}'\phi_1h_1 + \theta_{21}'\phi_2h_2 + \theta_{21}'\phi_3h_3] \\
h_3' &= \mathrm{a}[\theta_{30}' + \theta_{31}'y] &= \mathrm{a}[\theta_{30}' + \theta_{31}'\phi_0 + \theta_{31}'\phi_1h_1 + \theta_{31}'\phi_2h_2 + \theta_{31}'\phi_3h_3],
\end{aligned}
\tag{4.5}
$$

which we can rewrite as:

$$
\begin{aligned}
h_1' &= \mathrm{a}[\psi_{10} + \psi_{11}h_1 + \psi_{12}h_2 + \psi_{13}h_3] \\
h_2' &= \mathrm{a}[\psi_{20} + \psi_{21}h_1 + \psi_{22}h_2 + \psi_{23}h_3] \\
h_3' &= \mathrm{a}[\psi_{30} + \psi_{31}h_1 + \psi_{32}h_2 + \psi_{33}h_3],
\end{aligned}
\tag{4.6}
$$

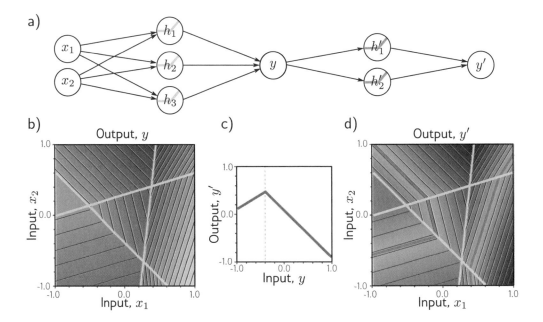

Figure 4.2 Composing neural networks with a 2D input. a) The first network (from figure 3.8) has three hidden units and takes two inputs x_1 and x_2 and returns a scalar output y. This is passed into a second network with two hidden units to produce y'. b) The first network produces a function consisting of seven linear regions, one of which is flat. c) The second network defines a function comprising two linear regions in $y \in [-1, 1]$. d) When these networks are composed, each of the six non-flat regions from the first network is divided into two new regions by the second network to create a total of 13 linear regions.

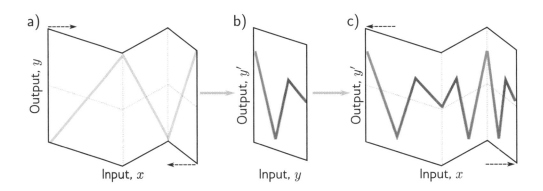

Figure 4.3 Deep networks as folding input space. a) One way to think about the first network from figure 4.1 is that it "folds" the input space back on top of itself. b) The second network applies its function to the folded space. c) The final output is revealed by "unfolding" again.

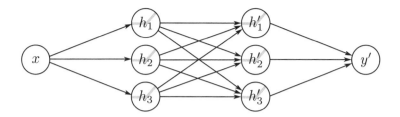

Figure 4.4 Neural network with one input, one output, and two hidden layers, each containing three hidden units.

where $\psi_{10} = \theta'_{10} + \theta'_{11}\phi_0, \psi_{11} = \theta'_{11}\phi_1, \psi_{12} = \theta'_{11}\phi_2$ and so on. The result is a network with two hidden layers (figure 4.4).

It follows that a network with two layers can represent the family of functions created by passing the output of one single-layer network into another. In fact, it represents a broader family because in equation 4.6, the nine slope parameters $\psi_{11}, \psi_{21}, \ldots, \psi_{33}$ can take arbitrary values, whereas, in equation 4.5, these parameters are constrained to be the outer product $[\theta'_{11}, \theta'_{21}, \theta'_{31}]^T[\phi_1, \phi_2, \phi_3]$.

4.3 Deep neural networks

In the previous section, we showed that composing two shallow networks yields a special case of a deep network with two hidden layers. Now we consider the general case of a deep network with two hidden layers, each containing three hidden units (figure 4.4). The first layer is defined by:

$$\begin{aligned} h_1 &= \text{a}[\theta_{10} + \theta_{11}x] \\ h_2 &= \text{a}[\theta_{20} + \theta_{21}x] \\ h_3 &= \text{a}[\theta_{30} + \theta_{31}x], \end{aligned} \tag{4.7}$$

the second layer by:

$$\begin{aligned} h'_1 &= \text{a}[\psi_{10} + \psi_{11}h_1 + \psi_{12}h_2 + \psi_{13}h_3] \\ h'_2 &= \text{a}[\psi_{20} + \psi_{21}h_1 + \psi_{22}h_2 + \psi_{23}h_3] \\ h'_3 &= \text{a}[\psi_{30} + \psi_{31}h_1 + \psi_{32}h_2 + \psi_{33}h_3], \end{aligned} \tag{4.8}$$

and the output by:

$$y' = \phi'_0 + \phi'_1 h'_1 + \phi'_2 h'_2 + \phi'_3 h'_3. \tag{4.9}$$

Notebook 4.2
Clipping
functions

Considering these equations leads to another way to think about how the network constructs an increasingly complicated function (figure 4.5):

1. The three hidden units h_1, h_2, and h_3 in the first layer are computed as usual by forming linear functions of the input and passing these through ReLU activation functions (equation 4.7).

2. The pre-activations at the second layer are computed by taking three new linear functions of these hidden units (arguments of the activation functions in equation 4.8). At this point, we effectively have a shallow network with three outputs; we have computed three piecewise linear functions with the "joints" between linear regions in the same places (see figure 3.6).

3. At the second hidden layer, another ReLU function $a[\bullet]$ is applied to each function (equation 4.8), which clips them and adds new "joints" to each.

4. The final output is a linear combination of these hidden units (equation 4.9).

In conclusion, we can either think of each layer as "folding" the input space or as creating new functions, which are clipped (creating new regions) and then recombined. The former view emphasizes the dependencies in the output function but not how clipping creates new joints, and the latter has the opposite emphasis. Ultimately, both descriptions provide only partial insight into how deep neural networks operate. Regardless, it's important not to lose sight of the fact that this is still merely an equation relating input x to output y'. Indeed, we can combine equations 4.7–4.9 to get one expression:

$$
\begin{aligned}
y' = \ & \phi_0' + \phi_1' a \left[\psi_{10} + \psi_{11} a[\theta_{10} + \theta_{11} x] + \psi_{12} a[\theta_{20} + \theta_{21} x] + \psi_{13} a[\theta_{30} + \theta_{31} x] \right] \\
& + \phi_2' a[\psi_{20} + \psi_{21} a[\theta_{10} + \theta_{11} x] + \psi_{22} a[\theta_{20} + \theta_{21} x] + \psi_{23} a[\theta_{30} + \theta_{31} x]] \\
& + \phi_3' a[\psi_{30} + \psi_{31} a[\theta_{10} + \theta_{11} x] + \psi_{32} a[\theta_{20} + \theta_{21} x] + \psi_{33} a[\theta_{30} + \theta_{31} x]],
\end{aligned}
$$

$$(4.10)$$

although this is admittedly rather difficult to understand.

4.3.1 Hyperparameters

We can extend the deep network construction to more than two hidden layers; modern networks might have more than a hundred layers with thousands of hidden units at each layer. The number of hidden units in each layer is referred to as the *width* of the network, and the number of hidden layers as the *depth*. The total number of hidden units is a measure of the network's *capacity*.

We denote the number of layers as K and the number of hidden units in each layer as $D_1, D_2, \ldots, D_K$. These are examples of *hyperparameters*. They are quantities chosen before we learn the model parameters (i.e., the slope and intercept terms). For fixed hyperparameters (e.g., $K = 2$ layers with $D_k = 3$ hidden units in each), the model describes a family of functions, and the parameters determine the particular function. Hence, when we also consider the hyperparameters, we can think of neural networks as representing a family of families of functions relating input to output.

Problem 4.2

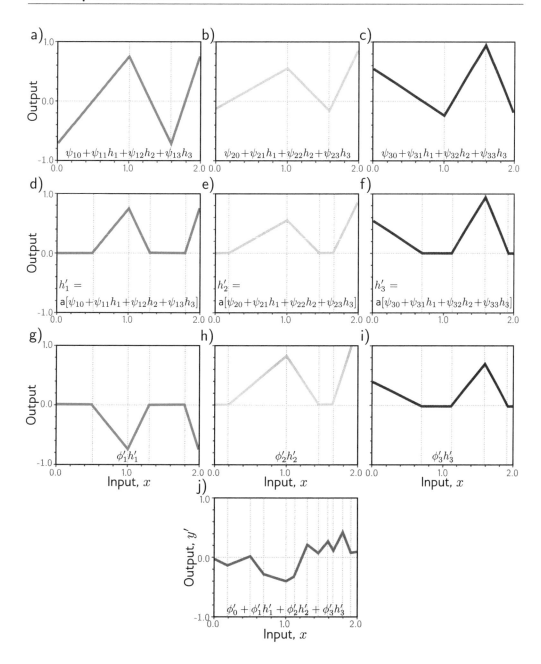

Figure 4.5 Computation for the deep network in figure 4.4. a–c) The inputs to the second hidden layer (i.e., the pre-activations) are three piecewise linear functions where the "joints" between the linear regions are at the same places (see figure 3.6). d–f) Each piecewise linear function is clipped to zero by the ReLU activation function. g–i) These clipped functions are then weighted with parameters ϕ'_1, ϕ'_2, and ϕ'_3, respectively. j) Finally, the clipped and weighted functions are summed and an offset ϕ'_0 that controls the overall height is added.

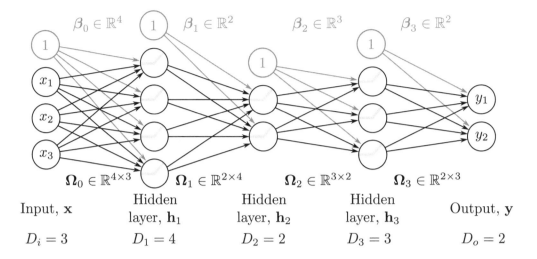

Figure 4.6 Matrix notation for network with $D_i = 3$-dimensional input $\mathbf{x}$, $D_o = 2$-dimensional output $\mathbf{y}$, and $K = 3$ hidden layers $\mathbf{h}_1, \mathbf{h}_2$, and $\mathbf{h}_3$ of dimensions $D_1 = 4$, $D_2 = 2$, and $D_3 = 3$ respectively. The weights are stored in matrices $\boldsymbol{\Omega}_k$ that pre-multiply the activations from the preceding layer to create the pre-activations at the subsequent layer. For example, the weight matrix $\boldsymbol{\Omega}_1$ that computes the pre-activations at $\mathbf{h}_2$ from the activations at $\mathbf{h}_1$ has dimension 2×4. It is applied to the four hidden units in layer one and creates the inputs to the two hidden units at layer two. The biases are stored in vectors $\boldsymbol{\beta}_k$ and have the dimension of the layer into which they feed. For example, the bias vector $\boldsymbol{\beta}_2$ is length three because layer $\mathbf{h}_3$ contains three hidden units.

4.4   Matrix notation

Appendix B.3
Matrices

We have seen that a deep neural network consists of linear transformations alternating with activation functions. We could equivalently describe equations 4.7–4.9 in matrix notation as:

$$\begin{bmatrix} h_1 \\ h_2 \\ h_3 \end{bmatrix} = \mathbf{a}\left[\begin{bmatrix} \theta_{10} \\ \theta_{20} \\ \theta_{30} \end{bmatrix} + \begin{bmatrix} \theta_{11} \\ \theta_{21} \\ \theta_{31} \end{bmatrix} x\right], \tag{4.11}$$

$$\begin{bmatrix} h'_1 \\ h'_2 \\ h'_3 \end{bmatrix} = \mathbf{a}\left[\begin{bmatrix} \psi_{10} \\ \psi_{20} \\ \psi_{30} \end{bmatrix} + \begin{bmatrix} \psi_{11} & \psi_{12} & \psi_{13} \\ \psi_{21} & \psi_{22} & \psi_{23} \\ \psi_{31} & \psi_{32} & \psi_{33} \end{bmatrix} \begin{bmatrix} h_1 \\ h_2 \\ h_3 \end{bmatrix}\right], \tag{4.12}$$

and

$$y' = \phi'_0 + \begin{bmatrix} \phi'_1 & \phi'_2 & \phi'_3 \end{bmatrix} \begin{bmatrix} h'_1 \\ h'_2 \\ h'_3 \end{bmatrix}, \tag{4.13}$$

or even more compactly in matrix notation as:

$$
\begin{aligned}
\mathbf{h} &= \mathbf{a}\left[\boldsymbol{\theta}_0 + \boldsymbol{\theta}x\right] \\
\mathbf{h}' &= \mathbf{a}\left[\boldsymbol{\psi}_0 + \boldsymbol{\Psi}\mathbf{h}\right] \\
y' &= \phi_0' + \boldsymbol{\phi}'\mathbf{h}',
\end{aligned}
\tag{4.14}
$$

where, in each case, the function $\mathbf{a}[\bullet]$ applies the activation function separately to every element of its vector input.

4.4.1 General formulation

This notation becomes cumbersome for networks with many layers. Hence, from now on, we will describe the vector of hidden units at layer k as $\mathbf{h}_k$, the vector of biases (intercepts) that contribute to hidden layer $k+1$ as $\boldsymbol{\beta}_k$, and the weights (slopes) that are applied to the kth layer and contribute to the $(k+1)^{th}$ layer as $\boldsymbol{\Omega}_k$. A general deep network $\mathbf{y} = \mathrm{f}[\mathbf{x}, \boldsymbol{\phi}]$ with K layers can now be written as:

$$
\begin{aligned}
\mathbf{h}_1 &= \mathbf{a}[\boldsymbol{\beta}_0 + \boldsymbol{\Omega}_0\mathbf{x}] \\
\mathbf{h}_2 &= \mathbf{a}[\boldsymbol{\beta}_1 + \boldsymbol{\Omega}_1\mathbf{h}_1] \\
\mathbf{h}_3 &= \mathbf{a}[\boldsymbol{\beta}_2 + \boldsymbol{\Omega}_2\mathbf{h}_2] \\
&\ \ \vdots \\
\mathbf{h}_K &= \mathbf{a}[\boldsymbol{\beta}_{K-1} + \boldsymbol{\Omega}_{K-1}\mathbf{h}_{K-1}] \\
\mathbf{y} &= \boldsymbol{\beta}_K + \boldsymbol{\Omega}_K\mathbf{h}_K.
\end{aligned}
\tag{4.15}
$$

The parameters $\boldsymbol{\phi}$ of this model comprise all of these weight matrices and bias vectors $\boldsymbol{\phi} = \{\boldsymbol{\beta}_k, \boldsymbol{\Omega}_k\}_{k=0}^K$.

If the kth layer has D_k hidden units, then the bias vector $\boldsymbol{\beta}_{k-1}$ will be of size D_k. The last bias vector $\boldsymbol{\beta}_K$ has the size D_o of the output. The first weight matrix $\boldsymbol{\Omega}_0$ has size $D_1 \times D_i$ where D_i is the size of the input. The last weight matrix $\boldsymbol{\Omega}_K$ is $D_o \times D_K$, and the remaining matrices $\boldsymbol{\Omega}_k$ are $D_{k+1} \times D_k$ (figure 4.6).

We can equivalently write the network as a single function:

$$
\mathbf{y} = \boldsymbol{\beta}_K + \boldsymbol{\Omega}_K\mathbf{a}\left[\boldsymbol{\beta}_{K-1} + \boldsymbol{\Omega}_{K-1}\mathbf{a}\left[\ldots \boldsymbol{\beta}_2 + \boldsymbol{\Omega}_2\mathbf{a}\left[\boldsymbol{\beta}_1 + \boldsymbol{\Omega}_1\mathbf{a}\left[\boldsymbol{\beta}_0 + \boldsymbol{\Omega}_0\mathbf{x}\right]\right]\ldots\right]\right].
\tag{4.16}
$$

Notebook 4.3 Deep networks

Problems 4.3–4.6

4.5 Shallow vs. deep neural networks

Chapter 3 discussed shallow networks (with a single hidden layer), and here we have described deep networks (with multiple hidden layers). We now compare these models.

4.5.1   Ability to approximate different functions

In section 3.2, we argued that shallow neural networks with enough capacity (hidden units) could model any continuous function arbitrarily closely. In this chapter, we saw that a deep network with two hidden layers could represent the composition of two shallow networks. If the second of these networks computes the identity function, then this deep network replicates a single shallow network. Hence, it can also approximate any continuous function arbitrarily closely given sufficient capacity.

Problem 4.7

4.5.2   Number of linear regions per parameter

Problems 4.8–4.11

A shallow network with one input, one output, and $D > 2$ hidden units can create up to $D + 1$ linear regions and is defined by $3D + 1$ parameters. A deep network with one input, one output, and K layers of $D > 2$ hidden units can create a function with up to $(D + 1)^K$ linear regions using $3D + 1 + (K - 1)D(D + 1)$ parameters.

Figure 4.7a shows how the maximum number of linear regions increases as a function of the number of parameters for networks mapping scalar input x to scalar output y. Deep neural networks create much more complex functions for a fixed parameter budget. This effect is magnified as the number of input dimensions D_i increases (figure 4.7b), although computing the maximum number of regions is less straightforward.

This seems attractive, but the flexibility of the functions is still limited by the number of parameters. Deep networks can create extremely large numbers of linear regions, but these contain complex dependencies and symmetries. We saw some of these when we considered deep networks as "folding" the input space (figure 4.3). So, it's not clear that the greater number of regions is an advantage unless (i) there are similar symmetries in the real-world functions that we wish to approximate or (ii) we have reason to believe that the mapping from input to output really does involve a composition of simpler functions.

4.5.3   Depth efficiency

Both deep and shallow networks can model arbitrary functions, but some functions can be approximated much more efficiently with deep networks. Functions have been identified that require a shallow network with exponentially more hidden units to achieve an equivalent approximation to that of a deep network. This phenomenon is referred to as the *depth efficiency* of neural networks. This property is also attractive, but it's not clear that the real-world functions that we want to approximate fall into this category.

4.5.4   Large, structured inputs

We have discussed fully connected networks where every element of each layer contributes to every element of the subsequent one. However, these are not practical for large,

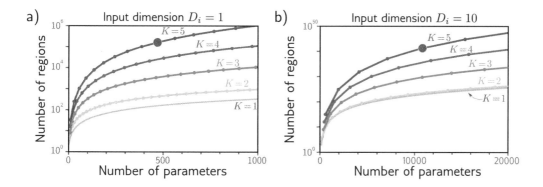

Figure 4.7 The maximum number of linear regions for neural networks increases rapidly with the network depth. a) Network with $D_i = 1$ input. Each curve represents a fixed number of hidden layers K, as we vary the number of hidden units D per layer. For a fixed parameter budget (horizontal position), deeper networks produce more linear regions than shallower ones. A network with $K = 5$ layers and $D = 10$ hidden units per layer has 471 parameters (highlighted point) and can produce 161,051 regions. b) Network with $D_i = 10$ inputs. Each subsequent point along a curve represents ten hidden units. Here, a model with $K = 5$ layers and $D = 50$ hidden units per layer has 10,801 parameters (highlighted point) and can create more than 10^{40} linear regions.

structured inputs like images, where the input might comprise $\sim 10^6$ pixels. The number of parameters would be prohibitive, and moreover, we want different parts of the image to be processed similarly; there is no point in independently learning to recognize the same object at every possible position in the image.

The solution is to process local image regions in parallel and then gradually integrate information from increasingly large regions. This kind of local-to-global processing is difficult to specify without using multiple layers (see chapter 10).

4.5.5 Training and generalization

A further possible advantage of deep networks over shallow networks is their ease of fitting; it is usually easier to train moderately deep networks than to train shallow ones (see figure 20.2). It may be that over-parameterized deep models (i.e., those with more parameters than training examples) have a large family of roughly equivalent solutions that are easy to find. However, as we add more hidden layers, training becomes more difficult again. Many methods have been developed to mitigate this problem (see chapter 11).

Deep neural networks also seem to generalize to new data better than shallow ones. In practice, the best results for most tasks have been achieved using networks with tens or hundreds of layers. Neither of these phenomena are well understood, and we return to them in chapter 20.

4.6   Summary

In this chapter, we first considered what happens when we compose two shallow networks. We argued that the first network "folds" the input space, and the second network then applies a piecewise linear function. The effects of the second network are duplicated where the input space is folded onto itself.

We then showed that this composition of shallow networks is a special case of a deep network with two layers. We interpreted the ReLU functions in each layer as clipping the input functions in multiple places and creating more "joints" in the output function. We introduced the idea of hyperparameters, which for the networks we've seen so far, comprise the number of hidden layers and the number of hidden units in each.

Finally, we compared shallow and deep networks. We saw that (i) both networks can approximate any function given enough capacity, (ii) deep networks produce many more linear regions per parameter, (iii) some functions can be approximated much more efficiently by deep networks, (iv) large, structured inputs like images are best processed in multiple stages, and (v) in practice, the best results for most tasks are achieved using deep networks with many layers.

Now that we understand deep and shallow network models, we turn our attention to training them. In the next chapter, we discuss loss functions. For any given parameter values ϕ, the loss function returns a single number that indicates the mismatch between the model outputs and the ground truth predictions for a training dataset. In chapters 6 and 7, we deal with the training process itself, in which we seek the parameter values that minimize this loss.

Notes

Deep learning: It has long been understood that it is possible to build more complex functions by composing shallow neural networks or developing networks with more than one hidden layer. Indeed, the term "deep learning" was first used by Dechter (1986). However, interest was limited due to practical concerns; it was not possible to train such networks well. The modern era of deep learning was kick-started by startling improvements in image classification reported by Krizhevsky et al. (2012). This sudden progress was arguably due to the confluence of four factors: larger training datasets, improved processing power for training, the use of the ReLU activation function, and the use of stochastic gradient descent (see chapter 6). LeCun et al. (2015) present an overview of early advances in the modern era of deep learning.

Number of linear regions: For deep networks using a total of D hidden units with ReLU activations, the upper bound on the number of regions is 2^D (Montúfar et al., 2014). The same authors show that a deep ReLU network with D_i-dimensional input and K layers, each containing $D \geq D_i$ hidden units, has $\mathcal{O}\left((D/D_i)^{(K-1)D_i}D^{D_i}\right)$ linear regions. Montúfar (2017), Arora et al. (2016) and Serra et al. (2018) all provide tighter upper bounds that consider the possibility that each layer has different numbers of hidden units. Serra et al. (2018) provide an algorithm that counts the number of linear regions in a neural network, although it is only practical for very small networks.

If the number of hidden units D in each of the K layers is the same, and D is an integer multiple of the input dimensionality D_i, then the maximum number of linear regions N_r can be computed exactly and is:

$$N_r = \left(\frac{D}{D_i} + 1 \right)^{D_i(K-1)} \cdot \sum_{j=0}^{D_i} \binom{D}{j}. \tag{4.17}$$

The first term in this expression corresponds to the first $K-1$ layers of the network, which can be thought of as repeatedly folding the input space. However, we now need to devote D/D_i hidden units to each input dimension to create these folds. The last term in this equation (a sum of binomial coefficients) is the number of regions that a shallow network can create and is attributable to the last layer. For further information, consult Montúfar et al. (2014), Pascanu et al. (2013), and Montúfar (2017).

Appendix B.2
Binomial coefficient

Universal approximation theorem: We argued in section 4.5.1 that if the layers of a deep network have enough hidden units, then the width version of the universal approximation theorem applies: there exists a network that can approximate any given continuous function on a compact subset of $\mathbb{R}^{D_i}$ to arbitrary accuracy. Lu et al. (2017) proved that there exists a network with ReLU activation functions and at least $D_i + 4$ hidden units in each layer can approximate any specified D_i-dimensional Lebesgue integrable function to arbitrary accuracy given enough layers. This is known as the *depth version* of the universal approximation theorem.

Depth efficiency: Several results show that there are functions that can be realized by deep networks but not by any shallow network whose capacity is bounded above exponentially. In other words, it would take an exponentially larger number of units in a shallow network to describe these functions accurately. This is known as the *depth efficiency* of neural networks.

Telgarsky (2016) shows that for any integer k, it is possible to construct networks with one input, one output, and $\mathcal{O}[k^3]$ layers of constant width, which cannot be realized with $\mathcal{O}[k]$ layers and less than 2^k width. Perhaps surprisingly, Eldan & Shamir (2016) showed that when there are multivariate inputs, there is a three-layer network that cannot be realized by any two-layer network if the capacity is sub-exponential in the input dimension. Cohen et al. (2016), Safran & Shamir (2017), and Poggio et al. (2017) also demonstrate functions that deep networks can approximate efficiently, but shallow ones cannot. Liang & Srikant (2016) show that for a broad class of functions, including univariate functions, shallow networks require exponentially more hidden units than deep networks for a given upper bound on the approximation error.

Width efficiency: Lu et al. (2017) investigate whether there are wide shallow networks (i.e., shallow networks with lots of hidden units) that cannot be realized by narrow networks whose depth is not substantially larger. They show that there exist classes of wide, shallow networks that can only be expressed by narrow networks with polynomial depth. This is known as the *width efficiency* of neural networks. This polynomial lower bound on width is less restrictive than the exponential lower bound on depth, suggesting that depth is more important. Vardi et al. (2022) subsequently showed that the price for making the width small is only a linear increase in the network depth for networks with ReLU activations.

Problems

Problem 4.1[*] Consider composing the two neural networks in figure 4.8. Draw a plot of the relationship between the input x and output y' for $x \in [-1, 1]$.

Problem 4.2 Identify the four hyperparameters in figure 4.6.

Problem 4.3 Using the non-negative homogeneity property of the ReLU function (see problem 3.5), show that:

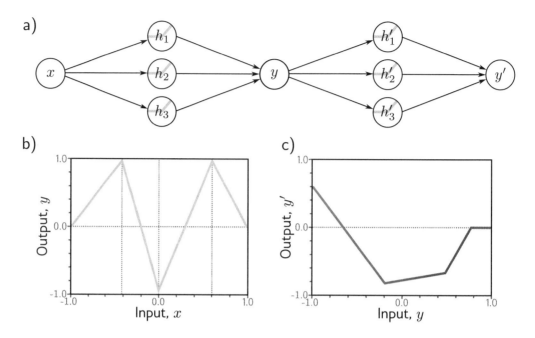

Figure 4.8 Composition of two networks for problem 4.1. a) The output y of the first network becomes the input to the second. b) The first network computes this function with output values $y \in [-1, 1]$. c) The second network computes this function on the input range $y \in [-1, 1]$.

$$\text{ReLU}\left[\boldsymbol{\beta}_1 + \lambda_1 \cdot \boldsymbol{\Omega}_1 \text{ReLU}\left[\boldsymbol{\beta}_0 + \lambda_0 \cdot \boldsymbol{\Omega}_0 \mathbf{x}\right]\right] = \lambda_0 \lambda_1 \cdot \text{ReLU}\left[\frac{1}{\lambda_0 \lambda_1}\boldsymbol{\beta}_1 + \boldsymbol{\Omega}_1 \text{ReLU}\left[\frac{1}{\lambda_0}\boldsymbol{\beta}_0 + \boldsymbol{\Omega}_0 \mathbf{x}\right]\right],$$
(4.18)

where λ_0 and λ_1 are non-negative scalars. From this, we see that the weight matrices can be rescaled by any magnitude as long as the biases are also adjusted, and the scale factors can be re-applied at the end of the network.

Problem 4.4 Write out the equations for a deep neural network that takes $D_i = 5$ inputs, $D_o = 4$ outputs and has three hidden layers of sizes $D_1 = 20$, $D_2 = 10$, and $D_3 = 7$, respectively, in both the forms of equations 4.15 and 4.16. What are the sizes of each weight matrix $\boldsymbol{\Omega}_\bullet$ and bias vector $\boldsymbol{\beta}_\bullet$?

Problem 4.5 Consider a deep neural network with $D_i = 5$ inputs, $D_o = 1$ output, and $K = 20$ hidden layers containing $D = 30$ hidden units each. What is the depth of this network? What is the width?

Problem 4.6 Consider a network with $D_i = 1$ input, $D_o = 1$ output, and $K = 10$ layers, with $D = 10$ hidden units in each. Would the number of weights increase more if we increased the depth by one or the width by one? Provide your reasoning.

Problem 4.7 Choose values for the parameters $\phi = \{\phi_0, \phi_1, \phi_2, \phi_3, \theta_{10}, \theta_{11}, \theta_{20}, \theta_{21}, \theta_{30}, \theta_{31}\}$ for the shallow neural network in equation 3.1 (with ReLU activation functions) that will define an identity function over a finite range $x \in [a, b]$.

Problem 4.8* Figure 4.9 shows the activations in the three hidden units of a shallow network (as in figure 3.3). The slopes in the hidden units are 1.0, 1.0, and -1.0, respectively, and the "joints" in the hidden units are at positions 1/6, 2/6, and 4/6. Find values of ϕ_0, ϕ_1, ϕ_2, and ϕ_3 that will combine the hidden unit activations as $\phi_0 + \phi_1 h_1 + \phi_2 h_2 + \phi_3 h_3$ to create a function with four linear regions that oscillate between output values of zero and one. The slope of the leftmost region should be positive, the next one negative, and so on. How many linear regions will we create if we compose this network with itself? How many will we create if we compose it with itself K times?

Problem 4.9* Following problem 4.8, is it possible to create a function with three linear regions that oscillates back and forth between output values of zero and one using a shallow network with two hidden units? Is it possible to create a function with five linear regions that oscillates in the same way using a shallow network with four hidden units?

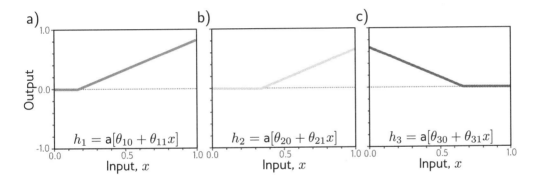

Figure 4.9 Hidden unit activations for problem 4.8. a) First hidden unit has a joint at position $x = 1/6$ and a slope of one in the active region. b) Second hidden unit has a joint at position $x = 2/6$ and a slope of one in the active region. c) Third hidden unit has a joint at position $x = 4/6$ and a slope of minus one in the active region.

Problem 4.10 Consider a deep neural network with a single input, a single output, and K hidden layers, each of which contains D hidden units. Show that this network will have a total of $3D + 1 + (K - 1)D(D + 1)$ parameters.

Problem 4.11* Consider two neural networks that map a scalar input x to a scalar output y. The first network is shallow and has $D = 95$ hidden units. The second is deep and has $K = 10$ layers, each containing $D = 5$ hidden units. How many parameters does each network have? How many linear regions can each network make (see equation 4.17)? Which would run faster?

Chapter 5

Loss functions

The last three chapters described linear regression, shallow neural networks, and deep neural networks. Each represents a family of functions that map input to output, where the particular member of the family is determined by the model parameters ϕ. When we train these models, we seek the parameters that produce the best possible mapping from input to output for the task we are considering. This chapter defines what is meant by the "best possible" mapping.

That definition requires a training dataset $\{\mathbf{x}_i, \mathbf{y}_i\}$ of input/output pairs. A *loss function* or *cost function* $L[\phi]$ returns a single number that describes the mismatch between the model predictions $\mathbf{f}[\mathbf{x}_i, \phi]$ and their corresponding ground-truth outputs $\mathbf{y}_i$. During training, we seek parameter values ϕ that minimize the loss and hence map the training inputs to the outputs as closely as possible. We saw one example of a loss function in chapter 2; the least squares loss function is suitable for univariate regression problems for which the target is a real number $y \in \mathbb{R}$. It computes the sum of the squares of the deviations between the model predictions $\mathrm{f}[\mathbf{x}_i, \phi]$ and the true values y_i.

Appendix A
Number sets

This chapter provides a framework that both justifies the choice of the least squares criterion for real-valued outputs and allows us to build loss functions for other prediction types. We consider *binary classification*, where the prediction $y \in \{0, 1\}$ is one of two categories, *multiclass classification*, where the prediction $y \in \{1, 2, \ldots, K\}$ is one of K categories, and more complex cases. In the following two chapters, we address model training, where the goal is to find the parameter values that minimize these loss functions.

5.1 Maximum likelihood

Appendix C.1.3
Conditional
probability

In this section, we develop a recipe for constructing loss functions. Consider a model $\mathbf{f}[\mathbf{x}, \phi]$ with parameters ϕ that computes an output from input $\mathbf{x}$. Until now, we have implied that the model directly computes a prediction $\mathbf{y}$. We now shift perspective and consider the model as computing a conditional probability distribution $Pr(\mathbf{y}|\mathbf{x})$ over possible outputs $\mathbf{y}$ given input $\mathbf{x}$. The loss encourages each training output $\mathbf{y}_i$ to have a high probability under the distribution $Pr(\mathbf{y}_i|\mathbf{x}_i)$ computed from the corresponding input $\mathbf{x}_i$ (figure 5.1).

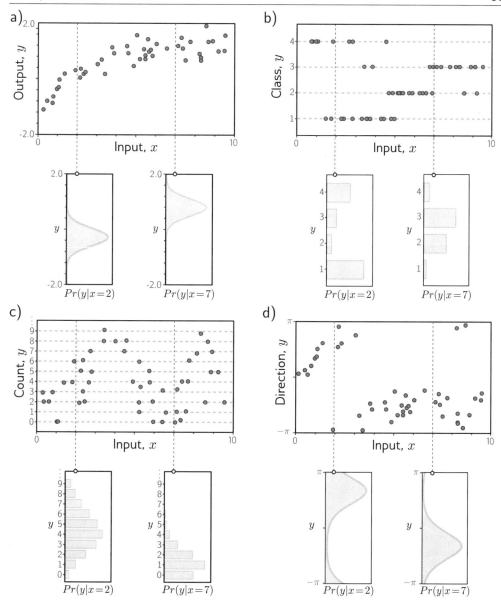

Figure 5.1 Predicting distributions over outputs. a) Regression task, where the goal is to predict a real-valued output y from the input x based on training data $\{x_i, y_i\}$ (orange points). For each input value x, the machine learning model predicts a distribution $Pr(y|x)$ over the output $y \in \mathbb{R}$ (cyan curves show distributions for $x = 2.0$ and $x = 7.0$). The loss function aims to maximize the probability of the observed training outputs y_i under the distribution predicted from the corresponding inputs x_i. b) To predict discrete classes $y \in \{1, 2, 3, 4\}$ in a classification task, we use a discrete probability distribution, so the model predicts a different histogram over the four possible values of y_i for each value of x_i. c) To predict counts $y \in \{0, 1, 2, \ldots\}$ and d) direction $y \in (-\pi, \pi]$, we use distributions defined over positive integers and circular domains, respectively.

5.1.1 Computing a distribution over outputs

This raises the question of exactly how a model $\mathbf{f}[\mathbf{x}, \phi]$ can be adapted to compute a probability distribution. The solution is simple. First, we choose a parametric distribution $Pr(\mathbf{y}|\theta)$ defined on the output domain $\mathbf{y}$. Then we use the network to compute one or more of the parameters θ of this distribution.

For example, suppose the prediction domain is the set of real numbers, so $y \in \mathbb{R}$. Here, we might choose the univariate normal distribution, which is defined on $\mathbb{R}$. This distribution is defined by the mean μ and variance σ^2, so $\theta = \{\mu, \sigma^2\}$. The machine learning model might predict the mean μ, and the variance σ^2 could be treated as an unknown constant.

5.1.2 Maximum likelihood criterion

The model now computes different distribution parameters $\theta_i = \mathbf{f}[\mathbf{x}_i, \phi]$ for each training input $\mathbf{x}_i$. Each observed training output $\mathbf{y}_i$ should have high probability under its corresponding distribution $Pr(\mathbf{y}_i|\theta_i)$. Hence, we choose the model parameters ϕ so that they maximize the combined probability across all I training examples:

$$
\begin{aligned}
\hat{\phi} &= \underset{\phi}{\operatorname{argmax}} \left[\prod_{i=1}^{I} Pr(\mathbf{y}_i|\mathbf{x}_i) \right] \\
&= \underset{\phi}{\operatorname{argmax}} \left[\prod_{i=1}^{I} Pr(\mathbf{y}_i|\theta_i) \right] \\
&= \underset{\phi}{\operatorname{argmax}} \left[\prod_{i=1}^{I} Pr(\mathbf{y}_i|\mathbf{f}[\mathbf{x}_i, \phi]) \right].
\end{aligned}
\tag{5.1}
$$

The combined probability term is the *likelihood* of the parameters, and hence equation 5.1 is known as the *maximum likelihood* criterion.[1]

Here we are implicitly making two assumptions. First, we assume that the data are identically distributed (the form of the probability distribution over the outputs $\mathbf{y}_i$ is the same for each data point). Second, we assume that the conditional distributions $Pr(\mathbf{y}_i|\mathbf{x}_i)$ of the output given the input are independent, so the total likelihood of the training data decomposes as:

Appendix C.1.5
Independence

$$
Pr(\mathbf{y}_1, \mathbf{y}_2, \ldots, \mathbf{y}_I|\mathbf{x}_1, \mathbf{x}_2, \ldots, \mathbf{x}_I) = \prod_{i=1}^{I} Pr(\mathbf{y}_i|\mathbf{x}_i).
\tag{5.2}
$$

In other words, we assume the data are *independent and identically distributed (i.i.d.)*.

---

[1] A conditional probability $Pr(z|\psi)$ can be considered in two ways. As a function of z, it is a probability distribution that sums to one. As a function of ψ, it is known as a *likelihood* and does not generally sum to one.

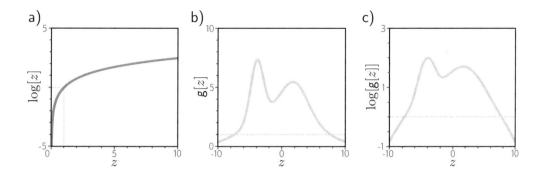

Figure 5.2 The log transform. a) The log function is monotonically increasing. If $z > z'$, then $\log[z] > \log[z']$. It follows that the maximum of any function $g[z]$ will be at the same position as the maximum of $\log[g[z]]$. b) A function $g[z]$. c) The logarithm of this function $\log[g[z]]$. All positions on $g[z]$ with a positive slope retain a positive slope after the log transform, and those with a negative slope retain a negative slope. The position of the maximum remains the same.

5.1.3 Maximizing log-likelihood

The maximum likelihood criterion (equation 5.1) is not very practical. Each term $Pr(\mathbf{y}_i|\mathbf{f}[\mathbf{x}_i, \boldsymbol{\phi}])$ can be small, so the product of many of these terms can be tiny. It may be difficult to represent this quantity with finite precision arithmetic. Fortunately, we can equivalently maximize the logarithm of the likelihood:

$$
\begin{aligned}
\hat{\boldsymbol{\phi}} &= \operatorname*{argmax}_{\boldsymbol{\phi}} \left[\prod_{i=1}^{I} Pr(\mathbf{y}_i|\mathbf{f}[\mathbf{x}_i, \boldsymbol{\phi}]) \right] \\
&= \operatorname*{argmax}_{\boldsymbol{\phi}} \left[\log \left[\prod_{i=1}^{I} Pr(\mathbf{y}_i|\mathbf{f}[\mathbf{x}_i, \boldsymbol{\phi}]) \right] \right] \\
&= \operatorname*{argmax}_{\boldsymbol{\phi}} \left[\sum_{i=1}^{I} \log \left[Pr(\mathbf{y}_i|\mathbf{f}[\mathbf{x}_i, \boldsymbol{\phi}]) \right] \right].
\end{aligned}
\tag{5.3}
$$

This *log-likelihood* criterion is equivalent because the logarithm is a monotonically increasing function: if $z > z'$, then $\log[z] > \log[z']$ and vice versa (figure 5.2). It follows that when we change the model parameters $\boldsymbol{\phi}$ to improve the log-likelihood criterion, we also improve the original maximum likelihood criterion. It also follows that the overall maxima of the two criteria must be in the same place, so the best model parameters $\hat{\boldsymbol{\phi}}$ are the same in both cases. However, the log-likelihood criterion has the practical advantage of using a sum of terms, not a product, so representing it with finite precision isn't problematic.

5.1.4   Minimizing negative log-likelihood

Finally, we note that, by convention, model fitting problems are framed in terms of minimizing a loss. To convert the maximum log-likelihood criterion to a minimization problem, we multiply by minus one, which gives us the *negative log-likelihood criterion*:

$$
\begin{aligned}
\hat{\phi} &= \underset{\phi}{\operatorname{argmin}} \left[-\sum_{i=1}^{I} \log\Big[Pr(\mathbf{y}_i | \mathbf{f}[\mathbf{x}_i, \phi]) \Big] \right] \\
&= \underset{\phi}{\operatorname{argmin}} \Big[L[\phi] \Big],
\end{aligned}
\tag{5.4}
$$

which is what forms the final loss function $L[\phi]$.

5.1.5   Inference

The network no longer directly predicts the outputs $\mathbf{y}$ but instead determines a probability distribution over $\mathbf{y}$. When we perform inference, we often want a point estimate rather than a distribution, so we return the maximum of the distribution:

$$
\hat{\mathbf{y}} = \underset{\mathbf{y}}{\operatorname{argmax}} \Big[Pr(\mathbf{y} | \mathbf{f}[\mathbf{x}, \hat{\phi}]) \Big].
\tag{5.5}
$$

It is usually possible to find an expression for this in terms of the distribution parameters $\boldsymbol{\theta}$ predicted by the model. For example, in the univariate normal distribution, the maximum occurs at the mean μ.

5.2   Recipe for constructing loss functions

The recipe for constructing loss functions for training data $\{\mathbf{x}_i, \mathbf{y}_i\}$ using the maximum likelihood approach is hence:

1. Choose a suitable probability distribution $Pr(\mathbf{y}|\boldsymbol{\theta})$ defined over the domain of the predictions $\mathbf{y}$ with distribution parameters $\boldsymbol{\theta}$.
2. Set the machine learning model $\mathbf{f}[\mathbf{x}, \phi]$ to predict one or more of these parameters, so $\boldsymbol{\theta} = \mathbf{f}[\mathbf{x}, \phi]$ and $Pr(\mathbf{y}|\boldsymbol{\theta}) = Pr(\mathbf{y}|\mathbf{f}[\mathbf{x}, \phi])$.
3. To train the model, find the network parameters $\hat{\phi}$ that minimize the negative log-likelihood loss function over the training dataset pairs $\{\mathbf{x}_i, \mathbf{y}_i\}$:

$$
\hat{\phi} = \underset{\phi}{\operatorname{argmin}} \Big[L[\phi] \Big] = \underset{\phi}{\operatorname{argmin}} \left[-\sum_{i=1}^{I} \log\Big[Pr(\mathbf{y}_i | \mathbf{f}[\mathbf{x}_i, \phi]) \Big] \right].
\tag{5.6}
$$

4. To perform inference for a new test example $\mathbf{x}$, return either the full distribution $Pr(\mathbf{y}|\mathbf{f}[\mathbf{x}, \hat{\phi}])$ or the maximum of this distribution.

We devote most of the rest of this chapter to constructing loss functions for common prediction types using this recipe.

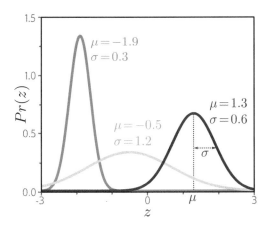

Figure 5.3 The univariate normal distribution (also known as the Gaussian distribution) is defined on the real line $z \in \mathbb{R}$ and has parameters μ and σ^2. The mean μ determines the position of the peak. The positive root of the variance σ^2 (the standard deviation) determines the width of the distribution. Since the total probability density sums to one, the peak becomes higher as the variance decreases and the distribution becomes narrower.

5.3 Example 1: univariate regression

We start by considering univariate regression models. Here the goal is to predict a single scalar output $y \in \mathbb{R}$ from input $\mathbf{x}$ using a model $f[\mathbf{x}, \phi]$ with parameters ϕ. Following the recipe, we choose a probability distribution over the output domain y. We select the univariate normal (figure 5.3), which is defined over $y \in \mathbb{R}$. This distribution has two parameters (mean μ and variance σ^2) and has a probability density function:

$$Pr(y|\mu, \sigma^2) = \frac{1}{\sqrt{2\pi\sigma^2}} \exp\left[-\frac{(y-\mu)^2}{2\sigma^2}\right]. \tag{5.7}$$

Second, we set the machine learning model $f[\mathbf{x}, \phi]$ to compute one or more of the parameters of this distribution. Here, we just compute the mean so $\mu = f[\mathbf{x}, \phi]$:

$$Pr(y|f[\mathbf{x}, \phi], \sigma^2) = \frac{1}{\sqrt{2\pi\sigma^2}} \exp\left[-\frac{(y-f[\mathbf{x}, \phi])^2}{2\sigma^2}\right]. \tag{5.8}$$

We aim to find the parameters ϕ that make the training data $\{\mathbf{x}_i, y_i\}$ most probable under this distribution (figure 5.4). To accomplish this, we choose a loss function $L[\phi]$ based on the negative log-likelihood:

$$\begin{aligned} L[\phi] &= -\sum_{i=1}^{I} \log\left[Pr(y_i|f[\mathbf{x}_i, \phi], \sigma^2)\right] \\ &= -\sum_{i=1}^{I} \log\left[\frac{1}{\sqrt{2\pi\sigma^2}} \exp\left[-\frac{(y_i - f[\mathbf{x}_i, \phi])^2}{2\sigma^2}\right]\right]. \end{aligned} \tag{5.9}$$

When we train the model, we seek parameters $\hat{\phi}$ that minimize this loss.

5.3.1 Least squares loss function

Now let's perform some algebraic manipulations on the loss function. We seek:

$$
\begin{aligned}
\hat{\phi} &= \underset{\phi}{\operatorname{argmin}} \left[-\sum_{i=1}^{I} \log \left[\frac{1}{\sqrt{2\pi\sigma^2}} \exp \left[-\frac{(y_i - \mathrm{f}[\mathbf{x}_i, \phi])^2}{2\sigma^2} \right] \right] \right] \\
&= \underset{\phi}{\operatorname{argmin}} \left[-\sum_{i=1}^{I} \left(\log \left[\frac{1}{\sqrt{2\pi\sigma^2}} \right] - \frac{(y_i - \mathrm{f}[\mathbf{x}_i, \phi])^2}{2\sigma^2} \right) \right] \\
&= \underset{\phi}{\operatorname{argmin}} \left[-\sum_{i=1}^{I} -\frac{(y_i - \mathrm{f}[\mathbf{x}_i, \phi])^2}{2\sigma^2} \right] \\
&= \underset{\phi}{\operatorname{argmin}} \left[\sum_{i=1}^{I} (y_i - \mathrm{f}[\mathbf{x}_i, \phi])^2 \right],
\end{aligned}
\tag{5.10}
$$

where we have removed the first term between the second and third lines because it does not depend on ϕ. We have removed the denominator between the third and fourth lines, as this is just a constant scaling factor that does not affect the position of the minimum.

The result of these manipulations is the least squares loss function that we originally introduced when we discussed linear regression in chapter 2:

$$
L[\phi] = \sum_{i=1}^{I} \big(y_i - \mathrm{f}[\mathbf{x}_i, \phi] \big)^2.
\tag{5.11}
$$

Notebook 5.1
Least squares
loss

We see that the least squares loss function follows naturally from the assumptions that the prediction errors are (i) independent and (ii) drawn from a normal distribution with mean $\mu = \mathrm{f}[\mathbf{x}_i, \phi]$ (figure 5.4).

5.3.2 Inference

The network no longer directly predicts y but instead predicts the mean $\mu = \mathrm{f}[\mathbf{x}, \phi]$ of the normal distribution over y. When we perform inference, we usually want a single "best" point estimate $\hat{y}$, so we take the maximum of the predicted distribution:

$$
\hat{y} = \underset{y}{\operatorname{argmax}} \left[Pr(y | \mathrm{f}[\mathbf{x}, \hat{\phi}, \sigma^2]) \right].
\tag{5.12}
$$

For the univariate normal, the maximum position is determined by the mean parameter μ (figure 5.3). This is precisely what the model computed, so $\hat{y} = \mathrm{f}[\mathbf{x}, \hat{\phi}]$.

5.3.3 Estimating variance

To formulate the least squares loss function, we assumed that the network predicted the mean of a normal distribution. The final expression in equation 5.11 (perhaps surpris-

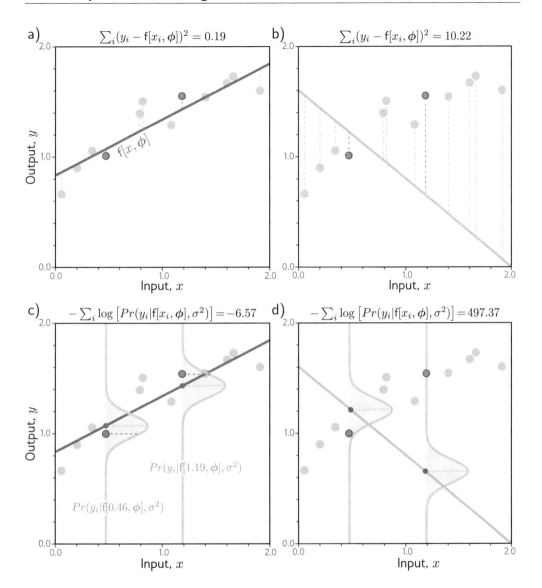

Figure 5.4 Equivalence of least squares and maximum likelihood loss for the normal distribution. a) Consider the linear model from figure 2.2. The least squares criterion minimizes the sum of the squares of the deviations (dashed lines) between the model prediction $f[x_i, \phi]$ (green line) and the true output values y_i (orange points). Here the fit is good, so these deviations are small (e.g., for the two highlighted points). b) For these parameters, the fit is bad, and the squared deviations are large. c) The least squares criterion follows from the assumption that the model predicts the mean of a normal distribution over the outputs and that we maximize the probability. For the first case, the model fits well, so the probability $Pr(y_i|x_i)$ of the data (horizontal orange dashed lines) is large (and the negative log probability is small). d) For the second case, the model fits badly, so the probability is small and the negative log probability is large.

ingly) does not depend on the variance σ^2. However, there is nothing to stop us from treating σ^2 as a parameter of the model and minimizing equation 5.9 with respect to both the model parameters ϕ and the distribution variance σ^2:

$$\hat{\phi}, \hat{\sigma}^2 = \underset{\phi, \sigma^2}{\mathrm{argmin}} \left[-\sum_{i=1}^{I} \log \left[\frac{1}{\sqrt{2\pi\sigma^2}} \exp \left[-\frac{(y_i - \mathrm{f}[\mathbf{x}_i, \phi])^2}{2\sigma^2} \right] \right] \right]. \tag{5.13}$$

In inference, the model predicts the mean $\mu = \mathrm{f}[\mathbf{x}, \hat{\phi}]$ from the input, and we learned the variance $\hat{\sigma}^2$ during the training process. The former is the best prediction. The latter tells us about the uncertainty of the prediction.

5.3.4 Heteroscedastic regression

The model above assumes that the variance of the data is constant everywhere. However, this might be unrealistic. When the uncertainty of the model varies as a function of the input data, we refer to this as *heteroscedastic* (as opposed to *homoscedastic*, where the uncertainty is constant).

A simple way to model this is to train a neural network $\mathbf{f}[\mathbf{x}, \phi]$ that computes both the mean and the variance. For example, consider a shallow network with two outputs. We denote the first output as $\mathrm{f}_1[\mathbf{x}, \phi]$ and use this to predict the mean, and we denote the second output as $\mathrm{f}_2[\mathbf{x}, \phi]$ and use it to predict the variance.

There is one complication; the variance must be positive, but we can't guarantee that the network will always produce a positive output. To ensure that the computed variance is positive, we pass the second network output through a function that maps an arbitrary value to a positive one. A suitable choice is the squaring function, giving:

$$\begin{aligned} \mu &= \mathrm{f}_1[\mathbf{x}, \phi] \\ \sigma^2 &= \mathrm{f}_2[\mathbf{x}, \phi]^2, \end{aligned} \tag{5.14}$$

which results in the loss function:

$$\hat{\phi} = \underset{\phi}{\mathrm{argmin}} \left[-\sum_{i=1}^{I} \left(\log \left[\frac{1}{\sqrt{2\pi \mathrm{f}_2[\mathbf{x}_i, \phi]^2}} \right] - \frac{(y_i - \mathrm{f}_1[\mathbf{x}_i, \phi])^2}{2\mathrm{f}_2[\mathbf{x}_i, \phi]^2} \right) \right]. \tag{5.15}$$

Homoscedastic and heteroscedastic models are compared in figure 5.5.

5.4 Example 2: binary classification

In *binary classification*, the goal is to assign the data $\mathbf{x}$ to one of two discrete classes $y \in \{0, 1\}$. In this context, we refer to y as a *label*. Examples of binary classification include (i) predicting whether a restaurant review is positive ($y = 1$) or negative ($y = 0$) from text data $\mathbf{x}$ and (ii) predicting whether a tumor is present ($y = 1$) or absent ($y = 0$) from an MRI scan $\mathbf{x}$.

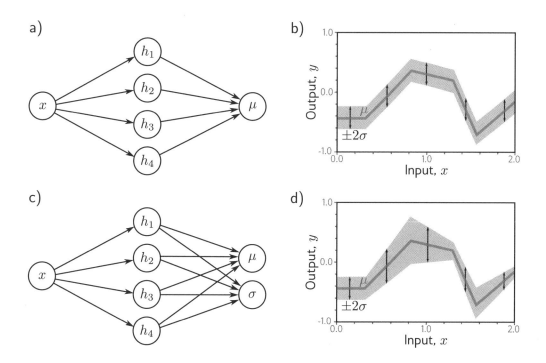

Figure 5.5 Homoscedastic vs. heteroscedastic regression. a) A shallow neural network for homoscedastic regression predicts just the mean μ of the output distribution from the input x. b) The result is that while the mean (blue line) is a piecewise linear function of the input x, the variance is constant everywhere (arrows and gray region show ± 2 standard deviations). c) A shallow neural network for heteroscedastic regression also predicts the variance σ^2 (or, more precisely, computes its square root, which we then square). d) The standard deviation now also becomes a piecewise linear function of the input x.

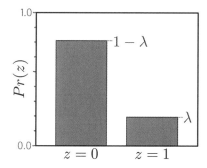

Figure 5.6 Bernoulli distribution. The Bernoulli distribution is defined on the domain $z \in \{0, 1\}$ and has a single parameter λ that denotes the probability of observing $z = 1$. It follows that the probability of observing $z = 0$ is $1 - \lambda$.

Figure 5.7 Logistic sigmoid function. This function maps the real line $z \in \mathbb{R}$ to numbers between zero and one, so $\text{sig}[z] \in [0, 1]$. An input of 0 is mapped to 0.5. Negative inputs are mapped to numbers below 0.5, and positive inputs to numbers above 0.5.

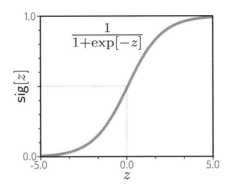

Once again, we follow the recipe from section 5.2 to construct the loss function. First, we choose a probability distribution over the output space $y \in \{0, 1\}$. A suitable choice is the Bernoulli distribution, which is defined on the domain $\{0, 1\}$. This has a single parameter $\lambda \in [0, 1]$ that represents the probability that y takes the value one (figure 5.6):

$$Pr(y|\lambda) = \begin{cases} 1 - \lambda & y = 0 \\ \lambda & y = 1 \end{cases}, \tag{5.16}$$

which can equivalently be written as:

$$Pr(y|\lambda) = (1 - \lambda)^{1-y} \cdot \lambda^y. \tag{5.17}$$

Second, we set the machine learning model $f[\mathbf{x}, \boldsymbol{\phi}]$ to predict the single distribution parameter λ. However, λ can only take values in the range $[0, 1]$, and we cannot guarantee that the network output will lie in this range. Consequently, we pass the network output through a function that maps the real numbers $\mathbb{R}$ to $[0, 1]$. A suitable function is the *logistic sigmoid* (figure 5.7):

Problem 5.1

$$\text{sig}[z] = \frac{1}{1 + \exp[-z]}. \tag{5.18}$$

Hence, we predict the distribution parameter as $\lambda = \text{sig}[f[\mathbf{x}, \boldsymbol{\phi}]]$. The likelihood is now:

$$Pr(y|\mathbf{x}) = (1 - \text{sig}[f[\mathbf{x}, \boldsymbol{\phi}]])^{1-y} \cdot \text{sig}[f[\mathbf{x}, \boldsymbol{\phi}]]^y. \tag{5.19}$$

This is depicted in figure 5.8 for a shallow neural network model. The loss function is the negative log-likelihood of the training set:

$$L[\boldsymbol{\phi}] = \sum_{i=1}^{I} -(1 - y_i) \log\Big[1 - \text{sig}[f[\mathbf{x}_i, \boldsymbol{\phi}]]\Big] - y_i \log\Big[\text{sig}[f[\mathbf{x}_i, \boldsymbol{\phi}]]\Big]. \tag{5.20}$$

Notebook 5.2
Binary
cross-entropy loss

Problem 5.2

For reasons to be explained in section 5.7, this is known as the *binary cross-entropy loss*.

The transformed model output $\text{sig}[f[\mathbf{x}, \boldsymbol{\phi}]]$ predicts the parameter λ of the Bernoulli distribution. This represents the probability that $y = 1$, and it follows that $1 - \lambda$ represents the probability that $y = 0$. When we perform inference, we may want a point estimate of y, so we set $y = 1$ if $\lambda > 0.5$ and $y = 0$ otherwise.

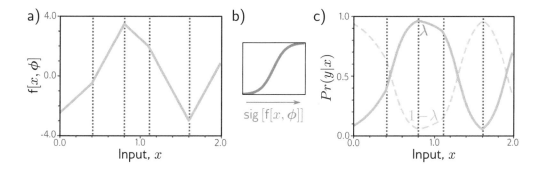

Figure 5.8 Binary classification model. a) The network output is a piecewise linear function that can take arbitrary real values. b) This is transformed by the logistic sigmoid function, which compresses these values to the range $[0, 1]$. c) The transformed output predicts the probability λ that $y = 1$ (solid line). The probability that $y = 0$ is hence $1 - \lambda$ (dashed line). For any fixed x (vertical slice), we retrieve the two values of a Bernoulli distribution similar to that in figure 5.6. The loss function favors model parameters that produce large values of λ at positions x_i that are associated with positive examples $y_i = 1$ and small values of λ at positions associated with negative examples $y_i = 0$.

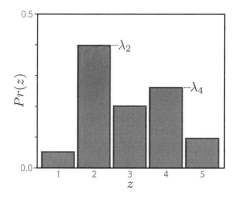

Figure 5.9 Categorical distribution. The categorical distribution assigns probabilities to $K > 2$ categories, with associated probabilities $\lambda_1, \lambda_2, \ldots, \lambda_K$. Here, there are five categories, so $K = 5$. To ensure that this is a valid probability distribution, each parameter λ_k must lie in the range $[0, 1]$, and all K parameters must sum to one.

5.5 Example 3: multiclass classification

The goal of *multiclass classification* is to assign an input data example $\mathbf{x}$ to one of $K > 2$ classes, so $y \in \{1, 2, \ldots, K\}$. Real-world examples include (i) predicting which of $K = 10$ digits y is present in an image $\mathbf{x}$ of a handwritten number and (ii) predicting which of K possible words y follows an incomplete sentence $\mathbf{x}$.

We once more follow the recipe from section 5.2. We first choose a distribution over the prediction space y. In this case, we have $y \in \{1, 2, \ldots, K\}$, so we choose the *categorical distribution* (figure 5.9), which is defined on this domain. This has K parameters $\lambda_1, \lambda_2, \ldots, \lambda_K$, which determine the probability of each category:

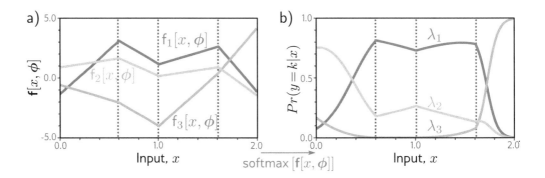

Figure 5.10 Multiclass classification for $K = 3$ classes. a) The network has three piecewise linear outputs, which can take arbitrary values. b) After the softmax function, these outputs are constrained to be non-negative and sum to one. Hence, for a given input $\mathbf{x}$, we compute valid parameters for the categorical distribution: any vertical slice of this plot produces three values sum to one and would form the heights of the bars in a categorical distribution similar to figure 5.9.

$$Pr(y = k) = \lambda_k. \tag{5.21}$$

The parameters are constrained to take values between zero and one, and they must collectively sum to one to ensure a valid probability distribution.

Then we use a network $\mathbf{f}[\mathbf{x}, \phi]$ with K outputs to compute these K parameters from the input $\mathbf{x}$. Unfortunately, the network outputs will not necessarily obey the aforementioned constraints. Consequently, we pass the K outputs of the network through a function that ensures these constraints are respected. A suitable choice is the *softmax* function (figure 5.10). This takes an arbitrary vector of length K and returns a vector of the same length but where the elements are now in the range $[0, 1]$ and sum to one. The kth output of the softmax function is:

$$\text{softmax}_k[\mathbf{z}] = \frac{\exp[z_k]}{\sum_{k'=1}^{K} \exp[z_{k'}]}, \tag{5.22}$$

Appendix B.1.3
Exponential
function

where the exponential functions ensure positivity, and the sum in the denominator ensures that the K numbers sum to one.

The likelihood that input $\mathbf{x}$ has label $y = k$ (figure 5.10) is hence:

$$Pr(y = k|\mathbf{x}) = \text{softmax}_k\Big[\mathbf{f}[\mathbf{x}, \phi]\Big]. \tag{5.23}$$

The loss function is the negative log-likelihood of the training data:

$$L[\phi] = -\sum_{i=1}^{I} \log\left[\text{softmax}_{y_i}\left[\mathbf{f}[\mathbf{x}_i, \phi]\right]\right]$$

$$= -\sum_{i=1}^{I}\left(f_{y_i}[\mathbf{x}_i, \phi] - \log\left[\sum_{k'=1}^{K} \exp[\,f_{k'}[\mathbf{x}_i, \phi]]\right]\right), \qquad (5.24)$$

where $f_k[\mathbf{x}, \phi]$ denotes the kth output of the neural network. For reasons that will be explained in section 5.7, this is known as the *multiclass cross-entropy loss*.

The transformed model output represents a categorical distribution over possible classes $y \in \{1, 2, \ldots, K\}$. For a point estimate, we take the most probable category $\hat{y} = \text{argmax}_k[Pr(y = k|\mathbf{f}[\mathbf{x}, \hat{\phi}])]$. This corresponds to whichever curve is highest for that value of $\mathbf{x}$ in figure 5.10.

Notebook 5.3
Multiclass
cross-entropy loss

5.5.1 Predicting other data types

In this chapter, we have focused on regression and classification because these problems are widespread. However, to make different types of predictions, we simply choose an appropriate distribution over that domain and apply the recipe in section 5.2. Figure 5.11 enumerates a series of probability distributions and their prediction domains. Some of these are explored in the problems at the end of the chapter.

Problems 5.3–5.6

5.6 Multiple outputs

Often, we wish to make more than one prediction with the same model, so the target output $\mathbf{y}$ is a vector. For example, we might want to predict a molecule's melting and boiling point (a multivariate regression problem, figure 1.2b) or the object class at every point in an image (a multivariate classification problem, figure 1.4a). While it is possible to define multivariate probability distributions and use a neural network to model their parameters as a function of the input, it is more usual to treat each prediction as *independent*.

Independence implies that we treat the probability $Pr(\mathbf{y}|\mathbf{f}[\mathbf{x}, \phi])$ as a product of univariate terms for each element $y_d \in \mathbf{y}$:

Appendix C.1.5
Independence

$$Pr(\mathbf{y}|\mathbf{f}[\mathbf{x}, \phi]) = \prod_d Pr(y_d|\mathbf{f}_d[\mathbf{x}, \phi]), \qquad (5.25)$$

where $\mathbf{f}_d[\mathbf{x}, \phi]$ is the dth set of network outputs, which describe the parameters of the distribution over y_d. For example, to predict multiple continuous variables $y_d \in \mathbb{R}$, we use a normal distribution for each y_d, and the network outputs $f_d[\mathbf{x}, \phi]$ predict the means of these distributions. To predict multiple discrete variables $y_d \in \{1, 2, \ldots, K\}$, we use a categorical distribution for each y_d. Here, each set of network outputs $\mathbf{f}_d[\mathbf{x}, \phi]$ predicts the K values that contribute to the categorical distribution for y_d.

Data Type	Domain	Distribution	Use
univariate, continuous, unbounded	$y \in \mathbb{R}$	univariate normal	regression
univariate, continuous, unbounded	$y \in \mathbb{R}$	Laplace or t-distribution	robust regression
univariate, continuous, unbounded	$y \in \mathbb{R}$	mixture of Gaussians	multimodal regression
univariate, continuous, bounded below	$y \in \mathbb{R}^+$	exponential or gamma	predicting magnitude
univariate, continuous, bounded	$y \in [0,1]$	beta	predicting proportions
multivariate, continuous, unbounded	$\mathbf{y} \in \mathbb{R}^K$	multivariate normal	multivariate regression
univariate, continuous, circular	$y \in (-\pi, \pi]$	von Mises	predicting direction
univariate, discrete, binary	$y \in \{0,1\}$	Bernoulli	binary classification
univariate, discrete, bounded	$y \in \{1, 2, \ldots, K\}$	categorical	multiclass classification
univariate, discrete, bounded below	$y \in [0, 1, 2, 3, \ldots]$	Poisson	predicting event counts
multivariate, discrete, permutation	$\mathbf{y} \in \mathrm{Perm}[1, 2, \ldots, K]$	Plackett-Luce	ranking

Figure 5.11 Distributions for loss functions for different prediction types.

When we minimize the negative log probability, this product becomes a sum of terms:

$$L[\phi] = -\sum_{i=1}^{I} \log\Big[Pr(\mathbf{y}_i | \mathbf{f}[\mathbf{x}_i, \phi])\Big] = -\sum_{i=1}^{I} \sum_{d} \log\Big[Pr(y_{id} | \mathbf{f}_d[\mathbf{x}_i, \phi])\Big]. \tag{5.26}$$

where y_{id} is the dth output from the ith training example.

To make two or more prediction types simultaneously, we similarly assume the errors in each are independent. For example, to predict wind direction and strength, we might choose the von Mises distribution (defined on circular domains) for the direction and the exponential distribution (defined on positive real numbers) for the strength. The independence assumption implies that the joint likelihood of the two predictions is the product of individual likelihoods. These terms will become additive when we compute the negative log-likelihood.

Problems 5.7–5.10

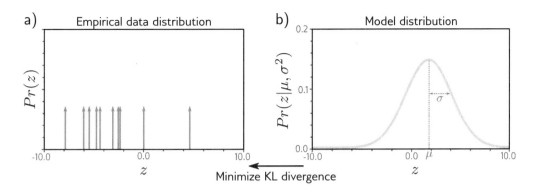

Figure 5.12 Cross-entropy method. a) Empirical distribution of training samples (arrows denote Dirac delta functions). b) Model distribution (a normal distribution with parameters $\boldsymbol{\theta} = \mu, \sigma^2$). In the cross-entropy approach, we minimize the distance (KL divergence) between these two distributions as a function of the model parameters $\boldsymbol{\theta}$.

5.7   Cross-entropy loss

In this chapter, we developed loss functions that minimize negative log-likelihood. However, the term *cross-entropy* loss is also commonplace. In this section, we describe the cross-entropy loss and show that it is equivalent to using negative log-likelihood.

The cross-entropy loss is based on the idea of finding parameters $\boldsymbol{\theta}$ that minimize the distance between the empirical distribution $q(y)$ of the observed data y and a model distribution $Pr(y|\boldsymbol{\theta})$ (figure 5.12). The distance between two probability distributions $q(z)$ and $p(z)$ can be evaluated using the Kullback-Leibler (KL) divergence:

Appendix C.5.1
KL Divergence

$$D_{KL}\big[q||p\big] = \int_{-\infty}^{\infty} q(z)\log\big[q(z)\big]dz - \int_{-\infty}^{\infty} q(z)\log\big[p(z)\big]dz. \qquad (5.27)$$

Now consider that we observe an empirical data distribution at points $\{y_i\}_{i=1}^{I}$. We can describe this as a weighted sum of point masses:

$$q(y) = \frac{1}{I}\sum_{i=1}^{I}\delta[y - y_i], \qquad (5.28)$$

where $\delta[\bullet]$ is the Dirac delta function. We want to minimize the KL divergence between the model distribution $Pr(y|\boldsymbol{\theta})$ and this empirical distribution:

Appendix B.1.3
Dirac delta
function

$$\begin{aligned}
\hat{\boldsymbol{\theta}} &= \operatorname*{argmin}_{\boldsymbol{\theta}}\left[\int_{-\infty}^{\infty} q(y)\log\big[q(y)\big]dy - \int_{-\infty}^{\infty} q(y)\log\big[Pr(y|\boldsymbol{\theta})\big]dy\right] \\
&= \operatorname*{argmin}_{\boldsymbol{\theta}}\left[-\int_{-\infty}^{\infty} q(y)\log\big[Pr(y|\boldsymbol{\theta})\big]dy\right], \qquad (5.29)
\end{aligned}$$

where the first term disappears, as it has no dependence on $\boldsymbol{\theta}$. The remaining second term is known as the *cross-entropy*. It can be interpreted as the amount of uncertainty that remains in one distribution after taking into account what we already know from the other. Now, we substitute in the definition of $q(y)$ from equation 5.28:

$$
\begin{aligned}
\hat{\boldsymbol{\theta}} &= \operatorname*{argmin}_{\boldsymbol{\theta}} \left[-\int_{-\infty}^{\infty} \left(\frac{1}{I} \sum_{i=1}^{I} \delta[y - y_i] \right) \log\left[Pr(y|\boldsymbol{\theta}) \right] dy \right] \\
&= \operatorname*{argmin}_{\boldsymbol{\theta}} \left[-\frac{1}{I} \sum_{i=1}^{I} \log\left[Pr(y_i|\boldsymbol{\theta}) \right] \right] \\
&= \operatorname*{argmin}_{\boldsymbol{\theta}} \left[-\sum_{i=1}^{I} \log\left[Pr(y_i|\boldsymbol{\theta}) \right] \right].
\end{aligned}
\tag{5.30}
$$

The product of the two terms in the first line corresponds to pointwise multiplying the point masses in figure 5.12a with the logarithm of the distribution in figure 5.12b. We are left with a finite set of weighted probability masses centered on the data points. In the last line, we have eliminated the constant scaling factor $1/I$, as this does not affect the position of the minimum.

In machine learning, the distribution parameters $\boldsymbol{\theta}$ are computed by the model $\mathbf{f}[\mathbf{x}_i, \boldsymbol{\phi}]$, so we have:

$$
\hat{\boldsymbol{\phi}} = \operatorname*{argmin}_{\boldsymbol{\phi}} \left[-\sum_{i=1}^{I} \log\left[Pr(y_i|\mathbf{f}[\mathbf{x}_i, \boldsymbol{\phi}]) \right] \right].
\tag{5.31}
$$

This is precisely the negative log-likelihood criterion from the recipe in section 5.2.

It follows that the negative log-likelihood criterion (from maximizing the data likelihood) and the cross-entropy criterion (from minimizing the distance between the model and empirical data distributions) are equivalent.

5.8 Summary

We previously considered neural networks as directly predicting outputs $\mathbf{y}$ from data $\mathbf{x}$. In this chapter, we shifted perspective to think about neural networks as computing the parameters $\boldsymbol{\theta}$ of probability distributions $Pr(\mathbf{y}|\boldsymbol{\theta})$ over the output space. This led to a principled approach to building loss functions. We selected model parameters $\boldsymbol{\phi}$ that maximized the likelihood of the observed data under these distributions. We saw that this is equivalent to minimizing the negative log-likelihood.

The least squares criterion for regression is a natural consequence of this approach; it follows from the assumption that y is normally distributed and that we are predicting the mean. We also saw how the regression model could be (i) extended to estimate the uncertainty over the prediction and (ii) extended to make that uncertainty dependent on the input (the heteroscedastic model). We applied the same approach to both binary and multiclass classification and derived loss functions for each. We discussed how to tackle more complex data types and how to deal with multiple outputs. Finally, we argued that cross-entropy is an equivalent way to think about fitting models.

In previous chapters, we developed neural network models. In this chapter, we developed loss functions for deciding how well a model describes the training data for a given set of parameters. The next chapter considers model training, in which we aim to find the model parameters that minimize this loss.

Notes

Losses based on the normal distribution: Nix & Weigend (1994) and Williams (1996) investigated heteroscedastic nonlinear regression in which both the mean and the variance of the output are functions of the input. In the context of unsupervised learning, Burda et al. (2016) use a loss function based on a multivariate normal distribution with diagonal covariance, and Dorta et al. (2018) use a loss function based on a normal distribution with full covariance.

Robust regression: Qi et al. (2020) investigate the properties of regression models that minimize mean absolute error rather than mean squared error. This loss function follows from assuming a Laplace distribution over the outputs and estimates the median output for a given input rather than the mean. Barron (2019) presents a loss function that parameterizes the degree of robustness. When interpreted in a probabilistic context, it yields a family of univariate probability distributions that includes the normal and Cauchy distributions as special cases.

Estimating quantiles: Sometimes, we may not want to estimate the mean or median in a regression task but may instead want to predict a quantile. For example, this is useful for risk models, where we want to know that the true value will be less than the predicted value 90% of the time. This is known as *quantile regression* (Koenker & Hallock, 2001). This could be done by fitting a heteroscedastic regression model and then estimating the quantile based on the predicted normal distribution. Alternatively, the quantiles can be estimated directly using *quantile loss* (also known as *pinball loss*). In practice, this minimizes the absolute deviations of the data from the model but weights the deviations in one direction more than the other. Recent work has investigated simultaneously predicting multiple quantiles to get an idea of the overall distribution shape (Rodrigues & Pereira, 2020).

Class imbalance and focal loss: Lin et al. (2017c) address data imbalance in classification problems. If the number of examples for some classes is much greater than for others, then the standard maximum likelihood loss does not work well; the model may concentrate on becoming more confident about well-classified examples from the dominant classes and classify less well-represented classes poorly. Lin et al. (2017c) introduce *focal loss*, which adds a single extra parameter that down-weights the effect of well-classified examples to improve performance.

Learning to rank: Cao et al. (2007), Xia et al. (2008), and Chen et al. (2009) all used the Plackett-Luce model in loss functions for learning to rank data. This is the *listwise* approach to learning to rank as the model ingests an entire list of objects to be ranked at once. Alternative approaches are the *pointwise* approach, in which the model ingests a single object, and the *pairwise* approach, where the model ingests pairs of objects. Chen et al. (2009) summarize different approaches for learning to rank.

Other data types: Fan et al. (2020) use a loss based on the beta distribution for predicting values between zero and one. Jacobs et al. (1991) and Bishop (1994) investigated *mixture density networks* for multimodal data. These model the output as a mixture of Gaussians

Figure 5.13 The von Mises distribution is defined over the circular domain $(-\pi, \pi]$. It has two parameters. The mean μ determines the position of the peak. The concentration $\kappa > 0$ acts like the inverse of the variance. Hence $1/\sqrt{\kappa}$ is roughly equivalent to the standard deviation in a normal distribution.

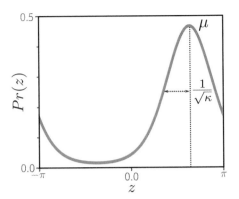

(see figure 5.14) that is conditional on the input. Prokudin et al. (2018) used the von Mises distribution to predict direction (see figure 5.13). Fallah et al. (2009) constructed loss functions for prediction counts using the Poisson distribution (see figure 5.15). Ng et al. (2017) used loss functions based on the gamma distribution to predict duration.

Non-probabilistic approaches: It is not strictly necessary to adopt the probabilistic approach discussed in this chapter, but this has become the default in recent years; any loss function that aims to reduce the distance between the model output and the training outputs will suffice, and distance can be defined in any way that seems sensible. There are several well-known non-probabilistic machine learning models for classification, including support vector machines (Vapnik, 1995; Cristianini & Shawe-Taylor, 2000), which use *hinge loss*, and AdaBoost (Freund & Schapire, 1997), which uses *exponential loss*.

Problems

Problem 5.1 Show that the logistic sigmoid function $\text{sig}[z]$ becomes 0 as $z \to -\infty$, is 0.5 when $z = 0$, and becomes 1 when $z \to \infty$, where:

$$\text{sig}[z] = \frac{1}{1 + \exp[-z]}. \tag{5.32}$$

Problem 5.2 The loss L for binary classification for a single training pair $\{\mathbf{x}, y\}$ is:

$$L = -(1 - y) \log\Big[1 - \text{sig}[\text{f}[\mathbf{x}, \boldsymbol{\phi}]]\Big] - y \log\Big[\text{sig}[\text{f}[\mathbf{x}, \boldsymbol{\phi}]]\Big], \tag{5.33}$$

where $\text{sig}[\bullet]$ is defined in equation 5.32. Plot this loss as a function of the transformed network output $\text{sig}[\text{f}[\mathbf{x}, \boldsymbol{\phi}]] \in [0, 1]$ (i) when the training label $y = 0$ and (ii) when $y = 1$.

Problem 5.3* Suppose we want to build a model that predicts the direction y in radians of the prevailing wind based on local measurements of barometric pressure $\mathbf{x}$. A suitable distribution over circular domains is the von Mises distribution (figure 5.13):

$$Pr(y|\mu, \kappa) = \frac{\exp\big[\kappa \cos[y - \mu]\big]}{2\pi \cdot \text{Bessel}_0[\kappa]}, \tag{5.34}$$

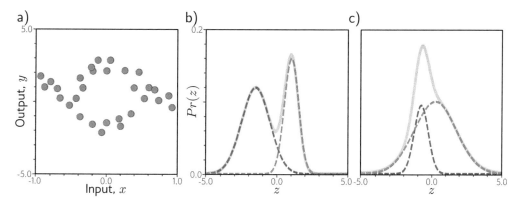

Figure 5.14 Multimodal data and mixture of Gaussians density. a) Example training data where, for intermediate values of the input x, the corresponding output y follows one of two paths. For example, at $x = 0$, the output y might be roughly -2 or $+3$ but is unlikely to be between these values. b) The mixture of Gaussians is a probability model suited to this kind of data. As the name suggests, the model is a weighted sum (solid cyan curve) of two or more normal distributions with different means and variances (here, two weighted distributions, dashed blue and orange curves). When the means are far apart, this forms a multimodal distribution. c) When the means are close, the mixture can model unimodal but non-normal densities.

where μ is a measure of the mean direction and κ is a measure of concentration (i.e., the inverse of the variance). The term $\text{Bessel}_0[\kappa]$ is a modified Bessel function of the first kind of order 0. Use the recipe from section 5.2 to develop a loss function for learning the parameter μ of a model $f[\mathbf{x}, \boldsymbol{\phi}]$ to predict the most likely wind direction. Your solution should treat the concentration κ as constant. How would you perform inference?

Problem 5.4* Sometimes, the outputs y for input $\mathbf{x}$ are multimodal (figure 5.14a); there is more than one valid prediction for a given input. Here, we might use a weighted sum of normal components as the distribution over the output. This is known as a *mixture of Gaussians* model. For example, a mixture of two Gaussians has parameters $\boldsymbol{\theta} = \{\lambda, \mu_1, \sigma_1^2, \mu_2, \sigma_2^2\}$:

$$Pr(y|\lambda, \mu_1, \mu_2, \sigma_1^2, \sigma_2^2) = \frac{\lambda}{\sqrt{2\pi\sigma_1^2}} \exp\left[\frac{-(y-\mu_1)^2}{2\sigma_1^2}\right] + \frac{1-\lambda}{\sqrt{2\pi\sigma_2^2}} \exp\left[\frac{-(y-\mu_2)^2}{2\sigma_2^2}\right], \quad (5.35)$$

where $\lambda \in [0, 1]$ controls the relative weight of the two components, which have means μ_1, μ_2 and variances σ_1^2, σ_2^2, respectively. This model can represent a distribution with two peaks (figure 5.14b) or a distribution with one peak but a more complex shape (figure 5.14c).

Use the recipe from section 5.2 to construct a loss function for training a model $\mathbf{f}[x, \boldsymbol{\phi}]$ that takes input x, has parameters $\boldsymbol{\phi}$, and predicts a mixture of two Gaussians. The loss should be based on I training data pairs $\{x_i, y_i\}$. What problems do you foresee when performing inference?

Problem 5.5 Consider extending the model from problem 5.3 to predict the wind direction using a mixture of two von Mises distributions. Write an expression for the likelihood $Pr(y|\boldsymbol{\theta})$ for this model. How many outputs will the network need to produce?

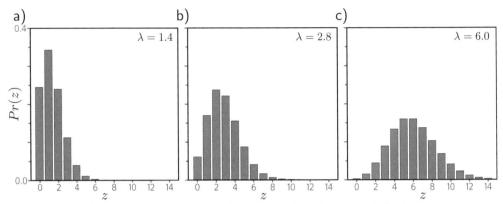

Figure 5.15 Poisson distribution. This discrete distribution is defined over non-negative integers $z \in \{0, 1, 2, \ldots\}$. It has a single parameter $\lambda \in \mathbb{R}^+$, which is known as the rate and is the mean of the distribution. a–c) Poisson distributions with rates of 1.4, 2.8, and 6.0, respectively.

Problem 5.6 Consider building a model to predict the number of pedestrians $y \in \{0, 1, 2, \ldots\}$ that will pass a given point in the city in the next minute, based on data $\mathbf{x}$ that contains information about the time of day, the longitude and latitude, and the type of neighborhood. A suitable distribution for modeling counts is the Poisson distribution (figure 5.15). This has a single parameter $\lambda > 0$ called the *rate* that represents the mean of the distribution. The distribution has probability density function:

$$Pr(y = k) = \frac{\lambda^k e^{-\lambda}}{k!}. \tag{5.36}$$

Design a loss function for this model assuming we have access to I training pairs $\{\mathbf{x}_i, y_i\}$.

Problem 5.7 Consider a multivariate regression problem where we predict ten outputs, so $\mathbf{y} \in \mathbb{R}^{10}$, and model each with an independent normal distribution where the means μ_d are predicted by the network, and variances σ^2 are constant. Write an expression for the likelihood $Pr(\mathbf{y}|\mathbf{f}[\mathbf{x}, \boldsymbol{\phi}])$. Show that minimizing the negative log-likelihood of this model is still equivalent to minimizing a sum of squared terms if we don't estimate the variance σ^2.

Problem 5.8* Construct a loss function for making multivariate predictions $\mathbf{y} \in \mathbb{R}^{D_o}$ based on independent normal distributions with different variances σ_d^2 for each dimension. Assume a heteroscedastic model so that both the means μ_d and variances σ_d^2 vary as a function of the data.

Problem 5.9* Consider a multivariate regression problem in which we predict the height of a person in meters and their weight in kilos from data $\mathbf{x}$. Here, the units take quite different ranges. What problems do you see this causing? Propose two solutions to these problems.

Problem 5.10 Extend the model from problem 5.3 to predict both the wind direction and the wind speed and define the associated loss function.

Chapter 6

Fitting models

Chapters 3 and 4 described shallow and deep neural networks. These represent families of piecewise linear functions, where the parameters determine the particular function. Chapter 5 introduced the loss — a single number representing the mismatch between the network predictions and the ground truth for a training set.

The loss depends on the network parameters, and this chapter considers how to find the parameter values that minimize this loss. This is known as *learning* the network's parameters or simply as *training* or *fitting* the model. The process is to choose initial parameter values and then iterate the following two steps: (i) compute the derivatives (gradients) of the loss with respect to the parameters, and (ii) adjust the parameters based on the gradients to decrease the loss. After many iterations, we hope to reach the overall minimum of the loss function.

This chapter tackles the second of these steps; we consider algorithms that adjust the parameters to decrease the loss. Chapter 7 discusses how to initialize the parameters and compute the gradients for neural networks.

6.1 Gradient descent

To fit a model, we need a training set $\{\mathbf{x}_i, \mathbf{y}_i\}$ of input/output pairs. We seek parameters ϕ for the model $\mathbf{f}[\mathbf{x}_i, \phi]$ that map the inputs $\mathbf{x}_i$ to the outputs $\mathbf{y}_i$ as well as possible. To this end, we define a loss function $L[\phi]$ that returns a single number that quantifies the mismatch in this mapping. The goal of an *optimization algorithm* is to find parameters $\hat{\phi}$ that minimize the loss:

$$\hat{\phi} = \underset{\phi}{\operatorname{argmin}}\Big[L[\phi]\Big]. \tag{6.1}$$

There are many families of optimization algorithms, but the standard methods for training neural networks are iterative. These algorithms initialize the parameters heuristically and then adjust them repeatedly in such a way that the loss decreases.

The simplest method in this class is *gradient descent*. This starts with initial parameters $\phi = [\phi_0, \phi_1, \ldots, \phi_N]^T$ and iterates two steps:

Step 1. Compute the derivatives of the loss with respect to the parameters:

$$\frac{\partial L}{\partial \phi} = \begin{bmatrix} \frac{\partial L}{\partial \phi_0} \\ \frac{\partial L}{\partial \phi_1} \\ \vdots \\ \frac{\partial L}{\partial \phi_N} \end{bmatrix}. \tag{6.2}$$

Step 2. Update the parameters according to the rule:

$$\phi \longleftarrow \phi - \alpha \cdot \frac{\partial L}{\partial \phi}, \tag{6.3}$$

where the positive scalar α determines the magnitude of the change.

The first step computes the gradient of the loss function at the current position. This determines the *uphill* direction of the loss function. The second step moves a small distance α *downhill* (hence the negative sign). The parameter α may be fixed (in which case, we call it a *learning rate*), or we may perform a *line search* where we try several values of α to find the one that most decreases the loss.

At the minimum of the loss function, the surface must be flat (or we could improve further by going downhill). Hence, the gradient will be zero, and the parameters will stop changing. In practice, we monitor the gradient magnitude and terminate the algorithm when it becomes too small.

Notebook 6.1
Line search

6.1.1 Linear regression example

Consider applying gradient descent to the 1D linear regression model from chapter 2. The model $f[x, \phi]$ maps a scalar input x to a scalar output y and has parameters $\phi = [\phi_0, \phi_1]^T$, which represent the y-intercept and the slope:

$$\begin{aligned} y &= f[x, \phi] \\ &= \phi_0 + \phi_1 x. \end{aligned} \tag{6.4}$$

Given a dataset $\{x_i, y_i\}$ containing I input/output pairs, we choose the least squares loss function:

$$\begin{aligned} L[\phi] &= \sum_{i=1}^{I} \ell_i = \sum_{i=1}^{I} (f[x_i, \phi] - y_i)^2 \\ &= \sum_{i=1}^{I} (\phi_0 + \phi_1 x_i - y_i)^2, \end{aligned} \tag{6.5}$$

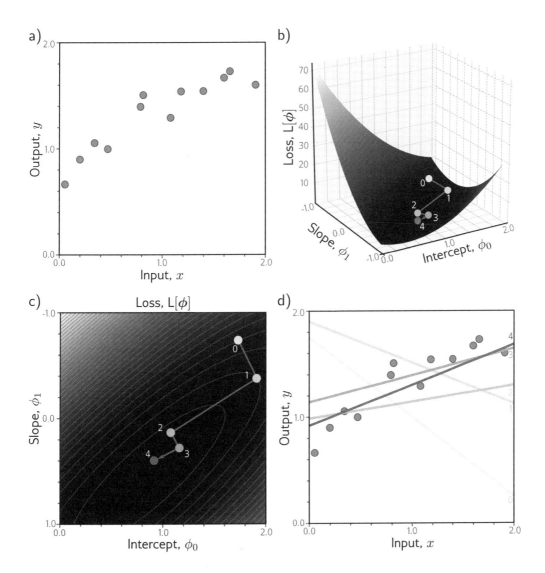

Figure 6.1 Gradient descent for the linear regression model. a) Training set of $I = 12$ input/output pairs $\{x_i, y_i\}$. b) Loss function showing iterations of gradient descent. We start at point 0 and move in the steepest downhill direction until we can improve no further to arrive at point 1. We then repeat this procedure. We measure the gradient at point 1 and move downhill to point 2 and so on. c) This can be visualized better as a heatmap, where the brightness represents the loss. After only four iterations, we are already close to the minimum. d) The model with the parameters at point 0 (lightest line) describes the data very badly, but each successive iteration improves the fit. The model with the parameters at point 4 (darkest line) is already a reasonable description of the training data.

where the term $\ell_i = (\phi_0 + \phi_1 x_i - y_i)^2$ is the individual contribution to the loss from the ith training example.

The derivative of the loss function with respect to the parameters can be decomposed into the sum of the derivatives of the individual contributions:

$$\frac{\partial L}{\partial \phi} = \frac{\partial}{\partial \phi} \sum_{i=1}^{I} \ell_i = \sum_{i=1}^{I} \frac{\partial \ell_i}{\partial \phi}, \tag{6.6}$$

Problem 6.1

where these are given by:

$$\frac{\partial \ell_i}{\partial \phi} = \begin{bmatrix} \frac{\partial \ell_i}{\partial \phi_0} \\ \frac{\partial \ell_i}{\partial \phi_1} \end{bmatrix} = \begin{bmatrix} 2(\phi_0 + \phi_1 x_i - y_i) \\ 2 x_i (\phi_0 + \phi_1 x_i - y_i) \end{bmatrix}. \tag{6.7}$$

Notebook 6.2
Gradient descent

Figure 6.1 shows the progression of this algorithm as we iteratively compute the derivatives according to equations 6.6 and 6.7 and then update the parameters using the rule in equation 6.3. In this case, we have used a line search procedure to find the value of α that decreases the loss the most at each iteration.

6.1.2 Gabor model example

Problem 6.2

Loss functions for linear regression problems (figure 6.1c) always have a single well-defined global minimum. More formally, they are *convex*, which means that no chord (line segment between two points on the surface) intersects the function. Convexity implies that wherever we initialize the parameters, we are bound to reach the minimum if we keep walking downhill; the training procedure can't fail.

Unfortunately, loss functions for most nonlinear models, including both shallow and deep networks, are *non-convex*. Visualizing neural network loss functions is challenging due to the number of parameters. Hence, we first explore a simpler nonlinear model with two parameters to gain insight into the properties of non-convex loss functions:

$$\mathrm{f}[x, \phi] = \sin[\phi_0 + 0.06 \cdot \phi_1 x] \cdot \exp\left(-\frac{(\phi_0 + 0.06 \cdot \phi_1 x)^2}{32.0}\right). \tag{6.8}$$

Problems 6.3–6.5

This *Gabor model* maps scalar input x to scalar output y and consists of a sinusoidal component (creating an oscillatory function) multiplied by a negative exponential component (causing the amplitude to decrease as we move from the center). It has two parameters $\phi = [\phi_0, \phi_1]^T$, where $\phi_0 \in \mathbb{R}$ determines the mean position of the function and $\phi_1 \in \mathbb{R}^+$ stretches or squeezes it along the x-axis (figure 6.2).

Consider a training set of I examples $\{x_i, y_i\}$ (figure 6.3). The least squares loss function for I training examples is defined as:

$$L[\phi] = \sum_{i=1}^{I} (\mathrm{f}[x_i, \phi] - y_i)^2. \tag{6.9}$$

Once more, the goal is to find the parameters $\hat{\phi}$ that minimize this loss.

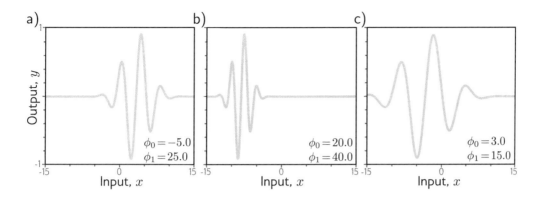

Figure 6.2 Gabor model. This nonlinear model maps scalar input x to scalar output y and has parameters $\phi = [\phi_0, \phi_1]^T$. It describes a sinusoidal function that decreases in amplitude with distance from its center. Parameter $\phi_0 \in \mathbb{R}$ determines the position of the center. As ϕ_0 increases, the function moves left. Parameter $\phi_1 \in \mathbb{R}^+$ squeezes the function along the x-axis relative to the center. As ϕ_1 increases, the function narrows. a–c) Model with different parameters.

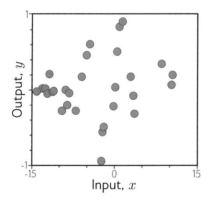

Figure 6.3 Training data for fitting the Gabor model. The training dataset contains 28 input/output examples $\{x_i, y_i\}$. These data were created by uniformly sampling $x_i \in [-15, 15]$, passing the samples through a Gabor model with parameters $\phi = [0.0, 16.6]^T$, and adding normally distributed noise.

6.1.3 Local minima and saddle points

Figure 6.4 depicts the loss function associated with the Gabor model for this dataset. There are numerous *local minima* (cyan circles). Here the gradient is zero, and the loss increases if we move in any direction, but we are *not* at the overall minimum of the function. The point with the lowest loss is known as the *global minimum* and is depicted by the gray circle.

Problem 6.6

If we start in a random position and use gradient descent to go downhill, there is no guarantee that we will wind up at the global minimum and find the best parameters (figure 6.5a). It's equally or even more likely that the algorithm will terminate in one of the local minima. Furthermore, there is no way of knowing whether there is a better solution elsewhere.

Problems 6.7–6.8

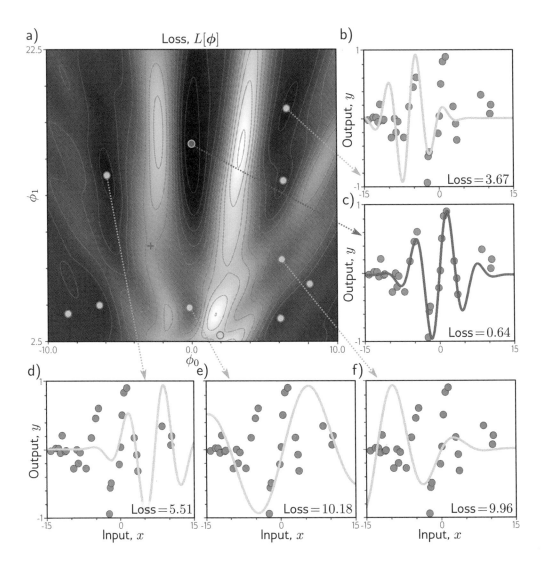

Figure 6.4 Loss function for the Gabor model. a) The loss function is non-convex, with multiple local minima (cyan circles) in addition to the global minimum (gray circle). It also contains saddle points where the gradient is locally zero, but the function increases in one direction and decreases in the other. The blue cross is an example of a saddle point; the function decreases as we move horizontally in either direction but increases as we move vertically. b–f) Models associated with the different minima. In each case, there is no small change that decreases the loss. Panel (c) shows the global minimum, which has a loss of 0.64.

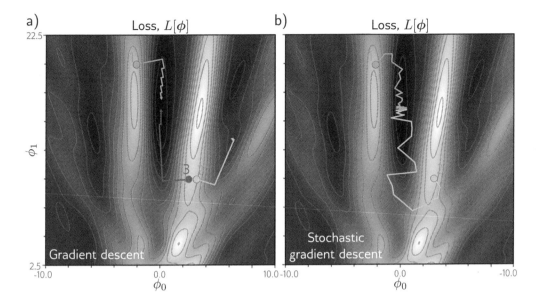

Figure 6.5 Gradient descent vs. stochastic gradient descent. a) Gradient descent with line search. As long as the gradient descent algorithm is initialized in the right "valley" of the loss function (e.g., points 1 and 3), the parameter estimate will move steadily toward the global minimum. However, if it is initialized outside this valley (e.g., point 2), it will descend toward one of the local minima. b) Stochastic gradient descent adds noise to the optimization process, so it is possible to escape from the wrong valley (e.g., point 2) and still reach the global minimum.

In addition, the loss function contains *saddle points* (e.g., the blue cross in figure 6.4). Here, the gradient is zero, but the function increases in some directions and decreases in others. If the current parameters are not exactly at the saddle point, then gradient descent can escape by moving downhill. However, the surface near the saddle point is flat, so it's hard to be sure that training hasn't converged; if we terminate the algorithm when the gradient is small, we may erroneously stop near a saddle point.

6.2 Stochastic gradient descent

The Gabor model has two parameters, so we could find the global minimum by either (i) exhaustively searching the parameter space or (ii) repeatedly starting gradient descent from different positions and choosing the result with the lowest loss. However, neural network models can have millions of parameters, so neither approach is practical. In short, using gradient descent to find the global optimum of a high-dimensional loss function is challenging. We can find *a* minimum, but there is no way to tell whether this

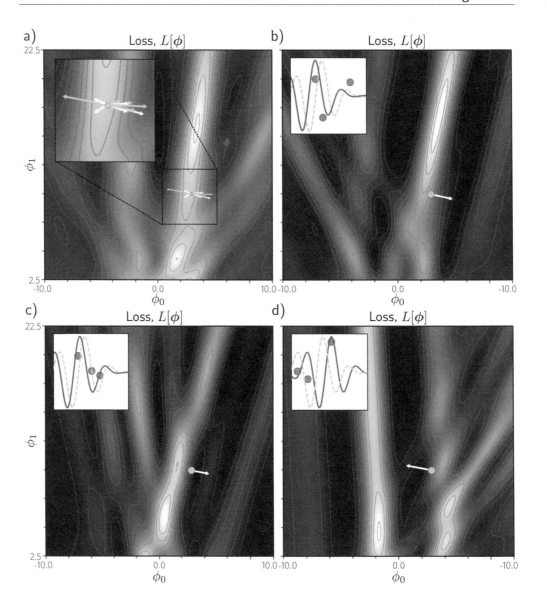

Figure 6.6 Alternative view of SGD for the Gabor model with a batch size of three. a) Loss function for the entire training dataset. At each iteration, there is a probability distribution of possible parameter changes (inset shows samples). These correspond to different choices of the three batch elements. b) Loss function for one possible batch. The SGD algorithm moves in the downhill direction on this function for a distance that is determined by the learning rate and the local gradient magnitude. The current model (dashed function in inset) changes to better fit the batch data (solid function). c) A different batch creates a different loss function and results in a different update. d) For this batch, the algorithm moves *downhill* with respect to the batch loss function but *uphill* with respect to the global loss function in panel (a). This is how SGD can escape local minima.

is the global minimum or even a good one.

One of the main problems is that the final destination of a gradient descent algorithm is entirely determined by the starting point. *Stochastic gradient descent (SGD)* attempts to remedy this problem by adding some noise to the gradient at each step. The solution still moves downhill on average, but at any given iteration, the direction chosen is not necessarily in the steepest downhill direction. Indeed, it might not be downhill at all. The SGD algorithm has the possibility of moving temporarily uphill and hence jumping from one "valley" of the loss function to another (figure 6.5b).

Notebook 6.3
Stochastic
gradient descent

6.2.1 Batches and epochs

The mechanism for introducing randomness is simple. At each iteration, the algorithm chooses a random subset of the training data and computes the gradient from these examples alone. This subset is known as a *minibatch* or *batch* for short. The update rule for the model parameters ϕ_t at iteration t is hence:

$$\phi_{t+1} \longleftarrow \phi_t - \alpha \cdot \sum_{i \in \mathcal{B}_t} \frac{\partial \ell_i[\phi_t]}{\partial \phi}, \tag{6.10}$$

where $\mathcal{B}_t$ is a set containing the indices of the input/output pairs in the current batch and, as before, ℓ_i is the loss due to the ith pair. The term α is the learning rate, and together with the gradient magnitude, determines the distance moved at each iteration. The learning rate is chosen at the start of the procedure and does not depend on the local properties of the function.

The batches are usually drawn from the dataset without replacement. The algorithm works through the training examples until it has used all the data, at which point it starts sampling from the full training dataset again. A single pass through the entire training dataset is referred to as an *epoch*. A batch may be as small as a single example or as large as the whole dataset. The latter case is called *full-batch gradient descent* and is identical to regular (non-stochastic) gradient descent.

Problem 6.9

An alternative interpretation of SGD is that it computes the gradient of a different loss function at each iteration; the loss function depends on both the model and the training data and hence will differ for each randomly selected batch. In this view, SGD performs deterministic gradient descent on a constantly changing loss function (figure 6.6). However, despite this variability, the expected loss and expected gradients at any point remain the same as for gradient descent.

6.2.2 Properties of stochastic gradient descent

SGD has several attractive features. First, although it adds noise to the trajectory, it still improves the fit to a subset of the data at each iteration. Hence, the updates tend to be sensible even if they are not optimal. Second, because it draws training examples without replacement and iterates through the dataset, the training examples all still contribute equally. Third, it is less computationally expensive to compute the gradient from just a subset of the training data. Fourth, it can (in principle) escape local minima. Fifth, it reduces the chances of getting stuck near saddle points; it is likely that at least some of the possible batches will have a significant gradient at any point on the loss function. Finally, there is some evidence that SGD finds parameters for neural networks that cause them to generalize well to new data in practice (see section 9.2).

SGD does not necessarily "converge" in the traditional sense. However, the hope is that when we are close to the global minimum, all the data points will be well described by the model. Consequently, the gradient will be small, whichever batch is chosen, and the parameters will cease to change much. In practice, SGD is often applied with a *learning rate schedule*. The learning rate α starts at a high value and is decreased by a constant factor every N epochs. The logic is that in the early stages of training, we want the algorithm to explore the parameter space, jumping from valley to valley to find a sensible region. In later stages, we are roughly in the right place and are more concerned with fine-tuning the parameters, so we decrease α to make smaller changes.

6.3 Momentum

A common modification to stochastic gradient descent is to add a *momentum* term. We update the parameters with a weighted combination of the gradient computed from the current batch and the direction moved in the previous step:

$$\mathbf{m}_{t+1} \quad \leftarrow \quad \beta \cdot \mathbf{m}_t + (1 - \beta) \sum_{i \in \mathcal{B}_t} \frac{\partial \ell_i[\phi_t]}{\partial \phi}$$

$$\phi_{t+1} \quad \leftarrow \quad \phi_t - \alpha \cdot \mathbf{m}_{t+1}, \tag{6.11}$$

where $\mathbf{m}_t$ is the momentum (which drives the update at iteration t), $\beta \in [0, 1)$ controls the degree to which the gradient is smoothed over time, and α is the learning rate.

The recursive formulation of the momentum calculation means that the gradient step is an infinite weighted sum of all the previous gradients, where the weights get smaller as we move back in time. The effective learning rate increases if all these gradients are aligned over multiple iterations but decreases if the gradient direction repeatedly changes as the terms in the sum cancel out. The overall effect is a smoother trajectory and reduced oscillatory behavior in valleys (figure 6.7).

Problem 6.10

6.3.1 Nesterov accelerated momentum

Notebook 6.4
Momentum

The momentum term can be considered a coarse prediction of where the SGD algorithm will move next. Nesterov accelerated momentum (figure 6.8) computes the gradients at this predicted point rather than at the current point:

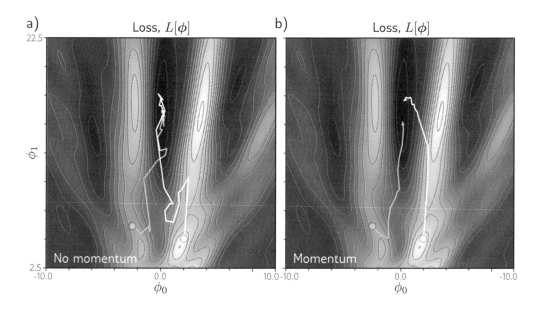

Figure 6.7 Stochastic gradient descent with momentum. a) Regular stochastic descent takes a very indirect path toward the minimum. b) With a momentum term, the change at the current step is a weighted combination of the previous change and the gradient computed from the batch. This smooths out the trajectory and increases the speed of convergence.

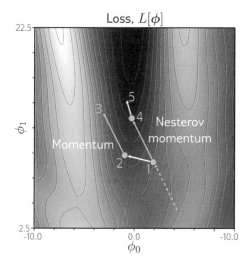

Figure 6.8 Nesterov accelerated momentum. The solution has traveled along the dashed line to arrive at point 1. A traditional momentum update measures the gradient at point 1, moves some distance in this direction to point 2, and then adds the momentum term from the previous iteration (i.e., in the same direction as the dashed line), arriving at point 3. The Nesterov momentum update first applies the momentum term (moving from point 1 to point 4) and then measures the gradient and applies an update to arrive at point 5.

$$\mathbf{m}_{t+1} \quad \leftarrow \quad \beta \cdot \mathbf{m}_t + (1 - \beta) \sum_{i \in \mathcal{B}_t} \frac{\partial \ell_i[\phi_t - \alpha\beta \cdot \mathbf{m}_t]}{\partial \phi}$$

$$\phi_{t+1} \quad \leftarrow \quad \phi_t - \alpha \cdot \mathbf{m}_{t+1}, \tag{6.12}$$

where now the gradients are evaluated at $\phi_t - \alpha\beta \cdot \mathbf{m}_t$. One way to think about this is that the gradient term now corrects the path provided by momentum alone.

6.4 Adam

Gradient descent with a fixed step size has the following undesirable property: it makes large adjustments to parameters associated with large gradients (where perhaps we should be more cautious) and small adjustments to parameters associated with small gradients (where perhaps we should explore further). When the gradient of the loss surface is much steeper in one direction than another, it is difficult to choose a learning rate that (i) makes good progress in both directions and (ii) is stable (figures 6.9a–b).

A straightforward approach is to normalize the gradients so that we move a fixed distance (governed by the learning rate) in each direction. To do this, we first measure the gradient $\mathbf{m}_{t+1}$ and the pointwise squared gradient $\mathbf{v}_{t+1}$:

$$\mathbf{m}_{t+1} \quad \leftarrow \quad \frac{\partial L[\phi_t]}{\partial \phi}$$

$$\mathbf{v}_{t+1} \quad \leftarrow \quad \left(\frac{\partial L[\phi_t]}{\partial \phi} \right)^2. \tag{6.13}$$

Then we apply the update rule:

$$\phi_{t+1} \quad \leftarrow \quad \phi_t - \alpha \cdot \frac{\mathbf{m}_{t+1}}{\sqrt{\mathbf{v}_{t+1}} + \epsilon}, \tag{6.14}$$

where the square root and division are both pointwise, α is the learning rate, and ϵ is a small constant that prevents division by zero when the gradient magnitude is zero. The term $\mathbf{v}_{t+1}$ is the squared gradient, and the positive root of this is used to normalize the gradient itself, so all that remains is the sign in each coordinate direction. The result is that the algorithm moves a fixed distance α along each coordinate, where the direction is determined by whichever way is downhill (figure 6.9c). This simple algorithm makes good progress in both directions but will not converge unless it happens to land exactly at the minimum. Instead, it will bounce back and forth around the minimum.

Adaptive moment estimation, or *Adam*, takes this idea and adds momentum to both the estimate of the gradient and the squared gradient:

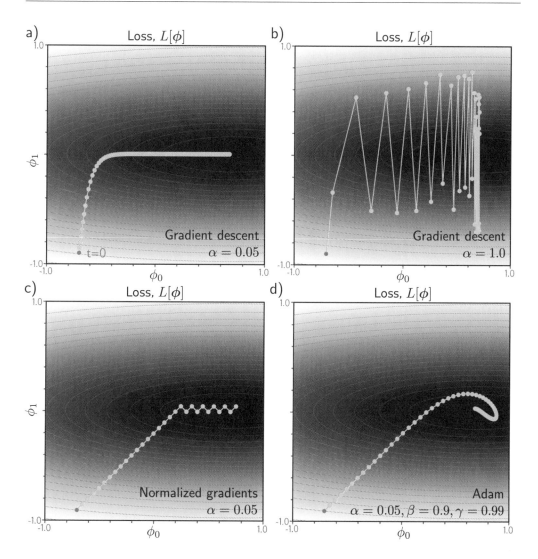

Figure 6.9 Adaptive moment estimation (Adam). a) This loss function changes quickly in the vertical direction but slowly in the horizontal direction. If we run full-batch gradient descent with a learning rate that makes good progress in the vertical direction, then the algorithm takes a long time to reach the final horizontal position. b) If the learning rate is chosen so that the algorithm makes good progress in the horizontal direction, it overshoots in the vertical direction and becomes unstable. c) A straightforward approach is to move a fixed distance along each axis at each step so that we move downhill in both directions. This is accomplished by normalizing the gradient magnitude and retaining only the sign. However, this does not usually converge to the exact minimum but instead oscillates back and forth around it (here between the last two points). d) The Adam algorithm uses momentum in both the estimated gradient and the normalization term, which creates a smoother path.

$$\mathbf{m}_{t+1} \;\leftarrow\; \beta \cdot \mathbf{m}_t + (1 - \beta)\frac{\partial L[\phi_t]}{\partial \phi}$$

$$\mathbf{v}_{t+1} \;\leftarrow\; \gamma \cdot \mathbf{v}_t + (1 - \gamma)\left(\frac{\partial L[\phi_t]}{\partial \phi}\right)^2, \tag{6.15}$$

where β and γ are the momentum coefficients for the two statistics.

Using momentum is equivalent to taking a weighted average over the history of each of these statistics. At the start of the procedure, all the previous measurements are effectively zero, resulting in unrealistically small estimates. Consequently, we modify these statistics using the rule:

$$\tilde{\mathbf{m}}_{t+1} \;\leftarrow\; \frac{\mathbf{m}_{t+1}}{1 - \beta^{t+1}}$$

$$\tilde{\mathbf{v}}_{t+1} \;\leftarrow\; \frac{\mathbf{v}_{t+1}}{1 - \gamma^{t+1}}. \tag{6.16}$$

Since β and γ are in the range $[0, 1)$, the terms with exponents $t+1$ become smaller with each time step, the denominators become closer to one, and this modification has a diminishing effect.

Finally, we update the parameters as before, but with the modified terms:

$$\phi_{t+1} \;\leftarrow\; \phi_t - \alpha \cdot \frac{\tilde{\mathbf{m}}_{t+1}}{\sqrt{\tilde{\mathbf{v}}_{t+1}} + \epsilon}. \tag{6.17}$$

Notebook 6.5
Adam

The result is an algorithm that can converge to the overall minimum and makes good progress in every direction in the parameter space. Note that Adam is usually used in a stochastic setting where the gradients and their squares are computed from mini-batches:

$$\mathbf{m}_{t+1} \;\leftarrow\; \beta \cdot \mathbf{m}_t + (1 - \beta)\sum_{i \in \mathcal{B}_t}\frac{\partial \ell_i[\phi_t]}{\partial \phi}$$

$$\mathbf{v}_{t+1} \;\leftarrow\; \gamma \cdot \mathbf{v}_t + (1 - \gamma)\left(\sum_{i \in \mathcal{B}_t}\frac{\partial \ell_i[\phi_t]}{\partial \phi}\right)^2, \tag{6.18}$$

and so the trajectory is noisy in practice.

As we shall see in chapter 7, the gradient magnitudes of neural network parameters can depend on their depth in the network. Adam helps compensate for this tendency and balances out changes across the different layers. In practice, Adam also has the advantage of being less sensitive to the initial learning rate because it avoids situations like those in figures 6.9a–b, so it doesn't need complex learning rate schedules.

6.5 Training algorithm hyperparameters

The choices of learning algorithm, batch size, learning rate schedule, and momentum coefficients are all considered *hyperparameters* of the training algorithm; these directly affect the final model performance but are distinct from the model parameters. Choosing these can be more art than science, and it's common to train many models with different hyperparameters and choose the best one. This is known as *hyperparameter search*. We return to this issue in chapter 8.

6.6 Summary

This chapter discussed model training. This problem was framed as finding parameters ϕ that corresponded to the minimum of a loss function $L[\phi]$. The gradient descent method measures the gradient of the loss function for the current parameters (i.e., how the loss changes when we make a small change to the parameters). Then it moves the parameters in the direction that decreases the loss fastest. This is repeated until convergence.

For nonlinear functions, the loss function may have both local minima (where gradient descent gets trapped) and saddle points (where gradient descent may appear to have converged but has not). Stochastic gradient descent helps mitigate these problems.[1] At each iteration, we use a different random subset of the data (a batch) to compute the gradient. This adds noise to the process and helps prevent the algorithm from getting trapped in a sub-optimal region of parameter space. Each iteration is also computationally cheaper since it only uses a subset of the data. We saw that adding a momentum term makes convergence more efficient. Finally, we introduced the Adam algorithm.

The ideas in this chapter apply to optimizing *any* model. The next chapter tackles two aspects of training specific to neural networks. First, we address how to compute the gradients of the loss with respect to the parameters of a neural network. This is accomplished using the famous backpropagation algorithm. Second, we discuss how to initialize the network parameters before optimization begins. Without careful initialization, the gradients used by the optimization can become extremely large or extremely small, which can hinder the training process.

Notes

Optimization algorithms: Optimization algorithms are used extensively throughout engineering, and it is generally more typical to use the term *objective function* rather than loss function or cost function. Gradient descent was invented by Cauchy (1847), and stochastic gradient descent dates back to at least Robbins & Monro (1951). A modern compromise between the two is stochastic variance-reduced descent (Johnson & Zhang, 2013), in which the full gradient is computed periodically, with stochastic updates interspersed. Reviews of optimization algorithms for neural networks can be found in Ruder (2016), Bottou et al. (2018), and Sun (2020). Bottou (2012) discusses best practice for SGD, including shuffling without replacement.

---

[1]Chapter 20 discusses the extent to which saddle points and local minima really *are* problems in deep learning. In practice, deep networks are surprisingly easy to train.

Convexity, minima, and saddle points: A function is convex if no chord (line segment between two points on the surface) intersects the function. This can be tested algebraically by considering the *Hessian matrix* (the matrix of second derivatives):

$$\mathbf{H}[\boldsymbol{\phi}] = \begin{bmatrix} \frac{\partial^2 L}{\partial \phi_0^2} & \frac{\partial^2 L}{\partial \phi_0 \partial \phi_1} & \cdots & \frac{\partial^2 L}{\partial \phi_0 \partial \phi_N} \\ \frac{\partial^2 L}{\partial \phi_1 \partial \phi_0} & \frac{\partial^2 L}{\partial \phi_1^2} & \cdots & \frac{\partial^2 L}{\partial \phi_1 \partial \phi_N} \\ \vdots & \vdots & \ddots & \vdots \\ \frac{\partial^2 L}{\partial \phi_N \partial \phi_0} & \frac{\partial^2 L}{\partial \phi_N \partial \phi_1} & \cdots & \frac{\partial^2 L}{\partial \phi_N^2} \end{bmatrix}. \tag{6.19}$$

Appendix B.3.7
Eigenvalues

If the Hessian matrix is positive definite (has positive eigenvalues) for all possible parameter values, then the function is convex; the loss function will look like a smooth bowl (as in figure 6.1c), so training will be relatively easy. There will be a single global minimum and no local minima or saddle points.

For any loss function, the eigenvalues of the Hessian matrix at places where the gradient is zero allow us to classify this position as (i) a minimum (the eigenvalues are all positive), (ii) a maximum (the eigenvalues are all negative), or (iii) a saddle point (positive eigenvalues are associated with directions in which we are at a minimum and negative ones with directions where we are at a maximum).

Line search: Gradient descent with a fixed step size is inefficient because the distance moved depends entirely on the magnitude of the gradient. It moves a long distance when the function is changing fast (where perhaps it should be more cautious) but a short distance when the function is changing slowly (where perhaps it should explore further). For this reason, gradient descent methods are usually combined with a line search procedure in which we sample the function along the desired direction to try to find the optimal step size. One such approach is bracketing (figure 6.10). Another problem with gradient descent is that it tends to lead to inefficient oscillatory behavior when descending valleys (e.g., path 1 in figure 6.5a).

Beyond gradient descent: Numerous algorithms have been developed that remedy the problems of gradient descent. Most notable is the Newton method, which takes the curvature of the surface into account using the inverse of the Hessian matrix; if the gradient of the function is changing quickly, then it applies a more cautious update. This method eliminates the need for line search and does not suffer from oscillatory behavior. However, it has its own problems; in its simplest form, it moves toward the nearest extremum, but this may be a maximum if we are closer to the top of a hill than we are to the bottom of a valley. Moreover, computing the inverse Hessian is intractable when the number of parameters is large, as in neural networks.

Problem 6.11

Properties of SGD: The limit of SGD as the learning rate tends to zero is a stochastic differential equation. Jastrzębski et al. (2018) showed that this equation relies on the learning-rate to batch size ratio and that there is a relation between the learning rate to batch size ratio and the width of the minimum found. Wider minima are considered more desirable; if the loss function for test data is similar, then small errors in the parameter estimates will have little effect on test performance. He et al. (2019) prove a generalization bound for SGD that has a positive correlation with the ratio of batch size to learning rate. They train a large number of models on different architectures and datasets and find empirical evidence that test accuracy improves when the ratio of batch size to learning rate is low. Smith et al. (2018) and Goyal et al. (2018) also identified the ratio of batch size to learning rate as being important for generalization (see figure 20.10).

Momentum: The idea of using momentum to speed up optimization dates to Polyak (1964). Goh (2017) presents an in-depth discussion of the properties of momentum. The Nesterov

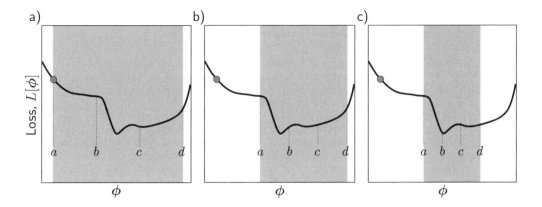

Figure 6.10 Line search using the bracketing approach. a) The current solution is at position a (orange point), and we wish to search the region $[a, d]$ (gray shaded area). We define two points b, c interior to the search region and evaluate the loss function at these points. Here $L[b] > L[c]$, so we eliminate the range $[a, b]$. b) We now repeat this procedure in the refined search region and find that $L[b] < L[c]$, so we eliminate the range $[c, d]$. c) We repeat this process until this minimum is closely bracketed.

accelerated gradient method was introduced by Nesterov (1983). Nesterov momentum was first applied in the context of stochastic gradient descent by Sutskever et al. (2013).

Adaptive training algorithms: AdaGrad (Duchi et al., 2011) is an optimization algorithm that addresses the possibility that some parameters may have to move further than others by assigning a different learning rate to each parameter. AdaGrad uses the cumulative squared gradient for each parameter to attenuate its learning rate. This has the disadvantage that the learning rates decrease over time, and learning can halt before the minimum is found. RMSProp (Hinton et al., 2012a) and AdaDelta (Zeiler, 2012) modified this algorithm to help prevent these problems by recursively updating the squared gradient term.

By far the most widely used adaptive training algorithm is adaptive moment optimization or Adam (Kingma & Ba, 2015). This combines the ideas of momentum (in which the gradient vector is averaged over time) and AdaGrad, AdaDelta, and RMSProp (in which a smoothed squared gradient term is used to modify the learning rate for each parameter). The original paper on the Adam algorithm provided a convergence proof for convex loss functions, but a counterexample was identified by Reddi et al. (2018), who developed a modification of Adam called AMSGrad, which does converge. Of course, in deep learning, the loss functions are non-convex, and Zaheer et al. (2018) subsequently developed an adaptive algorithm called YOGI and proved that it converges in this scenario. Regardless of these theoretical objections, the original Adam algorithm works well in practice and is widely used, not least because it works well over a broad range of hyperparameters and makes rapid initial progress.

One potential problem with adaptive training algorithms is that the learning rates are based on accumulated statistics of the observed gradients. At the start of training, when there are few samples, these statistics may be very noisy. This can be remedied by *learning rate warm-up* (Goyal et al., 2018), in which the learning rates are gradually increased over the first few thousand iterations. An alternative solution is rectified Adam (Liu et al., 2021a), which gradually changes the momentum term over time in a way that helps avoid high variance. Dozat (2016) incorporated Nesterov momentum into the Adam algorithm.

SGD vs. Adam: There has been a lively discussion about the relative merits of SGD and Adam. Wilson et al. (2017) provided evidence that SGD with momentum can find lower minima than Adam, which generalizes better over a variety of deep learning tasks. However, this is strange since SGD is a special case of Adam (when $\beta = \gamma = 0$) once the modification term (equation 6.16) becomes one, which happens quickly. It is hence more likely that SGD outperforms Adam *when we use Adam's default hyperparameters.* Loshchilov & Hutter (2019) proposed AdamW, which substantially improves the performance of Adam in the presence of L2 regularization (see section 9.1). Choi et al. (2019) provide evidence that if we search for the best Adam hyperparameters, it performs just as well as SGD and converges faster. Keskar & Socher (2017) proposed a method called SWATS that starts using Adam (to make rapid initial progress) and then switches to SGD (to get better final generalization performance).

Exhaustive search: All the algorithms discussed in this chapter are iterative. A completely different approach is to quantize the network parameters and exhaustively search the resulting discretized parameter space using SAT solvers (Mézard & Mora, 2009). This approach has the potential to find the global minimum and provide a guarantee that there is no lower loss elsewhere but is only practical for very small models.

Problems

Problem 6.1 Show that the derivatives of the least squares loss function in equation 6.5 are given by the expressions in equation 6.7.

Problem 6.2 A surface is convex if the eigenvalues of the Hessian $\mathbf{H}[\phi]$ are positive everywhere. In this case, the surface has a unique minimum, and optimization is easy. Find an algebraic expression for the Hessian matrix,

$$\mathbf{H}[\phi] = \begin{bmatrix} \frac{\partial^2 L}{\partial \phi_0^2} & \frac{\partial^2 L}{\partial \phi_0 \partial \phi_1} \\ \frac{\partial^2 L}{\partial \phi_1 \partial \phi_0} & \frac{\partial^2 L}{\partial \phi_1^2} \end{bmatrix}, \tag{6.20}$$

Appendix B.3.7
Eigenvalues

Appendix B.3.8
Trace

Appendix B.3.8
Determinant

for the linear regression model (equation 6.5). Prove that this function is convex by showing that the eigenvalues are always positive. This can be done by showing that both the trace and the determinant of the matrix are positive.

Problem 6.3 Compute the derivatives of the least squares loss $L[\phi]$ with respect to the parameters ϕ_0 and ϕ_1 for the Gabor model (equation 6.8).

Problem 6.4* The logistic regression model uses a linear function to assign an input $\mathbf{x}$ to one of two classes $y \in \{0, 1\}$. For a 1D input and a 1D output, it has two parameters, ϕ_0 and ϕ_1, and is defined by:

$$Pr(y = 1|x) = \text{sig}[\phi_0 + \phi_1 x], \tag{6.21}$$

where sig[•] is the logistic sigmoid function:

$$\text{sig}[z] = \frac{1}{1 + \exp[-z]}. \tag{6.22}$$

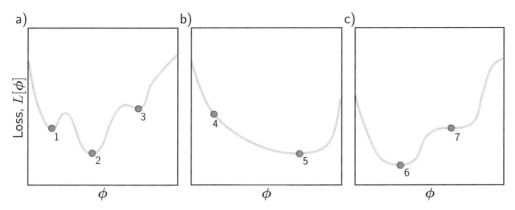

Figure 6.11 Three 1D loss functions for problem 6.6.

(i) Plot y against x for this model for different values of ϕ_0 and ϕ_1 and explain the qualitative meaning of each parameter. (ii) What is a suitable loss function for this model? (iii) Compute the derivatives of this loss function with respect to the parameters. (iv) Generate ten data points from a normal distribution with mean -1 and standard deviation 1 and assign them the label $y = 0$. Generate another ten data points from a normal distribution with mean 1 and standard deviation 1 and assign these the label $y = 1$. Plot the loss as a heatmap in terms of the two parameters ϕ_0 and ϕ_1. (v) Is this loss function convex? How could you prove this?

Problem 6.5* Compute the derivatives of the least squares loss with respect to the ten parameters of the simple neural network model introduced in equation 3.1:

$$\mathrm{f}[x, \boldsymbol{\phi}] = \phi_0 + \phi_1 \mathrm{a}[\theta_{10} + \theta_{11}x] + \phi_2 \mathrm{a}[\theta_{20} + \theta_{21}x] + \phi_3 \mathrm{a}[\theta_{30} + \theta_{31}x]. \tag{6.23}$$

Think carefully about what the derivative of the ReLU function $a[\bullet]$ will be.

Problem 6.6 Which of the functions in figure 6.11 is convex? Justify your answer. Characterize each of the points 1–7 as (i) a local minimum, (ii) the global minimum, or (iii) neither.

Problem 6.7* The gradient descent trajectory for path 1 in figure 6.5a oscillates back and forth inefficiently as it moves down the valley toward the minimum. It's also notable that it turns at right angles to the previous direction at each step. Provide a qualitative explanation for these phenomena. Propose a solution that might help prevent this behavior.

Problem 6.8* Can (non-stochastic) gradient descent with a *fixed* learning rate escape local minima?

Problem 6.9 We run the stochastic gradient descent algorithm for 1,000 iterations on a dataset of size 100 with a batch size of 20. For how many epochs did we train the model?

Problem 6.10 Show that the momentum term $\mathbf{m}_t$ (equation 6.11) is an infinite weighted sum of the gradients at the previous iterations and derive an expression for the coefficients (weights) of that sum.

Problem 6.11 What dimensions will the Hessian have if the model has one million parameters?

Chapter 7

Gradients and initialization

Chapter 6 introduced iterative optimization algorithms. These are general-purpose methods for finding the minimum of a function. In the context of neural networks, they find parameters that minimize the loss so that the model accurately predicts the training outputs from the inputs. The basic approach is to choose initial parameters randomly and then make a series of small changes that decrease the loss on average. Each change is based on the gradient of the loss with respect to the parameters at the current position.

This chapter discusses two issues that are specific to neural networks. First, we consider how to calculate the gradients efficiently. This is a serious challenge since the largest models at the time of writing have $\sim 10^{12}$ parameters, and the gradient needs to be computed for every parameter at every iteration of the training algorithm. Second, we consider how to initialize the parameters. If this is not done carefully, the initial losses and their gradients can be extremely large or small. In either case, this impedes the training process.

7.1 Problem definitions

Consider a network $\mathbf{f}[\mathbf{x}, \boldsymbol{\phi}]$ with multivariate input $\mathbf{x}$, parameters $\boldsymbol{\phi}$, and three hidden layers $\mathbf{h}_1, \mathbf{h}_2$, and $\mathbf{h}_3$:

$$
\begin{aligned}
\mathbf{h}_1 &= \mathbf{a}[\boldsymbol{\beta}_0 + \boldsymbol{\Omega}_0 \mathbf{x}] \\
\mathbf{h}_2 &= \mathbf{a}[\boldsymbol{\beta}_1 + \boldsymbol{\Omega}_1 \mathbf{h}_1] \\
\mathbf{h}_3 &= \mathbf{a}[\boldsymbol{\beta}_2 + \boldsymbol{\Omega}_2 \mathbf{h}_2] \\
\mathbf{f}[\mathbf{x}, \boldsymbol{\phi}] &= \boldsymbol{\beta}_3 + \boldsymbol{\Omega}_3 \mathbf{h}_3,
\end{aligned}
\tag{7.1}
$$

where the function $\mathbf{a}[\bullet]$ applies the activation function separately to every element of the input. The model parameters $\boldsymbol{\phi} = \{\boldsymbol{\beta}_0, \boldsymbol{\Omega}_0, \boldsymbol{\beta}_1, \boldsymbol{\Omega}_1, \boldsymbol{\beta}_2, \boldsymbol{\Omega}_2, \boldsymbol{\beta}_3, \boldsymbol{\Omega}_3\}$ consist of the bias vectors $\boldsymbol{\beta}_k$ and weight matrices $\boldsymbol{\Omega}_k$ between every layer (figure 7.1).

We also have individual loss terms ℓ_i, which return the negative log-likelihood of the ground truth label y_i given the model prediction $\mathbf{f}[\mathbf{x}_i, \boldsymbol{\phi}]$ for training input $\mathbf{x}_i$. For example, this might be the least squares loss $\ell_i = (\mathbf{f}[\mathbf{x}_i, \boldsymbol{\phi}] - y_i)^2$. The total loss is the sum of these terms over the training data:

$$L[\boldsymbol{\phi}] = \sum_{i=1}^{I} \ell_i. \tag{7.2}$$

The most commonly used optimization algorithm for training neural networks is stochastic gradient descent (SGD), which updates the parameters as:

$$\boldsymbol{\phi}_{t+1} \longleftarrow \boldsymbol{\phi}_t - \alpha \sum_{i \in \mathcal{B}_t} \frac{\partial \ell_i[\boldsymbol{\phi}_t]}{\partial \boldsymbol{\phi}}, \tag{7.3}$$

where α is the learning rate, and $\mathcal{B}_t$ contains the batch indices at iteration t. To compute this update, we need to calculate the derivatives:

$$\frac{\partial \ell_i}{\partial \boldsymbol{\beta}_k} \quad \text{and} \quad \frac{\partial \ell_i}{\partial \boldsymbol{\Omega}_k}, \tag{7.4}$$

for the parameters $\{\boldsymbol{\beta}_k, \boldsymbol{\Omega}_k\}$ at every layer $k \in \{0, 1, \ldots, K\}$ and for each index i in the batch. The first part of this chapter describes the *backpropagation algorithm*, which computes these derivatives efficiently.

Problem 7.1

In the second part of the chapter, we consider how to initialize the network parameters before we commence training. We describe methods to choose the initial weights $\boldsymbol{\Omega}_k$ and biases $\boldsymbol{\beta}_k$ so that training is stable.

7.2 Computing derivatives

The derivatives of the loss tell us how the loss changes when we make a small change to the parameters. Optimization algorithms exploit this information to manipulate the parameters so that the loss becomes smaller. The *backpropagation algorithm* computes these derivatives. The mathematical details are somewhat involved, so we first make two observations that provide some intuition.

Observation 1: Each weight (element of $\boldsymbol{\Omega}_k$) multiplies the activation at a source hidden unit and adds the result to a destination hidden unit in the next layer. It follows that the effect of any small change to the weight is amplified or attenuated by the activation at the source hidden unit. Hence, we run the network for each data example in the batch and store the activations of all the hidden units. This is known as the *forward pass* (figure 7.1). The stored activations will subsequently be used to compute the gradients.

Observation 2: A small change in a bias or weight causes a ripple effect of changes through the subsequent network. The change modifies the value of its destination hidden

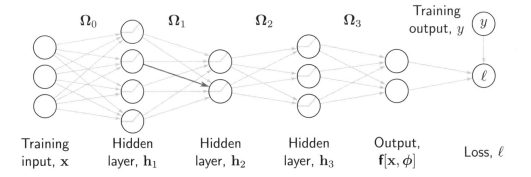

Figure 7.1 Backpropagation forward pass. The goal is to compute the derivatives of the loss ℓ with respect to each of the weights (arrows) and biases (not shown). In other words, we want to know how a small change to each parameter will affect the loss. Each weight multiplies the hidden unit at its source and contributes the result to the hidden unit at its destination. Consequently, the effects of any small change to the weight will be scaled by the activation of the source hidden unit. For example, the blue weight is applied to the second hidden unit at layer 1; if the activation of this unit doubles, then the effect of a small change to the blue weight will double too. Hence, to compute the derivatives of the weights, we need to calculate and store the activations at the hidden layers. This is known as the *forward pass* since it involves running the network equations sequentially.

unit. This, in turn, changes the values of the hidden units in the subsequent layer, which will change the hidden units in the layer after that, and so on, until a change is made to the model output and, finally, the loss.

Hence, to know how changing a parameter modifies the loss, we also need to know how changes to every subsequent hidden layer will, in turn, modify their successor. These same quantities are required when considering other parameters in the same or earlier layers. It follows that we can calculate them once and reuse them. For example, consider computing the effect of a small change in weights that feed into hidden layers $\mathbf{h}_3$, $\mathbf{h}_2$, and $\mathbf{h}_1$, respectively:

- To calculate how a small change in a weight or bias feeding into hidden layer $\mathbf{h}_3$ modifies the loss, we need to know (i) how a change in layer $\mathbf{h}_3$ changes the model output $\mathbf{f}$, and (ii) how a change in this output changes the loss ℓ (figure 7.2a).

- To calculate how a small change in a weight or bias feeding into hidden layer $\mathbf{h}_2$ modifies the loss, we need to know (i) how a change in layer $\mathbf{h}_2$ affects $\mathbf{h}_3$, (ii) how $\mathbf{h}_3$ changes the model output, and (iii) how this output changes the loss (figure 7.2b).

- To calculate how a small change in a weight or bias feeding into hidden layer $\mathbf{h}_1$ modifies the loss, we need to know (i) how a change in layer $\mathbf{h}_1$ affects layer $\mathbf{h}_2$, (ii) how a change in layer $\mathbf{h}_2$ affects layer $\mathbf{h}_3$, (iii) how layer $\mathbf{h}_3$ changes the model output, and (iv) how the model output changes the loss (figure 7.2c).

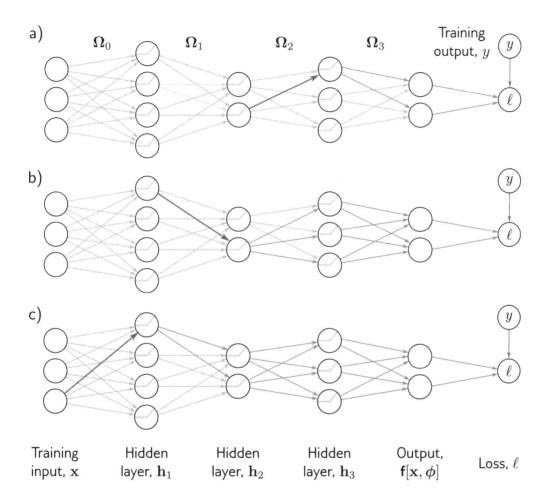

Figure 7.2 Backpropagation backward pass. a) To compute how a change to a weight feeding into layer $\mathbf{h}_3$ (blue arrow) changes the loss, we need to know how the hidden unit in $\mathbf{h}_3$ changes the model output $\mathbf{f}$ and how $\mathbf{f}$ changes the loss (orange arrows). b) To compute how a small change to a weight feeding into $\mathbf{h}_2$ (blue arrow) changes the loss, we need to know (i) how the hidden unit in $\mathbf{h}_2$ changes $\mathbf{h}_3$, (ii) how $\mathbf{h}_3$ changes $\mathbf{f}$, and (iii) how $\mathbf{f}$ changes the loss (orange arrows). c) Similarly, to compute how a small change to a weight feeding into $\mathbf{h}_1$ (blue arrow) changes the loss, we need to know how $\mathbf{h}_1$ changes $\mathbf{h}_2$ and how these changes propagate through to the loss (orange arrows). The backward pass first computes derivatives at the end of the network and then works backward to exploit the inherent redundancy of these computations.

As we move backward through the network, we see that most of the terms we need were already calculated in the previous step, so we do not need to re-compute them. Proceeding backward through the network in this way to compute the derivatives is known as the *backward pass*.

The ideas behind backpropagation are relatively easy to understand. However, the derivation requires matrix calculus because the bias and weight terms are vectors and matrices, respectively. To help grasp the underlying mechanics, the following section derives backpropagation for a simpler toy model with scalar parameters. We then apply the same approach to a deep neural network in section 7.4.

7.3 Toy example

Consider a model $f[x, \phi]$ with eight scalar parameters $\phi = \{\beta_0, \omega_0, \beta_1, \omega_1, \beta_2, \omega_2, \beta_3, \omega_3\}$ that consists of a composition of the functions $\sin[\bullet], \exp[\bullet]$, and $\cos[\bullet]$:

$$f[x, \phi] = \beta_3 + \omega_3 \cdot \cos\Big[\beta_2 + \omega_2 \cdot \exp\big[\beta_1 + \omega_1 \cdot \sin[\beta_0 + \omega_0 \cdot x]\big]\Big], \tag{7.5}$$

and a least squares loss function $L[\phi] = \sum_i \ell_i$ with individual terms:

$$\ell_i = (f[x_i, \phi] - y_i)^2, \tag{7.6}$$

where, as usual, x_i is the ith training input, and y_i is the ith training output. You can think of this as a simple neural network with one input, one output, one hidden unit at each layer, and different activation functions $\sin[\bullet], \exp[\bullet]$, and $\cos[\bullet]$ between each layer.

We aim to compute the derivatives:

$$\frac{\partial \ell_i}{\partial \beta_0}, \quad \frac{\partial \ell_i}{\partial \omega_0}, \quad \frac{\partial \ell_i}{\partial \beta_1}, \quad \frac{\partial \ell_i}{\partial \omega_1}, \quad \frac{\partial \ell_i}{\partial \beta_2}, \quad \frac{\partial \ell_i}{\partial \omega_2}, \quad \frac{\partial \ell_i}{\partial \beta_3}, \quad \text{and} \quad \frac{\partial \ell_i}{\partial \omega_3}.$$

Of course, we could find expressions for these derivatives by hand and compute them directly. However, some of these expressions are quite complex. For example:

$$
\begin{aligned}
\frac{\partial \ell_i}{\partial \omega_0} \;=\; & -2\left(\beta_3 + \omega_3 \cdot \cos\Big[\beta_2 + \omega_2 \cdot \exp\big[\beta_1 + \omega_1 \cdot \sin[\beta_0 + \omega_0 \cdot x_i]\big]\Big] - y_i\right) \\
& \cdot \omega_1 \omega_2 \omega_3 \cdot x_i \cdot \cos[\beta_0 + \omega_0 \cdot x_i] \cdot \exp\Big[\beta_1 + \omega_1 \cdot \sin[\beta_0 + \omega_0 \cdot x_i]\Big] \\
& \cdot \sin\Big[\beta_2 + \omega_2 \cdot \exp\big[\beta_1 + \omega_1 \cdot \sin[\beta_0 + \omega_0 \cdot x_i]\big]\Big]. \tag{7.7}
\end{aligned}
$$

Such expressions are awkward to derive and code without mistakes and do not exploit the inherent redundancy; notice that the three exponential terms are the same.

The backpropagation algorithm is an efficient method for computing all of these derivatives at once. It consists of (i) a forward pass, in which we compute and store a series of intermediate values and the network output, and (ii) a backward pass, in which

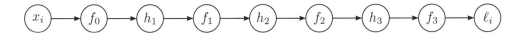

Figure 7.3 Backpropagation forward pass. We compute and store each of the intermediate variables in turn until we finally calculate the loss.

we calculate the derivatives of each parameter, starting at the end of the network, and reusing previous calculations as we move toward the start.

Forward pass: We treat the computation of the loss as a series of calculations:

$$
\begin{aligned}
f_0 &= \beta_0 + \omega_0 \cdot x_i \\
h_1 &= \sin[f_0] \\
f_1 &= \beta_1 + \omega_1 \cdot h_1 \\
h_2 &= \exp[f_1] \\
f_2 &= \beta_2 + \omega_2 \cdot h_2 \\
h_3 &= \cos[f_2] \\
f_3 &= \beta_3 + \omega_3 \cdot h_3 \\
\ell_i &= (f_3 - y_i)^2.
\end{aligned}
\tag{7.8}
$$

We compute and store the values of the intermediate variables f_k and h_k (figure 7.3).

Backward pass #1: We now compute the derivatives of ℓ_i with respect to these intermediate variables, but in reverse order:

$$
\frac{\partial \ell_i}{\partial f_3}, \quad \frac{\partial \ell_i}{\partial h_3}, \quad \frac{\partial \ell_i}{\partial f_2}, \quad \frac{\partial \ell_i}{\partial h_2}, \quad \frac{\partial \ell_i}{\partial f_1}, \quad \frac{\partial \ell_i}{\partial h_1}, \quad \text{and} \quad \frac{\partial \ell_i}{\partial f_0}.
\tag{7.9}
$$

The first of these derivatives is straightforward:

$$
\frac{\partial \ell_i}{\partial f_3} = 2(f_3 - y_i).
\tag{7.10}
$$

The next derivative can be calculated using the chain rule:

$$
\frac{\partial \ell_i}{\partial h_3} = \frac{\partial f_3}{\partial h_3} \frac{\partial \ell_i}{\partial f_3}.
\tag{7.11}
$$

The left-hand side asks how ℓ_i changes when h_3 changes. The right-hand side says we can decompose this into (i) how f_3 changes when h_3 changes and (ii) how ℓ_i changes when f_3 changes. In the original equations, h_3 changes f_3, which changes ℓ_i, and the derivatives

Figure 7.4 Backpropagation backward pass #1. We work backward from the end of the function computing the derivatives $\partial \ell_i / \partial f_k$ and $\partial \ell_i / \partial h_k$ of the loss with respect to the intermediate quantities. Each derivative is computed from the previous one by multiplying by terms of the form $\partial f_k / \partial h_k$ or $\partial h_k / \partial f_{k-1}$.

represent the effects of this chain. Notice that we already computed the second of these derivatives, and the other is the derivative of $\beta_3 + \omega_3 \cdot h_3$ with respect to h_3, which is ω_3.

We continue in this way, computing the derivatives of the output with respect to these intermediate quantities (figure 7.4):

$$
\begin{aligned}
\frac{\partial \ell_i}{\partial f_2} &= \frac{\partial h_3}{\partial f_2} \left(\frac{\partial f_3}{\partial h_3} \frac{\partial \ell_i}{\partial f_3} \right) \\
\frac{\partial \ell_i}{\partial h_2} &= \frac{\partial f_2}{\partial h_2} \left(\frac{\partial h_3}{\partial f_2} \frac{\partial f_3}{\partial h_3} \frac{\partial \ell_i}{\partial f_3} \right) \\
\frac{\partial \ell_i}{\partial f_1} &= \frac{\partial h_2}{\partial f_1} \left(\frac{\partial f_2}{\partial h_2} \frac{\partial h_3}{\partial f_2} \frac{\partial f_3}{\partial h_3} \frac{\partial \ell_i}{\partial f_3} \right) \\
\frac{\partial \ell_i}{\partial h_1} &= \frac{\partial f_1}{\partial h_1} \left(\frac{\partial h_2}{\partial f_1} \frac{\partial f_2}{\partial h_2} \frac{\partial h_3}{\partial f_2} \frac{\partial f_3}{\partial h_3} \frac{\partial \ell_i}{\partial f_3} \right) \\
\frac{\partial \ell_i}{\partial f_0} &= \frac{\partial h_1}{\partial f_0} \left(\frac{\partial f_1}{\partial h_1} \frac{\partial h_2}{\partial f_1} \frac{\partial f_2}{\partial h_2} \frac{\partial h_3}{\partial f_2} \frac{\partial f_3}{\partial h_3} \frac{\partial \ell_i}{\partial f_3} \right).
\end{aligned}
\tag{7.12}
$$

Problem 7.2

In each case, we have already computed the quantities in the brackets in the previous step, and the last term has a simple expression. These equations embody Observation 2 from the previous section (figure 7.2); we can reuse the previously computed derivatives if we calculate them in reverse order.

Backward pass #2: Finally, we consider how the loss ℓ_i changes when we change the parameters $\{\beta_k\}$ and $\{\omega_k\}$. Once more, we apply the chain rule (figure 7.5):

$$
\begin{aligned}
\frac{\partial \ell_i}{\partial \beta_k} &= \frac{\partial f_k}{\partial \beta_k} \frac{\partial \ell_i}{\partial f_k} \\
\frac{\partial \ell_i}{\partial \omega_k} &= \frac{\partial f_k}{\partial \omega_k} \frac{\partial \ell_i}{\partial f_k}.
\end{aligned}
\tag{7.13}
$$

In each case, the second term on the right-hand side was computed in equation 7.12. When $k > 0$, we have $f_k = \beta_k + \omega_k \cdot h_k$, so:

$$
\frac{\partial f_k}{\partial \beta_k} = 1 \qquad \text{and} \qquad \frac{\partial f_k}{\partial \omega_k} = h_k.
\tag{7.14}
$$

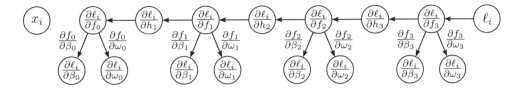

Figure 7.5 Backpropagation backward pass #2. Finally, we compute the derivatives $\partial \ell_i / \partial \beta_k$ and $\partial \ell_i / \partial \omega_k$. Each derivative is computed by multiplying the term $\partial \ell_i / \partial f_k$ by $\partial f_k / \partial \beta_k$ or $\partial f_k / \partial \omega_k$ as appropriate.

This is consistent with Observation 1 from the previous section; the effect of a change in the weight ω_k is proportional to the value of the source variable h_k (which was stored in the forward pass). The final derivatives from the term $f_0 = \beta_0 + \omega_0 \cdot x_i$ are:

Notebook 7.1
Backpropagation
in toy model

$$\frac{\partial f_0}{\partial \beta_0} = 1 \quad \text{and} \quad \frac{\partial f_0}{\partial \omega_0} = x_i. \tag{7.15}$$

Backpropagation is both simpler and more efficient than computing the derivatives individually, as in equation 7.7.[1]

7.4 Backpropagation algorithm

Now we repeat this process for a three-layer network (figure 7.1). The intuition and much of the algebra are identical. The main differences are that intermediate variables $\mathbf{f}_k, \mathbf{h}_k$ are vectors, the biases $\boldsymbol{\beta}_k$ are vectors, the weights $\boldsymbol{\Omega}_k$ are matrices, and we are using ReLU functions rather than simple algebraic functions like $\cos[\bullet]$.

Forward pass: We write the network as a series of sequential calculations:

$$
\begin{aligned}
\mathbf{f}_0 &= \boldsymbol{\beta}_0 + \boldsymbol{\Omega}_0 \mathbf{x}_i \\
\mathbf{h}_1 &= \mathbf{a}[\mathbf{f}_0] \\
\mathbf{f}_1 &= \boldsymbol{\beta}_1 + \boldsymbol{\Omega}_1 \mathbf{h}_1 \\
\mathbf{h}_2 &= \mathbf{a}[\mathbf{f}_1] \\
\mathbf{f}_2 &= \boldsymbol{\beta}_2 + \boldsymbol{\Omega}_2 \mathbf{h}_2 \\
\mathbf{h}_3 &= \mathbf{a}[\mathbf{f}_2] \\
\mathbf{f}_3 &= \boldsymbol{\beta}_3 + \boldsymbol{\Omega}_3 \mathbf{h}_3 \\
\ell_i &= \mathrm{l}[\mathbf{f}_3, y_i],
\end{aligned}
\tag{7.16}
$$

---

[1]Note that we did not actually need the derivatives $\partial l_i / \partial h_k$ of the loss with respect to the activations. In the final backpropagation algorithm, we will not compute these explicitly.

Figure 7.6 Derivative of rectified linear unit. The rectified linear unit (orange curve) returns zero when the input is less than zero and returns the input otherwise. Its derivative (cyan curve) returns zero when the input is less than zero (since the slope here is zero) and one when the input is greater than zero (since the slope here is one).

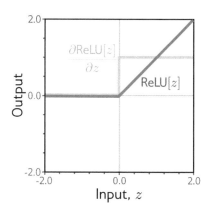

where $\mathbf{f}_{k-1}$ represents the pre-activations at the kth hidden layer (i.e., the values before the ReLU function $\mathbf{a}[\bullet]$) and $\mathbf{h}_k$ contains the activations at the kth hidden layer (i.e., after the ReLU function). The term $l[\mathbf{f}_3, y_i]$ represents the loss function (e.g., least squares or binary cross-entropy loss). In the forward pass, we work through these calculations and store all the intermediate quantities.

Backward pass #1: Now let's consider how the loss changes when we modify the pre-activations $\mathbf{f}_0, \mathbf{f}_1, \mathbf{f}_2$. Applying the chain rule, the expression for the derivative of the loss ℓ_i with respect to $\mathbf{f}_2$ is:

Appendix B.5
Matrix calculus

$$\frac{\partial \ell_i}{\partial \mathbf{f}_2} = \frac{\partial \mathbf{h}_3}{\partial \mathbf{f}_2} \frac{\partial \mathbf{f}_3}{\partial \mathbf{h}_3} \frac{\partial \ell_i}{\partial \mathbf{f}_3}. \tag{7.17}$$

The three terms on the right-hand side have sizes $D_3 \times D_3, D_3 \times D_f$, and $D_f \times 1$, respectively, where D_3 is the number of hidden units in the third layer, and D_f is the dimensionality of the model output $\mathbf{f}_3$.

Similarly, we can compute how the loss changes when we change $\mathbf{f}_1$ and $\mathbf{f}_0$:

$$\frac{\partial \ell_i}{\partial \mathbf{f}_1} = \frac{\partial \mathbf{h}_2}{\partial \mathbf{f}_1} \frac{\partial \mathbf{f}_2}{\partial \mathbf{h}_2} \left(\frac{\partial \mathbf{h}_3}{\partial \mathbf{f}_2} \frac{\partial \mathbf{f}_3}{\partial \mathbf{h}_3} \frac{\partial \ell_i}{\partial \mathbf{f}_3} \right) \tag{7.18}$$

$$\frac{\partial \ell_i}{\partial \mathbf{f}_0} = \frac{\partial \mathbf{h}_1}{\partial \mathbf{f}_0} \frac{\partial \mathbf{f}_1}{\partial \mathbf{h}_1} \left(\frac{\partial \mathbf{h}_2}{\partial \mathbf{f}_1} \frac{\partial \mathbf{f}_2}{\partial \mathbf{h}_2} \frac{\partial \mathbf{h}_3}{\partial \mathbf{f}_2} \frac{\partial \mathbf{f}_3}{\partial \mathbf{h}_3} \frac{\partial \ell_i}{\partial \mathbf{f}_3} \right). \tag{7.19}$$

Problem 7.3

Note that in each case, the term in brackets was computed in the previous step. By working backward through the network, we can reuse the previous computations.

Problems 7.4–7.5

Moreover, the terms themselves are simple. Working backward through the right-hand side of equation 7.17, we have:

- The derivative $\partial \ell_i / \partial \mathbf{f}_3$ of the loss ℓ_i with respect to the network output $\mathbf{f}_3$ will depend on the loss function but usually has a simple form.

- The derivative $\partial \mathbf{f}_3 / \partial \mathbf{h}_3$ of the network output with respect to hidden layer $\mathbf{h}_3$ is:

$$\frac{\partial \mathbf{f}_3}{\partial \mathbf{h}_3} = \frac{\partial}{\partial \mathbf{h}_3} \left(\boldsymbol{\beta}_3 + \boldsymbol{\Omega}_3 \mathbf{h}_3 \right) = \boldsymbol{\Omega}_3^T. \tag{7.20}$$

If you are unfamiliar with matrix calculus, this result is not obvious. It is explored in problem 7.6.

Problem 7.6

- The derivative $\partial \mathbf{h}_3 / \partial \mathbf{f}_2$ of the output $\mathbf{h}_3$ of the activation function with respect to its input $\mathbf{f}_2$ will depend on the activation function. It will be a diagonal matrix since each activation only depends on the corresponding pre-activation. For ReLU functions, the diagonal terms are zero everywhere $\mathbf{f}_2$ is less than zero and one otherwise (figure 7.6). Rather than multiply by this matrix, we extract the diagonal terms as a vector $\mathbb{I}[\mathbf{f}_2 > 0]$ and pointwise multiply, which is more efficient.

Problems 7.7–7.8

The terms on the right-hand side of equations 7.18 and 7.19 have similar forms. As we progress back through the network, we alternately (i) multiply by the transpose of the weight matrices $\boldsymbol{\Omega}_k^T$ and (ii) threshold based on the inputs $\mathbf{f}_{k-1}$ to the hidden layer. These inputs were stored during the forward pass.

Backward pass #2: Now that we know how to compute $\partial \ell_i / \partial \mathbf{f}_k$, we can focus on calculating the derivatives of the loss with respect to the weights and biases. To calculate the derivatives of the loss with respect to the biases $\boldsymbol{\beta}_k$, we again use the chain rule:

$$
\begin{aligned}
\frac{\partial \ell_i}{\partial \boldsymbol{\beta}_k} &= \frac{\partial \mathbf{f}_k}{\partial \boldsymbol{\beta}_k} \frac{\partial \ell_i}{\partial \mathbf{f}_k} \\
&= \frac{\partial}{\partial \boldsymbol{\beta}_k} \left(\boldsymbol{\beta}_k + \boldsymbol{\Omega}_k \mathbf{h}_k \right) \frac{\partial \ell_i}{\partial \mathbf{f}_k} \\
&= \frac{\partial \ell_i}{\partial \mathbf{f}_k},
\end{aligned}
\tag{7.21}
$$

which we already calculated in equations 7.17 and 7.18.

Similarly, the derivative for the weights matrix $\boldsymbol{\Omega}_k$, is given by:

$$
\begin{aligned}
\frac{\partial \ell_i}{\partial \boldsymbol{\Omega}_k} &= \frac{\partial \mathbf{f}_k}{\partial \boldsymbol{\Omega}_k} \frac{\partial \ell_i}{\partial \mathbf{f}_k} \\
&= \frac{\partial}{\partial \boldsymbol{\Omega}_k} \left(\boldsymbol{\beta}_k + \boldsymbol{\Omega}_k \mathbf{h}_k \right) \frac{\partial \ell_i}{\partial \mathbf{f}_k} \\
&= \frac{\partial \ell_i}{\partial \mathbf{f}_k} \mathbf{h}_k^T.
\end{aligned}
\tag{7.22}
$$

Again, the progression from line two to line three is not obvious and is explored in problem 7.9. However, the result makes sense. The final line is a matrix of the same size as $\boldsymbol{\Omega}_k$. It depends linearly on $\mathbf{h}_k$, which was multiplied by $\boldsymbol{\Omega}_k$ in the original expression. This is also consistent with the initial intuition that the derivative of the weights in $\boldsymbol{\Omega}_k$ will be proportional to the values of the hidden units $\mathbf{h}_k$ that they multiply. Recall that we already computed these during the forward pass.

Problem 7.9

7.4.1   Backpropagation algorithm summary

We now briefly summarize the final backpropagation algorithm. Consider a deep neural network $\mathbf{f}[\mathbf{x}_i, \boldsymbol{\phi}]$ that takes input $\mathbf{x}_i$, has K hidden layers with ReLU activations, and individual loss term $\ell_i = \mathrm{l}[\mathbf{f}[\mathbf{x}_i, \boldsymbol{\phi}], \mathbf{y}_i]$. The goal of backpropagation is to compute the derivatives $\partial \ell_i / \partial \boldsymbol{\beta}_k$ and $\partial \ell_i / \partial \boldsymbol{\Omega}_k$ with respect to the biases $\boldsymbol{\beta}_k$ and weights $\boldsymbol{\Omega}_k$.

Forward pass: We compute and store the following quantities:

$$
\begin{aligned}
\mathbf{f}_0 &= \boldsymbol{\beta}_0 + \boldsymbol{\Omega}_0 \mathbf{x}_i \\
\mathbf{h}_k &= \mathbf{a}[\mathbf{f}_{k-1}] & k \in \{1, 2, \ldots, K\} \\
\mathbf{f}_k &= \boldsymbol{\beta}_k + \boldsymbol{\Omega}_k \mathbf{h}_k. & k \in \{1, 2, \ldots, K\}
\end{aligned}
\tag{7.23}
$$

Backward pass: We start with the derivative $\partial \ell_i / \partial \mathbf{f}_K$ of the loss function ℓ_i with respect to the network output $\mathbf{f}_K$ and work backward through the network:

$$
\begin{aligned}
\frac{\partial \ell_i}{\partial \boldsymbol{\beta}_k} &= \frac{\partial \ell_i}{\partial \mathbf{f}_k} & k \in \{K, K-1, \ldots, 1\} \\
\frac{\partial \ell_i}{\partial \boldsymbol{\Omega}_k} &= \frac{\partial \ell_i}{\partial \mathbf{f}_k} \mathbf{h}_k^T & k \in \{K, K-1, \ldots, 1\} \\
\frac{\partial \ell_i}{\partial \mathbf{f}_{k-1}} &= \mathbb{I}[\mathbf{f}_{k-1} > 0] \odot \left(\boldsymbol{\Omega}_k^T \frac{\partial \ell_i}{\partial \mathbf{f}_k} \right), & k \in \{K, K-1, \ldots, 1\}
\end{aligned}
\tag{7.24}
$$

where $\odot$ denotes pointwise multiplication, and $\mathbb{I}[\mathbf{f}_{k-1} > 0]$ is a vector containing ones where $\mathbf{f}_{k-1}$ is greater than zero and zeros elsewhere. Finally, we compute the derivatives with respect to the first set of biases and weights:

$$
\begin{aligned}
\frac{\partial \ell_i}{\partial \boldsymbol{\beta}_0} &= \frac{\partial \ell_i}{\partial \mathbf{f}_0} \\
\frac{\partial \ell_i}{\partial \boldsymbol{\Omega}_0} &= \frac{\partial \ell_i}{\partial \mathbf{f}_0} \mathbf{x}_i^T.
\end{aligned}
\tag{7.25}
$$

We calculate these derivatives for every training example in the batch and sum them together to retrieve the gradient for the SGD update.

Note that the backpropagation algorithm is extremely efficient; the most demanding computational step in both the forward and backward pass is matrix multiplication (by $\boldsymbol{\Omega}$ and $\boldsymbol{\Omega}^T$, respectively) which only requires additions and multiplications. However, it is not memory efficient; the intermediate values in the forward pass must all be stored, and this can limit the size of the model we can train.

Problem 7.10

Notebook 7.2
Backpropagation

7.4.2   Algorithmic differentiation

Although it's important to understand the backpropagation algorithm, it's unlikely that you will need to code it in practice. Modern deep learning frameworks such as PyTorch and TensorFlow calculate the derivatives automatically, given the model specification. This is known as *algorithmic differentiation*.

Each functional component (linear transform, ReLU activation, loss function) in the framework knows how to compute its own derivative. For example, the PyTorch ReLU function $\mathbf{z}_{out} = \mathbf{relu}[\mathbf{z}_{in}]$ knows how to compute the derivative of its output $\mathbf{z}_{out}$ with respect to its input $\mathbf{z}_{in}$. Similarly, a linear function $\mathbf{z}_{out} = \boldsymbol{\beta} + \boldsymbol{\Omega}\mathbf{z}_{in}$ knows how to compute the derivatives of the output $\mathbf{z}_{out}$ with respect to the input $\mathbf{z}_{in}$ and with respect to the parameters $\boldsymbol{\beta}$ and $\boldsymbol{\Omega}$. The algorithmic differentiation framework also knows the sequence of operations in the network and thus has all the information required to perform the forward and backward passes.

These frameworks exploit the massive parallelism of modern graphics processing units (GPUs). Computations such as matrix multiplication (which features in both the forward and backward pass) are naturally amenable to parallelization. Moreover, it's possible to perform the forward and backward passes for the entire batch in parallel if the model and intermediate results in the forward pass do not exceed the available memory.

Problem 7.11

Since the training algorithm now processes the entire batch in parallel, the input becomes a multi-dimensional *tensor*. In this context, a tensor can be considered the generalization of a matrix to arbitrary dimensions. Hence, a vector is a 1D tensor, a matrix is a 2D tensor, and a 3D tensor is a 3D grid of numbers. Until now, the training data have been 1D, so the input for backpropagation would be a 2D tensor where the first dimension indexes the batch element and the second indexes the data dimension. In subsequent chapters, we will encounter more complex structured input data. For example, in models where the input is an RGB image, the original data examples are 3D (height × width × channel). Here, the input to the learning framework would be a 4D tensor, where the extra dimension indexes the batch element.

7.4.3 Extension to arbitrary computational graphs

We have described backpropagation in a deep neural network that is naturally sequential; we calculate the intermediate quantities $\mathbf{f}_0, \mathbf{h}_1, \mathbf{f}_1, \mathbf{h}_2 \ldots, \mathbf{f}_k$ in turn. However, models need not be restricted to sequential computation. Later in this book, we will meet models with branching structures. For example, we might take the values in a hidden layer and process them through two different sub-networks before recombining.

Problems 7.12–7.13

Fortunately, the ideas of backpropagation still hold if the computational graph is acyclic. Modern algorithmic differentiation frameworks such as PyTorch and TensorFlow can handle arbitrary acyclic computational graphs.

7.5 Parameter initialization

The backpropagation algorithm computes the derivatives that are used by stochastic gradient descent and Adam to train the model. We now address how to initialize the parameters before we start training. To see why this is crucial, consider that during the forward pass, each set of pre-activations $\mathbf{f}_k$ is computed as:

$$\begin{aligned}
\mathbf{f}_k &= \boldsymbol{\beta}_k + \boldsymbol{\Omega}_k \mathbf{h}_k \\
&= \boldsymbol{\beta}_k + \boldsymbol{\Omega}_k \mathbf{a}[\mathbf{f}_{k-1}],
\end{aligned} \tag{7.26}$$

where $\mathbf{a}[\bullet]$ applies the ReLU functions and $\boldsymbol{\Omega}_k$ and $\boldsymbol{\beta}_k$ are the weights and biases, respectively. Imagine that we initialize all the biases to zero and the elements of $\boldsymbol{\Omega}_k$ according to a normal distribution with mean zero and variance σ^2. Consider two scenarios:

- If the variance σ^2 is very small (e.g., 10^{-5}), then each element of $\boldsymbol{\beta}_k + \boldsymbol{\Omega}_k \mathbf{h}_k$ will be a weighted sum of $\mathbf{h}_k$ where the weights are very small; the result will likely have a smaller magnitude than the input. In addition, the ReLU function clips values less than zero, so the range of $\mathbf{h}_k$ will be half that of $\mathbf{f}_{k-1}$. Consequently, the magnitudes of the pre-activations at the hidden layers will get smaller and smaller as we progress through the network.

- If the variance σ^2 is very large (e.g., 10^5), then each element of $\boldsymbol{\beta}_k + \boldsymbol{\Omega}_k \mathbf{h}_k$ will be a weighted sum of $\mathbf{h}_k$ where the weights are very large; the result is likely to have a much larger magnitude than the input. The ReLU function halves the range of the inputs, but if σ^2 is large enough, the magnitudes of the pre-activations will still get larger as we progress through the network.

In these two situations, the values at the pre-activations can become so small or so large that they cannot be represented with finite precision floating point arithmetic.

Even if the forward pass is tractable, the same logic applies to the backward pass. Each gradient update (equation 7.24) consists of multiplying by $\boldsymbol{\Omega}^T$. If the values of $\boldsymbol{\Omega}$ are not initialized sensibly, then the gradient magnitudes may decrease or increase uncontrollably during the backward pass. These cases are known as the *vanishing gradient problem* and the *exploding gradient problem*, respectively. In the former case, updates to the model become vanishingly small. In the latter case, they become unstable.

7.5.1 Initialization for forward pass

We now present a mathematical version of the same argument. Consider the computation between adjacent pre-activations $\mathbf{f}$ and $\mathbf{f}'$ with dimensions D_h and $D_{h'}$, respectively:

$$\begin{aligned}
\mathbf{h} &= \mathbf{a}[\mathbf{f}], \\
\mathbf{f}' &= \boldsymbol{\beta} + \boldsymbol{\Omega}\mathbf{h}
\end{aligned} \tag{7.27}$$

where $\mathbf{f}$ represents the pre-activations, $\boldsymbol{\Omega}$, and $\boldsymbol{\beta}$ represent the weights and biases, and $\mathbf{a}[\bullet]$ is the activation function.

Assume the pre-activations f_j in the input layer $\mathbf{f}$ have variance σ_f^2. Consider initializing the biases β_i to zero and the weights Ω_{ij} as normally distributed with mean zero and variance σ_Ω^2. Now we derive expressions for the mean and variance of the pre-activations $\mathbf{f}'$ in the subsequent layer.

The expectation (mean) $\mathbb{E}[f_i']$ of the intermediate values f_i' is:

Appendix C.2
Expectation

$$
\begin{aligned}
\mathbb{E}[f_i'] &= \mathbb{E}\left[\beta_i + \sum_{j=1}^{D_h} \Omega_{ij} h_j\right] \\
&= \mathbb{E}[\beta_i] + \sum_{j=1}^{D_h} \mathbb{E}[\Omega_{ij} h_j] \\
&= \mathbb{E}[\beta_i] + \sum_{j=1}^{D_h} \mathbb{E}[\Omega_{ij}] \mathbb{E}[h_j] \\
&= 0 + \sum_{j=1}^{D_h} 0 \cdot \mathbb{E}[h_j] = 0,
\end{aligned}
\tag{7.28}
$$

where D_h is the dimensionality of the input layer $\mathbf{h}$. We have used the rules for manipulating expectations, and we have assumed that the distributions over the hidden units h_j and the network weights Ω_{ij} are independent between the second and third lines.

Appendix C.2.1
Expectation rules

Using this result, we see that the variance $\sigma_{f'}^2$ of the pre-activations f_i' is:

$$
\begin{aligned}
\sigma_{f'}^2 &= \mathbb{E}[f_i'^2] - \mathbb{E}[f_i']^2 \\
&= \mathbb{E}\left[\left(\beta_i + \sum_{j=1}^{D_h} \Omega_{ij} h_j\right)^2\right] - 0 \\
&= \mathbb{E}\left[\left(\sum_{j=1}^{D_h} \Omega_{ij} h_j\right)^2\right] \\
&= \sum_{j=1}^{D_h} \mathbb{E}[\Omega_{ij}^2] \mathbb{E}[h_j^2] \\
&= \sum_{j=1}^{D_h} \sigma_\Omega^2 \mathbb{E}[h_j^2] = \sigma_\Omega^2 \sum_{j=1}^{D_h} \mathbb{E}[h_j^2],
\end{aligned}
\tag{7.29}
$$

where we have used the variance identity $\sigma^2 = \mathbb{E}[(z - \mathbb{E}[z])^2] = \mathbb{E}[z^2] - \mathbb{E}[z]^2$. We have assumed once more that the distributions of the weights Ω_{ij} and the hidden units h_j are independent between lines three and four.

Appendix C.2.3
Variance identity

Assuming that the input distribution of pre-activations f_j is symmetric about zero, half of these pre-activations will be clipped by the ReLU function, and the second moment $\mathbb{E}[h_j^2]$ will be half the variance σ_f^2 of f_j (see problem 7.14):

Problem 7.14

$$
\sigma_{f'}^2 = \sigma_\Omega^2 \sum_{j=1}^{D_h} \frac{\sigma_f^2}{2} = \frac{1}{2} D_h \sigma_\Omega^2 \sigma_f^2.
\tag{7.30}
$$

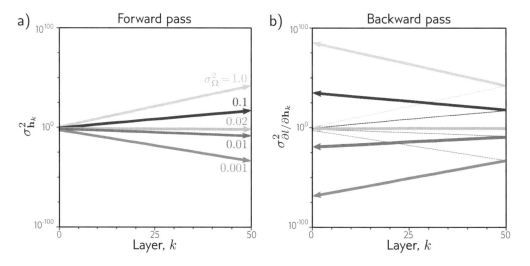

Figure 7.7 Weight initialization. Consider a deep network with 50 hidden layers and $D_h = 100$ hidden units per layer. The network has a 100-dimensional input $\mathbf{x}$ initialized from a standard normal distribution, a single fixed target $y = 0$, and a least squares loss function. The bias vectors $\boldsymbol{\beta}_k$ are initialized to zero, and the weight matrices $\boldsymbol{\Omega}_k$ are initialized with a normal distribution with mean zero and five different variances $\sigma^2_{\boldsymbol{\Omega}} \in \{0.001, 0.01, 0.02, 0.1, 1.0\}$. a) Variance of hidden unit activations computed in forward pass as a function of the network layer. For He initialization ($\sigma^2_{\boldsymbol{\Omega}} = 2/D_h = 0.02$), the variance is stable. However, for larger values, it increases rapidly, and for smaller values, it decreases rapidly (note log scale). b) The variance of the gradients in the backward pass (solid lines) continues this trend; if we initialize with a value larger than 0.02, the magnitude of the gradients increases rapidly as we pass back through the network. If we initialize with a value smaller, then the magnitude decreases. These are known as the *exploding gradient* and *vanishing gradient* problems, respectively.

This, in turn, implies that if we want the variance $\sigma^2_{f'}$ of the subsequent pre-activations $\mathbf{f}'$ to be the same as the variance σ^2_f of the original pre-activations $\mathbf{f}$ during the forward pass, we should set:

$$\sigma^2_{\boldsymbol{\Omega}} = \frac{2}{D_h}, \tag{7.31}$$

where D_h is the dimension of the original layer to which the weights were applied. This is known as *He initialization*.

7.5.2   Initialization for backward pass

A similar argument establishes how the variance of the gradients $\partial l/\partial f_k$ changes during the backward pass. During the backward pass, we multiply by the transpose $\boldsymbol{\Omega}^T$ of the weight matrix (equation 7.24), so the equivalent expression becomes:

$$\sigma_\Omega^2 = \frac{2}{D_{h'}}, \tag{7.32}$$

where $D_{h'}$ is the dimension of the layer that the weights feed into.

7.5.3 Initialization for both forward and backward pass

If the weight matrix $\mathbf{\Omega}$ is not square (i.e., there are different numbers of hidden units in the two adjacent layers, so D_h and $D_{h'}$ differ), then it is not possible to choose the variance to satisfy both equations 7.31 and 7.32 simultaneously. One possible compromise is to use the mean $(D_h + D_{h'})/2$ as a proxy for the number of terms, which gives:

$$\sigma_\Omega^2 = \frac{4}{D_h + D_{h'}}. \tag{7.33}$$

Figure 7.7 shows empirically that both the variance of the hidden units in the forward pass and the variance of the gradients in the backward pass remain stable when the parameters are initialized appropriately.

Problem 7.15

Notebook 7.3
Initialization

7.6 Example training code

The primary focus of this book is scientific; this is not a guide for implementing deep learning models. Nonetheless, in figure 7.8, we present PyTorch code that implements the ideas explored in this book so far. The code defines a neural network and initializes the weights. It creates random input and output datasets and defines a least squares loss function. The model is trained from the data using SGD with momentum in batches of size 10 over 100 epochs. The learning rate starts at 0.01 and halves every 10 epochs.

Problems 7.16–7.17

The takeaway is that although the underlying ideas in deep learning are quite complex, implementation is relatively simple. For example, all of the details of the backpropagation are hidden in the single line of code: `loss.backward()`.

7.7 Summary

The previous chapter introduced stochastic gradient descent (SGD), an iterative optimization algorithm that aims to find the minimum of a function. In the context of neural networks, this algorithm finds the parameters that minimize the loss function. SGD relies on the gradient of the loss function with respect to the parameters, which must be initialized before optimization. This chapter has addressed these two problems for deep neural networks.

The gradients must be evaluated for a very large number of parameters, for each member of the batch, and at each SGD iteration. It is hence imperative that the gradient

```
import torch, torch.nn as nn
from torch.utils.data import TensorDataset, DataLoader
from torch.optim.lr_scheduler import StepLR

# define input size, hidden layer size, output size
D_i, D_k, D_o = 10, 40, 5
# create model with two hidden layers
model = nn.Sequential(
    nn.Linear(D_i, D_k),
    nn.ReLU(),
    nn.Linear(D_k, D_k),
    nn.ReLU(),
    nn.Linear(D_k, D_o))

# He initialization of weights
def weights_init(layer_in):
    if isinstance(layer_in, nn.Linear):
        nn.init.kaiming_normal_(layer_in.weight)
        layer_in.bias.data.fill_(0.0)
model.apply(weights_init)

# choose least squares loss function
criterion = nn.MSELoss()
# construct SGD optimizer and initialize learning rate and momentum
optimizer = torch.optim.SGD(model.parameters(), lr = 0.1, momentum=0.9)
# object that decreases learning rate by half every 10 epochs
scheduler = StepLR(optimizer, step_size=10, gamma=0.5)

# create 100 random data points and store in data loader class
x = torch.randn(100, D_i)
y = torch.randn(100, D_o)
data_loader = DataLoader(TensorDataset(x,y), batch_size=10, shuffle=True)

# loop over the dataset 100 times
for epoch in range(100):
    epoch_loss = 0.0
    # loop over batches
    for i, data in enumerate(data_loader):
        # retrieve inputs and labels for this batch
        x_batch, y_batch = data
        # zero the parameter gradients
        optimizer.zero_grad()
        # forward pass
        pred = model(x_batch)
        loss = criterion(pred, y_batch)
        # backward pass
        loss.backward()
        # SGD update
        optimizer.step()
        # update statistics
        epoch_loss += loss.item()
    # print error
    print(f'Epoch {epoch:5d}, loss {epoch_loss:.3f}')
    # tell scheduler to consider updating learning rate
    scheduler.step()
```

Figure 7.8 Sample code for training two-layer network on random data.

computation is efficient, and to this end, the backpropagation algorithm was introduced. Careful parameter initialization is also critical. The magnitudes of the hidden unit activations can either decrease or increase exponentially in the forward pass. The same is true of the gradient magnitudes in the backward pass, where these behaviors are known as the vanishing gradient and exploding gradient problems. Both impede training but can be avoided with appropriate initialization.

We've now defined the model and the loss function, and we can train a model for a given task. The next chapter discusses how to measure the model performance.

Notes

Backpropagation: Efficient reuse of partial computations while calculating gradients in computational graphs has been repeatedly discovered, including by Werbos (1974), Bryson et al. (1979), LeCun (1985), and Parker (1985). However, the most celebrated description of this idea was by Rumelhart et al. (1985) and Rumelhart et al. (1986), who also coined the term "backpropagation." This latter work kick-started a new phase of neural network research in the eighties and nineties; for the first time, it was practical to train networks with hidden layers. However, progress stalled due (in retrospect) to a lack of training data, limited computational power, and the use of sigmoid activations. Areas such as natural language processing and computer vision did not rely on neural network models until the remarkable image classification results of Krizhevsky et al. (2012) ushered in the modern era of deep learning.

The implementation of backpropagation in modern deep learning frameworks such as PyTorch and TensorFlow is an example of reverse-mode algorithmic differentiation. This is distinguished from forward-mode algorithmic differentiation in which the derivatives from the chain rule are accumulated while moving forward through the computational graph (see problem 7.13). Further information about algorithmic differentiation can be found in Griewank & Walther (2008) and Baydin et al. (2018).

Initialization: He initialization was first introduced by He et al. (2015). It follows closely from *Glorot* or *Xavier* initialization (Glorot & Bengio, 2010), which is very similar but does not consider the effect of the ReLU layer and so differs by a factor of two. Essentially the same method was proposed much earlier by LeCun et al. (2012) but with a slightly different motivation; in this case, sigmoidal activation functions were used, which naturally normalize the range of outputs at each layer, and hence help prevent an exponential increase in the magnitudes of the hidden units. However, if the pre-activations are too large, they fall into the flat regions of the sigmoid function and result in very small gradients. Hence, it is still important to initialize the weights sensibly. Klambauer et al. (2017) introduce the scaled exponential linear unit (SeLU) and show that, within a certain range of inputs, this activation function tends to make the activations in network layers automatically converge to mean zero and unit variance.

A completely different approach is to pass data through the network and then normalize by the empirically observed variance. *Layer-sequential unit variance initialization* (Mishkin & Matas, 2016) is an example of this kind of method, in which the weight matrices are initialized as orthonormal. GradInit (Zhu et al., 2021) randomizes the initial weights and temporarily fixes them while it learns non-negative scaling factors for each weight matrix. These factors are selected to maximize the decrease in the loss for a fixed learning rate subject to a constraint on the maximum gradient norm. *Activation normalization* or *ActNorm* adds a learnable scaling and offset parameter after each network layer at each hidden unit. They run an initial batch through the network and then choose the offset and scale so that the mean of the activations is zero and the variance one. After this, these extra parameters are learned as part of the model.

Closely related to these methods are schemes such as *BatchNorm* (Ioffe & Szegedy, 2015), in which the network normalizes the variance of each batch as part of its processing at every step. BatchNorm and its variants are discussed in chapter 11. Other initialization schemes have been proposed for specific architectures, including the *ConvolutionOrthogonal* initializer (Xiao et al., 2018a) for convolutional networks, *Fixup* (Zhang et al., 2019a) for residual networks, and *TFixup* (Huang et al., 2020a) and *DTFixup* (Xu et al., 2021b) for transformers.

Reducing memory requirements: Training neural networks is memory intensive. We must store both the model parameters and the pre-activations at the hidden units for every member of the batch during the forward pass. Two methods that decrease memory requirements are *gradient checkpointing* (Chen et al., 2016a) and *micro-batching* (Huang et al., 2019). In gradient checkpointing, the activations are only stored every N layers during the forward pass. During the backward pass, the intermediate missing activations are recalculated from the nearest checkpoint. In this manner, we can drastically reduce the memory requirements at the computational cost of performing the forward pass twice (problem 7.11). In micro-batching, the batch is subdivided into smaller parts, and the gradient updates are aggregated from each sub-batch before being applied to the network. A completely different approach is to build a reversible network (e.g., Gomez et al., 2017), in which the activations at the previous layer can be computed from the activations at the current one, so there is no need to cache anything during the forward pass (see chapter 16). Sohoni et al. (2019) review approaches to reducing memory requirements.

Distributed training: For sufficiently large models, the memory requirements or total required time may be too much for a single processor. In this case, we must use *distributed training*, in which training takes place in parallel across multiple processors. There are several approaches to parallelism. In *data parallelism*, each processor or *node* contains a full copy of the model but runs a subset of the batch (see Xing et al., 2015; Li et al., 2020b). The gradients from each node are aggregated centrally and then redistributed back to each node to ensure that the models remain consistent. This is known as *synchronous training*. The synchronization required to aggregate and redistribute the gradients can be a performance bottleneck, and this leads to the idea of asynchronous training. For example, in the *Hogwild!* algorithm (Recht et al., 2011), the gradient from a node is used to update a central model whenever it is ready. The updated model is then redistributed to the node. This means that each node may have a slightly different version of the model at any given time, so the gradient updates may be stale; however, it works well in practice. Other decentralized schemes have also been developed. For example, in Zhang et al. (2016a), the individual nodes update one another in a ring structure.

Data parallelism methods still assume that the entire model can be held in the memory of a single node. *Pipeline model parallelism* stores different layers of the network on different nodes and hence does not have this requirement. In a naïve implementation, the first node runs the forward pass for the batch on the first few layers and passes the result to the next node, which runs the forward pass on the next few layers and so on. In the backward pass, the gradients are updated in the opposite order. The obvious disadvantage of this approach is that each machine lies idle for most of the cycle. Various schemes revolving around each node processing micro-batches sequentially have been proposed to reduce this inefficiency (e.g., Huang et al., 2019; Narayanan et al., 2021a). Finally, in *tensor model parallelism*, computation at a single network layer is distributed across nodes (e.g., Shoeybi et al., 2019). A good overview of distributed training methods can be found in Narayanan et al. (2021b), who combine tensor, pipeline, and data parallelism to train a language model with one trillion parameters on 3072 GPUs.

Problems

Problem 7.1 A two-layer network with two hidden units in each layer can be defined as:

$$
\begin{aligned}
y \;=\; & \phi_0 + \phi_1 a\Big[\psi_{01} + \psi_{11}a[\theta_{01} + \theta_{11}x] + \psi_{21}a[\theta_{02} + \theta_{12}x]\Big] \\
& +\phi_2 a\Big[\psi_{02} + \psi_{12}a[\theta_{01} + \theta_{11}x] + \psi_{22}a[\theta_{02} + \theta_{12}x]\Big],
\end{aligned}
\tag{7.34}
$$

where the functions $a[\bullet]$ are ReLU functions. Compute the derivatives of the output y with respect to each of the 13 parameters $\phi_\bullet, \theta_{\bullet\bullet}$, and $\psi_{\bullet\bullet}$ directly (i.e., not using the backpropagation algorithm). The derivative of the ReLU function with respect to its input $\partial a[z]/\partial z$ is the indicator function $\mathbb{I}[z > 0]$, which returns one if the argument is greater than zero and zero otherwise (figure 7.6).

Problem 7.2 Find an expression for the final term in each of the five chains of derivatives in equation 7.12.

Problem 7.3 What size are each of the terms in equation 7.19?

Problem 7.4 Calculate the derivative $\partial \ell_i / \partial f[\mathbf{x}_i, \boldsymbol{\phi}]$ for the least squares loss function:

$$
\ell_i = (y_i - f[\mathbf{x}_i, \boldsymbol{\phi}])^2.
\tag{7.35}
$$

Problem 7.5 Calculate the derivative $\partial \ell_i / \partial f[\mathbf{x}_i, \boldsymbol{\phi}]$ for the binary classification loss function:

$$
\ell_i = -(1 - y_i)\log\Big[1 - \mathrm{sig}\big[f[\mathbf{x}_i, \boldsymbol{\phi}]\big]\Big] - y_i \log\Big[\mathrm{sig}\big[f[\mathbf{x}_i, \boldsymbol{\phi}]\big]\Big],
\tag{7.36}
$$

where the function $\mathrm{sig}[\bullet]$ is the logistic sigmoid and is defined as:

$$
\mathrm{sig}[z] = \frac{1}{1 + \exp[-z]}.
\tag{7.37}
$$

Problem 7.6* Show that for $\mathbf{z} = \boldsymbol{\beta} + \boldsymbol{\Omega}\mathbf{h}$:

$$
\frac{\partial \mathbf{z}}{\partial \mathbf{h}} = \boldsymbol{\Omega}^T,
$$

where $\partial \mathbf{z}/\partial \mathbf{h}$ is a matrix containing the term $\partial z_i / \partial h_j$ in its ith column and j^{th} row. To do this, first find an expression for the constituent elements $\partial z_i / \partial h_j$, and then consider the form that the matrix $\partial \mathbf{z}/\partial \mathbf{h}$ must take.

Problem 7.7 Consider the case where we use the logistic sigmoid (see equation 7.37) as an activation function, so $h = \mathrm{sig}[f]$. Compute the derivative $\partial h/\partial f$ for this activation function. What happens to the derivative when the input takes (i) a large positive value and (ii) a large negative value?

Problem 7.8 Consider using (i) the Heaviside function and (ii) the rectangular function as activation functions:

$$
\mathrm{Heaviside}[z] = \begin{cases} 0 & z < 0 \\ 1 & z \geq 0 \end{cases},
\tag{7.38}
$$

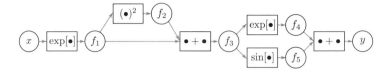

Figure 7.9 Computational graph for problem 7.12 and problem 7.13. Adapted from Domke (2010).

and

$$
\text{rect}[z] = \begin{cases} 0 & z < 0 \\ 1 & 0 \le z \le 1 \\ 0 & z > 1 \end{cases}.
\tag{7.39}
$$

Discuss why these functions are problematic for neural network training with gradient-based optimization methods.

Problem 7.9* Consider a loss function $\ell[\mathbf{f}]$, where $\mathbf{f} = \boldsymbol{\beta} + \boldsymbol{\Omega}\mathbf{h}$. We want to find how the loss ℓ changes when we change $\boldsymbol{\Omega}$, which we'll express with a matrix that contains the derivative $\partial\ell/\partial\Omega_{ij}$ at the ith row and j^{th} column. Find an expression for $\partial f_i/\partial\Omega_{ij}$ and, using the chain rule, show that:

$$
\frac{\partial\ell}{\partial\boldsymbol{\Omega}} = \frac{\partial\ell}{\partial\mathbf{f}}\mathbf{h}^T.
\tag{7.40}
$$

Problem 7.10* Derive the equations for the backward pass of the backpropagation algorithm for a network that uses leaky ReLU activations, which are defined as:

$$
\text{a}[z] = \text{ReLU}[z] = \begin{cases} \alpha \cdot z & z < 0 \\ z & z \ge 0 \end{cases},
\tag{7.41}
$$

where α is a small positive constant (typically 0.1).

Problem 7.11 Consider training a network with fifty layers, where we only have enough memory to store the pre-activations at every tenth hidden layer during the forward pass. Explain how to compute the derivatives in this situation using gradient checkpointing.

Problem 7.12* This problem explores computing derivatives on general acyclic computational graphs. Consider the function:

$$
y = \exp\left[\exp[x] + \exp[x]^2\right] + \sin[\exp[x] + \exp[x]^2].
\tag{7.42}
$$

We can break this down into a series of intermediate computations so that:

$$
\begin{aligned}
f_1 &= \exp[x] \\
f_2 &= f_1^2 \\
f_3 &= f_1 + f_2 \\
f_4 &= \exp[f_3] \\
f_5 &= \sin[f_3] \\
y &= f_4 + f_5.
\end{aligned}
\tag{7.43}
$$

The associated computational graph is depicted in figure 7.9. Compute the derivative $\partial y/\partial x$ by *reverse-mode differentiation*. In other words, compute in order:

$$
\frac{\partial y}{\partial f_5}, \frac{\partial y}{\partial f_4}, \frac{\partial y}{\partial f_3}, \frac{\partial y}{\partial f_2}, \frac{\partial y}{\partial f_1} \text{ and } \frac{\partial y}{\partial x},
\tag{7.44}
$$

using the chain rule in each case to make use of the derivatives already computed.

Problem 7.13* For the same function as in problem 7.12, compute the derivative $\partial y/\partial x$ by *forward-mode differentiation*. In other words, compute in order:

$$
\frac{\partial f_1}{\partial x}, \frac{\partial f_2}{\partial x}, \frac{\partial f_3}{\partial x}, \frac{\partial f_4}{\partial x}, \frac{\partial f_5}{\partial x}, \text{ and } \frac{\partial y}{\partial x},
\tag{7.45}
$$

using the chain rule in each case to make use of the derivatives already computed. Why do we not use forward-mode differentiation when we calculate the parameter gradients for deep networks?

Problem 7.14 Consider a random variable a with variance $\text{Var}[a] = \sigma^2$ and a symmetrical distribution around the mean $\mathbb{E}[a] = 0$. Prove that if we pass this variable through the ReLU function:

$$
b = \text{ReLU}[a] = \begin{cases} 0 & a < 0 \\ a & a \geq 0 \end{cases},
\tag{7.46}
$$

then the second moment of the transformed variable is $\mathbb{E}[b^2] = \sigma^2/2$.

Problem 7.15 What would you expect to happen if we initialized all of the weights and biases in the network to zero?

Problem 7.16 Implement the code in figure 7.8 in PyTorch and plot the training loss as a function of the number of epochs.

Problem 7.17 Change the code in figure 7.8 to tackle a binary classification problem. You will need to (i) change the targets y so they are binary, (ii) change the network to predict numbers between zero and one (iii) change the loss function appropriately.

Chapter 8

Measuring performance

Previous chapters described neural network models, loss functions, and training algorithms. This chapter considers how to measure the performance of the trained models. With sufficient capacity (i.e., number of hidden units), a neural network model will often perform perfectly on the training data. However, this does not necessarily mean it will generalize well to new test data.

We will see that the test errors have three distinct causes and that their relative contributions depend on (i) the inherent uncertainty in the task, (ii) the amount of training data, and (iii) the choice of model. The latter dependency raises the issue of hyperparameter search. We discuss how to select both the model hyperparameters (e.g., the number of hidden layers and the number of hidden units in each) and the learning algorithm hyperparameters (e.g., the learning rate and batch size).

8.1 Training a simple model

We explore model performance using the MNIST-1D dataset (figure 8.1). This consists of ten classes $y \in \{0, 1, \ldots, 9\}$, representing the digits 0–9. The data are derived from 1D templates for each of the digits. Each data example $\mathbf{x}$ is created by randomly transforming one of these templates and adding noise. The full training dataset $\{\mathbf{x}_i, y_i\}$ consists of $I = 4000$ training examples, each consisting of $D_i = 40$ dimensions representing the horizontal offset at 40 positions. The ten classes are drawn uniformly during data generation, so there are ~ 400 examples of each class.

We use a network with $D_i = 40$ inputs and $D_o = 10$ outputs which are passed through a softmax function to produce class probabilities (see section 5.5). The network has two hidden layers with $D = 100$ hidden units each. It is trained using stochastic gradient descent with batch size 100 and learning rate 0.1 for 6000 steps (150 epochs) with a multiclass cross-entropy loss (equation 5.24). Figure 8.2 shows that the training error decreases as training proceeds. The training data are classified perfectly after about 4000 steps. The training loss also decreases, eventually approaching zero.

However, this doesn't imply that the classifier is perfect; the model might have mem-

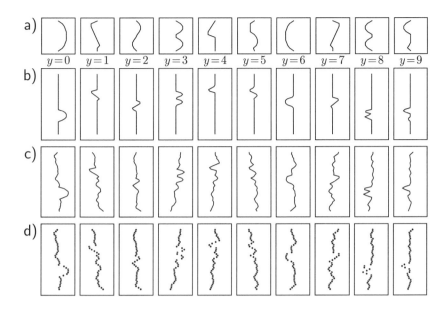

Figure 8.1 MNIST-1D. a) Templates for 10 classes $y \in \{0, \ldots, 9\}$, based on digits 0–9. b) Training examples $\mathbf{x}$ are created by randomly transforming a template and c) adding noise. d) The horizontal offset of the transformed template is then sampled at 40 vertical positions. Adapted from (Greydanus, 2020)

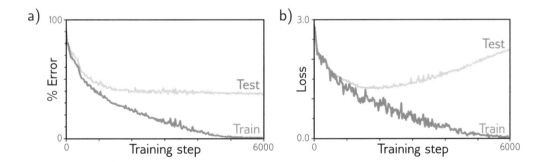

Figure 8.2 MNIST-1D results. a) Percent classification error as a function of the training step. The training set errors decrease to zero, but the test errors do not drop below $\sim 40\%$. This model doesn't generalize well to new test data. b) Loss as a function of the training step. The training loss decreases steadily toward zero. The test loss decreases at first but subsequently increases as the model becomes increasingly confident about its (wrong) predictions.

Figure 8.3 Regression function. Solid black line shows ground truth function. To generate I training examples $\{x_i, y_i\}$, the input space $x \in [0, 1]$ is divided into I equal segments and one sample x_i is drawn from a uniform distribution within each segment. The corresponding value y_i is created by evaluating the function at x_i and adding Gaussian noise (gray region shows ± 2 standard deviations). The test data are generated in the same way.

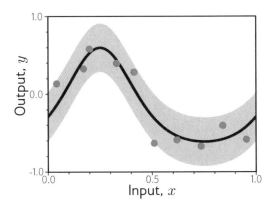

orized the training set but be unable to predict new examples. To estimate the true performance, we need a separate *test set* of input/output pairs $\{\mathbf{x}_i, y_i\}$. To this end, we generate 1000 more examples using the same process. Figure 8.2a also shows the errors for this test data as a function of the training step. These decrease as training proceeds, but only to around 40%. This is better than the chance error rate of 90% error rate but far worse than for the training set; the model has not *generalized* well to the test data.

Notebook 8.1
MNIST-1D
performance

The test loss (figure 8.2b) decreases for the first 1500 training steps but then increases again. At this point, the test error rate is fairly constant; the model makes the same mistakes but with increasing confidence. This decreases the probability of the correct answers and thus increases the negative log-likelihood. This increasing confidence is a side-effect of the softmax function; the pre-softmax activations are driven to increasingly extreme values to make the probability of the training data approach one (see figure 5.10).

8.2 Sources of error

We now consider the sources of the errors that occur when a model fails to generalize. To make this easier to visualize, we revert to a 1D linear least squares regression problem where we know exactly how the ground truth data were generated. Figure 8.3 shows a quasi-sinusoidal function; both training and test data are generated by sampling input values in the range $[0, 1]$, passing them through this function, and adding Gaussian noise with a fixed variance.

We fit a simplified shallow neural net to this data (figure 8.4). The weights and biases that connect the input layer to the hidden layer are chosen so that the "joints" of the function are evenly spaced across the interval. If there are D hidden units, then these joints will be at $0, 1/D, 2/D, \ldots, (D-1)/D$. This model can represent any piecewise linear function with D equally sized regions in the range $[0, 1]$. As well as being easy to understand, this model also has the advantage that it can be fit in closed form without the need for stochastic optimization algorithms (see problem 8.3). Consequently, we can

Problems 8.2–8.3

guarantee to find the global minimum of the loss function during training.

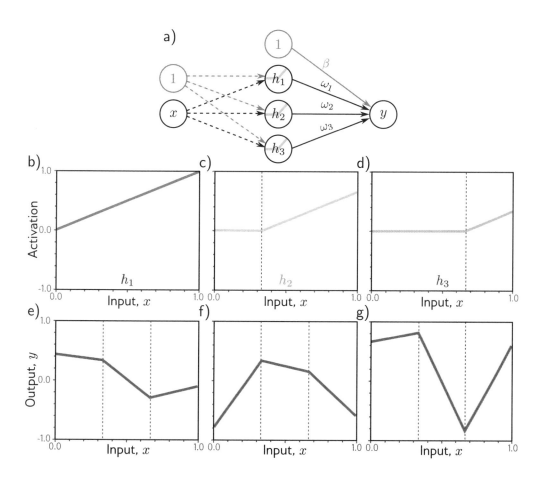

Figure 8.4 Simplified neural network with three hidden units. a) The weights and biases between the input and hidden layer are fixed (dashed arrows). b–d) They are chosen so that the hidden unit activations have slope one, and their joints are equally spaced across the interval, with joints at $x = 0$, $x = 1/3$, and $x = 2/3$, respectively. Modifying the remaining parameters $\phi = \{\beta, \omega_1, \omega_2, \omega_3\}$ can create any piecewise linear function over $x \in [0, 1]$ with joints at $1/3$ and $2/3$. e–g) Three example functions with different values of the parameters ϕ.

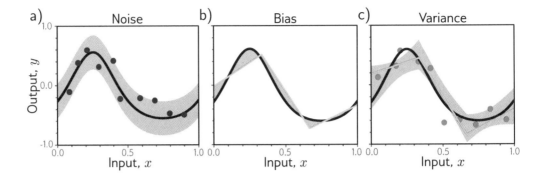

Figure 8.5 Sources of test error. a) Noise. Data generation is noisy, so even if the model exactly replicates the true underlying function (black line), the noise in the test data (gray points) means that some error will remain (gray region represents two standard deviations). b) Bias. Even with the best possible parameters, the three-region model (cyan line) cannot exactly fit the true function (black line). This bias is another source of error (gray regions represent signed error). c) Variance. In practice, we have limited noisy training data (orange points). When we fit the model, we don't recover the best possible function from panel (b) but a slightly different function (cyan line) that reflects idiosyncrasies of the training data. This provides an additional source of error (gray region represents two standard deviations). Figure 8.6 shows how this region was calculated.

8.2.1 Noise, bias, and variance

There are three possible sources of error, which are known as *noise*, *bias*, and *variance* respectively (figure 8.5):

Noise The data generation process includes the addition of noise, so there are multiple possible valid outputs y for each input x (figure 8.5a). This source of error is insurmountable for the test data. Note that it does not necessarily limit the training performance; we will likely never see the same input x twice during training, so it is still possible to fit the training data perfectly.

Noise may arise because there is a genuine stochastic element to the data generation process, because some of the data are mislabeled, or because there are further explanatory variables that were not observed. In rare cases, noise may be absent; for example, a network might approximate a function that is deterministic but requires significant computation to evaluate. However, noise is usually a fundamental limitation on the possible test performance.

Bias A second potential source of error may occur because the model is not flexible enough to fit the true function perfectly. For example, the three-region neural network model cannot exactly describe the quasi-sinusoidal function, even when the parameters are chosen optimally (figure 8.5b). This is known as *bias*.

Variance   We have limited training examples, and there is no way to distinguish systematic changes in the underlying function from noise in the underlying data. When we fit a model, we do not get the closest possible approximation to the true underlying function. Indeed, for different training datasets, the result will be slightly different each time. This additional source of variability in the fitted function is termed *variance* (figure 8.5c). In practice, there might also be additional variance due to the stochastic learning algorithm, which does not necessarily converge to the same solution each time.

8.2.2   Mathematical formulation of test error

We now make the notions of noise, bias, and variance mathematically precise. Consider a 1D regression problem where the data generation process has additive noise with variance σ^2 (e.g., figure 8.3); we can observe different outputs y for the same input x, so for each x, there is a distribution $Pr(y|x)$ with expected value (mean) $\mu[x]$:

Appendix C.2
Expectation

$$\mu[x] = \mathbb{E}_y[y[x]] = \int y[x] Pr(y|x) dy, \tag{8.1}$$

and fixed noise $\sigma^2 = \mathbb{E}_y\left[(\mu[x] - y[x])^2\right]$. Here we have used the notation $y[x]$ to specify that we are considering the output y at a given input position x.

Now consider a least squares loss between the model prediction $f[x, \phi]$ at position x and the observed value $y[x]$ at that position:

$$
\begin{aligned}
L[x] &= \left(f[x, \phi] - y[x]\right)^2 \\
&= \left(\left(f[x, \phi] - \mu[x]\right) + \left(\mu[x] - y[x]\right)\right)^2 \\
&= \left(f[x, \phi] - \mu[x]\right)^2 + 2\left(f[x, \phi] - \mu[x]\right)\left(\mu[x] - y[x]\right) + \left(\mu[x] - y[x]\right)^2,
\end{aligned} \tag{8.2}
$$

where we have both added and subtracted the mean $\mu[x]$ of the underlying function in the second line and have expanded out the squared term in the third line.

The underlying function is stochastic, so this loss depends on the particular $y[x]$ we observe. The expected loss is:

$$
\begin{aligned}
\mathbb{E}_y\left[L[x]\right] &= \mathbb{E}_y\left[\left(f[x, \phi] - \mu[x]\right)^2 + 2\left(f[x, \phi] - \mu[x]\right)\left(\mu[x] - y[x]\right) + \left(\mu[x] - y[x]\right)^2\right] \\
&= \left(f[x, \phi] - \mu[x]\right)^2 + 2\left(f[x, \phi] - \mu[x]\right)\left(\mu[x] - \mathbb{E}_y\left[y[x]\right]\right) + \mathbb{E}_y\left[(\mu[x] - y[x])^2\right] \\
&= \left(f[x, \phi] - \mu[x]\right)^2 + 2\left(f[x, \phi] - \mu[x]\right) \cdot 0 + \mathbb{E}_y\left[\left(\mu[x] - y[x]\right)^2\right] \\
&= \left(f[x, \phi] - \mu[x]\right)^2 + \sigma^2, \tag{8.3}
\end{aligned}
$$

where we have made use of the rules for manipulating expectations. In the second line, we have distributed the expectation operator and removed it from terms with no dependence on $y[x]$, and in the third line, we note that the second term is zero since $\mathbb{E}_y[y[x]] = \mu[x]$ by definition. Finally, in the fourth line, we have substituted in the definition of the

Appendix C.2.1
Expectation rules

noise σ^2. We can see that the expected loss has been broken down into two terms; the first term is the squared deviation between the model and the true function mean, and the second term is the noise.

The first term can be further partitioned into bias and variance. The parameters ϕ of the model $f[x, \phi]$ depend on the training dataset $\mathcal{D} = \{x_i, y_i\}$, so more properly, we should write $f[x, \phi[\mathcal{D}]]$. The training dataset is a random sample from the data generation process; with a different sample of training data, we would learn different parameter values. The expected model output $f_\mu[x]$ with respect to all possible datasets $\mathcal{D}$ is hence:

$$f_\mu[x] = \mathbb{E}_\mathcal{D}\Big[f[x, \phi[\mathcal{D}]]\Big]. \tag{8.4}$$

Returning to the first term of equation 8.3, we add and subtract $f_\mu[x]$ and expand:

$$\big(f[x, \phi[\mathcal{D}]] - \mu[x]\big)^2 \tag{8.5}$$
$$= \Big(\big(f[x, \phi[\mathcal{D}]] - f_\mu[x]\big) + \big(f_\mu[x] - \mu[x]\big)\Big)^2$$
$$= \big(f[x, \phi[\mathcal{D}]] - f_\mu[x]\big)^2 + 2\big(f[x, \phi[\mathcal{D}]] - f_\mu[x]\big)\big(f_\mu[x] - \mu[x]\big) + \big(f_\mu[x] - \mu[x]\big)^2.$$

We then take the expectation with respect to the training dataset $\mathcal{D}$:

$$\mathbb{E}_\mathcal{D}\Big[\big(f[x, \phi[\mathcal{D}]] - \mu[x]\big)^2\Big] = \mathbb{E}_\mathcal{D}\Big[\big(f[x, \phi[\mathcal{D}]] - f_\mu[x]\big)^2\Big] + \big(f_\mu[x] - \mu[x]\big)^2, \tag{8.6}$$

where we have simplified using similar steps as for equation 8.3. Finally, we substitute this result into equation 8.3:

$$\mathbb{E}_\mathcal{D}\Big[\mathbb{E}_y[L[x]]\Big] = \underbrace{\mathbb{E}_\mathcal{D}\Big[\big(f[x, \phi[\mathcal{D}]] - f_\mu[x]\big)^2\Big]}_{\text{variance}} + \underbrace{\big(f_\mu[x] - \mu[x]\big)^2}_{\text{bias}} + \underbrace{\sigma^2}_{\text{noise}}. \tag{8.7}$$

This equation says that the expected loss after considering the uncertainty in the training data $\mathcal{D}$ and the test data y consists of three additive components. The variance is uncertainty in the fitted model due to the particular training dataset we sample. The bias is the systematic deviation of the model from the mean of the function we are modeling. The noise is the inherent uncertainty in the true mapping from input to output. These three sources of error will be present for any task. They combine additively for linear regression with a least squares loss. However, their interaction can be more complex for other types of problems.

8.3 Reducing error

In the previous section, we saw that test error results from three sources: noise, bias, and variance. The noise component is insurmountable; there is nothing we can do to circumvent this, and it represents a fundamental limit on model performance. However, it is possible to reduce the other two terms.

8.3.1 Reducing variance

Recall that the variance results from limited noisy training data. Fitting the model to two different training sets results in slightly different parameters. It follows we can reduce the variance by increasing the quantity of training data. This averages out the inherent noise and ensures that the input space is well sampled.

Figure 8.6 shows the effect of training with 6, 10, and 100 samples. For each dataset size, we show the best-fitting model for three training datasets. With only six samples, the fitted function is quite different each time: the variance is significant. As we increase the number of samples, the fitted models become very similar, and the variance reduces. In general, adding training data almost always improves test performance.

8.3.2 Reducing bias

The bias term results from the inability of the model to describe the true underlying function. This suggests that we can reduce this error by making the model more flexible. This is usually done by increasing the model *capacity*. For neural networks, this means adding more hidden units and/or hidden layers.

In the simplified model, adding capacity corresponds to adding more hidden units so that the interval $[0, 1]$ is divided into more linear regions. Figures 8.7a–c show that (unsurprisingly) this does indeed reduce the bias; as we increase the number of linear regions to ten, the model becomes flexible enough to fit the true function closely.

8.3.3 Bias-variance trade-off

However, figures 8.7d–f show an unexpected side-effect of increasing the model capacity. For a fixed-size training dataset, the variance term increases as the model capacity increases. Consequently, increasing the model capacity does not necessarily reduce the test error. This is known as the *bias-variance trade-off*.

Figure 8.8 explores this phenomenon. In panels a–c), we fit the simplified three-region model to three different datasets of fifteen points. Although the datasets differ, the final model is much the same; the noise in the dataset roughly averages out in each linear region. In panels d–f), we fit a model with ten regions to the same three datasets. This model has more flexibility, but this is disadvantageous; the model certainly fits the data better, and the training error will be lower, but much of the extra descriptive power is devoted to modeling the noise. This phenomenon is known as *overfitting*.

We've seen that as we add capacity to the model, the bias decreases, but the variance increases for a fixed-size training dataset. This suggests that there is an optimal capacity where the bias is not too large and the variance is still relatively small. Figure 8.9 shows how these terms vary numerically for the toy model as we increase the capacity, using the data from figure 8.8. For regression models, the total expected error is the sum of the bias and the variance, and this sum is minimized when the model capacity is four (i.e., with four hidden units and four linear regions in the range of the data).

Notebook 8.2
Bias-variance
trade-off

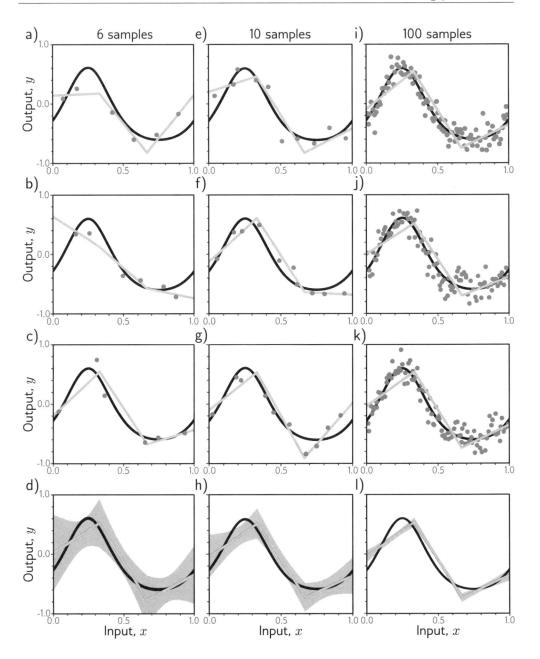

Figure 8.6 Reducing variance by increasing training data. a–c) The three-region model fitted to three different randomly sampled datasets of six points. The fitted model is quite different each time. d) We repeat this experiment many times and plot the mean model predictions (cyan line) and the variance of the model predictions (gray area shows two standard deviations). e–h) We do the same experiment, but this time with datasets of size ten. The variance of the predictions is reduced. i–l) We repeat this experiment with datasets of size 100. Now the fitted model is always similar, and the variance is small.

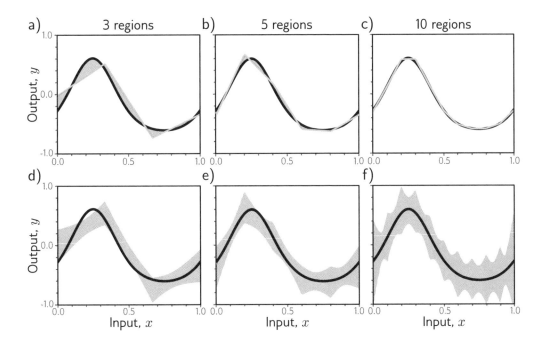

Figure 8.7 Bias and variance as a function of model capacity. a–c) As we increase the number of hidden units of the toy model, the number of linear regions increases, and the model becomes able to fit the true function closely; the bias (gray region) decreases. d–f) Unfortunately, increasing the model capacity has the side-effect of increasing the variance term (gray region). This is known as the bias-variance trade-off.

8.4 Double descent

In the previous section, we examined the bias-variance trade-off as we increased the capacity of a model. Let's now return to the MNIST-1D dataset and see whether this happens in practice. We use 10,000 training examples, test with another 5,000 examples and examine the training and test performance as we increase the capacity (number of parameters) in the model. We train the model with Adam and a step size of 0.005 using a full batch of 10,000 examples for 4000 steps.

Figure 8.10a shows the training and test error for a neural network with two hidden layers as the number of hidden units increases. The training error decreases as the capacity grows and quickly becomes close to zero. The vertical dashed line represents the capacity where the model has the same number of parameters as there are training examples, but the model memorizes the dataset before this point. The test error decreases as we add model capacity but does not increase as predicted by the bias-variance trade-off curve; it keeps decreasing.

In figure 8.10b, we repeat this experiment, but this time, we randomize 15% of the

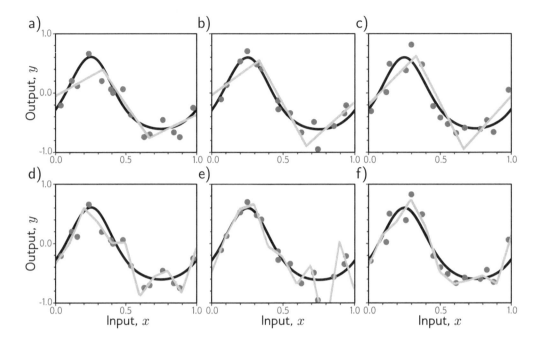

Figure 8.8 Overfitting. a–c) A model with three regions is fit to three different datasets of fifteen points each. The result is similar in all three cases (i.e., the variance is low). d–f) A model with ten regions is fit to the same datasets. The additional flexibility does not necessarily produce better predictions. While these three models each describe the training data better, they are not necessarily closer to the true underlying function (black curve). Instead, they overfit the data and describe the noise, and the variance (difference between fitted curves) is larger.

Figure 8.9 Bias-variance trade-off. The bias and variance terms from equation 8.7 are plotted as a function of the model capacity (number of hidden units / linear regions in range of data) in the simplified model using training data from figure 8.8. As the capacity increases, the bias (solid orange line) decreases, but the variance (solid cyan line) increases. The sum of these two terms (dashed gray line) is minimized when the capacity is four.

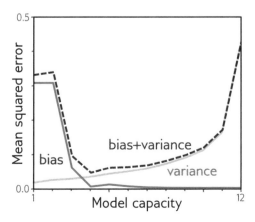

training labels. Once more, the training error decreases to zero. This time, there is more randomness, and the model requires almost as many parameters as there are data points to memorize the data. The test error does show the typical bias-variance trade-off as we increase the capacity to the point where the model fits the training data exactly. However, then it does something unexpected; it starts to decrease again. Indeed, if we add enough capacity, the test loss reduces to below the minimal level that we achieved in the first part of the curve.

This phenomenon is known as *double descent*. For some datasets like MNIST, it is present with the original data (figure 8.10c). For others, like MNIST-1D and CIFAR-100 (figure 8.10d), it emerges or becomes more prominent when we add noise to the labels. The first part of the curve is referred to as the *classical* or *under-parameterized regime*, and the second part as the *modern* or *over-parameterized regime*. The central part where the error increases is termed the *critical regime*.

Notebook 8.3
Double descent

8.4.1   Explanation

The discovery of double descent is recent, unexpected, and somewhat puzzling. It results from an interaction of two phenomena. First, the test performance becomes temporarily worse when the model has just enough capacity to memorize the data. Second, the test performance continues to improve with capacity even after the training performance is perfect. The first phenomenon is exactly as predicted by the bias-variance trade-off. The second phenomenon is more confusing; it's unclear why performance should be better in the over-parameterized regime, given that there are now not even enough training data points to constrain the model parameters uniquely.

To understand why performance continues to improve as we add more parameters, note that once the model has enough capacity to drive the training loss to near zero, the model fits the training data almost perfectly. This implies that further capacity cannot help the model fit the training data any better; any change must occur *between* the training points. The tendency of a model to prioritize one solution over another as it extrapolates between data points is known as its *inductive bias*.

Problems 8.4–8.5

The model's behavior between data points is critical because, in high-dimensional space, the training data are extremely sparse. The MNIST-1D dataset has 40 dimensions, and we trained with 10,000 examples. If this seems like plenty of data, consider what would happen if we quantized each input dimension into 10 bins. There would be 10^{40} bins in total, constrained by only 10^4 examples. Even with this coarse quantization, there will only be one data point in every 10^{35} bins! The tendency of the volume of high-dimensional space to overwhelm the number of training points is termed the *curse of dimensionality*.

The implication is that problems in high dimensions might look more like figure 8.11a; there are small regions of the input space where we observe data with significant gaps between them. The putative explanation for double descent is that as we add capacity to the model, it interpolates between the nearest data points increasingly smoothly. In the absence of information about what happens between the training points, assuming smoothness is sensible and will probably generalize reasonably to new data.

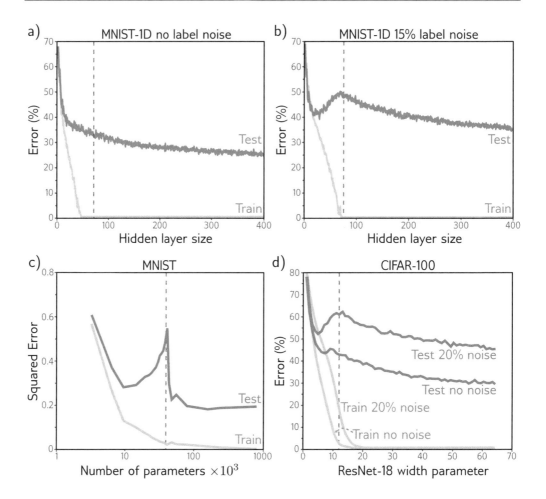

Figure 8.10 Double descent. a) Training and test loss on MNIST-1D for a two-hidden layer network as we increase the number of hidden units (and hence parameters) in each layer. The training loss decreases to zero as the number of parameters approaches the number of training examples (vertical dashed line). The test error does not show the expected bias-variance trade-off but continues to decrease even after the model has memorized the dataset. b) The same experiment is repeated with noisier training data. Again, the training error reduces to zero, although it now takes almost as many parameters as training points to memorize the dataset. The test error shows the predicted bias/variance trade-off; it decreases as the capacity increases but then increases again as we near the point where the training data is exactly memorized. However, it subsequently decreases again and ultimately reaches a better performance level. This is known as double descent. Depending on the loss, the model, and the amount of noise in the data, the double descent pattern can be seen to a greater or lesser degree across many datasets. c) Results on MNIST (without label noise) with shallow neural network from Belkin et al. (2019). d) Results on CIFAR-100 with ResNet18 network (see chapter 11) from Nakkiran et al. (2021). See original papers for details.

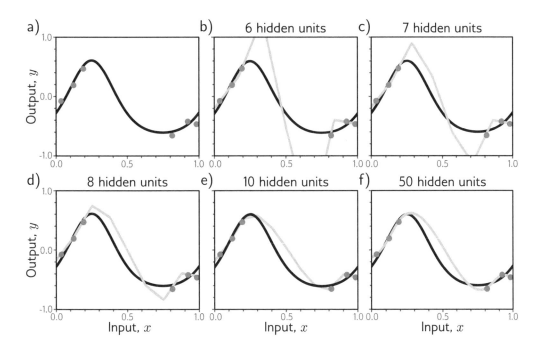

Figure 8.11 Increasing capacity (hidden units) allows smoother interpolation between sparse data points. a) Consider this situation where the training data (orange circles) are sparse; there is a large region in the center with no data examples to constrain the model to mimic the true function (black curve). b) If we fit a model with just enough capacity to fit the training data (cyan curve), then it has to contort itself to pass through the training data, and the output predictions will not be smooth. c–f) However, as we add more hidden units, the model has the *ability* to interpolate between the points more smoothly (smoothest possible curve plotted in each case). However, unlike in this figure, it is not obliged to.

This argument is plausible. It's certainly true that as we add more capacity to the model, it will have the capability to create smoother functions. Figures 8.11b–f show the smoothest possible functions that still pass through the data points as we increase the number of hidden units. When the number of parameters is very close to the number of training data examples (figure 8.11b), the model is forced to contort itself to fit the training data exactly, resulting in erratic predictions. This explains why the peak in the double descent curve is so pronounced. As we add more hidden units, the model has the ability to construct smoother functions that are likely to generalize better to new data.

However, this does not explain *why* over-parameterized models should produce smooth functions. Figure 8.12 shows three functions that can be created by the simplified model with 50 hidden units. In each case, the model fits the data exactly, so the loss is zero. If the modern regime of double descent is explained by increasing smoothness, then what exactly is encouraging this smoothness?

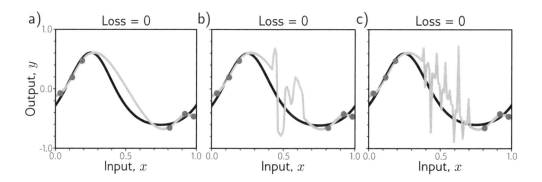

Figure 8.12 Regularization. a–c) Each of the three fitted curves passes through the data points exactly, so the training loss for each is zero. However, we might expect the smooth curve in panel (a) to generalize much better to new data than the erratic curves in panels (b) and (c). Any factor that biases a model toward a subset of the solutions with a similar training loss is known as a regularizer. It is thought that the initialization and/or fitting of neural networks have an implicit regularizing effect. Consequently, in the over-parameterized regime, more reasonable solutions, such as that in panel (a), are encouraged.

The answer to this question is uncertain, but there are two likely possibilities. First, the network initialization may encourage smoothness, and the model never departs from the sub-domain of smooth function during the training process. Second, the training algorithm may somehow "prefer" to converge to smooth functions. Any factor that biases a solution toward a subset of equivalent solutions is known as a *regularizer*, so one possibility is that the training algorithm acts as an implicit regularizer (see section 9.2).

8.5   Choosing hyperparameters

In the previous section, we discussed how test performance changes with model capacity. Unfortunately, in the classical regime, we don't have access to either the bias (which requires knowledge of the true underlying function) or the variance (which requires multiple independently sampled datasets to estimate). In the modern regime, there is no way to tell how much capacity should be added before the test error stops improving. This raises the question of exactly how we should choose model capacity in practice.

For a deep network, the model capacity depends on the numbers of hidden layers and hidden units per layer as well as other aspects of architecture that we have yet to introduce. Furthermore, the choice of learning algorithm and any associated parameters (learning rate, etc.) also affects the test performance. These elements are collectively termed *hyperparameters*. The process of finding the best hyperparameters is termed *hyperparameter search* or (when focused on network structure) *neural architecture search*.

Hyperparameters are typically chosen empirically; we train many models with different hyperparameters on the same training set, measure their performance, and retain the best model. However, we do not measure their performance on the test set; this would admit the possibility that these hyperparameters just happen to work well for the test set but don't generalize to further data. Instead, we introduce a third dataset known as a *validation set*. For every choice of hyperparameters, we train the associated model using the training set and evaluate performance on the validation set. Finally, we select the model that worked best on the validation set and measure its performance on the test set. In principle, this should give a reasonable estimate of the true performance.

The hyperparameter space is generally smaller than the parameter space but still too large to try every combination exhaustively. Unfortunately, many hyperparameters are discrete (e.g., the number of hidden layers), and others may be conditional on one another (e.g., we only need to specify the number of hidden units in the tenth hidden layer if there are ten or more layers). Hence, we cannot rely on gradient descent methods as we did for learning the model parameters. Hyperparameter optimization algorithms intelligently sample the space of hyperparameters, contingent on previous results. This procedure is computationally expensive since we must train an entire model and measure the validation performance for each combination of hyperparameters.

8.6   Summary

To measure performance, we use a separate test set. The degree to which performance is maintained on this test set is known as generalization. Test errors can be explained by three factors: noise, bias, and variance. These combine additively in regression problems with least squares losses. Adding training data decreases the variance. When the model capacity is less than the number of training examples, increasing the capacity decreases bias but increases variance. This is known as the bias-variance trade-off, and there is a capacity where the trade-off is optimal.

However, this is balanced against a tendency for performance to improve with capacity, even when the parameters exceed the training examples. Together, these two phenomena create the double descent curve. It is thought that the model interpolates more smoothly between the training data points in the over-parameterized "modern regime," although it is unclear what drives this. To choose the capacity and other model and training algorithm hyperparameters, we fit multiple models and evaluate their performance using a separate validation set.

Notes

Bias-variance trade-off: We showed that the test error for regression problems with least squares loss decomposes into the sum of noise, bias, and variance terms. These factors are all present for models with other losses, but their interaction is typically more complicated (Friedman, 1997; Domingos, 2000). For classification problems, there are some counter-intuitive predictions; for example, if the model is biased toward selecting the wrong class in a region of the input space, then increasing the variance can improve the classification rate as this pushes some of the predictions over the threshold to be classified correctly.

Cross-validation: We saw that it is typical to divide the data into three parts: training data (which is used to learn the model parameters), validation data (which is used to choose the hyperparameters), and test data (which is used to estimate the final performance). This approach is known as *cross-validation*. However, this division may cause problems where the total number of data examples is limited; if the number of training examples is comparable to the model capacity, then the variance will be large.

One way to mitigate this problem is to use *k-fold cross-validation*. The training and validation data are partitioned into K disjoint subsets. For example, we might divide these data into five parts. We train with four and validate with the fifth for each of the five permutations and choose the hyperparameters based on the average validation performance. The final test performance is assessed using the average of the predictions from the five models with the best hyperparameters on an entirely different test set. There are many variations of this idea, but all share the general goal of using a larger proportion of the data to train the model, thereby reducing variance.

Capacity: We have used the term *capacity* informally to mean the number of parameters or hidden units in the model (and hence indirectly, the ability of the model to fit functions of increasing complexity). The *representational capacity* of a model describes the space of possible functions it can construct when we consider all possible parameter values. When we take into account the fact that an optimization algorithm may not be able to reach all of these solutions, what is left is the *effective capacity*.

The Vapnik-Chervonenkis (VC) dimension (Vapnik & Chervonenkis, 1971) is a more formal measure of capacity. It is the largest number of training examples that a binary classifier can label arbitrarily. Bartlett et al. (2019) derive upper and lower bounds for the VC dimension in terms of the number of layers and weights. An alternative measure of capacity is the Rademacher complexity, which is the expected empirical performance of a classification model (with optimal parameters) for data with random labels. Neyshabur et al. (2017) derive a lower bound on the generalization error in terms of the Rademacher complexity.

Double descent: The term "double descent" was coined by Belkin et al. (2019), who demonstrated that the test error decreases again in the over-parameterized regime for two-layer neural networks and random features. They also claimed that this occurs in decision trees, although Buschjäger & Morik (2021) subsequently provided evidence to the contrary. Nakkiran et al. (2021) show that double descent occurs for various modern datasets (CIFAR-10, CIFAR-100, IWSLT'14 de-en), architectures (CNNs, ResNets, transformers), and optimizers (SGD, Adam). The phenomenon is more pronounced when noise is added to the target labels (Nakkiran et al., 2021) and when some regularization techniques are used (Ishida et al., 2020).

Nakkiran et al. (2021) also provide empirical evidence that test performance depends on *effective model capacity* (the largest number of samples for which a given model and training method can achieve zero training error). At this point, the model starts to devote its efforts to interpolating smoothly. As such, the test performance depends not just on the model but also on the training algorithm and length of training. They observe the same pattern when they study a model with fixed capacity and increase the number of training iterations. They term this *epoch-wise double descent*. This phenomenon has been modeled by Pezeshki et al. (2022) in terms of different features in the model being learned at different speeds.

Double descent makes the rather strange prediction that adding training data can sometimes worsen test performance. Consider an over-parameterized model in the second descending part of the curve. If we increase the training data to match the model capacity, we will now be in the critical region of the new test error curve, and the test loss may increase.

Bubeck & Sellke (2021) prove that overparameterization is necessary to interpolate data smoothly in high dimensions. They demonstrate a trade-off between the number of parameters and the Lipschitz constant of a model (the fastest the output can change for a small input change). A review of the theory of over-parameterized machine learning can be found in Dar et al. (2021).

Appendix B.1.1
Lipschitz constant

Curse of dimensionality: As dimensionality increases, the volume of space grows so fast that the amount of data needed to densely sample it increases exponentially. This phenomenon is known as the curse of dimensionality. High-dimensional space has many unexpected properties, and caution should be used when trying to reason about it based on low-dimensional examples. This book visualizes many aspects of deep learning in one or two dimensions, but these visualizations should be treated with healthy skepticism.

Surprising properties of high-dimensional spaces include: (i) Two randomly sampled data points from a standard normal distribution are very close to orthogonal to one another (relative to the origin) with high likelihood. (ii) The distance from the origin of samples from a standard normal distribution is roughly constant. (iii) Most of a volume of a high-dimensional sphere (hypersphere) is adjacent to its surface (a common metaphor is that most of the volume of a high-dimensional orange is in the peel, not in the pulp). (iv) If we place a unit-diameter hypersphere inside a hypercube with unit-length sides, then the hypersphere takes up a decreasing proportion of the volume of the cube as the dimension increases. Since the volume of the cube is fixed at size one, this implies that the volume of a high-dimensional hypersphere becomes close to zero. (v) For random points drawn from a uniform distribution in a high-dimensional hypercube, the ratio of the Euclidean distance between the nearest and furthest points becomes close to one. For further information, consult Beyer et al. (1999) and Aggarwal et al. (2001).

Problems 8.6–8.9

Notebook 8.4
High-dimensional
spaces

Real-world performance: In this chapter, we argued that model performance could be evaluated using a held-out test set. However, the result won't be indicative of real-world performance if the statistics of the test set don't match those of real-world data. Moreover, the statistics of real-world data may change over time, causing the model to become increasingly stale and performance to decrease. This is known as *data drift* and means that deployed models must be carefully monitored.

There are three main reasons why real-world performance may be worse than the test performance implies. First, the statistics of the input data $\mathbf{x}$ may change; we may now be observing parts of the function that were sparsely sampled or not sampled at all during training. This is known as *covariate shift*. Second, the statistics of the output data $\mathbf{y}$ may change; if some output values are infrequent during training, then the model may learn not to predict these in ambiguous situations and will make mistakes if they are more common in the real world. This is known as *prior shift*. Third, the relationship between input and output may change. This is known as *concept shift*. These issues are discussed in Moreno-Torres et al. (2012).

Hyperparameter search: Finding the best hyperparameters is a challenging optimization task. Testing a single configuration of hyperparameters is expensive; we must train an entire model and measure its performance. We have no easy way to access the derivatives (i.e., how performance changes when we make a small change to a hyperparameter). Moreover, many of the hyperparameters are discrete, so we cannot use gradient descent methods. There are multiple local minima and no way to tell if we are close to the global minimum. The noise level is high since each training/validation cycle uses a stochastic training algorithm; we expect different results if we train a model twice with the same hyperparameters. Finally, some variables are conditional and only exist if others are set. For example, the number of hidden units in the third hidden layer is only relevant if we have at least three hidden layers.

A simple approach is to sample the space randomly (Bergstra & Bengio, 2012). However, for continuous variables, it is better to build a model of performance as a function of the hyperparameters and the uncertainty in this function. This can be exploited to test where the uncertainty is great (explore the space) or home in on regions where performance looks promising (exploit previous knowledge). Bayesian optimization is a framework based on Gaussian processes that does just this, and its application to hyperparameter search is described in Snoek et al. (2012). The Beta-Bernoulli bandit (see Lattimore & Szepesvári, 2020) is a roughly equivalent model for describing uncertainty in results due to discrete variables.

The sequential model-based configuration (SMAC) algorithm (Hutter et al., 2011) can cope with continuous, discrete, and conditional parameters. The basic approach is to use a random forest to model the objective function where the mean of the tree predictions is the best guess about the objective function, and their variance represents the uncertainty. A completely different approach that can also cope with combinations of continuous, discrete, and conditional parameters is Tree-Parzen Estimators (Bergstra et al., 2011). The previous methods modeled the probability of the model performance given the hyperparameters. In contrast, the Tree-Parzen estimator models the probability of the hyperparameters given the model performance.

Hyperband (Li et al., 2017b) is a multi-armed bandit strategy for hyperparameter optimization. It assumes that there are computationally cheap but approximate ways to measure performance (e.g., by not training to completion) and that these can be associated with a budget (e.g., by training for a fixed number of iterations). A number of random configurations are sampled and run until the budget is used up. Then the best fraction η of runs is kept, and the budget is multiplied by $1/\eta$. This is repeated until the maximum budget is reached. This approach has the advantage of efficiency; for bad configurations, it does not need to run the experiment to the end. However, each sample is just chosen randomly, which is inefficient. The BOHB algorithm (Falkner et al., 2018) combines the efficiency of Hyperband with the more sensible choice of hyperparameters from Tree Parzen estimators to construct an even better method.

Problems

Problem 8.1 Will the multiclass cross-entropy training loss in figure 8.2 ever reach zero? Explain your reasoning.

Problem 8.2 What values should we choose for the three weights and biases in the first layer of the model in figure 8.4a so that the hidden unit's responses are as depicted in figures 8.4b–d?

Problem 8.3* Given a training dataset consisting of I input/output pairs $\{x_i, y_i\}$, show how the parameters $\{\beta, \omega_1, \omega_2, \omega_3\}$ for the model in figure 8.4a using the least squares loss function can be found in closed form.

Problem 8.4 Consider the curve in figure 8.10b at the point where we train a model with a hidden layer of size 200, which would have 50,410 parameters. What do you predict will happen to the training and test performance if we increase the number of training examples from 10,000 to 50,410?

Problem 8.5 Consider the case where the model capacity exceeds the number of training data points, and the model is flexible enough to reduce the training loss to zero. What are the implications of this for fitting a heteroscedastic model? Propose a method to resolve any problems that you identify.

Problem 8.6 Show that two random points drawn from a 1000-dimensional standard Gaussian distribution are orthogonal relative to the origin with high probability.

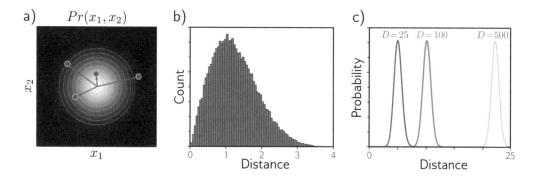

a) $Pr(x_1, x_2)$ b)   c)

Figure 8.13 Typical sets. a) Standard normal distribution in two dimensions. Circles are four samples from this distribution. As the distance from the center increases, the probability decreases, but the volume of space at that radius (i.e., the area between adjacent evenly spaced circles) increases. b) These factors trade off so that the histogram of distances of samples from the center has a pronounced peak. c) In higher dimensions, this effect becomes more extreme, and the probability of observing a sample close to the mean becomes vanishingly small. Although the most likely point is at the mean of the distribution, the *typical samples* are found in a relatively narrow shell.

Problem 8.7 The volume of a hypersphere with radius r in D dimensions is:

$$\text{Vol}[r] = \frac{r^D \pi^{D/2}}{\Gamma[D/2 + 1]},\tag{8.8}$$

where $\Gamma[\bullet]$ is the Gamma function. Show using Stirling's formula that the volume of a hypersphere of diameter one (radius $r = 0.5$) becomes zero as the dimension increases.

Appendix B.1.3
Gamma function

Appendix B.1.4
Stirling's formula

Problem 8.8* Consider a hypersphere of radius $r = 1$. Find an expression for the proportion of the total volume that lies in the outermost 1% of the distance from the center (i.e., in the outermost shell of thickness 0.01). Show that this becomes one as the dimension increases.

Problem 8.9 Figure 8.13c shows the distribution of distances of samples of a standard normal distribution as the dimension increases. Empirically verify this finding by sampling from the standard normal distributions in 25, 100, and 500 dimensions and plotting a histogram of the distances from the center. What closed-form probability distribution describes these distances?

Chapter 9

Regularization

Chapter 8 described how to measure model performance and identified that there could be a significant performance gap between the training and test data. Possible reasons for this discrepancy include: (i) the model describes statistical peculiarities of the training data that are not representative of the true mapping from input to output (overfitting), and (ii) the model is unconstrained in areas with no training examples, leading to suboptimal predictions.

This chapter discusses *regularization* techniques. These are a family of methods that reduce the generalization gap between training and test performance. Strictly speaking, regularization involves adding explicit terms to the loss function that favor certain parameter choices. However, in machine learning, this term is commonly used to refer to any strategy that improves generalization.

We start by considering regularization in its strictest sense. Then we show how the stochastic gradient descent algorithm itself favors certain solutions. This is known as implicit regularization. Following this, we consider a set of heuristic methods that improve test performance. These include early stopping, ensembling, dropout, label smoothing, and transfer learning.

9.1 Explicit regularization

Consider fitting a model $f[\mathbf{x}, \boldsymbol{\phi}]$ with parameters $\boldsymbol{\phi}$ using a training set $\{\mathbf{x}_i, \mathbf{y}_i\}$ of input/output pairs. We seek the minimum of the loss function $L[\boldsymbol{\phi}]$:

$$
\begin{aligned}
\hat{\boldsymbol{\phi}} &= \underset{\boldsymbol{\phi}}{\operatorname{argmin}}\left[L[\boldsymbol{\phi}]\right] \\
&= \underset{\boldsymbol{\phi}}{\operatorname{argmin}}\left[\sum_{i=1}^{I} \ell_i[\mathbf{x}_i, \mathbf{y}_i]\right],
\end{aligned}
\tag{9.1}
$$

where the individual terms $\ell_i[\mathbf{x}_i, \mathbf{y}_i]$ measure the mismatch between the network predictions $f[\mathbf{x}_i, \boldsymbol{\phi}]$ and output targets $\mathbf{y}_i$ for each training pair. To bias this minimization

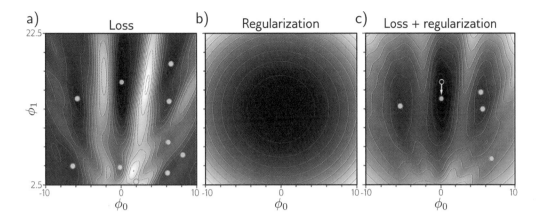

Figure 9.1 Explicit regularization. a) Loss function for Gabor model (see section 6.1.2). Cyan circles represent local minima. Gray circle represents the global minimum. b) The regularization term favors parameters close to the center of the plot by adding an increasing penalty as we move away from this point. c) The final loss function is the sum of the original loss function plus the regularization term. This surface has fewer local minima, and the global minimum has moved to a different position (arrow shows change).

toward certain solutions, we include an additional term:

$$\hat{\phi} = \underset{\phi}{\operatorname{argmin}} \left[\sum_{i=1}^{I} \ell_i[\mathbf{x}_i, \mathbf{y}_i] + \lambda \cdot \mathrm{g}[\phi] \right], \tag{9.2}$$

where $\mathrm{g}[\phi]$ is a function that returns a scalar that takes a larger value when the parameters are less preferred. The term λ is a positive scalar that controls the relative contribution of the original loss function and the regularization term. The minima of the regularized loss function usually differ from those in the original, so the training procedure converges to different parameter values (figure 9.1).

9.1.1 Probabilistic interpretation

Regularization can be viewed from a probabilistic perspective. Section 5.1 shows how loss functions are constructed from the maximum likelihood criterion:

$$\hat{\phi} = \underset{\phi}{\operatorname{argmax}} \left[\prod_{i=1}^{I} Pr(\mathbf{y}_i | \mathbf{x}_i, \phi) \right]. \tag{9.3}$$

The regularization term can be considered as a *prior* $Pr(\phi)$ that represents knowledge about the parameters before we observe the data and we now have the *maximum a posteriori* or *MAP* criterion:

$$\hat{\phi} = \underset{\phi}{\mathrm{argmax}} \left[\prod_{i=1}^{I} Pr(\mathbf{y}_i | \mathbf{x}_i, \phi) Pr(\phi) \right]. \tag{9.4}$$

Moving back to the negative log-likelihood loss function by taking the log and multiplying by minus one, we see that $\lambda \cdot g[\phi] = -\log[Pr(\phi)]$.

9.1.2   L2 regularization

This discussion has sidestepped the question of *which* solutions the regularization term should penalize (or equivalently that the prior should favor). Since neural networks are used in an extremely broad range of applications, these can only be very generic preferences. The most commonly used regularization term is the *L2 norm*, which penalizes the sum of the squares of the parameter values:

$$\hat{\phi} = \underset{\phi}{\mathrm{argmin}} \left[\sum_{i=1}^{I} \ell_i[\mathbf{x}_i, \mathbf{y}_i] + \lambda \sum_j \phi_j^2 \right], \tag{9.5}$$

Problems 9.1–9.2

where j indexes the parameters. This is also referred to as *Tikhonov regularization* or *ridge regression*, or (when applied to matrices) *Frobenius norm regularization*.

For neural networks, L2 regularization is usually applied to the weights but not the biases and is hence referred to as a *weight decay* term. The effect is to encourage smaller weights, so the output function is smoother. To see this, consider that the output prediction is a weighted sum of the activations at the last hidden layer. If the weights have a smaller magnitude, the output will vary less. The same logic applies to the computation of the pre-activations at the last hidden layer and so on, progressing backward through the network. In the limit, if we forced all the weights to be zero, the network would produce a constant output determined by the final bias parameter.

Notebook 9.1
L2 regularization

Figure 9.2 shows the effect of fitting the simplified network from figure 8.4 with weight decay and different values of the regularization coefficient λ. When λ is small, it has little effect. However, as λ increases, the fit to the data becomes less accurate, and the function becomes smoother. This might improve the test performance for two reasons:

- If the network is overfitting, then adding the regularization term means that the network must trade off slavish adherence to the data against the desire to be smooth. One way to think about this is that the error due to variance reduces (the model no longer needs to pass through every data point) at the cost of increased bias (the model can only describe smooth functions).
- When the network is over-parameterized, some of the extra model capacity describes areas with no training data. Here, the regularization term will favor functions that smoothly interpolate between the nearby points. This is reasonable behavior in the absence of knowledge about the true function.

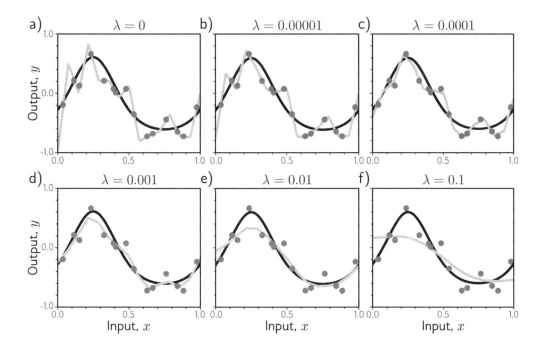

Figure 9.2 L2 regularization in simplified network (see figure 8.4). a–f) Fitted functions as we increase the regularization coefficient λ. The black curve is the true function, the orange circles are the noisy training data, and the cyan curve is the fitted model. For small λ (panels a–b), the fitted function passes exactly through the data points. For intermediate λ (panels c–d), the function is smoother and more similar to the ground truth. For large λ (panels e–f), the fitted function is smoother than the ground truth, so the fit is worse.

9.2 Implicit regularization

An intriguing recent finding is that neither gradient descent nor stochastic gradient descent moves neutrally to the minimum of the loss function; each exhibits a preference for some solutions over others. This is known as *implicit regularization*.

9.2.1 Implicit regularization in gradient descent

Consider a continuous version of gradient descent where the step size is infinitesimal. The change in parameters ϕ will be governed by the differential equation:

$$\frac{d\phi}{dt} = -\frac{\partial L}{\partial \phi}. \tag{9.6}$$

Gradient descent approximates this process with a series of discrete steps of size α:

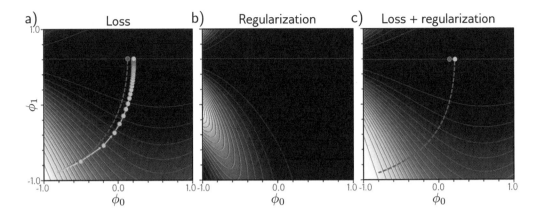

Figure 9.3 Implicit regularization in gradient descent. a) Loss function with family of global minima on horizontal line $\phi_1 = 0.61$. Dashed blue line shows continuous gradient descent path starting in bottom-left. Cyan trajectory shows discrete gradient descent with step size 0.1 (first few steps shown explicitly as arrows). The finite step size causes the paths to diverge and reach a different final position. b) This disparity can be approximated by adding a regularization term to the continuous gradient descent loss function that penalizes the squared gradient magnitude. c) After adding this term, the continuous gradient descent path converges to the same place that the discrete one did on the original function.

$$\phi_{t+1} = \phi_t - \alpha \frac{\partial L[\phi_t]}{\partial \phi}, \tag{9.7}$$

The discretization causes a deviation from the continuous path (figure 9.3).

This deviation can be understood by deriving a modified loss term $\tilde{L}$ for the continuous case that arrives at the same place as the discretized version on the original loss L. It can be shown (see end of chapter) that this modified loss is:

$$\tilde{L}_{GD}[\phi] = L[\phi] + \frac{\alpha}{4} \left\| \frac{\partial L}{\partial \phi} \right\|^2. \tag{9.8}$$

In other words, the discrete trajectory is repelled from places where the gradient norm is large (the surface is steep). This doesn't change the position of the minima where the gradients are zero anyway. However, it changes the effective loss function elsewhere and modifies the optimization trajectory, which potentially converges to a different minimum. Implicit regularization due to gradient descent may be responsible for the observation that full batch gradient descent generalizes better with larger step sizes (figure 9.5a).

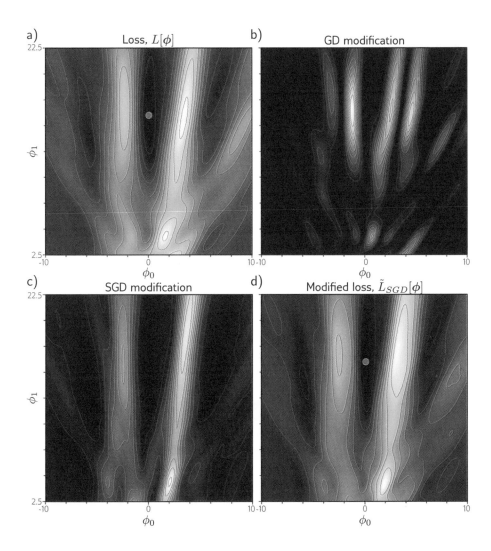

Figure 9.4 Implicit regularization for stochastic gradient descent. a) Original loss function for Gabor model (section 6.1.2). Blue point represents global minimum. b) Implicit regularization term from gradient descent penalizes the squared gradient magnitude. c) Additional implicit regularization from stochastic gradient descent penalizes the variance of the batch gradients. d) Modified loss function (sum of original loss plus two implicit regularization components). Blue point represents global minimum which may now be in a different place from panel (a).

9.2.2 Implicit regularization in stochastic gradient descent

A similar analysis can be applied to stochastic gradient descent. Now we seek a modified loss function such that the continuous version reaches the same place as the average of the possible random SGD updates. This can be shown to be:

$$
\begin{aligned}
\tilde{L}_{SGD}[\phi] &= \tilde{L}_{GD}[\phi] + \frac{\alpha}{4B} \sum_{b=1}^{B} \left\| \frac{\partial L_b}{\partial \phi} - \frac{\partial L}{\partial \phi} \right\|^2 \\
&= L[\phi] + \frac{\alpha}{4} \left\| \frac{\partial L}{\partial \phi} \right\|^2 + \frac{\alpha}{4B} \sum_{b=1}^{B} \left\| \frac{\partial L_b}{\partial \phi} - \frac{\partial L}{\partial \phi} \right\|^2 .
\end{aligned}
\tag{9.9}
$$

Here, L_b is the loss for the bth of the B batches in an epoch, and both L and L_b now represent the means of the I individual losses in the full dataset and the $|\mathcal{B}|$ individual losses in the batch, respectively:

$$
L = \frac{1}{I} \sum_{i=1}^{I} \ell_i[\mathbf{x}_i, y_i] \qquad \text{and} \qquad L_b = \frac{1}{|\mathcal{B}|} \sum_{i \in \mathcal{B}_b} \ell_i[\mathbf{x}_i, y_i].
\tag{9.10}
$$

Equation 9.9 reveals an extra regularization term, which corresponds to the variance of the gradients of the batch losses L_b. In other words, SGD implicitly favors places where the gradients are stable (where all the batches agree on the slope). Once more, this modifies the trajectory of the optimization process (figure 9.4) but does not necessarily change the position of the global minimum; if the model is over-parameterized, then it may fit all the training data exactly, so *all* of these gradient terms will all be zero at the global minimum.

SGD generalizes better than gradient descent, and smaller batch sizes generally perform better than larger ones (figure 9.5b). One possible explanation is that the inherent randomness allows the algorithm to reach different parts of the loss function. However, it's also possible that some or all of this performance increase is due to implicit regularization; this encourages solutions where all the data fits well (so the batch variance is small) rather than solutions where some of the data fit extremely well and other data less well (perhaps with the same overall loss, but with larger batch variance). The former solutions are likely to generalize better.

Notebook 9.2
Implicit
regularization

9.3 Heuristics to improve performance

We've seen that adding explicit regularization terms encourages the training algorithm to find a good solution by adding extra terms to the loss function. This also occurs implicitly as an unintended (but seemingly helpful) byproduct of stochastic gradient descent. This section describes other heuristic methods used to improve generalization.

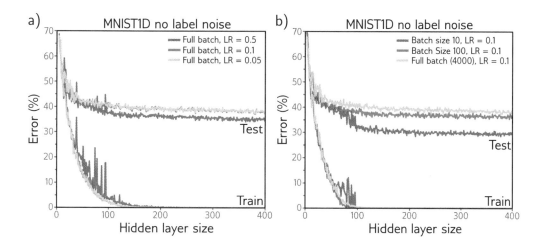

Figure 9.5 Effect of learning rate (LR) and batch size for 4000 training and 4000 test examples from MNIST-1D (see figure 8.1) for a neural network with two hidden layers. a) Performance is better for large learning rates than for intermediate or small ones. In each case, the number of iterations is 6000/LR, so each solution has the opportunity to move the same distance. b) Performance is superior for smaller batch sizes. In each case, the number of iterations was chosen so that the training data were memorized at roughly the same model capacity.

9.3.1   Early stopping

Early stopping refers to stopping the training procedure before it has fully converged. This can reduce overfitting if the model has already captured the coarse shape of the underlying function but has not yet had time to overfit to the noise (figure 9.6). One way of thinking about this is that since the weights are initialized to small values (see section 7.5), they simply don't have time to become large, so early stopping has a similar effect to explicit L2 regularization. A different view is that early stopping reduces the effective model complexity. Hence, we move back down the bias/variance trade-off curve from the critical region, and performance improves (see figures 8.9 and 8.10).

Early stopping has a single hyperparameter, the number of steps after which learning is terminated. As usual, this is chosen empirically using a validation set (section 8.5). However, for early stopping, the hyperparameter can be selected without the need to train multiple models. The model is trained once, the performance on the validation set is monitored every T iterations, and the associated models are stored. The stored model where the validation performance was best is selected.

9.3.2   Ensembling

Another approach to reducing the generalization gap between training and test data is to build several models and average their predictions. A group of such models is known

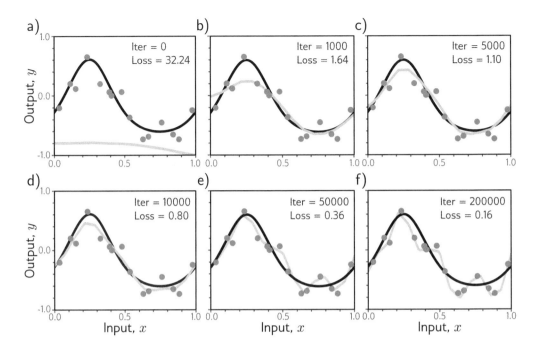

Figure 9.6 Early stopping. a) Simplified shallow network model with 14 linear regions (figure 8.4) is initialized randomly (cyan curve) and trained with SGD using a batch size of five and a learning rate of 0.05. b–d) As training proceeds, the function first captures the coarse structure of the true function (black curve) before e–f) overfitting to the noisy training data (orange points). Although the training loss continues to decrease throughout this process, the learned models in panels (c) and (d) are closest to the true underlying function. They will generalize better on average to test data than those in panels (e) or (f).

as an *ensemble*. This technique reliably improves test performance at the cost of training and storing multiple models and performing inference multiple times.

The models can be combined by taking the mean of the outputs (for regression problems) or the mean of the pre-softmax activations (for classification problems). The assumption is that model errors are independent and will cancel out. Alternatively, we can take the median of the outputs (for regression problems) or the most frequent predicted class (for classification problems) to make the predictions more robust.

One way to train different models is just to use different random initializations. This may help in regions of input space far from the training data. Here, the fitted function is relatively unconstrained, and different models may produce different predictions, so the average of several models may generalize better than any single model.

A second approach is to generate several different datasets by re-sampling the training data with replacement and training a different model from each. This is known as *bootstrap aggregating* or *bagging* for short (figure 9.7). It has the effect of smoothing out the data; if a data point is not present in one training set, the model will interpo-

Notebook 9.3
Ensembling

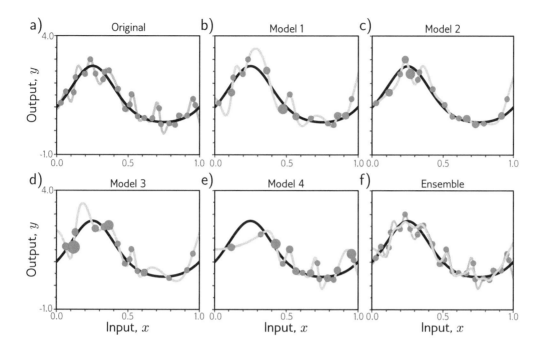

Figure 9.7 Ensemble methods. a) Fitting a single model (gray curve) to the entire dataset (orange points). b–e) Four models created by re-sampling the data with replacement (bagging) four times (size of orange point indicates number of times the data point was re-sampled). f) When we average the predictions of this ensemble, the result (cyan curve) is smoother than the result from panel (a) for the full dataset (gray curve) and will probably generalize better.

late from nearby points; hence, if that point was an outlier, the fitted function will be more moderate in this region. Other approaches include training models with different hyperparameters or training completely different families of models.

9.3.3 Dropout

Dropout randomly clamps a subset (typically 50%) of hidden units to zero at each iteration of SGD (figure 9.8). This makes the network less dependent on any given hidden unit and encourages the weights to have smaller magnitudes so that the change in the function due to the presence or absence of the hidden unit is reduced.

This technique has the positive benefit that it can eliminate undesirable "kinks" in the function that are far from the training data and don't affect the loss. For example, consider three hidden units that become active sequentially as we move along the curve (figure 9.9a). The first hidden unit causes a large increase in the slope. A second hidden

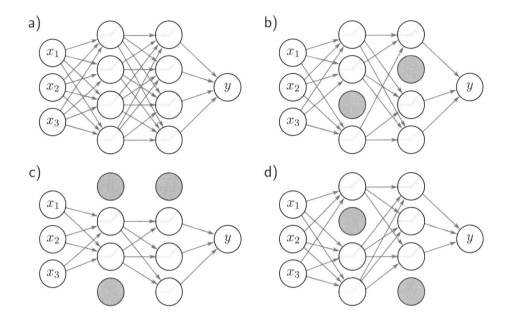

Figure 9.8 Dropout. a) Original network. b–d) At each training iteration, a random subset of hidden units is clamped to zero (gray nodes). The result is that the incoming and outgoing weights from these units have no effect, so we are training with a slightly different network each time.

unit decreases the slope, so the function goes back down. Finally, the third unit cancels out this decrease and returns the curve to its original trajectory. These three units conspire to make an undesirable local change in the function. This will not change the training loss but is unlikely to generalize well.

When several units conspire in this way, eliminating one (as would happen in dropout) causes a considerable change to the output function that is propagated to the half-space where that unit was active (figure 9.9b). A subsequent gradient descent step will attempt to compensate for the change that this induces, and such dependencies will be eliminated over time. The overall effect is that large unnecessary changes between training data points are gradually removed even though they contribute nothing to the loss (figure 9.9).

At test time, we can run the network as usual with all the hidden units active; however, the network now has more hidden units than it was trained with at any given iteration, so we multiply the weights by one minus the dropout probability to compensate. This is known as the *weight scaling inference rule*. A different approach to inference is to use *Monte Carlo dropout*, in which we run the network multiple times with different random subsets of units clamped to zero (as in training) and combine the results. This is closely related to ensembling in that every random version of the network is a different model; however, we do not have to train or store multiple networks here.

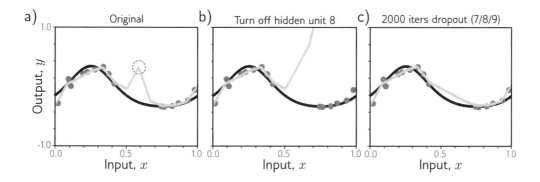

Figure 9.9 Dropout mechanism. a) An undesirable kink in the curve is caused by a sequential increase in the slope, decrease in the slope (at circled joint), and then another increase to return the curve to its original trajectory. Here we are using full-batch gradient descent, and the model (from figure 8.4) fits the data as well as possible, so further training won't remove the kink. b) Consider what happens if we remove the eighth hidden unit that produced the circled joint in panel (a), as might happen using dropout. Without the decrease in the slope, the right-hand side of the function takes an upwards trajectory, and a subsequent gradient descent step will aim to compensate for this change. c) Curve after 2000 iterations of (i) randomly removing one of the three hidden units that cause the kink and (ii) performing a gradient descent step. The kink does not affect the loss but is nonetheless removed by this approximation of the dropout mechanism.

9.3.4 Applying noise

Dropout can be interpreted as applying multiplicative Bernoulli noise to the network activations. This leads to the idea of applying noise to other parts of the network during training to make the final model more robust.

One option is to add noise to the input data; this smooths out the learned function (figure 9.10). For regression problems, it can be shown to be equivalent to adding a regularizing term that penalizes the derivatives of the network's output with respect to its input. An extreme variant is *adversarial training*, in which the optimization algorithm actively searches for small perturbations of the input that cause large changes to the output. These can be thought of as worst-case additive noise vectors.

Problem 9.3

A second possibility is to add noise to the weights. This encourages the network to make sensible predictions even for small perturbations of the weights. The result is that the training converges to local minima in the middle of wide, flat regions, where changing the individual weights does not matter much.

Finally, we can perturb the labels. The maximum-likelihood criterion for multiclass classification aims to predict the correct class with absolute certainty (equation 5.24). To this end, the final network activations (i.e., before the softmax function) are pushed to very large values for the correct class and very small values for the wrong classes. We could discourage this overconfident behavior by assuming that a proportion ρ of

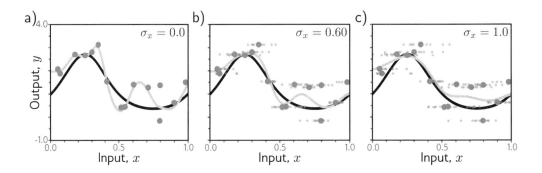

Figure 9.10 Adding noise to inputs. At each step of SGD, random noise with variance σ_x^2 is added to the batch data. a–c) Fitted model with different noise levels (small dots represent ten samples). Adding more noise smooths out the fitted function (cyan line).

the training labels are incorrect and belong with equal probability to the other classes. This could be done by randomly changing the labels at each training iteration. However, the same end can be achieved by changing the loss function to minimize the cross-entropy between the predicted distribution and a distribution where the true label has probability $1 - \rho$, and the other classes have equal probability. This is known as *label smoothing* and improves generalization in diverse scenarios.

Problem 9.4

9.3.5 Bayesian inference

The maximum likelihood approach is generally overconfident; in the training phase, it selects the most likely parameters and bases its predictions on the model defined by these. However, many parameter values may be broadly compatible with the data and only slightly less likely. The Bayesian approach treats the parameters as unknown variables and computes a distribution $Pr(\phi|\{\mathbf{x}_i, \mathbf{y}_i\})$ over these parameters ϕ conditioned on the training data $\{\mathbf{x}_i, \mathbf{y}_i\}$ using Bayes' rule:

Appendix C.1.4
Bayes' rule

$$Pr(\phi|\{\mathbf{x}_i, \mathbf{y}_i\}) = \frac{\prod_{i=1}^{I} Pr(\mathbf{y}_i|\mathbf{x}_i, \phi)Pr(\phi)}{\int \prod_{i=1}^{I} Pr(\mathbf{y}_i|\mathbf{x}_i, \phi)Pr(\phi)d\phi}, \tag{9.11}$$

where $Pr(\phi)$ is the prior probability of the parameters, and the denominator is a normalizing term. Hence, every parameter choice is assigned a probability (figure 9.11).

The prediction $\mathbf{y}$ for new input $\mathbf{x}$ is an infinite weighted sum (i.e., an integral) of the predictions for each parameter set, where the weights are the associated probabilities:

$$Pr(\mathbf{y}|\mathbf{x}, \{\mathbf{x}_i, \mathbf{y}_i\}) = \int Pr(\mathbf{y}|\mathbf{x}, \phi)Pr(\phi|\{\mathbf{x}_i, \mathbf{y}_i\})d\phi. \tag{9.12}$$

This is effectively an infinite weighted ensemble, where the weight depends on (i) the prior probability of the parameters and (ii) their agreement with the data.

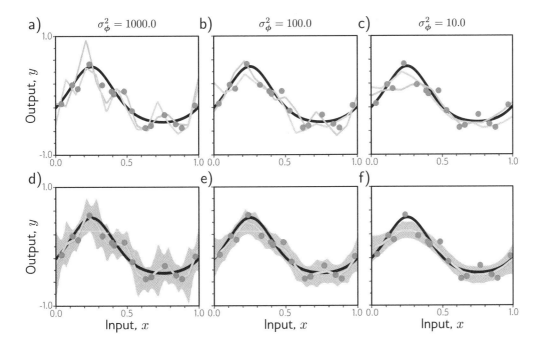

Figure 9.11 Bayesian approach for simplified network model (see figure 8.4). The parameters are treated as uncertain. The posterior probability $Pr(\phi|\{\mathbf{x}_i, \mathbf{y}_i\})$ for a set of parameters is determined by their compatibility with the data $\{\mathbf{x}_i, \mathbf{y}_i\}$ and a prior distribution $Pr(\phi)$. a–c) Two sets of parameters (cyan and gray curves) sampled from the posterior using normally distributed priors with mean zero and three variances. When the prior variance σ_ϕ^2 is small, the parameters also tend to be small, and the functions smoother. d–f) Inference proceeds by taking a weighted sum over all possible parameter values where the weights are the posterior probabilities. This produces both a prediction of the mean (cyan curves) and the associated uncertainty (gray region is two standard deviations).

The Bayesian approach is elegant and can provide more robust predictions than those that derive from maximum likelihood. Unfortunately, for complex models like neural networks, there is no practical way to represent the full probability distribution over the parameters or to integrate over it during the inference phase. Consequently, all current methods of this type make approximations of some kind, and typically these add considerable complexity to learning and inference.

Notebook 9.4
Bayesian
approach

9.3.6 Transfer learning and multi-task learning

When training data are limited, other datasets can be exploited to improve performance. In *transfer learning* (figure 9.12a), the network is *pre-trained* to perform a related secondary task for which data are more plentiful. The resulting model is then adapted to the original task. This is typically done by removing the last layer and adding one or more layers that produce a suitable output. The main model may be fixed, and the new layers trained for the original task, or we may *fine-tune* the entire model.

The principle is that the network will build a good internal representation of the data from the secondary task, which can subsequently be exploited for the original task. Equivalently, transfer learning can be viewed as initializing most of the parameters of the final network in a sensible part of the space that is likely to produce a good solution.

Multi-task learning (figure 9.12b) is a related technique in which the network is trained to solve several problems concurrently. For example, the network might take an image and simultaneously learn to segment the scene, estimate the pixel-wise depth, and predict a caption describing the image. All of these tasks require some understanding of the image and, when learned simultaneously, the model performance for each may improve.

9.3.7 Self-supervised learning

The above discussion assumes that we have plentiful data for a secondary task or data for multiple tasks to be learned concurrently. If not, we can create large amounts of "free" labeled data using *self-supervised* learning and use this for transfer learning. There are two families of methods for self-supervised learning: *generative* and *contrastive*.

In *generative self-supervised learning*, part of each data example is masked, and the secondary task is to predict the missing part (figure 9.12c). For example, we might use a corpus of unlabeled images and a secondary task that aims to *inpaint* (fill in) missing parts of the image (figure 9.12c). Similarly, we might use a large corpus of text and mask some words. We train the network to predict the missing words and then fine-tune it for the actual language task we are interested in (see chapter 12).

In *contrastive self-supervised learning*, pairs of examples with commonalities are compared to unrelated pairs. For images, the secondary task might be to identify whether a pair of images are transformed versions of one another or are unconnected. For text, the secondary task might be to determine whether two sentences followed one another in the original document. Sometimes, the precise relationship between a connected pair must be identified (e.g., finding the relative position of two patches from the same image).

9.3.8 Augmentation

Transfer learning improves performance by exploiting a different dataset. Multi-task learning improves performance using additional labels. A third option is to expand the dataset. We can often transform each input data example in such a way that the label stays the same. For example, we might aim to determine if there is a bird in an image (figure 9.13). Here, we could rotate, flip, blur, or manipulate the color balance of the image, and the label "bird" remains valid. Similarly, for tasks where the input is text, we can substitute synonyms or translate to another language and back again. For tasks where the input is audio, we can amplify or attenuate different frequency bands.

Notebook 9.5
Augmentation

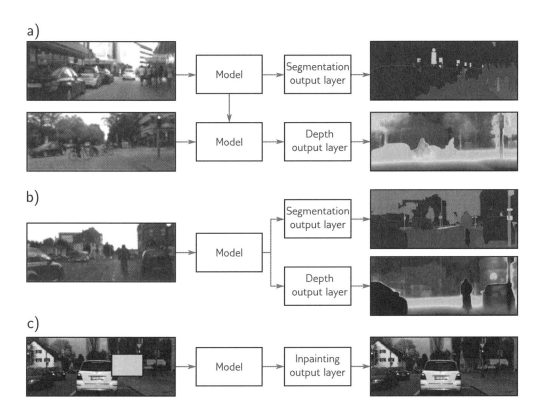

Figure 9.12 Transfer, multi-task, and self-supervised learning. a) Transfer learning is used when we have limited labeled data for the primary task (here depth estimation) but plentiful data for a secondary task (here segmentation). We train a model for the secondary task, remove the final layers, and replace them with new layers appropriate to the primary task. We then train only the new layers or fine-tune the entire network for the primary task. The network learns a good internal representation from the secondary task that is then exploited for the primary task. b) In multi-task learning, we train a model to perform multiple tasks simultaneously, hoping that performance on each will improve. c) In generative self-supervised learning, we remove part of the data and train the network to complete the missing information. Here, the task is to fill in (inpaint) a masked portion of the image. This permits transfer learning when no labels are available. Images from Cordts et al. (2016).

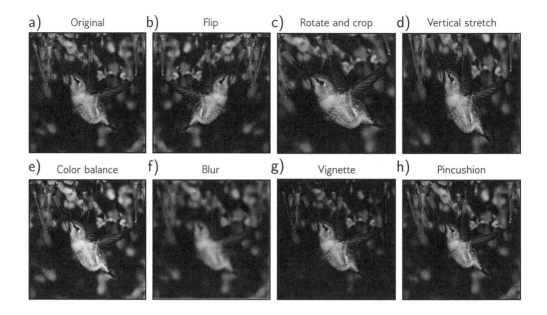

Figure 9.13 Data augmentation. For some problems, each data example can be transformed to augment the dataset. a) Original image. b–h) Various geometric and photometric transformations of this image. For image classification, all these images still have the same label, "bird." Adapted from Wu et al. (2015a).

Generating extra training data in this way is known as *data augmentation*. The aim is to teach the model to be indifferent to these irrelevant data transformations.

9.4 Summary

Explicit regularization involves adding an extra term to the loss function that changes the position of the minimum. The term can be interpreted as a prior probability over the parameters. Stochastic gradient descent with a finite step size does not neutrally descend to the minimum of the loss function. This bias can be interpreted as adding additional terms to the loss function, and this is known as implicit regularization.

There are also many heuristics for improving generalization, including early stopping, dropout, ensembling, the Bayesian approach, adding noise, transfer learning, multi-task learning, and data augmentation. There are four main principles behind these methods (figure 9.14). We can (i) encourage the function to be smoother (e.g., L2 regularization), (ii) increase the amount of data (e.g., data augmentation), (iii) combine models (e.g., ensembling), or (iv) search for wider minima (e.g., applying noise to network weights).

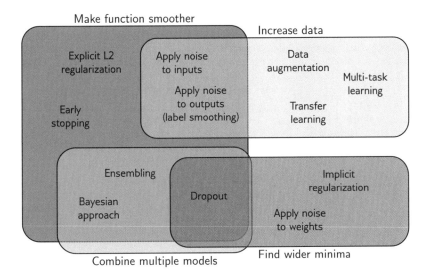

Figure 9.14 Regularization methods. The regularization methods discussed in this chapter aim to improve generalization by one of four mechanisms. Some methods aim to make the modeled function smoother. Other methods increase the effective amount of data. The third group of methods combine multiple models and hence mitigate against uncertainty in the fitting process. Finally, the fourth group of methods encourages the training process to converge to a wide minimum where small errors in the estimated parameters are less important (see also figure 20.11).

Another way to improve generalization is to choose the model architecture to suit the task. For example, in image segmentation, we can share parameters within the model, so we don't need to independently learn what a tree looks like at every image location. Chapters 10–13 consider architectural variations designed for different tasks.

Notes

An overview and taxonomy of regularization techniques in deep learning can be found in Kukačka et al. (2017). Notably missing from the discussion in this chapter is BatchNorm (Szegedy et al., 2016) at its variants, which are described in chapter 11.

Regularization: L2 regularization penalizes the sum of squares of the network weights. This encourages the output function to change slowly (i.e., become smoother) and is the most used regularization term. It is sometimes referred to as Frobenius norm regularization as it penalizes the Frobenius norms of the weight matrices. It is often also mistakenly referred to as "weight decay," although this is a separate technique devised by Hanson & Pratt (1988) in which the parameters ϕ are updated as:

$$\phi \longleftarrow (1 - \lambda')\phi - \alpha \frac{\partial L}{\partial \phi}, \tag{9.13}$$

where, as usual, α is the learning rate, and L is the loss. This is identical to gradient descent, except that the weights are reduced by a factor of $1 - \lambda'$ before the gradient update. For standard SGD, weight decay is equivalent to L2 regularization (equation 9.5) with coefficient $\lambda = \lambda'/2\alpha$. However, for Adam, the learning rate α is different for each parameter, so L2 regularization and weight decay differ. Loshchilov & Hutter (2019) present AdamW, which modifies Adam to implement weight decay correctly and show that this improves performance.

Other choices of vector norm encourage sparsity in the weights. The L0 regularization term applies a fixed penalty for every non-zero weight. The effect is to "prune" the network. L0 regularization can also be used to encourage group sparsity; this might apply a fixed penalty if any of the weights contributing to a given hidden unit are non-zero. If they are all zero, we can remove the unit, decreasing the model size and making inference faster.

Unfortunately, L0 regularization is challenging to implement since the derivative of the regularization term is not smooth, and more sophisticated fitting methods are required (see Louizos et al., 2018). Somewhere between L2 and L0 regularization is L1 regularization or *LASSO* (least absolute shrinkage and selection operator), which imposes a penalty on the absolute values of the weights. L2 regularization somewhat discourages sparsity in that the derivative of the squared penalty decreases as the weight becomes smaller, lowering the pressure to make it smaller still. L1 regularization does not have this disadvantage, as the derivative of the penalty is constant. This can produce sparser solutions than L2 regularization but is much easier to optimize than L0 regularization. Sometimes both L1 and L2 regularization terms are used, which is termed an *elastic net* penalty (Zou & Hastie, 2005).

A different approach to regularization is to modify the gradients of the learning algorithm without ever explicitly formulating a new loss function (e.g., equation 9.13). This approach has been used to promote sparsity during backpropagation (Schwarz et al., 2021).

The evidence on the effectiveness of explicit regularization is mixed. Zhang et al. (2017a) showed that L2 regularization contributes little to generalization. It has been proven that the Lipschitz constant of the network (how fast the function can change as we modify the input) bounds the generalization error (Bartlett et al., 2017; Neyshabur et al., 2018). However, the Lipschitz constant depends on the product of the spectral norms of the weight matrices Ω_k, which are only indirectly dependent on the magnitudes of the individual weights. Bartlett et al. (2017), Neyshabur et al. (2018), and Yoshida & Miyato (2017) all add terms that indirectly encourage the spectral norms to be smaller. Gouk et al. (2021) take a different approach and develop an algorithm that constrains the Lipschitz constant of the network to be below a particular value.

Implicit regularization in gradient descent: The gradient descent step is:

$$\phi_1 = \phi_0 + \alpha \cdot \mathbf{g}[\phi_0], \tag{9.14}$$

where $\mathbf{g}[\phi_0]$ is the negative of the gradient of the loss function, and α is the step size. As $\alpha \to 0$, the gradient descent process can be described by a differential equation:

$$\frac{d\phi}{dt} = \mathbf{g}[\phi]. \tag{9.15}$$

For typical step sizes α, the discrete and continuous versions converge to different solutions. We can use *backward error analysis* to find a correction $\mathbf{g}_1[\phi]$ to the continuous version:

$$\frac{d\phi}{dt} \approx \mathbf{g}[\phi] + \alpha\mathbf{g}_1[\phi] + \dots, \tag{9.16}$$

so that it gives the same result as the discrete version.

Consider the first two terms of a Taylor expansion of the modified continuous solution ϕ around initial position ϕ_0:

Problem 9.5

Appendix B.3.2
Vector norms

Problem 9.6

Appendix B.1.1
Lipschitz constant

Appendix B.3.7
Spectral norm

$$\begin{aligned}
\boldsymbol{\phi}[\alpha] \quad &\approx \quad \boldsymbol{\phi} + \alpha \frac{d\boldsymbol{\phi}}{dt} + \frac{\alpha^2}{2}\frac{d^2\boldsymbol{\phi}}{dt^2}\bigg|_{\boldsymbol{\phi}=\boldsymbol{\phi}_0} \\
&\approx \quad \boldsymbol{\phi} + \alpha\left(\mathbf{g}[\boldsymbol{\phi}] + \alpha\mathbf{g}_1[\boldsymbol{\phi}]\right) + \frac{\alpha^2}{2}\left(\frac{\partial\mathbf{g}[\boldsymbol{\phi}]}{\partial\boldsymbol{\phi}}\frac{d\boldsymbol{\phi}}{dt} + \alpha\frac{\partial\mathbf{g}_1[\boldsymbol{\phi}]}{\partial\boldsymbol{\phi}}\frac{d\boldsymbol{\phi}}{dt}\right)\bigg|_{\boldsymbol{\phi}=\boldsymbol{\phi}_0} \\
&= \quad \boldsymbol{\phi} + \alpha\left(\mathbf{g}[\boldsymbol{\phi}] + \alpha\mathbf{g}_1[\boldsymbol{\phi}]\right) + \frac{\alpha^2}{2}\left(\frac{\partial\mathbf{g}[\boldsymbol{\phi}]}{\partial\boldsymbol{\phi}}\mathbf{g}[\boldsymbol{\phi}] + \alpha\frac{\partial\mathbf{g}_1[\boldsymbol{\phi}]}{\partial\boldsymbol{\phi}}\mathbf{g}[\boldsymbol{\phi}]\right)\bigg|_{\boldsymbol{\phi}=\boldsymbol{\phi}_0} \\
&\approx \quad \boldsymbol{\phi} + \alpha\mathbf{g}[\boldsymbol{\phi}] + \alpha^2\left(\mathbf{g}_1[\boldsymbol{\phi}] + \frac{1}{2}\frac{\partial\mathbf{g}[\boldsymbol{\phi}]}{\partial\boldsymbol{\phi}}\mathbf{g}[\boldsymbol{\phi}]\right)\bigg|_{\boldsymbol{\phi}=\boldsymbol{\phi}_0} ,
\end{aligned} \tag{9.17}$$

where in the second line, we have introduced the correction term (equation 9.16), and in the final line, we have removed terms of greater order than α^2.

Note that the first two terms on the right-hand side $\boldsymbol{\phi}_0 + \alpha\mathbf{g}[\boldsymbol{\phi}_0]$ are the same as the discrete update (equation 9.14). Hence, to make the continuous and discrete versions arrive at the same place, the third term on the right-hand side must equal zero, allowing us to solve for $\mathbf{g}_1[\boldsymbol{\phi}]$:

$$\mathbf{g}_1[\boldsymbol{\phi}] = -\frac{1}{2}\frac{\partial\mathbf{g}[\boldsymbol{\phi}]}{\partial\boldsymbol{\phi}}\mathbf{g}[\boldsymbol{\phi}]. \tag{9.18}$$

During training, the evolution function $\mathbf{g}[\boldsymbol{\phi}]$ is the negative of the gradient of the loss:

$$\begin{aligned}
\frac{d\boldsymbol{\phi}}{dt} \quad &\approx \quad \mathbf{g}[\boldsymbol{\phi}] + \alpha\mathbf{g}_1[\boldsymbol{\phi}] \\
&= \quad -\frac{\partial L}{\partial\boldsymbol{\phi}} - \frac{\alpha}{2}\left(\frac{\partial^2 L}{\partial\boldsymbol{\phi}^2}\right)\frac{\partial L}{\partial\boldsymbol{\phi}}.
\end{aligned} \tag{9.19}$$

This is equivalent to performing continuous gradient descent on the loss function:

$$L_{GD}[\boldsymbol{\phi}] = L[\boldsymbol{\phi}] + \frac{\alpha}{4}\left\|\frac{\partial L}{\partial\boldsymbol{\phi}}\right\|^2, \tag{9.20}$$

because the right-hand side of equation 9.19 is the derivative of that in equation 9.20.

This formulation of implicit regularization was developed by Barrett & Dherin (2021) and extended to stochastic gradient descent by Smith et al. (2021). Smith et al. (2020) and others have shown that stochastic gradient descent with small or moderate batch sizes outperforms full batch gradient descent on the test set, and this may in part be due to implicit regularization.

Relatedly, Jastrzębski et al. (2021) and Cohen et al. (2021) both show that using a large learning rate reduces the tendency of typical optimization trajectories to move to "sharper" parts of the loss function (i.e., where at least one direction has high curvature). This implicit regularization effect of large learning rates can be approximated by penalizing the trace of the Fisher Information Matrix, which is closely related to penalizing the gradient norm in equation 9.20 (Jastrzębski et al., 2021).

Early stopping: Bishop (1995) and Sjöberg & Ljung (1995) argued that early stopping limits the effective solution space that the training procedure can explore; given that the weights are initialized to small values, this leads to the idea that early stopping helps prevent the weights from getting too large. Goodfellow et al. (2016) show that under a quadratic approximation of the loss function with parameters initialized to zero, early stopping is equivalent to L2 regularization in gradient descent. The effective regularization weight λ is approximately $1/(\tau\alpha)$ where α is the learning rate, and τ is the early stopping time.

Ensembling: Ensembles can be trained using different random seeds (Lakshminarayanan et al., 2017), hyperparameters (Wenzel et al., 2020b), or even entirely different families of models. The models can be combined by averaging their predictions, weighting the predictions, or *stacking* (Wolpert, 1992), in which the results are combined using another machine learning model. Lakshminarayanan et al. (2017) showed that averaging the output of independently trained networks can improve accuracy, calibration, and robustness. Conversely, Frankle et al. (2020) showed that if we average together the weights to make one model, the network fails. Fort et al. (2019) compared ensembling solutions that resulted from different initializations with ensembling solutions that were generated from the same original model. For example, in the latter case, they consider exploring around the solution in a limited subspace to find other good nearby points. They found that both techniques provide complementary benefits but that genuine ensembling from different random starting points provides a bigger improvement.

Appendix B.3.6
Subspaces

An efficient way of ensembling is to combine models from intermediate stages of training. To this end, Izmailov et al. (2018) introduce *stochastic weight averaging*, in which the model weights are sampled at different time steps and averaged together. As the name suggests, *snapshot ensembles* (Huang et al., 2017a) also store the models from different time steps and average their predictions. The diversity of these models can be improved by cyclically increasing and decreasing the learning rate. Garipov et al. (2018) observed that different minima of the loss function are often connected by a low-energy path (i.e., a path with a low loss everywhere along it). Motivated by this observation, they developed a method that explores low-energy regions around an initial solution to provide diverse models without retraining. This is known as *fast geometric ensembling*. A review of ensembling methods can be found in Ganaie et al. (2022).

Dropout: Dropout was first introduced by Hinton et al. (2012b) and Srivastava et al. (2014). Dropout is applied at the level of hidden units. Dropping a hidden unit has the same effect as temporarily setting all the incoming and outgoing weights and the bias to zero. Wan et al. (2013) generalized dropout by randomly setting individual weights to zero. Gal & Ghahramani (2016) and Kendall & Gal (2017) proposed Monte Carlo dropout, in which inference is computed with several dropout patterns, and the results are averaged together. Gal & Ghahramani (2016) argued that this could be interpreted as approximating Bayesian inference.

Dropout is equivalent to applying multiplicative Bernoulli noise to the hidden units. Similar benefits derive from using other distributions, including the normal (Srivastava et al., 2014; Shen et al., 2017), uniform (Shen et al., 2017), and beta distributions (Liu et al., 2019b).

Adding noise: Bishop (1995) and An (1996) added Gaussian noise to the network inputs to improve performance. Bishop (1995) showed that this is equivalent to weight decay. An (1996) also investigated adding noise to the weights. DeVries & Taylor (2017a) added Gaussian noise to the hidden units. The *randomized ReLU* (Xu et al., 2015) applies noise in a different way by making the activation functions stochastic.

Label smoothing: Label smoothing was introduced by Szegedy et al. (2016) for image classification but has since been shown to be helpful in speech recognition (Chorowski & Jaitly, 2017), machine translation (Vaswani et al., 2017), and language modeling (Pereyra et al., 2017). The precise mechanism by which label smoothing improves test performance isn't well understood, although Müller et al. (2019a) show that it improves the calibration of the predicted output probabilities. A closely related technique is *DisturbLabel* (Xie et al., 2016), in which a certain percentage of the labels in each batch are randomly switched at each training iteration.

Finding wider minima: It is thought that wider minima generalize better (see figure 20.11). Here, the exact values of the weights are less important, so performance should be robust to errors in their estimates. One of the reasons that applying noise to parts of the network during training is effective is that it encourages the network to be indifferent to their exact values.

Chaudhari et al. (2019) developed a variant of SGD that biases the optimization toward flat minima, which they call *entropy SGD*. The idea is to incorporate local entropy as a term in the loss function. In practice, this takes the form of one SGD-like update within another. Keskar et al. (2017) showed that SGD finds wider minima as the batch size is reduced. This may be because of the batch variance term that results from implicit regularization by SGD.

Ishida et al. (2020) use a technique named *flooding*, in which they intentionally prevent the training loss from becoming zero. This encourages the solution to perform a random walk over the loss landscape and drift into a flatter area with better generalization.

Bayesian approaches: For some models, including the simplified neural network model in figure 9.11, the Bayesian predictive distribution can be computed in closed form (see Bishop, 2006; Prince, 2012). For neural networks, the posterior distribution over the parameters cannot be represented in closed form and must be approximated. The two main approaches are variational Bayes (Hinton & van Camp, 1993; MacKay, 1995; Barber & Bishop, 1997; Blundell et al., 2015), in which the posterior is approximated by a simpler tractable distribution, and Markov Chain Monte Carlo (MCMC) methods, which approximate the distribution by drawing a set of samples (Neal, 1995; Welling & Teh, 2011; Chen et al., 2014; Ma et al., 2015; Li et al., 2016a). The generation of samples can be integrated into SGD, and this is known as stochastic gradient MCMC (see Ma et al., 2015). It has recently been discovered that "cooling" the posterior distribution over the parameters (making it sharper) improves predictions from these models (Wenzel et al., 2020a), but this is not currently fully understood (see Noci et al., 2021).

Transfer learning: Transfer learning for visual tasks works extremely well (Sharif Razavian et al., 2014) and has supported rapid progress in computer vision, including the original AlexNet results (Krizhevsky et al., 2012). Transfer learning has also impacted natural language processing (NLP), where many models are based on pre-trained features from the BERT model (Devlin et al., 2019). More information can be found in Zhuang et al. (2020) and Yang et al. (2020b).

Self-supervised learning: Self-supervised learning techniques for images have included inpainting masked image regions (Pathak et al., 2016), predicting the relative position of patches in an image (Doersch et al., 2015), re-arranging permuted image tiles back into their original configuration (Noroozi & Favaro, 2016), colorizing grayscale images (Zhang et al., 2016b), and transforming rotated images back to their original orientation (Gidaris et al., 2018). In SimCLR (Chen et al., 2020c), a network is learned that maps versions of the same image that have been photometrically and geometrically transformed to the same representation while repelling versions of different images, with the goal of becoming indifferent to irrelevant image transformations. Jing & Tian (2020) present a survey of self-supervised learning in images.

Self-supervised learning in NLP can be based on predicting masked words(Devlin et al., 2019), predicting the next word in a sentence (Radford et al., 2019; Brown et al., 2020), or predicting whether two sentences follow one another (Devlin et al., 2019). In automatic speech recognition, the Wav2Vec model (Schneider et al., 2019) aims to distinguish an original audio sample from one where 10ms of audio has been swapped out from elsewhere in the clip. Self-supervision has also been applied to graph neural networks (chapter 13). Tasks include recovering masked features (You et al., 2020) and recovering the adjacency structure of the graph (Kipf & Welling, 2016). Liu et al. (2023a) review self-supervised learning for graph models.

Data augmentation: Data augmentation for images dates back to at least LeCun et al. (1998) and contributed to the success of AlexNet (Krizhevsky et al., 2012), in which the dataset was increased by a factor of 2048. Image augmentation approaches include geometric transformations, changing or manipulating the color space, noise injection, and applying spatial filters. More elaborate techniques include randomly mixing images (Inoue, 2018; Summers & Dinneen, 2019), randomly erasing parts of the image (Zhong et al., 2020), style transfer (Jackson et al., 2019), and randomly swapping image patches (Kang et al., 2017). In addition, many studies have used generative adversarial networks or GANs (see chapter 15) to produce novel but plausible data examples (e.g., Calimeri et al., 2017). In other cases, the data have been augmented with adversarial examples (Goodfellow et al., 2015a), which are minor perturbations of the training data that cause the example to be misclassified. A review of data augmentation for images can be found in Shorten & Khoshgoftaar (2019).

Augmentation methods for acoustic data include pitch shifting, time stretching, dynamic range compression, and adding random noise (e.g., Abeßer et al., 2017; Salamon & Bello, 2017; Xu et al., 2015; Lasseck, 2018), as well as mixing data pairs (Zhang et al., 2017c; Yun et al., 2019), masking features (Park et al., 2019), and using GANs to generate new data (Mun et al., 2017). Augmentation for speech data includes vocal tract length perturbation (Jaitly & Hinton, 2013; Kanda et al., 2013), style transfer (Gales, 1998; Ye & Young, 2004), adding noise (Hannun et al., 2014), and synthesizing speech (Gales et al., 2009).

Augmentation methods for text include adding noise at a character level by switching, deleting, and inserting letters (Belinkov & Bisk, 2018; Feng et al., 2020), or by generating adversarial examples (Ebrahimi et al., 2018), using common spelling mistakes (Coulombe, 2018), randomly swapping or deleting words (Wei & Zou, 2019), using synonyms (Kolomiyets et al., 2011), altering adjectives (Li et al., 2017c), passivization (Min et al., 2020), using generative models to create new data (Qiu et al., 2020), and round-trip translation to another language and back (Aiken & Park, 2010). Augmentation methods for text are reviewed by Bayer et al. (2022).

Problems

Problem 9.1 Consider a model where the prior distribution over the parameters is a normal distribution with mean zero and variance σ_ϕ^2 so that

$$Pr(\boldsymbol{\phi}) = \prod_{j=1}^{J} \text{Norm}_{\phi_j}[0, \sigma_\phi^2], \tag{9.21}$$

where j indexes the model parameters. We now maximize $\prod_{i=1}^{I} Pr(\mathbf{y}_i|\mathbf{x}_i, \boldsymbol{\phi})Pr(\boldsymbol{\phi})$. Show that the associated loss function of this model is equivalent to L2 regularization.

Problem 9.2 How do the gradients of the loss function change when L2 regularization (equation 9.5) is added?

Problem 9.3* Consider a linear regression model $y = \phi_0 + \phi_1 x$ with input x, output y, and parameters ϕ_0 and ϕ_1. Assume we have I training examples $\{x_i, y_i\}$ and use a least squares loss. Consider adding Gaussian noise with mean zero and variance σ_x^2 to the inputs x_i at each training iteration. What is the expected gradient update?

Problem 9.4* Derive the loss function for multiclass classification when we use label smoothing so that the target probability distribution has 0.9 at the correct class and the remaining probability mass of 0.1 is divided between the remaining $D_o - 1$ classes.

Problem 9.5 Show that the weight decay parameter update with decay rate λ:

$$\boldsymbol{\phi} \longleftarrow (1 - \lambda)\boldsymbol{\phi} - \alpha \frac{\partial L}{\partial \boldsymbol{\phi}}, \tag{9.22}$$

on the original loss function $L[\boldsymbol{\phi}]$ is equivalent to a standard gradient update using L2 regularization so that the modified loss function $\tilde{L}[\boldsymbol{\phi}]$ is:

$$\tilde{L}[\boldsymbol{\phi}] = L[\boldsymbol{\phi}] + \frac{\lambda}{2\alpha} \sum_k \phi_k^2, \tag{9.23}$$

where $\boldsymbol{\phi}$ are the parameters, and α is the learning rate.

Problem 9.6 Consider a model with parameters $\boldsymbol{\phi} = [\phi_0, \phi_1]^T$. Draw the L0, $L\frac{1}{2}$, and L1 regularization terms in a similar form to figure 9.1b. The LP regularization term is $\sum_{d=1}^{D} |\phi_d|^P$.

Chapter 10

Convolutional networks

Chapters 2–9 introduced the supervised learning pipeline for deep neural networks. However, these chapters only considered fully connected networks with a single path from input to output. Chapters 10–13 introduce more specialized network components with sparser connections, shared weights, and parallel processing paths. This chapter describes *convolutional layers*, which are mainly used for processing image data.

Images have three properties that suggest the need for specialized model architecture. First, they are high-dimensional. A typical image for a classification task contains 224×224 RGB values (i.e., 150,528 input dimensions). Hidden layers in fully connected networks are generally larger than the input size, so even for a shallow network, the number of weights would exceed $150,528^2$, or 22 billion. This poses obvious practical problems in terms of the required training data, memory, and computation.

Second, nearby image pixels are statistically related. However, fully connected networks have no notion of "nearby" and treat the relationship between every input equally. If the pixels of the training and test images were randomly permuted in the same way, the network could still be trained with no practical difference. Third, the interpretation of an image is stable under geometric transformations. An image of a tree is still an image of a tree if we shift it leftwards by a few pixels. However, this shift changes every input to the network. Hence, a fully connected model must learn the patterns of pixels that signify a tree separately at every position, which is clearly inefficient.

Convolutional layers process each local image region independently, using parameters shared across the whole image. They use fewer parameters than fully connected layers, exploit the spatial relationships between nearby pixels, and don't have to re-learn the interpretation of the pixels at every position. A network predominantly consisting of convolutional layers is known as a *convolutional neural network* or *CNN*.

10.1 Invariance and equivariance

We argued above that some properties of images (e.g., tree texture) are stable under transformations. In this section, we make this idea more mathematically precise. A

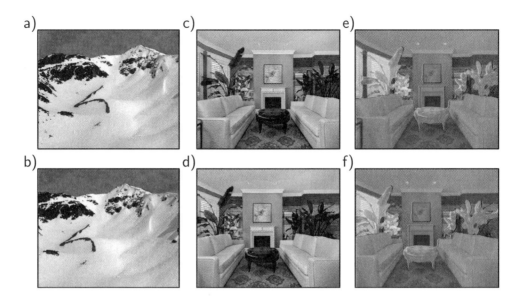

Figure 10.1 Invariance and equivariance for translation. a–b) In image classification, the goal is to categorize both images as "mountain" regardless of the
horizontal shift that has occurred. In other words, we require the network prediction to be invariant to translation. c,e) The goal of semantic segmentation is
to associate a label with each pixel. d,f) When the input image is translated, we
want the output (colored overlay) to translate in the same way. In other words,
we require the output to be equivariant with respect to translation. Panels c–f)
adapted from Bousselham et al. (2021).

function f[$\mathbf{x}$] of an image $\mathbf{x}$ is *invariant* to a transformation $\mathbf{t}[\mathbf{x}]$ if:

$$\mathbf{f}\big[\mathbf{t}[\mathbf{x}]\big] = \mathbf{f}[\mathbf{x}]. \tag{10.1}$$

In other words, the output of the function f[$\mathbf{x}$] is the same regardless of the transformation $\mathbf{t}[\mathbf{x}]$. Networks for image classification should be invariant to geometric transformations of the image (figure 10.1a–b). The network $\mathbf{f}[\mathbf{x}]$ should identify an image as
containing the same object, even if it has been translated, rotated, flipped, or warped.

A function f[$\mathbf{x}$] of an image $\mathbf{x}$ is *equivariant* or *covariant* to a transformation $\mathbf{t}[\mathbf{x}]$ if:

$$\mathbf{f}\big[\mathbf{t}[\mathbf{x}]\big] = \mathbf{t}\big[\mathbf{f}[\mathbf{x}]\big]. \tag{10.2}$$

In other words, $\mathbf{f}[\mathbf{x}]$ is equivariant to the transformation $\mathbf{t}[\mathbf{x}]$ if its output changes in
the same way under the transformation as the input. Networks for per-pixel image
segmentation should be equivariant to transformations (figure 10.1c–f); if the image is
translated, rotated, or flipped, the network $\mathbf{f}[\mathbf{x}]$ should return a segmentation that has
been transformed in the same way.

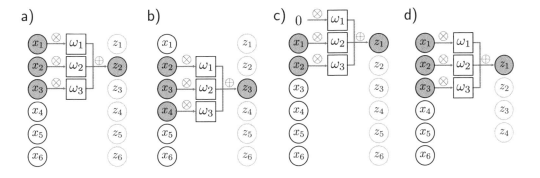

Figure 10.2 1D convolution with kernel size three. Each output z_i is a weighted sum of the nearest three inputs x_{i-1}, x_i, and x_{i+1}, where the weights are $\boldsymbol{\omega} = [\omega_1, \omega_2, \omega_3]$. a) Output z_2 is computed as $z_2 = \omega_1 x_1 + \omega_2 x_2 + \omega_3 x_3$. b) Output z_3 is computed as $z_3 = \omega_1 x_2 + \omega_2 x_3 + \omega_3 x_4$. c) At position z_1, the kernel extends beyond the first input x_1. This can be handled by zero padding, in which we assume values outside the input are zero. The final output is treated similarly. d) Alternatively, we could only compute outputs where the kernel fits within the input range ("valid" convolution); now, the output will be smaller than the input.

10.2 Convolutional networks for 1D inputs

Convolutional networks consist of a series of convolutional layers, each of which is equivariant to translation. They also typically include pooling mechanisms that induce partial invariance to translation. For clarity of exposition, we first consider convolutional networks for 1D data, which are easier to visualize. In section 10.3, we progress to 2D convolution, which can be applied to image data.

10.2.1 1D convolution operation

Convolutional layers are network layers based on the *convolution* operation. In 1D, a convolution transforms an input vector $\mathbf{x}$ into an output vector $\mathbf{z}$ so that each output z_i is a weighted sum of nearby inputs. The same weights are used at every position and are collectively called the *convolution kernel* or *filter*. The size of the region over which inputs are combined is termed the *kernel size*. For a kernel size of three, we have:

$$z_i = \omega_1 x_{i-1} + \omega_2 x_i + \omega_3 x_{i+1}, \tag{10.3}$$

where $\boldsymbol{\omega} = [\omega_1, \omega_2, \omega_3]^T$ is the kernel (figure 10.2).[1] Notice that the convolution operation is equivariant with respect to translation. If we translate the input x, then the corresponding output z is translated in the same way.

Problem 10.1

---

[1]Strictly speaking, this is a cross-correlation and not a convolution, in which the weights would be flipped relative to the input (so we would switch x_{i-1} with x_{i+1}). Regardless, this (incorrect) definition is the usual convention in machine learning.

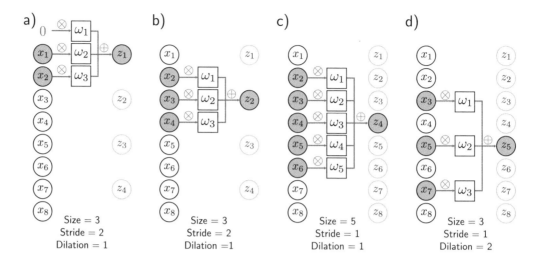

Figure 10.3 Stride, kernel size, and dilation. a) With a stride of two, we evaluate the kernel at every other position, so the first output z_1 is computed from a weighted sum centered at x_1, and b) the second output z_2 is computed from a weighted sum centered at x_3 and so on. c) The kernel size can also be changed. With a kernel size of five, we take a weighted sum of the nearest five inputs. d) In dilated or atrous convolution (from the French "à trous" – with holes), we intersperse zeros in the weight vector to allow us to combine information over a large area using fewer weights.

10.2.2 Padding

Equation 10.3 shows that each output is computed by taking a weighted sum of the previous, current, and subsequent positions in the input. This begs the question of how to deal with the first output (where there is no previous input) and the final output (where there is no subsequent input).

There are two common approaches. The first is to pad the edges of the inputs with new values and proceed as usual. *Zero padding* assumes the input is zero outside its valid range (figure 10.2c). Other possibilities include treating the input as circular or reflecting it at the boundaries. The second approach is to discard the output positions where the kernel exceeds the range of input positions. These *valid convolutions* have the advantage of introducing no extra information at the edges of the input. However, they have the disadvantage that the representation decreases in size.

10.2.3 Stride, kernel size, and dilation

In the example above, each output was a sum of the nearest three inputs. However, this is just one of a larger family of convolution operations, the members of which are distinguished by their *stride, kernel size,* and *dilation rate.* When we evaluate the output at every position, we term this a *stride* of one. However, it is also possible to shift the kernel by a stride greater than one. If we have a stride of two, we create roughly half the number of outputs (figure 10.3a–b).

The *kernel size* can be increased to integrate over a larger area (figure 10.3c). However, it typically remains an odd number so that it can be centered around the current position. Increasing the kernel size has the disadvantage of requiring more weights. This leads to the idea of *dilated* or *atrous* convolutions, in which the kernel values are interspersed with zeros. For example, we can turn a kernel of size five into a dilated kernel of size three by setting the second and fourth elements to zero. We still integrate information from a larger input region but only require three weights to do this (figure 10.3d). The number of zeros we intersperse between the weights determines the *dilation rate.*

Problems 10.2–10.4

10.2.4 Convolutional layers

A convolutional layer computes its output by convolving the input, adding a bias β, and passing each result through an activation function $a[\bullet]$. With kernel size three, stride one, and dilation rate one, the ith hidden unit h_i would be computed as:

$$
\begin{aligned}
h_i &= a\left[\beta + \omega_1 x_{i-1} + \omega_2 x_i + \omega_3 x_{i+1}\right] \\
&= a\left[\beta + \sum_{j=1}^{3} \omega_j x_{i+j-2}\right],
\end{aligned} \tag{10.4}
$$

where the bias β and kernel weights $\omega_1, \omega_2, \omega_3$ are trainable parameters, and (with zero padding) we treat the input x as zero when it is out of the valid range. This is a special case of a fully connected layer that computes the ith hidden unit as:

$$
h_i = a\left[\beta_i + \sum_{j=1}^{D} \omega_{ij} x_j\right]. \tag{10.5}
$$

If there are D inputs $x_\bullet$ and D hidden units $h_\bullet$, this fully connected layer would have D^2 weights $\omega_{\bullet\bullet}$ and D biases $\beta_\bullet$. The convolutional layer only uses three weights and one bias. A fully connected layer can reproduce this exactly if most weights are set to zero and others are constrained to be identical (figure 10.4).

Problem 10.5

10.2.5 Channels

If we only apply a single convolution, information will inevitably be lost; we are averaging nearby inputs, and the ReLU activation function clips results that are less than zero. Hence, it is usual to compute several convolutions in parallel. Each convolution produces a new set of hidden variables, termed a *feature map* or *channel.*

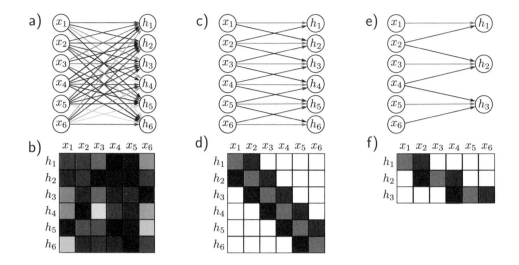

Figure 10.4 Fully connected vs. convolutional layers. a) A fully connected layer has a weight connecting each input x to each hidden unit h (colored arrows) and a bias for each hidden unit (not shown). b) Hence, the associated weight matrix Ω contains 36 weights relating the six inputs to the six hidden units. c) A convolutional layer with kernel size three computes each hidden unit as the same weighted sum of the three neighboring inputs (arrows) plus a bias (not shown). d) The weight matrix is a special case of the fully connected matrix where many weights are zero and others are repeated (same colors indicate same value, white indicates zero weight). e) A convolutional layer with kernel size three and stride two computes a weighted sum at every other position. f) This is also a special case of a fully connected network with a different sparse weight structure.

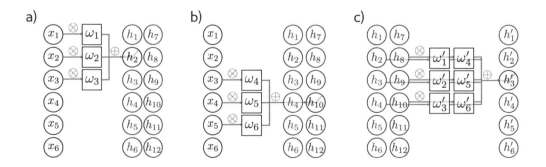

Figure 10.5 Channels. Typically, multiple convolutions are applied to the input $\mathbf{x}$ and stored in channels. a) A convolution is applied to create hidden units h_1 to h_6, which form the first channel. b) A second convolution operation is applied to create hidden units h_7 to h_{12}, which form the second channel. The channels are stored in a 2D array $\mathbf{H}_1$ that contains all the hidden units in the first hidden layer. c) If we add a further convolutional layer, there are now two channels at each input position. Here, the 1D convolution defines a weighted sum over both input channels at the three closest positions to create each new output channel.

Figure 10.5a–b illustrates this with two convolution kernels of size three and with zero padding. The first kernel computes a weighted sum of the nearest three pixels, adds a bias, and passes the results through the activation function to produce hidden units h_1 to h_6. These comprise the first channel. The second kernel computes a different weighted sum of the nearest three pixels, adds a different bias, and passes the results through the activation function to create hidden units h_7 to h_{12}. These comprise the second channel.

In general, the input and the hidden layers all have multiple channels (figure 10.5c). If the incoming layer has C_i channels and kernel size K, the hidden units in each output channel are computed as a weighted sum over all C_i channels and K kernel positions using a weight matrix $\boldsymbol{\Omega} \in \mathbb{R}^{C_i \times K}$ and one bias. Hence, if there are C_o channels in the next layer, then we need $\boldsymbol{\Omega} \in \mathbb{R}^{C_i \times C_o \times K}$ weights and $\boldsymbol{\beta} \in \mathbb{R}^{C_o}$ biases.

Problems 10.6–10.8

Notebook 10.1
1D convolution

10.2.6 Convolutional networks and receptive fields

Chapter 4 described deep networks, which consisted of a sequence of fully connected layers. Similarly, convolutional networks comprise a sequence of convolutional layers. The *receptive field* of a hidden unit in the network is the region of the original input that feeds into it. Consider a convolutional network where each convolutional layer has kernel size three. The hidden units in the first layer take a weighted sum of the three closest inputs, so have receptive fields of size three. The units in the second layer take a weighted sum of the three closest positions in the first layer, which are themselves weighted sums of three inputs. Hence, the hidden units in the second layer have a receptive field of size five. In this way, the receptive field of units in successive layers increases, and information from across the input is gradually integrated (figure 10.6).

Problems 10.9–10.11

10.2.7 Example: MNIST-1D

We now apply a convolutional network to the MNIST-1D data (see figure 8.1). The input $\mathbf{x}$ is a 40D vector, and the output $\mathbf{f}$ is a 10D vector that is passed through a softmax layer to produce class probabilities. We use a network with three hidden layers (figure 10.7). The fifteen channels of the first hidden layer $\mathbf{H}_1$ are each computed using a kernel size of three and a stride of two with "valid" padding, giving nineteen spatial positions. The second hidden layer $\mathbf{H}_2$ is also computed using a kernel size of three, a stride of two, and "valid" padding. The third hidden layer is computed similarly. At this stage, the representation has four spatial positions and fifteen channels. These values are reshaped into a vector of size sixty, which is mapped by a fully connected layer to the ten output activations.

This network was trained for 100,000 steps using SGD without momentum, a learning rate of 0.01, and a batch size of 100 on a dataset of 4,000 examples. We compare this to a fully connected network with the same number of layers and hidden units (i.e., three hidden layers with 285, 135, and 60 hidden units, respectively). The convolutional network has 2,050 parameters, and the fully connected network has 59,065 parameters. By the logic of figure 10.4, the convolutional network is a special case of the fully connected

Problem 10.12

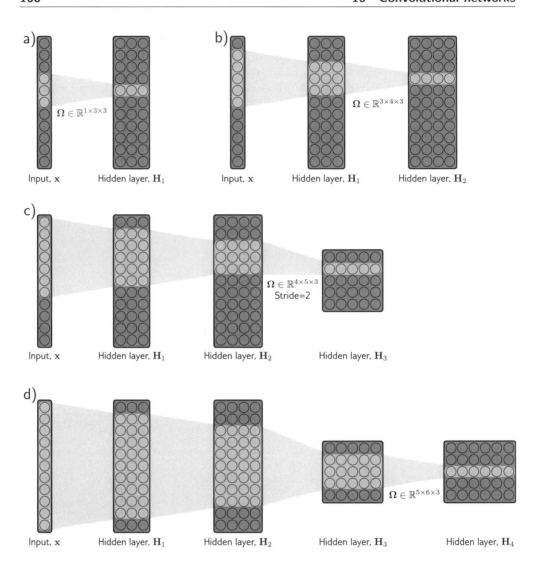

Figure 10.6 Receptive fields for network with kernel width of three. a) An input with eleven dimensions feeds into a hidden layer with three channels and convolution kernel of size three. The pre-activations of the three highlighted hidden units in the first hidden layer $\mathbf{H}_1$ are different weighted sums of the nearest three inputs, so the receptive field in $\mathbf{H}_1$ has size three. b) The pre-activations of the four highlighted hidden units in layer $\mathbf{H}_2$ each take a weighted sum of the three channels in layer $\mathbf{H}_1$ at each of the three nearest positions. Each hidden unit in layer $\mathbf{H}_1$ weights the nearest three input positions. Hence, hidden units in $\mathbf{H}_2$ have a receptive field size of five. c) The hidden units in the third layer (kernel size three, stride two) increases the receptive field size to seven. d) By the time we add a fourth layer, the receptive field of the hidden units at position three have a receptive field that covers the entire input.

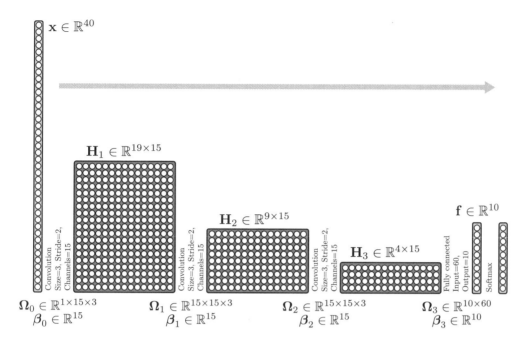

Figure 10.7 Convolutional network for classifying MNIST-1D data (see figure 8.1). The MNIST-1D input has dimension $D_i = 40$. The first convolutional layer has fifteen channels, kernel size three, stride two, and only retains "valid" positions to make a representation with nineteen positions and fifteen channels. The following two convolutional layers have the same settings, gradually reducing the representation size. Finally, a fully connected layer takes all sixty hidden units from the third hidden layer. It outputs ten activations that are subsequently passed through a softmax layer to produce the ten class probabilities.

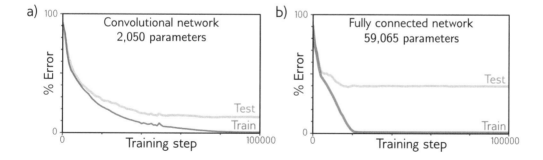

Figure 10.8 MNIST-1D results. a) The convolutional network from figure 10.7 eventually fits the training data perfectly and has $\sim17\%$ test error. b) A fully connected network with the same number of hidden layers and the number of hidden units in each learns the training data faster but fails to generalize well with $\sim40\%$ test error. The latter model can reproduce the convolutional model but fails to do so. The convolutional structure restricts the possible mappings to those that process every position similarly, and this restriction improves performance.

Notebook 10.2
Convolution
for MNIST-1D

one. The latter has enough flexibility to replicate the former exactly. Figure 10.8 shows both models fit the training data perfectly. However, the test error for the convolutional network is much less than for the fully connected network.

This discrepancy is probably not due to the difference in the number of parameters; we know overparameterization usually improves performance (section 8.4.1). The likely explanation is that the convolutional architecture has a superior inductive bias (i.e., interpolates between the training data better) because we have embodied some prior knowledge in the architecture; we have forced the network to process each position in the input in the same way. We know that the data were created by starting with a template that is (among other operations) randomly translated, so this is sensible.

The fully connected network has to learn what each digit template looks like at every position. In contrast, the convolutional network shares information across positions and hence learns to identify each category more accurately. Another way of thinking about this is that when we train the convolutional network, we search through a smaller family of input/output mappings, all of which are plausible. Alternatively, the convolutional structure can be considered a regularizer that applies an infinite penalty to most of the solutions that a fully connected network can describe.

10.3   Convolutional networks for 2D inputs

The previous section described convolutional networks for processing 1D data. Such networks can be applied to financial time series, audio, and text. However, convolutional networks are more usually applied to 2D image data. The convolutional kernel is now a 2D object. A 3×3 kernel $\mathbf{\Omega} \in \mathbb{R}^{3 \times 3}$ applied to a 2D input comprising of elements x_{ij} computes a single layer of hidden units h_{ij} as:

$$
h_{ij} \;=\; \mathrm{a}\left[\beta + \sum_{m=1}^{3}\sum_{n=1}^{3}\omega_{mn}x_{i+m-2,j+n-2}\right], \tag{10.6}
$$

Problem 10.13

where ω_{mn} are the entries of the convolutional kernel. This is simply a weighted sum over a square 3×3 input region. The kernel is translated both horizontally and vertically across the 2D input (figure 10.9) to create an output at each position.

Notebook 10.3
2D convolution

Problem 10.14

Appendix B.3
Tensors

Often the input is an RGB image, which is treated as a 2D signal with three channels (figure 10.10). Here, a 3×3 kernel would have 3×3×3 weights and be applied to the three input channels at each of the 3×3 positions to create a 2D output that is the same height and width as the input image (assuming zero padding). To generate multiple output channels, we repeat this process with different kernel weights and append the results to form a 3D tensor. If the kernel is size $K \times K$, and there are C_i input channels, each output channel is a weighted sum of $C_i \times K \times K$ quantities plus one bias. It follows that to compute C_o output channels, we need $C_i \times C_o \times K \times K$ weights and C_o biases.

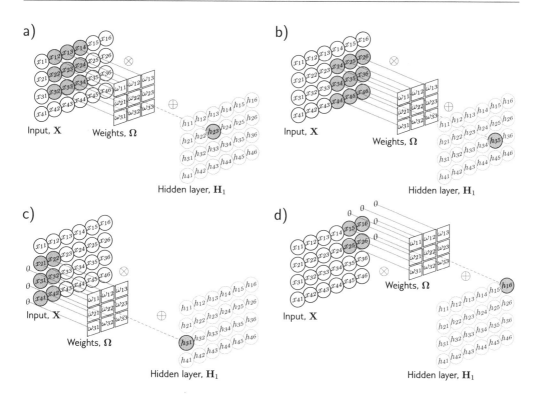

Figure 10.9 2D convolutional layer. Each output h_{ij} computes a weighted sum of the 3×3 nearest inputs, adds a bias, and passes the result through an activation function. a) Here, the output h_{23} (shaded output) is a weighted sum of the nine positions from x_{12} to x_{34} (shaded inputs). b) Different outputs are computed by translating the kernel across the image grid in two dimensions. c–d) With zero padding, positions beyond the image's edge are considered to be zero.

10.4 Downsampling and upsampling

The network in figure 10.7 increased receptive field size by scaling down the representation at each layer using stride two convolutions. We now consider methods for scaling down or *downsampling* 2D input representations. We also describe methods for scaling them back up (*upsampling*), which is useful when the output is also an image. Finally, we consider methods to change the number of channels between layers. This is helpful when recombining representations from two branches of a network (chapter 11).

10.4.1 Downsampling

There are three main approaches to scaling down a 2D representation. Here, we consider the most common case of scaling down both dimensions by a factor of two. First, we

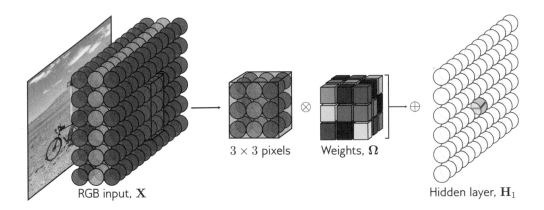

RGB input, $\mathbf{X}$ 3×3 pixels   Weights, $\mathbf{\Omega}$ Hidden layer, $\mathbf{H}_1$

Figure 10.10 2D convolution applied to an image. The image is treated as a 2D input with three channels corresponding to the red, green, and blue components. With a 3×3 kernel, each pre-activation in the first hidden layer is computed by pointwise multiplying the 3×3×3 kernel weights with the 3×3 RGB image patch centered at the same position, summing, and adding the bias. To calculate all the pre-activations in the hidden layer, we "slide" the kernel over the image in both horizontal and vertical directions. The output is a 2D layer of hidden units. To create multiple output channels, we would repeat this process with multiple kernels, resulting in a 3D tensor of hidden units at hidden layer $\mathbf{H}_1$.

Problem 10.15

can sample every other position. When we use a stride of two, we effectively apply this method simultaneously with the convolution operation (figure 10.11a).

Second, *max pooling* retains the maximum of the 2×2 input values (figure 10.11b). This induces some invariance to translation; if the input is shifted by one pixel, many of these maximum values remain the same. Finally, *mean pooling* or *average pooling* averages the inputs. For all approaches, we apply downsampling separately to each channel, so the output has half the width and height but the same number of channels.

10.4.2 Upsampling

The simplest way to scale up a network layer to double the resolution is to duplicate all the channels at each spatial position four times (figure 10.12a). A second method is max unpooling; this is used where we have previously used a max pooling operation for downsampling, and we distribute the values to the positions they originated from (figure 10.12b). A third approach uses bilinear interpolation to fill in the missing values between the points where we have samples. (figure 10.12c).

Notebook 10.4
Downsampling
& upsampling

A fourth approach is roughly analogous to downsampling using a stride of two. In that method, there were half as many outputs as inputs, and for kernel size three, each output was a weighted sum of the three closest inputs (figure 10.13a). In *transposed convolution*, this picture is reversed (figure 10.13c). There are twice as many outputs

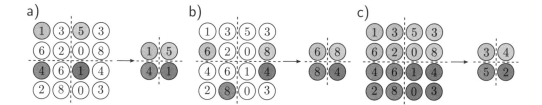

Figure 10.11 Methods for scaling down representation size (downsampling). a) Sub-sampling. The original 4×4 representation (left) is reduced to size 2×2 (right) by retaining every other input. Colors on the left indicate which inputs contribute to the outputs on the right. This is effectively what happens with a kernel of stride two, except that the intermediate values are never computed. b) Max pooling. Each output comprises the maximum value of the corresponding 2×2 block. c) Mean pooling. Each output is the mean of the values in the 2×2 block.

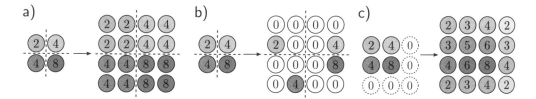

Figure 10.12 Methods for scaling up representation size (upsampling). a) The simplest way to double the size of a 2D layer is to duplicate each input four times. b) In networks where we have previously used a max pooling operation (figure 10.11b), we can redistribute the values to the same positions they originally came from (i.e., where the maxima were). This is known as max unpooling. c) A third option is bilinear interpolation between the input values.

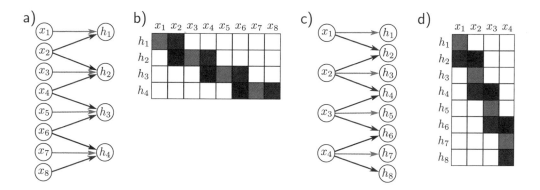

Figure 10.13 Transposed convolution in 1D. a) Downsampling with kernel size three, stride two, and zero padding. Each output is a weighted sum of three inputs (arrows indicate weights). b) This can be expressed by a weight matrix (same color indicates shared weight). c) In transposed convolution, each input contributes three values to the output layer, which has twice as many outputs as inputs. d) The associated weight matrix is the transpose of that in panel (b).

as inputs, and each input contributes to three of the outputs. When we consider the associated weight matrix of this upsampling mechanism (figure 10.13d), we see that it is the transpose of the matrix for the downsampling mechanism (figure 10.13b).

10.4.3   Changing the number of channels

Sometimes we want to change the number of channels between one hidden layer and the next without further spatial pooling. This is usually so we can combine the representation with another parallel computation (see chapter 11). To accomplish this, we apply a convolution with kernel size one. Each element of the output layer is computed by taking a weighted sum of all the channels at the same position (figure 10.14). We can repeat this multiple times with different weights to generate as many output channels as we need. The associated convolution weights have size $1 \times 1 \times C_i \times C_o$. Hence, this is known as *1×1 convolution*. Combined with a bias and activation function, it is equivalent to running the same fully connected network on the channels at every position.

10.5   Applications

We conclude by describing three computer vision applications. We describe convolutional networks for image classification where the goal is to assign the image to one of a predetermined set of categories. Then we consider object detection, where the goal is to identify multiple objects in an image and find the bounding box around each. Finally, we describe an early system for semantic segmentation where the goal is to assign a label to each pixel according to which object is present.

10.5.1   Image classification

Much of the pioneering work on deep learning in computer vision focused on image classification using the ImageNet dataset (figure 10.15). This contains 1,281,167 training images, 50,000 validation images, and 100,000 test images, and every image is labeled as belonging to one of 1000 possible categories.

Most methods reshape the input images to a standard size; in a typical system, the input $\mathbf{x}$ to the network is a 224×224 RGB image, and the output is a probability distribution over the 1000 classes. The task is challenging; there are a large number of classes, and they exhibit considerable variation (figure 10.15). In 2011, before deep networks were applied, the state-of-the-art method classified the test images with $\sim 25\%$ errors for the correct class being in the top five suggestions. Five years later, the best deep learning models eclipsed human performance.

In 2012, *AlexNet* was the first convolutional network to perform well on this task. It consists of eight hidden layers with ReLU activation functions, of which the first five are convolutional and the rest fully connected (figure 10.16). The network starts by

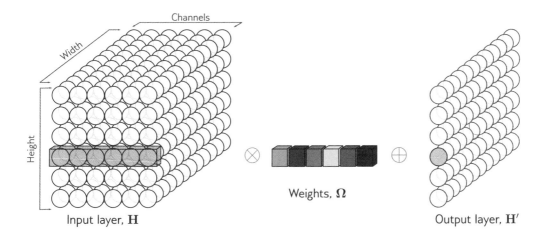

Figure 10.14 1×1 convolution. To change the number of channels without spatial pooling, we apply a 1×1 kernel. Each output channel is computed by taking a weighted sum of all of the channels at the same position, adding a bias, and passing through an activation function. Multiple output channels are created by repeating this operation with different weights and biases.

Figure 10.15 Example ImageNet classification images. The model aims to assign an input image to one of 1000 classes. This task is challenging because the images vary widely along different attributes (columns). These include rigidity (monkey < canoe), number of instances in image (lizard < strawberry), clutter (compass < steel drum), size (candle < spiderweb), texture (screwdriver < leopard), distinctiveness of color (mug < red wine), and distinctiveness of shape (headland < bell). Adapted from Russakovsky et al. (2015).

Figure 10.16 AlexNet (Krizhevsky et al., 2012). The network maps a 224×224 color image to a 1000-dimensional vector representing class probabilities. The network first convolves with 11×11 kernels and stride 4 to create 96 channels. It decreases the resolution again using a max pool operation and applies a 5×5 convolutional layer. Another max pooling layer follows, and three 3×3 convolutional layers are applied. After a final max pooling operation, the result is vectorized and passed through three fully connected (FC) layers and finally the softmax layer.

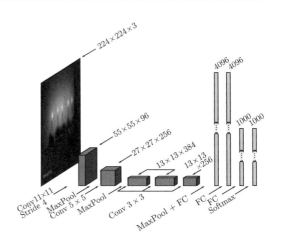

downsampling the input using an 11×11 kernel with a stride of four to create 96 channels. It then downsamples again using a max pooling layer before applying a 5×5 kernel to create 256 channels. There are three more convolutional layers with kernel size 3×3, eventually resulting in a 13×13 representation with 256 channels. A final max-pooling layer yields a 6×6 representation with 256 channels which is resized into a vector of length $9,216$ and passed through three fully connected layers containing 4096, 4096, and 1000 hidden units, respectively. The last layer is passed through the softmax function to output a probability distribution over the 1000 classes. The complete network contains ~ 60 million parameters, most of which are in the fully connected layers.

The dataset size was augmented by a factor of 2048 using (i) spatial transformations and (ii) modifications of the input intensities. At test time, five different cropped and mirrored versions of the image were run through the network, and their predictions averaged. The system was learned using SGD with a momentum coefficient of 0.9 and a batch size of 128. Dropout was applied in the fully connected layers, and an L2 (weight decay) regularizer was used. This system achieved a 16.4% top-5 error rate and a 38.1% top-1 error rate. At the time, this was an enormous leap forward in performance at a task considered far beyond the capabilities of contemporary methods. This result revealed the potential of deep learning and kick-started the modern era of AI research.

The *VGG network* was also targeted at classification in the ImageNet task and achieved a considerably better performance of 6.8% top-5 error rate and a 23.7% top-1 error rate. This network is similarly composed of a series of interspersed convolutional and max pooling layers, where the spatial size of the representation gradually decreases, but the number of channels increase. These are followed by three fully connected layers (figure 10.17). The VGG network was also trained using data augmentation, weight decay, and dropout.

Although there were various minor differences in the training regime, the most important change between AlexNet and VGG was the depth of the network. The latter used 19 hidden layers and 144 million parameters. The networks in figures 10.16 and 10.17 are depicted at the same scale for comparison. There was a general trend for several years for performance on this task to improve as the depth of the networks increased, and this is evidence that depth is important in neural networks.

Problems 10.16–10.17

Notebook 10.5
Convolution
for MNIST

Problem 10.18

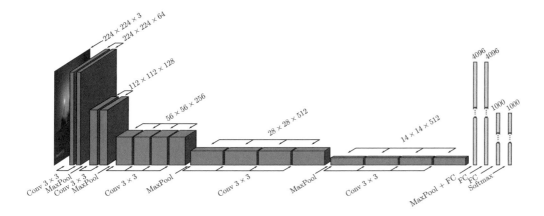

Figure 10.17 VGG network (Simonyan & Zisserman, 2014) depicted at the same scale as AlexNet (see figure 10.16). This network consists of a series of convolutional layers and max pooling operations, in which the spatial scale of the representation gradually decreases, but the number of channels gradually increases. The hidden layer after the last convolutional operation is resized to a 1D vector and three fully connected layers follow. The network outputs 1000 activations corresponding to the class labels that are passed through a softmax function to create class probabilities.

10.5.2 Object detection

In *object detection*, the goal is to identify and localize multiple objects within the image. An early method based on convolutional networks was *You Only Look Once*, or *YOLO* for short. The input to the YOLO network is a 448×448 RGB image. This is passed through 24 convolutional layers that gradually decrease the representation size using max pooling operations while concurrently increasing the number of channels, similarly to the VGG network. The final convolutional layer is of size 7×7 and has 1024 channels. This is reshaped to a vector, and a fully connected layer maps it to 4096 values. One further fully connected layer maps this representation to the output.

The output values encode which class is present at each of a 7×7 grid of locations (figure 10.18a–b). For each location, the output values also encode a fixed number of bounding boxes. Five parameters define each box: the x- and y-positions of the center, the height and width of the box, and the confidence of the prediction (figure 10.18c). The confidence estimates the overlap between the predicted and ground truth bounding boxes. The system is trained using momentum, weight decay, dropout, and data augmentation. Transfer learning is employed; the network is initially trained on the ImageNet classification task and is then fine-tuned for object detection.

After the network is run, a heuristic process is used to remove rectangles with low confidence and to suppress predicted bounding boxes that correspond to the same object so only the most confident one is retained.

Figure 10.18 YOLO object detection. a) The input image is reshaped to 448×448 and divided into a regular 7×7 grid. b) The system predicts the most likely class at each grid cell. c) It also predicts two bounding boxes per cell, and a confidence value (represented by thickness of line). d) During inference, the most likely bounding boxes are retained, and boxes with lower confidence values that belong to the same object are suppressed. Adapted from Redmon et al. (2016).

10.5.3   Semantic segmentation

The goal of semantic segmentation is to assign a label to each pixel according to the object that it belongs to or no label if that pixel does not correspond to anything in the training database. An early network for semantic segmentation is depicted in figure 10.19. The input is a 224×224 RGB image, and the output is a 224×224×21 array that contains the probability of each of 21 possible classes at each position.

The first part of the network is a smaller version of VGG (figure 10.17) that contains thirteen rather than sixteen convolutional layers and downsizes the representation to size 14×14. There is then one more max pooling operation, followed by two fully connected layers that map to two 1D representations of size 4096. These layers do not represent spatial position but instead, combine information from across the whole image.

Here, the architecture diverges from VGG. Another fully connected layer reconstitutes the representation into 7×7 spatial positions and 512 channels. This is followed

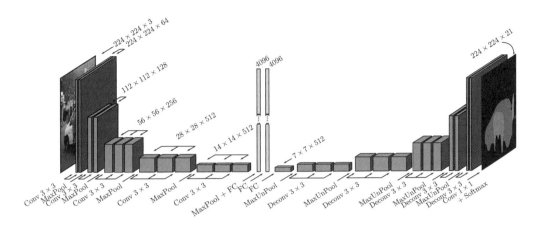

Figure 10.19 Semantic segmentation network of Noh et al. (2015). The input is a 224×224 image, which is passed through a version of the VGG network and eventually transformed into a representation of size 4096 using a fully connected layer. This contains information about the entire image. This is then reformed into a representation of size 7×7 using another fully connected layer, and the image is upsampled and deconvolved (transposed convolutions without upsampling) in a mirror image of the VGG network. The output is a 224×224×21 representation that gives the output probabilities for the 21 classes at each position.

by a series of max unpooling layers (see figure 10.12b) and *deconvolution* layers. These are transposed convolutions (see figure 10.13) but in 2D and without the upsampling. Finally, there is a 1×1 convolution to create 21 channels representing the possible classes and a softmax operation at each spatial position to map the activations to class probabilities. The downsampling side of the network is sometimes referred to as an *encoder*, and the upsampling side as a *decoder*, so networks of this type are sometimes called *encoder-decoder networks* or *hourglass networks* due to their shape.

The final segmentation is generated using a heuristic method that greedily searches for the class that is most represented and infers its region, taking into account the probabilities but also encouraging connectedness. Then the next most-represented class is added where it dominates at the remaining unlabeled pixels. This continues until there is insufficient evidence to add more (figure 10.20).

10.6 Summary

In convolutional layers, each hidden unit is computed by taking a weighted sum of the nearby inputs, adding a bias, and applying an activation function. The weights and the bias are the same at every spatial position, so there are far fewer parameters than in a fully connected network, and the number of parameters doesn't increase with the input image size. To ensure that information is not lost, this operation is repeated with

Input   Ground truth   Result

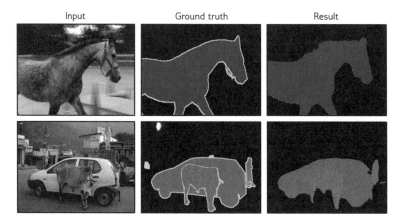

Figure 10.20 Semantic segmentation results. The final result is created from the 21 probability maps by greedily selecting the best class and using a heuristic method to find a sensible binary map based on the probabilities and their spatial proximity. If there is enough evidence, subsequent classes are added, and their segmentation maps are combined. Adapted from Noh et al. (2015).

different weights and biases to create multiple channels at each spatial position.

Typical convolutional networks consist of convolutional layers interspersed with layers that downsample by a factor of two. As the network progresses, the spatial dimensions usually decrease by factors of two, and the number of channels increases by factors of two. At the end of the network, there are typically one or more fully connected layers that integrate information from across the entire input and create the desired output. If the output is an image, a mirrored "decoder" upsamples back to the original size.

The translational equivariance of convolutional layers imposes a useful inductive bias that increases performance for image-based tasks relative to fully connected networks. We described image classification, object detection, and semantic segmentation networks. Image classification performance was shown to improve as the network became deeper. However, subsequent experiments showed that increasing the network depth indefinitely doesn't continue to help; after a certain depth, the system becomes difficult to train. This is the motivation for *residual connections*, which are the topic of the next chapter.

Notes

Dumoulin & Visin (2016) present an overview of the mathematics of convolutions that expands on the brief treatment in this chapter.

Convolutional networks: Early convolutional networks were developed by Fukushima & Miyake (1982), LeCun et al. (1989a), and LeCun et al. (1989b). Initial applications included handwriting recognition (LeCun et al., 1989a; Martin, 1993), face recognition (Lawrence et al., 1997), phoneme recognition (Waibel et al., 1989), spoken word recognition (Bottou et al., 1990), and signature verification (Bromley et al., 1993). However, convolutional networks were popularized by LeCun et al. (1998), who built a system called LeNet for classifying 28×28 grayscale images of handwritten digits. This is immediately recognizable as a precursor of modern networks; it uses a series of convolutional layers, followed by fully connected layers, sigmoid activations rather than ReLUs, and average pooling rather than max pooling. AlexNet (Krizhevsky et al., 2012) is widely considered the starting point for modern deep convolutional networks.

ImageNet Challenge: Deng et al. (2009) collated the ImageNet database and the associated classification challenge drove progress in deep learning for several years after AlexNet. Notable subsequent winners of this challenge include the *network-in-network* architecture (Lin et al., 2014), which alternated convolutions with fully connected layers that operated independently on all of the channels at each position (i.e., 1×1 convolutions). Zeiler & Fergus (2014) and Simonyan & Zisserman (2014) trained larger and deeper architectures that were fundamentally similar to AlexNet. Szegedy et al. (2017) developed an architecture called *GoogLeNet*, which introduced *inception blocks*. These use several parallel paths with different filter sizes, which are then recombined. This effectively allowed the system to learn the filter size.

The trend was for performance to improve with increasing depth. However, it ultimately became difficult to train deeper networks without modifications; these include residual connections and normalization layers, both of which are described in the next chapter. Progress in the ImageNet challenges is summarized in Russakovsky et al. (2015). A more general survey of image classification using convolutional networks can be found in Rawat & Wang (2017). The improvement of image classification networks over time is visualized in figure 10.21.

Types of convolutional layers: Atrous or dilated convolutions were introduced by Chen et al. (2018c) and Yu & Koltun (2015). Transposed convolutions were introduced by Long et al. (2015). Odena et al. (2016) pointed out that they can lead to checkerboard artifacts and should be used with caution. Lin et al. (2014) is an early example of convolution with 1×1 filters.

Many variants of the standard convolutional layer aim to reduce the number of parameters. These include *depthwise* or *channel-separate convolution* (Howard et al., 2017; Tran et al., 2018), in which a different filter convolves each channel separately to create a new set of channels. For a kernel size of $K \times K$ with C input channels and C output channels, this requires $K \times K \times C$ parameters rather than the $K \times K \times C \times C$ parameters in a regular convolutional layer. A related approach is *grouped convolutions* (Xie et al., 2017), where each convolution kernel is only applied to a subset of the channels with a commensurate reduction in the parameters. In fact, grouped convolutions were used in AlexNet for computational reasons; the whole network could not run on a single GPU, so some channels were processed on one GPU and some on another, with limited interaction points. *Separable convolutions* treat each kernel as an outer product of 1D vectors; they use $C + K + K$ parameters for each of the C channels. *Partial convolutions* (Liu et al., 2018a) are used when inpainting missing pixels and account for the partial masking of the input. *Gated convolutions* learn the mask from the previous layer (Yu et al., 2019; Chang et al., 2019b). Hu et al. (2018b) propose squeeze-and-excitation networks which re-weight the channels using information pooled across all spatial positions.

Downsampling and upsampling: Average pooling dates back to at least LeCun et al. (1989a) and max pooling to Zhou & Chellappa (1988). Scherer et al. (2010) compared these methods and concluded that max pooling was superior. The max unpooling method was introduced by Zeiler et al. (2011) and Zeiler & Fergus (2014). Max pooling can be thought of as applying

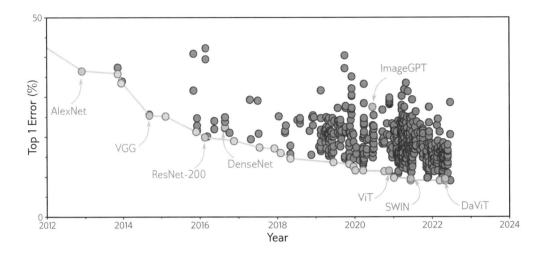

Figure 10.21 ImageNet performance. Each circle represents a different published model. Blue circles represent models that were state-of-the-art. Models discussed in this book are also highlighted. The AlexNet and VGG networks were remarkable for their time but are now far from state of the art. ResNet-200 and DenseNet are discussed in chapter 11. ImageGPT, ViT, SWIN, and DaViT are discussed in chapter 12. Adapted from https://paperswithcode.com/sota/image-classification-on-imagenet.

Appendix B.3.2
Vector norms

an L_∞ norm to the hidden units that are to be pooled. This led to applying other L_k norms (Springenberg et al., 2015; Sainath et al., 2013), although these require more computation and are not widely used. Zhang (2019) introduced *max-blur-pooling*, in which a low-pass filter is applied before downsampling to prevent aliasing, and showed that this improves generalization over translation of the inputs and protects against adversarial attacks (see section 20.4.6).

Shi et al. (2016) introduced *PixelShuffle*, which used convolutional filters with a stride of $1/s$ to scale up 1D signals by a factor of s. Only the weights that lie exactly on positions are used to create the outputs, and the ones that fall between positions are discarded. This can be implemented by multiplying the number of channels in the kernel by a factor of s, where the sth output position is computed from just the sth subset of channels. This can be trivially extended to 2D convolution, which requires s^2 channels.

Convolution in 1D and 3D: Convolutional networks are usually applied to images but have also been applied to 1D data in applications that include speech recognition (Abdel-Hamid et al., 2012), sentence classification (Zhang et al., 2015; Conneau et al., 2017), electrocardiogram classification (Kiranyaz et al., 2015), and bearing fault diagnosis (Eren et al., 2019). A survey of 1D convolutional networks can be found in Kiranyaz et al. (2021). Convolutional networks have also been applied to 3D data, including video (Ji et al., 2012; Saha et al., 2016; Tran et al., 2015) and volumetric measurements (Wu et al., 2015b; Maturana & Scherer, 2015).

Invariance and equivariance: Part of the motivation for convolutional layers is that they are approximately equivariant with respect to translation, and part of the motivation for max pooling is to induce invariance to small translations. Zhang (2019) considers the degree to which convolutional networks really have these properties and proposes the max-blur-pooling modification that demonstrably improves them. There is considerable interest in making networks equivariant or invariant to other types of transformations, such as reflections, rotations, and scaling. Sifre & Mallat (2013) constructed a system based on wavelets that induced both translational and rotational invariance in image patches and applied this to texture classification. Kanazawa et al. (2014) developed locally scale-invariant convolutional neural networks. Cohen & Welling (2016) exploited group theory to construct *group CNNs*, which are equivariant to larger families of transformations, including reflections and rotations. Esteves et al. (2018) introduced *polar transformer networks*, which are invariant to translations and equivariant to rotation and scale. Worrall et al. (2017) developed *harmonic networks*, the first example of a group CNN that was equivariant to continuous rotations.

Initialization and regularization: Convolutional networks are typically initialized using Xavier initialization (Glorot & Bengio, 2010) or He initialization (He et al., 2015), as described in section 7.5. However, the *ConvolutionOrthogonal* initializer (Xiao et al., 2018a) is specialized for convolutional networks (Xiao et al., 2018a). Networks of up to 10,000 layers can be trained using this initialization without the need for residual connections.

Problem 10.19

Dropout is effective for fully connected networks but less so for convolutional layers (Park & Kwak, 2016). This may be because neighboring image pixels are highly correlated, so if a hidden unit drops out, the same information is passed on via adjacent positions. This is the motivation for spatial dropout and cutout. In spatial dropout (Tompson et al., 2015), entire feature maps are discarded instead of individual pixels. This circumvents the problem of neighboring pixels carrying the same information. Similarly, DeVries & Taylor (2017b) propose *cutout*, in which a square patch of each input image is masked at training time. Wu & Gu (2015) modified max pooling for dropout layers using a method that involves sampling from a probability distribution over the constituent elements rather than always taking the maximum.

Adaptive Kernels: The *inception block* (Szegedy et al., 2017) applies convolutional filters of different sizes in parallel and, as such, provides a crude mechanism by which the network can learn the appropriate filter size. Other work has investigated learning the scale of convolutions as part of the training process (e.g., Pintea et al., 2021; Romero et al., 2021) or the stride of downsampling layers (Riad et al., 2022).

In some systems, the kernel size is changed adaptively based on the data. This is sometimes in the context of guided convolution, where one input is used to help guide the computation from another input. For example, an RGB image might be used to help upsample a low-resolution depth map. Jia et al. (2016) directly predicted the filter weights themselves using a different network branch. Xiong et al. (2020b) change the kernel size adaptively. Su et al. (2019a) moderate weights of fixed kernels by a function learned from another modality. Dai et al. (2017) learn offsets of weights so that they do not have to be applied in a regular grid.

Object detection and semantic segmentation: Object detection methods can be divided into *proposal-based* and *proposal-free* schemes. In the former case, processing occurs in two stages. A convolutional network ingests the whole image and proposes regions that might contain objects. These proposal regions are then resized, and a second network analyzes them to establish whether there is an object there and what it is. An early example of this approach was *R-CNN* (Girshick et al., 2014). This was subsequently extended to allow end-to-end training (Girshick, 2015) and to reduce the cost of the region proposals (Ren et al., 2015). Subsequent work on *feature pyramid networks* improved both performance and speed by combining features across multiple scales Lin et al. (2017b). In contrast, proposal-free schemes perform all the processing in a single pass. YOLO Redmon et al. (2016), which was described in section 10.5.2, is the most celebrated example of a proposal-free scheme. The most recent iteration of this framework at the time of writing is YOLOv7 (Wang et al., 2022a). A recent review of object detection can be found in Zou et al. (2023).

The semantic segmentation network described in section 10.5.3 was developed by Noh et al. (2015). Many subsequent approaches have been variations of U-Net (Ronneberger et al., 2015), which is described in section 11.5.3. Recent surveys of semantic segmentation can be found in Minaee et al. (2021) and Ulku & Akagündüz (2022).

Visualizing Convolutional Networks: The dramatic success of convolutional networks led to a series of efforts to visualize the information they extract from the image (see Qin et al., 2018, for a review). Erhan et al. (2009) visualized the optimal stimulus that activated a hidden unit by starting with an image containing noise and then optimizing the input to make the hidden unit most active using gradient ascent. Zeiler & Fergus (2014) trained a network to reconstruct the input and then set all the hidden units to zero except the one they were interested in; the reconstruction then provides information about what drives the hidden unit. Mahendran & Vedaldi (2015) visualized an entire layer of a network. Their *network inversion* technique aimed to find an image that resulted in the activations at that layer but also incorporates prior knowledge that encourages this image to have similar statistics to natural images.

Finally, Bau et al. (2017) introduced *network dissection*. Here, a series of images with known pixel labels capturing color, texture, and object type are passed through the network, and the correlation of a hidden unit with each property is measured. This method has the advantage that it only uses the forward pass of the network and does not require optimization. These methods did provide some partial insight into how the network processes images. For example, Bau et al. (2017) showed that earlier layers correlate more with texture and color and later layers with the object type. However, it is fair to say that fully understanding the processing of networks containing millions of parameters is currently not possible.

Problems

Problem 10.1[*] Show that the operation in equation 10.3 is equivariant with respect to translation.

Problem 10.2 Equation 10.3 defines 1D convolution with a kernel size of three, stride of one, and dilation one. Write out the equivalent equation for the 1D convolution with a kernel size of three and a stride of two as pictured in figure 10.3a–b.

Problem 10.3 Write out the equation for the 1D dilated convolution with a kernel size of three and a dilation rate of two, as pictured in figure 10.3d.

Problem 10.4 Write out the equation for a 1D convolution with kernel size of seven, a dilation rate of three, and a stride of three. You may assume that the input is padded with zeros at positions x_{-2}, x_{-1} and x_0.

Problem 10.5 Draw weight matrices in the style of figure 10.4d for (i) the strided convolution in figure 10.3a–b, (ii) the convolution with kernel size 5 in figure 10.3c, and (iii) the dilated convolution in figure 10.3d.

Problem 10.6* Draw a 6×12 weight matrix in the style of figure 10.4d relating inputs $x_1, \ldots, x_6$ to outputs $h_1, \ldots, h_{12}$ in the multi-channel convolution as depicted in figures 10.5a–b.

Problem 10.7* Draw a 12×6 weight matrix in the style of figure 10.4d relating inputs $h_1, \ldots, h_{12}$ to outputs $h'_1, \ldots, h'_6$ in the multi-channel convolution in figure 10.5c.

Problem 10.8 Consider a 1D convolutional network where the input has three channels. The first hidden layer is computed using a kernel size of three and has four channels. The second hidden layer is computed using a kernel size of five and has ten channels. How many biases and how many weights are needed for each of these two convolutional layers?

Problem 10.9 A network consists of three 1D convolutional layers. At each layer, a zero-padded convolution with kernel size three, stride one, and dilation one is applied. What size is the receptive field of the hidden units in the third layer?

Problem 10.10 A network consists of three 1D convolutional layers. At each layer, a zero-padded convolution with kernel size seven, stride one, and dilation one is applied. What size is the receptive field of hidden units in the third layer?

Problem 10.11 Consider a convolutional network with 1D input $\mathbf{x}$. The first hidden layer $\mathbf{H}_1$ is computed using a convolution with kernel size five, stride two, and a dilation rate of one. The second hidden layer $\mathbf{H}_2$ is computed using a convolution with kernel size three, stride one, and a dilation rate of one. The third hidden layer $\mathbf{H}_3$ is computed using a convolution with kernel size five, stride one, and a dilation rate of two. What are the receptive field sizes at each hidden layer?

Problem 10.12 The 1D convolutional network in figure 10.7 was trained using stochastic gradient descent with a learning rate of 0.01 and a batch size of 100 on a training dataset of 4,000 examples for 100,000 steps. How many epochs was the network trained for?

Problem 10.13 Draw a weight matrix in the style of figure 10.4d that shows the relationship between the 24 inputs and the 24 outputs in figure 10.9.

Problem 10.14 Consider a 2D convolutional layer with kernel size 5×5 that takes 3 input channels and returns 10 output channels. How many convolutional weights are there? How many biases?

Problem 10.15 Draw a weight matrix in the style of figure 10.4d that samples every other variable in a 1D input (i.e., the 1D analog of figure 10.11a). Show that the weight matrix for 1D convolution with kernel size and stride two is equivalent to composing the matrices for 1D convolution with kernel size one and this sampling matrix.

Problem 10.16* Consider the AlexNet network (figure 10.16). How many parameters are used in each convolutional and fully connected layer? What is the total number of parameters?

Problem 10.17 What is the receptive field size at each of the first three layers of AlexNet (figure 10.16)?

Problem 10.18 How many weights and biases are there at each convolutional layer and fully connected layer in the VGG architecture (figure 10.17)?

Problem 10.19* Consider two hidden layers of size 224×224 with C_1 and C_2 channels, respectively, connected by a 3×3 convolutional layer. Describe how to initialize the weights using He initialization.

Chapter 11

Residual networks

The previous chapter described how image classification performance improved as the depth of convolutional networks was extended from eight layers (AlexNet) to eighteen layers (VGG). This led to experimentation with even deeper networks. However, performance decreased again when many more layers were added.

This chapter introduces *residual blocks*. Here, each network layer computes an additive change to the current representation instead of transforming it directly. This allows deeper networks to be trained but causes an exponential increase in the activation magnitudes at initialization. Residual blocks employ *batch normalization* to compensate for this, which re-centers and rescales the activations at each layer.

Residual blocks with batch normalization allow much deeper networks to be trained, and these networks improve performance across a variety of tasks. Architectures that combine residual blocks to tackle image classification, medical image segmentation, and human pose estimation are described.

11.1 Sequential processing

Every network we have seen so far processes the data sequentially; each layer receives the previous layer's output and passes the result to the next (figure 11.1). For example, a three-layer network is defined by:

$$
\begin{aligned}
\mathbf{h}_1 &= \mathbf{f}_1[\mathbf{x}, \boldsymbol{\phi}_1] \\
\mathbf{h}_2 &= \mathbf{f}_2[\mathbf{h}_1, \boldsymbol{\phi}_2] \\
\mathbf{h}_3 &= \mathbf{f}_3[\mathbf{h}_2, \boldsymbol{\phi}_3] \\
\mathbf{y} &= \mathbf{f}_4[\mathbf{h}_3, \boldsymbol{\phi}_4],
\end{aligned}
\tag{11.1}
$$

where $\mathbf{h}_1$, $\mathbf{h}_2$, and $\mathbf{h}_3$ denote the intermediate hidden layers, $\mathbf{x}$ is the network input, $\mathbf{y}$ is the output, and the functions $\mathbf{f}_k[\bullet, \boldsymbol{\phi}_k]$ perform the processing.

In a standard neural network, each layer consists of a linear transformation followed by an activation function, and the parameters $\boldsymbol{\phi}_k$ comprise the weights and biases of the

Figure 11.1 Sequential processing. Standard neural networks pass the output of each layer directly into the next layer.

linear transformation. In a convolutional network, each layer consists of a set of convolutions followed by an activation function, and the parameters comprise the convolutional kernels and biases.

Since the processing is sequential, we can equivalently think of this network as a series of nested functions:

$$\mathbf{y} = \mathbf{f}_4 \Big[\mathbf{f}_3 \Big[\mathbf{f}_2 \big[\mathbf{f}_1[\mathbf{x}, \boldsymbol{\phi}_1], \boldsymbol{\phi}_2 \big], \boldsymbol{\phi}_3 \Big], \boldsymbol{\phi}_4 \Big]. \tag{11.2}$$

11.1.1 Limitations of sequential processing

In principle, we can add as many layers as we want, and in the previous chapter, we saw that adding more layers to a convolutional network does improve performance; the VGG network (figure 10.17), which has eighteen layers, outperforms AlexNet (figure 10.16), which has eight layers. However, image classification performance decreases again as further layers are added (figure 11.2). This is surprising since models generally perform better as more capacity is added (figure 8.10). Indeed, the decrease is present for both the training set and the test set, which implies that the problem is training deeper networks rather than the inability of deeper networks to generalize.

This phenomenon is not completely understood. One conjecture is that at initialization, the loss gradients change unpredictably when we modify parameters in early network layers. With appropriate initialization of the weights (see section 7.5), the gradient of the loss with respect to these parameters will be reasonable (i.e., no exploding or vanishing gradients). However, the derivative assumes an infinitesimal change in the parameter, whereas optimization algorithms use a finite step size. Any reasonable choice of step size may move to a place with a completely different and unrelated gradient; the loss surface looks like an enormous range of tiny mountains rather than a single smooth structure that is easy to descend. Consequently, the algorithm doesn't make progress in the way that it does when the loss function gradient changes more slowly.

This conjecture is supported by empirical observations of gradients in networks with a single input and output. For a shallow network, the gradient of the output with respect to the input changes slowly as we change the input (figure 11.3a). However, for a deep network, a tiny change in the input results in a completely different gradient (figure 11.3b). This is captured by the autocorrelation function of the gradient (figure 11.3c). Nearby gradients are correlated for shallow networks, but this correlation quickly drops to zero for deep networks. This is termed the *shattered gradients* phenomenon.

Notebook 11.1
Shattered
gradients

Appendix B.2.1
Autocorrelation
function

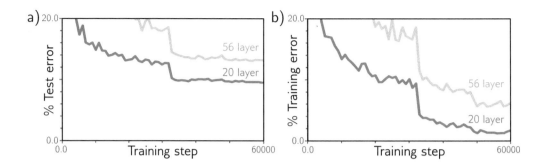

Figure 11.2 Decrease in performance when adding more convolutional layers. a) A 20-layer convolutional network outperforms a 56-layer neural network for image classification on the test set of the CIFAR-10 dataset (Krizhevsky & Hinton, 2009). b) This is also true for the training set, which suggests that the problem relates to training the original network rather than a failure to generalize to new data. Adapted from He et al. (2016a).

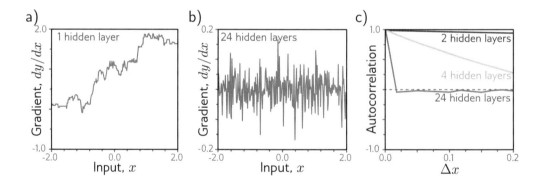

Figure 11.3 Shattered gradients. a) Consider a shallow network with 200 hidden units and Glorot initialization (He initialization without the factor of two) for both the weights and biases. The gradient $\partial y/\partial x$ of the scalar network output y with respect to the scalar input x changes relatively slowly as we change the input x. b) For a deep network with 24 layers and 200 hidden units per layer, this gradient changes very quickly and unpredictably. c) The autocorrelation function of the gradient shows that nearby gradients become unrelated (have autocorrelation close to zero) for deep networks. This *shattered gradients* phenomenon may explain why it is hard to train deep networks. Gradient descent algorithms rely on the loss surface being relatively smooth, so the gradients should be related before and after each update step. Adapted from Balduzzi et al. (2017).

Shattered gradients presumably arise because changes in early network layers modify the output in an increasingly complex way as the network becomes deeper. The derivative of the output $\mathbf{y}$ with respect to the first layer $\mathbf{f}_1$ of the network in equation 11.1 is:

$$\frac{\partial \mathbf{y}}{\partial \mathbf{f}_1} = \frac{\partial \mathbf{f}_2}{\partial \mathbf{f}_1} \frac{\partial \mathbf{f}_3}{\partial \mathbf{f}_2} \frac{\partial \mathbf{f}_4}{\partial \mathbf{f}_3}. \tag{11.3}$$

Appendix B.5
Matrix calculus

When we change the parameters that determine $\mathbf{f}_1$, *all* of the derivatives in this sequence can change since layers $\mathbf{f}_2, \mathbf{f}_3$, and $\mathbf{f}_4$ are themselves computed from $\mathbf{f}_1$. Consequently, the updated gradient at each training example may be completely different, and the loss function becomes badly behaved.[1]

11.2   Residual connections and residual blocks

Residual or *skip connections* are branches in the computational path, whereby the input to each network layer $\mathbf{f}[\bullet]$ is added back to the output (figure 11.4a). By analogy to equation 11.1, the residual network is defined as:

$$\begin{aligned}
\mathbf{h}_1 &= \mathbf{x} + \mathbf{f}_1[\mathbf{x}, \boldsymbol{\phi}_1] \\
\mathbf{h}_2 &= \mathbf{h}_1 + \mathbf{f}_2[\mathbf{h}_1, \boldsymbol{\phi}_2] \\
\mathbf{h}_3 &= \mathbf{h}_2 + \mathbf{f}_3[\mathbf{h}_2, \boldsymbol{\phi}_3] \\
\mathbf{y} &= \mathbf{h}_3 + \mathbf{f}_4[\mathbf{h}_3, \boldsymbol{\phi}_4],
\end{aligned} \tag{11.4}$$

where the first term on the right-hand side of each line is the residual connection. Each function $\mathbf{f}_k$ learns an additive change to the current representation. It follows that their outputs must be the same size as their inputs. Each additive combination of the input and the processed output is known as a *residual block* or *residual layer*.

Once more, we can write this as a single function by substituting in the expressions for the intermediate quantities $\mathbf{h}_k$:

Problem 11.1

$$\begin{aligned}
\mathbf{y} = \mathbf{x} +\ & \mathbf{f}_1[\mathbf{x}] \\
+\ & \mathbf{f}_2\big[\mathbf{x} + \mathbf{f}_1[\mathbf{x}]\big] \\
+\ & \mathbf{f}_3\Big[\mathbf{x} + \mathbf{f}_1[\mathbf{x}] + \mathbf{f}_2\big[\mathbf{x} + \mathbf{f}_1[\mathbf{x}]\big]\Big] \\
+\ & \mathbf{f}_4\Big[\mathbf{x} + \mathbf{f}_1[\mathbf{x}] + \mathbf{f}_2\big[\mathbf{x} + \mathbf{f}_1[\mathbf{x}]\big] + \mathbf{f}_3\big[\mathbf{x} + \mathbf{f}_1[\mathbf{x}] + \mathbf{f}_2\big[\mathbf{x} + \mathbf{f}_1[\mathbf{x}]\big]\big]\Big],
\end{aligned} \tag{11.5}$$

where we have omitted the parameters $\boldsymbol{\phi}_\bullet$ for clarity. We can think of this equation as "unraveling" the network (figure 11.4b). We see that the final network output is a sum of the input and four smaller networks, corresponding to each line of the equation; one

---

[1]In equations 11.3 and 11.6, we overload notation to define $\mathbf{f}_k$ as the output of the function $\mathbf{f}_k[\bullet]$.

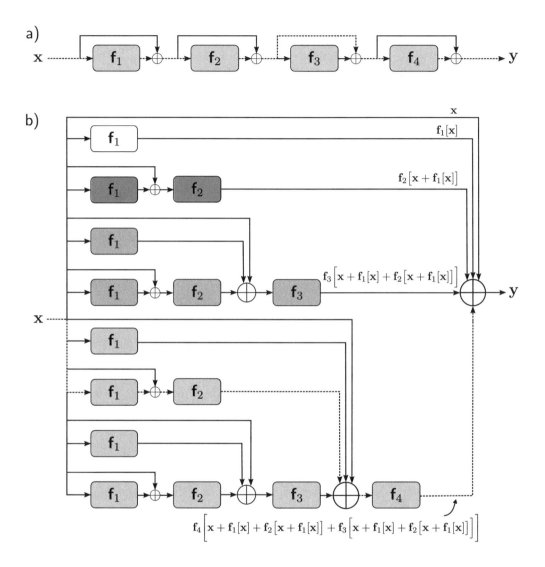

Figure 11.4 Residual connections. a) The output of each function $\mathbf{f}_k[\mathbf{x}, \phi_k]$ is added back to its input, which is passed via a parallel computational path called a residual or skip connection. Hence, the function computes an additive change to the representation. b) Upon expanding (unraveling) the network equations, we find that the output is the sum of the input plus four smaller networks (depicted in white, orange, gray, and cyan, respectively, and corresponding to terms in equation 11.5); we can think of this as an ensemble of networks. Moreover, the output from the cyan network is itself a transformation $\mathbf{f}_4[\bullet, \phi_4]$ of another ensemble, and so on. Alternatively, we can consider the network as a combination of 16 different paths through the computational graph. One example is the dashed path from input $\mathbf{x}$ to output $\mathbf{y}$, which is the same in panels (a) and (b).

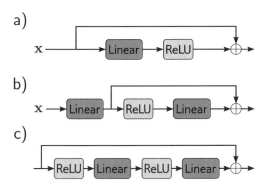

a)

b)

c)

Figure 11.5 Order of operations in residual blocks. a) The usual order of linear transformation or convolution followed by a ReLU nonlinearity means that each residual block can only add non-negative quantities. b) With the reverse order, both positive and negative quantities can be added. However, we must add a linear transformation at the start of the network in case the input is all negative. c) In practice, it's common for a residual block to contain several network layers.

interpretation is that residual connections turn the original network into an ensemble of these smaller networks whose outputs are summed to compute the result.

A complementary way of thinking about this residual network is that it creates sixteen paths of different lengths from input to output. For example, the first function $\mathbf{f}_1[\mathbf{x}]$ occurs in eight of these sixteen paths, including as a direct additive term (i.e., a path length of one), and the analogous derivative to equation 11.3 is:

Problem 11.2

Problem 11.3

$$\frac{\partial \mathbf{y}}{\partial \mathbf{f}_1} = \mathbf{I} + \frac{\partial \mathbf{f}_2}{\partial \mathbf{f}_1} + \left(\frac{\partial \mathbf{f}_3}{\partial \mathbf{f}_1} + \frac{\partial \mathbf{f}_2}{\partial \mathbf{f}_1} \frac{\partial \mathbf{f}_3}{\partial \mathbf{f}_2} \right) + \left(\frac{\partial \mathbf{f}_4}{\partial \mathbf{f}_1} + \frac{\partial \mathbf{f}_2}{\partial \mathbf{f}_1} \frac{\partial \mathbf{f}_4}{\partial \mathbf{f}_2} + \frac{\partial \mathbf{f}_3}{\partial \mathbf{f}_1} \frac{\partial \mathbf{f}_4}{\partial \mathbf{f}_3} + \frac{\partial \mathbf{f}_2}{\partial \mathbf{f}_1} \frac{\partial \mathbf{f}_3}{\partial \mathbf{f}_2} \frac{\partial \mathbf{f}_4}{\partial \mathbf{f}_3} \right), \quad (11.6)$$

where there is one term for each of the eight paths. The identity term on the right-hand side shows that changes in the parameters $\boldsymbol{\phi}_1$ in the first layer $\mathbf{f}_1[\mathbf{x}, \boldsymbol{\phi}_1]$ contribute directly to changes in the network output $\mathbf{y}$. They also contribute indirectly through the other chains of derivatives of varying lengths. In general, gradients through shorter paths will be better behaved. Since both the identity term and various short chains of derivatives will contribute to the derivative for each layer, networks with residual links suffer less from shattered gradients.

Notebook 11.2
Residual
networks

11.2.1 Order of operations in residual blocks

Until now, we have implied that the additive functions $\mathbf{f}[\mathbf{x}]$ could be any valid network layer (e.g., fully connected or convolutional). This is technically true, but the order of operations in these functions is important. They must contain a nonlinear activation function like a ReLU, or the entire network will be linear. However, in a typical network layer (figure 11.5a), the ReLU function is at the end, so the output is non-negative. If we adopt this convention, then each residual block can only increase the input values.

Hence, it is typical to change the order of operations so that the activation function is applied first, followed by the linear transformation (figure 11.5b). Sometimes there may be several layers of processing within the residual block (figure 11.5c), but these usually terminate with a linear transformation. Finally, we note that when we start these blocks with a ReLU operation, they will do nothing if the initial network input is negative since the ReLU will clip the entire signal to zero. Hence, it's typical to start the network with a linear transformation rather than a residual block, as in figure 11.5b.

11.2.2   Deeper networks with residual connections

Adding residual connections roughly doubles the depth of a network that can be practically trained before performance degrades. However, we would like to increase the depth further. To understand why residual connections do not allow us to increase the depth arbitrarily, we must consider how the variance of the activations changes during the forward pass and how the gradient magnitudes change during the backward pass.

11.3   Exploding gradients in residual networks

In section 7.5, we saw that initializing the network parameters is critical. Without careful initialization, the magnitudes of the intermediate values during the forward pass of backpropagation can increase or decrease exponentially. Similarly, the gradients during the backward pass can explode or vanish as we move backward through the network.

Hence, we initialize the network parameters so that the expected variance of the activations (in the forward pass) and gradients (in the backward pass) remains the same between layers. He initialization (section 7.5) achieves this for ReLU activations by initializing the biases β to zero and choosing normally distributed weights Ω with mean zero and variance $2/D_h$ where D_h is the number of hidden units in the previous layer.

Now consider a residual network. We do not have to worry about the intermediate values or gradients vanishing with network depth since there exists a path whereby each layer directly contributes to the network output (equation 11.5 and figure 11.4b). However, even if we use He initialization within the residual block, the values in the forward pass increase exponentially as we move through the network.

Problem 11.4

To see why, consider that we add the result of the processing in the residual block back to the input. Each branch has some (uncorrelated) variability. Hence, the overall variance increases when we recombine them. With ReLU activations and He initialization, the expected variance is unchanged by the processing in each block. Consequently, when we recombine with the input, the variance doubles (figure 11.6a), growing exponentially with the number of residual blocks. This limits the possible network depth before floating point precision is exceeded in the forward pass. A similar argument applies to the gradients in the backward pass of the backpropagation algorithm.

Hence, residual networks still suffer from unstable forward propagation and exploding gradients even with He initialization. One approach that would stabilize the forward and backward passes would be to use He initialization and then multiply the combined output of each residual block by $1/\sqrt{2}$ to compensate for the doubling (figure 11.6b). However, it is more usual to use *batch normalization*.

11.4   Batch normalization

Batch normalization or *BatchNorm* shifts and rescales each activation h so that its mean and variance across the batch $\mathcal{B}$ become values that are learned during training. First, the empirical mean m_h and standard deviation s_h are computed:

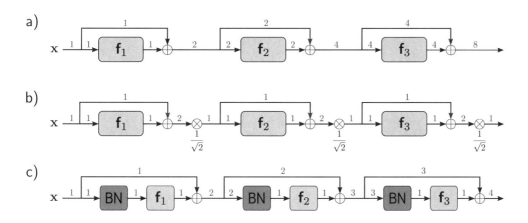

Figure 11.6 Variance in residual networks. a) He initialization ensures that the expected variance remains unchanged after a linear plus ReLU layer $\mathbf{f}_k$. Unfortunately, in residual networks, the input of each block is added back to the output, so the variance doubles at each layer (gray numbers indicate variance) and grows exponentially. b) One approach would be to rescale the signal by $1/\sqrt{2}$ between each residual block. c) A second method uses batch normalization (BN) as the first step in the residual block and initializes the associated offset δ to zero and scale γ to one. This transforms the input to each layer to have unit variance, and with He initialization, the output variance will also be one. Now the variance increases linearly with the number of residual blocks. A side-effect is that, at initialization, later network layers are dominated by the residual connection and are hence close to computing the identity.

$$
\begin{aligned}
m_h &= \frac{1}{|\mathcal{B}|}\sum_{i\in\mathcal{B}} h_i \\
s_h &= \sqrt{\frac{1}{|\mathcal{B}|}\sum_{i\in\mathcal{B}}(h_i - m_h)^2},
\end{aligned}
\tag{11.7}
$$

where all quantities are scalars. Then we use these statistics to standardize the batch activations to have mean zero and unit variance:

Appendix C.2.4
Standardization

$$
h_i \leftarrow \frac{h_i - m_h}{s_h + \epsilon} \qquad\qquad \forall i \in \mathcal{B},
\tag{11.8}
$$

where ϵ is a small number that prevents division by zero if h_i is the same for every member of the batch and $s_h = 0$.

Finally, the normalized variable is scaled by γ and shifted by δ:

$$
h_i \leftarrow \gamma h_i + \delta \qquad\qquad \forall i \in \mathcal{B}.
\tag{11.9}
$$

Problem 11.5
After this operation, the activations have mean δ and standard deviation γ across all members of the batch. Both of these quantities are learned during training.

Batch normalization is applied independently to each hidden unit. In a standard neural network with K layers, each containing D hidden units, there would be KD

Problem 11.6
learned offsets δ and KD learned scales γ. In a convolutional network, the normalizing statistics are computed over both the batch and the spatial position. If there were K

Notebook 11.3
BatchNorm
layers, each containing C channels, there would be KC offsets and KC scales. At test time, we do not have a batch from which we can gather statistics. To resolve this, the statistics m_h and s_h are calculated across the whole training dataset (rather than just a batch) and frozen in the final network.

11.4.1 Costs and benefits of batch normalization

Batch normalization makes the network invariant to rescaling the weights and biases that contribute to each activation; if these are doubled, then the activations also double, the estimated standard deviation s_h doubles, and the normalization in equation 11.8 compensates for these changes. This happens separately for each hidden unit. Consequently, there will be a large family of weights and biases that all produce the same effect. Batch normalization also adds two parameters, γ and δ, at every hidden unit, which makes the model somewhat larger. Hence, it both creates redundancy in the weight parameters and adds extra parameters to compensate for that redundancy. This is obviously inefficient, but batch normalization also provides several benefits.

Stable forward propagation: If we initialize the offsets δ to zero and the scales γ to one, then each output activation will have unit variance. In a regular network, this ensures the variance is stable during forward propagation at initialization. In a residual network, the variance must still increase as we add a new source of variation to the input at each layer. However, it will increase linearly with each residual block; the kth layer adds one unit of variance to the existing variance of k (figure 11.6c).

At initialization, this has the side-effect that later layers make a smaller change to the overall variation than earlier ones. The network is effectively less deep at the start of training since later layers are close to computing the identity. As training proceeds, the network can increase the scales γ in later layers and can control its own effective depth.

Higher learning rates: Empirical studies and theory both show that batch normalization makes the loss surface and its gradient change more smoothly (i.e., reduces shattered gradients). This means we can use higher learning rates as the surface is more predictable. We saw in section 9.2 that higher learning rates improve test performance.

Regularization: We also saw in chapter 9 that adding noise to the training process can improve generalization. Batch normalization injects noise because the normalization depends on the batch statistics. The activations for a given training example are normalized by an amount that depends on the other members of the batch and will be slightly different at each training iteration.

11.5   Common residual architectures

Residual connections are now a standard part of deep learning pipelines. This section reviews some well-known architectures that incorporate them.

11.5.1   ResNet

Residual blocks were first used in convolutional networks for image classification. The resulting networks are known as residual networks, or *ResNets* for short. In ResNets, each residual block contains a batch normalization operation, a ReLU activation function, and a convolutional layer. This is followed by the same sequence again before being added back to the input (figure 11.7a). Trial and error have shown that this order of operations works well for image classification.

Problem 11.7

For very deep networks, the number of parameters may become undesirably large. *Bottleneck residual blocks* make more efficient use of parameters using three convolutions. The first has a 1×1 kernel and reduces the number of channels. The second is a regular 3×3 kernel, and the third is another 1×1 kernel to increase the number of channels back to the original amount (figure 11.7b). In this way, we can integrate information over a 3×3 pixel area using fewer parameters.

Problem 11.8

The ResNet-200 model (figure 11.8) contains 200 layers and was used for image classification on the ImageNet database (figure 10.15). The architecture resembles AlexNet and VGG but uses bottleneck residual blocks instead of vanilla convolutional layers. As with AlexNet and VGG, these are periodically interspersed with decreases in spatial resolution and simultaneous increases in the number of channels. Here, the resolution is decreased by downsampling using convolutions with stride two. The number of channels is increased either by appending zeros to the representation or by using an extra 1×1 convolution. At the start of the network is a 7×7 convolutional layer, followed by a downsampling operation. At the end, a fully connected layer maps the block to a vector of length 1000. This is passed through a softmax layer to generate class probabilities.

The ResNet-200 model achieved a remarkable 4.8% error rate for the correct class being in the top five and 20.1% for identifying the correct class correctly. This compared favorably with AlexNet (16.4%, 38.1%) and VGG (6.8%, 23.7%) and was one of the first networks to exceed human performance (5.1% for being in the top five guesses). However, this model was conceived in 2016 and is far from state-of-the-art. At the time of writing, the best-performing model on this task has a 9.0% error for identifying the class correctly (see figure 10.21). This and all the other current top-performing models for image classification are now based on transformers (see chapter 12).

11.5.2   DenseNet

Residual blocks receive the output from the previous layer, modify it by passing it through some network layers, and add it back to the original input. An alternative is to concatenate the modified and original signals. This increases the representation size

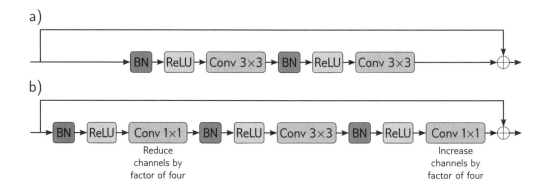

Figure 11.7 ResNet blocks. a) A standard block in the ResNet architecture contains a batch normalization operation, followed by an activation function, and a 3×3 convolutional layer. Then, this sequence is repeated. b). A bottleneck ResNet block still integrates information over a 3×3 region but uses fewer parameters. It contains three convolutions. The first 1×1 convolution reduces the number of channels. The second 3×3 convolution is applied to the smaller representation. A final 1×1 convolution increases the number of channels again so that it can be added back to the input.

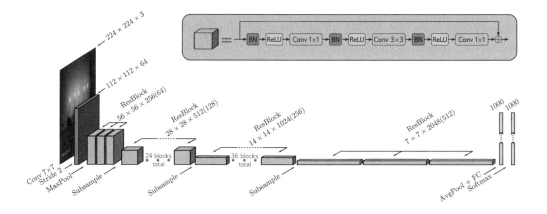

Figure 11.8 ResNet-200 model. A standard 7×7 convolutional layer with stride two is applied, followed by a MaxPool operation. A series of bottleneck residual blocks follow (number in brackets is channels after first 1×1 convolution), with periodic downsampling and accompanying increases in the number of channels. The network concludes with average pooling across all spatial positions and a fully connected layer that maps to pre-softmax activations.

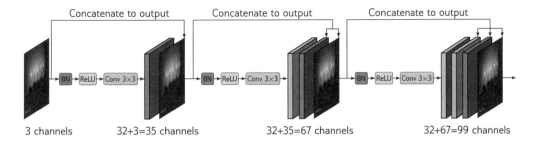

Figure 11.9 DenseNet. This architecture uses residual connections to concatenate the outputs of earlier layers to later ones. Here, the three-channel input image is processed to form a 32-channel representation. The input image is concatenated to this to give a total of 35 channels. This combined representation is processed to create another 32-channel representation, and both earlier representations are concatenated to this to create a total of 67 channels and so on.

(in terms of channels for a convolutional network), but an optional subsequent linear transformation can map back to the original size (a 1×1 convolution for a convolutional network). This allows the model to add the representations together, take a weighted sum, or combine them in a more complex way.

The DenseNet architecture uses concatenation so that the input to a layer comprises the concatenated outputs from *all* previous layers (figure 11.9). These are processed to create a new representation that is itself concatenated with the previous representation and passed to the next layer. This concatenation means there is a direct contribution from earlier layers to the output, so the loss surface behaves reasonably.

In practice, this can only be sustained for a few layers because the number of channels (and hence the number of parameters required to process them) becomes increasingly large. This problem can be alleviated by applying a 1×1 convolution to reduce the number of channels before the next 3×3 convolution is applied. In a convolutional network, the input is periodically downsampled. Concatenation across the downsampling makes no sense since the representations have different sizes. Consequently, the chain of concatenation is broken at this point, and a smaller representation starts a new chain. In addition, another bottleneck 1×1 convolution can be applied when the downsampling occurs to control the representation size further.

This network performs competitively with ResNet models on image classification (see figure 10.21); indeed, it can perform better for a comparable parameter count. This is presumably because it can reuse processing from earlier layers more flexibly.

11.5.3 U-Nets and hourglass networks

Section 10.5.3 described a semantic segmentation network that had an encoder-decoder or hourglass structure. The encoder repeatedly downsamples the image until the receptive fields are large and information is integrated from across the image. Then the decoder

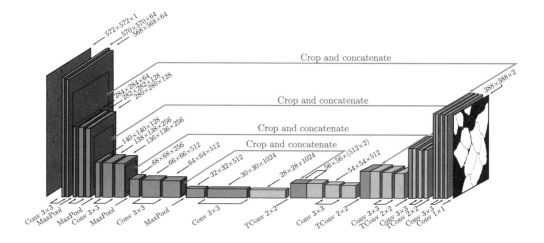

Figure 11.10 U-Net for segmenting HeLa cells. The U-Net has an encoder-decoder structure, in which the representation is downsampled (orange blocks) and then re-upsampled (blue blocks). The encoder uses regular convolutions, and the decoder uses transposed convolutions. Residual connections append the last representation at each scale in the encoder to the first representation at the same scale in the decoder (orange arrows). The original U-Net used "valid" convolutions, so the size decreased slightly with each layer, even without downsampling. Hence, the representations from the encoder were cropped (dashed squares) before appending to the decoder. Adapted from Ronneberger et al. (2015).

upsamples it back to the size of the original image. The final output is a probability over possible object classes at each pixel. One drawback of this architecture is that the low-resolution representation in the middle of the network must "remember" the high-resolution details to make the final result accurate. This is unnecessary if residual connections transfer the representations from the encoder to their partner in the decoder.

The *U-Net* (figure 11.10) is an encoder-decoder architecture where the earlier representations are concatenated to the later ones. The original implementation used "valid" convolutions, so the spatial size decreases by two pixels each time a 3×3 convolutional layer is applied. This means that the upsampled version is smaller than its counterpart in the encoder, which must be cropped before concatenation. Subsequent implementations have used zero padding, where this cropping is unnecessary. Note that the U-Net is completely convolutional, so after training, it can be run on an image of *any size*.

Problem 11.9

The U-Net was intended for segmenting medical images (figure 11.11) but has found many other uses in computer graphics and vision. *Hourglass networks* are similar but apply further convolutional layers in the skip connections and add the result back to the decoder rather than concatenating it. A series of these models form a *stacked hourglass network* that alternates between considering the image at local and global levels. Such networks are used for pose estimation (figure 11.12). The system is trained to predict one "heatmap" for each joint, and the estimated position is the maximum of each heatmap.

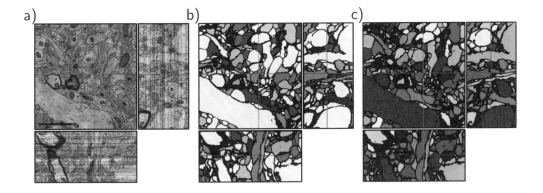

Figure 11.11 Segmentation using U-Net in 3D. a) Three slices through a 3D volume of mouse cortex taken by scanning electron microscope. b) A single U-Net is used to classify voxels as being inside or outside neurites. Connected regions are identified with different colors. c) For a better result, an ensemble of five U-Nets is trained, and a voxel is only classified as belonging to the cell if all five networks agree. Adapted from Falk et al. (2019).

11.6 Why do nets with residual connections perform so well?

Residual networks allow much deeper networks to be trained; it's possible to extend the ResNet architecture to 1000 layers and still train effectively. The improvement in image classification performance was initially attributed to the additional network depth, but two pieces of evidence contradict this viewpoint.

First, shallower, wider residual networks sometimes outperform deeper, narrower ones with a comparable parameter count. In other words, better performance can sometimes be achieved with a network with fewer layers but more channels per layer. Second, there is evidence that the gradients during training do not propagate effectively through very long paths in the unraveled network (figure 11.4b). In effect, a very deep network may act more like a combination of shallower networks.

The current view is that residual connections add some value of their own, as well as allowing deeper networks to be trained. This perspective is supported by the fact that the loss surfaces of residual networks around a minimum tend to be smoother and more predictable than those for the same network when the skip connections are removed (figure 11.13). This may make it easier to learn a good solution that generalizes well.

11.7 Summary

Increasing network depth indefinitely causes both training and test performance for image classification to decrease. This may be because the gradient of the loss with respect to

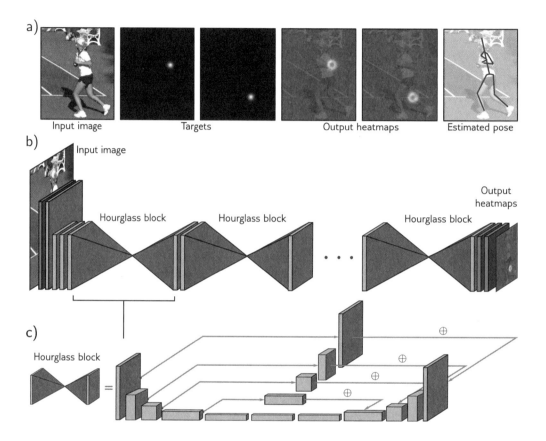

Figure 11.12 Stacked hourglass networks for pose estimation. a) The network input is an image containing a person, and the output is a set of heatmaps, with one heatmap for each joint. This is formulated as a regression problem where the targets are heatmap images with small, highlighted regions at the ground-truth joint positions. The peak of the estimated heatmap is used to establish each final joint position. b) The architecture consists of initial convolutional and residual layers followed by a series of hourglass blocks. c) Each hourglass block consists of an encoder-decoder network similar to the U-Net except that the convolutions use zero padding, some further processing is done in the residual links, and these links add this processed representation rather than concatenate it. Each blue cuboid is itself a bottleneck residual block (figure 11.7b). Adapted from Newell et al. (2016).

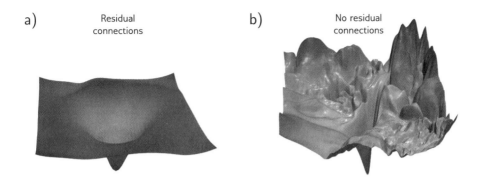

Figure 11.13 Visualizing neural network loss surfaces. Each plot shows the loss surface in two random directions in parameter space around the minimum found by SGD for an image classification task on the CIFAR-10 dataset. These directions are normalized to facilitate side-by-side comparison. a) Residual net with 56 layers. b) Results from the same network without skip connections. The surface is smoother with the skip connections. This facilitates learning and makes the final network performance more robust to minor errors in the parameters, so it will likely generalize better. Adapted from Li et al. (2018b).

parameters early in the network changes quickly and unpredictably relative to the update step size. Residual connections add the processed representation back to their own input. Now each layer contributes directly to the output as well as indirectly, so propagating gradients through many layers is not mandatory, and the loss surface is smoother.

Residual networks don't suffer from vanishing gradients but introduce an exponential increase in the variance of the activations during forward propagation and corresponding problems with exploding gradients. This is usually handled by adding batch normalization, which compensates for the empirical mean and variance of the batch and then shifts and rescales using learned parameters. If these parameters are initialized judiciously, very deep networks can be trained. There is evidence that both residual links and batch normalization make the loss surface smoother, which permits larger learning rates. Moreover, the variability in the batch statistics adds a source of regularization.

Residual blocks have been incorporated into convolutional networks. They allow deeper networks to be trained with commensurate increases in image classification performance. Variations of residual networks include the DenseNet architecture, which concatenates outputs of all prior layers to feed into the current layer, and U-Nets, which incorporate residual connections into encoder-decoder models.

Notes

Residual connections: Residual connections were introduced by He et al. (2016a), who built a network with 152 layers, which was eight times larger than VGG (figure 10.17), and achieved state-of-the-art performance on the ImageNet classification task. Each residual block consisted of a convolutional layer followed by batch normalization, a ReLU activation, a second convolutional layer, and second batch normalization. A second ReLU function was applied after this block was added back to the main representation. This architecture was termed *ResNet v1*. He et al. (2016b) investigated different variations of residual architectures, in which either (i) processing could also be applied along the skip connection or (ii) after the two branches had recombined. They concluded neither was necessary, leading to the architecture in figure 11.7, which is sometimes termed a *pre-activation residual block* and is the backbone of *ResNet v2*. They trained a network with 200 layers that improved further on the ImageNet classification task (see figure 11.8). Since this time, new methods for regularization, optimization, and data augmentation have been developed, and Wightman et al. (2021) exploit these to present a more modern training pipeline for the ResNet architecture.

Why residual connections help: Residual networks certainly allow deeper networks to be trained. Presumably, this is related to reducing shattered gradients (Balduzzi et al., 2017) at the start of training and the smoother loss surface near the minima as depicted in figure 11.13 (Li et al., 2018b). Residual connections alone (i.e., without batch normalization) increase the trainable depth of a network by roughly a factor of two (Sankararaman et al., 2020). With batch normalization, very deep networks can be trained, but it is unclear that depth is critical for performance. Zagoruyko & Komodakis (2016) showed that wide residual networks with only 16 layers outperformed all residual networks of the time for image classification. Orhan & Pitkow (2017) propose a different explanation for why residual connections improve learning in terms of eliminating singularities (places on the loss surface where the Hessian is degenerate).

Related architectures: Residual connections are a special case of *highway networks* (Srivastava et al., 2015) which also split the computation into two branches and additively recombine. Highway networks use a gating function that weights the inputs to the two branches in a way that depends on the data itself, whereas residual networks send the data down both branches in a straightforward manner. Xie et al. (2017) introduced the ResNeXt architecture, which places a residual connection around multiple parallel convolutional branches.

Residual networks as ensembles: Veit et al. (2016) characterized residual networks as ensembles of shorter networks and depicted the "unraveled network" interpretation (figure 11.4b). They provide evidence that this interpretation is valid by showing that deleting layers in a trained network (and hence a subset of paths) only has a modest effect on performance. Conversely, removing a layer in a purely sequential network like VGG is catastrophic. They also looked at the gradient magnitudes along paths of different lengths and showed that the gradient vanishes in longer paths. In a residual network consisting of 54 blocks, almost all of the gradient updates during training were from paths of length 5 to 17 blocks long, even though these only constitute 0.45% of the total paths. It seems that adding more blocks effectively adds more parallel shorter paths rather than creating a network that is truly deeper.

Regularization for residual networks: L2 regularization of the weights has a fundamentally different effect in vanilla networks and residual networks without BatchNorm. In the former, it encourages the output of the layer to be a constant function determined by the biases. In the latter, it encourages the residual block to compute the identity plus a constant determined by the biases.

Several regularization methods have been developed that are targeted specifically at residual architectures. ResDrop (Yamada et al., 2016), stochastic depth (Huang et al., 2016), and RandomDrop (Yamada et al., 2019) all regularize residual networks by randomly dropping residual blocks during the training process. In the latter case, the propensity for dropping a block is determined by a Bernoulli variable, whose parameter is linearly decreased during training. At test time, the residual blocks are added back in with their expected probability. These methods are effectively versions of dropout, in which all the hidden units in a block are simultaneously dropped in concert. In the multiple paths view of residual networks (figure 11.4b), they simply remove some of the paths at each training step. Wu et al. (2018b) developed BlockDrop, which analyzes an existing network and decides which residual blocks to use at runtime with the goal of improving the efficiency of inference.

Other regularization methods have been developed for networks with multiple paths inside the residual block. Shake-shake (Gastaldi, 2017a,b) randomly re-weights the paths during the forward and backward passes. In the forward pass, this can be viewed as synthesizing random data, and in the backward pass, as injecting another form of noise into the training method. ShakeDrop (Yamada et al., 2019) draws a Bernoulli variable that decides whether each block will be subject to Shake-Shake or behave like a standard residual unit on this training step.

Batch normalization: Batch normalization was introduced by Ioffe & Szegedy (2015) outside of the context of residual networks. They showed empirically that it allowed higher learning rates, increased convergence speed, and made sigmoid activation functions more practical (since the distribution of outputs is controlled, so examples are less likely to fall in the saturated extremes of the sigmoid). Balduzzi et al. (2017) investigated the activation of hidden units in later layers of deep networks with ReLU functions at initialization. They showed that many such hidden units were always active or always inactive regardless of the input but that BatchNorm reduced this tendency.

Although batch normalization helps stabilize the forward propagation of signals through a network, Yang et al. (2019) showed that it causes gradient explosion in ReLU networks without skip connections, with each layer increasing the magnitude of the gradients by $\sqrt{\pi/(\pi-1)} \approx$ 1.21. This argument is summarized by Luther (2020). Since a residual network can be seen as a combination of paths of different lengths (figure 11.4), this effect must also be present in residual networks. Presumably, however, the benefit of removing the 2^K increases in magnitude in the forward pass of a network with K layers outweighs the harm done by increasing the gradients by 1.21^K in the backward pass, so overall BatchNorm makes training more stable.

Variations of batch normalization: Several variants of BatchNorm have been proposed (figure 11.14). BatchNorm normalizes each channel separately based on statistics gathered across the batch. *Ghost batch normalization* or *GhostNorm* (Hoffer et al., 2017) uses only part of the batch to compute the normalization statistics, which makes them noisier and increases the amount of regularization when the batch size is very large (figure 11.14b).

When the batch size is very small or the fluctuations within a batch are very large (as is often the case in natural language processing), the statistics in BatchNorm may become unreliable. Ioffe (2017) proposed *batch renormalization*, which keeps a running average of the batch statistics and modifies the normalization of any batch to ensure that it is more representative. Another problem is that batch normalization is unsuitable for use in recurrent neural networks (networks for processing sequences, in which the previous output is fed back as an additional input as we move through the sequence (see figure 12.19). Here, the statistics must be stored at each step in the sequence, and it's unclear what to do if a test sequence is longer than the training sequences. A third problem is that batch normalization needs access to the whole batch. However, this may not be easily available when training is distributed across several machines.

Layer normalization or *LayerNorm* (Ba et al., 2016) avoids using batch statistics by normalizing each data example separately, using statistics gathered across the channels and spatial position (figure 11.14c). However, there is still a separate learned scale γ and offset δ per channel. *Group normalization* or *GroupNorm* (Wu & He, 2018) is similar to LayerNorm but divides the channels into groups and computes the statistics for each group separately across the within-group channels and the spatial positions (figure 11.14d). Again, there are still separate scale and offset parameters per channel. *Instance normalization* or *InstanceNorm* (Ulyanov et al., 2016) takes this to the extreme where the number of groups is the same as the number of channels, so each channel is normalized separately (figure 11.14e), using statistics gathered across spatial

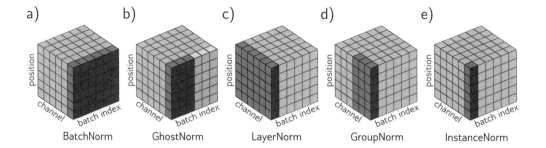

Figure 11.14 Normalization schemes. BatchNorm modifies each channel separately but adjusts each batch member in the same way based on statistics gathered across the batch and spatial position. Ghost BatchNorm computes these statistics from only part of the batch to make them more variable. LayerNorm computes statistics for each batch member separately, based on statistics gathered across the channels and spatial position. It retains a separate learned scaling factor for each channel. GroupNorm normalizes within each group of channels and also retains a separate scale and offset parameter for each channel. InstanceNorm normalizes within each channel separately, computing the statistics only across spatial position. Adapted from Wu & He (2018).

position alone. Salimans & Kingma (2016) investigated normalizing the network weights rather than the activations, but this has been less empirically successful. Teye et al. (2018) introduced *Monte Carlo batch normalization*, which can provide meaningful estimates of uncertainty in the predictions of neural networks. A recent comparison of the properties of different normalization schemes can be found in Lubana et al. (2021).

Why BatchNorm helps: BatchNorm helps control the initial gradients in a residual network (figure 11.6c). However, the mechanism by which BatchNorm improves performance is not well understood. The stated goal of Ioffe & Szegedy (2015) was to reduce problems caused by *internal covariate shift*, which is the change in the distribution of inputs to a layer caused by updating preceding layers during the backpropagation update. However, Santurkar et al. (2018) provided evidence against this view by artificially inducing covariate shift and showing that networks with and without BatchNorm performed equally well.

Motivated by this, they searched for another explanation for why BatchNorm should improve performance. They showed empirically for the VGG network that adding batch normalization decreases the variation in both the loss and its gradient as we move in the gradient direction. In other words, the loss surface is both smoother and changes more slowly, which is why larger learning rates are possible. They also provide theoretical proofs for both these phenomena and show that for any parameter initialization, the distance to the nearest optimum is less for networks with batch normalization. Bjorck et al. (2018) also argue that BatchNorm improves the properties of the loss landscape and allows larger learning rates.

Other explanations of why BatchNorm improves performance include decreasing the importance of tuning the learning rate (Ioffe & Szegedy, 2015; Arora et al., 2018). Indeed Li & Arora (2019) show that using an exponentially increasing learning rate schedule is possible with batch normalization. Ultimately, this is because batch normalization makes the network invariant to the scales of the weight matrices (see Huszár, 2019, for an intuitive visualization).

Hoffer et al. (2017) identified that BatchNorm has a regularizing effect due to statistical fluctuations from the random composition of the batch. They proposed using a *ghost batch size*, in which the mean and standard deviation statistics are computed from a subset of the batch. Large batches can now be used without losing the regularizing effect of the extra noise in smaller batch sizes. Luo et al. (2018) investigate the regularization effects of batch normalization.

Alternatives to batch normalization: Although BatchNorm is widely used, it is not strictly necessary to train deep residual nets; there are other ways of making the loss surface tractable. Balduzzi et al. (2017) proposed the rescaling by $\sqrt{1/2}$ in figure 11.6b; they argued that it prevents gradient explosion but does not resolve the problem of shattered gradients.

Other work has investigated rescaling the function's output in the residual block before adding it back to the input. For example, De & Smith (2020) introduce SkipInit, in which a learnable scalar multiplier is placed at the end of each residual branch. This helps if this multiplier is initialized to less than $\sqrt{1/K}$, where K is the number of residual blocks. In practice, they suggest initializing this to zero. Similarly, Hayou et al. (2021) introduce Stable ResNet, which rescales the output of the function in the kth residual block (before addition to the main branch) by a constant λ_k. They prove that in the limit of infinite width, the expected gradient norm of the weights in the first layer is lower bounded by the sum of squares of the scalings λ_k. They investigate setting these to a constant $\sqrt{1/K}$, where K is the number of residual blocks and show that it is possible to train networks with up to 1000 blocks.

Zhang et al. (2019a) introduce *FixUp*, in which every layer is initialized using He normalization, but the last linear/convolutional layer of every residual block is set to zero. Now the initial forward pass is stable (since each residual block contributes nothing), and the gradients do not explode in the backward pass (for the same reason). They also rescale the branches so that the magnitude of the total expected change in the parameters is constant regardless of the number of residual blocks. These methods allow training of deep residual networks but don't usually achieve the same test performance as when using BatchNorm. This is probably because they do not benefit from the regularization induced by the noisy batch statistics. De & Smith (2020) modify their method to induce regularization via dropout, which helps close this gap.

DenseNet and U-Net: DenseNet was first introduced by Huang et al. (2017b), U-Net was developed by Ronneberger et al. (2015), and stacked hourglass networks by Newell et al. (2016). Of these architectures, U-Net has been the most extensively adapted. Çiçek et al. (2016) introduced 3D U-Net, and Milletari et al. (2016) introduced V-Net, both of which extend U-Net to process 3D data. Zhou et al. (2018) combine the ideas of DenseNet and U-Net in an architecture that downsamples and re-upsamples the image but also repeatedly uses intermediate representations. U-Nets are commonly used in medical image segmentation (see Siddique et al., 2021, for a review). However, they have been applied to other areas, including depth estimation (Garg et al., 2016), semantic segmentation (Iglovikov & Shvets, 2018), inpainting (Zeng et al., 2019), pansharpening (Yao et al., 2018), and image-to-image translation (Isola et al., 2017). U-Nets are also a key component in diffusion models (chapter 18).

Problems

Problem 11.1 Derive equation 11.5 from the network definition in equation 11.4.

Problem 11.2 Unraveling the four-block network in figure 11.4a produces one path of length zero, four paths of length one, six paths of length two, four paths of length three, and one path of length four. How many paths of each length would there be if with (i) three residual blocks and (ii) five residual blocks? Deduce the rule for K residual blocks.

Problem 11.3 Show that the derivative of the network in equation 11.5 with respect to the first layer $\mathbf{f}_1[\mathbf{x}]$ is given by equation 11.6.

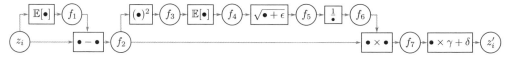

Figure 11.15 Computational graph for batch normalization (see problem 11.5).

Problem 11.4[*] Explain why the values in the two branches of the residual blocks in figure 11.6a are uncorrelated. Show that the variance of the sum of uncorrelated variables is the sum of their individual variances.

Problem 11.5[*] The forward pass for batch normalization given a batch of scalar values $\{z_i\}_{i=1}^{I}$ consists of the following operations (figure 11.15):

$$
\begin{aligned}
f_1 &= \mathbb{E}[z_i] & f_5 &= \sqrt{f_4 + \epsilon} \\
f_{2i} &= z_i - f_1 & f_6 &= 1/f_5 \\
f_{3i} &= f_{2i}^2 & f_{7i} &= f_{2i} \times f_6 \\
f_4 &= \mathbb{E}[f_{3i}] & z_i' &= f_{7i} \times \gamma + \delta,
\end{aligned}
\tag{11.10}
$$

where $\mathbb{E}[z_i] = \frac{1}{I}\sum_i z_i$. Write Python code to implement the forward pass. Now derive the algorithm for the backward pass. Work backward through the computational graph computing the derivatives to generate a set of operations that computes $\partial z_i'/\partial z_i$ for every element in the batch. Write Python code to implement the backward pass.

Problem 11.6 Consider a fully connected neural network with one input, one output, and ten hidden layers, each of which contains twenty hidden units. How many parameters does this network have? How many parameters will it have if we place a batch normalization operation between each linear transformation and ReLU?

Problem 11.7[*] Consider applying an L2 regularization penalty to the weights in the convolutional layers in figure 11.7a, but not to the scaling parameters of the subsequent BatchNorm layers. What do you expect will happen as training proceeds?

Problem 11.8 Consider a convolutional residual block that contains a batch normalization operation, followed by a ReLU activation function, and then a 3×3 convolutional layer. If the input and output both have 512 channels, how many parameters are needed to define this block? Now consider a bottleneck residual block that contains three batch normalization/ReLU/convolution sequences. The first uses a 1×1 convolution to reduce the number of channels from 512 to 128. The second uses a 3×3 convolution with the same number of input and output channels. The third uses a 1×1 convolution to increase the number of channels from 128 to 512 (see figure 11.7b). How many parameters are needed to define this block?

Problem 11.9 The U-Net is completely convolutional and can be run with any sized image after training. Why do we not train with a collection of arbitrarily-sized images?

Chapter 12

Transformers

Chapter 10 introduced convolutional networks, which are specialized for processing data that lie on a regular grid. They are particularly suited to processing images, which have a very large number of input variables, precluding the use of fully connected networks. Each layer of a convolutional network employs parameter sharing so that local image patches are processed similarly at every position in the image.

This chapter introduces transformers. These were initially targeted at natural language processing (NLP) problems, where the network input is a series of high-dimensional embeddings representing words or word fragments. Language datasets share some of the characteristics of image data. The number of input variables can be very large, and the statistics are similar at every position; it's not sensible to re-learn the meaning of the word dog at every possible position in a body of text. However, language datasets have the complication that text sequences vary in length, and unlike images, there is no easy way to resize them.

12.1 Processing text data

To motivate the transformer, consider the following passage:

The restaurant refused to serve me a ham sandwich because it only cooks vegetarian food. In the end, they just gave me two slices of bread. Their ambiance was just as good as the food and service.

The goal is to design a network to process this text into a representation suitable for downstream tasks. For example, it might be used to classify the review as positive or negative or to answer questions such as "Does the restaurant serve steak?".

We can make three immediate observations. First, the encoded input can be surprisingly large. In this case, each of the 37 words might be represented by an embedding vector of length 1024, so the encoded input would be of length $37 \times 1024 = 37888$ even for this small passage. A more realistically sized body of text might have hundreds or even thousands of words, so fully connected neural networks are impractical.

Second, one of the defining characteristics of NLP problems is that each input (one or more sentences) is of a different length; hence, it's not even obvious how to apply a fully connected network. These observations suggest that the network should share parameters across words at different input positions, similarly to how convolutional networks share parameters across different image positions.

Third, language is ambiguous; it is unclear from the syntax alone that the pronoun it refers to the restaurant and not to the ham sandwich. To understand the text, the word it should somehow be connected to the word restaurant. In the parlance of transformers, the former word should pay *attention* to the latter. This implies that there must be connections between the words and that the strength of these connections will depend on the words themselves. Moreover, these connections need to extend across large text spans. For example, the word their in the last sentence also refers to the restaurant.

12.2   Dot-product self-attention

The previous section argued that a model for processing text will (i) use parameter sharing to cope with long input passages of differing lengths and (ii) contain connections between word representations that depend on the words themselves. The transformer acquires both properties by using *dot-product self-attention*.

A standard neural network layer $\mathbf{f}[\mathbf{x}]$, takes a $D \times 1$ input $\mathbf{x}$ and applies a linear transformation followed by an activation function like a ReLU, so:

$$\mathbf{f}[\mathbf{x}] = \mathbf{ReLU}[\boldsymbol{\beta} + \boldsymbol{\Omega}\mathbf{x}], \tag{12.1}$$

where $\boldsymbol{\beta}$ contains the biases, and $\boldsymbol{\Omega}$ contains the weights.

A self-attention block $\mathbf{sa}[\bullet]$ takes N inputs $\mathbf{x}_1, \ldots, \mathbf{x}_N$, each of dimension $D \times 1$, and returns N output vectors of the same size. In the context of NLP, each input represents a word or word fragment. First, a set of *values* are computed for each input:

$$\mathbf{v}_m = \boldsymbol{\beta}_v + \boldsymbol{\Omega}_v \mathbf{x}_m, \tag{12.2}$$

where $\boldsymbol{\beta}_v \in \mathbb{R}^{D \times 1}$ and $\boldsymbol{\Omega}_v \in \mathbb{R}^{D \times D}$ represent biases and weights, respectively.

Then the nth output $\mathbf{sa}_n[\mathbf{x}_1, \ldots, \mathbf{x}_N]$ is a weighted sum of all the values $\mathbf{v}_1, \ldots, \mathbf{v}_N$:

$$\mathbf{sa}_n[\mathbf{x}_1, \ldots, \mathbf{x}_N] = \sum_{m=1}^{N} a[\mathbf{x}_m, \mathbf{x}_n]\mathbf{v}_m. \tag{12.3}$$

The scalar weight $a[\mathbf{x}_m, \mathbf{x}_n]$ is the *attention* that the nth output pays to input $\mathbf{x}_m$. The N weights $a[\bullet, \mathbf{x}_n]$ are non-negative and sum to one. Hence, self-attention can be thought of as *routing* the values in different proportions to create each output (figure 12.1).

The following sections examine dot-product self-attention in more detail. First, we consider the computation of the values and their subsequent weighting (equation 12.3). Then we describe how to compute the attention weights $a[\mathbf{x}_m, \mathbf{x}_n]$ themselves.

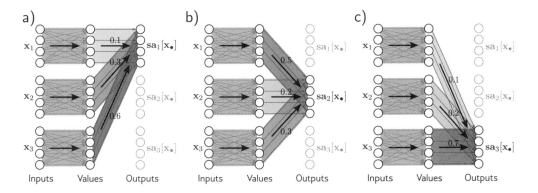

Figure 12.1 Self-attention as routing. The self-attention mechanism takes N inputs $\mathbf{x}_1, \ldots, \mathbf{x}_N \in \mathbb{R}^D$ (here $N = 3$ and $D = 4$) and processes each separately to compute N value vectors. The nth output $\mathbf{sa}_n[\mathbf{x}_1, \ldots \mathbf{x}_N]$ (written as $\mathbf{sa}_n[\mathbf{x}_\bullet]$ for short) is then computed as a weighted sum of the N value vectors, where the weights are positive and sum to one. a) Output $\mathbf{sa}_1[\mathbf{x}_\bullet]$ is computed as $a[\mathbf{x}_1, \mathbf{x}_1] = 0.1$ times the first value vector, $a[\mathbf{x}_2, \mathbf{x}_1] = 0.3$ times the second value vector, and $a[\mathbf{x}_3, \mathbf{x}_1] = 0.6$ times the third value vector. b) Output $\mathbf{sa}_2[\mathbf{x}_\bullet]$ is computed in the same way, but this time with weights of 0.5, 0.2, and 0.3. c) The weighting for output $\mathbf{sa}_3[\mathbf{x}_\bullet]$ is different again. Each output can hence be thought of as a different routing of the N values.

12.2.1 Computing and weighting values

Equation 12.2 shows that the same weights $\boldsymbol{\Omega}_v \in \mathbb{R}^{D \times D}$ and biases $\boldsymbol{\beta}_v \in \mathbb{R}^D$ are applied to each input $\mathbf{x}_\bullet \in \mathbb{R}^D$. This computation scales linearly with the sequence length N, so it requires fewer parameters than a fully connected network relating all DN inputs to all DN outputs. The value computation can be viewed as a sparse matrix operation with shared parameters (figure 12.2b).

The attention weights $a[\mathbf{x}_m, \mathbf{x}_n]$ combine the values from different inputs. They are also sparse since there is only one weight for each ordered pair of inputs $(\mathbf{x}_m, \mathbf{x}_n)$, regardless of the size of these inputs (figure 12.2c). It follows that the number of attention weights has a quadratic dependence on the sequence length N, but is independent of the length D of each input.

Problem 12.1

12.2.2 Computing attention weights

In the previous section, we saw that the outputs result from two chained linear transformations; the value vectors $\boldsymbol{\beta}_v + \boldsymbol{\Omega}_v\mathbf{x}_m$ are computed independently for each input $\mathbf{x}_m$, and these vectors are combined linearly by the attention weights $a[\mathbf{x}_m, \mathbf{x}_n]$. However, the overall self-attention computation is *nonlinear*. As we'll see shortly, the attention weights are themselves nonlinear functions of the input. This is an example of a *hypernetwork*, where one network branch computes the weights of another.

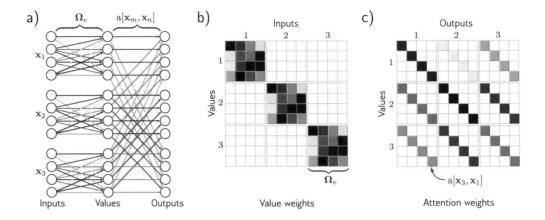

Figure 12.2 Self-attention for $N = 3$ inputs $\mathbf{x}_n$, each with dimension $D = 4$.
a) Each input $\mathbf{x}_n$ is operated on independently by the same weights $\boldsymbol{\Omega}_v$ (same color equals same weight) and biases $\boldsymbol{\beta}_v$ (not shown) to form the values $\boldsymbol{\beta}_v + \boldsymbol{\Omega}_v \mathbf{x}_n$. Each output is a linear combination of the values, with a shared attention weight $a[\mathbf{x}_m, \mathbf{x}_n]$ defining the contribution of the mth value to the nth output.
b) Matrix showing block sparsity of linear transformation $\boldsymbol{\Omega}_v$ between inputs and values. c) Matrix showing sparsity of attention weights relating values and outputs.

To compute the attention, we apply two more linear transformations to the inputs:

$$
\begin{aligned}
\mathbf{q}_n &= \boldsymbol{\beta}_q + \boldsymbol{\Omega}_q \mathbf{x}_n \\
\mathbf{k}_m &= \boldsymbol{\beta}_k + \boldsymbol{\Omega}_k \mathbf{x}_m,
\end{aligned}
\tag{12.4}
$$

Appendix B.3.4
Dot product

where $\{\mathbf{q}_n\}$ and $\{\mathbf{k}_m\}$ are termed *queries* and *keys*, respectively. Then we compute dot products between the queries and keys and pass the results through a softmax function:

$$
\begin{aligned}
a[\mathbf{x}_m, \mathbf{x}_n] &= \text{softmax}_m \left[\mathbf{k}_\bullet^T \mathbf{q}_n \right] \\
&= \frac{\exp \left[\mathbf{k}_m^T \mathbf{q}_n \right]}{\sum_{m'=1}^{N} \exp \left[\mathbf{k}_{m'}^T \mathbf{q}_n \right]},
\end{aligned}
\tag{12.5}
$$

so for each $\mathbf{x}_n$, they are positive and sum to one (figure 12.3). For obvious reasons, this is known as *dot-product self-attention*.

The names "queries" and "keys" were inherited from the field of information retrieval and have the following interpretation: the dot product operation returns a measure of similarity between its inputs, so the weights $a[\mathbf{x}_\bullet, \mathbf{x}_n]$ depend on the relative similarities between the nth query and all of the keys. The softmax function means that the key vectors "compete" with one another to contribute to the final result. The queries and keys must have the same dimensions. However, these can differ from the dimension of

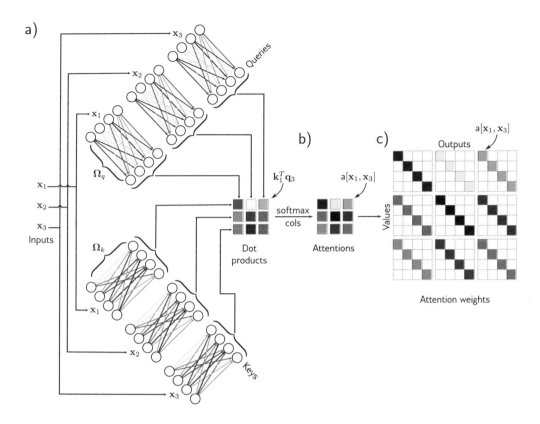

Figure 12.3 Computing attention weights. a) Query vectors $\mathbf{q}_n = \boldsymbol{\beta}_q + \boldsymbol{\Omega}_q\mathbf{x}_n$ and key vectors $\mathbf{k}_n = \boldsymbol{\beta}_k + \boldsymbol{\Omega}_k\mathbf{x}_n$ are computed for each input $\mathbf{x}_n$. b) The dot products between each query and the three keys are passed through a softmax function to form non-negative attentions that sum to one. c) These route the value vectors (figure 12.1) via the sparse matrix from figure 12.2c.

the values, which is usually the same size as the input, so the representation doesn't change size.

Problem 12.2

12.2.3 Self-attention summary

The nth output is a weighted sum of the same linear transformation $\mathbf{v}_\bullet = \boldsymbol{\beta}_v + \boldsymbol{\Omega}_v\mathbf{x}_\bullet$ applied to all of the inputs, where these attention weights are positive and sum to one. The weights depend on a measure of similarity between input $\mathbf{x}_n$ and the other inputs. There is no activation function, but the mechanism is nonlinear due to the dot-product and a softmax operation used to compute the attention weights.

Note that this mechanism fulfills the initial requirements. First, there is a single shared set of parameters $\boldsymbol{\phi} = \{\boldsymbol{\beta}_v, \boldsymbol{\Omega}_v, \boldsymbol{\beta}_q, \boldsymbol{\Omega}_q, \boldsymbol{\beta}_k, \boldsymbol{\Omega}_k\}$. This is independent of the

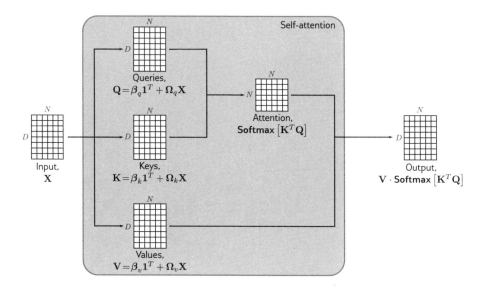

Figure 12.4 Self-attention in matrix form. Self-attention can be implemented efficiently if we store the N input vectors $\mathbf{x}_n$ in the columns of the $D{\times}N$ matrix $\mathbf{X}$. The input $\mathbf{X}$ is operated on separately by the query matrix $\mathbf{Q}$, key matrix $\mathbf{K}$, and value matrix $\mathbf{V}$. The dot products are then computed using matrix multiplication, and a softmax operation is applied independently to each column of the resulting matrix to calculate the attentions. Finally, the values are post-multiplied by the attentions to create an output of the same size as the input.

number of inputs N, so the network can be applied to different sequence lengths. Second, there are connections between the inputs (words), and the strength of these connections depends on the inputs themselves via the attention weights.

12.2.4 Matrix form

The above computation can be written in a compact form if the N inputs $\mathbf{x}_n$ form the columns of the $D \times N$ matrix $\mathbf{X}$. The values, queries, and keys can be computed as:

$$
\begin{aligned}
\mathbf{V}[\mathbf{X}] &= \boldsymbol{\beta}_v \mathbf{1^T} + \boldsymbol{\Omega}_v \mathbf{X} \\
\mathbf{Q}[\mathbf{X}] &= \boldsymbol{\beta}_q \mathbf{1^T} + \boldsymbol{\Omega}_q \mathbf{X} \\
\mathbf{K}[\mathbf{X}] &= \boldsymbol{\beta}_k \mathbf{1^T} + \boldsymbol{\Omega}_k \mathbf{X},
\end{aligned}
\tag{12.6}
$$

where $\mathbf{1}$ is an $N \times 1$ vector containing ones. The self-attention computation is then:

$$
\mathbf{Sa}[\mathbf{X}] = \mathbf{V}[\mathbf{X}] \cdot \mathbf{Softmax}\Big[\mathbf{K}[\mathbf{X}]^T \mathbf{Q}[\mathbf{X}]\Big],
\tag{12.7}
$$

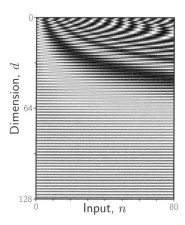

Figure 12.5 Positional encodings. The self-attention architecture is equivariant to permutations of the inputs. To ensure that inputs at different positions are treated differently, a positional encoding matrix $\boldsymbol{\Pi}$ can be added to the data matrix. Each column is different, so the positions can be distinguished. Here, the position encodings use a predefined procedural sinusoidal pattern (which can be extended to larger values of N if necessary). However, in other cases, they are learned.

where the function **Softmax**[•] takes a matrix and performs the softmax operation independently on each of its columns (figure 12.4). In this formulation, we have explicitly included the dependence of the values, queries, and keys on the input $\mathbf{X}$ to emphasize that self-attention computes a kind of triple product based on the inputs. However, from now on, we will drop this dependence and just write:

Notebook 12.1
Self-attention

$$\mathbf{Sa}[\mathbf{X}] = \mathbf{V} \cdot \mathbf{Softmax}[\mathbf{K}^T \mathbf{Q}]. \tag{12.8}$$

12.3 Extensions to dot-product self-attention

In the previous section, we described self-attention. Here, we introduce three extensions that are almost always used in practice.

12.3.1 Positional encoding

Observant readers will have noticed that the self-attention mechanism discards important information: the computation is the same regardless of the order of the inputs $\mathbf{x}_n$. More precisely, it is equivariant with respect to input permutations. However, order *is* important when the inputs correspond to the words in a sentence. The sentence The woman ate the raccoon has a different meaning than The raccoon ate the woman. There are two main approaches to incorporating position information.

Problem 12.3

Absolute positional encodings: A matrix $\boldsymbol{\Pi}$ is added to the input $\mathbf{X}$ that encodes positional information (figure 12.5). Each column of $\boldsymbol{\Pi}$ is unique and hence contains information about the absolute position in the input sequence. This matrix can be chosen by hand or learned. It may be added to the network inputs or at every network layer. Sometimes it is added to $\mathbf{X}$ in the computation of the queries and keys but not to the values.

Relative positional encodings: The input to a self-attention mechanism may be an entire sentence, many sentences, or just a fragment of a sentence, and the absolute position of a word is much less important than the relative position between two inputs. Of course, this can be recovered if the system knows the absolute position of both, but relative positional encodings encode this information directly. Each element of the attention matrix corresponds to a particular offset between key position a and query position b. Relative positional encodings learn a parameter $\pi_{a,b}$ for each offset and use this to modify the attention matrix by adding these values, multiplying by them, or using them to alter the attention matrix in some other way.

12.3.2 Scaled dot-product self-attention

The dot products in the attention computation can have large magnitudes and move the arguments to the softmax function into a region where the largest value completely dominates. Small changes to the inputs to the softmax function now have little effect on the output (i.e., the gradients are very small), making the model difficult to train. To prevent this, the dot products are scaled by the square root of the dimension D_q of the queries and keys (i.e., the number of rows in $\mathbf{\Omega}_q$ and $\mathbf{\Omega}_k$, which must be the same):

Problem 12.4

$$\mathbf{Sa}[\mathbf{X}] = \mathbf{V} \cdot \mathbf{Softmax}\left[\frac{\mathbf{K}^T\mathbf{Q}}{\sqrt{D_q}}\right]. \tag{12.9}$$

This is known as *scaled dot-product self-attention*.

12.3.3 Multiple heads

Multiple self-attention mechanisms are usually applied in parallel, and this is known as *multi-head self-attention*. Now H different sets of values, keys, and queries are computed:

$$\begin{aligned}
\mathbf{V}_h &= \boldsymbol{\beta}_{vh}\mathbf{1}^{\mathbf{T}} + \mathbf{\Omega}_{vh}\mathbf{X} \\
\mathbf{Q}_h &= \boldsymbol{\beta}_{qh}\mathbf{1}^{\mathbf{T}} + \mathbf{\Omega}_{qh}\mathbf{X} \\
\mathbf{K}_h &= \boldsymbol{\beta}_{kh}\mathbf{1}^{\mathbf{T}} + \mathbf{\Omega}_{kh}\mathbf{X}.
\end{aligned} \tag{12.10}$$

The hth self-attention mechanism or *head* can be written as:

$$\mathbf{Sa}_h[\mathbf{X}] = \mathbf{V}_h \cdot \mathbf{Softmax}\left[\frac{\mathbf{K}_h^T\mathbf{Q}_h}{\sqrt{D_q}}\right], \tag{12.11}$$

where we have different parameters $\{\boldsymbol{\beta}_{vh}, \mathbf{\Omega}_{vh}\}$, $\{\boldsymbol{\beta}_{qh}, \mathbf{\Omega}_{qh}\}$, and $\{\boldsymbol{\beta}_{kh}, \mathbf{\Omega}_{kh}\}$ for each head. Typically, if the dimension of the inputs $\mathbf{x}_m$ is D and there are H heads, the values, queries, and keys will all be of size D/H, as this allows for an efficient implementation. The outputs of these self-attention mechanisms are vertically concatenated, and another linear transform $\mathbf{\Omega}_c$ is applied to combine them (figure 12.6):

Problem 12.5

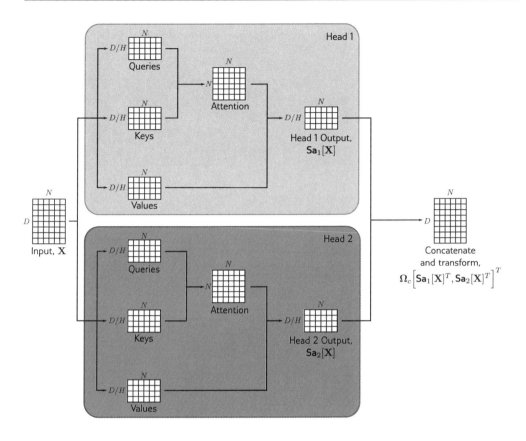

Figure 12.6 Multi-head self-attention. Self-attention occurs in parallel across multiple "heads." Each has its own queries, keys, and values. Here two heads are depicted, in the cyan and orange boxes, respectively. The outputs are vertically concatenated, and another linear transformation $\mathbf{\Omega}_c$ is used to recombine them.

$$\mathbf{MhSa}[\mathbf{X}] = \mathbf{\Omega}_c \Big[\mathbf{Sa}_1[\mathbf{X}]^T, \mathbf{Sa}_2[\mathbf{X}]^T, \dots, \mathbf{Sa}_H[\mathbf{X}]^T \Big]^T. \tag{12.12}$$

Multiple heads seem to be necessary to make self-attention work well. It has been speculated that they make the self-attention network more robust to bad initializations.

Notebook 12.2
Multi-head
self-attention

12.4 Transformer layers

Self-attention is just one part of a larger *transformer* layer. This consists of a multi-head self-attention unit (which allows the word representations to interact with each other)

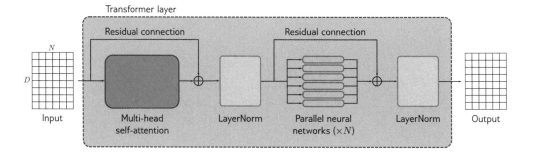

Figure 12.7 Transformer layer. The input consists of a $D \times N$ matrix containing the D-dimensional word embeddings for each of the N input tokens. The output is a matrix of the same size. The transformer layer consists of a series of operations. First, there is a multi-head attention block, allowing the word embeddings to interact with one another. This forms the processing of a residual block, so the inputs are added back to the output. Second, a LayerNorm operation is applied. Third, there is a second residual layer where the same fully connected neural network is applied separately to each of the N word representations (columns). Finally, LayerNorm is applied again.

followed by a fully connected network $\mathbf{mlp}[\mathbf{x}_\bullet]$ (that operates separately on each word). Both units are residual networks (i.e., their output is added back to the original input). In addition, it is typical to add a LayerNorm operation after both the self-attention and fully connected networks. This is similar to BatchNorm but uses statistics across the tokens within a single input sequence to perform the normalization (section 11.4 and figure 11.14). The complete layer can be described by the following series of operations (figure 12.7):

$$
\begin{aligned}
\mathbf{X} &\leftarrow \mathbf{X} + \mathbf{MhSa}[\mathbf{X}] \\
\mathbf{X} &\leftarrow \mathbf{LayerNorm}[\mathbf{X}] \\
\mathbf{x}_n &\leftarrow \mathbf{x}_n + \mathbf{mlp}[\mathbf{x}_n] \qquad\qquad \forall\, n \in \{1, \ldots, N\} \\
\mathbf{X} &\leftarrow \mathbf{LayerNorm}[\mathbf{X}],
\end{aligned}
\tag{12.13}
$$

where the column vectors $\mathbf{x}_n$ are separately taken from the full data matrix $\mathbf{X}$. In a real network, the data passes through a series of these transformer layers.

12.5 Transformers for natural language processing

The previous section described the transformer layer. This section describes how it is used in natural language processing (NLP) tasks. A typical NLP pipeline starts with a *tokenizer* that splits the text into words or word fragments. Then each of these tokens

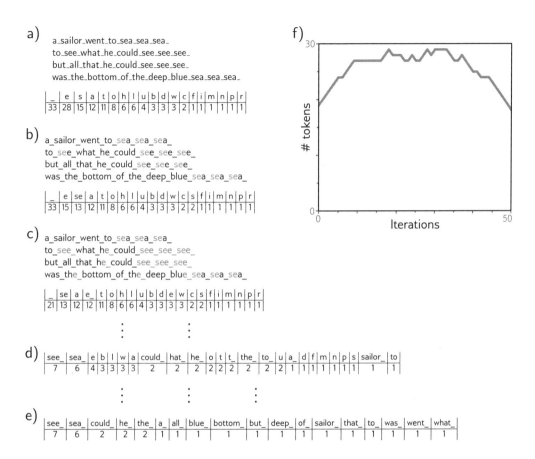

Figure 12.8 Sub-word tokenization. a) A passage of text from a nursery rhyme. The tokens are initially just the characters and whitespace (represented by an underscore), and their frequencies are displayed in the table. b) At each iteration, the sub-word tokenizer looks for the most commonly occurring adjacent pair of tokens (in this case, se) and merges them. This creates a new token and decreases the counts for the original tokens s and e. c) At the second iteration, the algorithm merges e and the whitespace character_. Note that the last character of the first token to be merged cannot be whitespace, which prevents merging across words. d) After 22 iterations, the tokens consist of a mix of letters, word fragments, and commonly occurring words. e) If we continue this process indefinitely, the tokens eventually represent the full words. f) Over time, the number of tokens increases as we add word fragments to the letters and then decreases again as we merge these fragments. In a real situation, there would be a very large number of words, and the algorithm would terminate when the vocabulary size (number of tokens) reached a predetermined value. Punctuation and capital letters would also be treated as separate input characters.

is mapped to a learned embedding. These embeddings are passed through a series of transformer layers. We now consider each of these stages in turn.

12.5.1 Tokenization

A text processing pipeline begins with a *tokenizer*. This splits the text into smaller constituent units (tokens) from a *vocabulary* of possible tokens. In the discussion above, we have implied that these tokens represent words, but there are several difficulties.

- Inevitably, some words (e.g., names) will not be in the vocabulary.
- It's unclear how to handle punctuation, but this is important. If a sentence ends in a question mark, we must encode this information.
- The vocabulary would need different tokens for versions of the same word with different suffixes (e.g., walk, walks, walked, walking), and there is no way to clarify that these variations are related.

One approach would be to use letters and punctuation marks as the vocabulary, but this would mean splitting text into very small parts and requiring the subsequent network to re-learn the relations between them.

Notebook 12.3
Tokenization

In practice, a compromise between letters and full words is used, and the final vocabulary includes both common words and word fragments from which larger and less frequent words can be composed. The vocabulary is computed using a *sub-word tokenizer* such as *byte pair encoding* (figure 12.8) that greedily merges commonly occurring sub-strings based on their frequency.

12.5.2 Embeddings

Each token in the vocabulary $\mathcal{V}$ is mapped to a unique *word embedding*, and the embeddings for the whole vocabulary are stored in a matrix $\mathbf{\Omega}_e \in \mathbb{R}^{D \times |\mathcal{V}|}$. To accomplish this, the N input tokens are first encoded in the matrix $\mathbf{T} \in \mathbb{R}^{|\mathcal{V}| \times N}$, where the nth column corresponds to the nth token and is a $|\mathcal{V}| \times 1$ *one-hot vector* (i.e., a vector where every entry is zero except for the entry corresponding to the token, which is set to one). The input embeddings are computed as $\mathbf{X} = \mathbf{\Omega}_e \mathbf{T}$, and $\mathbf{\Omega}_e$ is learned like any other network parameter (figure 12.9). A typical embedding size D is 1024, and a typical total vocabulary size $|\mathcal{V}|$ is 30,000, so even before the main network, there are many parameters in $\mathbf{\Omega}_e$ to learn.

12.5.3 Transformer model

Finally, the embedding matrix $\mathbf{X}$ representing the text is passed through a series of K transformer layers, called a *transformer model*. There are three types of transformer models. An *encoder* transforms the text embeddings into a representation that can support a variety of tasks. A *decoder* predicts the next token to continue the input

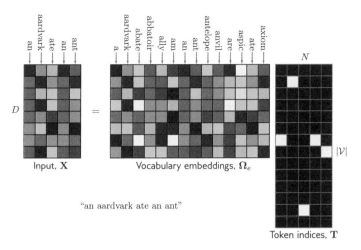

Figure 12.9 The input embedding matrix $\mathbf{X} \in \mathbb{R}^{D \times N}$ contains N embeddings of length D and is created by multiplying a matrix $\mathbf{\Omega}_e$ containing the embeddings for the entire vocabulary with a matrix containing one-hot vectors in its columns that correspond to the word or sub-word indices. The vocabulary matrix $\mathbf{\Omega}_e$ is considered a parameter of the model and is learned along with the other parameters. Note that the two embeddings for the word an in $\mathbf{X}$ are the same.

text. *Encoder-decoders* are used in *sequence-to-sequence tasks*, where one text string is converted into another (e.g., machine translation). These variations are described in sections 12.6–12.8, respectively.

12.6 Encoder model example: BERT

BERT is an encoder model that uses a vocabulary of 30,000 tokens. Input tokens are converted to 1024-dimensional word embeddings and passed through 24 transformer layers. Each contains a self-attention mechanism with 16 heads. The queries, keys, and values for each head are of dimension 64 (i.e., the matrices $\mathbf{\Omega}_{vh}, \mathbf{\Omega}_{qh}, \mathbf{\Omega}_{kh}$ are 1024×64). The dimension of the single hidden layer in the fully connected networks is 4096. The total number of parameters is ~ 340 million. When BERT was introduced, this was considered large, but it is now much smaller than state-of-the-art models.

Encoder models like BERT exploit *transfer learning* (section 9.3.6). During *pre-training*, the parameters of the transformer architecture are learned using *self-supervision* from a large corpus of text. The goal here is for the model to learn general information about the statistics of language. In the *fine-tuning stage*, the resulting network is adapted to solve a particular task using a smaller body of supervised training data.

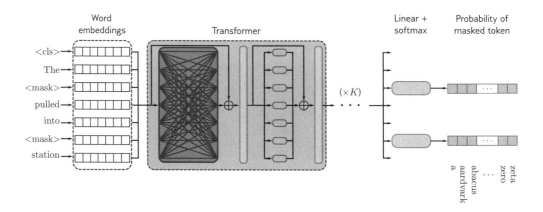

Figure 12.10 Pre-training for BERT-like encoder. The input tokens (and a special <cls> token denoting the start of the sequence) are converted to word embeddings. Here, these are represented as rows rather than columns, so the box labeled "word embeddings" is $\mathbf{X}^T$. These embeddings are passed through a series of transformer layers (orange connections indicate that every token attends to every other token in these layers) to create a set of output embeddings. A small fraction of the input tokens are randomly replaced with a generic <mask> token. In pre-training, the goal is to predict the missing word from the associated output embedding. As such, the output embeddings are passed through a softmax function, and the multiclass classification loss (section 5.24) is used. This task has the advantage that it uses both the left and right context to predict the missing word but has the disadvantage that it does not make efficient use of data; here, seven tokens need to be processed to add two terms to the loss function.

12.6.1 Pre-training

In the pre-training stage, the network is trained using self-supervision. This allows the use of enormous amounts of data without the need for manual labels. For BERT, the self-supervision task consists of predicting missing words from sentences from a large internet corpus (figure 12.10).[1] During training, the maximum input length is 512 tokens, and the batch size is 256. The system is trained for a million steps, corresponding to roughly 50 epochs of the 3.3-billion word corpus.

Predicting missing words forces the transformer network to understand some syntax. For example, it might learn that the adjective red is often found before nouns like house or car but never before a verb like shout. It also allows the model to learn superficial *common sense* about the world. For example, after training, the model will assign a higher probability to the missing word train in the sentence The <mask> pulled into the station than it would to the word peanut. However, the degree of "understanding" this type of model can ever have is limited.

Problem 12.6

---

[1]BERT also uses a secondary task that predicts whether two sentences were originally adjacent in the text or not, but this only marginally improves performance.

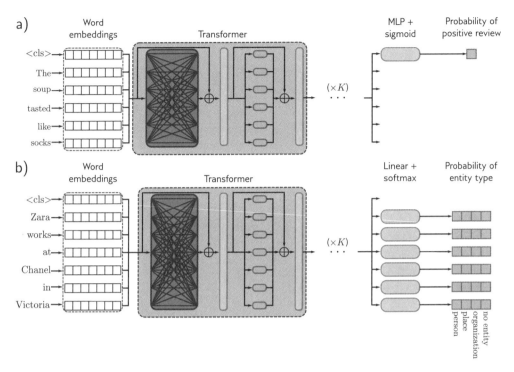

Figure 12.11 After pre-training, the encoder is fine-tuned using manually labeled data to solve a particular task. Usually, a linear transformation or a multi-layer perceptron (MLP) is appended to the encoder to produce whatever output is required. a) Example text classification task. In this sentiment classification task, the <cls> token embedding is used to predict the probability that the review is positive. b) Example word classification task. In this named entity recognition problem, the embedding for each word is used to predict whether the word corresponds to a person, place, or organization, or is not an entity.

12.6.2 Fine-tuning

In the fine-tuning stage, the model parameters are adjusted to specialize the network to a particular task. An extra layer is appended onto the transformer network to convert the output vectors to the desired output format. Examples include:

Text classification: In BERT, a special token known as the classification or <cls> token is placed at the start of each string during pre-training. For text classification tasks like *sentiment analysis* (in which the passage is labeled as having a positive or negative emotional tone), the vector associated with the <cls> token is mapped to a single number and passed through a logistic sigmoid (figure 12.11a). This contributes to a standard binary cross-entropy loss (section 5.4).

Word classification: The goal of *named entity recognition* is to classify each word as an entity type (e.g., person, place, organization, or no-entity). To this end, each input embedding $\mathbf{x}_n$ is mapped to an $E \times 1$ vector where the E entries correspond to the E entity types. This is passed through a softmax function to create probabilities for each class, which contribute to a multiclass cross-entropy loss (figure 12.11b).

Text span prediction: In the SQuAD 1.1 question answering task, the question and a passage from Wikipedia containing the answer are concatenated and tokenized. BERT is then used to predict the text span in the passage that contains the answer. Each token maps to two numbers indicating how likely it is that the text span begins and ends at this location. The resulting two sets of numbers are put through two softmax functions. The likelihood of any text span being the answer can be derived by combining the probability of starting and ending at the appropriate places.

12.7   Decoder model example: GPT3

This section presents a high-level description of GPT3, an example of a decoder model. The basic architecture is extremely similar to the encoder model and comprises a series of transformer layers that operate on learned word embeddings. However, the goal is different. The encoder aimed to build a representation of the text that could be fine-tuned to solve a variety of more specific NLP tasks. Conversely, the decoder has one purpose: to generate the next token in a sequence. It can generate a coherent text passage by feeding the extended sequence back into the model.

12.7.1   Language modeling

GPT3 constructs an autoregressive language model. This is easiest to understand with a concrete example. Consider the sentence It takes great courage to let yourself appear weak. For simplicity, let's assume that the tokens are the full words. The probability of the full sentence is:

$$
\begin{aligned}
Pr(\text{It takes great courage to let yourself appear weak}) \quad =& \\
Pr(\text{It}) \times Pr(\text{takes}|\text{It}) \times Pr(\text{great}|\text{It takes}) \times Pr(\text{courage}|\text{It takes great}) \times& \\
Pr(\text{to}|\text{It takes great courage}) \times Pr(\text{let}|\text{It takes great courage to}) \times& \\
Pr(\text{yourself}|\text{It takes great courage to let}) \times& \\
Pr(\text{appear}|\text{It takes great courage to let yourself}) \times& \\
Pr(\text{weak}|\text{It takes great courage to let yourself appear}).&
\end{aligned}
\tag{12.14}
$$

More formally, an autoregressive model factors the joint probability $Pr(t_1, t_2, \dots, t_N)$ of the N observed tokens into an autoregressive sequence:

$$Pr(t_1, t_2, \ldots, t_N) = Pr(t_1) \prod_{n=2}^{N} Pr(t_n | t_1, \ldots, t_{n-1}). \qquad (12.15)$$

The autoregressive formulation demonstrates the connection between maximizing the log probability of the tokens in the loss function and the next token prediction task.

12.7.2   Masked self-attention

To train a decoder, we maximize the log probability of the input text under the autoregressive model. Ideally, we would pass in the whole sentence and compute all the log probabilities and gradients simultaneously. However, this poses a problem; if we pass in the full sentence, the term computing $\log[Pr(\text{great}|\text{It takes})]$ has access to both the answer great and the right context courage to let yourself appear weak. Hence, the system can cheat rather than learn to predict the following words and will not train properly.

Fortunately, the tokens only interact in the self-attention layers in a transformer network. Hence, the problem can be resolved by ensuring that the attention to the answer and the right context is zero. This can be achieved by setting the corresponding dot products in the self-attention computation (equation 12.5) to negative infinity before they are passed through the **softmax**[•] function. This is known as *masked self-attention*. The effect is to make the weight of all the upward-angled arrows in figure 12.1 zero.

The entire decoder network operates as follows. The input text is tokenized, and the tokens are converted to embeddings. The embeddings are passed into the transformer network, but now the transformer layers use masked self-attention so that they can only attend to the current and previous tokens. Each of the output embeddings can be thought of as representing a partial sentence, and for each, the goal is to predict the next token in the sequence. Consequently, after the transformer layers, a linear layer maps each word embedding to the size of the vocabulary, followed by a **softmax**[•] function that converts these values to probabilities. During training, we aim to maximize the sum of the log probabilities of the next token in the ground truth sequence at every position using a standard multiclass cross-entropy loss (figure 12.12).

12.7.3   Generating text from a decoder

The autoregressive language model is the first example of a *generative model* discussed in this book. Since it defines a probability model over text sequences, it can be used to sample new examples of plausible text. To generate from the model, we start with an input sequence of text (which might be just a special <start> token indicating the beginning of the sequence) and feed this into the network, which then outputs the probabilities over possible subsequent tokens. We can then either pick the most likely token or sample from this probability distribution. The new extended sequence can be fed back into the decoder network that outputs the probability distribution over the next token. By repeating this process, we can generate large bodies of text. The computation can be made quite efficient as prior embeddings do not depend on subsequent ones due to

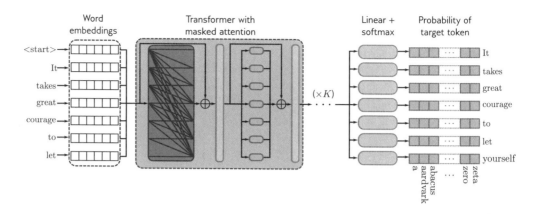

Figure 12.12 Training GPT3-type decoder network. The tokens are mapped to word embeddings with a special <start> token at the beginning of the sequence. The embeddings are passed through a series of transformer layers that use masked self-attention. Here, each position in the sentence can only attend to its own embedding and those of tokens earlier in the sequence (orange connections). The goal at each position is to maximize the probability of the following ground truth token in the sequence. In other words, at position one, we want to maximize the probability of the token It; at position two, we want to maximize the probability of the token takes; and so on. Masked self-attention ensures the system cannot cheat by looking at subsequent inputs. The autoregressive task has the advantage of making efficient use of the data since every word contributes a term to the loss function. However, it only exploits the left context of each word.

Problem 12.7

Notebook 12.4
Decoding
strategies

the masked self-attention. Hence, much of the earlier computation can be recycled as we generate subsequent tokens.

In practice, many strategies can make the output text more coherent. For example, *beam search* keeps track of multiple possible sentence completions to find the overall most likely (which is not necessarily found by greedily choosing the most likely next word at each step). *Top-K sampling* randomly draws the next word from only the top-K most likely possibilities to prevent the system from accidentally choosing from the long tail of low-probability tokens and leading to an unnecessary linguistic dead end.

12.7.4 GPT3 and few-shot learning

Large language models like GPT3 apply these ideas on a massive scale. In GPT3, the sequence lengths are 2048 tokens long, and the total batch size is 3.2 million tokens. There are 96 transformer layers (some of which implement a sparse version of attention), each processing a word embedding of size 12288. There are 96 heads in the self-attention layers, and the value, query, and key dimension is 128. It is trained with 300 billion tokens and contains 175 billion parameters.

Here's an example of completing text from the GPT3 model where the text provided to the model is in orange, and the generated text is in cyan:

Understanding Deep Learning is a new textbook from MIT Press by Simon Prince that's designed to offer an accessible, broad introduction to the field. Deep learning is a branch of machine learning that is concerned with algorithms that learn from data that is unstructured or unlabeled. The book is divided into four sections:

1. Introduction to deep learning

2. Deep learning architecture

3. Deep learning algorithms

4. Applications of deep learning

The first section offers an introduction to deep learning, including its history and origins. The second section covers deep learning architecture, discussing various types of neural networks and their applications. The third section dives into deep learning algorithms, including supervised and unsupervised learning, reinforcement learning, and more. The fourth section applies deep learning to various domains, such as computer vision, natural language processing, and robotics.

This continuation is plausible, albeit only partially accurate.

One surprising property of learning models on this scale is that they can perform many tasks without fine-tuning. If we provide several examples of correct question/answer pairs and then another question, they often answer the final question correctly by completing the sequence. One example is correcting English grammar:

Poor English input: I eated the purple berries.
Good English output: I ate the purple berries.
Poor English input: Thank you for picking me as your designer. I'd appreciate it.
Good English output: Thank you for choosing me as your designer. I appreciate it.
Poor English input: The mentioned changes have done. or I did the alteration that you requested. or I changed things you wanted and did the modifications.
Good English output: The requested changes have been made. or I made the alteration that you requested. or I changed things you wanted and made the modifications.
Poor English input: I'd be more than happy to work with you in another project.
Good English output: I'd be more than happy to work with you on another project.

(result from Brown et al., 2020)

Here, the text containing the paired examples in orange was provided as context for GPT3, and the system then generated the correct answer in cyan. This phenomenon extends to many situations, including generating code snippets based on natural language descriptions, arithmetic, translating between languages, and answering questions about text passages. Consequently, it is argued that enormous language models are *few-shot learners*; they can learn to do novel tasks based on just a few examples. However, performance is erratic in practice, and the extent to which it is extrapolating from learned examples rather than merely interpolating or copying verbatim is unclear.

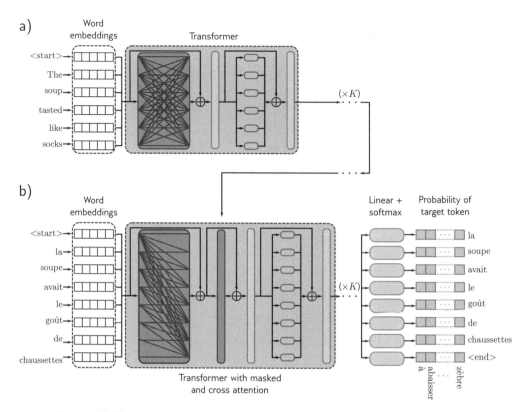

Figure 12.13 Encoder-decoder architecture. Two sentences are passed to the system with the goal of translating the first into the second. a) The first sentence is passed through a standard encoder. b) The second sentence is passed through a decoder that uses masked self-attention but also attends to the output embeddings of the encoder using cross-attention (orange rectangle). The loss function is the same as for the decoder model; we want to maximize the probability of the next word in the output sequence.

12.8 Encoder-decoder model example: machine translation

Translation between languages is an example of a *sequence-to-sequence* task. This requires an encoder (to compute a good representation of the source sentence) and a decoder (to generate the sentence in the target language). This task can be tackled using an *encoder-decoder* model.

Consider translating from English to French. The encoder receives the sentence in English and processes it through a series of transformer layers to create an output representation for each token. During training, the decoder receives the ground truth translation in French and passes it through a series of transformer layers that use masked self-attention and predict the following word at each position. However, the decoder layers also attend to the output of the encoder. Consequently, each French output word is

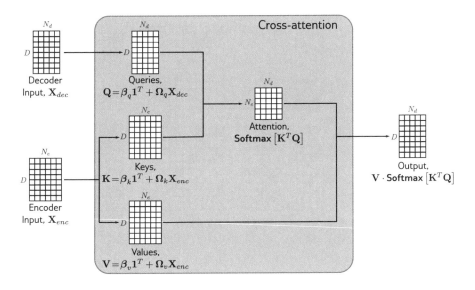

Figure 12.14 Cross-attention. The flow of computation is the same as in standard self-attention. However, the queries are calculated from the decoder embeddings $\mathbf{X}_{dec}$, and the keys and values from the encoder embeddings $\mathbf{X}_{enc}$. In the context of translation, the encoder contains information about the source language, and the decoder contains information about the target language statistics.

conditioned on the previous output words *and* the source English sentence (figure 12.13).

This is achieved by modifying the transformer layers in the decoder. Originally, these consisted of a masked self-attention layer followed by a neural network applied individually to each embedding (figure 12.12). A new self-attention layer is added between these two components, in which the decoder embeddings attend to the encoder embeddings. This uses a version of self-attention known as *encoder-decoder attention* or *cross-attention*, where the queries are computed from the decoder embeddings and the keys and values from the encoder embeddings (figure 12.14).

12.9 Transformers for long sequences

Since each token in a transformer encoder model interacts with every other token, the computational complexity scales quadratically with the length of the sequence. For a decoder model, each token only interacts with previous tokens, so there are roughly half the number of interactions, but the complexity still scales quadratically. These relationships can be visualized as interaction matrices (figure 12.15a–b).

This quadratic increase in the amount of computation ultimately limits the length of sequences that can be used. Many methods have been developed to extend the trans-

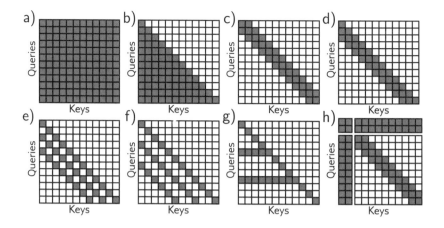

Figure 12.15 Interaction matrices for self-attention. a) In an encoder, every token interacts with every other token, and computation expands quadratically with the number of tokens. b) In a decoder, each token only interacts with the previous tokens, but complexity is still quadratic. c) Complexity can be reduced by using a convolutional structure (encoder case). d) Convolutional structure for decoder case. e–f) Convolutional structure with dilation rate of two and three (decoder case). g) Another strategy is to allow selected tokens to interact with all the other tokens (encoder case) or all the previous tokens (decoder case pictured). h) Alternatively, global tokens can be introduced (left two columns and top two rows). These interact with all of the tokens as well as with each other.

former to cope with longer sequences. One approach is to prune the self-attention interactions or, equivalently, to sparsify the interaction matrix (figures 12.15c-h). For example, this can be restricted to a convolutional structure so that each token only interacts with a few neighboring tokens. Across multiple layers, tokens still interact at larger distances as the receptive field expands. As for convolution in images, the kernel can vary in size and dilation rate.

A pure convolutional approach requires many layers to integrate information over large distances. One way to speed up this process is to allow select tokens (perhaps at the start of every sentence) to attend to all other tokens (encoder model) or all previous tokens (decoder model). A similar idea is to have a small number of global tokens that connect to all the other tokens and themselves. Like the <cls> token, these do not represent any word but serve to provide long-distance connections.

12.10 Transformers for images

Transformers were initially developed for text data. Their enormous success in this area led to experimentation on images. This was not obviously a promising idea for two reasons. First, there are many more pixels in an image than words in a sentence, so the quadratic complexity of self-attention poses a practical bottleneck. Second, convolutional nets have a good inductive bias because each layer is equivariant to spatial translation, and they take into account the 2D structure of the image. However, this must be learned in a transformer network.

Regardless of these apparent disadvantages, transformer networks for images have now eclipsed the performance of convolutional networks for image classification and other tasks. This is partly because of the enormous scale at which they can be constructed and the large amounts of data that can be used to pre-train the networks. This section describes transformer models for images.

2.10.1 ImageGPT

ImageGPT is a transformer decoder; it builds an autoregressive model of image pixels that ingests a partial image and predicts the subsequent pixel value. The quadratic complexity of the transformer network means that the largest model (which contained 6.8 billion parameters) could still only operate on 64×64 images. Moreover, to make this tractable, the original 24-bit RGB color space had to be quantized into a nine-bit color space, so the system ingests (and predicts) one of 512 possible tokens at each position.

Images are naturally 2D objects, but ImageGPT simply learns a different positional encoding at each pixel. Hence it must learn that each pixel has a close relationship with its preceding neighbors and also with nearby pixels in the row above. Figure 12.16 shows example generation results.

The internal representation of this decoder was used as a basis for image classification. The final pixel embeddings are averaged, and a linear layer maps these to activations which are passed through a softmax layer to predict class probabilities. The system is pre-trained on a large corpus of web images and then fine-tuned on the ImageNet database resized to 48×48 pixels using a loss function that contains both a cross-entropy term for image classification and a generative loss term for predicting the pixels. Despite using a large amount of external training data, the system achieved only a 27.4% top-1 error rate on ImageNet (figure 10.15). This was less than convolutional architectures of the time (see figure 10.21) but is still impressive given the small input image size; unsurprisingly, it fails to classify images where the target object is small or thin.

2.10.2 Vision Transformer (ViT)

The *Vision Transformer* tackled the problem of image resolution by dividing the image into 16×16 patches (figure 12.17). Each patch is mapped to a lower dimension via a learned linear transformation, and these representations are fed into the transformer network. Once again, standard 1D positional encodings are learned.

Problem 12.8

This is an encoder model with a <cls> token (see figures 12.10–12.11). However, unlike BERT, it uses *supervised* pre-training on a large database of 303 million labeled images from 18,000 classes. The <cls> token is mapped via a final network layer to create activations that are fed into a softmax function to generate class probabilities. After pre-training, the system is applied to the final classification task by replacing this

a)   b)

Figure 12.16 ImageGPT. a) Images generated from the autoregressive ImageGPT model. The top-left pixel is drawn from the estimated empirical distribution at this position. Subsequent pixels are generated in turn, conditioned on the previous ones, working along the rows until the bottom-right of the image is reached. For each pixel, the transformer decoder generates a conditional distribution as in equation 12.15, and a sample is drawn. The extended sequence is then fed back into the network to generate the next pixel, and so on. b) Image completion. In each case, the lower half of the image is removed (top row), and ImageGPT completes the remaining part pixel by pixel (three different completions shown). Adapted from https://openai.com/blog/image-gpt/.

final layer with one that maps to the desired number of classes and is fine-tuned.

For the ImageNet benchmark, this system achieved an 11.45% top-1 error rate. However, it did not perform as well as the best contemporary convolutional networks without supervised pre-training. The strong inductive bias of convolutional networks can only be superseded by employing extremely large amounts of training data.

12.10.3 Multi-scale vision transformers

The Vision Transformer differs from convolutional architectures in that it operates on a single scale. Several transformer models that process the image at multiple scales have been proposed. Similarly to convolutional networks, these generally start with high-resolution patches and few channels and gradually decrease the resolution while simultaneously increasing the number of channels.

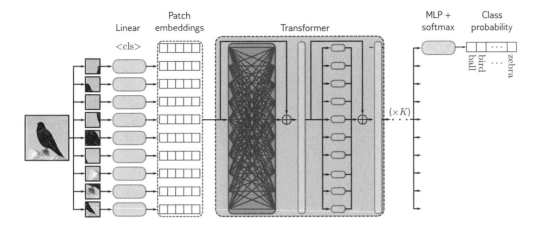

Figure 12.17 Vision transformer. The Vision Transformer (ViT) breaks the image into a grid of patches (16×16 in the original implementation). Each of these is projected via a learned linear transformation to become a patch embedding. These patch embeddings are fed into a transformer encoder network, and the <cls> token is used to predict the class probabilities.

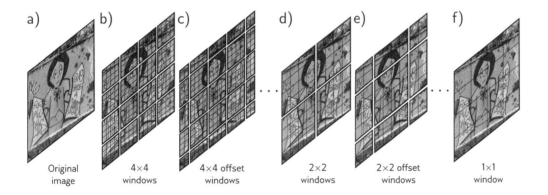

Figure 12.18 Shifted window (SWin) transformer (Liu et al., 2021c). a) Original image. b) The SWin transformer breaks the image into a grid of windows and each of these windows into a sub-grid of patches. The transformer network applies self-attention to the patches within each window independently. c) Each alternate layer shifts the windows so that the subsets of patches that interact with one another change, and information can propagate across the whole image. d) After several layers, the 2×2 blocks of patch representations are concatenated to increase the effective patch (and window) size. e) Alternate layers use shifted windows at this new lower resolution. f) Eventually, the resolution is such that there is just a single window, and the patches span the entire image.

A representative example of a multi-scale transformer is the *shifted-window* or *SWin* transformer. This is an encoder transformer that divides the image into patches and groups these patches into a grid of windows within which self-attention is applied independently (figure 12.18). These windows are shifted in adjacent transformers, so the effective receptive field at a given patch can expand beyond the window border.

The scale is reduced periodically by concatenating features from non-overlapping 2×2 patches and applying a linear transformation that maps these concatenated features to twice the original number of channels. This architecture does not have a `<cls>` token but instead averages the output features at the last layer. These are then mapped via a linear layer to the desired number of classes and passed through a softmax function to output class probabilities. At the time of writing, the most sophisticated version of this architecture achieves a 9.89% top-1 error rate on the ImageNet database.

A related idea is periodically to integrate information from across the whole image. *Dual attention vision transformers* (DaViT) alternate two types of transformers. In the first, image patches attend to one another, and the self-attention computation uses all the channels. In the second, the channels attend to one another, and the self-attention computation uses all the image patches. This architecture reaches a 9.60% top-1 error rate on ImageNet and is close to the state-of-the-art at the time of writing.

Problem 12.9

12.11   Summary

This chapter introduced self-attention and the transformer architecture. Encoder, decoder, and encoder-decoder models were then described. The transformer operates on sets of high-dimensional embeddings. It has a low computational complexity per layer, and much of the computation can be performed in parallel using the matrix form. Since every input embedding interacts with every other, it can describe long-range dependencies in text. Ultimately, the computation scales quadratically with the sequence length; one approach to reducing the complexity is sparsifying the interaction matrix.

The training of transformers with very large unlabeled datasets is the first example of *unsupervised learning* (learning without labels) in this book. Encoders learn a representation that can be used for other tasks by predicting missing tokens. Decoders build an autoregressive model over the inputs and are the first example of a *generative model* in this book. The generative decoders can be used to create new data examples.

Chapter 13 considers networks for processing graph data. These have connections with transformers in that the nodes of the graph attend to one another in each network layer. Chapters 14–18 return to unsupervised learning and generative models.

Notes

Natural language processing: Transformers were developed for natural language processing (NLP) tasks. This is an enormous area that deals with text analysis, categorization, generation, and manipulation. Example tasks include part of speech tagging, translation, text classification, entity recognition (people, places, companies, etc.), text summarization, question answering,

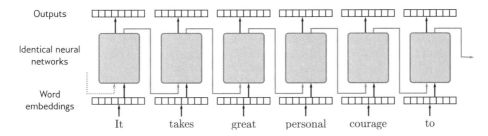

Outputs

Identical neural networks

Word embeddings

It   takes   great   personal   courage   to

Figure 12.19 Recurrent neural networks (RNNs). The word embeddings are passed sequentially through a series of identical neural networks. Each network has two outputs; one is the output embedding, and the other (orange arrows) feeds back into the next neural network, along with the next word embedding. Each output embedding contains information about the word itself and its context in the preceding sentence fragment. In principle, the final output contains information about the entire sentence and could be used to support classification tasks similarly to the <cls> token in a transformer encoder model. However, RNNs sometimes gradually "forget" about tokens that are further back in time.

word sense disambiguation, and document clustering. NLP was initially tackled by rule-based methods that exploited the structure and statistics of grammar. See Manning & Schutze (1999) and Jurafsky & Martin (2000) for early approaches.

Recurrent neural networks: Before the introduction of transformers, many state-of-the-art NLP applications used *recurrent neural networks*, or *RNNs* for short (figure 12.19). The term "recurrent" was introduced by Rumelhart et al. (1985), but the main idea dates to at least Minsky & Papert (1969). RNNs ingest a sequence of inputs (words in NLP) one at a time. At each step, the network receives both the new input and a hidden representation computed from the previous time step (the recurrent connection). The final output contains information about the whole input. This representation can then support NLP tasks like classification or translation. They have also been used in a decoding context in which generated tokens are fed back into the model to form the next input to the sequence. For example, the PixelRNN (Van den Oord et al., 2016c) used RNNs to build an autoregressive model of images.

From RNNs to transformers: One of the problems with RNNs is that they can forget information that is further back in the sequence. More sophisticated versions of this architecture, such as *long short-term memory networks* or *LSTMs* (Hochreiter & Schmidhuber, 1997b) and *gated recurrent units* or *GRUs* (Cho et al., 2014; Chung et al., 2014) partially addressed this problem. However, in machine translation, the idea emerged that all of the intermediate representations in the RNN could be exploited to produce the output sentence. Moreover, certain output words should *attend* more to certain input words according to their relation (Bahdanau et al., 2015). This ultimately led to dispensing with the recurrent structure and replacing it with the encoder-decoder transformer (Vaswani et al., 2017). Here input tokens attend to one another (self-attention), output tokens attend to those earlier in the sequence (masked self-attention), and output tokens also attend to the input tokens (cross-attention). A formal algorithmic description of the transformer can be found in Phuong & Hutter (2022), and a survey of work can be found in Lin et al. (2022). The literature should be approached with caution, as many enhancements to transformers do not make meaningful performance improvements when carefully assessed in controlled experiments (Narang et al., 2021).

Applications: Models based on self-attention and/or the transformer architecture have been applied to text sequences (Vaswani et al., 2017), image patches (Dosovitskiy et al., 2021), protein sequences (Rives et al., 2021), graphs (Veličković et al., 2019), database schema (Xu et al., 2021b), speech (Wang et al., 2020c), mathematical integration when formulated as a translation problem (Lample & Charton, 2020), and time series (Wu et al., 2020b). However, their most celebrated successes have been in building language models and, more recently, as a replacement for convolutional networks in computer vision.

Large language models: Vaswani et al. (2017) targeted translation tasks, but transformers are now more usually used to build either pure encoder or pure decoder models, the most famous of which are BERT (Devlin et al., 2019) and GPT2/GPT3 (Radford et al., 2019; Brown et al., 2020), respectively. These models are usually tested against benchmarks like GLUE (Wang et al., 2019b), which includes the SQuAD question-answering task (Rajpurkar et al., 2016) described in section 12.6.2, SuperGLUE (Wang et al., 2019a) and BIG-bench (Srivastava et al., 2022), which combine many NLP tasks to create an aggregate score for measuring language ability. Decoder models are generally not fine-tuned for these tasks but can perform well anyway when given a few examples of questions and answers and asked to complete the text from the next question. This is referred to as *few-shot learning* (Brown et al., 2020).

Since GPT3, many decoder language models have been released with steady improvement in few-shot results. These include GLaM (Du et al., 2022), Gopher (Rae et al., 2021), Chinchilla (Hoffmann et al., 2023), Megatron-Turing NLG (Smith et al., 2022), and LaMDa (Thoppilan et al., 2022). Most of the performance improvement is attributable to increased model size, using sparsely activated modules, and exploiting larger datasets. At the time of writing, the most recent model is PaLM (Chowdhery et al., 2022), which has 540 billion parameters and was trained on 780 billion tokens across 6144 processors. Interestingly, since text is highly compressible, this model has more than enough capacity to memorize the entire training dataset. This is true for many language models. Many bold statements have been made about how large language models exceed human performance. This is probably true for some tasks, but such statements should be treated with caution (see Ribeiro et al.,2021; McCoy et al., 2019; Bowman & Dahl, 2021; and Dehghani et al., 2021).

These models have considerable world knowledge. For example, in section 12.7.4, the model knows key facts about deep learning, including that it is a type of machine learning with associated algorithms and applications. Indeed, one such model has been mistakenly identified as being sentient (Clark, 2022). However, there are persuasive arguments that the degree of "understanding" this type of model can ever have is limited (Bender & Koller, 2020).

Tokenizers: Schuster & Nakajima (2012) and Sennrich et al. (2015) introduced *WordPiece* and *byte pair encoding* (*BPE*), respectively. Both methods greedily merge pairs of tokens based on their frequency of adjacency (figure 12.8), with the main difference being how the initial tokens are chosen. For example, in BPE, the initial tokens are characters or punctuation with a special token to denote whitespace. The merges cannot occur over the whitespace. As the algorithm proceeds, new tokens are formed by combining characters recursively so that sub-word and word tokens emerge. The unigram language model (Kudo, 2018) generates several possible candidate merges and chooses the best one based on the likelihood in a language model. Provilkov et al. (2020) develop BPE dropout, which generates the candidates more efficiently by introducing randomness into the process of counting frequencies. Versions of both byte pair encoding and the unigram language model are included in the SentencePiece library (Kudo & Richardson, 2018), which works directly on Unicode characters and can work with any language. He et al. (2020) introduce a method that treats the sub-word segmentation as a latent variable that should be marginalized out for learning and inference.

Decoding algorithms: Transformer decoder models take a body of text and return a probability over the next token. This is then added to the preceding text, and the model is run again. The process of choosing tokens from these probability distributions is known as *decoding*. Näive ways to do this would be to either (i) greedily choose the most likely token or (ii) choose a token randomly according to the distribution. However, neither of these methods works well in practice. In the former case, the results may be very generic, and the latter case may lead to degraded quality outputs (Holtzman et al., 2020). This is partly because, during training, the model was only exposed to sequences of ground truth tokens (known as *teacher forcing*) but sees its own output when deployed.

It is not computationally feasible to try every combination of tokens in the output sequence, but it is possible to maintain a fixed number of parallel hypotheses and choose the most likely overall sequence. This is known as *beam search*. Beam search tends to produce many similar hypotheses and has been modified to investigate more diverse sequences (Vijayakumar et al., 2016; Kulikov et al., 2018). One possible problem with random sampling is that there is a very long tail of unlikely following words that collectively have a significant probability. This has led to the development of *top-K sampling*, in which tokens are sampled from only the K most likely hypotheses (Fan et al., 2018). Top-K sampling still sometimes allows unreasonable token choices when there are only a few high-probability choices. To resolve this problem, Holtzman et al. (2020) proposed *nucleus sampling*, in which tokens are sampled from a fixed proportion of the total probability mass. El Asri & Prince (2020) discuss decoding algorithms in more depth.

Types of attention: Scaled dot-product attention (Vaswani et al., 2017) is just one of a family of attention mechanisms that includes additive attention (Bahdanau et al., 2015), multiplicative attention (Luong et al., 2015), key-value attention (Daniluk et al., 2017), and memory-compressed attention (Liu et al., 2019c). Zhai et al. (2021) constructed "attention-free" transformers, in which the tokens interact in a way that does not have quadratic complexity. Multihead attention was also introduced by Vaswani et al. (2017). Interestingly, it appears that most of the heads can be pruned after training without critically affecting the performance (Voita et al., 2019); it has been suggested that their role is to guard against bad initializations. Hu et al. (2018b) propose squeeze-and-excitation networks, attention-like mechanisms that re-weight the channels in a convolutional layer based on globally computed features.

Relationship of self-attention to other models: The self-attention computation has close connections to other models. First, it is an example of a hypernetwork (Ha et al., 2017) in that it uses one part of the network to choose the weights of another part: the attention matrix forms the weights of a sparse network layer that maps the values to the outputs (figure 12.3). The *synthesizer* (Tay et al., 2021) simplifies this idea by simply using a neural network to create each row of the attention matrix from the corresponding input. Even though the input tokens no longer interact with each other to create the attention weights, this works surprisingly well. Wu et al. (2019) present a similar system that produces an attention matrix with a convolutional structure so the tokens attend to their neighbors. The gated multi-layer perceptron (Wu et al., 2019) computes a matrix that pointwise multiplies the values and hence modifies them without mixing them. Transformers are also closely related to *fast weight memory systems*, which were the intellectual forerunners of hypernetworks (Schlag et al., 2021).

Self-attention can also be thought of as a routing mechanism (figure 12.1), and from this viewpoint, there is a connection to capsule networks (Sabour et al., 2017). These capture hierarchical relations in images; lower network levels might detect facial parts (noses, mouths), which are then combined (routed) in higher-level capsules that represent a face. However, capsule networks use *routing by agreement*. In self-attention, the inputs compete with each other for how much they contribute to a given output (via the softmax operation). In capsule networks, the outputs of the layer compete with each other for inputs from earlier layers. Once we consider self-attention as a routing network, we can question whether making this routing dynamic (i.e., dependent on the data) is necessary. The random synthesizer (Tay et al., 2021) removed the dependence of the attention matrix on the inputs entirely and either used predetermined random values or learned values. This performed surprisingly well across a variety of tasks.

Multi-head self-attention also has close connections to graph neural networks (see chapter 13), convolution (Cordonnier et al., 2020), recurrent neural networks (Choromanski et al., 2020), and memory retrieval in Hopfield networks (Ramsauer et al., 2021). For more information on the relationships between transformers and other models, consult Prince (2021a).

Positional encoding: The original transformer paper (Vaswani et al., 2017) experimented with predefining the positional encoding matrix $\mathbf{\Pi}$, and learning the positional encoding $\mathbf{\Pi}$. It might seem odd to *add* the positional encodings to the $D \times N$ data matrix $\mathbf{X}$ rather than concatenate them. However, the data dimension D is usually greater than the number of tokens N, so the positional encoding lies in a subspace. The word embeddings in $\mathbf{X}$ are learned, so the system can theoretically keep the two components in orthogonal subspaces and retrieve the positional encodings as required. The predefined embeddings chosen by Vaswani et al. (2017) were a family of sinusoidal components with two attractive properties: (i) the relative position of two embeddings is easy to recover using a linear operation and (ii) their dot product generally decreased as the distance between positions increased (see Prince, 2021a, for more details). Many systems, such as GPT3 and BERT, learn positional encodings. Wang et al. (2020a) examined the cosine similarities of the positional encodings in these models and showed that they generally decline with relative distance, although they also have a periodic component.

Much subsequent work has modified just the attention matrix so that in the scaled dot-product self-attention equation:

$$\mathbf{Sa[X]} = \mathbf{V} \cdot \mathbf{Softmax}\left[\frac{\mathbf{K}^T\mathbf{Q}}{\sqrt{D_q}}\right], \tag{12.16}$$

only the queries and keys contain position information:

$$\begin{aligned} \mathbf{V} &= \boldsymbol{\beta}_v\mathbf{1}^\mathbf{T} + \mathbf{\Omega}_v\mathbf{X} \\ \mathbf{Q} &= \boldsymbol{\beta}_q\mathbf{1}^\mathbf{T} + \mathbf{\Omega}_q(\mathbf{X} + \mathbf{\Pi}) \\ \mathbf{K} &= \boldsymbol{\beta}_k\mathbf{1}^\mathbf{T} + \mathbf{\Omega}_k(\mathbf{X} + \mathbf{\Pi}). \end{aligned} \tag{12.17}$$

This has led to the idea of multiplying out the quadratic component in the numerator of equation 12.16 and retaining only some of the terms. For example, Ke et al. (2021) decouple or *untie* the content and position information by retaining only the content-content and position-position terms and using different projection matrices $\mathbf{\Omega}_\bullet$ for each.

Another modification is to inject information directly about the relative position. This is more important than absolute position since a batch of text can start at an arbitrary place in a document. Shaw et al. (2018), Raffel et al. (2020), and Huang et al. (2020b) all developed systems where a single term was learned for each relative position offset, and the attention matrix was modified in various ways using these *relative positional encodings*. Wei et al. (2019) investigated relative positional encodings based on predefined sinusoidal embeddings rather than learned values. DeBERTa (He et al., 2021) combines these ideas; they retain only a subset of terms from the quadratic expansion, apply different projection matrices to them, and use relative positional encodings. Other work has explored sinusoidal embeddings that encode absolute and relative position information in more complex ways (Su et al., 2021).

Wang et al. (2020a) compare the performance of transformers in BERT with different positional encodings. They found that relative positional encodings perform better than absolute positional encodings, but there was little difference between using sinusoidal and learned embeddings. A survey of positional encodings can be found in Dufter et al. (2021).

Extending transformers to longer sequences: The complexity of the self-attention mechanism increases quadratically with the sequence length. Some tasks like summarization or question answering may require long inputs, so this quadratic dependence limits performance. Three lines of work have attempted to address this problem. The first decreases the size of the attention matrix, the second makes the attention sparse, and the third modifies the attention mechanism to make it more efficient.

To decrease the size of the attention matrix, Liu et al. (2018b) introduced *memory-compressed attention*. This applies strided convolution to the keys and values, which reduces the number of positions in a very similar way to downsampling in a convolutional network. Attention is now applied between weighted combinations of neighboring positions, where the weights are learned. Along similar lines, Wang et al. (2020b) observed that the quantities in the attention mechanism are often low rank in practice and developed the *LinFormer*, which projects the keys and values onto a smaller subspace before computing the attention matrix.

To make attention sparse, Liu et al. (2018b) proposed *local attention*, in which neighboring blocks of tokens only attend to one another. This creates a block diagonal interaction matrix (see figure 12.15). Information cannot pass from block to block, so such layers are typically alternated with full attention. Along the same lines, GPT3 (Brown et al., 2020) uses a convolutional interaction matrix and alternates this with full attention. Child et al. (2019) and Beltagy et al. (2020) experimented with various interaction matrices, including convolutional structures with different dilation rates but allowing some queries to interact with every other key. Ainslie et al. (2020) introduced the *extended transformer construction* (figure 12.15h), which uses a set of global embeddings that interact with every other token. This can only be done in the encoder version, or these implicitly allow the system to "look ahead." When combined with relative position encoding, this scheme requires special encodings for mapping to, from, and between these global embeddings. *BigBird* (Ainslie et al., 2020) combined global embeddings and a convolutional structure with a random sampling of possible connections. Other work has investigated learning the sparsity pattern of the attention matrix (Roy et al., 2021; Kitaev et al., 2020; Tay et al., 2020).

Finally, it has been noted that the terms in the numerator and denominator of the softmax operation that computes attention have the form $\exp[\mathbf{k}^T\mathbf{q}]$. This can be treated as a kernel function and, as such, can be expressed as the dot product $\mathbf{g}[\mathbf{k}]^T\mathbf{g}[\mathbf{q}]$ where $\mathbf{g}[\bullet]$ is a nonlinear transformation. This formulation decouples the queries and keys, making the attention computation more efficient. Unfortunately, to replicate the form of the exponential terms, the transformation $\mathbf{g}[\bullet]$ must map the inputs to the infinite space. The linear transformer (Katharopoulos et al., 2020) recognizes this and replaces the exponential term with a different similarity measure. The *Performer* (Choromanski et al., 2020) approximates this infinite mapping with a finite-dimensional one. More details about extending transformers to longer sequences can be found in Tay et al. (2023) and Prince (2021a).

Problem 12.10

Training transformers: Training transformers is challenging and requires both learning rate warm-up (Goyal et al., 2018) and Adam (Kingma & Ba, 2015). Indeed Xiong et al. (2020a) and Huang et al. (2020a) show that the gradients vanish, and the Adam updates decrease in magnitude without learning rate warm-up. Several interacting factors cause this problem. Residual connections cause the exploding gradients (figure 11.6), but normalization layers prevent this. Vaswani et al. (2017) used LayerNorm rather than BatchNorm because NLP statistics are highly variable between batches, although subsequent work has modified BatchNorm for transformers (Shen et al., 2020a). The positioning of the LayerNorm outside of the residual block causes gradients to shrink as they pass back through the network (Xiong et al., 2020a). In addition, the relative weight of the residual connections and main self-attention mechanism varies as we move through the network upon initialization (see figure 11.6c). There is the additional complication that the gradients for the query and key parameters are smaller than for the value parameters (Liu et al., 2020), which necessitates the use of Adam. These factors interact in a complex way, making training unstable and necessitating learning rate warm-up.

There have been various attempts to stabilize training, including (i) a variation of FixUp called *TFixup* (Huang et al., 2020a) that allows the LayerNorm components to be removed, (ii) changing the position of the LayerNorm components in the network (Liu et al., 2020), and (iii) re-weighting the two paths in the residual branches (Liu et al., 2020; Bachlechner et al., 2021). Xu et al. (2021b) introduced an initialization scheme called *DTFixup* that allows transformers to be trained with smaller datasets. A detailed discussion can be found in Prince (2021b).

Applications in vision: ImageGPT (Chen et al., 2020a) and the Vision Transformer (Dosovitskiy et al., 2021) were both early transformer architectures applied to images. Transformers have been used for image classification (Dosovitskiy et al., 2021; Touvron et al., 2021), object detection (Carion et al., 2020; Zhu et al., 2020b; Fang et al., 2021), semantic segmentation (Ye et al., 2019; Xie et al., 2021; Gu et al., 2022), super-resolution (Yang et al., 2020a), action recognition (Sun et al., 2019; Girdhar et al., 2019), image generation (Chen et al., 2021b; Nash et al., 2021), visual question answering (Su et al., 2019b; Tan & Bansal, 2019), inpainting (Wan et al., 2021; Zheng et al., 2021; Zhao et al., 2020b; Li et al., 2022), colorization (Kumar et al., 2021), and many other vision tasks (Khan et al., 2022; Liu et al., 2023b).

Transformers and convolutional networks: Transformers have been combined with convolutional neural networks for many tasks, including image classification (Wu et al., 2020a), object detection (Hu et al., 2018a; Carion et al., 2020), video processing (Wang et al., 2018c; Sun et al., 2019), unsupervised object discovery (Locatello et al., 2020) and various text/vision tasks (Chen et al., 2020d; Lu et al., 2019; Li et al., 2019). Transformers can outperform convolutional networks for vision tasks but usually require large quantities of data to achieve superior performance. Often, they are pre-trained on enormous datasets like JRT (Sun et al., 2017) and LAION (Schuhmann et al., 2021). The transformer doesn't have the inductive bias of convolutional networks, but by using huge amounts of data, it can surmount this disadvantage.

From pixels to video: Non-local networks (Wang et al., 2018c) were an early application of self-attention to image data. Transformers were initially applied to pixels in local neighborhoods (Parmar et al., 2018; Hu et al., 2019; Parmar et al., 2019; Zhao et al., 2020a). ImageGPT (Chen et al., 2020a) scaled this to model all pixels in a small image. The Vision Transformer (ViT) (Dosovitskiy et al., 2021) used non-overlapping patches to analyze bigger images.

Since then, many multi-scale systems have been developed, including the SWin transformer (Liu et al., 2021c), SWinV2 (Liu et al., 2022), multi-scale transformers (MViT) (Fan et al., 2021), and pyramid vision transformers (Wang et al., 2021). The Crossformer (Wang et al., 2022b) models interactions between spatial scales. Ali et al. (2021) introduced cross-covariance image transformers, in which the channels rather than spatial positions attend to one another, hence making the size of the attention matrix indifferent to the image size. The dual attention vision transformer (DaViT) was developed by Ding et al. (2022) and alternates between local spatial attention within sub-windows and spatially global attention between channels. Chu et al. (2021) similarly alternate between local attention within sub-windows and global attention by subsampling the spatial domain. Dong et al. (2022) adapt the ideas of figure 12.15, in which the interactions between elements are sparsified to the 2D image domain.

Transformers were subsequently adapted to video processing (Arnab et al., 2021; Bertasius et al., 2021; Liu et al., 2021c; Neimark et al., 2021; Patrick et al., 2021). A survey of transformers applied to video can be found in Selva et al. (2022).

Combining images and text: CLIP (Radford et al., 2021) learns a joint encoder for images and their captions using a contrastive pre-training task. The system ingests N images and their captions and produces a matrix of compatibility between images and captions. The loss function encourages the correct pairs to have a high score and the incorrect pairs to have a low score. Ramesh et al. (2021) and Ramesh et al. (2022) train a diffusion decoder to invert the CLIP image encoder for text-conditional image generation (see chapter 18).

Problems

Problem 12.1 Consider a self-attention mechanism that processes N inputs of length D to produce N outputs of the same size. How many weights and biases are used to compute the queries, keys, and values? How many attention weights $a[\bullet, \bullet]$ will there be? How many weights and biases would there be in a fully connected shallow network relating all DN inputs to all DN outputs?

Problem 12.2 Why might we want to ensure that the input to the self-attention mechanism is the same size as the output?

Problem 12.3* Show that the self-attention mechanism (equation 12.8) is equivariant to a permutation $\mathbf{XP}$ of the data $\mathbf{X}$, where $\mathbf{P}$ is a permutation matrix. In other words, show that:

$$\mathbf{Sa}[\mathbf{XP}] = \mathbf{Sa}[\mathbf{X}]\mathbf{P}. \tag{12.18}$$

Appendix B.4.4
Permutation
matrix

Problem 12.4 Consider the softmax operation:

$$y_i = \text{softmax}_i[\mathbf{z}] = \frac{\exp[z_i]}{\sum_{j=1}^{5} \exp[z_j]}, \tag{12.19}$$

in the case where there are five inputs with values: $z_1 = -3$, $z_2 = 1$, $z_3 = 100$, $z_4 = 5$, $z_5 = -1$. Compute the 25 derivatives, $\partial y_i / \partial z_j$ for all $i, j \in \{1, 2, 3, 4, 5\}$. What do you conclude?

Problem 12.5 Why is implementation more efficient if the values, queries, and keys in each of the H heads each have dimension D/H where D is the original dimension of the data?

Problem 12.6 BERT was pre-trained using two tasks. The first task requires the system to predict missing (masked) words. The second task requires the system to classify pairs of sentences as being adjacent or not in the original text. Identify whether each of these tasks is generative or contrastive (see section 9.3.6). Why do you think they used two tasks? Propose two novel contrastive tasks that could be used to pre-train a language model.

Problem 12.7 Consider adding a new token to a precomputed masked self-attention mechanism with N tokens. Describe the *extra* computation that must be done to incorporate this new token.

Problem 12.8 Computation in vision transformers expands quadratically with the number of patches. Devise two methods to reduce the computation using the principles from figure 12.15.

Problem 12.9 Consider representing an image with a grid of 16×16 patches, each represented by a patch embedding of length 512. Compare the amount of computation required in the DaViT transformer to perform attention (i) between the patches, using all of the channels, and (ii) between the channels, using all of the patches.

Problem 12.10* Attention weights are usually computed as:

$$a[\mathbf{x}_m, \mathbf{x}_n] = \text{softmax}_m \left[\mathbf{k}_\bullet^T \mathbf{q}_n \right] = \frac{\exp\left[\mathbf{k}_m^T \mathbf{q}_n\right]}{\sum_{m'=1}^{N} \exp\left[\mathbf{k}_{m'}^T \mathbf{q}_n\right]}. \tag{12.20}$$

Consider replacing $\exp\left[\mathbf{k}_m^T \mathbf{q}_n\right]$ with the dot product $\mathbf{g}[\mathbf{k}_m]^T \mathbf{g}[\mathbf{q}_n]$ where $\mathbf{g}[\bullet]$ is a nonlinear transformation. Show how this makes the computation of the attention weights more efficient.

Chapter 13

Graph neural networks

Chapter 10 described convolutional networks, which specialize in processing regular arrays of data (e.g., images). Chapter 12 described transformers, which specialize in processing sequences of variable length (e.g., text). This chapter describes *graph neural networks*. As the name suggests, these are neural architectures that process graphs (i.e., sets of nodes connected by edges).

There are three novel challenges associated with processing graphs. First, their topology is variable, and it is hard to design networks that are both sufficiently expressive and can cope with this variation. Second, graphs may be enormous; a graph representing connections between users of a social network might have a billion nodes. Third, there may only be a single monolithic graph available, so the usual protocol of training with many data examples and testing with new data is not always appropriate.

This chapter starts by presenting real-world examples of graphs. It then describes how to encode these graphs and how to formulate supervised learning problems for graphs. The algorithmic requirements for processing graphs are discussed, and these lead naturally to *graph convolutional networks*, a particular type of graph neural network.

13.1 What is a graph?

A graph is a very general structure and consists of a set of *nodes* or *vertices*, where pairs of nodes are connected by *edges* or *links*. Graphs are typically sparse; only a small subset of the possible edges are present.

Some objects in the real world naturally take the form of graphs. For example, road networks can be considered graphs where the nodes are physical locations, and the edges represent roads between them (figure 13.1a). Chemical molecules are small graphs where the nodes represent atoms, and the edges represent chemical bonds (figure 13.1b). Electrical circuits are graphs where the nodes represent components and junctions, and the edges are electrical connections (figure 13.1c).

Furthermore, many datasets can also be represented by graphs, even if this is not their obvious surface form. For example:

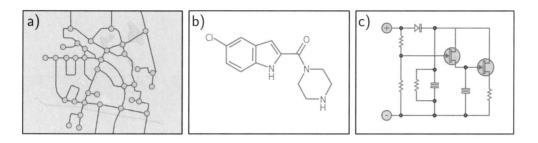

Figure 13.1 Real-world graphs. Some objects, such as a) road networks, b) molecules, and c) electrical circuits, are naturally structured as graphs.

- Social networks are graphs where nodes are people, and the edges represent friendships between them.
- The scientific literature can be viewed as a graph where the nodes are papers, and the edges represent citations.
- Wikipedia can be considered a graph where the nodes are articles, and the edges represent hyperlinks between articles.
- Computer programs can be represented as graphs where the nodes are syntax tokens (variables at different points in the program flow), and the edges represent computations involving these variables.
- Geometric point clouds can be represented as graphs. Here, each point is a node with edges connecting to other nearby points.
- Protein interactions in a cell can be expressed as graphs, where the nodes are the proteins, and there is an edge between two proteins if they interact.

In addition, a set (an unordered list) can be treated as a graph in which every member is a node and connects to every other. An image can be treated as a graph with regular topology, in which each pixel is a node with edges to the adjacent pixels.

13.1.1 Types of graphs

Graphs can be categorized in various ways. The social network in figure 13.2a contains *undirected edges*; each pair of individuals with a connection between them have mutually agreed to be friends, so there is no sense that the relationship is directional. In contrast, the citation network in figure 13.2b contains *directed edges*. Each paper cites other papers, and this relationship is inherently one-way.

Figure 13.2c depicts a *knowledge graph* that encodes a set of facts about objects by defining relations between them. Technically, this is a *directed heterogeneous multigraph*. It is heterogeneous because the nodes can represent different types of entities (e.g., people, countries, companies). It is a multigraph because there can be multiple edges of different types between any two nodes.

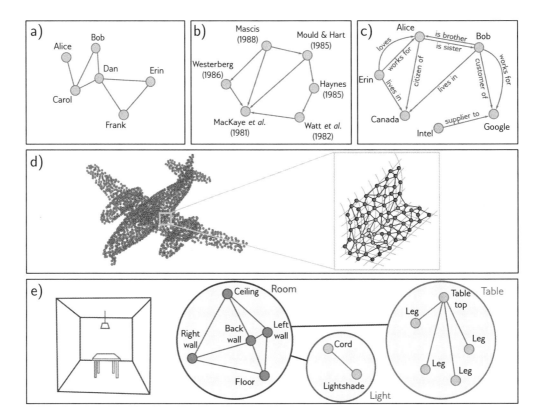

Figure 13.2 Types of graphs. a) A social network is an undirected graph; the connections between people are symmetric. b) A citation network is a directed graph; one publication cites another, so the relationship is asymmetric. c) A knowledge graph is a directed heterogeneous multigraph. The nodes are heterogeneous in that they represent different object types (people, places, companies) and multiple edges may represent different relations between each node. d) A point set can be converted to a graph by forming edges between nearby points. Each node has an associated position in 3D space, and this is termed a geometric graph (adapted from Hu et al., 2022). e) The scene on the left can be represented by a hierarchical graph. The topology of the room, table, and light are all represented by graphs. These graphs form nodes in a larger graph representing object adjacency (adapted from Fernández-Madrigal & González, 2002).

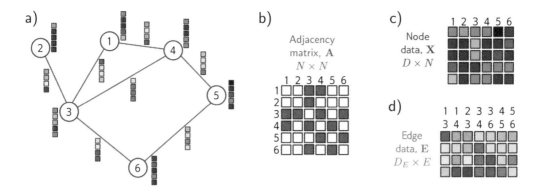

Figure 13.3 Graph representation. a) Example graph with six nodes and seven edges. Each node has an associated embedding of length five (brown vectors). Each edge has an associated embedding of length four (blue vectors). This graph can be represented by three matrices. b) The adjacency matrix is a binary matrix where element (m, n) is set to one if node m connects to node n. c) The node data matrix $\mathbf{X}$ contains the concatenated node embeddings. d) The edge data matrix $\mathbf{E}$ contains the edge embeddings.

The point set representing the airplane in figure 13.2d can be converted into a graph by connecting each point to its K nearest neighbors. The result is a *geometric graph* where each point is associated with a position in 3D space. Figure 13.2e represents a *hierarchical graph*. The table, light, and room are each described by graphs representing the adjacency of their respective components. These three graphs are themselves nodes in another graph that represents the topology of the objects in a larger model.

All types of graphs can be processed using deep learning. However, this chapter focuses on undirected graphs like the social network in figure 13.2a.

13.2 Graph representation

In addition to the graph structure itself, information is typically associated with each node. For example, in a social network, each individual might be characterized by a fixed-length vector representing their interests. Sometimes, the edges also have information attached. For example, in the road network example, each edge might be characterized by its length, number of lanes, frequency of accidents, and speed limit. The information at a node is stored in a *node embedding*, and the information at an edge is stored in an *edge embedding*.

More formally, a graph consists of a set of N nodes connected by a set of E edges. The graph can be encoded by three matrices $\mathbf{A}$, $\mathbf{X}$, and $\mathbf{E}$, representing the graph structure, node embeddings, and edge embeddings, respectively (figure 13.3).

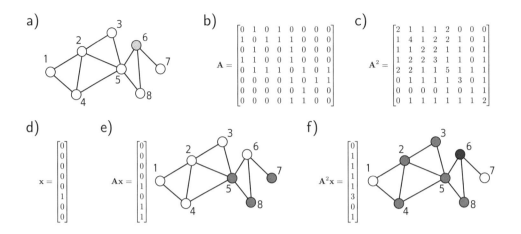

Figure 13.4 Properties of the adjacency matrix. a) Example graph. b) Position (m, n) of the adjacency matrix $\mathbf{A}$ contains the number of walks of length one from node m to node n. c) Position (m, n) of the squared adjacency matrix $\mathbf{A}^2$ contains the number of walks of length two from node n to node m. d) One hot vector representing node six, which was highlighted in panel (a). e) When we pre-multiply this vector by $\mathbf{A}$, the result contains the number of walks of length one from node six to each node; we can reach nodes five, seven, and eight in one move. f) When we pre-multiply this vector by $\mathbf{A}^2$, the resulting vector contains the number of walks of length two from node six to each node; we can reach nodes two, three, four, five, and eight in two moves, and we can return to the original node in three different ways (via nodes five, seven, and eight).

Problems 13.1–13.2

The graph structure is represented by the *adjacency matrix*, $\mathbf{A}$. This is an $N \times N$ matrix where entry (m, n) is set to one if there is an edge between nodes m and n and zero otherwise. For undirected graphs, this matrix is always symmetric. For large sparse graphs, it can be stored as a list of connections (m, n) to save memory.

The nth node has an associated node embedding $\mathbf{x}^{(n)}$ of length D. These embeddings are concatenated and stored in the $D \times N$ node data matrix $\mathbf{X}$. Similarly, the eth edge has an associated edge embedding $\mathbf{e}^{(e)}$ of length D_E. These edge embeddings are collected into the $D_E \times E$ matrix $\mathbf{E}$. For simplicity, we initially consider graphs that only have node embeddings and return to edge embeddings in section 13.9.

13.2.1 Properties of the adjacency matrix

The adjacency matrix can be used to find the neighbors of a node using linear algebra. Consider encoding the nth node as a one-hot column vector (a vector with only one non-zero entry at position n, which is set to one). When we pre-multiply this vector by the adjacency matrix, it extracts the nth column of the adjacency matrix and returns a vector with ones at the positions of the neighbors (i.e., all the places we can reach in a walk of length one from the nth node). If we repeat this procedure (i.e., pre-multiply by $\mathbf{A}$ again), the resulting vector contains the number of walks of length two from node n to every node (figures 13.4d–f).

Problems 13.3–13.4

In general, if we raise the adjacency matrix to the power of L, the entry at position (m, n) of $\mathbf{A}^L$ contains the number of unique *walks* of length L from node n to node m (figures 13.4a–c). This is not the same as the number of unique paths since it includes routes that visit the same node more than once. Nonetheless, $\mathbf{A}^L$ still contains valuable information about the graph connectivity; a non-zero entry at position (m, n) indicates that the distance from m to n must be less than or equal to L.

Notebook 13.1
Encoding
graphs

13.2.2   Permutation of node indices

Node indexing in graphs is arbitrary; permuting the node indices results in a permutation of the columns of the node data matrix $\mathbf{X}$ and a permutation of both the rows and columns of the adjacency matrix $\mathbf{A}$. However, the underlying graph is unchanged (figure 13.5). This is in contrast to images, where permuting the pixels creates a different image, and to text, where permuting the words creates a different sentence.

The operation of exchanging node indices can be expressed mathematically by a *permutation matrix*, $\mathbf{P}$. This is a matrix where exactly one entry in each row and column take the value one, and the remaining values are zero. When position (m, n) of the permutation matrix is set to one, it indicates that node m will become node n after the permutation. To map from one indexing to another, we use the operations:

Problem 13.5

$$\begin{aligned} \mathbf{X}' &= \mathbf{X}\mathbf{P} \\ \mathbf{A}' &= \mathbf{P}^T\mathbf{A}\mathbf{P}, \end{aligned} \tag{13.1}$$

where post-multiplying by $\mathbf{P}$ permutes the columns and pre-multiplying by $\mathbf{P}^T$ permutes the rows. It follows that any processing applied to the graph should also be indifferent to these permutations. Otherwise, the result will depend on the choice of node indices.

13.3   Graph neural networks, tasks, and loss functions

A graph neural network is a model that takes the node embeddings $\mathbf{X}$ and the adjacency matrix $\mathbf{A}$ as inputs and passes them through a series of K layers. The node embeddings are updated at each layer to create intermediate "hidden" representations $\mathbf{H}_k$ before finally computing output embeddings $\mathbf{H}_K$.

At the start of this network, each column of the input node embeddings $\mathbf{X}$ just contains information about the node itself. At the end, each column of the model output $\mathbf{H}_K$ includes information about the node and its context within the graph. This is similar to word embeddings passing through a transformer network. These represent words at the start, but represent the word meanings in the context of the sentence at the end.

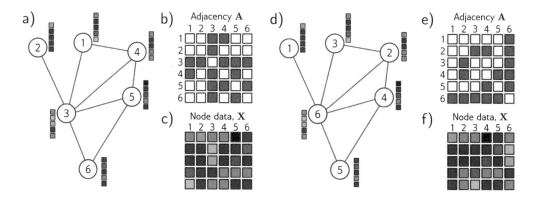

Figure 13.5 Permutation of node indices. a) Example graph, b) associated adjacency matrix and c) node embeddings. d) The same graph where the (arbitrary) order of the indices has been changed. e) The adjacency matrix and f) node matrix are now different. Consequently, any network layer that operates on the graph should be indifferent to the ordering of the nodes.

13.3.1 Tasks and loss functions

We defer discussion of graph neural network models until section 13.4 and first describe the types of problems these networks tackle and their associated loss functions. Supervised graph problems usually fall into one of three categories (figure 13.6).

Graph-level tasks: The network assigns a label or estimates one or more values from the entire graph, exploiting both the structure and node embeddings. For example, we might want to predict the temperature at which a molecule becomes liquid (a regression task) or whether a molecule is poisonous to human beings or not (a classification task).

For graph-level tasks, the output node embeddings are combined (e.g., by averaging), and the resulting vector is mapped via a linear transformation or neural network to a fixed-size vector. For regression, the mismatch between the result and the ground truth values is computed using the least squares loss. For binary classification, the output is passed through a sigmoid function, and the mismatch is calculated using the binary cross-entropy loss. Here, the probability that the graph belongs to class one might be given by:

$$Pr(y = 1|\mathbf{X}, \mathbf{A}) = \text{sig}\left[\beta_K + \boldsymbol{\omega}_K \mathbf{H}_K \mathbf{1}/N\right], \tag{13.2}$$

where the scalar β_K and $1 \times D$ vector $\boldsymbol{\omega}_K$ are learned parameters. Post-multiplying the output embedding matrix $\mathbf{H}_K$ by the column vector $\mathbf{1}$ that contains ones has the effect of summing together all the embeddings and subsequently dividing by the number of nodes N computes the average. This is known as *mean pooling* (see figure 10.11).

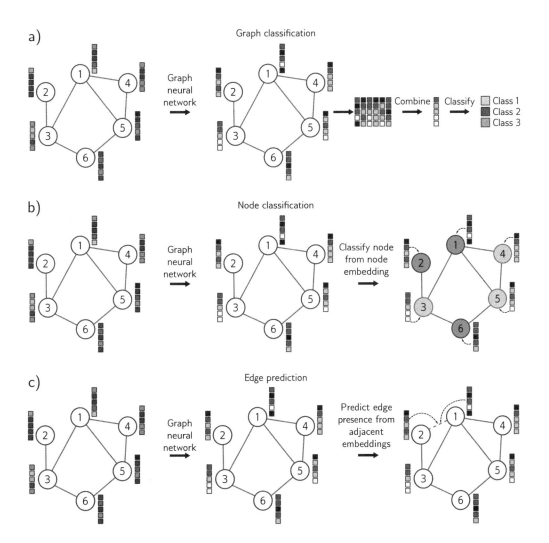

Figure 13.6 Common tasks for graphs. In each case, the input is a graph represented by its adjacency matrix and node embeddings. The graph neural network processes the node embeddings by passing them through a series of layers. The node embeddings at the last layer contain information about both the node and its context in the graph. a) Graph classification. The node embeddings are combined (e.g., by averaging) and then mapped to a fixed-size vector that is passed through a softmax function to produce class probabilities. b) Node classification. Each node embedding is used individually as the basis for classification (cyan and orange colors represent assigned node classes). c) Edge prediction. Node embeddings adjacent to the edge are combined (e.g., by taking the dot product) to compute a single number that is mapped via a sigmoid function to produce a probability that a missing edge should be present.

Node-level tasks: The network assigns a label (classification) or one or more values (regression) to each node of the graph, using both the graph structure and node embeddings. For example, given a graph constructed from a 3D point cloud similar to figure 13.2d, the goal might be to classify the nodes according to whether they belong to the wings or fuselage. Loss functions are defined in the same way as for graph-level tasks, except that now this is done independently at each node n:

$$Pr(y^{(n)} = 1|\mathbf{X}, \mathbf{A}) = \text{sig}\left[\beta_K + \boldsymbol{\omega}_K \mathbf{h}_K^{(n)}\right]. \tag{13.3}$$

Edge prediction tasks: The network predicts whether or not there should be an edge between nodes n and m. For example, in the social network setting, the network might predict whether two people know and like each other and suggest that they connect if that is the case. This is a binary classification task where the two node embeddings must be mapped to a single number representing the probability that the edge is present. One possibility is to take the dot product of the node embeddings and pass the result through a sigmoid function to create the probability:

$$Pr(y^{(mn)} = 1|\mathbf{X}, \mathbf{A}) = \text{sig}\left[\mathbf{h}^{(m)T}\mathbf{h}^{(n)}\right]. \tag{13.4}$$

13.4   Graph convolutional networks

There are many types of graph neural networks, but here we focus on *spatial-based convolutional graph neural networks*, or *GCNs* for short. These models are convolutional in that they update each node by aggregating information from nearby nodes. As such, they induce a *relational inductive bias* (i.e., a bias toward prioritizing information from neighbors). They are spatial-based because they use the original graph structure. This contrasts with *spectral-based methods*, which apply convolutions in the Fourier domain.

Each layer of the GCN is a function $\mathbf{F}[\bullet]$ with parameters $\boldsymbol{\Phi}$ that takes the node embeddings and adjacency matrix and outputs new node embeddings. The network can hence be written as:

$$
\begin{aligned}
\mathbf{H}_1 &= \mathbf{F}[\mathbf{X}, \mathbf{A}, \boldsymbol{\phi}_0] \\
\mathbf{H}_2 &= \mathbf{F}[\mathbf{H}_1, \mathbf{A}, \boldsymbol{\phi}_1] \\
\mathbf{H}_3 &= \mathbf{F}[\mathbf{H}_2, \mathbf{A}, \boldsymbol{\phi}_2] \\
\vdots\; &= \;\vdots \\
\mathbf{H}_K &= \mathbf{F}[\mathbf{H}_{K-1}, \mathbf{A}, \boldsymbol{\phi}_{K-1}],
\end{aligned}
\tag{13.5}
$$

where $\mathbf{X}$ is the input, $\mathbf{A}$ is the adjacency matrix, $\mathbf{H}_k$ contains the modified node embeddings at the kth layer, and $\boldsymbol{\phi}_k$ denotes the parameters that map from layer k to layer $k+1$.

13.4.1 Equivariance and invariance

We noted before that the indexing of the nodes in the graph is arbitrary, and any permutation of the node indices does not change the graph. It is hence imperative that any model respects this property. It follows that each layer must be equivariant (see section 10.1) with respect to permutations of the node indices. In other words, if we permute the node indices, the node embeddings at each stage will be permuted in the same way. In mathematical terms, if $\mathbf{P}$ is a permutation matrix, then we must have:

$$\mathbf{H}_{k+1}\mathbf{P} = \mathbf{F}[\mathbf{H}_k\mathbf{P}, \mathbf{P}^T\mathbf{A}\mathbf{P}, \phi_k]. \tag{13.6}$$

For node classification and edge prediction tasks, the output should also be equivariant with respect to permutations of the node indices. However, for graph-level tasks, the final layer aggregates information from across the graph, so the output is invariant to the node order. In fact, the output layer from equation 13.2 achieves this because:

Problem 13.6

$$y = \mathrm{sig}\left[\beta_K + \boldsymbol{\omega}_K\mathbf{H}_K\mathbf{1}/N\right] = \mathrm{sig}\left[\beta_K + \boldsymbol{\omega}_K\mathbf{H}_K\mathbf{P1}/N\right], \tag{13.7}$$

for any permutation matrix $\mathbf{P}$ (see problem 13.6).

This mirrors the case for images, where segmentation should be equivariant to geometric transformations, and image classification should be invariant (figure 10.1). Here, convolutional and pooling layers partially achieve this with respect to translations, but there is no known way to guarantee these properties exactly for more general transformations. However, for graphs, it is possible to define networks that ensure equivariance or invariance to permutations.

13.4.2 Parameter sharing

Chapter 10 argued applying fully connected networks to images isn't sensible because this requires the network to learn how to recognize an object separately at every image position. Instead, we used convolutional layers that processed every position in the image identically. This reduced the number of parameters and introduced an inductive bias that forced the model to treat every part of the image in the same way.

The same argument can be made about nodes in a graph. We could learn a model with separate parameters associated with each node. However, now the network must independently learn the meaning of the connections in the graph at each position, and training would require many graphs with the same topology. Instead, we build a model that uses the same parameters at every node, reducing the number of parameters and sharing what the network learns at each node across the entire graph.

Recall that a convolution (equation 10.3) updates a variable by taking a weighted sum of information from its neighbors. One way to think of this is that each neighbor sends a message to the variable of interest, which aggregates these messages to form the update. When we considered images, the neighbors were pixels from a fixed-size square region around the current position, so the spatial relationships at each position are the same. However, in a graph, each node may have a different number of neighbors, and there are no consistent relationships; there is no sense that we can weight information

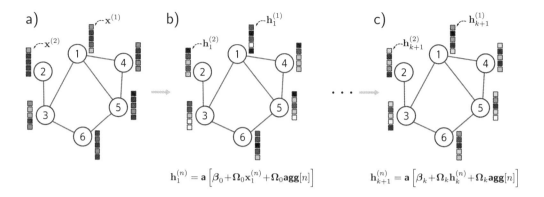

$$\mathbf{h}_1^{(n)} = \mathbf{a}\left[\boldsymbol{\beta}_0 + \boldsymbol{\Omega}_0 \mathbf{x}_1^{(n)} + \boldsymbol{\Omega}_0 \mathbf{agg}[n]\right] \qquad\qquad \mathbf{h}_{k+1}^{(n)} = \mathbf{a}\left[\boldsymbol{\beta}_k + \boldsymbol{\Omega}_k \mathbf{h}_k^{(n)} + \boldsymbol{\Omega}_k \mathbf{agg}[n]\right]$$

Figure 13.7 Simple Graph CNN layer. a) Input graph consists of structure (embodied in graph adjacency matrix $\mathbf{A}$, not shown) and node embeddings (stored in columns of $\mathbf{X}$). b) Each node in the first hidden layer is updated by (i) aggregating the neighboring nodes to form a single vector, (ii) applying a linear transformation $\boldsymbol{\Omega}_0$ to the aggregated nodes, (iii) applying the same linear transformation $\boldsymbol{\Omega}_0$ to the original node, (iv) adding these together with a bias $\boldsymbol{\beta}_0$, and finally (v) applying a nonlinear activation function $\mathbf{a}[\bullet]$ like a ReLU. c) This process is repeated at subsequent layers (but with different parameters for each layer) until we produce the final embeddings at the end of the network.

from a node that is "above" the node of interest differently to information from a node that is "below" it.

13.4.3 Example GCN layer

These considerations lead to a simple GCN layer (figure 13.7). At each node n in layer k, we aggregate information from neighboring nodes by summing their node embeddings $\mathbf{h}_\bullet$:

$$\mathbf{agg}[n, k] = \sum_{m \in \mathrm{ne}[n]} \mathbf{h}_k^{(m)}, \tag{13.8}$$

where $\mathrm{ne}[n]$ returns the set of indices of the neighbors of node n. Then we apply a linear transformation $\boldsymbol{\Omega}_k$ to the embedding $\mathbf{h}_k^{(n)}$ at the current node and to this aggregated value, add a bias term $\boldsymbol{\beta}_k$, and pass the result through a nonlinear activation function $\mathbf{a}[\bullet]$, which is applied independently to every member of its vector argument:

$$\mathbf{h}_{k+1}^{(n)} = \mathbf{a}\left[\boldsymbol{\beta}_k + \boldsymbol{\Omega}_k \cdot \mathbf{h}_k^{(n)} + \boldsymbol{\Omega}_k \cdot \mathbf{agg}[n, k]\right]. \tag{13.9}$$

We can write this more succinctly by noting that post-multiplication of a matrix by a vector returns a weighted sum of its columns. The nth column of the adjacency matrix $\mathbf{A}$ contains ones at the positions of the neighbors. Hence, if we collect the node embeddings into the $D \times N$ matrix $\mathbf{H}_k$ and post-multiply by the adjacency matrix $\mathbf{A}$, the nth column of the result is $\mathbf{agg}[n, k]$. The update for the nodes is now:

$$
\begin{aligned}
\mathbf{H}_{k+1} &= \mathbf{a}\left[\boldsymbol{\beta}_k \mathbf{1}^T + \boldsymbol{\Omega}_k \mathbf{H}_k + \boldsymbol{\Omega}_k \mathbf{H}_k \mathbf{A}\right] \\
&= \mathbf{a}\left[\boldsymbol{\beta}_k \mathbf{1}^T + \boldsymbol{\Omega}_k \mathbf{H}_k (\mathbf{A} + \mathbf{I})\right],
\end{aligned}
\tag{13.10}
$$

where $\mathbf{1}$ is an $N \times 1$ vector containing ones. Here, the nonlinear activation function $\mathbf{a}[\bullet]$ is applied independently to every member of its matrix argument.

This layer satisfies the design considerations: it is equivariant to permutations of the node indices, can cope with any number of neighbors, exploits the graph structure to provide a relational inductive bias, and shares parameters throughout the graph.

Problem 13.7

13.5 Example: graph classification

We now combine these ideas to describe a network that classifies molecules as toxic or harmless. The network inputs are the adjacency matrix and node embedding matrix $\mathbf{X}$. The adjacency matrix $\mathbf{A} \in \mathbb{R}^{N \times N}$ derives from the molecular structure. The columns of the node embedding matrix $\mathbf{X} \in \mathbb{R}^{118 \times N}$ are one-hot vectors indicating which of the 118 elements of the periodic table are present. In other words, they are vectors of length 118 where every position is zero except for the position corresponding to the relevant element, which is set to one. The node embeddings can be transformed to an arbitrary size D by the first weight matrix $\boldsymbol{\Omega}_0 \in \mathbb{R}^{D \times 118}$.

Notebook 13.2
Graph classification

The network equations are:

$$
\begin{aligned}
\mathbf{H}_1 &= \mathbf{a}\left[\boldsymbol{\beta}_0 \mathbf{1}^T + \boldsymbol{\Omega}_0 \mathbf{X}(\mathbf{A} + \mathbf{I})\right] \\
\mathbf{H}_2 &= \mathbf{a}\left[\boldsymbol{\beta}_1 \mathbf{1}^T + \boldsymbol{\Omega}_1 \mathbf{H}_1 (\mathbf{A} + \mathbf{I})\right] \\
&\vdots = \vdots \\
\mathbf{H}_K &= \mathbf{a}\left[\boldsymbol{\beta}_{K-1} \mathbf{1}^T + \boldsymbol{\Omega}_{K-1} \mathbf{H}_{K-1} (\mathbf{A} + \mathbf{I})\right] \\
\mathrm{f}[\mathbf{X}, \mathbf{A}, \boldsymbol{\Phi}] &= \mathrm{sig}\left[\beta_K + \boldsymbol{\omega}_K \mathbf{H}_K \mathbf{1} / N\right],
\end{aligned}
\tag{13.11}
$$

where the network output $\mathrm{f}[\mathbf{X}, \mathbf{A}, \boldsymbol{\Phi}]$ is a single value that determines the probability that the molecule is toxic (see equation 13.2).

13.5.1 Training with batches

Given I training graphs $\{\mathbf{X}_i, \mathbf{A}_i\}$ and their labels y_i, the parameters $\boldsymbol{\Phi} = \{\boldsymbol{\beta}_k, \boldsymbol{\Omega}_k\}_{k=0}^{K}$ can be learned using SGD and the binary cross-entropy loss (equation 5.19). Fully connected networks, convolutional networks, and transformers all exploit the parallelism of modern hardware to process an entire batch of training examples concurrently. To this end, the batch elements are concatenated into a higher-dimensional tensor (section 7.4.2).

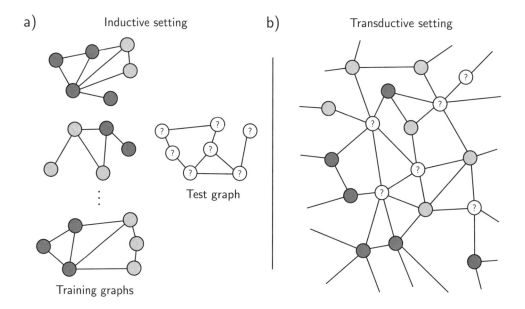

Figure 13.8 Inductive vs. transductive problems. a) Node classification task in the inductive setting. We are given a set of I training graphs, where the node labels (orange and cyan colors) are known. After training, we are given a test graph and must assign labels to each node. b) Node classification in the transductive setting. There is one large graph in which some nodes have labels (orange and cyan colors), and others are unknown. We train the model to predict the known labels correctly and then examine the predictions at the unknown nodes.

However, each graph may have a different number of nodes. Hence, the matrices $\mathbf{X}_i$ and $\mathbf{A}_i$ have different sizes, and there is no way to concatenate them into 3D tensors.

Luckily, a simple trick allows us to process the whole batch in parallel. The graphs in the batch are treated as disjoint components of a single large graph. The network can then be run as a single instance of the network equations. The mean pooling is carried out only over the individual graphs to make a single representation per graph that can be fed into the loss function.

13.6 Inductive vs. transductive models

Until this point, all of the models in this book have been *inductive*: we exploit a training set of labeled data to learn the relation between the inputs and outputs. Then we apply this to new test data. One way to think of this is that we are learning the rule that maps inputs to outputs and then applying it elsewhere.

By contrast, a *transductive* model considers both the labeled and unlabeled data at the same time. It does not produce a rule but merely a labeling for the unknown outputs. This is sometimes termed *semi-supervised learning*. It has the advantage that it can use patterns in the unlabeled data to help make its decisions. However, it has the disadvantage that the model needs to be retrained when extra unlabeled data are added.

Both problem types are commonly encountered for graphs (figure 13.8). Sometimes, we have many labeled graphs and learn a mapping between the graph and the labels. For example, we might have many molecules, each labeled according to whether it is toxic to humans. We learn the rule that maps the graph to the toxic/non-toxic label and then apply this rule to new molecules. However, sometimes there is a single monolithic graph. In the graph of scientific paper citations, we might have labels indicating the field (physics, biology, etc.) for some nodes and wish to label the remaining nodes. Here, the training and test data are irrevocably connected.

Graph-level tasks only occur in the inductive setting where there are training and test graphs. However, node-level tasks and edge prediction tasks can occur in either setting. In the transductive case, the loss function minimizes the mismatch between the model output and the ground truth where this is known. New predictions are computed by running the forward pass and retrieving the results where the ground truth is unknown.

13.7 Example: node classification

As a second example, consider a binary node classification task in a transductive setting. We start with a commercial-sized graph with millions of nodes. Some nodes have ground truth binary labels, and the goal is to label the remaining unlabeled nodes. The body of the network will be the same as in the previous example (equation 13.11) but with a different final layer that produces an output vector of size $1 \times N$:

$$\mathbf{f}[\mathbf{X}, \mathbf{A}, \mathbf{\Phi}] = \mathbf{sig}\left[\beta_K \mathbf{1}^T + \boldsymbol{\omega}_K \mathbf{H}_K\right], \tag{13.12}$$

where the function $\mathbf{sig}[\bullet]$ applies the sigmoid function independently to every element of the row vector input. As usual, we use the binary cross-entropy loss, but now only at nodes where we know the ground truth label y. Note that equation 13.12 is just a vectorized version of the node classification loss from equation 13.3.

Training this network raises two problems. First, it is logistically difficult to train a graph neural network of this size. Consider that we must store the node embeddings at every network layer in the forward pass. This will involve both storing and processing a structure several times the size of the entire graph, and this may not be practical. Second, we have only a single graph, so it's not obvious how to perform stochastic gradient descent. How can we form a batch if there is only a single object?

13.7.1 Choosing batches

One way to form a batch is to choose a random subset of labeled nodes at each training step. Each node depends on its neighbors in the previous layer. These, in turn, depend

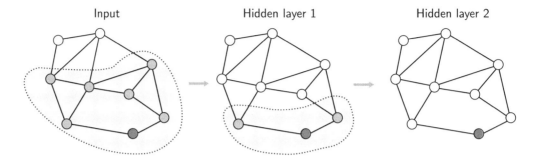

Figure 13.9 Receptive fields in graph neural networks. Consider the orange node in hidden layer two (right). This receives input from the nodes in the 1-hop neighborhood in hidden layer one (shaded region in center). These nodes in hidden layer one receive inputs from their neighbors in turn, and the orange node in layer two receives inputs from all the input nodes in the 2-hop neighborhood (shaded area on left). The region of the graph that contributes to a given node is equivalent to the notion of a receptive field in convolutional neural networks.

on their neighbors in the layer before, so each node has the equivalent of a receptive field (figure 13.9). The size of the receptive field is termed the *k-hop neighborhood*. We can hence perform a gradient descent step using the graph that forms the union of the k-hop neighborhoods of the batch nodes; the remaining inputs do not contribute.

Unfortunately, if there are many layers and the graph is densely connected, every input node may be in the receptive field of every output, and this may not reduce the graph size at all. This is known as the *graph expansion problem*. Two approaches that tackle this problem are *neighborhood sampling* and *graph partitioning*.

Neighborhood sampling: The full graph that feeds into the batch of nodes is sampled, thereby reducing the connections at each network layer (figure 13.10). For example, we might start with the batch nodes and randomly sample a fixed number of their neighbors in the previous layer. Then, we randomly sample a fixed number of *their* neighbors in the layer before, and so on. The graph still increases in size with each layer but in a much more controlled way. This is done anew for each batch, so the contributing neighbors differ even if the same batch is drawn twice. This is also reminiscent of dropout (section 9.3.3) and adds some regularization.

Graph partitioning: A second approach is to cluster the original graph into disjoint subsets of nodes (i.e., smaller graphs that are not connected to one another) before processing (figure 13.11). There are standard algorithms to choose these subsets to maximize the number of internal links. These smaller graphs can each be treated as batches, or a random subset of them can be combined to form a batch (reinstating any edges between them from the original graph).

Given one of the above methods to form batches, we can now train the network parameters in the same way as for the inductive setting, dividing the labeled nodes into

Notebook 13.3
Neighborhood
sampling

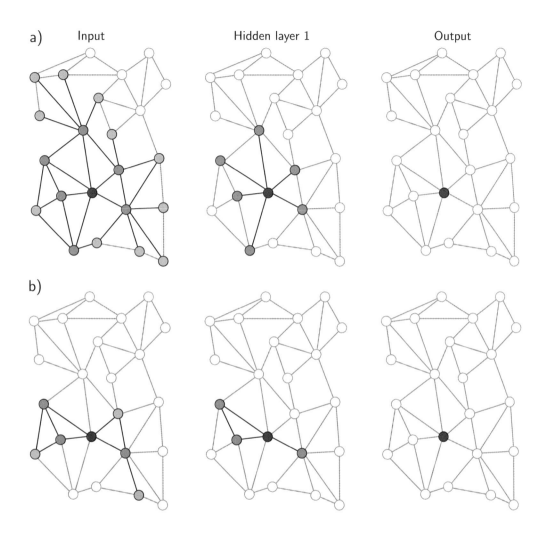

Figure 13.10 Neighborhood sampling. a) One way of forming batches on large graphs is to choose a subset of labeled nodes in the output layer (here, just one node in layer two, right) and then working back to find all of the nodes in the K-hop neighborhood (receptive field). Only this sub-graph is needed to train this batch. Unfortunately, if the graph is densely connected, this may retain a large proportion of the graph. b) One solution is neighborhood sampling. As we work back from the final layer, we select a subset of neighbors (here, three) in the layer before and a subset of the neighbors of these in the layer before that. This restricts the size of the graph for training the batch. In all panels, the brightness represents the distance from the original node.

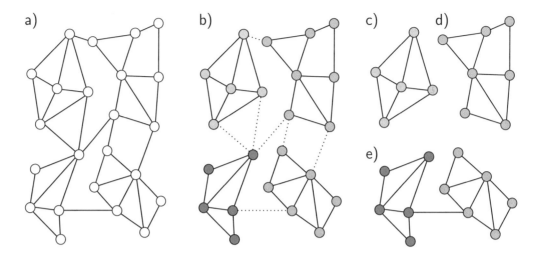

Figure 13.11 Graph partitioning. a) Input graph. b) The input graph is partitioned into smaller subgraphs using a principled method that removes the fewest edges. c-d) We can now use these subgraphs as batches to train in a transductive setting, so here, there are four possible batches. e) Alternatively, we can use combinations of the subgraphs as batches, reinstating the edges between them. If we use pairs of subgraphs, there would be six possible batches here.

train, test, and validation sets as desired; we have effectively converted a transductive problem to an inductive one. To perform inference, we compute predictions for the unknown nodes based on their k-hop neighborhood. Unlike training, this does not require storing the intermediate representations, so it is much more memory efficient.

13.8   Layers for graph convolutional networks

In the previous examples, we combined messages from adjacent nodes by summing them together with the transformed current node. This was accomplished by post-multiplying the node embedding matrix $\mathbf{H}$ by the adjacency matrix plus the identity $\mathbf{A} + \mathbf{I}$. We now consider different approaches to both (i) the combination of the current embedding with the aggregated neighbors and (ii) the aggregation process itself.

13.8.1   Combining current node and aggregated neighbors

In the example GCN layer above, we combined the aggregated neighbors $\mathbf{HA}$ with the current nodes $\mathbf{H}$ by just summing them:

$$\mathbf{H}_{k+1} = \mathbf{a}\Big[\boldsymbol{\beta}_k\mathbf{1}^T + \boldsymbol{\Omega}_k\mathbf{H}_k(\mathbf{A}+\mathbf{I})\Big]. \tag{13.13}$$

In another variation, the current node is multiplied by a factor of $(1 + \epsilon_k)$ before contributing to the sum, where ϵ_k is a learned scalar that is different for each layer:

$$\mathbf{H}_{k+1} = \mathbf{a}\Big[\boldsymbol{\beta}_k\mathbf{1}^T + \boldsymbol{\Omega}_k\mathbf{H}_k(\mathbf{A}+(1+\epsilon_k)\mathbf{I})\Big]. \tag{13.14}$$

This is known as *diagonal enhancement*. A related variation applies a different linear transform $\boldsymbol{\Psi}_k$ to the current node:

$$
\begin{aligned}
\mathbf{H}_{k+1} &= \mathbf{a}\Big[\boldsymbol{\beta}_k\mathbf{1}^T + \boldsymbol{\Omega}_k\mathbf{H}_k\mathbf{A} + \boldsymbol{\Psi}_k\mathbf{H}_k\Big] \\
&= \mathbf{a}\Big[\boldsymbol{\beta}_k\mathbf{1}^T + \begin{bmatrix}\boldsymbol{\Omega}_k & \boldsymbol{\Psi}_k\end{bmatrix}\begin{bmatrix}\mathbf{H}_k\mathbf{A} \\ \mathbf{H}_k\end{bmatrix}\Big] \\
&= \mathbf{a}\Big[\boldsymbol{\beta}_k\mathbf{1}^T + \boldsymbol{\Omega}'_k\begin{bmatrix}\mathbf{H}_k\mathbf{A} \\ \mathbf{H}_k\end{bmatrix}\Big],
\end{aligned} \tag{13.15}
$$

where we have defined $\boldsymbol{\Omega}'_k = \begin{bmatrix}\boldsymbol{\Omega}_k & \boldsymbol{\Psi}_k\end{bmatrix}$ in the third line.

13.8.2 Residual connections

With residual connections, the aggregated representation from the neighbors is transformed and passed through the activation function before summation or concatenation with the current node. For the latter case, the associated network equations are:

$$\mathbf{H}_{k+1} = \begin{bmatrix}\mathbf{a}\Big[\boldsymbol{\beta}_k\mathbf{1}^T + \boldsymbol{\Omega}_k\mathbf{H}_k\mathbf{A}\Big] \\ \mathbf{H}_k\end{bmatrix}. \tag{13.16}$$

13.8.3 Mean aggregation

The above methods aggregate the neighbors by summing the node embeddings. However, it's possible to combine the embeddings in different ways. Sometimes it's better to take the average of the neighbors rather than the sum; this can be superior if the embedding information is more important and the structural information less so since the magnitude of the neighborhood contributions will not depend on the number of neighbors:

$$\mathbf{agg}[n] = \frac{1}{|\text{ne}[n]|}\sum_{m\in\text{ne}[n]}\mathbf{h}_m, \tag{13.17}$$

where as before, ne[n] denotes a set containing the indices of the neighbors of the nth node. Equation 13.17 can be computed neatly in matrix form by introducing the diagonal $N \times N$ degree matrix $\mathbf{D}$. Each non-zero element of this matrix contains the number of neighbors for the associated node. It follows that each diagonal element in the inverse

Problem 13.8

matrix $\mathbf{D}^{-1}$ contains the denominator that we need to compute the average. The new GCN layer can be written as:

$$\mathbf{H}_{k+1} = \mathbf{a}\Big[\boldsymbol{\beta}_k \mathbf{1}^T + \boldsymbol{\Omega}_k \mathbf{H}_k (\mathbf{A}\mathbf{D}^{-1} + \mathbf{I})\Big].\tag{13.18}$$

13.8.4 Kipf normalization

Problem 13.9

There are many variations of graph neural networks based on mean aggregation. Sometimes the current node is included with its neighbors in the mean computation rather than treated separately. In Kipf normalization, the sum of the node representations is normalized as:

$$\mathbf{agg}[n] = \sum_{m \in \mathrm{ne}[n]} \frac{\mathbf{h}_m}{\sqrt{|\mathrm{ne}[n]||\mathrm{ne}[m]|}},\tag{13.19}$$

with the logic that information coming from nodes with a very large number of neighbors should be down-weighted since there are many connections and they provide less unique information. This can also be expressed in matrix form using the degree matrix:

$$\mathbf{H}_{k+1} = \mathbf{a}\Big[\boldsymbol{\beta}_k \mathbf{1}^T + \boldsymbol{\Omega}_k \mathbf{H}_k (\mathbf{D}^{-1/2}\mathbf{A}\mathbf{D}^{-1/2} + \mathbf{I})\Big].\tag{13.20}$$

13.8.5 Max pooling aggregation

An alternative operation that is also invariant to permutation is computing the maximum of a set of objects. The *max pooling* aggregation operator is:

$$\mathbf{agg}[n] = \max_{m \in \mathrm{ne}[n]}\big[\mathbf{h}_m\big],\tag{13.21}$$

where the operator $\mathbf{max}[\bullet]$ returns the element-wise maximum of the vectors $\mathbf{h}_m$ that are neighbors to the current node n.

13.8.6 Aggregation by attention

The aggregation methods discussed so far either weight the contribution of the neighbors equally or in a way that depends on the graph topology. Conversely, in *graph attention layers*, the weights depend on the data at the nodes. A linear transform is applied to the current node embeddings so that:

$$\mathbf{H}'_k = \boldsymbol{\beta}_k \mathbf{1}^T + \boldsymbol{\Omega}_k \mathbf{H}_k.\tag{13.22}$$

Then the similarity s_{mn} of each transformed node embedding $\mathbf{h}'_m$ to the transformed node embedding $\mathbf{h}'_n$ is computed by concatenating the pairs, taking a dot product with a column vector $\boldsymbol{\phi}_k$ of learned parameters, and applying an activation function:

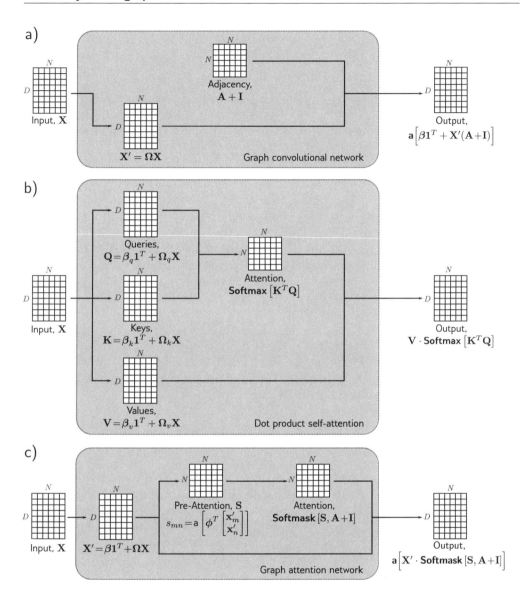

Figure 13.12 Comparison of graph convolutional network, dot product attention, and graph attention network. In each case, the mechanism maps N embeddings of size D stored in a $D \times N$ matrix $\mathbf{X}$ to an output of the same size. a) The graph convolutional network applies a linear transformation $\mathbf{X}' = \boldsymbol{\Omega}\mathbf{X}$ to the data matrix. It then computes a weighted sum of the transformed data, where the weighting is based on the adjacency matrix. A bias $\boldsymbol{\beta}$ is added, and the result is passed through an activation function. b) The outputs of the self-attention mechanism are also weighted sums of the transformed inputs, but this time the weights depend on the data itself via the attention matrix. c) The graph attention network combines both of these mechanisms; the weights are both computed from the data and based on the adjacency matrix.

$$s_{mn} = \mathrm{a}\left[\boldsymbol{\phi}_k^T \begin{bmatrix} \mathbf{h}'_m \\ \mathbf{h}'_n \end{bmatrix}\right]. \tag{13.23}$$

These variables are stored in an $N \times N$ matrix $\mathbf{S}$, where each element represents the similarity of every node to every other. As in dot-product self-attention, the attention weights contributing to each output embedding are normalized to be positive and sum to one using the softmax operation. However, only those values corresponding to the current node and its neighbors should contribute. The attention weights are applied to the transformed embeddings:

$$\mathbf{H}_{k+1} = \mathbf{a}\left[\mathbf{H}'_k \cdot \mathbf{Softmask}[\mathbf{S}, \mathbf{A} + \mathbf{I}]\right], \tag{13.24}$$

Notebook 13.4
Graph
attention

Problem 13.10

where $\mathbf{a}[\bullet]$ is a second activation function. The function $\mathbf{Softmask}[\bullet, \bullet]$ computes the attention values by applying softmax operation separately to each column of its first argument $\mathbf{S}$, but only after setting values where the second argument $\mathbf{A} + \mathbf{I}$ is zero to negative infinity, so they do not contribute. This ensures that the attention to non-neighboring nodes is zero.

This is very similar to the self-attention computation in transformers (see figure 13.12), except that (i) The keys, queries, and values are all the same, (ii) The measure of similarity is different, and (iii) The attentions are masked so that each node only attends to itself and its neighbors. As in transformers, this system can be extended to use multiple heads that are run in parallel and recombined.

13.9   Edge graphs

Until now, we have focused on processing node embeddings. These evolve as they are passed through the network so that by the end of the network, they represent both the node and its context in the graph. We now consider the case where the information is associated with the edges of the graph.

It is easy to adapt the machinery for node embeddings to process edge embeddings using the *edge graph* (also known as the *adjoint graph* or *line graph*). This is a complementary graph, in which each edge in the original graph becomes a node, and every two edges with a common node in the original graph create an edge in the new graph (figure 13.13). In general, a graph can be recovered from its edge graph, so it's possible to swap between these two representations.

Problems 13.11–13.13

To process edge embeddings, the graph is translated to its edge graph. Then we use exactly the same techniques, aggregating information at each new node from its neighbors and combining this with the current representation. When both node and edge embeddings are present, we can translate back and forth between the two graphs. Now there are four possible updates (nodes update nodes, nodes update edges, edges update nodes, and edges update edges), and these can be alternated as desired, or with minor modifications, nodes can be updated simultaneously from both nodes and edges.

Problem 13.14

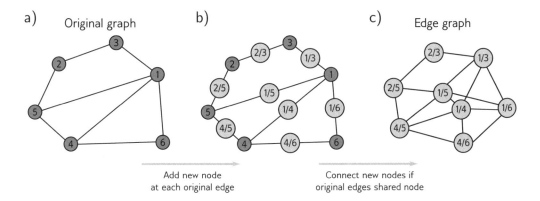

Figure 13.13 Edge graph. a) Graph with six nodes. b) To create the edge graph, we assign one node for each original edge (cyan circles), and c) connect the new nodes if the edges they represent connect to the same node in the original graph.

13.10 Summary

Graphs consist of a set of nodes, where pairs of these nodes are connected by edges. Both nodes and edges can have data attached, and these are referred to as node embeddings and edge embeddings, respectively. Many real-world problems can be framed in terms of graphs, where the goal is to establish a property of the entire graph, properties of each node or edge, or the presence of additional edges in the graph.

Graph neural networks are deep learning models that are applied to graphs. Since the node order in graphs is arbitrary, the layers of graph neural networks must be equivariant to permutations of the node indices. Spatial-based convolutional networks are a family of graph neural networks that aggregate information from the neighbors of a node and then use this to update the node embeddings.

One challenge of processing graphs is that they often occur in the transductive setting, where there is only one partially labeled graph rather than sets of training and test graphs. This graph can be extremely large, which adds further challenges in terms of training and has led to sampling and partitioning algorithms. The edge graph has a node for every edge in the original graph. By converting to this representation, graph neural networks can be used to update the edge embeddings.

Notes

Sanchez-Lengeling et al. (2021) and Daigavane et al. (2021) present good introductory articles on graph processing using neural networks. Recent surveys of research in graph neural networks can be found in articles by Zhou et al. (2020a), Wu et al. (2020c), and Veličković (2023), and the books of Hamilton (2020) and Ma & Tang (2021). GraphEDM (Chami et al., 2020) unifies many existing graph algorithms into a single framework. In this chapter, we have related graphs to convolutional networks following Bruna et al. (2013), but there are also strong connections with belief propagation (Dai et al., 2016) and graph isomorphism tests (Hamilton et al., 2017a). Zhang et al. (2019c) provide a review focusing specifically on graph convolutional networks. Bronstein et al. (2021) provide a general overview of geometric deep learning, including learning on graphs. Loukas (2020) discusses what types of functions graph neural networks can learn.

Applications: Applications include graph classification (e.g., Zhang et al., 2018b), node classification (e.g., Kipf & Welling, 2017), edge prediction (e.g., Zhang & Chen, 2018), graph clustering (e.g., Tsitsulin et al., 2020), and recommender systems (e.g., Wu et al., 2023). Methods for node classification are reviewed by Xiao et al. (2022a), methods for graph classification by Errica et al. (2019), and methods for edge prediction by Mutlu et al. (2020) and Kumar et al. (2020a).

Graph neural networks: Graph neural networks were introduced by Gori et al. (2005) and Scarselli et al. (2008), who formulated them as a generalization of recursive neural networks. The latter model used the iterative update:

$$\mathbf{h}_n \leftarrow \mathbf{f}\left[\mathbf{x}_n, \mathbf{x}_{m \in \text{ne}[n]}, \mathbf{e}_{e \in \text{nee}[n]}, \mathbf{h}_{m \in \text{ne}[n]}, \boldsymbol{\phi}\right], \tag{13.25}$$

in which each node embedding $\mathbf{h}_n$ is updated from the initial embedding $\mathbf{x}_n$, initial embeddings $\mathbf{x}_{m \in \text{ne}[n]}$ at the adjacent nodes, initial embeddings $\mathbf{e}_{e \in \text{nee}[n]}$ at the adjacent edges, and adjacent node embeddings $\mathbf{h}_{m \in \text{ne}[n]}$. For convergence, the function $\mathbf{f}[\bullet, \bullet, \bullet, \bullet, \boldsymbol{\phi}]$ must be a contraction mapping (see figure 16.9). If we unroll this equation in time for K steps and allow different parameters $\boldsymbol{\phi}_k$ at each time K, then equation 13.25 becomes similar to the graph convolutional network. Subsequent work extended graph neural networks to use gated recurrent units (Li et al., 2016b) and long short-term memory networks (Selsam et al., 2019).

Spectral methods: Bruna et al. (2013) applied the convolution operation in the Fourier domain. The Fourier basis vectors can be found by taking the eigendecomposition of the *graph Laplacian matrix*, $\mathbf{L} = \mathbf{D} - \mathbf{A}$ where $\mathbf{D}$ is the degree matrix and $\mathbf{A}$ is the adjacency matrix. This has disadvantages: the filters are not localized, and the decomposition is prohibitively expensive for large graphs. Henaff et al. (2015) tackled the first problem by forcing the Fourier representation to be smooth (and hence the spatial domain to be localized). Defferrard et al. (2016) introduced ChebNet, which approximates the filters efficiently by using the recursive properties of Chebyshev polynomials. This both provides spatially localized filters and reduces the computation. Kipf & Welling (2017) simplified this further to construct filters that use only a 1-hop neighborhood, resulting in a formulation similar to the spatial methods described in this chapter and providing a bridge between spectral and spatial methods.

Spatial methods: Spectral methods are ultimately based on the Graph Laplacian, so if the graph changes, the model must be retrained. This problem spurred the development of spatial methods. Duvenaud et al. (2015) defined convolutions in the spatial domain, using a different weight matrix to combine the adjacent embeddings for each node degree. This has the disadvantage that it becomes impractical if some nodes have a very large number of connections. Diffusion convolutional neural networks (Atwood & Towsley, 2016) use powers of the normalized adjacency matrix to blend features across different scales, sum these, pointwise multiply by weights, and pass through an activation function to create the node embeddings. Gilmer et al. (2017) introduced *message-passing neural networks*, which defined convolutions on the graph as propagating messages from spatial neighbors. The "aggregate and combine" formulation of *GraphSAGE* (Hamilton et al., 2017a) fits into this framework.

Aggregate and combine: *Graph convolutional networks* (Kipf & Welling, 2017) take a weighted average of the neighbors and current node and then apply a linear mapping and ReLU. *GraphSAGE* (Hamilton et al., 2017a) applies a neural network layer to each neighbor, taking the elementwise maximum to aggregate. Chiang et al. (2019) propose *diagonal enhancement* in which the previous embedding is weighted more than the neighbors. Kipf & Welling (2017) introduced Kipf normalization, which normalizes the sum of the neighboring embeddings based on the degrees of the current node and its neighbors (see equation 13.19).

The *mixture model network* or *MoNet* (Monti et al., 2017) takes this one step further by *learning* a weighting based on the degrees of the current node and the neighbor. They associate a pseudo-coordinate system with each node, where the positions of the neighbors depend on these two quantities. They then learn a continuous function based on a mixture of Gaussians and sample this at the pseudo-coordinates of the neighbors to get the weights. In this way, they can learn the weightings for nodes and neighbors with arbitrary degrees. Pham et al. (2017) use a linear interpolation of the node embedding and neighbors with a different weighted combination for each dimension. The weight of this gating mechanism is generated as a function of the data.

Higher-order convolutional layers: Zhou & Li (2017) used higher-order convolutions by replacing the adjacency matrix $\mathbf{A}$ with $\tilde{\mathbf{A}} = \mathbf{Min}[\mathbf{A}^L + \mathbf{I}, \mathbf{1}]$ where L is the maximum walk-length, $\mathbf{1}$ is a matrix containing only ones, and $\mathbf{Min}[\bullet]$ takes the pointwise minimum of its two matrix arguments; the updates now sum together contributions from any nodes where there is at least one walk of length L. Abu-El-Haija et al. (2019) proposed *MixHop*, which computes node updates from the neighbors (using the adjacency matrix $\mathbf{A}$), the neighbors of the neighbors (using $\mathbf{A}^2$), and so on. They concatenate these updates at each layer. Lee et al. (2018) combined information from nodes beyond the immediate neighbors using geometric *motifs*, which are small local geometric patterns in the graph (e.g., a fully connected clique of five nodes).

Residual connections: Kipf & Welling (2017) proposed a residual connection in which the original embeddings are added to the updated ones. Hamilton et al. (2017b) concatenate the previous embedding to the output of the next layer (see equation 13.16). Rossi et al. (2020) present an inception-style network where the node embedding is concatenated to not only the aggregation of its neighbors but also the aggregation of all neighbors within a walk of two (via computing powers of the adjacency matrix). Xu et al. (2018) introduced *jump knowledge connections* in which the final output at each node consists of the concatenated node embeddings throughout the network. Zhang & Meng (2019) present a general formulation of residual embeddings called *GResNet* and investigate several variations in which the embeddings from the previous layer are added, the input embeddings are added, or versions of these that aggregate information from their neighbors (without further transformation) are added.

Attention in graph neural networks: Veličković et al. (2019) developed the *graph attention network* (figure 13.12c). Their formulation uses multiple heads whose outputs are combined symmetrically. *Gated Attention Networks* (Zhang et al., 2018a) weight the output of the different heads in a way that depends on the data itself. *Graph-BERT* (Zhang et al., 2020) performs node classification using self-attention alone; the graph's structure is captured by adding position embeddings to the data, similarly to how the absolute or relative position of words is captured in the transformer (chapter 12). For example, they add positional information that depends on the number of hops between nodes in the graph.

Permutation invariance: In *DeepSets*, Zaheer et al. (2017) presented a general permutation invariant operator for processing sets. Janossy pooling (Murphy et al., 2018) accepts that many functions are not permutation equivariant and instead uses a permutation-sensitive function and averages the results across many permutations.

Edge graphs: The notation of the *edge graph*, *line graph*, or *adjoint graph* dates to Whitney (1932). The idea of "weaving" layers that update node embeddings from node embeddings, node embeddings from edge embeddings, edge embeddings from edge embeddings, and edge embeddings from node embeddings was proposed by Kearnes et al. (2016). However, here the node-node and edge-edge updates do not involve the neighbors. Monti et al. (2018) introduced the *dual-primal graph CNN*, a modern formulation in a CNN framework that alternates between updates in the original and edge graphs.

Power of graph neural networks: Xu et al. (2019) argue that a neural network should be able to distinguish different graph structures; it is undesirable to map two graphs to the same output if they have the same initial node embeddings but different adjacency matrices. They identified graph structures that could not be distinguished by previous approaches such as GCNs (Kipf & Welling, 2017) and GraphSAGE (Hamilton et al., 2017a). They developed a more powerful architecture with the same discriminative power as the Weisfeiler-Lehman graph isomorphism test (Weisfeiler & Leman, 1968), which is known to discriminate a broad class of graphs. This resulting *graph isomorphism network* was based on the aggregation operation:

$$\mathbf{h}_{k+1}^{(n)} = \mathbf{mlp}\left[(1 + \epsilon_k) \, \mathbf{h}_k^{(n)} + \sum_{m \in \mathrm{ne}[n]} \mathbf{h}_k^{(m)} \right]. \tag{13.26}$$

Batches: The original paper on graph convolutional networks (Kipf & Welling, 2017) used full-batch gradient descent. This has memory requirements proportional to the number of nodes, embedding size, and number of layers during training. Since then, three types of methods have been proposed to reduce the memory requirements and create batches for SGD in the transductive setting: node sampling, layer sampling, and sub-graph sampling.

Node sampling methods start by randomly selecting a subset of target nodes and then work back through the network, adding a subset of the nodes in the receptive field at each stage. GraphSAGE (Hamilton et al., 2017a) proposed a fixed number of neighborhood samples as in figure 13.10b. Chen et al. (2018b) introduce a variance reduction technique, but this uses historical activations of nodes and so still has a high memory requirement. *PinSAGE* (Ying et al., 2018a) uses random walks from the target nodes and chooses the K nodes with the highest visit count. This prioritizes ancestors that are more closely connected.

Node sampling still requires increasing numbers of nodes as we pass back through the graph. *Layer sampling methods* address this by directly sampling the receptive field in each layer independently. Examples of layer sampling include FastGCN (Chen et al., 2018a), adaptive sampling (Huang et al., 2018b), and layer-dependent importance sampling (Zou et al., 2019).

Subgraph sampling methods randomly draw subgraphs or divide the original graph into subgraphs. These are then trained as independent data examples. Examples of these approaches include *GraphSAINT* (Zeng et al., 2020), which samples sub-graphs during training using random walks and then runs a full GCN on the subgraph while also correcting for the bias and variance of the minibatch. *Cluster GCN* (Chiang et al., 2019) partitions the graph into clusters (by maximizing the embedding utilization or number of within-batch edges) in a pre-processing stage and randomly selects clusters to form minibatches. To create more randomness, they train random subsets of these clusters plus the edges between them (see figure 13.11).

Wolfe et al. (2021) proposed a distributed training method that both partitions the graph and trains narrower GCNs in parallel by partitioning the feature space at different layers. More information about sampling graphs can be found in Rozemberczki et al. (2020).

Regularization and normalization: Rong et al. (2020) proposed *DropEdge*, which randomly drops edges from the graph during each training iteration by masking the adjacency matrix. This can be done for the whole neural network or differently in each layer (layer-wise DropEdge). In a sense, this is similar to dropout in that it breaks connections in the flow of data, but it can also be considered an augmentation method since changing the graph is similar to perturbing the data. Schlichtkrull et al. (2018), Teru et al. (2020), and Veličković et al. (2019) also proposed randomly dropping edges from the graph as a form of regularization similar to dropout. Node sampling methods (Hamilton et al., 2017a; Huang et al., 2018b; Chen et al., 2018a) can also be considered regularizers. Hasanzadeh et al. (2020) present a general framework called *DropConnect* that unifies many of the above approaches.

There are also many proposed normalization schemes for graph neural networks, including *PairNorm* (Zhao & Akoglu, 2020), *weight normalization* (Oono & Suzuki, 2019), *differentiable group normalization* (Zhou et al., 2020b), and *GraphNorm* (Cai et al., 2021).

Multi-relational graphs: Schlichtkrull et al. (2018) proposed a variation of graph convolutional networks for multi-relational graphs (i.e., graphs with more than one edge type). Their scheme separately aggregates information from each edge type using different parameters. If there are many edge types, the number of parameters may become large, and to combat this, they propose that each edge type uses a different weighting of a basis set of parameters.

Hierarchical representations and pooling: CNNs for image classification gradually decrease the representation size but increase the number of channels as the network progresses. However, the GCNs for graph classification in this chapter maintain the entire graph until the last layer and then combine all the nodes to compute the final prediction. Ying et al. (2018b) proposed *DiffPool*, which clusters graph nodes to make a graph that gets progressively smaller as the depth increases in a way that is differentiable, and so can be learned. This can be done based on the graph structure alone or adaptively based on the graph structure and the embeddings. Other pooling methods include *SortPool* (Zhang et al., 2018b) and *self-attention graph pooling* (Lee et al., 2019). A comparison of pooling layers for graph neural networks can be found in Grattarola et al. (2022). Gao & Ji (2019) propose an encoder-decoder structure for graphs based on the U-Net (see figure 11.10).

Geometric graphs: The *MoNet* model (Monti et al., 2017) can exploit geometric information because neighboring nodes have well-defined spatial positions. They learn a mixture of Gaussians function and sample from this based on the relative coordinates of the neighbor. In this way, they can weight neighboring nodes based on their relative positions as in standard convolutional neural networks, even though these positions are not constant. The *geodesic CNN* (Masci et al., 2015) and *anisotropic CNN* (Boscaini et al., 2016) both adapt convolution to manifolds (i.e., surfaces) as represented by triangular meshes. They locally approximate the surface as a plane and define a coordinate system on this plane around the current node.

Oversmoothing and suspended animation: Unlike other deep learning models, graph neural networks did not, until recently, benefit significantly from increasing depth. Indeed, the original GCN paper (Kipf & Welling, 2017) and GraphSAGE (Hamilton et al., 2017a) both only use two layers, and Chiang et al. (2019) trained a five-layer Cluster-GCN to get state-of-the-art performance on the PPI dataset. One possible explanation is *over-smoothing* (Li et al., 2018c); at each layer, the network incorporates information from a larger neighborhood, and it may be that this ultimately results in the dissolution of (important) local information. Indeed (Xu et al., 2018) prove that the influence of one node on another is proportional to the probability of reaching that node in a K-step random walk. This approaches the stationary distribution of walks over the graph with increasing K, causing the local neighborhood to be washed out.

Alon & Yahav (2021) proposed another explanation for why performance doesn't improve with network depth. They argue that adding depth allows information to be aggregated from longer paths. However, in practice, the exponential growth in the number of neighbors means there is a bottleneck whereby too much information is "squashed" into the fixed-size node embeddings.

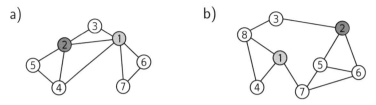

Figure 13.14 Graphs for problems 13.1, 13.3, and 13.8.

Ying et al. (2018a) also note that when the depth of the network exceeds a certain limit, the gradients no longer propagate back, and learning fails for both the training and test data. They term this effect *suspended animation*. This is similar to when many layers are naïvely added to convolutional neural networks (figure 11.2). They propose a family of residual connections that allow deeper networks to be trained. Vanishing gradients (section 7.5) have also been identified as a limitation by Li et al. (2021b).

It has recently become possible to train deeper graph neural networks using various forms of residual connection (Xu et al., 2018; Li et al., 2020a; Gong et al., 2020; Chen et al., 2020b; Xu et al., 2021a). Li et al. (2021a) train a state-of-the-art model with more than 1000 layers using an invertible network to reduce the memory requirements of training (see chapter 16).

Problems

Problem 13.1 Write out the adjacency matrices for the two graphs in figure 13.14.

Problem 13.2* Draw graphs that correspond to the following adjacency matrices:

$$\mathbf{A}_1 = \begin{bmatrix} 0 & 1 & 1 & 0 & 0 & 0 & 0 \\ 1 & 0 & 0 & 1 & 1 & 1 & 0 \\ 1 & 0 & 0 & 0 & 0 & 1 & 1 \\ 0 & 1 & 0 & 0 & 0 & 1 & 1 \\ 0 & 1 & 0 & 0 & 0 & 0 & 1 \\ 0 & 1 & 1 & 1 & 0 & 0 & 0 \\ 0 & 0 & 1 & 1 & 1 & 0 & 0 \end{bmatrix} \quad \text{and} \quad \mathbf{A}_2 = \begin{bmatrix} 0 & 0 & 1 & 1 & 0 & 0 & 1 \\ 0 & 0 & 1 & 1 & 1 & 0 & 0 \\ 1 & 1 & 0 & 0 & 0 & 0 & 0 \\ 1 & 1 & 0 & 0 & 1 & 1 & 1 \\ 0 & 1 & 0 & 1 & 0 & 0 & 1 \\ 0 & 0 & 0 & 1 & 0 & 0 & 1 \\ 1 & 0 & 0 & 1 & 1 & 1 & 0 \end{bmatrix}.$$

Problem 13.3* Consider the two graphs in figure 13.14. How many ways are there to walk from node one to node two in (i) three steps and (ii) seven steps?

Problem 13.4 The diagonal of $\mathbf{A}^2$ in figure 13.4c contains the number of edges that connect to each corresponding node. Explain this phenomenon.

Appendix B.4.4
Permutation
matrix

Problem 13.5 What permutation matrix is responsible for the transformation between the graphs in figures 13.5a–c and figure 13.5d–f?

Problem 13.6 Prove that:

$$\text{sig}\left[\beta_K + \boldsymbol{\omega}_K \mathbf{H}_K \mathbf{1}\right] = \text{sig}\left[\beta_K + \boldsymbol{\omega}_K \mathbf{H}_K \mathbf{P} \mathbf{1}\right], \tag{13.27}$$

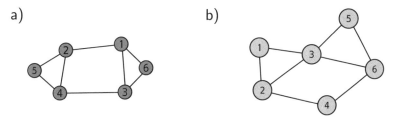

Figure 13.15 Graphs for problems 13.11–13.13.

where $\mathbf{P}$ is an $N \times N$ permutation matrix (a matrix that is all zeros except for exactly one entry in each row and each column, which is one), and $\mathbf{1}$ is an $N \times 1$ vector of ones.

Problem 13.7* Consider the simple GNN layer:

$$
\begin{aligned}
\mathbf{H}_{k+1} &= \text{GraphLayer}[\mathbf{H}_k, \mathbf{A}] \\
&= \mathbf{a}\left[\boldsymbol{\beta}_k \mathbf{1}^T + \boldsymbol{\Omega}_k \begin{bmatrix} \mathbf{H}_k \\ \mathbf{H}_k \mathbf{A} \end{bmatrix}\right],
\end{aligned}
\tag{13.28}
$$

where $\mathbf{H}$ is a $D \times N$ matrix containing the N node embeddings in its columns, $\mathbf{A}$ is the $N \times N$ adjacency matrix, $\boldsymbol{\beta}$ is the bias vector, and $\boldsymbol{\Omega}$ is the weight matrix. Show that this layer is equivariant to permutations of the node order so that:

$$
\text{GraphLayer}[\mathbf{H}_k, \mathbf{A}]\mathbf{P} = \text{GraphLayer}[\mathbf{H}_k \mathbf{P}, \mathbf{P}^T \mathbf{A} \mathbf{P}],
\tag{13.29}
$$

where $\mathbf{P}$ is an $N \times N$ permutation matrix.

Problem 13.8 What is the degree matrix $\mathbf{D}$ for each graph in figure 13.14?

Problem 13.9 The authors of GraphSAGE (Hamilton et al., 2017a) propose a pooling method in which the node embedding is averaged together with its neighbors so that:

$$
\mathbf{agg}[n] = \frac{1}{1 + |\text{ne}[n]|}\left(\mathbf{h}_n + \sum_{m \in \text{ne}[n]} \mathbf{h}_m\right).
\tag{13.30}
$$

Show how this operation can be computed simultaneously for all node embeddings in the $D \times N$ embedding matrix $\mathbf{H}$ using linear algebra. You will need to use both the adjacency matrix $\mathbf{A}$ and the degree matrix $\mathbf{D}$.

Problem 13.10* Devise a graph attention mechanism based on dot-product self-attention and draw its mechanism in the style of figure 13.12.

Problem 13.11* Draw the edge graph associated with the graph in figure 13.15a.

Problem 13.12* Draw the node graph corresponding to the edge graph in figure 13.15b.

Problem 13.13 For a general undirected graph, describe how the adjacency matrix of the node graph relates to the adjacency matrix of the corresponding edge graph.

Problem 13.14* Design a layer that updates a node embedding $\mathbf{h}_n$ based on its neighboring node embeddings $\{\mathbf{h}_m\}_{m \in \text{ne}[n]}$ and neighboring edge embeddings $\{\mathbf{e}_m\}_{m \in \text{nee}[n]}$. You should consider the possibility that the edge embeddings are not the same size as the node embeddings.

Chapter 14

Unsupervised learning

Chapters 2–9 walked through the *supervised learning* pipeline. We defined models that mapped observed data $\mathbf{x}$ to output values $\mathbf{y}$ and introduced loss functions that measured the quality of that mapping for a training dataset $\{\mathbf{x}_i, \mathbf{y}_i\}$. Then we discussed how to fit and measure the performance of these models. Chapters 10–13 introduced more sophisticated model architectures incorporating parameter sharing and allowing parallel computational paths.

The defining characteristic of *unsupervised learning models* is that they are learned from a set of observed data $\{\mathbf{x}_i\}$ in the absence of labels. All unsupervised models share this property, but they have diverse goals. They may be used to generate plausible new samples from the dataset or to manipulate, denoise, interpolate between, or compress examples. They can also be used to reveal the internal structure of a dataset (e.g., by dividing it into coherent clusters) or to distinguish whether new examples belong to the same dataset or are outliers.

This chapter introduces a taxonomy of unsupervised learning models and then discusses the desirable properties of models and how to measure their performance. The four subsequent chapters discuss four particular models: generative adversarial networks (GANs), variational autoencoders (VAEs), normalizing flows, and diffusion models.[1]

14.1 Taxonomy of unsupervised learning models

A common strategy in unsupervised learning is to define a mapping between the data examples $\mathbf{x}$ and a set of unseen *latent* variables $\mathbf{z}$. These latent variables capture underlying structure in the dataset and usually have a lower dimension than the original data; in this sense, a latent variable $\mathbf{z}$ can be considered a compressed version of a data example $\mathbf{x}$ that captures its essential qualities (figures 1.9–1.10).

In principle, the mapping between the observed and latent variables can be in either direction. Some models map from the data $\mathbf{x}$ to latent variables $\mathbf{z}$. For example, the

---

[1]Until this point, almost all of the relevant math has been embedded in the text. However, the following four chapters require a solid knowledge of probability. Appendix C covers the relevant material.

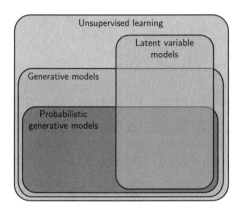

Figure 14.1 Taxonomy of unsupervised learning models. Unsupervised learning refers to any model trained on datasets without labels. Generative models can synthesize (generate) new examples with similar statistics to the training data. A subset of these are probabilistic and define a distribution over the data. We draw samples from this distribution to generate new examples. Latent variable models define a mapping between an underlying explanatory (latent) variable and the data. They may fall into any of the above categories.

famous *k-means* algorithm maps the data $\mathbf{x}$ to a cluster assignment $z \in \{1, 2, \ldots, K\}$. Other models map from the latent variables $\mathbf{z}$ to the data $\mathbf{x}$. Consider defining a distribution $Pr(\mathbf{z})$ over the latent variable $\mathbf{z}$ in these models. New examples can now be *generated* by (i) drawing from this distribution and (ii) mapping the sample to the data space $\mathbf{x}$. Accordingly, these are termed *generative models* (see figure 14.1).

The four models in chapters 15 to 18 are all generative models that use latent variables. *Generative adversarial networks* (chapter 15) learn to generate data examples $\mathbf{x}^*$ from latent variables $\mathbf{z}$, using a loss that encourages the generated samples to be indistinguishable from real examples (figure 14.2a).

Normalizing flows, *variational autoencoders*, and *diffusion models* (chapters 16–18) are *probabilistic generative models*. In addition to generating new examples, they assign a probability $Pr(\mathbf{x}|\boldsymbol{\phi})$ to each data point $\mathbf{x}$. This will depend on the model parameters $\boldsymbol{\phi}$, and in training, we maximize the probability of the observed data $\{\mathbf{x}_i\}$, so the loss is the sum of the negative log-likelihoods (figure 14.2b):

$$L[\boldsymbol{\phi}] = -\sum_{i=1}^{I} \log\left[Pr(\mathbf{x}_i|\boldsymbol{\phi})\right]. \tag{14.1}$$

Since probability distributions must sum to one, this implicitly reduces the probability of examples that lie far from the observed data. As well as providing a training criterion, assigning probabilities is useful in its own right; the probability on a test set can be used to compare two models quantitatively, and the probability for an example can be thresholded to determine if it belongs to the same dataset or is an *outlier*.[2]

14.2 What makes a good generative model?

Generative models based on latent variables should have the following properties:

---

[2]Note that not all probabilistic generative models rely on latent variables. The transformer decoder (section 12.7) was learned without labels, can generate new examples, and can assign a probability to these examples but is based on an autoregressive formulation (equation 12.15).

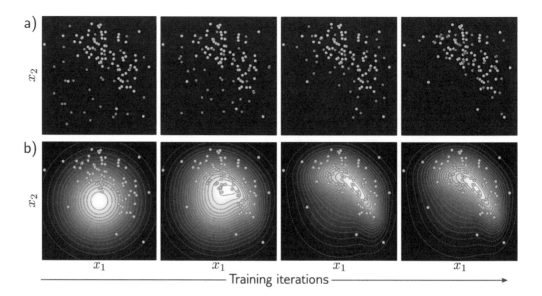

Figure 14.2 Fitting generative models a) Generative adversarial models provide a mechanism for generating samples (orange points). As training proceeds (left to right), the loss function encourages these samples to become progressively less distinguishable from real examples (cyan points). b) Probabilistic models (including variational autoencoders, normalizing flows, and diffusion models) learn a probability distribution over the training data. As training proceeds (left to right), the likelihood of the real examples increases under this distribution, which can be used to draw new samples and assess the probability of new data points.

- **Efficient sampling:** Generating samples from the model should be computationally inexpensive and take advantage of the parallelism of modern hardware.
- **High-quality sampling:** The samples should be indistinguishable from the real data with which the model was trained.
- **Coverage:** Samples should represent the entire training distribution. It is insufficient to generate samples that all look like a subset of the training examples.
- **Well-behaved latent space:** Every latent variable $\mathbf{z}$ corresponds to a plausible data example $\mathbf{x}$. Smooth changes in $\mathbf{z}$ correspond to smooth changes in $\mathbf{x}$.
- **Disentangled latent space:** Manipulating each dimension of $\mathbf{z}$ should correspond to changing an interpretable property of the data. For example, in a model of language, it might change the topic, tense, or verbosity.
- **Efficient likelihood computation:** If the model is probabilistic, we would like to be able to calculate the probability of new examples efficiently and accurately.

This naturally leads to the question of whether the generative models that we consider satisfy these properties. The answer is subjective, but figure 14.3 provides guidance. The precise assignments are disputable, but most practitioners would agree that there is no single model that satisfies all of these characteristics.

Model	Efficient	Sample quality	Coverage	Well-behaved latent space	Disentangled latent space	Efficient likelihood
GANs	✓	✓	✗	✓	?	n/a
VAEs	✓	✗	?	✓	?	✗
Flows	✓	✗	?	✓	?	✓
Diffusion	✗	✓	?	✗	✗	✗

Figure 14.3 Properties of four generative models. Neither generative adversarial networks (GANs), variational autoencoders (VAEs), normalizing flows (Flows), nor diffusion models (diffusion) have the full complement of desirable properties.

14.3 Quantifying performance

The previous section discussed the desirable properties of generative models. We now consider quantitative measures of success for generative models. Much experimentation with generative models has used images due to the widespread availability of that data and the ease of qualitatively judging the samples. Consequently, some of these metrics only apply to images.

Test likelihood: One way to compare probabilistic models is to measure their likelihood for a test dataset. It is ineffective to measure the training data likelihood because a model could assign a very high probability to each training point and very low probabilities in between. This model would have a very high training likelihood but could only reproduce the training data. The test likelihood captures how well the model generalizes from the training data and also the coverage; if the model assigns a high probability to just a subset of the training data, it must assign lower probabilities elsewhere, so a portion of the test examples will have low probability.

Test likelihood is a sensible way to quantify probabilistic models, but unfortunately, it is not relevant for generative adversarial models (which do not assign a probability) and is expensive to estimate for variational autoencoders and diffusion models (although it is possible to compute a lower bound on the log-likelihood). Normalizing flows are the only type of model for which the likelihood can be computed exactly and efficiently.

Inception score: The inception score (IS) is specialized for images and ideally for generative models trained on the ImageNet database. The score is calculated using a pre-trained classification model – usually the "Inception" model, from which the name is derived. It is based on two criteria. First, each generated image $\mathbf{x}^*$ should look like one and only one of the 1000 possible classes y in the ImageNet database. Hence, the probability distribution $Pr(y_i|\mathbf{x}_i^*)$ should be highly peaked at the correct class. Second, the entire set of generated images should be assigned to the classes with equal probability, so $Pr(y)$ should be flat when averaged over all generated examples.

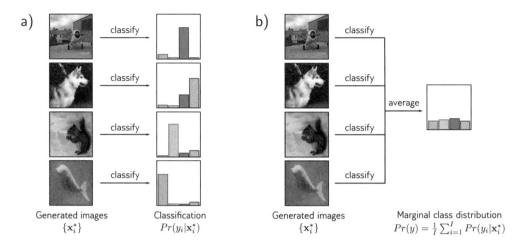

Figure 14.4 Inception score. a) A pretrained network classifies the generated images. If the images are realistic, the resulting class probabilities $Pr(y_i|\mathbf{x}_i^*)$ should be peaked at the correct class. b) If the model generates all classes equally frequently, the marginal (average) class probabilities should be flat. The inception score measures the average distance between the distributions in (a) and the distribution in (b). Images from Deng et al. (2009).

The inception score measures the average distance between these two distributions over the generated set. This distance will be large if one is peaked and the other flat (figure 14.4). More precisely, it returns the exponential of the expected KL-divergence between $Pr(y_i|\mathbf{x}_i^*)$ and $Pr(y)$:

Appendix C.5.1
KL divergence

$$IS = \exp\left[\frac{1}{I}\sum_{i=1}^{I} D_{KL}\Big[Pr(y_i|\mathbf{x}_i^*)||Pr(y)\Big]\right], \qquad (14.2)$$

where I is the number of generated examples and:

$$Pr(y) = \frac{1}{I}\sum_{i=1}^{I} Pr(y_i|\mathbf{x}_i^*). \qquad (14.3)$$

This metric is only sensible for generative models of the ImageNet database and is sensitive to the particular classification model; retraining this model can give quite different numerical results. Moreover, it does not reward diversity within an object class; it returns a high value if the model only generates one realistic example of each class.

Fréchet inception distance: This measure is also intended for images and computes a symmetric distance between the distributions of generated samples and real examples. This must be approximate since it is hard to characterize either distribution (indeed, characterizing the distribution of real examples is the job of generative models in the first place). Hence, the Fréchet inception distance approximates both distributions by multivariate Gaussians and (as the name suggests) estimates the distance between them using the Fréchet distance.

Appendix C.5.4
Fréchet distance

However, it does not model the distance with respect to the original data but rather the activations in the deepest layer of the inception classification network. These hidden units are the ones most associated with object classes, so the comparison occurs at a semantic level, ignoring the more fine-grained details of the images. This metric does take account of diversity within classes but relies heavily on the information retained by the features in the inception network; any information discarded by the network does not contribute to the result. Some of this discarded information may still be important to generate realistic samples.

Manifold precision/recall: Fréchet inception distance is sensitive both to the realism of the samples and their diversity but does not distinguish between these factors. To disentangle these qualities, we consider the overlap between the data *manifold* (i.e., the subset of the data space where the real examples lie) and the model manifold (i.e., where the generated samples lie). The *precision* is the fraction of model samples that fall into the data manifold. This measures the proportion of generated samples that are realistic. The *recall* is the fraction of data examples that fall within the model manifold. This measures the proportion of the real data the model can generate (figure 14.5).

To estimate the manifold, we place a hypersphere around each data example, whose radius is the distance to the kth nearest neighbor. The union of these spheres is an approximation of the manifold, and it's easy to determine if a new point lies within it. This manifold is also typically computed in the feature space of a classifier with the advantages and disadvantages that entails.

14.4   Summary

Unsupervised models learn about the structure of a dataset in the absence of labels. A subset of these models is generative and can synthesize new data examples. A further subset is probabilistic in that they can both generate new examples and assign a probability to observed data. The models considered in the following four chapters start with a latent variable $\mathbf{z}$ which has a known distribution. A deep neural network then maps from the latent variable to the observed data space. We considered desirable properties of generative models and introduced metrics that attempt to quantify their performance.

Notes

Popular generative models include generative adversarial networks (Goodfellow et al., 2014), variational autoencoders (Kingma & Welling, 2014), normalizing flows (Rezende & Mohamed,

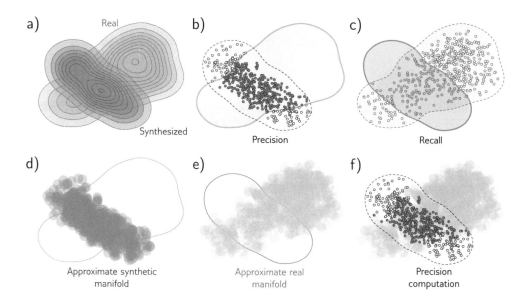

Figure 14.5 Manifold precision/recall. a) True distributions of real examples and samples synthesized by the generative model. b) The overlap can be summarized by the *precision* (the proportion of synthesized samples that overlap with the distribution or *manifold* of real examples), and c) *recall* (the proportion of real examples that overlap with the manifold of the synthesized samples). d) The manifold of synthesized samples can be approximated by taking the union of a set of hyperspheres centered on each sample. Here, these have constant radius, but more commonly, the radius is based on the distance to the kth nearest neighbor. e) The manifold for real examples is approximated similarly. f) The precision can be computed as the proportion of real examples that lie within the approximated manifold of samples. Similarly, the recall is computed as the proportion of samples that lie within the approximated manifold of real examples (not shown). Adapted from Kynkäänniemi et al. (2019).

2015), diffusion models (Sohl-Dickstein et al., 2015; Ho et al., 2020), autoregressive models (Bengio et al., 2000; Van den Oord et al., 2016b), and energy-based models (LeCun et al., 2006). All except energy models are discussed in this book. Bond-Taylor et al. (2022) provide a recent survey of generative models.

Evaluation: Salimans et al. (2016) introduced the inception score, and Heusel et al. (2017) introduced the Fréchet inception distance, both of which are based on the Pool-3 layer of the Inception V3 model (Szegedy et al., 2016). Nash et al. (2021) used earlier layers of the same network that retain more spatial information to ensure that the spatial statistics of images are also replicated. Kynkäänniemi et al. (2019) introduced the manifold precision/recall method. Barratt & Sharma (2018) discuss the inception score in detail and point out its weaknesses. Borji (2022) discusses the pros and cons of different methods for assessing generative models.

Chapter 15

Generative Adversarial Networks

A *generative adversarial network* or *GAN* is an unsupervised model that aims to generate new samples that are indistinguishable from a set of training examples. GANs are just mechanisms to create new samples; they do not build a probability distribution over the modeled data and hence cannot evaluate the probability that a new data point belongs to the same distribution.

In a GAN, the main *generator* network creates samples by mapping random noise to the output data space. If a second *discriminator* network cannot distinguish between the generated samples and the real examples, the samples must be plausible. If this network *can* tell the difference, this provides a training signal that can be fed back to improve the quality of the samples. This idea is simple, but training GANs is difficult: the learning algorithm can be unstable, and although GANs may learn to generate realistic samples, this does not imply that they learn to generate *all* possible samples.

GANs have been applied to many types of data, including audio, 3D models, text, video, and graphs. However, they have found the most success in the image domain, where they can produce samples that are almost indistinguishable from real pictures. Accordingly, the examples in this chapter focus on synthesizing images.

15.1 Discrimination as a signal

We aim to generate new samples $\{\mathbf{x}_j^*\}$ that are drawn from the same distribution as a set of real training data $\{\mathbf{x}_i\}$. A single new sample $\mathbf{x}_j^*$ is generated by (i) choosing a *latent variable* $\mathbf{z}_j$ from a simple base distribution (e.g., a standard normal) and then (ii) passing this data through a network $\mathbf{x}_j^* = \mathbf{g}[\mathbf{z}_j, \boldsymbol{\theta}]$ with parameters $\boldsymbol{\theta}$. This network is known as the *generator*. During the learning process, the goal is to find parameters $\boldsymbol{\theta}$ so that the samples $\{\mathbf{x}_j^*\}$ look "similar" to the real data $\{\mathbf{x}_i\}$ (see figure 14.2a).

Similarity can be defined in many ways, but the GAN uses the principle that the samples should be statistically indistinguishable from the true data. To this end, a second network $\mathbf{f}[\bullet, \boldsymbol{\phi}]$ with parameters $\boldsymbol{\phi}$ called the *discriminator* is introduced. This network aims to classify its input as being a real example or a generated sample. If this

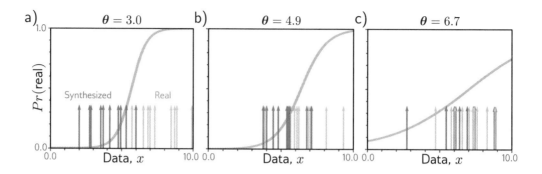

Figure 15.1 GAN mechanism. a) Given a parameterized function (a generator) that synthesizes samples (orange arrows) and a batch of real examples (cyan arrows), we train a discriminator to distinguish the real examples from the generated samples (sigmoid curve indicates the estimated probability that the data point is real). b) The generator is trained by modifying its parameters so that the discriminator becomes less confident the samples were synthetic (in this case, by moving the orange samples to the right). The discriminator is then updated. c) Alternating updates to the generator and discriminator cause the generated samples to become indistinguishable from real examples and the impetus to change the generator (i.e., the slope of the sigmoid function) to diminish.

proves impossible, the generated samples are indistinguishable from the real examples, and we have succeeded. If it is possible, the discriminator provides a signal that can be used to improve the generation process.

Figure 15.1 illustrates this scheme. We start with a training set $\{x_i\}$ of real 1D examples. A different batch of ten of these examples $\{x_i\}_{i=1}^{10}$ is shown in each panel (cyan arrows). To create a batch of samples $\{x_j^*\}$, we use the simple generator:

$$x_j^* = g[z_j, \theta] = z_j + \theta, \tag{15.1}$$

where latent variables $\{z_j\}$ are drawn from a standard normal distribution, and the parameter θ translates the generated samples along the x-axis (figure 15.1).

At initialization, $\theta = 3.0$, and the generated samples (orange arrows) lie to the left of the real examples (cyan arrows). The discriminator is trained to distinguish the generated samples from the real examples (the sigmoid curve indicates the probability that a data point is real). During training, the generator parameters θ are manipulated to increase the probability that its samples are classified as real. Here, this means increasing θ so that the samples move rightwards where the sigmoid curve is higher.

We alternate between updating the discriminator and the generator. Figures 15.1b–c show two iterations of this process. It gradually becomes harder to classify the data, so the impetus to change θ becomes weaker (i.e., the sigmoid becomes flatter). At the end of the process, there is no way to distinguish the two sets of data; the discriminator, which now has chance performance, is discarded, and we are left with a generator that makes plausible samples.

Notebook 15.1
GAN toy example

15.1.1 GAN loss function

We now define the loss function for training GANs more precisely. The discriminator $f[\mathbf{x}, \boldsymbol{\phi}]$ takes input $\mathbf{x}$, has parameters $\boldsymbol{\phi}$, and returns a scalar that is higher when it believes the input is a real example. This is a binary classification task, so we adapt the binary cross-entropy loss function (section 5.4), which originally had the form:

$$\hat{\boldsymbol{\phi}} = \underset{\boldsymbol{\phi}}{\operatorname{argmin}} \left[\sum_i -(1 - y_i) \log\left[1 - \operatorname{sig}[f[\mathbf{x}_i, \boldsymbol{\phi}]]\right] - y_i \log\left[\operatorname{sig}[f[\mathbf{x}_i, \boldsymbol{\phi}]]\right] \right], \quad (15.2)$$

where $y_i \in \{0, 1\}$ is the label, and $\operatorname{sig}[\bullet]$ is the logistic sigmoid function (figure 5.7).

In this case, we assume that the real examples $\mathbf{x}$ have label $y = 1$ and the generated samples $\mathbf{x}^*$ have label $y = 0$ so that:

$$\hat{\boldsymbol{\phi}} = \underset{\boldsymbol{\phi}}{\operatorname{argmin}} \left[\sum_j - \log\left[1 - \operatorname{sig}[f[\mathbf{x}_j^*, \boldsymbol{\phi}]]\right] - \sum_i \log\left[\operatorname{sig}[f[\mathbf{x}_i, \boldsymbol{\phi}]]\right] \right], \quad (15.3)$$

where i and j index the real examples and generated samples, respectively.

Now we substitute the definition for the generator $\mathbf{x}_j^* = \mathbf{g}[\mathbf{z}_j, \boldsymbol{\theta}]$ and note that we must maximize with respect to $\boldsymbol{\theta}$ since we want the generated samples to be misclassified (i.e., have low likelihood of being synthetic or high negative log-likelihood):

$$\hat{\boldsymbol{\theta}} = \underset{\boldsymbol{\theta}}{\operatorname{argmax}} \left[\underset{\boldsymbol{\phi}}{\operatorname{min}} \left[\sum_j - \log\left[1 - \operatorname{sig}[f[\mathbf{g}[\mathbf{z}_j, \boldsymbol{\theta}], \boldsymbol{\phi}]]\right] - \sum_i \log\left[\operatorname{sig}[f[\mathbf{x}_i, \boldsymbol{\phi}]]\right] \right] \right]. \quad (15.4)$$

15.1.2 Training GANs

Equation 15.4 is a more complex loss function than we have seen before; the discriminator parameters $\boldsymbol{\phi}$ are manipulated to minimize the loss function, and the generative parameters $\boldsymbol{\theta}$ are manipulated to maximize the loss function. GAN training is characterized as a *minimax game*; the generator tries to find new ways to fool the discriminator, which in turn searches for new ways to distinguish generated samples from real examples. Technically, the solution is a *Nash equilibrium* — the optimization algorithm searches for a position that is simultaneously a minimum of one function and a maximum of the other. If training proceeds as planned, then upon convergence, $\mathbf{g}[\mathbf{z}, \boldsymbol{\theta}]$ will be drawn from the same distribution as the data, and $\operatorname{sig}[f[\bullet, \boldsymbol{\phi}]]$ will be at chance (i.e., 0.5).

To train the GAN, we can divide equation 15.4 into two loss functions:

$$\begin{aligned}
L[\boldsymbol{\phi}] &= \sum_j - \log\left[1 - \operatorname{sig}[f[\mathbf{g}[\mathbf{z}_j, \boldsymbol{\theta}], \boldsymbol{\phi}]]\right] - \sum_i \log\left[\operatorname{sig}[f[\mathbf{x}_i, \boldsymbol{\phi}]]\right] \\
L[\boldsymbol{\theta}] &= \sum_j \log\left[1 - \operatorname{sig}[f[\mathbf{g}[\mathbf{z}_j, \boldsymbol{\theta}], \boldsymbol{\phi}]]\right],
\end{aligned} \quad (15.5)$$

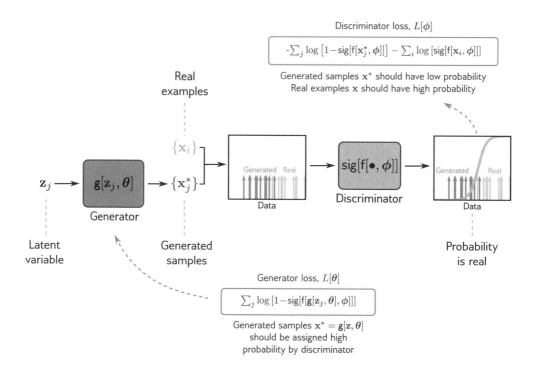

Figure 15.2 GAN loss functions. A latent variable $\mathbf{z}_j$ is drawn from the base distribution and passed through the generator to create a sample $\mathbf{x}^*$. A batch $\{\mathbf{x}_j^*\}$ of samples and a batch of real examples $\{\mathbf{x}_i\}$ are passed to the discriminator, which assigns a probability that each is real. The discriminator parameters ϕ are modified to assign high probability to the real examples and low probability to the generated samples. The generator parameters $\boldsymbol{\theta}$ are modified to "fool" the discriminator into assigning the generated samples a high probability.

where we multiplied the second function by minus one to convert to a minimization problem and dropped the second term, which has no dependence on $\boldsymbol{\theta}$. Minimizing the first loss function trains the discriminator. Minimizing the second trains the generator.

At each step, we draw a batch of latent variables $\mathbf{z}_j$ from the base distribution and pass these through the generator to create samples $\mathbf{x}_j^* = \mathbf{g}[\mathbf{z}_j, \boldsymbol{\theta}]$. Then we choose a batch of real training examples $\mathbf{x}_i$. Given the two batches, we can now perform one or more gradient descent steps on each loss function (figure 15.2).

15.1.3 Deep convolutional GAN

The *deep convolutional GAN* or *DCGAN* was an early GAN architecture specialized for generating images (figure 15.3). The input to the generator $\mathbf{g}[\mathbf{z}, \boldsymbol{\theta}]$ is a 100D latent

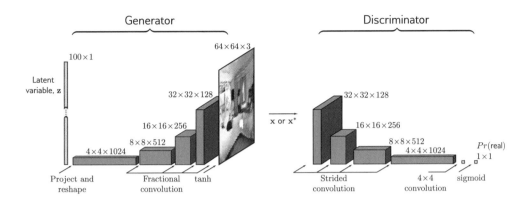

Figure 15.3 DCGAN architecture. In the generator, a 100D latent variable **z** is drawn from a uniform distribution and mapped by a linear transformation to a 4×4 representation with 1024 channels. This is then passed through a series of convolutional layers that gradually upsample the representation and decrease the number of channels. At the end is a tanh function that maps the 64×64×3 representation to a fixed range so that it can represent an image. The discriminator consists of a standard convolutional net that classifies the input as either a real example or a generated sample.

variable **z** sampled from a uniform distribution. This is then mapped to a 4×4 spatial representation with 1024 channels using a linear transformation. Four convolutional layers follow, each of which uses a fractionally-strided convolution that doubles the resolution (i.e., a convolution with a stride of 0.5). At the final layer, the 64×64×3 signal is passed through a tanh function to generate an image $\mathbf{x}^*$ in the range $[-1, 1]$. The discriminator $f[\bullet, \phi]$ is a standard convolutional network where the final convolutional layer reduces the size to 1×1 with one channel. This single number is passed through a sigmoid function $\text{sig}[\bullet]$ to create the output probability.

After training, the discriminator is discarded. To create new samples, latent variables **z** are drawn from the base distribution and passed through the generator. Example results are shown in figure 15.4.

15.1.4 Difficulty training GANs

Theoretically, the GAN is fairly straightforward. However, GANs are notoriously difficult to train. For example, to get the DCGAN to train reliably, it was necessary to (i) use strided convolutions for upsampling and downsampling; (ii) use BatchNorm in both generator and discriminator except in the last and first layers, respectively; (iii) use the leaky ReLU activation function (figure 3.13) in the discriminator; and (iv) use the Adam optimizer but with a lower momentum coefficient than usual. This is unusual. Most deep learning models are relatively robust to such choices.

a)   b)   c)

Figure 15.4 Synthesized images from the DCGAN model. a) Random samples drawn from DCGAN trained on a faces dataset. b) Random samples using the ImageNet database (see figure 10.15). c) Random samples drawn from the LSUN scene understanding dataset. Adapted from Radford et al. (2015).

Figure 15.5 Mode collapse. Synthesized images from a GAN trained on the LSUN scene understanding dataset using an MLP generator with a similar number of parameters and layers to the DCGAN. The samples are low quality, and many are similar. Adapted from Arjovsky et al. (2017).

A common failure mode is that the generator makes plausible samples, but these only represent a subset of the data (e.g., for faces, it might never generate faces with beards). This is known as *mode dropping*. An extreme version of this phenomenon can occur where the generator entirely or mostly ignores the latent variables $\mathbf{z}$ and collapses all samples to one or a few points; this is known as *mode collapse* (figure 15.5).

15.2   Improving stability

To understand *why* GANs are difficult to train, it's necessary to understand exactly *what* the loss function represents.

15.2.1 Analysis of GAN loss function

If we divide the two sums in the first line of equation 15.5 by the numbers I, J of real and generated samples, then the loss function can be written in terms of expectations:

$$
L[\phi] = -\frac{1}{J}\sum_{j=1}^{J}\left(\log\left[1 - \text{sig}[f[\mathbf{x}_j^*, \phi]]\right]\right) - \frac{1}{I}\sum_{i=1}^{I}\left(\log\left[\text{sig}[f[\mathbf{x}_i, \phi]]\right]\right) \tag{15.6}
$$

$$
\approx -\mathbb{E}_{\mathbf{x}^*}\left[\log\left[1 - \text{sig}[f[\mathbf{x}^*, \phi]]\right]\right] - \mathbb{E}_{\mathbf{x}}\left[\log\left[\text{sig}[f[\mathbf{x}, \phi]]\right]\right]
$$

$$
= -\int Pr(\mathbf{x}^*)\log\left[1 - \text{sig}[f[\mathbf{x}^*, \phi]]\right]d\mathbf{x}^* - \int Pr(\mathbf{x})\log\left[\text{sig}[f[\mathbf{x}, \phi]]\right]d\mathbf{x},
$$

where $Pr(\mathbf{x}^*)$ is the probability distribution over the generated samples, and $Pr(\mathbf{x})$ is the true probability distribution over the real examples.

When $I = J$, the optimal discriminator for an example $\tilde{\mathbf{x}}$ of unknown origin is:

$$
Pr(\text{real}|\tilde{\mathbf{x}}) = \text{sig}\left[f[\tilde{\mathbf{x}}, \phi]\right] = \frac{Pr(\tilde{\mathbf{x}}|\text{real})}{Pr(\tilde{\mathbf{x}}|\text{generated}) + Pr(\tilde{\mathbf{x}}|\text{real})} = \frac{Pr(\mathbf{x})}{Pr(\mathbf{x}^*) + Pr(\mathbf{x})}, \tag{15.7}
$$

where on the right hand side, we evaluate $\tilde{\mathbf{x}}$ against the generated distribution $Pr(\mathbf{x}^*)$ and the real distribution $Pr(\mathbf{x})$. Substituting into equation 15.6, we get:

$$
L[\phi] = -\int Pr(\mathbf{x}^*)\log\left[1 - \text{sig}[f[\mathbf{x}^*, \phi]]\right]d\mathbf{x}^* - \int Pr(\mathbf{x})\log\left[\text{sig}[f[\mathbf{x}, \phi]]\right]d\mathbf{x} \tag{15.8}
$$

$$
= -\int Pr(\mathbf{x}^*)\log\left[1 - \frac{Pr(\mathbf{x})}{Pr(\mathbf{x}^*) + Pr(\mathbf{x})}\right]d\mathbf{x}^* - \int Pr(\mathbf{x})\log\left[\frac{Pr(\mathbf{x})}{Pr(\mathbf{x}^*) + Pr(\mathbf{x})}\right]d\mathbf{x}
$$

$$
= -\int Pr(\mathbf{x}^*)\log\left[\frac{Pr(\mathbf{x}^*)}{Pr(\mathbf{x}^*) + Pr(\mathbf{x})}\right]d\mathbf{x}^* - \int Pr(\mathbf{x})\log\left[\frac{Pr(\mathbf{x})}{Pr(\mathbf{x}^*) + Pr(\mathbf{x})}\right]d\mathbf{x}.
$$

Disregarding additive and multiplicative constants, this is the Jensen-Shannon divergence between the synthesized distribution $Pr(x^*)$ and the true distribution $Pr(x)$:

Problems 15.1–15.2

Appendix C.5.2
Jensen-Shannon
divergence

$$
D_{JS}\left[Pr(\mathbf{x}^*)\,\|\,Pr(\mathbf{x})\right] \tag{15.9}
$$

$$
= \frac{1}{2}D_{KL}\left[Pr(\mathbf{x}^*)\,\left\|\,\frac{Pr(\mathbf{x}^*) + Pr(\mathbf{x})}{2}\right.\right] + \frac{1}{2}D_{KL}\left[Pr(\mathbf{x})\,\left\|\,\frac{Pr(\mathbf{x}^*) + Pr(\mathbf{x})}{2}\right.\right]
$$

$$
= \underbrace{\frac{1}{2}\int Pr(\mathbf{x}^*)\log\left[\frac{2Pr(\mathbf{x}^*)}{Pr(\mathbf{x}^*) + Pr(\mathbf{x})}\right]d\mathbf{x}^*}_{\text{quality}} + \underbrace{\frac{1}{2}\int Pr(\mathbf{x})\log\left[\frac{2Pr(\mathbf{x})}{Pr(\mathbf{x}^*) + Pr(\mathbf{x})}\right]d\mathbf{x}}_{\text{coverage}}.
$$

where $D_{KL}[\bullet\|\bullet]$ is the Kullback-Leibler divergence.

The first term indicates the distance will be small if, wherever the sample density $Pr(\mathbf{x}^*)$ is high, the mixture $(Pr(\mathbf{x}^*) + Pr(\mathbf{x}))/2$ has high probability. In other words, it penalizes regions with samples $\mathbf{x}^*$ but no real examples $\mathbf{x}$; it enforces *quality*. The second term says that the distance will be small if, wherever the true density $Pr(\mathbf{x})$

Appendix C.5.1
Kullback-Leibler
divergence

Figure 15.6 Problem with GAN loss function. If the generated samples (orange arrows) are easy to distinguish from the real examples (cyan arrows), then the discriminator (sigmoid) may have a very shallow slope at the positions of the samples; hence, the gradient to update the parameter of the generator may be tiny.

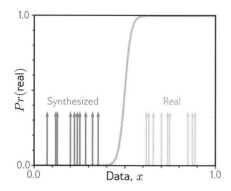

is high, the mixture $(Pr(\mathbf{x}^*) + Pr(\mathbf{x}))/2$ has high probability. In other words, it penalizes regions with real examples but no samples. It enforces *coverage*. Referring to equation 15.6, we see that the second term does not depend on the generator, which consequently doesn't care about coverage; it is happy to generate a subset of possible examples accurately. This is the putative reason for mode dropping.

15.2.2   Vanishing gradients

In the previous section, we saw that when the discriminator is optimal, the loss function minimizes a measure of the distance between the generated and real samples. However, there is a potential problem with using this distance between probability distributions as the criterion for optimizing GANs. If the probability distributions are completely disjoint, this distance is infinite, and any small change to the generator will not decrease the loss. The same phenomenon can be seen when we consider the original formulation; if the discriminator can perfectly separate the generated and real samples, no small change to the generated data will change the classification score (figure 15.6).

Unfortunately, the distributions of generated samples and real examples may *really be* disjoint; the generated samples lie in a subspace that is the size of the latent variable $\mathbf{z}$, and the real examples also lie in a low-dimensional subspace due to the physical processes that created the data (figure 1.9). There may be little or no overlap between these subspaces, and the result is very small or no gradients.

Figure 15.7 provides empirical evidence to support this hypothesis. If the DCGAN generator is frozen and the discriminator is updated repeatedly so that its classification performance improves, the generator gradients decrease. In short, there is a very fine balance between the quality of the discriminator and the generator; if the discriminator becomes too good, the training updates of the generator are attenuated.

15.2.3   Wasserstein distance

The previous sections showed that (i) the GAN loss can be interpreted in terms of distances between probability distributions and that (ii) the gradient of this distance

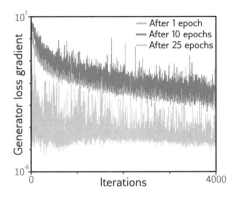

Figure 15.7 Vanishing gradients in the generator of a DCGAN. The generator is frozen after 1, 10, and 25 epochs, and the discriminator is trained further. The gradient of the generator decreases rapidly (note log scale); if the discriminator becomes too accurate, the gradients for the generator vanish. Adapted from Arjovsky & Bottou (2017).

becomes zero when the generated samples are too easy to distinguish from the real examples. The obvious way forward is to choose a distance metric with better properties.

The *Wasserstein* or (for discrete distributions) *earth mover's* distance is the quantity of work required to transport the probability mass from one distribution to create the other. Here, "work" is defined as the mass multiplied by the distance moved. This immediately sounds more promising; the Wasserstein distance is well-defined even when the distributions are disjoint and decreases smoothly as they become closer to one another.

15.2.4 Wasserstein distance for discrete distributions

The Wasserstein distance is easiest to understand for discrete distributions (figure 15.8). Consider distributions $Pr(x = i)$ and $q(x = j)$ defined over K bins. Assume there is a cost C_{ij} associated with moving one unit of mass from bin i in the first distribution to bin j in the second; this cost might be the absolute difference $|i - j|$ between the indices. The amounts that are moved form the *transport plan* and are stored in a matrix $\mathbf{P}$.

The Wasserstein distance is defined as:

$$D_w\Big[Pr(x)||q(x)\Big] = \min_{\mathbf{P}} \left[\sum_{i,j} P_{ij} \cdot |i - j| \right], \qquad (15.10)$$

subject to the constraints that:

$$\begin{array}{rcll} \sum_j P_{ij} &=& Pr(x = i) & \text{initial distribution of } Pr(x) \\ \sum_i P_{ij} &=& q(x = j) & \text{initial distribution of } q(x) \\ P_{ij} &\geq& 0 & \text{non-negative masses.} \end{array} \qquad (15.11)$$

In other words, the Wasserstein distance is the solution to a constrained minimization problem that maps the mass of one distribution to the other. This is inconvenient as we must solve this minimization problem over the elements P_{ij} every time we want to compute the distance. Fortunately, this is a standard problem that is easily solved for small systems of equations. It is a *linear programming problem* in its *primal form*.

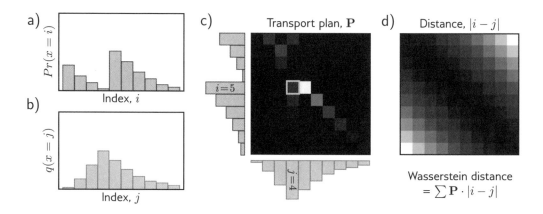

Figure 15.8 Wasserstein or earth mover's distance. a) Consider the discrete distribution $Pr(x = i)$. b) We wish to move the probability mass to create the target distribution $q(x = j)$. c) The transport plan $\mathbf{P}$ identifies how much mass will be moved from i to j. For example, the cyan highlighted square p_{54} indicates how much mass will be moved from $i = 5$ to $j = 4$. The elements of the transport plan must be non-negative, the sum over j must be $Pr(x = i)$, and the sum over i must be $q(x = j)$. Hence $\mathbf{P}$ is a joint probability distribution. d) The distance matrix between elements i and j. The optimal transport plan $\mathbf{P}$ minimizes the sum of the pointwise product of $\mathbf{P}$ and the distance matrix (termed the Wasserstein distance). Hence, the elements of $\mathbf{P}$ tend to lie close to the diagonal where the distance cost is lowest. Adapted from Hermann (2017).

primal form			dual form			
minimize	$\mathbf{c}^T\mathbf{p}$,		maximize	$\mathbf{b}^T\mathbf{f}$,		
such that	$\mathbf{Ap}$	$= \quad \mathbf{b}$	such that	$\mathbf{A}^T\mathbf{f}$	$\leq$	$\mathbf{c}$
and	$\mathbf{p}$	$\geq \quad \mathbf{0}$				

Problem 15.3

where $\mathbf{p}$ contains the vectorized elements P_{ij} that determine the amount of mass moved, $\mathbf{c}$ contains the distances, $\mathbf{Ap} = \mathbf{b}$ contains the initial distribution constraints, and $\mathbf{p} \geq 0$ ensures the masses moved are non-negative.[1]

As for all linear programming problems, there is an equivalent *dual problem* with the same solution. Here, we maximize with respect to a variable $\mathbf{f}$ that is applied to the initial distributions, subject to constraints that depend on the distances $\mathbf{c}$. The solution to this dual problem is:

Notebook 15.2
Wasserstein
distance

$$D_w\Big[Pr(x)||q(x)\Big] = \max_{\mathbf{f}} \left[\sum_i Pr(x = i)f_i - \sum_j q(x = j)f_j \right], \qquad (15.12)$$

[1]The mathematical background is omitted due to space constraints. Linear programming is a standard problem with well-known algorithms for finding the minimum.

subject to the constraint that:

$$|f_{i+1} - f_i| < 1. \tag{15.13}$$

In other words, we optimize over a new set of variables $\{f_i\}$ where adjacent values cannot change by more than one.

15.2.5 Wasserstein distance for continuous distributions

Translating these results back to the continuous multi-dimensional domain, the equivalent of the primal form (equation 15.10) is:

Problems 15.4–15.5

$$D_w\Big[Pr(\mathbf{x}), q(\mathbf{x})\Big] = \min_{\pi[\bullet,\bullet]} \left[\iint \pi(\mathbf{x}_1, \mathbf{x}_2) \cdot ||\mathbf{x}_1 - \mathbf{x}_2|| d\mathbf{x}_1 d\mathbf{x}_2 \right], \tag{15.14}$$

subject to constraints similar to equation 15.11 on the transport plan $\pi(\mathbf{x}_1, \mathbf{x}_2)$ representing the mass moved from position $\mathbf{x}_1$ to $\mathbf{x}_2$. The equivalent of the dual form (equation 15.12) is:

$$D_w\Big[Pr(\mathbf{x}), q(\mathbf{x})\Big] = \max_{f[\mathbf{x}]} \left[\int Pr(\mathbf{x})f[\mathbf{x}]d\mathbf{x} - \int q(\mathbf{x})f[\mathbf{x}]d\mathbf{x} \right], \tag{15.15}$$

subject to the constraint that the Lipschitz constant of the function $f[\mathbf{x}]$ is less than one (i.e., the absolute gradient of the function is less than one).

Appendix B.1.1 Lipschitz constant

15.2.6 Wasserstein GAN loss function

In the context of neural networks, we maximize over the space of functions $f[\mathbf{x}]$ by optimizing the parameters ϕ in a neural network $f[\mathbf{x}, \phi]$, and we approximate these integrals using generated samples $\mathbf{x}_i^*$ and real examples $\mathbf{x}_i$:

$$
\begin{aligned}
L[\phi] &= \sum_j f[\mathbf{x}_j^*, \phi] - \sum_i f[\mathbf{x}_i, \phi] \\
&= \sum_j f[\mathbf{g}[\mathbf{z}_j, \boldsymbol{\theta}], \phi] - \sum_i f[\mathbf{x}_i, \phi],
\end{aligned}
\tag{15.16}
$$

where we must constrain the neural network discriminator $\mathbf{f}[\mathbf{x}_i, \phi]$ to have an absolute gradient norm of less than one at every position $\mathbf{x}$:

$$\left| \frac{\partial f[\mathbf{x}, \phi]}{\partial \mathbf{x}} \right| < 1. \tag{15.17}$$

One way to achieve this is to clip the discriminator weights to a small range (e.g., $[-0.01, 0.01]$). An alternative is the *gradient penalty Wasserstein GAN* or *WGAN-GP*, which adds a regularization term that increases as the gradient norm deviates from unity.

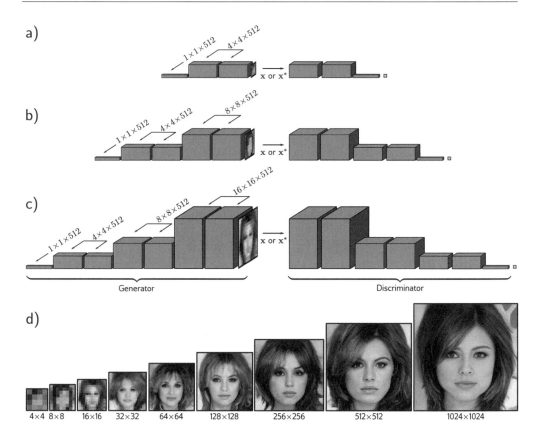

Figure 15.9 Progressive growing. a) The generator is initially trained to create very small (4×4) images, and the discriminator to identify if these images are synthesized or downsampled real images. b) After training at this low-resolution terminates, subsequent layers are added to the generator to generate (8×8) images. Similar layers are added to the discriminator to downsample back again. c) This process continues to create (16×16) images and so on. In this way, a GAN that produces very realistic high-resolution images can be trained. d) Images of increasing resolution generated at different stages from the same latent variable. Adapted from Wolf (2021), using method of Karras et al. (2018).

15.3 Progressive growing, minibatch discrimination, and truncation

The Wasserstein formulation makes GAN training more stable. However, further machinery is needed to generate high-quality images. We now review *progressive growing*, *minibatch discrimination*, and *truncation*, which all improve output quality.

In *progressive growing* (figure 15.9), we first train a GAN that synthesizes 4×4 images using an architecture similar to the DCGAN. Then we add subsequent layers to the generator, which upsample the representation and perform further processing to create

a)

b)

c)

d)

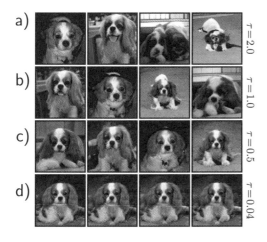

$\tau = 2.0$

$\tau = 1.0$

$\tau = 0.5$

$\tau = 0.04$

Figure 15.10 Truncation. The quality of GAN samples can be traded off against diversity by rejecting samples from the latent variable **z** that fall further than τ standard deviations from the mean. a) If this threshold is large ($\tau = 2.0$), the samples are visually varied but may have defects. b–c) As this threshold is decreased, the average visual quality improves, but the diversity decreases. d) With a very small threshold, the samples look almost identical. By judiciously choosing this threshold, it's possible to increase the average quality of GAN results. Adapted from Brock et al. (2019).

Figure 15.11 Progressive growing. This method generates realistic images of faces when trained on the CELEBA-HQ dataset and more complex, variable objects when trained on LSUN categories. Adapted from Karras et al. (2018).

Figure 15.12 Traversing latent space of progressive GAN trained on LSUN cars. Moving in the latent space produces car images that change smoothly. This usually only works for short trajectories; eventually, the latent variable moves to somewhere that produces unrealistic images. Adapted from Karras et al. (2018).

an 8×8 image. The discriminator also has extra layers added to it so that it can receive the higher-resolution images and classify them as either being generated samples or real examples. In practice, the higher-resolution layers gradually "fade in" over time; initially, the higher-resolution image is an upsampled version of the previous result, passed via a residual connection, and the new layers gradually take over.

Mini-batch discrimination ensures that the samples have sufficient variety and hence helps prevent mode collapse. This can be done by computing feature statistics across the mini-batches of synthesized and real data. These can be summarized and added as a feature map (usually toward the end of the discriminator). This allows the discriminator to send a signal back to the generator, encouraging it to include a similar amount of variation in the synthesized data as in the original dataset.

Another trick to improve generation results is *truncation* (figure 15.10), in which only latent variables $\mathbf{z}$ with high probability (i.e., close to the mean) are chosen during sampling. This reduces the variation in the samples but improves their quality. Careful normalization and regularization schemes also improve sample quality. Using combinations of these methods, GANs can synthesize varied and realistic images (figure 15.11). Moving smoothly through the latent space can also sometimes produce realistic interpolations from one synthesized image to another (figure 15.12).

Problem 15.6

15.4   Conditional generation

GANs produce realistic images but don't specify their attributes: we can't choose the hair color, ethnicity, or age of faces, without training separate GANs for each combination of characteristics. *Conditional generation* models provide us with this control.

15.4.1   Conditional GAN

The *conditional GAN* passes a vector $\mathbf{c}$ of attributes to both the generator and discriminator, which are now written as $\mathbf{g}[\mathbf{z}, \mathbf{c}, \boldsymbol{\theta}]$ and $\mathrm{f}[\mathbf{x}, \mathbf{c}, \boldsymbol{\phi}]$, respectively. The generator aims to transform the latent variable $\mathbf{z}$ into a data sample $\mathbf{x}$ with the correct attribute $\mathbf{c}$. The discriminator's goal is to distinguish between (i) the generated sample with the target attribute or (ii) a real example with the real attribute (figure 15.13a).

For the generator, the attribute $\mathbf{c}$ can be appended to the latent vector $\mathbf{z}$. For the discriminator, it may be appended to the input if the data are 1D. If the data comprise images, the attribute can be linearly transformed to a 2D representation and appended as an extra channel to the discriminator input or to one of its intermediate hidden layers.

15.4.2   Auxiliary classifier GAN

The *auxiliary classifier GAN* or *ACGAN* simplifies conditional generation by requiring that the discriminator correctly predicts the attribute (figure 15.13b). For a discrete

a) Conditional GAN

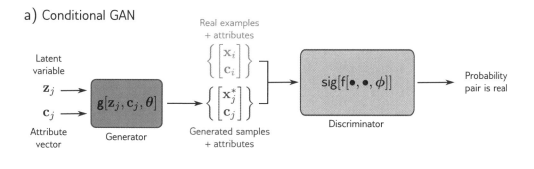

b) Auxiliary classifier GAN

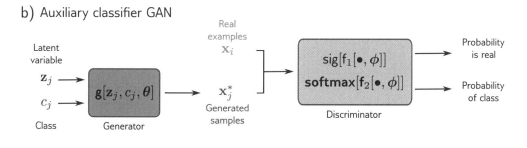

c) InfoGAN

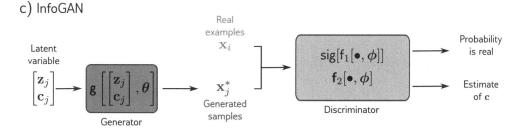

Figure 15.13 Conditional generation. a) The generator of the conditional GAN also receives an attribute vector **c** describing some aspect of the image. As usual, the discriminator receives either a real example or a generated sample, but now it also receives the attribute vector; this encourages the samples both to be realistic and compatible with the attribute. b) The generator of the auxiliary classifier GAN (ACGAN) takes a discrete attribute variable. The discriminator must both (i) determine if its input is real or synthetic and (ii) identify the class correctly. c) The InfoGAN splits the latent variable into noise **z** and unspecified random attributes **c**. The discriminator must distinguish if its input is real and also reconstruct these attributes. In practice, this means that the variables **c** correspond to salient aspects of the data with real-world interpretations (i.e., the latent space is *disentangled*).

Figure 15.14 Auxiliary classifier GAN. The generator takes a class label as well as the latent vector. The discriminator must both identify if the data point is real *and* predict the class label. This model was trained on ten ImageNet classes. Left to right: generated examples of monarch butterflies, goldfinches, daisies, redshanks, and gray whales. Adapted from Odena et al. (2017).

attribute with C categories, the discriminator takes the real/synthesized image as input and has $C + 1$ outputs; the first is passed through a sigmoid function and predicts if the sample is generated or real. The remaining outputs are passed through a softmax function to predict the probability that the data belongs to each of the C classes. Networks trained with this method can synthesize multiple classes from ImageNet (figure 15.14).

15.4.3 InfoGAN

The conditional GAN and ACGAN both generate samples that have predetermined attributes. By contrast, InfoGAN (figure 15.13c) attempts to identify important attributes automatically. The generator takes a vector consisting of random noise variables $\mathbf{z}$ and *random* attribute variables $\mathbf{c}$. The discriminator both predicts whether the image is real or synthesized and estimates the attribute variables.

The insight is that interpretable real-world characteristics should be easiest to predict and hence will be represented in the attribute variables $\mathbf{c}$. The attributes in $\mathbf{c}$ may be discrete (and a binary or multiclass cross-entropy loss would be used) or continuous (and a least squares loss would be used). The discrete variables identify categories in the data, and the continuous ones identify gradual modes of variation (figure 15.15).

15.5 Image translation

Although the adversarial discriminator was first used in the context of the GAN for generating random samples, it can also be used as a prior that favors realism in tasks that translate one data example into another. This is most commonly done with images,

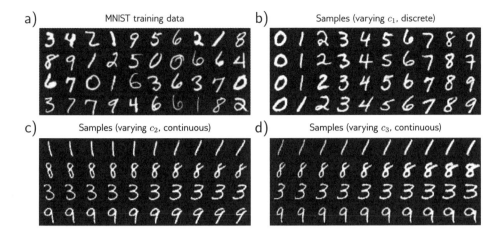

Figure 15.15 InfoGAN for MNIST. a) Training examples from the MNIST database, which consists of 28×28 pixel images of handwritten digits. b) The first attribute c_1 is categorical with 10 categories; each column shows samples generated with one of these categories. The InfoGAN recovers the ten digits. The attribute vectors c_2 and c_3 are continuous. c) Moving from left to right, each column represents a different value of c_2 while keeping the other latent variables constant. This attribute seems to correspond to the orientation of the character. d) The third attribute seems to correspond to the thickness of the stroke. Adapted from Chen et al. (2016b).

where we might want to translate a grayscale image to color, a noisy image to a clean one, a blurry image to a sharp one, or a sketch to a photo-realistic image.

This section discusses three image translation models that use different amounts of manual labeling. The Pix2Pix model uses before/after pairs for training. Models with adversarial losses use before/after pairs for the main model but also exploit unpaired "after" images in the discriminator. The CycleGAN model uses unpaired images.

15.5.1 Pix2Pix

The Pix2Pix model (figure 15.16) is a network $\mathbf{x} = \mathbf{g}[\mathbf{c}, \boldsymbol{\theta}]$ that maps one image $\mathbf{c}$ to a different style image $\mathbf{x}$ using a U-Net (figure 11.10) with parameters $\boldsymbol{\theta}$. A typical use case would be colorization, where the input is grayscale, and the output is color. The output should be similar to the input, and this is encouraged using a *content loss* that penalizes the ℓ_1 norm $||\mathbf{x} - \mathbf{g}[\mathbf{c}, \boldsymbol{\theta}]||_1$ between the input and output.

However, the output image should also look like a realistic conversion of the input. This is encouraged by using an adversarial discriminator $\mathrm{f}[\mathbf{c}, \mathbf{x}, \boldsymbol{\phi}]$, which ingests the before and after images $\mathbf{c}$ and $\mathbf{x}$. At each step, the discriminator tries to distinguish between a real before/after pair and a before/synthesized pair. To the extent that these

Appendix B.3.2
ℓ_1 norm

can be distinguished successfully, a feedback signal is provided to modify the U-Net to make its output more realistic. Since the content loss ensures that the large-scale image structure is correct, the discriminator is mainly needed to ensure that the local texture is plausible. To this end, the *PatchGAN* loss is based on a purely convolutional classifier. At the last layer, each hidden unit indicates whether the region within its receptive field is real or synthesized. These responses are averaged to provide the final output.

One way to think of this model is that it is a conditional GAN where the U-Net is the generator and is conditioned on an image rather than a label. Notice, though, that the U-Net input does not include noise and so is not really a "generator" in the conventional sense. Interestingly, the original authors experimented with adding noise $\mathbf{z}$ to the U-Net in addition to the input image $\mathbf{c}$. However, the network just learned to ignore it.

15.5.2 Adversarial loss

The discriminator of the Pix2Pix model attempted to distinguish whether before/after pairs in an image translation task were plausible. This has the disadvantage that we need ground truth before/after pairs to exploit the discriminator loss. Fortunately, there is a simpler way to exploit the power of adversarial discriminators in the context of supervised learning without the need for additional labeled training data.

An *adversarial loss* adds a penalty if a discriminator can distinguish the output of a supervised network from a real example from its output domain. Accordingly, the supervised model changes its predictions to decrease this penalty. This may be done at the scale of the entire output or at the level of patches, as in the Pix2Pix algorithm. This helps improve the *realism* of complex structured outputs. However, it doesn't necessarily lead to a better solution in terms of the original loss function.

The *super-resolution GAN* or *SRGAN* uses this approach (figure 15.17). The main model consists of a convolutional network with residual connections that ingests a low-resolution image and converts this via upsampling layers to a high-resolution image. The network is trained with three losses. The content loss measures the squared difference between the output and the true high-resolution image. The *VGG loss* or *perceptual loss* passes the synthesized and ground truth outputs through the VGG network and measures the squared difference between their activations. This encourages the image to be semantically similar to the target. Finally, the adversarial loss uses a discriminator that attempts to distinguish whether this is a real high-resolution image or an upsampled one. This encourages the output to be indistinguishable from real examples.

15.5.3 CycleGAN

The adversarial loss assumes that we have labeled before/after images for the main supervised network. The *CycleGAN* addresses the situation where we have two sets of data with distinct styles but *no* matching pairs. An example is converting a photo to the artistic style of Monet. There exist many photos and many Monet paintings, but no correspondence between them. CycleGAN exploits the idea that converting an image in

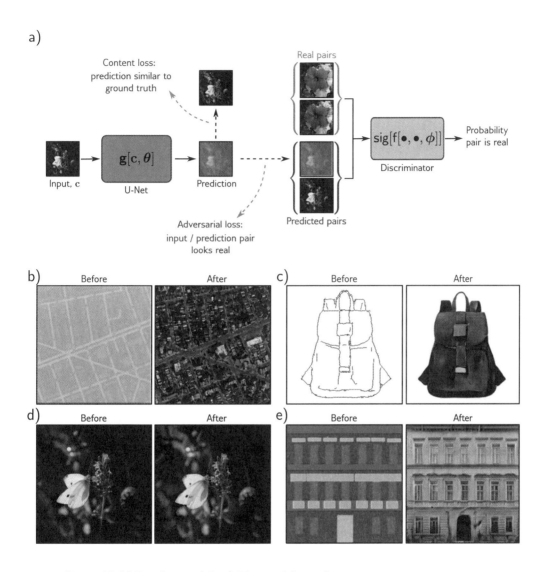

Figure 15.16 Pix2Pix model. a) The model translates an input image to a prediction in a different style using a U-Net (see figure 11.10). In this case, it maps a grayscale image to a plausibly colored version. The U-Net is trained with two losses. First, the content loss encourages the output image to have a similar structure to the input image. Second, the adversarial loss encourages the grayscale/color image pair to be indistinguishable from a real pair in each local region of these images. This framework can be adapted to many tasks, including b) translating maps to satellite imagery, c) converting sketches of bags to photorealistic examples, d) colorization, and e) converting label maps to photorealistic building facades. Adapted from Isola et al. (2017).

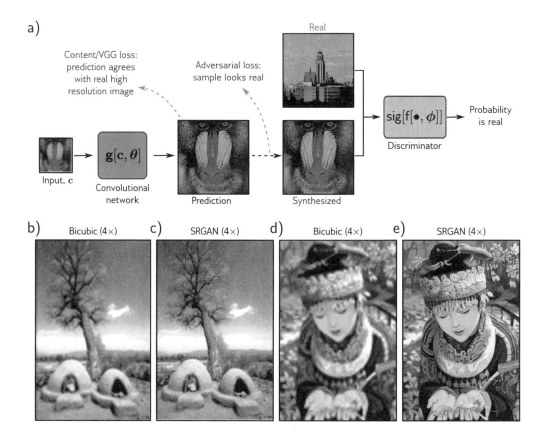

Figure 15.17 Super-resolution generative adversarial network (SRGAN). a) A convolutional network with residual connections is trained to increase the resolution of images by a factor of four. The model has losses that encourage the content to be close to the true high-resolution image. However, it also includes an adversarial loss, which penalizes results that can be distinguished from real high-resolution images. b) Upsampled image using bicubic interpolation. c) Upsampled image using SRGAN. d) Upsampled image using bicubic interpolation. e) Upsampled image using SRGAN. Adapted from Ledig et al. (2017).

one direction (e.g., photo→Monet) and then back again should recover the original.

The CycleGAN loss function is a weighted sum of three losses (figure 15.18). The content loss encourages the before and after images to be similar and is based on the ℓ_1 norm. The adversarial loss uses a discriminator to encourage the output to be indistinguishable from real examples of the target domain. Finally, the *cycle-consistency* loss encourages the mapping to be reversible. Here, two models are trained together. One maps from the first domain to the second, and the other in the opposite direction. The cycle-consistency loss will be low if the translated image can be itself translated successfully back to the image in the original domain. The model combines these three losses to train networks to translate images from one style to another and back again.

15.6 StyleGAN

StyleGAN is a more contemporary GAN that partitions the variation in a dataset into meaningful components, each of which is controlled by a subset of the latent variables. In particular, StyleGAN controls the output image at different scales and separates style from noise. For face images, large-scale changes include face shape and head pose, medium-scale changes include the shape and details of facial features, and fine-scale changes include hair and skin color. The style components represent aspects of the image that are salient to human beings, and the noise aspects represent unimportant variation such as the exact placement of hairs, stubble, freckles, or skin pores.

The GANs that we have seen until now started from a latent variable $\mathbf{z}$ which is drawn from a standard base distribution. This was passed through a series of convolutional layers to produce the output image. However, the latent variable inputs to the generator can (i) be introduced at various points in the architecture and (ii) modify the current representation at these points in different ways. StyleGAN makes these choices judiciously to control scale and to separate style from noise (figure 15.19).

The main generative branch of StyleGAN starts with a learned constant 4×4 representation with 512 channels. This passes through a series of convolutional layers that gradually upsample the representation to generate the image at its final resolution. Two sets of random latent variables representing style and noise are introduced at each scale; the closer that they are to the output, the finer scale details they represent.

The latent variables that represent noise are independently sampled Gaussian vectors $\mathbf{z}_1, \mathbf{z}_2 \dots$ and are injected additively after each convolution operation in the main generative pipeline. They are the same spatial size as the main representation at the point that they are added but are multiplied by learned per-channel scaling factors $\boldsymbol{\psi}_1, \boldsymbol{\psi}_2 \dots$ and so contribute in different amounts to each channel. As the resolution of the network increases, this noise contributes at finer scales.

The latent variables that represent style begin as a 1×1×512 noise tensor, which is passed through a seven-layer fully connected network to create an intermediate variable $\mathbf{w}$. This allows the network to decorrelate aspects of style so that each dimension of $\mathbf{w}$ can represent an independent real-world factor such as head pose or hair color. This variable $\mathbf{w}$ is linearly transformed to a 2×1×512 tensor $\mathbf{y}$, which is used to set the per-channel mean and variance of the representation across spatial positions in the

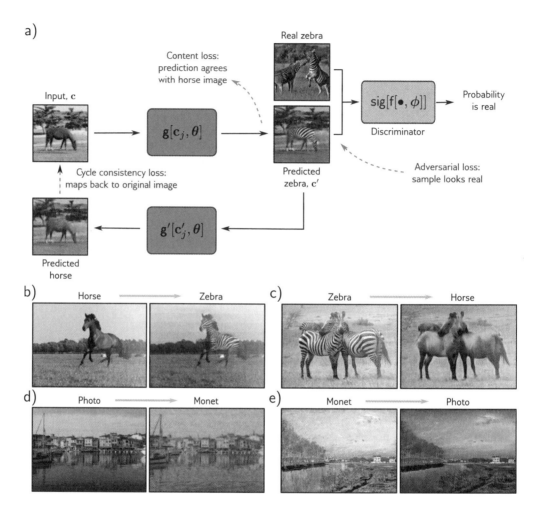

Figure 15.18 CycleGAN. Two models are trained simultaneously. The first $\mathbf{c}' = \mathbf{g}[\mathbf{c}_j, \boldsymbol{\theta}]$ translates from an image $\mathbf{c}$ in the first style (horse) to an image $\mathbf{c}'$ in the second style (zebra). The second model $\mathbf{c} = \mathbf{g}'[\mathbf{c}', \boldsymbol{\theta}]$ learns the opposite mapping. The cycle consistency loss penalizes both models if they cannot successfully convert an image to the other domain and back to the original. In addition, two adversarial losses encourage the translated images to look like realistic examples of the target domain (shown here for zebra only). Two content losses encourage the details and layout of the images before and after each mapping to be similar (i.e., the zebra is in the same position and pose that the horse was and against the same background and vice versa). Adapted from Zhu et al. (2017).

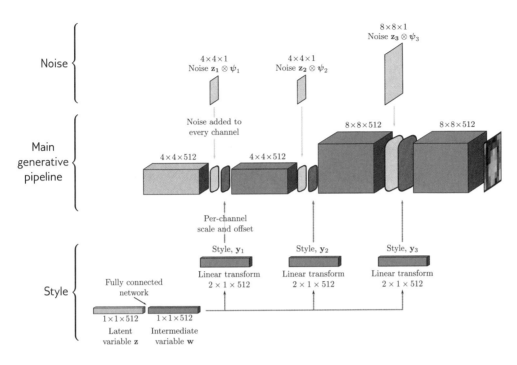

Figure 15.19 StyleGAN. The main pipeline (center row) starts with a constant learned representation (gray box). This is passed through a series of convolutional layers and gradually upsampled to create the output. Noise (top row) is added at different scales by periodically adding Gaussian variables $\mathbf{z}_\bullet$ with per-channel scaling $\psi_\bullet$. The Gaussian style variable $\mathbf{z}$ is passed through a fully connected network to create intermediate variable $\mathbf{w}$ (bottom row). This is used to set the mean and variance of each channel at various points in the pipeline.

main branch after noise addition. This is termed *adaptive instance normalization* (figure 11.14e). A series of vectors $\mathbf{y}_1, \mathbf{y}_2, \ldots$ are injected in this way at several different points in the main branch, so the same style contributes at different scales. Figure 15.20 shows examples of manipulating the style and noise vectors are different scales.

15.7   Summary

GANs learn a generator network that transforms random noise into data that is indistinguishable from a training set. To this end, the generator is trained using a discriminator network that tries to distinguish real examples from generated samples. The generator is then updated so that the data that it creates is identified as being more "real" by the discriminator. The original formulation of this idea has the flaw that the training signal is weak when it's easy to determine if the samples are real or generated. This led to the

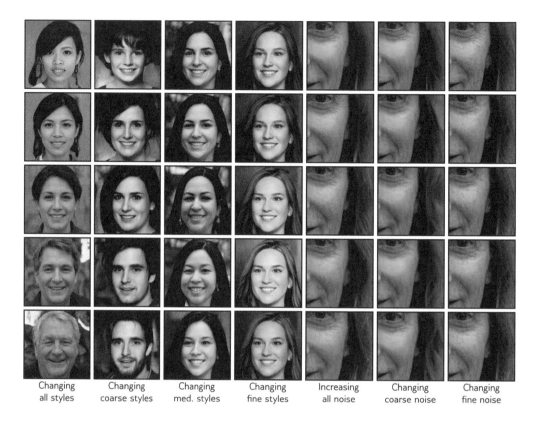

Changing all styles   Changing coarse styles   Changing med. styles   Changing fine styles   Increasing all noise   Changing coarse noise   Changing fine noise

Figure 15.20 StyleGAN results. First four columns show systematic changes in style at various scales. Fifth column shows the effect of increasing noise magnitude. Last two columns show different noise vectors at two different scales.

Wasserstein GAN, which provides a more consistent training signal.

We reviewed convolutional GANs for generating images and a series of tricks that improve the quality of the generated images, including progressive growing, mini-batch discrimination, and truncation. Conditional GAN architectures introduce an auxiliary vector that allows control over the output (e.g., the choice of object class). Image translation tasks retain this conditional information in the form of an image but dispense with the random noise. The GAN discriminator now works as an additional loss term that favors "realistic" looking images. Finally, we described StyleGAN, which injects noise into the generator strategically to control the style and noise at different scales.

Notes

Goodfellow et al. (2014) introduced generative adversarial networks. An early review of progress can be found in Goodfellow (2016). More recent overviews include Creswell et al. (2018) and

Gui et al. (2021). Park et al. (2021) present a review of GAN models that focuses on computer vision applications. Hindupur (2022) maintains a list of named GAN models (numbering 501 at the time of writing) from ABC-GAN (Susmelj et al., 2017) right through to ZipNet-GAN (Zhang et al., 2017b). Odena (2019) lists open problems concerning GANs.

Data: GANs have primarily been developed for image data. Examples include the deep convolutional GAN (Radford et al., 2015), progressive GAN (Karras et al., 2018), and StyleGAN (Karras et al., 2019) models presented in this chapter. For this reason, most GANs are based on convolutional layers, although more recently, GANs that exploit transformers in the generator and discriminator to capture long-range correlations have been developed (e.g., SAGAN, Zhang et al., 2019b). However, GANs have also been used to generate molecular graphs (De Cao & Kipf, 2018), voice data (Saito et al., 2017; Donahue et al., 2018b; Kaneko & Kameoka, 2017; Fang et al., 2018), EEG data (Hartmann et al., 2018), text (Lin et al., 2017a; Fedus et al., 2018), music (Mogren, 2016; Guimaraes et al., 2017; Yu et al., 2017), 3D models (Wu et al., 2016), DNA (Killoran et al., 2017), and video data (Vondrick et al., 2016; Wang et al., 2018a).

GAN loss functions: It was originally claimed that GANs converged to Nash equilibria during training. However, more recent evidence suggests that this isn't always the case (Farnia & Ozdaglar, 2020; Jin et al., 2020; Berard et al., 2019). (Arjovsky et al., 2017; Metz et al., 2017; Qi, 2020) identified that the original GAN loss function was unstable, and this led to different formulations. Mao et al. (2017) introduced the least squares GAN. For some parameter choices, this implicitly minimizes the Pearson χ^2 divergence. Nowozin et al. (2016) argue that the Jensen-Shannon divergence is a special case of a larger family of f-divergences and show that any f-divergence can be used for training GANs. Jolicoeur-Martineau (2019) introduces the relativistic GAN in which the discriminator estimates the probability that a real data example is more realistic than a generated one rather than the absolute probability that it is real. Zhao et al. (2017a) reformulate the GAN into a general energy-based framework in which the discriminator is a function that attributes low energies to real data and higher energies elsewhere. As an example, they use an autoencoder and base the energy on reconstruction error.

Arjovsky & Bottou (2017) analyzed vanishing gradients in GANs, and this led to the Wasserstein GAN (Arjovsky et al., 2017), which is based on earth mover's distance/optimal transport. The Wasserstein formulation requires that the Lipschitz constant of the discriminator is less than one; the original paper proposed to clip the weights in the discriminator, but subsequent work imposed a gradient penalty (Gulrajani et al., 2016) or applied spectral normalization (Miyato et al., 2018) to limit the Lipschitz constant. Other variations of the Wasserstein GAN were introduced by Wu et al. (2018a), Bellemare et al. (2017b), and Adler & Lunz (2018). Hermann (2017) presents an excellent blog post discussing duality and the Wasserstein GAN. For more information about optimal transport, consult the book by Peyré et al. (2019). Lucic et al. (2018) present an empirical comparison of GAN loss functions of the time.

Tricks for training GANs: Many heuristics improve the stability of training GANs and the quality of the final results. Marchesi (2017) first used the truncation trick (figure 15.10) to trade off the variability of GAN outputs relative to their quality. This was also proposed by Pieters & Wiering (2018) and Brock et al. (2019), who added a regularizer that encourages the weight matrices in the generator to be orthogonal. This means that truncating the latent variable has a closer relationship to truncating the output variance and improves sample quality.

Other tricks include only using the gradients from the top K most realistic images (Sinha et al., 2020), label smoothing in the discriminator (Salimans et al., 2016), updating the discriminator using a history of generated images rather than the ones produced by the latest generator to avoid model "oscillation" (Salimans et al., 2016), and adding noise to the discriminator input (Arjovsky & Bottou, 2017). Kurach et al. (2019) present an overview of normalization and regularization in GANs. Chintala et al. (2020) provide further suggestions for training GANs.

Sample diversity: The original GAN paper (Goodfellow et al., 2014) argued that given enough capacity, training samples, and computation time, a GAN can learn to minimize the Jensen-Shannon divergence between the generated samples and the true distribution. However, subsequent work has cast doubt on whether this happens in practice. Arora et al. (2017) suggest that the finite capacity of the discriminator means that the GAN training objective can approach its optimum value even when the variation in the output distribution is limited. Wu et al. (2017) approximated the log-likelihoods of the distributions produced by GANs using annealed importance sampling and found a mismatch between the generated and real distributions. Arora & Zhang (2017) ask human observers to identify GAN samples that are (near-)duplicates and infer the diversity of images from the frequency of these duplicates. They found that for DCGAN, a duplicate occurs with probability >50% with 400 samples; this implies that the support size was ∼ 400,000, which is smaller than the training set. They also showed that the diversity increased as a function of the discriminator size. Bau et al. (2019) take a different approach and investigate the parts of the data space that GANs *cannot* generate.

Increasing diversity and preventing mode collapse: The extreme case of lack of diversity is *mode collapse*, in which the network repeatedly produces the same image (Salimans et al., 2016). This is a particular problem for conditional GANs, where the latent variable is sometimes completely ignored, and the output depends only on the conditional information. Mao et al. (2019) introduce a regularization term to help prevent mode collapse in conditional GANs, which maximizes the ratio of the distance between generated images with respect to the corresponding latent variables and hence encourages diversity in the outputs. Other work that aims to reduce mode collapse includes VEEGAN (Srivastava et al., 2017), which introduces a reconstruction network that maps the generated image back to the original noise and hence discourages many-to-one mappings from noise to images.

Salimans et al. (2016) suggested computing statistics across the mini-batch and using the discriminator to ensure that these are indistinguishable from the statistics of batches of real images. This is known as *mini-batch discrimination* and is implemented by adding a layer toward the end of the discriminator that learns a tensor for each image that captures the statistics of the batch. This was simplified by Karras et al. (2018), who computed a standard deviation for each feature in each spatial location over the mini-batch. Then they average over spatial locations and features to get a single estimate. This is replicated to get a single feature map, which is appended to a layer near the end of the discriminator network. Lin et al. (2018) pass concatenated (real or generated) samples to the discriminator and provide a theoretical analysis of how presenting multiple samples to the discriminator increases diversity. MAD-GAN (Ghosh et al., 2018) increases the diversity of GAN samples by using multiple generators and requiring the single discriminator to identify which generator created the samples, thus providing a signal to help push the generators to create different samples from one another.

Multiple scales: Wang et al. (2018b) used multiple discriminators at different scales to help ensure that image quality is high in all frequency bands. Other work defined both generators and discriminators at different resolutions (Denton et al., 2015; Zhang et al., 2017d; Huang et al., 2017c). Karras et al. (2018) introduced the progressive growing method (figure 15.9), which is somewhat simpler and faster to train.

StyleGAN: Karras et al. (2019) introduced the StyleGAN framework (section 15.6). In subsequent work (Karras et al., 2020b), they improved the quality of generated images by (i) redesigning the normalization layers in the generator to remove "water droplet" artifacts and (ii) reducing artifacts where fine details do not follow the coarse details by changing the progressive growing framework. Further improvements include developing methods to train GANs with limited data (Karras et al., 2020a) and fixing aliasing artifacts (Karras et al., 2021). A large body of work finds and manipulates the latent variables in the StyleGAN to edit images (e.g., Abdal et al., 2021; Collins et al., 2020; Härkönen et al., 2020; Patashnik et al., 2021; Shen et al., 2020b; Tewari et al., 2020; Wu et al., 2021; Roich et al., 2022).

Conditional GANs: The conditional GAN was developed by Mirza & Osindero (2014), the auxiliary classifier GAN by Odena et al. (2017), and the InfoGAN by Chen et al. (2016b). The discriminators of these models usually append the conditional information to the discriminator input (Mirza & Osindero, 2014; Denton et al., 2015; Saito et al., 2017) or to an intermediate hidden layer in the discriminator (Reed et al., 2016a; Zhang et al., 2017d; Perarnau et al., 2016). However, Miyato & Koyama (2018) experimented with taking the inner product between embedded conditional information with a layer of the discriminator, motivated by the role of the class information in the underlying probabilistic model. Images generated by GANs have variously been conditioned on classes (e.g., Odena et al., 2017), input text (Reed et al., 2016a; Zhang et al., 2017d), attributes (Yan et al., 2016; Donahue et al., 2018a; Xiao et al., 2018b), bounding boxes and keypoints (Reed et al., 2016b), and images (e.g., Isola et al., 2017)).

Image translation: Isola et al. (2017) developed the Pix2Pix algorithm (figure 15.16), and a similar system with higher-resolution results was subsequently developed by Wang et al. (2018b). StarGAN (Choi et al., 2018) performs image-to-image translation across multiple domains using only a single model. The idea of cycle consistency loss was introduced by Zhou et al. (2016b) in DiscoGAN and Zhu et al. (2017) in CycleGAN (figure 15.18).

Adversarial loss: In many image translation tasks, there is no "generator"; such models can be considered supervised learning tasks with an adversarial loss that encourages realism. The super-resolution algorithm of Ledig et al. (2017) is a good example of this (figure 15.17). Esser et al. (2021) used an autoencoder with an adversarial loss. This network takes an image, reduces the representation size to create a "bottleneck," and then reconstructs the image from this reduced data space. In practice, the architecture is similar to encoder-decoder networks (e.g., figure 10.19). After training, the autoencoder reproduces something that is both close to the image and looks highly realistic. They vector quantize (discretize) the bottleneck of the autoencoder and then learn a probability distribution over the discrete variables using a transformer decoder. By sampling from this transformer decoder, they can produce extremely large high-quality images.

Inverting GANs: One way to edit real images is to project them to the latent space, manipulate the latent variable, and then re-project them to image space. This process is known as *resynthesis*. Unfortunately, GANs only map from the latent variable to the observed data, not vice versa. This has led to methods to *invert* GANs (i.e., find the latent variable that corresponds as closely as possible to an observed image). These methods fall into two classes. The first learns a network that maps in the opposite direction (Donahue et al., 2018b; Luo et al., 2017a; Perarnau et al., 2016; Dumoulin et al., 2017; Guan et al., 2020). This is known as an *encoder*. The second approach is to start with some latent variable $\mathbf{z}$ and optimize it until it reconstructs the image as closely as possible (Creswell & Bharath, 2018; Karras et al., 2020b; Abdal et al., 2019; Lipton & Tripathi, 2017). Zhu et al. (2020a) combine both approaches.

There has been particular interest in inversion for StyleGAN because it produces excellent results and can control the image at different scales. Unfortunately, Abdal et al. (2020) showed that it is not possible to invert StyleGAN without artifacts and proposed inverting to an extended style space, and Richardson et al. (2021) trained an encoder that reliably maps to this space. Even after inverting to the extended space, editing images that are out of domain may still not work well. Roich et al. (2022) address this issue by fine-tuning the generator of StyleGAN so that it reconstructs the image exactly and show that the result can be edited well. They also add extra terms that reconstruct nearby points exactly so that the modification is local. This technique is known as *pivotal tuning*. A survey of GAN inversion techniques can be found in Xia et al. (2022).

Editing images with GANs: The iGAN (Zhu et al., 2016) allows users to make interactive edits by scribbling or warping parts of an existing image. The tool then adjusts the output image to be both realistic and to fit these new constraints. It does this by finding a latent vector that produces an image that is similar to the edited image and obeys the edge map of any added lines. It is typical also to add a mask so that only parts of the image close to the edits are changed. EditGAN (Ling et al., 2021) jointly models images and their semantic segmentation masks and allows edits to that mask.

Problems

Problem 15.1 What will the loss be in equation 15.8 when $q(\mathbf{x}) = Pr(\mathbf{x})$?

Problem 15.2[*] Write an equation relating the loss L in equation 15.8 to the Jensen-Shannon distance $D_{JS}[q(\mathbf{x}) \| Pr(\mathbf{x})]$ in equation 15.9.

Problem 15.3 Consider computing the earth mover's distance using linear programming in the primal form. The discrete distributions $Pr(x{=}i)$ and $q(x{=}j)$ are defined on $x = 1, 2, 3, 4$ and:

$$\mathbf{b} = \left[Pr(x{=}1), Pr(x{=}2), Pr(x{=}3), Pr(x{=}4), q(x{=}1), q(x{=}2), q(x{=}3), q(x{=}4) \right]^T. \quad (15.18)$$

Write out the contents of the $8{\times}16$ matrix $\mathbf{A}$. You may assume that the contents of $\mathbf{P}$ have been vectorized into $\mathbf{p}$ column-first.

Problem 15.4[*] Calculate (i) the KL divergence, (ii) the reverse KL divergence, (iii) the Jensen-Shannon divergence, and (iv) the Wasserstein distance between the distributions:

$$Pr(z) = \begin{cases} 0 & z < 0 \\ 1 & 0 \leq z \leq 1 \\ 0 & z > 1 \end{cases}, \quad \text{and} \quad Pr(z) = \begin{cases} 0 & z < a \\ 1 & a \leq z \leq a + 1 \\ 0 & z > a \end{cases}. \quad (15.19)$$

for the range $a \in [-3, 3]$. To get a formula for the Wasserstein distance for this special case, consider the total "earth" (i.e., probability mass) that must be moved and multiply this by the squared distance it must move.

Problem 15.5 The KL distance and Wasserstein distances between univariate Gaussian distributions are given by:

$$D_{kl} = \log \left[\frac{\sigma_2}{\sigma_1} \right] + \frac{\sigma_1^2 + (\mu_1 - \mu_2)^2}{2\sigma_2^2} - \frac{1}{2}, \quad (15.20)$$

and

$$D_w = (\mu_1 - \mu_2)^2 + \sigma_1 + \sigma_2 - 2\sqrt{\sigma_1 \sigma_2}, \quad (15.21)$$

respectively. Plot these distances as a function of $\mu_1 - \mu_2$ for the case when $\sigma_1 = \sigma_2 = 1$.

Problem 15.6 Consider a latent variable $\mathbf{z}$ with dimension 100. Consider truncating the values of this variable to (i) $\tau = 2.0$, (ii) $\tau = 1.0$, (iii) $\tau = 0.5$, (iv) $\tau = 0.04$ standard deviations. What proportion of the original probability distribution is disregarded in each case?

Chapter 16

Normalizing flows

Chapter 15 introduced generative adversarial networks (GANs). These are generative models that pass a latent variable through a deep network to create a new sample. GANs are trained using the principle that the samples should be indistinguishable from real data. However, they don't define a distribution over data examples. Hence, assessing the probability that a new example belongs to the same dataset isn't straightforward.

In this chapter, we describe *normalizing flows*. These learn a probability model by transforming a simple distribution into a more complicated one using a deep network. Normalizing flows can both sample from this distribution and evaluate the probability of new examples. However, they require specialized architecture: each layer must be *invertible*. In other words, it must be able to transform data in both directions.

16.1 1D example

Normalizing flows are probabilistic generative models: they fit a probability distribution to training data (figure 14.2b). Consider modeling a 1D distribution $Pr(x)$. Normalizing flows start with a simple tractable *base* distribution $Pr(z)$ over a latent variable z and apply a function $x = \mathrm{f}[z, \phi]$, where the parameters ϕ are chosen so that $Pr(x)$ has the desired distribution (figure 16.1). Generating a new example x^* is easy; we draw z^* from the base density and pass this through the function so that $x^* = \mathrm{f}[z^*, \phi]$.

16.1.1 Measuring probability

Measuring the probability of a data point x is more challenging. Consider applying a function $\mathrm{f}[z, \phi]$ to random variable z with known density $Pr(z)$. The probability density will decrease in areas that are stretched by the function and increase in areas that are compressed so that the area under the new distribution remains one. The degree to which a function $\mathrm{f}[z, \phi]$ stretches or compresses its input depends on the magnitude of its gradient. If a small change to the input causes a larger change in the output, it

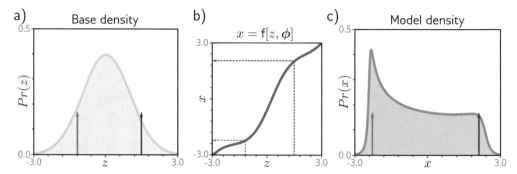

Figure 16.1 Transforming probability distributions. a) The base density is a standard normal defined on a latent variable z. b) This variable is transformed by a function $x = \mathsf{f}[z, \boldsymbol{\phi}]$ to a new variable x, which c) has a new distribution. To sample from this model, we draw values z from the base density (green and brown arrows in panel (a) show two examples). We pass these through the function $\mathsf{f}[z, \boldsymbol{\phi}]$ as shown by dotted arrows in panel (b) to generate the values of x, which are indicated as arrows in panel (c).

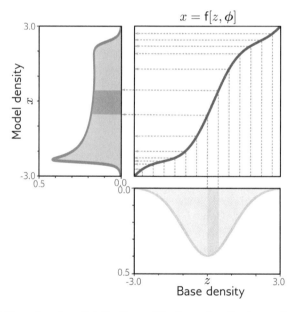

Figure 16.2 Transforming distributions. The base density (cyan, bottom) passes through a function (blue curve, top right) to create the model density (orange, left). Consider dividing the base density into equal intervals (gray vertical lines). The probability mass between adjacent lines must remain the same after transformation. The cyan-shaded region passes through a part of the function where the gradient is larger than one, so this region is stretched. Consequently, the height of the orange-shaded region must be lower so that it retains the same area as the cyan-shaded region. In other places (e.g., $z = -2$), the gradient is less than one, and the model density increases relative to the base density.

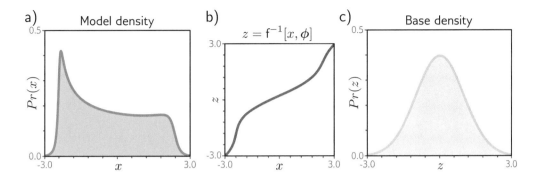

Figure 16.3 Inverse mapping (normalizing direction). If the function is invertible, then it's possible to transform the model density back to the original base density. The probability of a point x under the model density depends partly on the probability of the equivalent point z under the base density (see equation 16.1).

stretches the function. If a small change to the input causes a smaller change in the output, it compresses the function (figure 16.2).

More precisely, the probability of data x under the transformed distribution is:

$$Pr(x|\boldsymbol{\phi}) \quad = \quad \left| \frac{\partial f[z, \boldsymbol{\phi}]}{\partial z} \right|^{-1} \cdot Pr(z), \tag{16.1}$$

where $z = f^{-1}[x, \boldsymbol{\phi}]$ is the latent variable that created x. The term $Pr(z)$ is the original probability of this latent variable under the base density. This is moderated according to the magnitude of the derivative of the function. If this is greater than one, then the probability decreases. If it is smaller, the probability increases.

Notebook 16.1
1D normalizing
flows

16.1.2   Forward and inverse mappings

To draw samples from the distribution, we need the forward mapping $x = f[z, \boldsymbol{\phi}]$, but to measure the likelihood, we need to compute the inverse $z = f^{-1}[x, \boldsymbol{\phi}]$. Hence, we need to choose $f[z, \boldsymbol{\phi}]$ judiciously so that it is *invertible*.

Problems 16.1–16.2

The forward mapping is sometimes termed the *generative direction*. The base density is usually chosen to be a standard normal distribution. Hence, the inverse mapping is termed the *normalizing direction* since this takes the complex distribution over x and turns it into a normal distribution over z (figure 16.3).

16.1.3   Learning

To learn the distribution, we find parameters ϕ that maximize the likelihood of the training data $\{x_i\}_{i=1}^{I}$ or equivalently minimize the negative log-likelihood:

$$
\begin{aligned}
\hat{\phi} &= \underset{\phi}{\operatorname{argmax}}\left[\prod_{i=1}^{I} Pr(x_i|\phi)\right] \\
&= \underset{\phi}{\operatorname{argmin}}\left[\sum_{i=1}^{I} -\log\Big[Pr(x_i|\phi)\Big]\right] \\
&= \underset{\phi}{\operatorname{argmin}}\left[\sum_{i=1}^{I} \log\left[\left|\frac{\partial \mathrm{f}[z_i,\phi]}{\partial z_i}\right|\right] - \log\big[Pr(z_i)\big]\right],
\end{aligned}
\tag{16.2}
$$

where we have assumed that the data are independent and identically distributed in the first line and used the likelihood definition from equation 16.1 in the third line.

16.2   General case

The previous section developed a simple 1D example that modeled a probability distribution $Pr(x)$ by transforming a simpler base density $Pr(z)$. We now extend this to multivariate distributions $Pr(\mathbf{x})$ and $Pr(\mathbf{z})$ and add the complication that the transformation is defined by a deep neural network.

Consider applying a function $\mathbf{x} = \mathbf{f}[\mathbf{z},\phi]$ to a random variable $\mathbf{z} \in \mathbb{R}^D$ with base density $Pr(\mathbf{z})$, where $\mathbf{f}[\mathbf{z},\phi]$ is a deep network. The resulting variable $\mathbf{x} \in \mathbb{R}^D$ has a new distribution. A new sample $\mathbf{x}^*$ can be drawn from this distribution by (i) drawing a sample $\mathbf{z}^*$ from the base density and (ii) passing this through the neural network so that $\mathbf{x}^* = \mathbf{f}[\mathbf{z}^*,\phi]$.

By analogy with equation 16.1, the likelihood of a sample under this distribution is:

$$
Pr(\mathbf{x}|\phi) = \left|\frac{\partial \mathbf{f}[\mathbf{z},\phi]}{\partial \mathbf{z}}\right|^{-1} \cdot Pr(\mathbf{z}),
\tag{16.3}
$$

Appendix B.3.8
Determinant

Appendix B.5
Jacobian

where $\mathbf{z} = \mathbf{f}^{-1}[\mathbf{x},\phi]$ is the latent variable $\mathbf{z}$ that created $\mathbf{x}$. The first term is the inverse of the determinant of the $D \times D$ Jacobian matrix $\partial \mathbf{f}[\mathbf{z},\phi]/\partial \mathbf{z}$, which contains elements $\partial \mathrm{f}_i[\mathbf{z},\phi]/\partial z_j$ at position (i,j). Just as the absolute derivative measured the change of area at a point on a 1D function when the function was applied, the absolute determinant measures the change in volume at a point in the multivariate function. The second term is the probability of the latent variable under the base density.

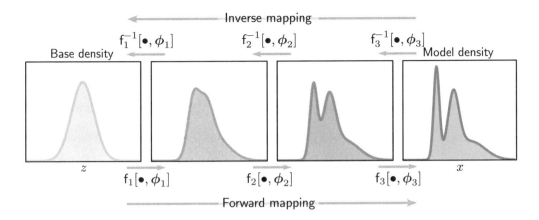

Figure 16.4 Forward and inverse mappings for a deep neural network. The base density (left) is gradually transformed by the network layers $f_1[\bullet, \phi_1], f_2[\bullet, \phi_2], \ldots$ to create the model density. Each layer is invertible, and we can equivalently think of the inverse of the layers as gradually transforming (or "flowing") the model density back to the base density.

16.2.1 Forward mapping with a deep neural network

In practice, the forward mapping $\mathbf{f}[\mathbf{z}, \phi]$ is usually defined by a neural network, consisting of a series of layers $\mathbf{f}_k[\bullet, \phi_k]$ with parameters ϕ_k, which are composed together as:

$$\mathbf{x} = \mathbf{f}[\mathbf{z}, \phi] = \mathbf{f}_K\left[\mathbf{f}_{K-1}\left[\ldots \mathbf{f}_2\left[\mathbf{f}_1[\mathbf{z}, \phi_1], \phi_2\right], \ldots \phi_{K-1}\right], \phi_K\right]. \tag{16.4}$$

The inverse mapping (normalizing direction) is defined by the composition of the inverse of each layer $\mathbf{f}_k^{-1}[\bullet, \phi_k]$ applied in the opposite order:

$$\mathbf{z} = \mathbf{f}^{-1}[\mathbf{x}, \phi] = \mathbf{f}_1^{-1}\left[\mathbf{f}_2^{-1}\left[\ldots \mathbf{f}_{K-1}^{-1}\left[\mathbf{f}_K^{-1}[\mathbf{x}, \phi_K], \phi_{K-1}\right], \ldots \phi_2\right], \phi_1\right]. \tag{16.5}$$

The base density $Pr(\mathbf{z})$ is usually defined as a multivariate standard normal (i.e., with mean zero and identity covariance). Hence, the effect of each subsequent inverse layer is to gradually move or "flow" the data density toward this normal distribution (figure 16.4). This gives rise to the name "normalizing flows."

The Jacobian of the forward mapping can be expressed as:

$$\frac{\partial \mathbf{f}[\mathbf{z}, \phi]}{\partial \mathbf{z}} = \frac{\partial \mathbf{f}_K[\mathbf{f}_{K-1}, \phi_K]}{\partial \mathbf{f}_{K-1}} \cdot \frac{\partial \mathbf{f}_{K-1}[\mathbf{f}_{K-2}, \phi_{K-1}]}{\partial \mathbf{f}_{K-2}} \cdots \frac{\partial \mathbf{f}_2[\mathbf{f}_1, \phi_2]}{\partial \mathbf{f}_1} \cdot \frac{\partial \mathbf{f}_1[\mathbf{z}, \phi_1]}{\partial \mathbf{z}}, \tag{16.6}$$

where we have overloaded the notation to make $\mathbf{f}_k$ the output of the function $\mathbf{f}_k[\bullet, \phi_k]$. The absolute determinant of this Jacobian can be computed by taking the product of the individual absolute determinants:

$$\left| \frac{\partial \mathbf{f}[\mathbf{z}, \boldsymbol{\phi}]}{\partial \mathbf{z}} \right| = \left| \frac{\partial \mathbf{f}_K[\mathbf{f}_{K-1}, \boldsymbol{\phi}_K]}{\partial \mathbf{f}_{K-1}} \right| \cdot \left| \frac{\partial \mathbf{f}_{K-1}[\mathbf{f}_{K-2}, \boldsymbol{\phi}_{K-1}]}{\partial \mathbf{f}_{K-2}} \right| \cdots \left| \frac{\partial \mathbf{f}_2[\mathbf{f}_1, \boldsymbol{\phi}_2]}{\partial \mathbf{f}_1} \right| \cdot \left| \frac{\partial \mathbf{f}_1[\mathbf{z}, \boldsymbol{\phi}_1]}{\partial \mathbf{z}} \right|.$$

$$(16.7)$$

Problem 16.3

The absolute determinant of the Jacobian of the inverse mapping is found by applying the same rule to equation 16.5. It is the reciprocal of the absolute determinant in the forward mapping.

We train normalizing flows with a dataset $\{\mathbf{x}_i\}$ of I training examples using the negative log-likelihood criterion:

$$\hat{\boldsymbol{\phi}} = \underset{\boldsymbol{\phi}}{\operatorname{argmax}} \left[\prod_{i=1}^{I} Pr(\mathbf{z}_i) \cdot \left| \frac{\partial \mathbf{f}[\mathbf{z}_i, \boldsymbol{\phi}]}{\partial \mathbf{z}_i} \right|^{-1} \right]$$

$$= \underset{\boldsymbol{\phi}}{\operatorname{argmin}} \left[\sum_{i=1}^{I} \log \left[\left| \frac{\partial \mathbf{f}[\mathbf{z}_i, \boldsymbol{\phi}]}{\partial \mathbf{z}_i} \right| \right] - \log \left[Pr(\mathbf{z}_i) \right] \right], \qquad (16.8)$$

where $\mathbf{z}_i = \mathbf{f}^{-1}[\mathbf{x}_i, \boldsymbol{\phi}]$, $Pr(\mathbf{z}_i)$ is measured under the base distribution, and the absolute determinant $|\partial \mathbf{f}[\mathbf{z}_i, \boldsymbol{\phi}]/\partial \mathbf{z}_i|$ is given by equation 16.7.

16.2.2 Desiderata for network layers

The theory of normalizing flows is straightforward. However, for this to be practical, we need neural network layers $\mathbf{f}_k$ that have four properties.

1. Collectively, the set of network layers must be sufficiently *expressive* to map a multivariate standard normal distribution to an arbitrary density.

2. The network layers must be *invertible*; each must define a unique one-to-one mapping from any input point to an output point (a *bijection*). If multiple inputs were mapped to the same output, the inverse would be ambiguous.

3. It must be possible to compute the *inverse* of each layer *efficiently*. We need to do this every time we evaluate the likelihood. This happens repeatedly during training, so there must be a closed-form solution or a fast algorithm for the inverse.

4. It also must be possible to evaluate the *determinant* of the Jacobian *efficiently* for either the forward or inverse mapping.

Appendix B.1
Bijection

16.3 Invertible network layers

We now describe different invertible network layers or *flows* for use in these models. We start with linear and elementwise flows. These are easy to invert, and it's possible to compute the determinant of their Jacobians, but neither is sufficiently expressive to describe arbitrary transformations of the base density. However, they form the building blocks of coupling, autoregressive, and residual flows, which are all more expressive.

16.3.1 Linear flows

A linear flow has the form $\mathbf{f}[\mathbf{h}] = \boldsymbol{\beta} + \boldsymbol{\Omega}\mathbf{h}$. If the matrix $\boldsymbol{\Omega}$ is invertible, the linear transform is invertible. For $\boldsymbol{\Omega} \in \mathbb{R}^{D \times D}$, the computation of the inverse is $\mathcal{O}[D^3]$. The determinant of the Jacobian is just the determinant of $\boldsymbol{\Omega}$, which can also be computed in $\mathcal{O}[D^3]$. This means that linear flows become expensive as the dimension D increases.

Appendix A
Big O notation

If the matrix $\boldsymbol{\Omega}$ takes a special form, then inversion and computation of the determinant can become more efficient, but the transformation becomes less general. For example, diagonal matrices require only $\mathcal{O}[D]$ computation for the inversion and determinant, but the elements of $\mathbf{h}$ don't interact. Orthogonal matrices are also more efficient to invert, and their determinant is fixed, but they do not allow scaling of the individual dimensions. Triangular matrices are more practical; they are invertible using a process known as back-substitution, which is $\mathcal{O}[D^2]$, and the determinant is just the product of the diagonal values.

Appendix B.4
Matrix types

Problem 16.4

One way to make a linear flow that is general, efficient to invert, and for which the Jacobian can be computed efficiently is to parameterize it directly in terms of the LU decomposition. In other words, we use:

$$\boldsymbol{\Omega} = \mathbf{PL}(\mathbf{U} + \mathbf{D}), \tag{16.9}$$

where $\mathbf{P}$ is a predetermined permutation matrix, $\mathbf{L}$ is a lower triangular matrix, $\mathbf{U}$ is an upper triangular matrix with zeros on the diagonal, and $\mathbf{D}$ is a diagonal matrix that supplies those missing diagonal elements. This can be inverted in $\mathcal{O}[D^2]$, and the log determinant is just the sum of the log of the absolute values on the diagonal of $\mathbf{D}$.

Unfortunately, linear flows are not sufficiently expressive. When a linear function $\mathbf{f}[\mathbf{h}] = \boldsymbol{\beta} + \boldsymbol{\Omega}\mathbf{h}$ is applied to normally distributed input $\text{Norm}_{\mathbf{h}}[\boldsymbol{\mu}, \boldsymbol{\Sigma}]$, then the result is also normally distributed with mean and variance, $\boldsymbol{\beta} + \boldsymbol{\Omega}\boldsymbol{\mu}$ and $\boldsymbol{\Omega}\boldsymbol{\Sigma}\boldsymbol{\Omega}^T$, respectively. Hence, it is not possible to map a normal distribution to an arbitrary density using linear flows alone.

Problems 16.5–16.6

16.3.2 Elementwise flows

Since linear flows are not sufficiently expressive, we must turn to nonlinear flows. The simplest of these are elementwise flows, which apply a pointwise nonlinear function $\mathrm{f}[\bullet, \boldsymbol{\phi}]$ with parameters $\boldsymbol{\phi}$ to each element of the input so that:

$$\mathbf{f}[\mathbf{h}] = \Big[\mathrm{f}[h_1, \boldsymbol{\phi}], \mathrm{f}[h_2, \boldsymbol{\phi}], \dots \mathrm{f}[h_D, \boldsymbol{\phi}]\Big]^T. \tag{16.10}$$

The Jacobian $\partial \mathbf{f}[\mathbf{h}]/\partial \mathbf{h}$ is diagonal since the dth input to $\mathbf{f}[\mathbf{h}]$ only affects the dth output. Its determinant is the product of the entries on the diagonal, so:

$$\left|\frac{\partial \mathbf{f}[\mathbf{h}]}{\partial \mathbf{h}}\right| = \prod_{d=1}^{D} \left|\frac{\partial \mathrm{f}[h_d]}{\partial h_d}\right|. \tag{16.11}$$

The function $\mathrm{f}[\bullet, \boldsymbol{\phi}]$ could be a fixed invertible nonlinearity like the leaky ReLU (figure 3.13), in which case there are no parameters, or it may be any parameterized

Problem 16.7

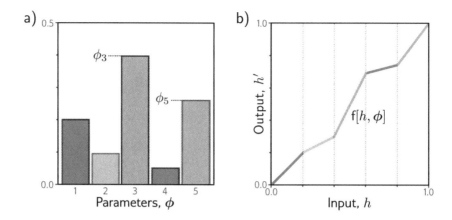

Figure 16.5 Piecewise linear mapping. An invertible piecewise linear mapping $h' = f[h, \phi]$ can be created by dividing the input domain $h \in [0, 1]$ into K equally sized regions (here $K = 5$). Each region has a slope with parameter, ϕ_k. a) If these parameters are positive and sum to one, then b) the function will be invertible and map to the output domain $h' \in [0, 1]$.

invertible one-to-one mapping. A simple example is a piecewise linear function with K regions (figure 16.5) which maps $[0, 1]$ to $[0, 1]$ as:

$$f[h, \phi] = \left(\sum_{k=1}^{b-1} \phi_k \right) + (hK - b)\phi_b, \qquad (16.12)$$

where the parameters $\phi_1, \phi_2, \ldots, \phi_K$ are positive and sum to 1, and $b = \lfloor Kh \rfloor$ is the index of the bin that contains h. The first term is the sum of all the preceding bins, and the second term represents the proportion of the way through the current bin that h lies. This function is easy to invert, and its gradient can be calculated almost everywhere. There are many similar schemes for creating smooth functions, often using splines with parameters that ensure the function is monotonic and hence invertible.

Problems 16.8–16.9

Elementwise flows are nonlinear but don't mix input dimensions, so they can't create correlations between variables. When alternated with linear flows (which do mix dimensions), more complex transformations can be modeled. However, in practice, elementwise flows are used as components of more complex layers like *coupling flows*.

16.3.3   Coupling flows

Coupling flows divide the input $\mathbf{h}$ into two parts so that $\mathbf{h} = [\mathbf{h}_1^T, \mathbf{h}_2^T]^T$ and define the flow $\mathbf{f}[\mathbf{h}, \phi]$ as:

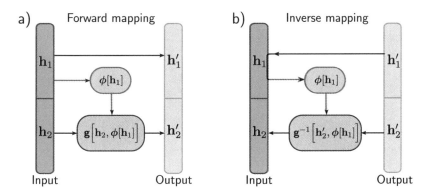

Figure 16.6 Coupling flows. a) The input (orange vector) is divided into $\mathbf{h}_1$ and $\mathbf{h}_2$. The first part $\mathbf{h}_1'$ of the output (cyan vector) is a copy of $\mathbf{h}_1$. The output $\mathbf{h}_2'$ is created by applying an invertible transformation $\mathbf{g}[\bullet, \phi]$ to $\mathbf{h}_2$, where the parameters ϕ are themselves a (not necessarily invertible) function of $\mathbf{h}_1$. b) In the inverse mapping, $\mathbf{h}_1 = \mathbf{h}_1'$. This allows us to calculate the parameters $\phi[\mathbf{h}_1]$ and then apply the inverse $\mathbf{g}^{-1}[\mathbf{h}_2', \phi]$ to retrieve $\mathbf{h}_2$.

$$\begin{aligned} \mathbf{h}_1' &= \mathbf{h}_1 \\ \mathbf{h}_2' &= \mathbf{g}\Big[\mathbf{h}_2, \phi[\mathbf{h}_1]\Big]. \end{aligned} \tag{16.13}$$

Here $\mathbf{g}[\bullet, \phi]$ is an elementwise flow (or other invertible layer) with parameters $\phi[\mathbf{h}_1]$ that are themselves a nonlinear function of the inputs $\mathbf{h}_1$ (figure 16.6). The function $\phi[\bullet]$ is usually a neural network of some kind and does not have to be invertible. The original variables can be recovered as:

$$\begin{aligned} \mathbf{h}_1 &= \mathbf{h}_1' \\ \mathbf{h}_2 &= \mathbf{g}^{-1}\Big[\mathbf{h}_2', \phi[\mathbf{h}_1]\Big]. \end{aligned} \tag{16.14}$$

If the function $\mathbf{g}[\bullet, \phi]$ is an elementwise flow, the Jacobian will be diagonal with the identity matrix in the top-left quadrant and the derivatives of the elementwise transformation in the bottom right. Its determinant is the product of these diagonal values.

The inverse and Jacobian can be computed efficiently, but this approach only transforms the second half of the parameters in a way that depends on the first half. To make a more general transformation, the elements of $\mathbf{h}$ are randomly shuffled using permutation matrices between layers, so every variable is ultimately transformed by every other. In practice, these permutation matrices are difficult to learn. Hence, they are initialized randomly and then frozen. For structured data like images, the channels are divided into two halves $\mathbf{h}_1$ and $\mathbf{h}_2$ and permuted between layers using $1{\times}1$ convolutions.

Appendix B.4.4
Permutation matrix

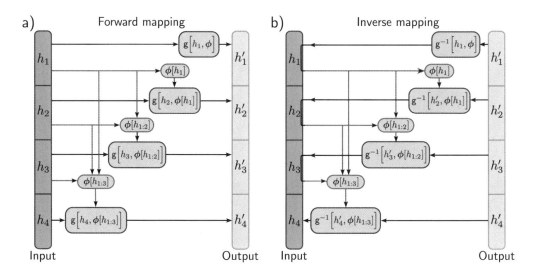

Figure 16.7 Autoregressive flows. The input $\mathbf{h}$ (orange column) and output $\mathbf{h}'$ (cyan column) are split into their constituent dimensions (here four dimensions). a) Output h_1' is an invertible transformation of input h_1. Output h_2' is an invertible function of input h_2 where the parameters depend on h_1. Output h_3' is an invertible function of input h_3 where the parameters depend on previous inputs h_1 and h_2, and so on. None of the outputs depend on one another, so they can be computed in parallel. b) The inverse of the autoregressive flow is computed using a similar method as for coupling flows. However, notice that to compute h_2 we must already know h_1, to compute h_3, we must already know h_1 and h_2, and so on. Consequently, the inverse cannot be computed in parallel.

16.3.4   Autoregressive flows

Autoregressive flows are a generalization of coupling flows that treat each input dimension as a separate "block" (figure 16.7). They compute the dth dimension of the output $\mathbf{h}'$ based on the first $d-1$ dimensions of the input $\mathbf{h}$:

$$h_d' = \mathrm{g}\Big[h_d, \boldsymbol{\phi}[\mathbf{h}_{1:d-1}]\Big]. \qquad (16.15)$$

The function $\mathrm{g}[\bullet, \bullet]$ is termed the *transformer*,[1] and the parameters $\boldsymbol{\phi}$, $\boldsymbol{\phi}[h_1]$, $\boldsymbol{\phi}[h_1, h_2], \ldots$ are termed *conditioners*. As for coupling flows, the transformer $\mathrm{g}[\bullet, \boldsymbol{\phi}]$ must be invertible, but the conditioners $\boldsymbol{\phi}[\bullet]$ can take any form and are usually neural networks. If the transformer and conditioner are sufficiently flexible, autoregressive flows are *universal approximators* in that they can represent any probability distribution.

It's possible to compute all of the entries of the output $\mathbf{h}'$ in parallel using a network with appropriate masks so that the parameters $\boldsymbol{\phi}$ at position d only depend on previous

---

[1]This is nothing to do with the transformer layers discussed in chapter 12.

positions. This is known as a *masked autoregressive flow*. The principle is very similar to masked self-attention (section 12.7.2); connections that relate inputs to previous outputs are pruned.

Inverting the transformation is less efficient. Consider the forward mapping:

$$
\begin{aligned}
h_1' &= \mathrm{g}\Big[h_1, \phi\Big] \\
h_2' &= \mathrm{g}\Big[h_2, \phi[h_1]\Big] \\
h_3' &= \mathrm{g}\Big[h_3, \phi[h_{1:2}]\Big] \\
h_4' &= \mathrm{g}\Big[h_4, \phi[h_{1:3}]\Big].
\end{aligned}
\tag{16.16}
$$

This must be inverted sequentially using a similar principle as for coupling flows:

$$
\begin{aligned}
h_1 &= \mathrm{g}^{-1}\Big[h_1', \phi\Big] \\
h_2 &= \mathrm{g}^{-1}\Big[h_2', \phi[h_1]\Big] \\
h_3 &= \mathrm{g}^{-1}\Big[h_3', \phi[h_{1:2}]\Big] \\
h_4 &= \mathrm{g}^{-1}\Big[h_4', \phi[h_{1:3}]\Big].
\end{aligned}
\tag{16.17}
$$

This can't be done in parallel as the computation for h_d depends on $h_{1:d-1}$ (i.e., the partial results so far). Hence, inversion is time-consuming when the input is large.

Notebook 16.2
Autoregressive flows

16.3.5 Inverse autoregressive flows

Masked autoregressive flows are defined in the normalizing (inverse) direction. This is required to evaluate the likelihood efficiently and hence to learn the model. However, sampling requires the forward direction, in which each variable must be computed sequentially at each layer, which is slow. If we use an autoregressive flow for the forward (generative) transformation, then sampling is efficient, but computing the likelihood (and training) is slow. This is known as an *inverse autoregressive flow*.

A trick that allows fast learning and also fast (but approximate) sampling is to build a masked autoregressive flow to learn the distribution (the teacher) and then use this to train an inverse autoregressive flow from which we can sample efficiently (the student). This requires a different formulation of normalizing flows that learns from another function rather than a set of samples (see section 16.5.3).

16.3.6 Residual flows: iRevNet

Residual flows take their inspiration from residual networks. They divide the input into two parts $\mathbf{h} = [\mathbf{h}_1^T, \mathbf{h}_2^T]^T$ (as for coupling flows) and define the outputs as:

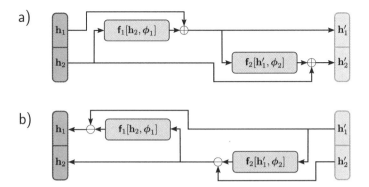

Figure 16.8 Residual flows. a) An invertible function is computed by splitting the input into $\mathbf{h}_1$ and $\mathbf{h}_2$ and creating two residual layers. In the first, $\mathbf{h}_2$ is processed and $\mathbf{h}_1$ is added. In the second, the result is processed, and $\mathbf{h}_2$ is added. b) In the reverse mechanism the functions are computed in the opposite order, and the addition operation becomes subtraction.

$$
\begin{aligned}
\mathbf{h}_1' &= \mathbf{h}_1 + \mathbf{f}_1[\mathbf{h}_2, \boldsymbol{\phi}_1] \\
\mathbf{h}_2' &= \mathbf{h}_2 + \mathbf{f}_2[\mathbf{h}_1', \boldsymbol{\phi}_2],
\end{aligned}
\tag{16.18}
$$

where $\mathbf{f}_1[\bullet, \boldsymbol{\phi}_1]$ and $\mathbf{f}_2[\bullet, \boldsymbol{\phi}_2]$ are two functions that do not necessarily have to be invertible (figure 16.8). The inverse can be computed by reversing the order of computation:

$$
\begin{aligned}
\mathbf{h}_2 &= \mathbf{h}_2' - \mathbf{f}_2[\mathbf{h}_1', \boldsymbol{\phi}_2] \\
\mathbf{h}_1 &= \mathbf{h}_1' - \mathbf{f}_1[\mathbf{h}_2, \boldsymbol{\phi}_1].
\end{aligned}
\tag{16.19}
$$

As for coupling flows, the division into blocks restricts the family of transformations that can be represented. Hence, the inputs are permuted between layers so that the variables can mix in arbitrary ways.

This formulation can be inverted easily, but for general functions $\mathbf{f}_1[\bullet, \boldsymbol{\phi}_1]$ and $\mathbf{f}_2[\bullet, \boldsymbol{\phi}_2]$, there is no efficient way to compute the Jacobian. This formulation is sometimes used to save memory when training residual networks; because the network is invertible, storing the activations at each layer in the forward pass is unnecessary.

Problem 16.10

16.3.7   Residual flows and contraction mappings: iResNet

A different approach to exploiting residual networks is to utilize the *Banach fixed point theorem* or *contraction mapping theorem*, which states that every contraction mapping has a fixed point. A contraction mapping f[•] has the property that:

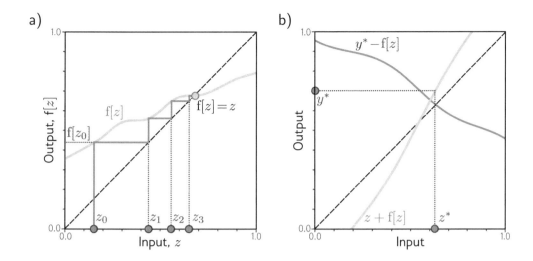

Figure 16.9 Contraction mappings. If a function has an absolute slope of less than one everywhere, iterating the function converges to a fixed point $f[z] = z$. a) Starting at z_0, we evaluate $z_1 = f[z_0]$. We then pass z_1 back into the function and iterate. Eventually, the process converges to the point where $f[z] = z$ (i.e., where the function crosses the dashed diagonal identity line). b) This can be used to invert equations of the form $y = z + f[z]$ for a value y^* by noticing that the fixed point of $y^* - f[z]$ (where the orange line crosses the dashed identity line) is at the same position as where $y^* = z + f[z]$.

$$\text{dist}\Big[f[z'], f[z]\Big] < \beta \cdot \text{dist}\Big[z', z\Big] \qquad \forall\, z, z', \qquad (16.20)$$

where $\text{dist}[\bullet, \bullet]$ is a distance function and $0 < \beta < 1$. When a function with this property is iterated (i.e., the output is repeatedly passed back in as an input), the result converges to a fixed point where $f[z] = z$ (figure 16.9). To understand this, consider applying the function to both the fixed point and the current position; the fixed point remains static, but the distance between the two must become smaller, so the current position must get closer to the fixed point.

Notebook 16.3
Contraction mappings

This theorem can be exploited to invert an equation of the form:

$$y = z + f[z] \qquad (16.21)$$

if $f[z]$ is a contraction mapping. In other words, it can be used to find the z^* that maps to a given value, y^*. This can be done by starting with any point z_0 and iterating $z_{k+1} = y^* - f[z_k]$. This has a fixed point at $z + f[z] = y^*$ (figure 16.9b).

The same principle can be used to invert residual network layers of the form $\mathbf{h}' = \mathbf{h} + \mathbf{f}[\mathbf{h}, \phi]$ if we ensure that $\mathbf{f}[\mathbf{h}, \phi]$ is a contraction mapping. In practice, this means that the Lipschitz constant must be less than one. Assuming that the slope of the activation functions is not greater than one, this is equivalent to ensuring the largest eigenvalue of

Appendix B.1.1
Lipschitz constant

Appendix B.3.7
Eigenvalues

each weight matrix $\boldsymbol{\Omega}$ must be less than one. A crude way to do this is to ensure that the absolute magnitudes of the weights $\boldsymbol{\Omega}$ are small by clipping them.

The Jacobian determinant cannot be computed easily, but its logarithm can be approximated using a series of tricks.

$$
\begin{aligned}
\log\left[\left|\mathbf{I} + \frac{\partial\mathbf{f}[\mathbf{h},\boldsymbol{\phi}]}{\partial\mathbf{h}}\right|\right] &= \text{trace}\left[\log\left[\mathbf{I} + \frac{\partial\mathbf{f}[\mathbf{h},\boldsymbol{\phi}]}{\partial\mathbf{h}}\right]\right] \\
&= \sum_{k=1}^{\infty}(-1)^{k-1}\text{trace}\left[\frac{\partial\mathbf{f}[\mathbf{h},\boldsymbol{\phi}]}{\partial\mathbf{h}}\right]^{k},
\end{aligned} \tag{16.22}
$$

where we have used the identity $\log[|\mathbf{A}|] = \text{trace}[\log[\mathbf{A}]]$ in the first line and expanded this into a power series in the second line.

Appendix B.3.8
Trace

Even when we truncate this series, it's still computationally expensive to compute the trace of the constituent terms. Hence, we approximate this using *Hutchinson's trace estimator*. Consider a normal random variable $\boldsymbol{\epsilon}$ with mean $\mathbf{0}$ and variance $\mathbf{I}$. The trace of a matrix $\mathbf{A}$ can be estimated as:

$$
\begin{aligned}
\text{trace}[\mathbf{A}] &= \text{trace}\left[\mathbf{A}\mathbb{E}\left[\boldsymbol{\epsilon}\boldsymbol{\epsilon}^{T}\right]\right] \\
&= \text{trace}\left[\mathbb{E}\left[\mathbf{A}\boldsymbol{\epsilon}\boldsymbol{\epsilon}^{T}\right]\right] \\
&= \mathbb{E}\left[\text{trace}\left[\mathbf{A}\boldsymbol{\epsilon}\boldsymbol{\epsilon}^{T}\right]\right] \\
&= \mathbb{E}\left[\text{trace}\left[\boldsymbol{\epsilon}^{T}\mathbf{A}\boldsymbol{\epsilon}\right]\right] \\
&= \mathbb{E}\left[\boldsymbol{\epsilon}^{T}\mathbf{A}\boldsymbol{\epsilon}\right],
\end{aligned} \tag{16.23}
$$

where the first line is true because $\mathbb{E}[\boldsymbol{\epsilon}\boldsymbol{\epsilon}^{T}] = \mathbf{I}$. The second line derives from the properties of the expectation operator. The third line comes from the linearity of the trace operator. The fourth line is due to the invariance of the trace to cyclic permutation. The final line is true because the argument in the fourth line is now a scalar. We estimate the trace by drawing samples $\boldsymbol{\epsilon}_i$ from $Pr(\boldsymbol{\epsilon})$:

$$
\begin{aligned}
\text{trace}[\mathbf{A}] &= \mathbb{E}\left[\boldsymbol{\epsilon}^{T}\mathbf{A}\boldsymbol{\epsilon}\right] \\
&\approx \frac{1}{I}\sum_{i=1}^{I}\boldsymbol{\epsilon}_{i}^{T}\mathbf{A}\boldsymbol{\epsilon}_{i}.
\end{aligned} \tag{16.24}
$$

In this way, we can approximate the trace of the powers of the Taylor expansion (equation 16.22) and evaluate the log probability.

16.4 Multi-scale flows

In normalizing flows, the latent space $\mathbf{z}$ must be the same size as the data space $\mathbf{x}$, but we know that natural datasets can often be described by fewer underlying variables. At

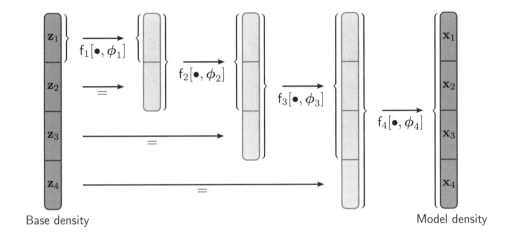

Figure 16.10 Multiscale flows. The latent space **z** must be the same size as the model density in normalizing flows. However, it can be partitioned into several components, which can be gradually introduced at different layers. This makes both density estimation and sampling faster. For the inverse process, the black arrows are reversed, and the last part of each block skips the remaining processing. For example, $\mathbf{f}_3^{-1}[\bullet, \boldsymbol{\phi}_3]$ only operates on the first three blocks, and the fourth block becomes $\mathbf{z}_4$ and is assessed against the base density.

some point, we have to introduce all of these variables, but it is inefficient to pass them through the entire network. This leads to the idea of *multi-scale flows* (figure 16.10).

In the generative direction, multi-scale flows partition the latent vector into $\mathbf{z} = [\mathbf{z}_1, \mathbf{z}_2, \ldots, \mathbf{z}_N]$. The first partition $\mathbf{z}_1$ is processed by a series of reversible layers with the same dimension as $\mathbf{z}_1$ until, at some point, $\mathbf{z}_2$ is appended and combined with the first partition. This continues until the network is the same size as the data $\mathbf{x}$. In the normalizing direction, the network starts at the full dimension of $\mathbf{x}$, but when it reaches the point where $\mathbf{z}_n$ was added, this is assessed against the base distribution.

16.5 Applications

We now describe three applications of normalizing flows. First, we consider modeling probability densities. Second, we consider the GLOW model for synthesizing images. Finally, we discuss using normalizing flows to approximate other distributions.

16.5.1 Modeling densities

Of the four generative models discussed in this book, normalizing flows is the only model that can compute the exact log-likelihood of a new sample. Generative adversarial

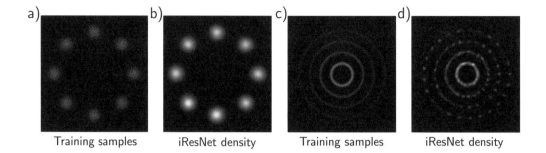

a) Training samples   b) iResNet density   c) Training samples   d) iResNet density

Figure 16.11 Modeling densities. a) Toy 2D data samples. b) Modeled density using iResNet. c–d) Second example. Adapted from Behrmann et al. (2019)

networks are not probabilistic, and both variational autoencoders and diffusion models can only return a lower bound on the likelihood.[2] Figure 16.11 depicts the estimated probability distributions in two toy problems using i-ResNet. One application of density estimation is anomaly detection; the data distribution of a clean dataset is described using a normalizing flow model. New examples with low probability are flagged as outliers. However, caution must be used as there may exist outliers with high probability that don't fall in the typical set (see figure 8.13).

16.5.2 Synthesis

Generative flows, or *GLOW*, is a normalizing flow model that can create high-fidelity images (figure 16.12) and uses many of the ideas from this chapter. It is easiest understood in the normalizing direction. GLOW starts with a $256 \times 256 \times 3$ tensor containing an RGB image. It uses coupling layers, in which the channels are partitioned into two halves. The second half is subject to a different affine transform at each spatial position, where the parameters of the affine transformation are computed by a 2D convolutional neural network run on the other half of the channels. The coupling layers are alternated with 1×1 convolutions, parameterized as LU decompositions which mix the channels.

Periodically, the resolution is halved by combining each 2×2 patch into one position with four times as many channels. GLOW is a multi-scale flow, and some of the channels are periodically removed to become part of the latent vector $\mathbf{z}$. Images are discrete (due to the quantization of RGB values), so noise is added to the inputs to prevent the training likelihood increasing without bound. This is known as *dequantization*.

To sample more realistic images, the GLOW model samples from the base density raised to a positive power. This chooses examples that are closer to the center of the density rather than from the tails. This is similar to the truncation trick in GANs

---

[2]The lower bound on the likelihood for diffusion models can actually exceed the exact computation in normalizing flows, but data generation is much slower (see chapter 18).

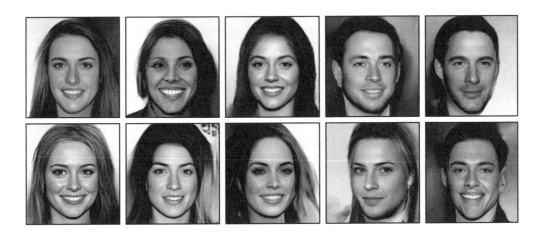

Figure 16.12 Samples from GLOW trained on the CelebA HQ dataset (Karras et al., 2018). The samples are of reasonable quality, although GANs and diffusion models produce superior results. Adapted from Kingma & Dhariwal (2018).

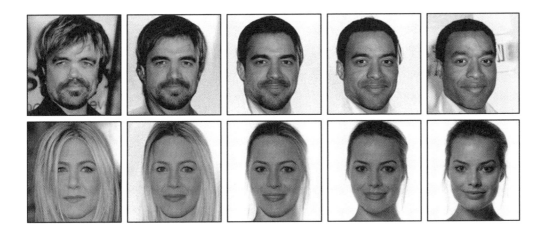

Figure 16.13 Interpolation using GLOW model. The left and right images are real people. The intermediate images were computed by projecting the real images to the latent space, interpolating, and then projecting the interpolated points back to image space. Adapted from Kingma & Dhariwal (2018).

(figure 15.10). Notably, the samples are not as good as those from GANs or diffusion models. It is unknown whether this is due to a fundamental restriction associated with invertible layers or merely because less research effort has been invested in this goal.

Figure 16.13 shows an example of interpolation using GLOW. Two latent vectors are computed by transforming two real images in the normalizing direction. Intermediate points between these latent vectors are computed by linear interpolation, and these are projected back to image space using the network in the generative direction. The result is a set of images that interpolate realistically between the two real ones.

16.5.3   Approximating other density models

Normalizing flows can also learn to generate samples that approximate an existing density which is easy to evaluate but difficult to sample from. In this context, we denote the normalizing flow $Pr(\mathbf{x}|\boldsymbol{\phi})$ as the *student* and the target density $q(\mathbf{x})$ as the *teacher*.

To make progress, we generate samples $\mathbf{x}_i = \text{f}[\mathbf{z}_i, \boldsymbol{\phi}]$ from the student. Since we generated these samples ourselves, we know their corresponding latent variables $\mathbf{z}_i$, and we can calculate their likelihood in the student model without inversion. Thus, we can use a model like a masked-autoregressive flow where inversion is slow. We define a loss function based on the reverse KL divergence that encourages the student and teacher likelihood to be identical and use this to train the student model (figure 16.14):

Problem 16.11

$$\hat{\boldsymbol{\phi}} = \underset{\boldsymbol{\phi}}{\operatorname{argmin}}\left[\text{KL}\left[\frac{1}{I}\sum_{i=1}^{I}\delta\big[\mathbf{x} - \text{f}[\mathbf{z}_i, \boldsymbol{\phi}]\big]\,\Big|\Big|\,q(\mathbf{x})\right]\right]. \tag{16.25}$$

This approach contrasts with the typical use of normalizing flows to build a probability model $Pr(\mathbf{x}_i, \boldsymbol{\phi})$ of data that came from an unknown distribution with samples $\mathbf{x}_i$ using maximum likelihood, which relies on the cross-entropy term from the forward KL divergence (section 5.7):

$$\hat{\boldsymbol{\phi}} = \underset{\boldsymbol{\phi}}{\operatorname{argmin}}\left[\text{KL}\left[\frac{1}{I}\sum_{i=1}^{I}\delta[\mathbf{x} - \mathbf{x}_i]\,\Big|\Big|\,Pr(\mathbf{x}_i, \boldsymbol{\phi})\right]\right]. \tag{16.26}$$

Normalizing flows can model the posterior in VAEs using this trick (see chapter 17).

16.6   Summary

Normalizing flows transform a base distribution (usually a normal distribution) to create a new density. They have the advantage that they can both evaluate the likelihood of samples exactly and generate new samples. However, they have the architectural constraint that each layer must be invertible; we need the forward transformation to generate samples and the backward transformation to evaluate the likelihoods.

It's also important that the Jacobian can be estimated efficiently to evaluate the likelihood; this must be done repeatedly to learn the density. However, invertible layers

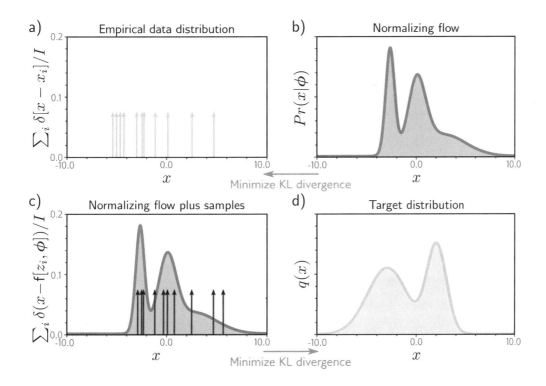

Figure 16.14 Approximating density models. a) Training data. b) Usually, we modify the flow model parameters to minimize the KL divergence from the training data to the flow model. This is equivalent to maximum likelihood fitting (section 5.7). c) Alternatively, we can modify the flow parameters ϕ to minimize the KL divergence from the flow samples $x_i = f[z_i, \phi]$ to d) a target density.

are still useful in their own right even when the Jacobian cannot be estimated efficiently; they reduce the memory requirements of training a K-layer network from $\mathcal{O}[K]$ to $\mathcal{O}[1]$.

This chapter reviewed invertible network layers or flows. We considered linear flows and elementwise flows, which are simple but insufficiently expressive. Then we described more complex flows, such as coupling, autoregressive, and residual flows. Finally, we showed how normalizing flows can be used to estimate likelihoods, generate and interpolate between images, and approximate other distributions.

Notes

Normalizing flows were first introduced by Rezende & Mohamed (2015) but had intellectual antecedents in the work of Tabak & Vanden-Eijnden (2010), Tabak & Turner (2013), and Rippel & Adams (2013). Reviews of normalizing flows can be found in Kobyzev et al. (2020) and Papamakarios et al. (2021). Kobyzev et al. (2020) presented a quantitative comparison of many normalizing flow approaches. They concluded that the Flow++ model (a coupling flow with a novel elementwise transformation and other innovations) performed best at the time.

Invertible network layers: Invertible layers decrease the memory requirements of the back-propagation algorithm; the activations in the forward pass no longer need to be stored since they can be recomputed in the backward pass. In addition to the regular network layers and residual layers (Gomez et al., 2017; Jacobsen et al., 2018) discussed in this chapter, invertible layers have been developed for graph neural networks (Li et al., 2021a), recurrent neural networks (MacKay et al., 2018), masked convolutions (Song et al., 2019), U-Nets (Brügger et al., 2019; Etmann et al., 2020), and transformers (Mangalam et al., 2022).

Radial and planar flows: The original normalizing flows paper (Rezende & Mohamed, 2015) used planar flows (which contract or expand the distribution along certain dimensions) and radial flows (which expand or contract around a certain point). Inverses for these flows can't be computed easily, but they are useful for approximating distributions where sampling is slow or where the likelihood can only be evaluated up to an unknown scaling factor (figure 16.14).

Applications: Applications include image generation (Ho et al., 2019; Kingma & Dhariwal, 2018), noise modeling (Abdelhamed et al., 2019), video generation (Kumar et al., 2019b), audio generation (Esling et al., 2019; Kim et al., 2018; Prenger et al., 2019), graph generation (Madhawa et al., 2019), image classification (Kim et al., 2021; Mackowiak et al., 2021), image steganography (Lu et al., 2021), super-resolution (Yu et al., 2020; Wolf et al., 2021; Liang et al., 2021), style transfer (An et al., 2021), motion style transfer (Wen et al., 2021), 3D shape modeling (Paschalidou et al., 2021), compression (Zhang et al., 2021b), sRGB to RAW image conversion (Xing et al., 2021), denoising (Liu et al., 2021b), anomaly detection (Yu et al., 2021), image-to-image translation (Ardizzone et al., 2020), synthesizing cell microscopy images under different molecular interventions (Yang et al., 2021), and light transport simulation (Müller et al., 2019b). For applications using image data, noise must be added before learning since the inputs are quantized and hence discrete (see Theis et al., 2016).

Rezende & Mohamed (2015) used normalizing flows to model the posterior in VAEs. Abdal et al. (2021) used normalizing flows to model the distribution of attributes in the latent space of StyleGAN and then used these distributions to change specified attributes in real images. Wolf et al. (2021) use normalizing flows to learn the conditional image of a noisy input image given a clean one and hence simulate noisy data that can be used to train denoising or super-resolution models.

Normalizing flows have also found diverse uses in physics (Kanwar et al., 2020; Köhler et al., 2020; Noé et al., 2019; Wirnsberger et al., 2020; Wong et al., 2020), natural language processing (Tran et al., 2019; Ziegler & Rush, 2019; Zhou et al., 2019; He et al., 2018; Jin et al., 2019), and reinforcement learning (Schroecker et al., 2019; Haarnoja et al., 2018a; Mazoure et al., 2020; Ward et al., 2019; Touati et al., 2020).

Linear flows: Diagonal linear flows can represent normalization transformations like Batch-Norm (Dinh et al., 2016) and ActNorm (Kingma & Dhariwal, 2018). Tomczak & Welling (2016) investigated combining triangular matrices and using orthogonal transformations parameterized by the Householder transform. Kingma & Dhariwal (2018) proposed the LU parameterization described in section 16.5.2. Hoogeboom et al. (2019b) proposed using the QR decomposition instead, which does not require predetermined permutation matrices. Convolutions are linear transformations (figure 10.4) that are widely used in deep learning, but their inverse and determinant are not straightforward to compute. Kingma & Dhariwal (2018) used 1×1 convolutions, which is effectively a full linear transformation applied separately at each position. Zheng et al. (2017) introduced ConvFlow, which was restricted to 1D convolutions. Hoogeboom et al. (2019b) provided more general solutions for modeling 2D convolutions either by stacking together masked autoregressive convolutions or by operating in the Fourier domain.

Elementwise flows and coupling functions: Elementwise flows transform each variable independently using the same function (but with different parameters for each variable). The same flows can be used to form the coupling functions in coupling and autoregressive flows, in which case their parameters depend on the preceding variables. To be invertible, these functions must be monotone.

An additive coupling function (Dinh et al., 2015) just adds an offset to the variable. Affine coupling functions scale the variable and add an offset and were used by Dinh et al. (2015), Dinh et al. (2016), Kingma & Dhariwal (2018), Kingma et al. (2016), and Papamakarios et al. (2017). Ziegler & Rush (2019) propose the nonlinear squared flow, which is an invertible ratio of polynomials with five parameters. Continuous mixture CDFs (Ho et al., 2019) apply a monotone transformation based on the cumulative density function (CDF) of a mixture of K logistics, post-composed by an inverse logistic sigmoid, scaled, and offset.

The piecewise linear coupling function (figure 16.5) was developed by Müller et al. (2019b). Since then, systems based on cubic splines (Durkan et al., 2019a) and rational quadratic splines (Durkan et al., 2019b) have been proposed. Huang et al. (2018a) introduced neural autoregressive flows, in which the function is represented by a neural network that produces a monotonic function. A sufficient condition is that the weights are all positive and the activation functions are monotone. It is hard to train a network with the constraint that the weights are positive, so this led to unconstrained monotone neural networks (Wehenkel & Louppe, 2019), which model strictly positive functions and then integrate them numerically to get a monotone function. Jaini et al. (2019) construct positive functions that can be integrated in closed form based on a classic result that all positive single-variable polynomials are the sum of squares of polynomials. Finally, Dinh et al. (2019) investigated piecewise monotonic coupling functions.

Coupling flows: Dinh et al. (2015) introduced coupling flows in which the dimensions were split in half (figure 16.6). Dinh et al. (2016) introduced *RealNVP*, which partitioned the image input by taking alternating pixels or blocks of channels. Das et al. (2019) proposed selecting features for the propagated part based on the magnitude of the derivatives. Dinh et al. (2016) interpreted multi-scale flows (in which dimensions are gradually introduced) as coupling flows in which the parameters ϕ have no dependence on the other half of the data. Kruse et al. (2021) introduce a hierarchical formulation of coupling flows in which each partition is recursively divided into two. GLOW (figures 16.12–16.13) was designed by Kingma & Dhariwal (2018) and uses coupling flows, as do NICE (Dinh et al., 2015), RealNVP (Dinh et al., 2016), FloWaveNet (Kim et al., 2018), WaveGlOW (Prenger et al., 2019), and Flow++ (Ho et al., 2019).

Autoregressive flows: Kingma et al. (2016) used autoregressive models for normalizing flows. Germain et al. (2015) developed a general method for masking previous variables. This was exploited by Papamakarios et al. (2017) to compute all of the outputs in the forward direction simultaneously in masked autoregressive flows. Kingma et al. (2016) introduced the inverse autoregressive flow. Parallel WaveNet (Van den Oord et al., 2018) distilled WaveNet (Van den Oord et al., 2016a), which is a different type of generative model for audio, into an inverse autoregressive flow so that sampling would be fast (see figure 16.14c–d).

Residual flows: Residual flows are based on residual networks (He et al., 2016a). RevNets (Gomez et al., 2017) and iRevNets (Jacobsen et al., 2018) divide the input into two sections (figure 16.8), each of which passes through a residual network. These networks are invertible, but the determinant of the Jacobian cannot be computed easily. The residual connection can be interpreted as the discretization of an ordinary differential equation, and this perspective led to different invertible architectures (Chang et al., 2018, 2019a). However, the Jacobian of these networks could still not be computed efficiently. Behrmann et al. (2019) noted that the network can be inverted using fixed point iterations if its Lipschitz constant is less than one. This led to iResNet, in which the log determinant of the Jacobian can be estimated using Hutchinson's trace estimator (Hutchinson, 1989). Chen et al. (2019) removed the bias induced by the truncation of the power series in equation 16.22 by using the Russian Roulette estimator.

Infinitesimal flows: If residual networks can be viewed as a discretization of an ordinary differential equation (ODE), then the next logical step is to represent the change in the variables directly by an ODE. The neural ODE was explored by Chen et al. (2018e) and exploits standard methods for forward and backward propagation in ODEs. The Jacobian is no longer required to compute the likelihood; this is represented by a different ODE in which the change in log probability is related to the trace of the derivative of the forward propagation. Grathwohl et al. (2019) used the Hutchinson estimator to estimate the trace and simplified this further. Finlay et al. (2020) added regularization terms to the loss function that make training easier, and Dupont et al. (2019) augmented the representation to allow the neural ODE to represent a broader class of diffeomorphisms. Tzen & Raginsky (2019) and Peluchetti & Favaro (2020) replaced the ODEs with stochastic differential equations.

Universality: The universality property refers to the ability of a normalizing flow to model any probability distribution arbitrarily well. Some flows (e.g., planar, elementwise) do not have this property. Autoregressive flows can be shown to have the universality property when the coupling function is a neural monotone network (Huang et al., 2018a), based on monotone polynomials (Jaini et al., 2020) or based on splines (Kobyzev et al., 2020). For dimension D, a series of D coupling flows can form an autoregressive flow. To understand why, note that the partitioning into two parts $\mathbf{h}_1$ and $\mathbf{h}_2$ means that at any given layer $\mathbf{h}_2$ depends only on the previous variables (figure 16.6). Hence, if we increase the size of $\mathbf{h}_1$ by one at every layer, we can reproduce an autoregressive flow, and the result is universal. It is not known whether coupling flows can be universal with fewer than D layers. However, they work well in practice (e.g., GLOW) without the need for this induced autoregressive structure.

Other work: Active areas of research in normalizing flows include the investigation of *discrete flows* (Hoogeboom et al., 2019a; Tran et al., 2019), normalizing flows on non-Euclidean manifolds (Gemici et al., 2016; Wang & Wang, 2019), and *equivariant flows* (Köhler et al., 2020; Rezende et al., 2019) which aim to create densities that are invariant to families of transformations.

Problems

Problem 16.1 Consider transforming a uniform base density defined on $z \in [0, 1]$ using the function $x = \mathrm{f}[z] = z^2$. Find an expression for the transformed distribution $Pr(x)$.

Problem 16.2[*] Consider transforming a standard normal distribution:

$$Pr(z) = \frac{1}{\sqrt{2\pi}} \exp\left[\frac{-z^2}{2}\right], \tag{16.27}$$

with the function:

$$x = \mathrm{f}[z] = \frac{1}{1 + \exp[-z]}. \tag{16.28}$$

Find an expression for the transformed distribution $Pr(x)$.

Problem 16.3[*] Write expressions for the Jacobian of the inverse mapping $\mathbf{z} = \mathbf{f}^{-1}[\mathbf{x}, \boldsymbol{\phi}]$ and the absolute determinant of that Jacobian in forms similar to equations 16.6 and 16.7.

Problem 16.4 Compute the inverse and the determinant of the following matrices by hand:

$$
\Omega_1 = \begin{bmatrix} 2 & 0 & 0 & 0 \\ 0 & -5 & 0 & 0 \\ 0 & 0 & 1 & 0 \\ 0 & 0 & 0 & 2 \end{bmatrix} \qquad \Omega_2 = \begin{bmatrix} 1 & 0 & 0 & 0 \\ 2 & 4 & 0 & 0 \\ 1 & -1 & 2 & 0 \\ 4 & -2 & -2 & 1 \end{bmatrix}. \tag{16.29}
$$

Problem 16.5 Consider a random variable $\mathbf{z}$ with mean $\boldsymbol{\mu}$ and covariance $\boldsymbol{\Sigma}$ that is transformed as $\mathbf{x} = \mathbf{A}\mathbf{z} + \mathbf{b}$. Show that the expected value of $\mathbf{x}$ is $\mathbf{A}\boldsymbol{\mu} + \mathbf{b}$ and that the covariance of $\mathbf{x}$ is $\mathbf{A}\boldsymbol{\Sigma}\mathbf{A}^T$.

Problem 16.6* Prove that if $\mathbf{x} = \mathbf{f}[\mathbf{z}] = \mathbf{A}\mathbf{z} + \mathbf{b}$ and $Pr(\mathbf{z}) = \mathrm{Norm}_{\mathbf{z}}[\boldsymbol{\mu}, \boldsymbol{\Sigma}]$, then $Pr(\mathbf{x}) = \mathrm{Norm}_{\mathbf{x}}[\mathbf{A}\boldsymbol{\mu} + \mathbf{b}, \mathbf{A}\boldsymbol{\Sigma}\mathbf{A}^T]$ using the relation:

$$
Pr(\mathbf{x}) = Pr(\mathbf{z}) \cdot \left| \frac{\partial \mathbf{f}[\mathbf{z}]}{\partial \mathbf{z}} \right|^{-1}. \tag{16.30}
$$

Problem 16.7 The Leaky ReLU is defined as:

$$
\mathrm{LReLU}[z] = \begin{cases} 0.1z & z < 0 \\ z & z \geq 0 \end{cases}. \tag{16.31}
$$

Write an expression for the inverse of the leaky ReLU. Write an expression for the inverse absolute determinant of the Jacobian $|\partial \mathbf{f}[\mathbf{z}]/\partial \mathbf{z}|^{-1}$ for an elementwise transformation $\mathbf{x} = \mathbf{f}[z]$ of the multivariate variable $\mathbf{z}$ where:

$$
\mathbf{f}[\mathbf{z}] = \Big[\mathrm{LReLU}[z_1], \mathrm{LReLU}[z_2], \dots, \mathrm{LReLU}[z_D] \Big]^T. \tag{16.32}
$$

Problem 16.8 Consider applying the piecewise linear function $\mathrm{f}[h, \boldsymbol{\phi}]$ defined in equation 16.12 for the domain $h' \in [0, 1]$ elementwise to an input $\mathbf{h} = [h_1, h_2, \dots, h_D]^T$ so that $\mathbf{f}[\mathbf{h}] = [\mathrm{f}[h_1, \boldsymbol{\phi}], \mathrm{f}[h_2, \boldsymbol{\phi}], \dots, \mathrm{f}[h_D, \boldsymbol{\phi}]]$. What is the Jacobian $\partial \mathbf{f}[\mathbf{h}]/\partial \mathbf{h}$? What is the determinant of the Jacobian?

Problem 16.9* Consider constructing an element-wise flow based on a conical combination of square root functions in equally spaced bins:

$$
\mathbf{h}' = \mathrm{f}[h, \boldsymbol{\phi}] = \sqrt{[Kh - b]\, \phi_b} + \sum_{k=1}^{b} \sqrt{\phi_k}, \tag{16.33}
$$

where $b = \lfloor Kh \rfloor$ is the bin that h falls into, and the parameters ϕ_k are positive, and sum to one. Consider the case where $K = 5$ and $\phi_1 = 0.1, \phi_2 = 0.2, \phi_3 = 0.5, \phi_4 = 0.1, \phi_5 = 0.1$. Draw the function $\mathrm{f}[h, \boldsymbol{\phi}]$. Draw the inverse function $\mathrm{f}^{-1}[h', \boldsymbol{\phi}]$.

Problem 16.10 Draw the structure of the Jacobian (indicating which elements are zero) for the forward mapping of the residual flow in figure 16.8 for the cases where $\mathbf{f}_1[\bullet, \boldsymbol{\phi}_1]$ and $\mathbf{f}_2[\bullet, \boldsymbol{\phi}_2]$ are (i) a fully connected neural network, (ii) an elementwise flow.

Problem 16.11* Write out the expression for the KL divergence in equation 16.25. Why does it not matter if we can only evaluate the probability $q(\mathbf{x})$ up to a scaling factor κ? Does the network have to be invertible to minimize this loss function? Explain your reasoning.

Chapter 17

Variational autoencoders

Generative adversarial networks learn a mechanism for creating samples that are statistically indistinguishable from the training data $\{\mathbf{x}_i\}$. In contrast, like normalizing flows, *variational autoencoders*, or *VAEs*, are *probabilistic generative models*; they aim to learn a distribution $Pr(\mathbf{x})$ over the data (see figure 14.2). After training, it is possible to draw (generate) samples from this distribution. However, the properties of the VAE mean that it is unfortunately *not* possible to evaluate the probability of new examples $\mathbf{x}^*$ exactly.

It is common to talk about the VAE as if it *is* the model of $Pr(\mathbf{x})$, but this is misleading; the VAE is a neural architecture that is designed to help *learn* the model for $Pr(\mathbf{x})$. The final model for $Pr(\mathbf{x})$ contains neither the "variational" nor the "autoencoder" parts and might be better described as a *nonlinear latent variable model*.

This chapter starts by introducing latent variable models in general and then considers the specific case of the nonlinear latent variable model. It will become clear that maximum likelihood learning of this model is not straightforward. Nevertheless, it is possible to define a lower bound on the likelihood, and the VAE architecture approximates this bound using a Monte Carlo (sampling) method. The chapter concludes by presenting several applications of the VAE.

17.1 Latent variable models

Appendix C.1.2
Marginalization

Latent variable models take an indirect approach to describing a probability distribution $Pr(\mathbf{x})$ over a multi-dimensional variable $\mathbf{x}$. Instead of directly writing the expression for $Pr(\mathbf{x})$, they model a joint distribution $Pr(\mathbf{x}, \mathbf{z})$ of the data $\mathbf{x}$ and an unobserved *hidden* or *latent variable* $\mathbf{z}$. They then describe the probability of $Pr(\mathbf{x})$ as a marginalization of this joint probability so that:

$$Pr(\mathbf{x}) = \int Pr(\mathbf{x}, \mathbf{z}) d\mathbf{z}. \tag{17.1}$$

Appendix C.1.3
Conditional
probability

Typically, the joint probability $Pr(\mathbf{x}, \mathbf{z})$ is broken down using the rules of conditional probability into the *likelihood* of the data with respect to the latent variables term $Pr(\mathbf{x}|\mathbf{z})$ and the *prior* $Pr(\mathbf{z})$:

$$Pr(\mathbf{x}) = \int Pr(\mathbf{x}|\mathbf{z})Pr(\mathbf{z})d\mathbf{z}. \tag{17.2}$$

This is a rather indirect approach to describing $Pr(\mathbf{x})$, but it is useful because relatively simple expressions for $Pr(\mathbf{x}|\mathbf{z})$ and $Pr(\mathbf{z})$ can define complex distributions $Pr(\mathbf{x})$.

17.1.1 Example: mixture of Gaussians

In a 1D mixture of Gaussians (figure 17.1a), the latent variable z is discrete, and the prior $Pr(z)$ is a categorical distribution (figure 5.9) with one probability λ_n for each possible value of z. The likelihood $Pr(x|z = n)$ of the data x given that the latent variable z takes value n is normally distributed with mean μ_n and variance σ_n^2:

Problem 17.1

$$
\begin{aligned}
Pr(z = n) &= \lambda_n \\
Pr(x|z = n) &= \text{Norm}_x\left[\mu_n, \sigma_n^2\right].
\end{aligned} \tag{17.3}
$$

As in equation 17.2, the likelihood $Pr(x)$ is given by the marginalization over the latent variable z (figure 17.1b). Here, the latent variable is discrete, so we sum over its possible values to marginalize:

$$
\begin{aligned}
Pr(x) &= \sum_{n=1}^{N} Pr(x, z = n) \\
&= \sum_{n=1}^{N} Pr(x|z = n) \cdot Pr(z = n) \\
&= \sum_{n=1}^{N} \lambda_n \cdot \text{Norm}_x\left[\mu_n, \sigma_n^2\right].
\end{aligned} \tag{17.4}
$$

From simple expressions for the likelihood and prior, we describe a complex multi-modal probability distribution.

17.2 Nonlinear latent variable model

In the nonlinear latent variable model, both the data $\mathbf{x}$ and the latent variable $\mathbf{z}$ are continuous and multivariate. The prior $Pr(\mathbf{z})$ is a standard multivariate normal:

Appendix C.3.2
Multivariate
normal

$$Pr(\mathbf{z}) = \text{Norm}_\mathbf{z}[\mathbf{0}, \mathbf{I}]. \tag{17.5}$$

The likelihood $Pr(\mathbf{x}|\mathbf{z}, \boldsymbol{\phi})$ is also normally distributed; its mean is a nonlinear function $\mathbf{f}[\mathbf{z}, \boldsymbol{\phi}]$ of the latent variable, and its covariance $\sigma^2\mathbf{I}$ is spherical:

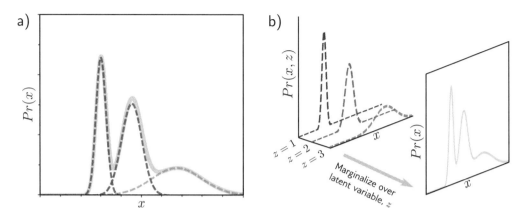

Figure 17.1 Mixture of Gaussians (MoG). a) The MoG describes a complex probability distribution (cyan curve) as a weighted sum of Gaussian components (dashed curves). b) This sum is the marginalization of the joint density $Pr(x, z)$ between the continuous observed data x and a discrete latent variable z.

$$Pr(\mathbf{x}|\mathbf{z}, \boldsymbol{\phi}) = \text{Norm}_{\mathbf{x}}\Big[\mathbf{f}[\mathbf{z}, \boldsymbol{\phi}], \sigma^2\mathbf{I}\Big]. \tag{17.6}$$

The function $\mathbf{f}[\mathbf{z}, \boldsymbol{\phi}]$ is described by a deep network with parameters $\boldsymbol{\phi}$. The latent variable $\mathbf{z}$ is lower dimensional than the data $\mathbf{x}$. The model $\mathbf{f}[\mathbf{z}, \boldsymbol{\phi}]$ describes the important aspects of the data, and the remaining unmodeled aspects are ascribed to the noise $\sigma^2\mathbf{I}$.

Notebook 17.1
Latent variable
models

The data probability $Pr(\mathbf{x}|\boldsymbol{\phi})$ is found by marginalizing over the latent variable $\mathbf{z}$:

$$
\begin{aligned}
Pr(\mathbf{x}|\boldsymbol{\phi}) &= \int Pr(\mathbf{x}, \mathbf{z}|\boldsymbol{\phi})d\mathbf{z} \\
&= \int Pr(\mathbf{x}|\mathbf{z}, \boldsymbol{\phi}) \cdot Pr(\mathbf{z})d\mathbf{z} \\
&= \int \text{Norm}_{\mathbf{x}}\Big[\mathbf{f}[\mathbf{z}, \boldsymbol{\phi}], \sigma^2\mathbf{I}\Big] \cdot \text{Norm}_{\mathbf{z}}\left[\mathbf{0}, \mathbf{I}\right] d\mathbf{z}.
\end{aligned}
\tag{17.7}
$$

This can be viewed as an infinite weighted sum (i.e., an infinite mixture) of spherical Gaussians with different means, where the weights are $Pr(\mathbf{z})$ and the means are the network outputs $\mathbf{f}[\mathbf{z}, \boldsymbol{\phi}]$ (figure 17.2).

17.2.1 Generation

Appendix C.4.2
Ancestral sampling

A new example $\mathbf{x}^*$ can be generated using ancestral sampling (figure 17.3). We draw $\mathbf{z}^*$ from the prior $Pr(\mathbf{z})$ and pass this through the network $\mathbf{f}[\mathbf{z}^*, \boldsymbol{\phi}]$ to compute the mean of the likelihood $Pr(\mathbf{x}|\mathbf{z}^*, \boldsymbol{\phi})$ (equation 17.6), from which we draw $\mathbf{x}^*$. Both the prior and likelihood are normal distributions, so this is straightforward.

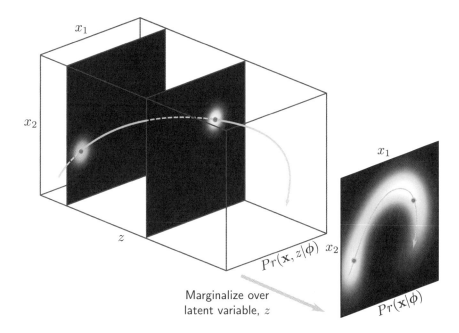

Figure 17.2 Nonlinear latent variable model. A complex 2D density $Pr(\mathbf{x})$ (right) is created as the marginalization of the joint distribution $Pr(\mathbf{x}, z)$ (left) over the latent variable z; to create $Pr(\mathbf{x})$, we integrate the 3D volume over the dimension z. For each z, the distribution over $\mathbf{x}$ is a spherical Gaussian (two slices shown) with a mean $\mathbf{f}[z, \boldsymbol{\phi}]$ that is a nonlinear function of z and depends on parameters $\boldsymbol{\phi}$. The distribution $Pr(\mathbf{x})$ is a weighted sum of these Gaussians.

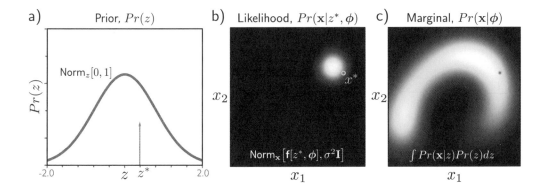

Figure 17.3 Generation from nonlinear latent variable model. a) We draw a sample z^* from the prior probability $Pr(z)$ over the latent variable. b) A sample $\mathbf{x}^*$ is then drawn from $Pr(\mathbf{x}|z^*, \boldsymbol{\phi})$. This is a spherical Gaussian with a mean that is a nonlinear function $\mathbf{f}[\bullet, \boldsymbol{\phi}]$ of z^* and a fixed variance $\sigma^2 \mathbf{I}$. c) If we repeat this process many times, we recover the density $Pr(\mathbf{x}|\boldsymbol{\phi})$.

Figure 17.4 Jensen's inequality (discrete case). The logarithm (black curve) is a concave function; you can draw a straight line between any two points on the curve, and this line will always lie underneath it. It follows that any convex combination (weighted sum with positive weights that sum to one) of the six points on the log function must lie in the gray region under the curve. Here, we have weighted the points equally (i.e., taken the mean) to yield the cyan point. Since this point lies below the curve, $\log[\mathbb{E}[y]] > \mathbb{E}[\log[y]]$.

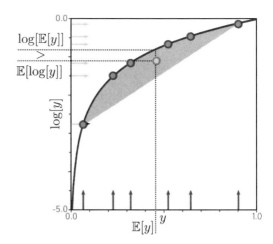

17.3   Training

To train the model, we maximize the log-likelihood over a training dataset $\{\mathbf{x}_i\}_{i=1}^{I}$ with respect to the model parameters. For simplicity, we assume that the variance term σ^2 in the likelihood expression is known and concentrate on learning ϕ:

$$\hat{\phi} \;=\; \underset{\phi}{\mathrm{argmax}}\left[\sum_{i=1}^{I}\log\Big[Pr(\mathbf{x}_i|\phi)\Big]\right], \tag{17.8}$$

where:

$$Pr(\mathbf{x}_i|\phi) \;=\; \int \mathrm{Norm}_{\mathbf{x}_i}[\mathbf{f}[\mathbf{z},\phi],\sigma^2\mathbf{I}]\cdot\mathrm{Norm}_{\mathbf{z}}[\mathbf{0},\mathbf{I}]d\mathbf{z}. \tag{17.9}$$

Unfortunately, this is intractable. There is no closed-form expression for the integral and no easy way to evaluate it for a particular value of $\mathbf{x}$.

17.3.1   Evidence lower bound (ELBO)

To make progress, we define a *lower bound* on the log-likelihood. This is a function that is always less than or equal to the log-likelihood for a given value of ϕ and will also depend on some other parameters $\boldsymbol{\theta}$. Eventually, we will build a network to compute this lower bound and optimize it. To define this lower bound, we need *Jensen's inequality*.

17.3.2   Jensen's inequality

Appendix B.1.2
Concave functions

Jensen's inequality says that a concave function $g[\bullet]$ of the expectation of data y is greater than or equal to the expectation of the function of the data:

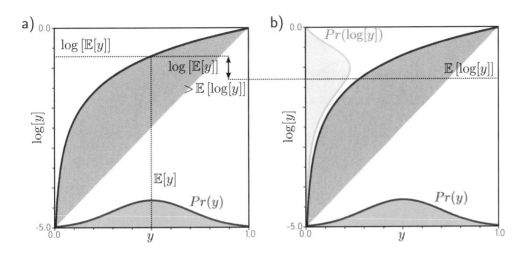

Figure 17.5 Jensen's inequality (continuous case). For a concave function, computing the expectation of a distribution $Pr(y)$ and passing it through the function gives a result greater than or equal to transforming the variable y by the function and then computing the expectation of the new variable. In the case of the logarithm, we have $\log[\mathbb{E}[y]] \geq \mathbb{E}[\log[y]]$. The left-hand side of the figure corresponds to the left-hand side of this inequality and the right-hand side of the figure to the right-hand side. One way of thinking about this is to consider that we are taking a convex combination of the points in the orange distribution defined over $y \in [0, 1]$. By the logic of figure 17.4, this must lie under the curve. Alternatively, we can think about the concave function as compressing the high values of y relative to the low values, so the expected value is lower when we pass y through the function first.

$$g[\mathbb{E}[y]] \geq \mathbb{E}\big[g[y]\big]. \tag{17.10}$$

In this case, the concave function is the logarithm, so we have:

Problems 17.2–17.3

$$\log\big[\mathbb{E}[y]\big] \geq \mathbb{E}\big[\log[y]\big], \tag{17.11}$$

or writing out the expression for the expectation in full, we have:

$$\log\left[\int Pr(y)y\,dy\right] \geq \int Pr(y)\log[y]dy. \tag{17.12}$$

This is explored in figures 17.4–17.5. In fact, the slightly more general statement is true:

$$\log\left[\int Pr(y)h[y]dy\right] \geq \int Pr(y)\log[h[y]]dy. \tag{17.13}$$

where $h[y]$ is a function of y. This follows because $h[y]$ is another random variable with a new distribution. Since we never specified $Pr(y)$, the relation remains true.

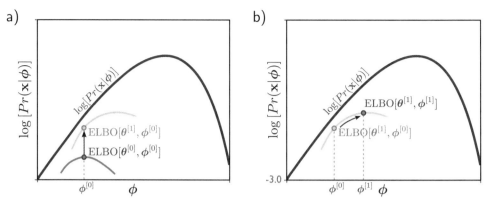

Figure 17.6 Evidence lower bound (ELBO). The goal is to maximize the log-likelihood $\log[Pr(\mathbf{x}|\boldsymbol{\phi})]$ (black curve) with respect to the parameters $\boldsymbol{\phi}$. The ELBO is a function that lies everywhere below the log-likelihood. It is a function of both $\boldsymbol{\phi}$ and a second set of parameters $\boldsymbol{\theta}$. For fixed $\boldsymbol{\theta}$, we get a function of $\boldsymbol{\phi}$ (two colored curves for different values of $\boldsymbol{\theta}$). Consequently, we can increase the log-likelihood by either improving the ELBO with respect to a) the new parameters $\boldsymbol{\theta}$ (moving from colored curve to colored curve) or b) the original parameters $\boldsymbol{\phi}$ (moving along the current colored curve).

17.3.3 Deriving the bound

We now use Jensen's inequality to derive the lower bound for the log-likelihood. We start by multiplying and dividing the log-likelihood by an arbitrary probability distribution $q(\mathbf{z})$ over the latent variables:

$$
\begin{aligned}
\log[Pr(\mathbf{x}|\boldsymbol{\phi})] &= \log\left[\int Pr(\mathbf{x},\mathbf{z}|\boldsymbol{\phi})d\mathbf{z}\right] \\
&= \log\left[\int q(\mathbf{z})\frac{Pr(\mathbf{x},\mathbf{z}|\boldsymbol{\phi})}{q(\mathbf{z})}d\mathbf{z}\right],
\end{aligned}
\tag{17.14}
$$

We then use Jensen's inequality for the logarithm (equation 17.12) to find a lower bound:

$$
\log\left[\int q(\mathbf{z})\frac{Pr(\mathbf{x},\mathbf{z}|\boldsymbol{\phi})}{q(\mathbf{z})}d\mathbf{z}\right] \geq \int q(\mathbf{z})\log\left[\frac{Pr(\mathbf{x},\mathbf{z}|\boldsymbol{\phi})}{q(\mathbf{z})}\right]d\mathbf{z},
\tag{17.15}
$$

where the right-hand side is termed the *evidence lower bound* or *ELBO*. It gets this name because $Pr(\mathbf{x}|\boldsymbol{\phi})$ is called the *evidence* in the context of Bayes' rule (equation 17.19).

In practice, the distribution $q(\mathbf{z})$ has parameters $\boldsymbol{\theta}$, so the ELBO can be written as:

$$
\text{ELBO}[\boldsymbol{\theta},\boldsymbol{\phi}] = \int q(\mathbf{z}|\boldsymbol{\theta})\log\left[\frac{Pr(\mathbf{x},\mathbf{z}|\boldsymbol{\phi})}{q(\mathbf{z}|\boldsymbol{\theta})}\right]d\mathbf{z}.
\tag{17.16}
$$

To learn the nonlinear latent variable model, we maximize this quantity as a function of both ϕ and θ. The neural architecture that computes this quantity is the VAE.

17.4 ELBO properties

When first encountered, the ELBO is a somewhat mysterious object, so we now provide some intuition about its properties. Consider that the original log-likelihood of the data is a function of the parameters ϕ and that we want to find its maximum. For any fixed θ, the ELBO is still a function of the parameters but one that must lie below the original likelihood function. When we change θ, we modify this function, and depending on our choice, the lower bound may move closer or further from the log-likelihood. When we change ϕ, we move along the lower bound function (figure 17.6).

17.4.1 Tightness of bound

The ELBO is *tight* when, for a fixed value of ϕ, the ELBO and the likelihood function coincide. To find the distribution $q(\mathbf{z}|\theta)$ that makes the bound tight, we factor the numerator of the log term in the ELBO using the definition of conditional probability:

Appendix C.1.3
Conditional
probability

$$
\begin{aligned}
\mathrm{ELBO}[\theta, \phi] &= \int q(\mathbf{z}|\theta) \log\left[\frac{Pr(\mathbf{x}, \mathbf{z}|\phi)}{q(\mathbf{z}|\theta)}\right] d\mathbf{z} \\
&= \int q(\mathbf{z}|\theta) \log\left[\frac{Pr(\mathbf{z}|\mathbf{x}, \phi)Pr(\mathbf{x}|\phi)}{q(\mathbf{z}|\theta)}\right] d\mathbf{z} \\
&= \int q(\mathbf{z}|\theta) \log\left[Pr(\mathbf{x}|\phi)\right] d\mathbf{z} + \int q(\mathbf{z}|\theta) \log\left[\frac{Pr(\mathbf{z}|\mathbf{x}, \phi)}{q(\mathbf{z}|\theta)}\right] d\mathbf{z} \\
&= \log\left[Pr(\mathbf{x}|\phi)\right] + \int q(\mathbf{z}|\theta) \log\left[\frac{Pr(\mathbf{z}|\mathbf{x}, \phi)}{q(\mathbf{z}|\theta)}\right] d\mathbf{z} \\
&= \log\left[Pr(\mathbf{x}|\phi)\right] - \mathrm{D}_{KL}\left[q(\mathbf{z}|\theta)\,\middle\|\,Pr(\mathbf{z}|\mathbf{x}, \phi)\right].
\end{aligned}
\tag{17.17}
$$

Here, the first integral disappears between lines three and four since $\log[Pr(\mathbf{x}|\phi)]$ does not depend on $\mathbf{z}$, and the integral of the probability distribution $q(\mathbf{z}|\theta)$ is one. In the last line, we have just used the definition of the Kullback-Leibler (KL) divergence.

Appendix C.5.1
KL divergence

This equation shows that the ELBO is the original log-likelihood minus the KL divergence $\mathrm{D}_{KL}[q(\mathbf{z}|\theta)||Pr(\mathbf{z}|\mathbf{x}, \phi)]$. The KL divergence measures the "distance" between distributions and can only take non-negative values. It follows the ELBO is a lower bound on $\log[Pr(\mathbf{x}|\phi)]$. The KL distance will be zero, and the bound will be *tight* when $q(\mathbf{z}|\theta) = Pr(\mathbf{z}|\mathbf{x}, \phi)$. This is the posterior distribution over the latent variables $\mathbf{z}$ given observed data $\mathbf{x}$; it indicates which values of the latent variable could have been responsible for the data point (figure 17.7).

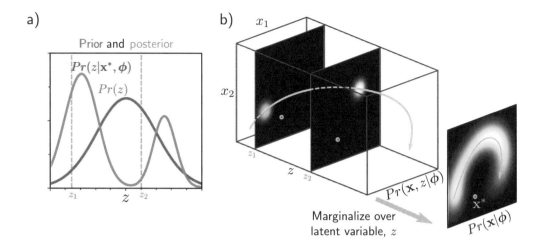

Figure 17.7 Posterior distribution over latent variable. a) The posterior distribution $Pr(z|\mathbf{x}^*, \phi)$ is the distribution over the values of the latent variable z that could be responsible for a data point $\mathbf{x}^*$. We calculate this via Bayes' rule $Pr(z|\mathbf{x}^*, \phi) \propto Pr(\mathbf{x}^*|z, \phi)Pr(z)$. b) We compute the first term on the right-hand side (the likelihood) by assessing the probability of $\mathbf{x}^*$ against the symmetric Gaussian associated with each value of z. Here, it was more likely to have been created from z_1 than z_2. The second term is the prior probability $Pr(z)$ over the latent variable. Combining these two factors and normalizing so the distribution sums to one gives us the posterior $Pr(z|\mathbf{x}^*, \phi)$.

17.4.2   ELBO as reconstruction loss minus KL distance to prior

Equations 17.16 and 17.17 are two different ways to express the ELBO. A third way is to consider the bound as reconstruction error minus the distance to the prior:

$$
\begin{aligned}
\mathrm{ELBO}[\boldsymbol{\theta}, \boldsymbol{\phi}] &= \int q(\mathbf{z}|\boldsymbol{\theta}) \log \left[\frac{Pr(\mathbf{x}, \mathbf{z}|\boldsymbol{\phi})}{q(\mathbf{z}|\boldsymbol{\theta})} \right] d\mathbf{z} \\
&= \int q(\mathbf{z}|\boldsymbol{\theta}) \log \left[\frac{Pr(\mathbf{x}|\mathbf{z}, \boldsymbol{\phi})Pr(\mathbf{z})}{q(\mathbf{z}|\boldsymbol{\theta})} \right] d\mathbf{z} \\
&= \int q(\mathbf{z}|\boldsymbol{\theta}) \log \left[Pr(\mathbf{x}|\mathbf{z}, \boldsymbol{\phi}) \right] d\mathbf{z} + \int q(\mathbf{z}|\boldsymbol{\theta}) \log \left[\frac{Pr(\mathbf{z})}{q(\mathbf{z}|\boldsymbol{\theta})} \right] d\mathbf{z} \\
&= \int q(\mathbf{z}|\boldsymbol{\theta}) \log \left[Pr(\mathbf{x}|\mathbf{z}, \boldsymbol{\phi}) \right] d\mathbf{z} - \mathrm{D}_{KL} \left[q(\mathbf{z}|\boldsymbol{\theta}) \middle\| Pr(\mathbf{z}) \right], \quad (17.18)
\end{aligned}
$$

Problem 17.4

where the joint distribution $Pr(\mathbf{x}, \mathbf{z}|\boldsymbol{\phi})$ has been factored into conditional probability $Pr(\mathbf{x}|\mathbf{z}, \boldsymbol{\phi})Pr(\mathbf{z})$ between the first and second lines, and the definition of KL divergence is used again in the last line.

In this formulation, the first term measures the average agreement $Pr(\mathbf{x}|\mathbf{z}, \boldsymbol{\phi})$ of the latent variable and the data. This is termed the *reconstruction loss*. The second term measures the degree to which the auxiliary distribution $q(\mathbf{z}|\boldsymbol{\theta})$ matches the prior. This formulation is the one that is used in the variational autoencoder.

17.5 Variational approximation

We saw in equation 17.17 that the ELBO is tight when $q(\mathbf{z}|\boldsymbol{\theta})$ is the posterior $Pr(\mathbf{z}|\mathbf{x}, \boldsymbol{\phi})$. In principle, we can compute the posterior using Bayes' rule:

$$Pr(\mathbf{z}|\mathbf{x}, \boldsymbol{\phi}) = \frac{Pr(\mathbf{x}|\mathbf{z}, \boldsymbol{\phi})Pr(\mathbf{z})}{Pr(\mathbf{x}|\boldsymbol{\phi})}, \tag{17.19}$$

but in practice, this is intractable because we can't evaluate the evidence term $Pr(\mathbf{x}|\boldsymbol{\phi})$ in the denominator (see section 17.3).

One solution is to make a variational approximation: we choose a simple parametric form for $q(\mathbf{z}|\boldsymbol{\theta})$ and use this to approximate the true posterior. Here, we choose a multivariate normal distribution with mean $\boldsymbol{\mu}$ and diagonal covariance $\boldsymbol{\Sigma}$. This will not always match the posterior well but will be better for some values of $\boldsymbol{\mu}$ and $\boldsymbol{\Sigma}$ than others. During training, we will find the normal distribution that is "closest" to the true posterior $Pr(\mathbf{z}|\mathbf{x})$ (figure 17.8). This corresponds to minimizing the KL divergence in equation 17.17 and moving the colored curves in figure 17.6 upwards.

Since the optimal choice for $q(\mathbf{z}|\boldsymbol{\theta})$ was the posterior $Pr(\mathbf{z}|\mathbf{x})$, and this depends on the data example $\mathbf{x}$, the variational approximation should do the same, so we choose:

$$q(\mathbf{z}|\mathbf{x}, \boldsymbol{\theta}) = \text{Norm}_{\mathbf{z}}\Big[\mathbf{g}_{\boldsymbol{\mu}}[\mathbf{x}, \boldsymbol{\theta}], \mathbf{g}_{\boldsymbol{\Sigma}}[\mathbf{x}, \boldsymbol{\theta}]\Big], \tag{17.20}$$

where $\mathbf{g}[\mathbf{x}, \boldsymbol{\theta}]$ is a second neural network with parameters $\boldsymbol{\theta}$ that predicts the mean $\boldsymbol{\mu}$ and variance $\boldsymbol{\Sigma}$ of the normal variational approximation.

Appendix C.3.2
Multivariate
normal

17.6 The variational autoencoder

Finally, we can describe the VAE. We build a network that computes the ELBO:

$$\text{ELBO}[\boldsymbol{\theta}, \boldsymbol{\phi}] = \int q(\mathbf{z}|\mathbf{x}, \boldsymbol{\theta}) \log\big[Pr(\mathbf{x}|\mathbf{z}, \boldsymbol{\phi})\big] d\mathbf{z} - \text{D}_{KL}\Big[q(\mathbf{z}|\mathbf{x}, \boldsymbol{\theta})\big|\big|Pr(\mathbf{z})\Big], \tag{17.21}$$

where the distribution $q(\mathbf{z}|\mathbf{x}, \boldsymbol{\theta})$ is the approximation from equation 17.20.

The first term still involves an intractable integral, but since it is an expectation with respect to $q(\mathbf{z}|\mathbf{x}, \boldsymbol{\theta})$, we can approximate it by sampling. For any function a[•] we have:

Appendix C.2
Expectation

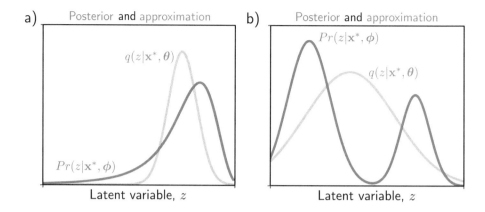

Figure 17.8 Variational approximation. The posterior $Pr(\mathbf{z}|\mathbf{x}^*, \boldsymbol{\phi})$ can't be computed in closed form. The variational approximation chooses a family of distributions $q(\mathbf{z}|\mathbf{x}, \boldsymbol{\theta})$ (here Gaussians) and tries to find the closest member of this family to the true posterior. a) Sometimes, the approximation (cyan curve) is good and lies close to the true posterior (orange curve). b) However, if the posterior is multi-modal (as in figure 17.7), then the Gaussian approximation will be poor.

$$\mathbb{E}_{\mathbf{z}}\big[\mathrm{a}[\mathbf{z}]\big] = \int \mathrm{a}[\mathbf{z}]q(\mathbf{z}|\mathbf{x}, \boldsymbol{\theta})d\mathbf{z} \approx \frac{1}{N}\sum_{n=1}^{N}\mathrm{a}[\mathbf{z}_n^*], \qquad (17.22)$$

where $\mathbf{z}_n^*$ is the nth sample from $q(\mathbf{z}|\mathbf{x}, \boldsymbol{\theta})$. This is known as a *Monte Carlo estimate*. For a very approximate estimate, we can just use a single sample $\mathbf{z}^*$ from $q(\mathbf{z}|\mathbf{x}, \boldsymbol{\theta})$:

$$\mathrm{ELBO}[\boldsymbol{\theta}, \boldsymbol{\phi}] \;\approx\; \log\big[Pr(\mathbf{x}|\mathbf{z}^*, \boldsymbol{\phi})\big] - \mathrm{D}_{KL}\Big[q(\mathbf{z}|\mathbf{x}, \boldsymbol{\theta})\Big|\Big|Pr(\mathbf{z})\Big]. \qquad (17.23)$$

Appendix C.5.4
KL divergence
between normal
distributions

The second term is the KL divergence between the variational distribution $q(\mathbf{z}|\mathbf{x}, \boldsymbol{\theta}) = \mathrm{Norm}_{\mathbf{z}}[\boldsymbol{\mu}, \boldsymbol{\Sigma}]$ and the prior $Pr(\mathbf{z}) = \mathrm{Norm}_{\mathbf{z}}[\mathbf{0}, \mathbf{I}]$. The KL divergence between two normal distributions can be calculated in closed form. For the special case where one distribution has parameters $\boldsymbol{\mu}, \boldsymbol{\Sigma}$ and the other is a standard normal, it is given by:

$$\mathrm{D}_{KL}\Big[q(\mathbf{z}|\mathbf{x}, \boldsymbol{\theta})\Big|\Big|Pr(\mathbf{z})\Big] = \frac{1}{2}\bigg(\mathrm{Tr}[\boldsymbol{\Sigma}] + \boldsymbol{\mu}^T\boldsymbol{\mu} - D_{\mathbf{z}} - \log\Big[\det[\boldsymbol{\Sigma}]\Big]\bigg). \qquad (17.24)$$

where $D_{\mathbf{z}}$ is the dimensionality of the latent space.

17.6.1   VAE algorithm

To summarize, we aim to build a model that computes the evidence lower bound for a point $\mathbf{x}$. Then we use an optimization algorithm to maximize this lower bound over the

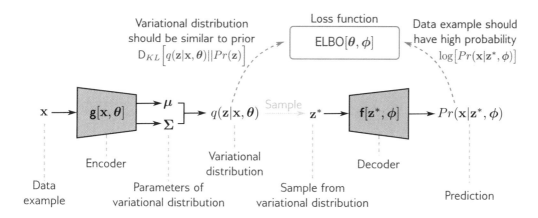

Figure 17.9 Variational autoencoder. The encoder $\mathbf{g}[\mathbf{x}, \boldsymbol{\theta}]$ takes a training example $\mathbf{x}$ and predicts the parameters $\boldsymbol{\mu}, \boldsymbol{\Sigma}$ of the variational distribution $q(\mathbf{z}|\mathbf{x}, \boldsymbol{\theta})$. We sample from this distribution and then use the decoder $\mathbf{f}[\mathbf{z}, \boldsymbol{\phi}]$ to predict the data $\mathbf{x}$. The loss function is the negative ELBO, which depends on how accurate this prediction is and how similar the variational distribution $q(\mathbf{z}|\mathbf{x}, \boldsymbol{\theta})$ is to the prior $Pr(\mathbf{z})$ (equation 17.21).

dataset and hence improve the log-likelihood. To compute the ELBO we:

- compute the mean $\boldsymbol{\mu}$ and variance $\boldsymbol{\Sigma}$ of the variational posterior distribution $q(\mathbf{z}|\boldsymbol{\theta}, \mathbf{x})$ for this data point $\mathbf{x}$ using the network $\mathbf{g}[\mathbf{x}, \boldsymbol{\theta}]$,

- draw a sample $\mathbf{z}^*$ from this distribution, and

- compute the ELBO using equation 17.23.

The associated architecture is shown in figure 17.9. It should now be clear why this is called a variational autoencoder. It is variational because it computes a Gaussian approximation to the posterior distribution. It is an autoencoder because it starts with a data point $\mathbf{x}$, computes a lower-dimensional latent vector $\mathbf{z}$ from this, and then uses this vector to recreate the data point $\mathbf{x}$ as closely as possible. In this context, the mapping from the data to the latent variable by the network $\mathbf{g}[\mathbf{x}, \boldsymbol{\theta}]$ is called the *encoder*, and the mapping from the latent variable to the data by the network $\mathbf{f}[\mathbf{z}, \boldsymbol{\phi}]$ is called the *decoder*.

The VAE computes the ELBO as a function of both $\boldsymbol{\phi}$ and $\boldsymbol{\theta}$. To maximize this bound, we run mini-batches of samples through the network and update these parameters with an optimization algorithm such as SGD or Adam. The gradients of the ELBO with respect to the parameters are computed as usual using automatic differentiation. During this process, we are both moving between the colored curves (changing $\boldsymbol{\theta}$) and along them (changing $\boldsymbol{\phi}$) in figure 17.10. During this process, the parameters $\boldsymbol{\phi}$ change to assign the data a higher likelihood in the nonlinear latent variable model.

Figure 17.10 The VAE updates both factors that determine the lower bound at each iteration. Both the parameters ϕ of the decoder and the parameters θ of the encoder are manipulated to increase this lower bound.

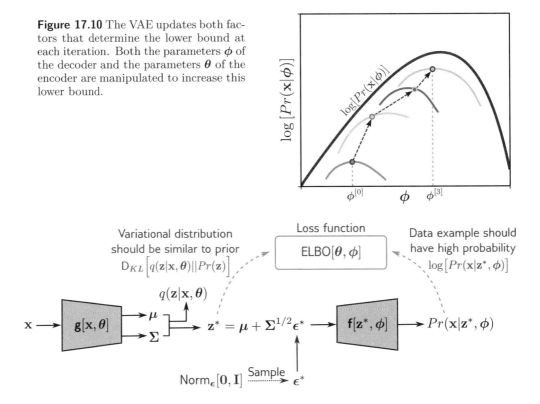

Figure 17.11 Reparameterization trick. With the original architecture (figure 17.9), we cannot easily backpropagate through the sampling step. The reparameterization trick removes the sampling step from the main pipeline; we draw from a standard normal and combine this with the predicted mean and covariance to get a sample from the variational distribution.

17.7 The reparameterization trick

There is one more complication; the network involves a sampling step, and it is difficult to differentiate through this stochastic component. However, differentiating past this step is necessary to update the parameters θ that precede it in the network.

Problem 17.5

Fortunately, there is a simple solution; we can move the stochastic part into a branch of the network that draws a sample $\boldsymbol{\epsilon}^*$ from $\text{Norm}_{\boldsymbol{\epsilon}}[\mathbf{0}, \mathbf{I}]$ and then use the relation:

$$\mathbf{z}^* = \boldsymbol{\mu} + \boldsymbol{\Sigma}^{1/2}\boldsymbol{\epsilon}^*, \tag{17.25}$$

Notebook 17.2
Reparameterization
trick

to draw from the intended Gaussian. Now we can compute the derivatives as usual because the backpropagation algorithm does not need to pass down the stochastic branch. This is known as the *reparameterization trick* (figure 17.11).

17.8 Applications

Variational autoencoders have many uses, including denoising, anomaly detection, and compression. This section reviews several applications for image data.

17.8.1 Approximating sample probability

In section 17.3, we argued that it is not possible to evaluate the probability of a sample with the VAE, which describes this probability as:

$$
\begin{aligned}
Pr(\mathbf{x}) &= \int Pr(\mathbf{x}|\mathbf{z})Pr(\mathbf{z})d\mathbf{z} \\
&= \mathbb{E}_{\mathbf{z}}\Big[Pr(\mathbf{x}|\mathbf{z})\Big] \\
&= \mathbb{E}_{\mathbf{z}}\Big[\text{Norm}_{\mathbf{x}}[\mathbf{f}[\mathbf{z},\boldsymbol{\phi}],\sigma^2\mathbf{I}]\Big].
\end{aligned}
\tag{17.26}
$$

In principle, we could *approximate* this probability using equation 17.22 by drawing samples from $Pr(\mathbf{z}) = \text{Norm}_{\mathbf{z}}[\mathbf{0},\mathbf{I}]$ and computing:

$$
Pr(\mathbf{x}) \approx \frac{1}{N}\sum_{n=1}^{N} Pr(\mathbf{x}|\mathbf{z}_n).
\tag{17.27}
$$

However, the curse of dimensionality means that almost all values of $\mathbf{z}_n$ that we draw would have a very low probability; we would have to draw an enormous number of samples to get a reliable estimate. A better approach is to use *importance sampling*. Here, we sample $\mathbf{z}$ from an auxiliary distribution $q(\mathbf{z})$, evaluate $Pr(\mathbf{x}|\mathbf{z}_n)$, and rescale the resulting values by the probability $q(\mathbf{z})$ under the new distribution:

$$
\begin{aligned}
Pr(\mathbf{x}) &= \int Pr(\mathbf{x}|\mathbf{z})Pr(\mathbf{z})d\mathbf{z} \\
&= \int \frac{Pr(\mathbf{x}|\mathbf{z})Pr(\mathbf{z})}{q(\mathbf{z})}q(\mathbf{z})d\mathbf{z} \\
&= \mathbb{E}_{q(\mathbf{z})}\left[\frac{Pr(\mathbf{x}|\mathbf{z})Pr(\mathbf{z})}{q(\mathbf{z})}\right] \\
&\approx \frac{1}{N}\sum_{n=1}^{N}\frac{Pr(\mathbf{x}|\mathbf{z}_n)Pr(\mathbf{z}_n)}{q(\mathbf{z}_n)},
\end{aligned}
\tag{17.28}
$$

where now we draw the samples from $q(\mathbf{z})$. If $q(\mathbf{z})$ is close to the region of $\mathbf{z}$ where the $Pr(\mathbf{x}|\mathbf{z})$ has high likelihood, then we will focus the sampling on the relevant area of space and estimate $Pr(\mathbf{x})$ much more efficiently.

Notebook 17.3
Importance
sampling

The product $Pr(\mathbf{x}|\mathbf{z})Pr(\mathbf{z})$ that we are trying to integrate is proportional to the posterior distribution $Pr(\mathbf{z}|\mathbf{x})$ (by Bayes' rule). Hence, a sensible choice of auxiliary distribution $q(\mathbf{z})$ is the variational posterior $q(\mathbf{z}|\mathbf{x})$ computed by the encoder.

Figure 17.12 Sampling from a standard VAE trained on CELEBA. In each column, a latent variable $\mathbf{z}^*$ is drawn and passed through the model to predict the mean $\mathbf{f}[\mathbf{z}^*, \phi]$ before adding independent Gaussian noise (see figure 17.3). a) A set of samples that are the sum of b) the predicted means and c) spherical Gaussian noise vectors. The images look too smooth before we add the noise and too noisy afterward. This is typical, and usually, the noise-free version is shown since the noise is considered to represent aspects of the image that are not modeled. Adapted from Dorta et al. (2018). d) It is now possible to generate high-quality images from VAEs using hierarchical priors, specialized architecture, and careful regularization. Adapted from Vahdat & Kautz (2020).

In this way, we can approximate the probability of new samples. With sufficient samples, this will provide a better estimate than the lower bound and could be used to evaluate the quality of the model by evaluating the log-likelihood of test data. Alternatively, it could be used as a criterion for determining whether new examples belong to the distribution or are anomalous.

17.8.2 Generation

VAEs build a probabilistic model, and it's easy to sample from this model by drawing from the prior $Pr(\mathbf{z})$ over the latent variable, passing this result through the decoder $\mathbf{f}[\mathbf{z}, \phi]$, and adding noise according to $Pr(\mathbf{x}|\mathbf{f}[\mathbf{z}, \phi])$. Unfortunately, samples from vanilla VAEs are generally low-quality (figure 17.12a–c). This is partly because of the naïve spherical Gaussian noise model and partly because of the Gaussian models used for the prior and variational posterior. One trick to improve generation quality is to sample from the *aggregated posterior* $q(\mathbf{z}|\boldsymbol{\theta}) = (1/I)\sum_i q(\mathbf{z}|\mathbf{x}_i, \boldsymbol{\theta})$ rather than the prior; this is the average posterior over all samples and is a mixture of Gaussians that is more representative of true distribution in latent space.

Modern VAEs can produce high-quality samples (figure 17.12d), but only by using hierarchical priors and specialized network architecture and regularization techniques. Diffusion models (chapter 18) can be viewed as VAEs with hierarchical priors. These also create very high-quality samples.

7.8.3 Resynthesis

VAEs can also be used to modify real data. A data point $\mathbf{x}$ can be projected into the latent space by either (i) taking the mean of the distribution predicted by the encoder or (ii) by using an optimization procedure to find the latent variable $\mathbf{z}$ that maximizes the posterior probability, which Bayes' rule tells us is proportional to $Pr(\mathbf{x}|\mathbf{z})Pr(\mathbf{z})$.

In figure 17.13, multiple images labeled as "neutral" or "smiling" are projected into latent space. The vector representing this change is estimated by taking the difference in latent space between the means of these two groups. A second vector is estimated to represent "mouth closed" versus "mouth open."

Now the image of interest is projected into the latent space, and then the representation is modified by adding or subtracting these vectors. To generate intermediate images, *spherical linear interpolation* or *Slerp* is used rather than linear interpolation. In 3D, this would be the difference between interpolating along the surface of a sphere versus digging a straight tunnel through its body.

The process of encoding (and possibly modifying) input data before decoding again is known as *resynthesis*. This can also be done with GANs and normalizing flows. However, in GANs, there is no encoder, so a separate procedure must be used to find the latent variable that corresponds to the observed data.

Problem 17.6

7.8.4 Disentanglement

In the resynthesis example above, the directions in space representing interpretable properties had to be estimated using labeled training data. Other work attempts to improve the characteristics of the latent space so that its coordinate directions correspond to real-world properties. When each dimension represents an independent real-world factor, the latent space is described as *disentangled*. For example, when modeling face images, we might hope to uncover head pose or hair color as independent factors.

Methods to encourage disentanglement typically add regularization terms to the loss function based on either (i) the posterior $q(\mathbf{z}|\mathbf{x}, \boldsymbol{\theta})$ over the latent variables $\mathbf{z}$, or (ii) the aggregated posterior $q(\mathbf{z}|\boldsymbol{\theta}) = (1/I)\sum_i q(\mathbf{z}|\mathbf{x}_i, \boldsymbol{\theta})$:

$$L_{\text{new}} = -\text{ELBO}[\boldsymbol{\theta}, \boldsymbol{\phi}] + \lambda_1 \mathbb{E}_{Pr(\mathbf{x})}\Big[\text{r}_1\big[q(\mathbf{z}|\mathbf{x}, \boldsymbol{\theta})\big]\Big] + \lambda_2 \text{r}_2\big[q(\mathbf{z}|\boldsymbol{\theta})\big]. \tag{17.29}$$

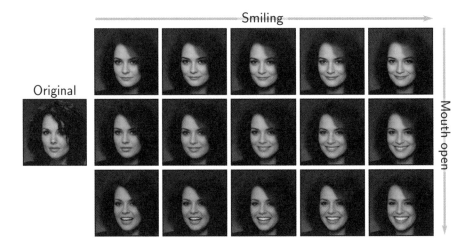

Figure 17.13 Resynthesis. The original image on the left is projected into the latent space using the encoder, and the mean of the predicted Gaussian is chosen to represent the image. The center-left image in the grid is the reconstruction of the input. The other images are reconstructions after manipulating the latent space in directions representing smiling/neutral (horizontal) and mouth open/closed (vertical). Adapted from White (2016).

Here the regularization term $r_1[\bullet]$ is a function of the posterior and is weighted by λ_1. The term $r_2[\bullet]$ is a function of the aggregated posterior and is weighted by λ_2.

For example, the *beta VAE* upweights the second term in the ELBO (equation 17.18):

$$\text{ELBO}[\boldsymbol{\theta}, \boldsymbol{\phi}] \quad \approx \quad \log\big[Pr(\mathbf{x}|\mathbf{z}^*, \boldsymbol{\phi})\big] - \beta \cdot \text{D}_{KL}\Big[q(\mathbf{z}|\mathbf{x}, \boldsymbol{\theta})\big\|Pr(\mathbf{z})\Big], \qquad (17.30)$$

where $\beta > 1$ determines how much more the deviation from the prior $Pr(\mathbf{z})$ is weighted relative to the reconstruction error. Since the prior is usually a multivariate normal with a spherical covariance matrix, its dimensions are independent. Hence, up-weighting this term encourages the posterior distributions to be less correlated. Another variant is the total correlation VAE, which adds a term to decrease the total correlation between variables in the latent space (figure 17.14) and maximizes the mutual information between a small subset of the latent variables and the observations.

17.9 Summary

The VAE is an architecture that helps to learn a nonlinear latent variable model over $\mathbf{x}$. This model can generate new examples by sampling from the latent variable, passing the result through a deep network, and then adding independent Gaussian noise.

a)   Rotation   b)   Size   c)   Legs

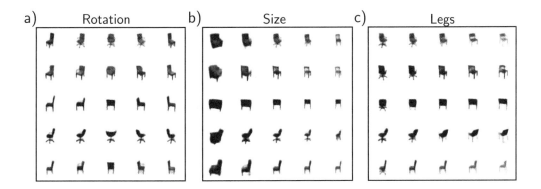

Figure 17.14 Disentanglement in the total correlation VAE. The VAE model is modified so that the loss function encourages the total correlation of the latent variables to be minimized and hence encourages disentanglement. When trained on a dataset of images of chairs, several of the latent dimensions have clear real-world interpretations, including a) rotation, b) overall size, and c) legs (swivel chair versus normal). In each case, the central column depicts samples from the model, and as we move left to right, we are subtracting or adding a coordinate vector in latent space. Adapted from Chen et al. (2018d).

It is not possible to compute the likelihood of a data point in closed form, and this poses problems for training with maximum likelihood. However, we can define a lower bound on the likelihood and maximize this bound. Unfortunately, for the bound to be tight, we need to compute the posterior probability of the latent variable given the observed data, which is also intractable. The solution is to make a variational approximation. This is a simpler distribution (usually a Gaussian) that approximates the posterior and whose parameters are computed by a second encoder network.

To create high-quality samples from the VAE, it seems to be necessary to model the latent space with more sophisticated probability distributions than the Gaussian prior and posterior. One option is to use hierarchical priors (in which one latent variable generates another). The next chapter discusses diffusion models, which produce very high-quality examples and can be viewed as hierarchical VAEs.

Notes

The VAE was originally introduced by Kingma & Welling (2014). A comprehensive introduction to variational autoencoders can be found in Kingma et al. (2019).

Applications: The VAE and variants thereof have been applied to images (Kingma & Welling, 2014; Gregor et al., 2016; Gulrajani et al., 2016; Akuzawa et al., 2018), speech (Hsu et al., 2017b), text (Bowman et al., 2015; Hu et al., 2017; Xu et al., 2020), molecules (Gómez-Bombarelli et al.,

2018; Sultan et al., 2018), graphs (Kipf & Welling, 2016; Simonovsky & Komodakis, 2018), robotics (Hernández et al., 2018; Inoue et al., 2018; Park et al., 2018), reinforcement learning (Heess et al., 2015; Van Hoof et al., 2016), 3D scenes (Eslami et al., 2016, 2018; Rezende Jimenez et al., 2016), and handwriting (Chung et al., 2015).

Applications include resynthesis and interpolation (White, 2016; Bowman et al., 2015), collaborative filtering (Liang et al., 2018), and compression (Gregor et al., 2016). Gómez-Bombarelli et al. (2018) use the VAE to construct a continuous representation of chemical structures that can then be optimized for desirable properties. Ravanbakhsh et al. (2017) simulate astronomical observations for calibrating measurements.

Relation to other models: The autoencoder (Rumelhart et al., 1985; Hinton & Salakhutdinov, 2006) passes data through an encoder to a bottleneck layer and then reconstructs it using a decoder. The bottleneck is similar to latent variables in the VAE, but the motivation differs. Here, the goal is not to learn a probability distribution but to create a low-dimensional representation that captures the essence of the data. Autoencoders also have various applications, including denoising (Vincent et al., 2008) and anomaly detection (Zong et al., 2018).

If the encoder and decoder are linear transformations, the autoencoder is just principal component analysis (PCA). Hence, the nonlinear autoencoder is a generalization of PCA. There are also probabilistic forms of PCA. Probabilistic PCA (Tipping & Bishop, 1999) adds spherical Gaussian noise to the reconstruction to create a probability model, and factor analysis adds diagonal Gaussian noise (see Rubin & Thayer, 1982). If we make the encoder and decoder of these probabilistic variants nonlinear, we return to the variational autoencoder.

Architectural variations: The conditional VAE (Sohn et al., 2015) passes class information c into both the encoder and decoder. The result is that the latent space does not need to encode the class information. For example, when MNIST data are conditioned on the digit label, the latent variables might encode the orientation and width of the digit rather than the digit category itself. Sønderby et al. (2016a) introduced ladder variational autoencoders, which recursively correct the generative distribution with a data-dependent approximate likelihood term.

Modifying likelihood: Other work investigates more sophisticated likelihood models $Pr(\mathbf{x}|\mathbf{z})$. The PixelVAE (Gulrajani et al., 2016) used an autoregressive model over the output variables. Dorta et al. (2018) modeled the covariance of the decoder output as well as the mean. Lamb et al. (2016) improved the quality of reconstruction by adding extra regularization terms that encourage the reconstruction to be similar to the original image in the space of activations of a layer of an image classification model. This model encourages semantic information to be retained and was used to generate the results in figure 17.13. Larsen et al. (2016) use an adversarial loss for reconstruction, which also improves results.

Latent space, prior, and posterior: Many different forms for the variational approximation to the posterior have been investigated, including normalizing flows (Rezende & Mohamed, 2015; Kingma et al., 2016), directed graphical models (Maaløe et al., 2016), undirected models (Vahdat et al., 2020), and recursive models for temporal data (Gregor et al., 2016, 2019).

Other authors have investigated using a discrete latent space (Van Den Oord et al., 2017; Razavi et al., 2019b; Rolfe, 2017; Vahdat et al., 2018a,b) For example, Razavi et al. (2019b) use a vector quantized latent space and model the prior with an autoregressive model (equation 12.15). This is slow to sample from but can describe very complex distributions.

Jiang et al. (2016) use a mixture of Gaussians for the posterior, allowing clustering. This is a hierarchical latent variable model that adds a discrete latent variable to improve the flexibility of the posterior. Other authors (Salimans et al., 2015; Ranganath et al., 2016; Maaløe et al., 2016; Vahdat & Kautz, 2020) have experimented with hierarchical models that use continuous variables. These have a close connection with diffusion models (chapter 18).

Combination with other models: Gulrajani et al. (2016) combined VAEs with an autoregressive model to produce more realistic images. Chung et al. (2015) combine the VAE with recurrent neural networks to model time-varying measurements.

As discussed above, adversarial losses have been used to inform the likelihood term directly. However, other models have combined ideas from generative adversarial networks (GANs) with VAEs in different ways. Makhzani et al. (2015) use an adversarial loss in the latent space; the idea is that the discriminator will ensure that the aggregated posterior distribution $q(\mathbf{z})$ is indistinguishable from the prior distribution $Pr(\mathbf{z})$. Tolstikhin et al. (2018) generalize this to a broader family of distances between the prior and aggregated posterior. Dumoulin et al. (2017) introduced adversarially learned inference which uses an adversarial loss to distinguish two pairs of latent/observed data points. In one case, the latent variable is drawn from the latent posterior distribution and, in the other, from the prior. Other hybrids of VAEs and GANs were proposed by Larsen et al. (2016), Brock et al. (2016), and Hsu et al. (2017a).

Posterior collapse: One potential problem in training is *posterior collapse*, in which the encoder always predicts the prior distribution. This was identified by Bowman et al. (2015) and can be mitigated by gradually increasing the term that encourages the KL distance between the posterior and the prior to be small during training. Several other methods have been proposed to prevent posterior collapse (Razavi et al., 2019a; Lucas et al., 2019b,a), and this is also part of the motivation for using a discrete latent space (Van Den Oord et al., 2017).

Blurry reconstructions: Zhao et al. (2017c) provide evidence that the blurry reconstructions are partly due to Gaussian noise and also because of the sub-optimal posterior distributions induced by the variational approximation. It is perhaps not coincidental that some of the best synthesis results have come from using a discrete latent space modeled by a sophisticated autoregressive model (Razavi et al., 2019b) or from using hierarchical latent spaces (Vahdat & Kautz, 2020; see figure 17.12d). Figure 17.12a-c used a VAE that was trained on the CELEBA database (Liu et al., 2015). Figure 17.12d uses a hierarchical VAE that was trained on the CELEBA HQ dataset (Karras et al., 2018).

Other problems: Chen et al. (2017) noted that when more complex likelihood terms are used, such as the PixelCNN (Van den Oord et al., 2016c), the output can cease to depend on the latent variables at all. They term this the *information preference* problem. This was addressed by Zhao et al. (2017b) in the InfoVAE, which added an extra term that maximized the mutual information between the latent and observed distributions.

Another problem with the VAE is that there can be "holes" in the latent space that do not correspond to any realistic sample. Xu et al. (2020) introduce the constrained posterior VAE, which helps prevent these vacant regions in latent space by adding a regularization term. This allows for better interpolation from real samples.

Disentangling latent representation: Methods to "disentangle" the latent representation include the beta VAE (Higgins et al., 2017) and others (e.g., Kim & Mnih, 2018; Kumar et al.,

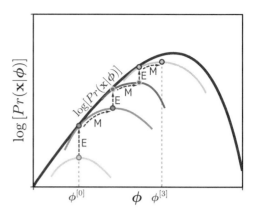

Figure 17.15 Expectation maximization (EM) algorithm. The EM algorithm alternately adjusts the auxiliary parameters $\boldsymbol{\theta}$ (moves between colored curves) and model parameters $\boldsymbol{\phi}$ (moves along colored curves) until the a maximum is reached. These adjustments are known as the E-step and the M-step, respectively. Because the E-Step uses the posterior distribution $Pr(h|\mathbf{x},\boldsymbol{\phi})$ for $q(h|\mathbf{x},\boldsymbol{\theta})$, the bound is tight, and the colored curve touches the black likelihood curve after each E-Step.

2018). Chen et al. (2018d) further decomposed the ELBO to show the existence of a term measuring the total correlation between the latent variables (i.e., the distance between the aggregate posterior and the product of its marginals). They use this to motivate the total correlation VAE, which attempts to minimize this quantity. The Factor VAE (Kim & Mnih, 2018) uses a different approach to minimize the total correlation. Mathieu et al. (2019) discuss the factors that are important in disentangling representations.

Reparameterization trick: Consider computing an expectation of some function, where the probability distribution with which the expectation is taken depends on some parameters. The reparameterization trick computes the derivative of this expectation with respect to these parameters. This chapter introduced this as a method to differentiate through the sampling procedure approximating the expectation; there are alternative approaches (see problem 17.5), but the reparameterization trick gives an estimator that (usually) has low variance. This issue is discussed in Rezende et al. (2014), Kingma et al. (2015), and Roeder et al. (2017).

Lower bound and the EM algorithm: VAE training is based on optimizing the evidence lower bound (sometimes also referred to as the ELBO, variational lower bound, or negative variational free energy). Hoffman & Johnson (2016) and Lücke et al. (2020) re-express this lower bound in several ways that elucidate its properties. Other work has aimed to make this bound tighter (Burda et al., 2016; Li & Turner, 2016; Bornschein et al., 2016; Masrani et al., 2019). For example, Burda et al. (2016) use a modified bound based on using multiple importance-weighted samples from the approximate posterior to form the objective function.

The ELBO is tight when the distribution $q(\mathbf{z}|\boldsymbol{\theta})$ matches the posterior $Pr(\mathbf{z}|\mathbf{x},\boldsymbol{\phi})$. This is the basis of the *expectation maximization* (*EM*) algorithm (Dempster et al., 1977). Here, we alternately (i) choose $\boldsymbol{\theta}$ so that $q(\mathbf{z}|\boldsymbol{\theta})$ equals the posterior $Pr(\mathbf{z}|\mathbf{x},\boldsymbol{\phi})$ and (ii) change $\boldsymbol{\phi}$ to maximize the lower bound (figure 17.15). This is viable for models like the mixture of Gaussians, where we can compute the posterior distribution in closed form. Unfortunately, this is not the case for the nonlinear latent variable model, so this method cannot be used.

Problem 17.7

Problems

Problem 17.1 How many parameters are needed to create a 1D mixture of Gaussians with $n = 5$

components (equation 17.4)? State the possible range of values that each parameter could take.

Problem 17.2 A function is concave if its second derivative is less than or equal to zero everywhere. Show that this is true for the function $g[x] = \log[x]$.

Problem 17.3 For convex functions, Jensen's inequality works the other way around.

$$g\big[\mathbb{E}[y]\big] \leq \mathbb{E}\big[g[y]\big]. \tag{17.31}$$

A function is convex if its second derivative is greater than or equal to zero everywhere. Show that the function $g[x] = x^{2n}$ is convex for arbitrary $n \in [1, 2, 3, \ldots]$. Use this result with Jensen's inequality to show that the square of the mean $\mathbb{E}[x]$ of a distribution $Pr(x)$ must be less than or equal to its second moment $\mathbb{E}[x^2]$.

Problem 17.4[*] Show that the ELBO, as expressed in equation 17.18, can alternatively be derived from the KL divergence between the variational distribution $q(\mathbf{z}|\mathbf{x})$ and the true posterior distribution $Pr(\mathbf{z}|\mathbf{x}, \boldsymbol{\phi})$:

$$\mathrm{D}_{KL}\Big[q(\mathbf{z}|\mathbf{x})\Big|\Big|Pr(\mathbf{z}|\mathbf{x}, \boldsymbol{\phi})\Big] = \int q(\mathbf{z}|\mathbf{x}) \log\left[\frac{q(\mathbf{z}|\mathbf{x})}{Pr(\mathbf{z}|\mathbf{x}, \boldsymbol{\phi})}\right] d\mathbf{z}. \tag{17.32}$$

Start by using Bayes' rule (equation 17.19).

Problem 17.5 The reparameterization trick computes the derivative of an expectation of a function $f[x]$:

$$\frac{\partial}{\partial \boldsymbol{\phi}} \mathbb{E}_{Pr(x|\boldsymbol{\phi})}\big[f[x]\big], \tag{17.33}$$

with respect to the parameters $\boldsymbol{\phi}$ of the distribution $Pr(x|\boldsymbol{\phi})$ that the expectation is over. Show that this derivative can also be computed as:

$$
\begin{aligned}
\frac{\partial}{\partial \boldsymbol{\phi}} \mathbb{E}_{Pr(x|\boldsymbol{\phi})}\big[f[x]\big] &= \mathbb{E}_{Pr(x|\boldsymbol{\phi})}\left[f[x]\frac{\partial}{\partial \boldsymbol{\phi}} \log\big[Pr(x|\boldsymbol{\phi})\big]\right] \\
&\approx \frac{1}{I} \sum_{i=1}^{I} f[x_i]\frac{\partial}{\partial \boldsymbol{\phi}} \log\big[Pr(x_i|\boldsymbol{\phi})\big].
\end{aligned}
\tag{17.34}
$$

This method is known as the *REINFORCE algorithm* or *score function estimator*.

Problem 17.6 Why is it better to use spherical linear interpolation rather than regular linear interpolation when moving between points in the latent space? Hint: consider figure 8.13.

Problem 17.7[*] Derive the EM algorithm for the 1D mixture of Gaussians algorithm with N components. To do this, you need to (i) find an expression for the posterior distribution $Pr(z|x)$ over the latent variable $z \in \{1, 2, \ldots, N\}$ for a data point x and (ii) find an expression that updates the evidence lower bound given the posterior distributions for all of the data points. You will need to use Lagrange multipliers to ensure that the weights $\lambda_1, \ldots, \lambda_N$ of the Gaussians sum to one.

Chapter 18

Diffusion models

Chapter 15 described generative adversarial models, which produce plausible-looking samples but do not define a probability distribution over the data. Chapter 16 discussed normalizing flows. These do define such a probability distribution but must place architectural constraints on the network; each layer must be invertible, and the determinant of its Jacobian must be easy to calculate. Chapter 17 introduced variational autoencoders, which also have a solid probabilistic foundation but where the computation of the likelihood is intractable and must be approximated by a lower bound.

This chapter introduces diffusion models. Like normalizing flows, these are probabilistic models that define a nonlinear mapping from latent variables to the observed data where both quantities have the same dimension. Like variational autoencoders, they approximate the data likelihood using a lower bound based on an encoder that maps *to* the latent variable. However, in diffusion models, this encoder is predetermined; the goal is to learn a decoder that is the inverse of this process and can be used to produce samples. Diffusion models are easy to train and can produce very high-quality samples that exceed the realism of those produced by GANs. The reader should be familiar with variational autoencoders (chapter 17) before reading this chapter.

18.1 Overview

A diffusion model consists of an *encoder* and a *decoder*. The encoder takes a data sample $\mathbf{x}$ and maps it through a series of intermediate latent variables $\mathbf{z}_1 \ldots \mathbf{z}_T$. The decoder reverses this process; it starts with $\mathbf{z}_T$ and maps back through $\mathbf{z}_{T-1}, \ldots, \mathbf{z}_1$ until it finally (re-)creates a data point $\mathbf{x}$. In both encoder and decoder, the mappings are stochastic rather than deterministic.

The encoder is prespecified; it gradually blends the input with samples of white noise (figure 18.1). With enough steps, the conditional distribution $q(\mathbf{z}_T|\mathbf{x})$ and marginal distribution $q(\mathbf{z}_T)$ of the final latent variable both become the standard normal distribution. Since this process is prespecified, all the learned parameters are in the decoder.

In the decoder, a series of networks are trained to map backward between each

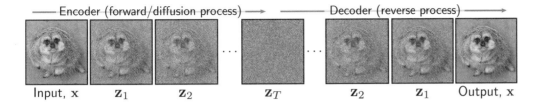

Encoder (forward/diffusion process) ⟶   ⟵ Decoder (reverse process) ⟶

Input, $\mathbf{x}$ $\mathbf{z}_1$ $\mathbf{z}_2$ $\mathbf{z}_T$ $\mathbf{z}_2$ $\mathbf{z}_1$ Output, $\mathbf{x}$

Figure 18.1 Diffusion models. The encoder (forward, or diffusion process) maps the input $\mathbf{x}$ through a series of latent variables $\mathbf{z}_1 \ldots \mathbf{z}_T$. This process is pre-specified and gradually mixes the data with noise until only noise remains. The decoder (reverse process) is learned and passes the data back through the latent variables, removing noise at each stage. After training, new examples are generated by sampling noise vectors $\mathbf{z}_T$ and passing them through the decoder.

adjacent pair of latent variables $\mathbf{z}_t$ and $\mathbf{z}_{t-1}$. The loss function encourages each network to invert the corresponding encoder step. The result is that noise is gradually removed from the representation until a realistic-looking data example remains. To generate a new data example $\mathbf{x}$, we draw a sample from $q(\mathbf{z}_T)$ and pass it through the decoder.

In section 18.2, we consider the encoder in detail. Its properties are non-obvious but are critical for the learning algorithm. In section 18.3, we discuss the decoder. Section 18.4 derives the training algorithm, and section 18.5 reformulates it to be more practical. Section 18.6 discusses implementation details, including how to make the generation conditional on text prompts.

18.2   Encoder (forward process)

The *diffusion* or *forward* process[1] (figure 18.2) maps a data example $\mathbf{x}$ through a series of intermediate variables $\mathbf{z}_1, \mathbf{z}_2, \ldots, \mathbf{z}_T$ with the same size as $\mathbf{x}$ according to:

$$
\begin{aligned}
\mathbf{z}_1 &= \sqrt{1-\beta_1} \cdot \mathbf{x} + \sqrt{\beta_1} \cdot \boldsymbol{\epsilon}_1 \\
\mathbf{z}_t &= \sqrt{1-\beta_t} \cdot \mathbf{z}_{t-1} + \sqrt{\beta_t} \cdot \boldsymbol{\epsilon}_t \qquad \forall\, t \in 2, \ldots, T,
\end{aligned}
\tag{18.1}
$$

where $\boldsymbol{\epsilon}_t$ is noise drawn from a standard normal distribution. The first term attenuates the data plus any noise added so far, and the second adds more noise. The hyperparameters $\beta_t \in [0,1]$ determine how quickly the noise is blended and are collectively known as the *noise schedule*. The forward process can equivalently be written as:

---

[1]Note, this is the opposite nomenclature to normalizing flows, where the inverse mapping moves from the data to the latent variable, and the forward mapping moves back again.

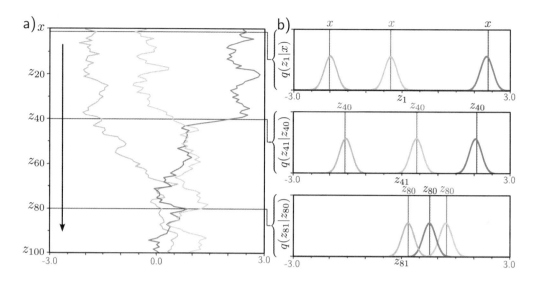

Figure 18.2 Forward process. a) We consider one-dimensional data x with $T = 100$ latent variables $z_1, \ldots, z_{100}$ and $\beta = 0.03$ at all steps. Three values of x (gray, cyan, and orange) are initialized (top row). These are propagated through $z_1, \ldots, z_{100}$. At each step, the variable is updated by attenuating its value by $\sqrt{1 - \beta}$ and adding noise with mean zero and variance β (equation 18.1). Accordingly, the three examples noisily propagate through the variables with a tendency to move toward zero. b) The conditional probabilities $Pr(z_1|x)$ and $Pr(z_t|z_{t-1})$ are normal distributions with a mean that is slightly closer to zero than the current point and a fixed variance β_t (equation 18.2).

$$
\begin{aligned}
q(\mathbf{z}_1|\mathbf{x}) &= \text{Norm}_{\mathbf{z}_1}\left[\sqrt{1 - \beta_1}\mathbf{x}, \beta_1\mathbf{I}\right] & (18.2)\\
q(\mathbf{z}_t|\mathbf{z}_{t-1}) &= \text{Norm}_{\mathbf{z}_t}\left[\sqrt{1 - \beta_t}\mathbf{z}_{t-1}, \beta_t\mathbf{I}\right] & \forall\, t \in \{2, \ldots, T\}.
\end{aligned}
$$

This is a *Markov chain* because the probability of $\mathbf{z}_t$ is determined entirely by the value of the immediately preceding variable $\mathbf{z}_{t-1}$. With sufficient steps T, all traces of the original data are removed, and $q(\mathbf{z}_T|\mathbf{x}) = q(\mathbf{z}_T)$ becomes a standard normal distribution.[2]

Problem 18.1

The joint distribution of all of the latent variables $\mathbf{z}_1, \mathbf{z}_2, \ldots, \mathbf{z}_T$ given input $\mathbf{x}$ is:

$$
q(\mathbf{z}_{1\ldots T}|\mathbf{x}) = q(\mathbf{z}_1|\mathbf{x}) \prod_{t=2}^{T} q(\mathbf{z}_t|\mathbf{z}_{t-1}). \tag{18.3}
$$

---

[2]We use $q(\mathbf{z}_t|\mathbf{z}_{t-1})$ rather than $Pr(\mathbf{z}_t|\mathbf{z}_{t-1})$ to match the notation in the description of the VAE encoder in the previous chapter.

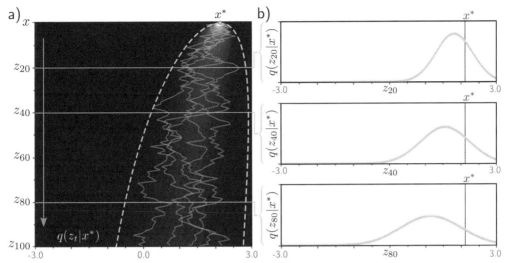

Figure 18.3 Diffusion kernel. a) The point $x^* = 2.0$ is propagated through the latent variables using equation 18.1 (five paths shown in gray). The diffusion kernel $q(z_t|x^*)$ is the probability distribution over variable z_t given that we started from x^*. It can be computed in closed-form and is a normal distribution whose mean moves toward zero and whose variance increases as t increases. Heatmap shows $q(z_t|x^*)$ for each variable. Cyan lines show ± 2 standard deviations from the mean. b) The diffusion kernel $q(z_t|x^*)$ is shown explicitly for $t = 20, 40, 80$. In practice, the diffusion kernel allows us to sample a latent variable z_t corresponding to a given x^* without computing the intermediate variables $z_1, \ldots, z_{t-1}$. When t becomes very large, the diffusion kernel becomes a standard normal.

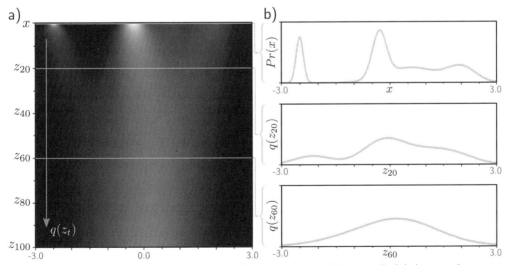

Figure 18.4 Marginal distributions. a) Given an initial density $Pr(x)$ (top row), the diffusion process gradually blurs the distribution as it passes through the latent variables z_t and moves it toward a standard normal distribution. Each subsequent horizontal line of heatmap represents a marginal distribution $q(z_t)$. b) The top graph shows the initial distribution $Pr(x)$. The other two graphs show the marginal distributions $q(z_{20})$ and $q(z_{60})$, respectively.

18.2.1 Diffusion kernel $q(\mathbf{z}_t|\mathbf{x})$

To train the decoder to invert this process, we use multiple samples $\mathbf{z}_t$ at time t for the same example $\mathbf{x}$. However, generating these sequentially using equation 18.1 is time-consuming when t is large. Fortunately, there is a closed-form expression for $q(\mathbf{z}_t|\mathbf{x})$, which allows us to directly draw samples $\mathbf{z}_t$ given initial data point $\mathbf{x}$ without computing the intermediate variables $\mathbf{z}_1 \dots \mathbf{z}_{t-1}$. This is known as the *diffusion kernel* (figure 18.3).

To derive an expression for $q(\mathbf{z}_t|\mathbf{x})$, consider the first two steps of the forward process:

$$
\begin{aligned}
\mathbf{z}_1 &= \sqrt{1-\beta_1} \cdot \mathbf{x} + \sqrt{\beta_1} \cdot \boldsymbol{\epsilon}_1 \\
\mathbf{z}_2 &= \sqrt{1-\beta_2} \cdot \mathbf{z}_1 + \sqrt{\beta_2} \cdot \boldsymbol{\epsilon}_2.
\end{aligned}
\tag{18.4}
$$

Substituting the first equation into the second, we get:

$$
\begin{aligned}
\mathbf{z}_2 &= \sqrt{1-\beta_2}\left(\sqrt{1-\beta_1} \cdot \mathbf{x} + \sqrt{\beta_1} \cdot \boldsymbol{\epsilon}_1\right) + \sqrt{\beta_2} \cdot \boldsymbol{\epsilon}_2 \\
&= \sqrt{1-\beta_2}\left(\sqrt{1-\beta_1} \cdot \mathbf{x} + \sqrt{1-(1-\beta_1)} \cdot \boldsymbol{\epsilon}_1\right) + \sqrt{\beta_2} \cdot \boldsymbol{\epsilon}_2 \\
&= \sqrt{(1-\beta_2)(1-\beta_1)} \cdot \mathbf{x} + \sqrt{1-\beta_2-(1-\beta_2)(1-\beta_1)} \cdot \boldsymbol{\epsilon}_1 + \sqrt{\beta_2} \cdot \boldsymbol{\epsilon}_2.
\end{aligned}
\tag{18.5}
$$

The last two terms are independent samples from mean-zero normal distributions with variances $1-\beta_2-(1-\beta_2)(1-\beta_1)$ and β_2, respectively. The mean of this sum is zero, and its variance is the sum of the component variances (see problem 18.2), so:

$$
\mathbf{z}_2 = \sqrt{(1-\beta_2)(1-\beta_1)} \cdot \mathbf{x} + \sqrt{1-(1-\beta_2)(1-\beta_1)} \cdot \boldsymbol{\epsilon},
\tag{18.6}
$$

where $\boldsymbol{\epsilon}$ is also a sample from a standard normal distribution.

If we continue this process by substituting this equation into the expression for $\mathbf{z}_3$ and so on, we can show that:

$$
\mathbf{z}_t = \sqrt{\alpha_t} \cdot \mathbf{x} + \sqrt{1-\alpha_t} \cdot \boldsymbol{\epsilon},
\tag{18.7}
$$

where $\alpha_t = \prod_{s=1}^{t} 1-\beta_s$. We can equivalently write this in probabilistic form:

$$
q(\mathbf{z}_t|\mathbf{x}) = \text{Norm}_{\mathbf{z}_t}\left[\sqrt{\alpha_t} \cdot \mathbf{x}, (1-\alpha_t)\mathbf{I}\right].
\tag{18.8}
$$

For any starting data point $\mathbf{x}$, variable $\mathbf{z}_t$ is normally distributed with a known mean and variance. Consequently, if we don't care about the history of the evolution through the intermediate variables $\mathbf{z}_1 \dots \mathbf{z}_{t-1}$, it is easy to generate samples from $q(\mathbf{z}_t|\mathbf{x})$.

18.2.2 Marginal distributions $q(\mathbf{z}_t)$

The marginal distribution $q(\mathbf{z}_t)$ is the probability of observing a value of $\mathbf{z}_t$ given the distribution of possible starting points $\mathbf{x}$ and the possible diffusion paths for each starting

Problem 18.2

Problem 18.3

point (figure 18.4). It can be computed by considering the joint distribution $q(\mathbf{x}, \mathbf{z}_{1...t})$ and marginalizing over all the variables except $\mathbf{z}_t$:

Appendix C.1.2
Marginalization

$$
\begin{aligned}
q(\mathbf{z}_t) &= \iint q(\mathbf{z}_{1...t}, \mathbf{x})d\mathbf{z}_{1...t-1}d\mathbf{x} \\
&= \iint q(\mathbf{z}_{1...t}|\mathbf{x})Pr(\mathbf{x})d\mathbf{z}_{1...t-1}d\mathbf{x},
\end{aligned}
\tag{18.9}
$$

where $q(\mathbf{z}_{1...t}|\mathbf{x})$ was defined in equation 18.3.

However, since we now have an expression for the diffusion kernel $q(\mathbf{z}_t|\mathbf{x})$ that "skips" the intervening variables, we can equivalently write:

$$
q(\mathbf{z}_t) = \int q(\mathbf{z}_t|\mathbf{x})Pr(\mathbf{x})d\mathbf{x}.
\tag{18.10}
$$

Hence, if we repeatedly sample from the data distribution $Pr(\mathbf{x})$ and superimpose the diffusion kernel $q(\mathbf{z}_t|\mathbf{x})$ on each sample, the result is the marginal distribution $q(\mathbf{z}_t)$ (figure 18.4). However, the marginal distribution cannot be written in closed form because we don't know the original data distribution $Pr(\mathbf{x})$.

Notebook 18.1
Diffusion encoder

18.2.3 Conditional distribution $q(\mathbf{z}_{t-1}|\mathbf{z}_t)$

We defined the conditional probability $q(\mathbf{z}_t|\mathbf{z}_{t-1})$ as the mixing process (equation 18.2). To reverse this process, we apply Bayes' rule:

Appendix C.1.4
Bayes' rule

$$
q(\mathbf{z}_{t-1}|\mathbf{z}_t) = \frac{q(\mathbf{z}_t|\mathbf{z}_{t-1})q(\mathbf{z}_{t-1})}{q(\mathbf{z}_t)}.
\tag{18.11}
$$

This is intractable since we cannot compute the marginal distribution $q(\mathbf{z}_{t-1})$.

For this simple 1D example, it's possible to evaluate $q(\mathbf{z}_{t-1}|\mathbf{z}_t)$ numerically (figure 18.5). In general, their form is complex, but in many cases, they are well-approximated by a normal distribution. This is important because when we build the decoder, we will approximate the reverse process using a normal distribution.

18.2.4 Conditional diffusion distribution $q(\mathbf{z}_{t-1}|\mathbf{z}_t, \mathbf{x})$

There is one final distribution related to the encoder to consider. We noted above that we could not find the conditional distribution $q(\mathbf{z}_{t-1}|\mathbf{z}_t)$ because we do not know the marginal distribution $q(\mathbf{z}_{t-1})$. However, if we know the starting variable $\mathbf{x}$, then we *do* know the distribution $q(\mathbf{z}_{t-1}|\mathbf{x})$ at the time before. This is just the diffusion kernel (figure 18.3), and it is normally distributed.

Hence, it is possible to compute the conditional diffusion distribution $q(\mathbf{z}_{t-1}|\mathbf{z}_t, \mathbf{x})$ in closed form (figure 18.6). This distribution is used to train the decoder. It is the distribution over $\mathbf{z}_{t-1}$ when we know the current latent variable $\mathbf{z}_t$ and the training

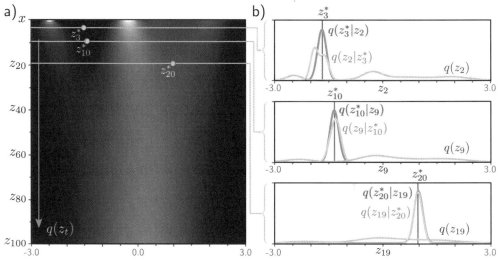

Figure 18.5 Conditional distribution $q(z_{t-1}|z_t)$. a) The marginal densities $q(z_t)$ with three points z_t^* highlighted. b) The probability $q(z_{t-1}|z_t^*)$ (cyan curves) is computed via Bayes' rule and is proportional to $q(z_t^*|z_{t-1})q(z_{t-1})$. In general, it is not normally distributed (top graph), although often the normal is a good approximation (bottom two graphs). The first likelihood term $q(z_t^*|z_{t-1})$ is normal in z_{t-1} (equation 18.2) with a mean that is slightly further from zero than z_t^* (brown curves). The second term is the marginal density $q(z_{t-1})$ (gray curves).

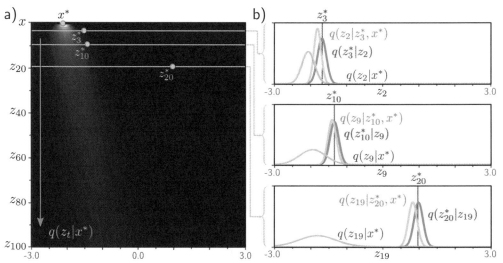

Figure 18.6 Conditional distribution $q(z_{t-1}|z_t, x)$. a) Diffusion kernel for $x^* = -2.1$ with three points z_t^* highlighted. b) The probability $q(z_{t-1}|z_t^*, x^*)$ is computed via Bayes' rule and is proportional to $q(z_t^*|z_{t-1})q(z_{t-1}|x^*)$. This *is* normally distributed and can be computed in closed form. The first likelihood term $q(z_t^*|z_{t-1})$ is normal in z_{t-1} (equation 18.2) with a mean that is slightly further from zero than z_t^* (brown curves). The second term is the diffusion kernel $q(z_{t-1}|x^*)$ (gray curves).

data example $\mathbf{x}$ (which, of course, we do when training). To compute an expression for $q(\mathbf{z}_{t-1}|\mathbf{z}_t, \mathbf{x})$ we start with Bayes' rule:

$$
\begin{aligned}
q(\mathbf{z}_{t-1}|\mathbf{z}_t, \mathbf{x}) &= \frac{q(\mathbf{z}_t|\mathbf{z}_{t-1}, \mathbf{x})q(\mathbf{z}_{t-1}|\mathbf{x})}{q(\mathbf{z}_t|\mathbf{x})} \qquad (18.12) \\
&\propto q(\mathbf{z}_t|\mathbf{z}_{t-1})q(\mathbf{z}_{t-1}|\mathbf{x}) \\
&= \text{Norm}_{\mathbf{z}_t}\left[\sqrt{1-\beta_t}\cdot\mathbf{z}_{t-1}, \beta_t\mathbf{I}\right]\text{Norm}_{\mathbf{z}_{t-1}}\left[\sqrt{\alpha_{t-1}}\cdot\mathbf{x}, (1-\alpha_{t-1})\mathbf{I}\right] \\
&\propto \text{Norm}_{\mathbf{z}_{t-1}}\left[\frac{1}{\sqrt{1-\beta_t}}\mathbf{z}_t, \frac{\beta_t}{1-\beta_t}\mathbf{I}\right]\text{Norm}_{\mathbf{z}_{t-1}}\left[\sqrt{\alpha_{t-1}}\cdot\mathbf{x}, (1-\alpha_{t-1})\mathbf{I}\right]
\end{aligned}
$$

where between the first two lines, we have used the fact that $q(\mathbf{z}_t|\mathbf{z}_{t-1}, \mathbf{x}) = q(\mathbf{z}_t|\mathbf{z}_{t-1})$ because the diffusion process is Markov, and all information about $\mathbf{z}_t$ is captured by $\mathbf{z}_{t-1}$. Between lines three and four, we use the Gaussian change of variables identity:

Appendix C.3.4
Gaussian change
of variables

$$
\text{Norm}_{\mathbf{v}}\left[\mathbf{A}\mathbf{w}, \mathbf{B}\right] \propto \text{Norm}_{\mathbf{w}}\left[\left(\mathbf{A}^T\mathbf{B}^{-1}\mathbf{A}\right)^{-1}\mathbf{A}^T\mathbf{B}^{-1}\mathbf{v}, \left(\mathbf{A}^T\mathbf{B}^{-1}\mathbf{A}\right)^{-1}\right], \qquad (18.13)
$$

to rewrite the first distribution in terms of $\mathbf{z}_{t-1}$. We then use a second Gaussian identity:

Problems 18.4–18.5

$$
\begin{aligned}
\text{Norm}_{\mathbf{w}}[\mathbf{a}, \mathbf{A}]\cdot\text{Norm}_{\mathbf{w}}[\mathbf{b}, \mathbf{B}] &\propto \qquad\qquad (18.14) \\
&\text{Norm}_{\mathbf{w}}\left[\left(\mathbf{A}^{-1}+\mathbf{B}^{-1}\right)^{-1}(\mathbf{A}^{-1}\mathbf{a}+\mathbf{B}^{-1}\mathbf{b}), \left(\mathbf{A}^{-1}+\mathbf{B}^{-1}\right)^{-1}\right],
\end{aligned}
$$

to combine the two normal distributions in $\mathbf{z}_{t-1}$, which gives:

Problem 18.6

$$
q(\mathbf{z}_{t-1}|\mathbf{z}_t, \mathbf{x}) = \text{Norm}_{\mathbf{z}_{t-1}}\left[\frac{(1-\alpha_{t-1})}{1-\alpha_t}\sqrt{1-\beta_t}\mathbf{z}_t + \frac{\sqrt{\alpha_{t-1}}\beta_t}{1-\alpha_t}\mathbf{x}, \frac{\beta_t(1-\alpha_{t-1})}{1-\alpha_t}\mathbf{I}\right]. \quad (18.15)
$$

Note that the constants of proportionality in equations 18.12, 18.13, and 18.14 must cancel out since the final result is already a correctly normalized probability distribution.

18.3 Decoder model (reverse process)

When we learn a diffusion model, we learn the *reverse process*. In other words, we learn a series of probabilistic mappings back from latent variable $\mathbf{z}_T$ to $\mathbf{z}_{T-1}$, from $\mathbf{z}_{T-1}$ to $\mathbf{z}_{T-2}$, and so on, until we reach the data $\mathbf{x}$. The true reverse distributions $q(\mathbf{z}_{t-1}|\mathbf{z}_t)$ of the diffusion process are complex multi-modal distributions (figure 18.5) that depend on the data distribution $Pr(\mathbf{x})$. We approximate these as normal distributions:

$$
\begin{aligned}
Pr(\mathbf{z}_T) &= \text{Norm}_{\mathbf{z}_T}[\mathbf{0}, \mathbf{I}] \\
Pr(\mathbf{z}_{t-1}|\mathbf{z}_t, \boldsymbol{\phi}_t) &= \text{Norm}_{\mathbf{z}_{t-1}}\left[\mathbf{f}_t[\mathbf{z}_t, \boldsymbol{\phi}_t], \sigma_t^2\mathbf{I}\right] \\
Pr(\mathbf{x}|\mathbf{z}_1, \boldsymbol{\phi}_1) &= \text{Norm}_{\mathbf{x}}\left[\mathbf{f}_1[\mathbf{z}_1, \boldsymbol{\phi}_1], \sigma_1^2\mathbf{I}\right], \qquad (18.16)
\end{aligned}
$$

where $\mathbf{f}_t[\mathbf{z}_t, \boldsymbol{\phi}_t]$ is a neural network that computes the mean of the normal distribution in the estimated mapping from $\mathbf{z}_t$ to the preceding latent variable $\mathbf{z}_{t-1}$. The terms $\{\sigma_t^2\}$ are predetermined. If the hyperparameters β_t in the diffusion process are close to zero (and the number of time steps T is large), then this normal approximation will be reasonable.

We generate new examples from $Pr(\mathbf{x})$ using ancestral sampling. We start by drawing $\mathbf{z}_T$ from $Pr(\mathbf{z}_T)$. Then we sample $\mathbf{z}_{T-1}$ from $Pr(\mathbf{z}_{T-1}|\mathbf{z}_T, \boldsymbol{\phi}_T)$, sample $\mathbf{z}_{T-2}$ from $Pr(\mathbf{z}_{T-2}|\mathbf{z}_{T-1}, \boldsymbol{\phi}_{T-1})$ and so on until we finally generate $\mathbf{x}$ from $Pr(\mathbf{x}|\mathbf{z}_1, \boldsymbol{\phi}_1)$.

18.4   Training

The joint distribution of the observed variable $\mathbf{x}$ and the latent variables $\{\mathbf{z}_t\}$ is:

$$Pr(\mathbf{x}, \mathbf{z}_{1...T}|\boldsymbol{\phi}_{1...T}) = Pr(\mathbf{x}|\mathbf{z}_1, \boldsymbol{\phi}_1) \prod_{t=2}^{T} Pr(\mathbf{z}_{t-1}|\mathbf{z}_t, \boldsymbol{\phi}_t) \cdot Pr(\mathbf{z}_T). \tag{18.17}$$

Appendix C.1.2
Marginalization

The likelihood of the observed data $Pr(\mathbf{x}|\boldsymbol{\phi}_{1...T})$ is found by marginalizing over the latent variables:

$$Pr(\mathbf{x}|\boldsymbol{\phi}_{1...T}) = \int Pr(\mathbf{x}, \mathbf{z}_{1...T}|\boldsymbol{\phi}_{1...T}) d\mathbf{z}_{1...T}. \tag{18.18}$$

To train the model, we maximize the log-likelihood of the training data $\{\mathbf{x}_i\}$ with respect to the parameters $\boldsymbol{\phi}$:

$$\hat{\boldsymbol{\phi}}_{1...T} = \underset{\boldsymbol{\phi}_{1...T}}{\operatorname{argmax}} \left[\sum_{i=1}^{I} \log \left[Pr(\mathbf{x}_i|\boldsymbol{\phi}_{1...T}) \right] \right]. \tag{18.19}$$

We can't maximize this directly because the marginalization in equation 18.18 is intractable. Hence, we use Jensen's inequality to define a lower bound on the likelihood and optimize the parameters $\boldsymbol{\phi}_{1...T}$ with respect to this bound exactly as we did for the VAE (see section 17.3.1).

18.4.1   Evidence lower bound (ELBO)

To derive the lower bound, we multiply and divide the log-likelihood by the encoder distribution $q(\mathbf{z}_{1...T}|\mathbf{x})$ and apply Jensen's inequality (see section 17.3.2):

$$
\begin{aligned}
\log \left[Pr(\mathbf{x}|\boldsymbol{\phi}_{1...T}) \right] &= \log \left[\int Pr(\mathbf{x}, \mathbf{z}_{1...T}|\boldsymbol{\phi}_{1...T}) d\mathbf{z}_{1...T} \right] \\
&= \log \left[\int q(\mathbf{z}_{1...T}|\mathbf{x}) \frac{Pr(\mathbf{x}, \mathbf{z}_{1...T}|\boldsymbol{\phi}_{1...T})}{q(\mathbf{z}_{1...T}|\mathbf{x})} d\mathbf{z}_{1...T} \right] \\
&\geq \int q(\mathbf{z}_{1...T}|\mathbf{x}) \log \left[\frac{Pr(\mathbf{x}, \mathbf{z}_{1...T}|\boldsymbol{\phi}_{1...T})}{q(\mathbf{z}_{1...T}|\mathbf{x})} \right] d\mathbf{z}_{1...T}. \quad (18.20)
\end{aligned}
$$

This gives us the evidence lower bound (ELBO):

$$\text{ELBO}\big[\phi_{1...T}\big] = \int q(\mathbf{z}_{1...T}|\mathbf{x}) \log \left[\frac{Pr(\mathbf{x}, \mathbf{z}_{1...T}|\phi_{1...T})}{q(\mathbf{z}_{1...T}|\mathbf{x})}\right] d\mathbf{z}_{1...T}. \tag{18.21}$$

In the VAE, the encoder $q(\mathbf{z}|\mathbf{x})$ approximates the posterior distribution over the latent variables to make the bound tight, and the decoder maximizes this bound (figure 17.10). In diffusion models, the decoder must do all the work since the encoder has no parameters. It makes the bound tighter by both (i) changing its parameters so that the static encoder does approximate the posterior $Pr(\mathbf{z}_{1...T}|\mathbf{x}, \phi_{1...T})$ and (ii) optimizing its own parameters with respect to that bound (see figure 17.6).

18.4.2 Simplifying the ELBO

We now manipulate the log term from the ELBO into the final form that we will optimize. We first substitute in the definitions for the numerator and denominator from equations 18.17 and 18.3, respectively:

$$\log\left[\frac{Pr(\mathbf{x}, \mathbf{z}_{1...T}|\phi_{1...T})}{q(\mathbf{z}_{1...T}|\mathbf{x})}\right] = \log\left[\frac{Pr(\mathbf{x}|\mathbf{z}_1, \phi_1)\prod_{t=2}^{T} Pr(\mathbf{z}_{t-1}|\mathbf{z}_t, \phi_t) \cdot Pr(\mathbf{z}_T)}{q(\mathbf{z}_1|\mathbf{x})\prod_{t=2}^{T} q(\mathbf{z}_t|\mathbf{z}_{t-1})}\right] \tag{18.22}$$

$$= \log\left[\frac{Pr(\mathbf{x}|\mathbf{z}_1, \phi_1)}{q(\mathbf{z}_1|\mathbf{x})}\right] + \log\left[\frac{\prod_{t=2}^{T} Pr(\mathbf{z}_{t-1}|\mathbf{z}_t, \phi_t)}{\prod_{t=2}^{T} q(\mathbf{z}_t|\mathbf{z}_{t-1})}\right] + \log\big[Pr(\mathbf{z}_T)\big].$$

Then we expand the denominator of the second term:

$$q(\mathbf{z}_t|\mathbf{z}_{t-1}) = q(\mathbf{z}_t|\mathbf{z}_{t-1}, \mathbf{x}) = \frac{q(\mathbf{z}_{t-1}|\mathbf{z}_t, \mathbf{x})q(\mathbf{z}_t|\mathbf{x})}{q(\mathbf{z}_{t-1}|\mathbf{x})}, \tag{18.23}$$

where the first equality follows because all of the information about variable $\mathbf{z}_t$ is encompassed in $\mathbf{z}_{t-1}$, so the extra conditioning on the data $\mathbf{x}$ is irrelevant. The second equality is a straightforward application of Bayes' rule.

Appendix C.1.4
Bayes' rule

Substituting in this result gives:

$$\log\left[\frac{Pr(\mathbf{x}, \mathbf{z}_{1...T}|\phi_{1...T})}{q(\mathbf{z}_{1...T}|\mathbf{x})}\right]$$

$$= \log\left[\frac{Pr(\mathbf{x}|\mathbf{z}_1, \phi_1)}{q(\mathbf{z}_1|\mathbf{x})}\right] + \log\left[\frac{\prod_{t=2}^{T} Pr(\mathbf{z}_{t-1}|\mathbf{z}_t, \phi_t) \cdot q(\mathbf{z}_{t-1}|\mathbf{x})}{\prod_{t=2}^{T} q(\mathbf{z}_{t-1}|\mathbf{z}_t, \mathbf{x}) \cdot q(\mathbf{z}_t|\mathbf{x})}\right] + \log\big[Pr(\mathbf{z}_T)\big]$$

$$= \log\big[Pr(\mathbf{x}|\mathbf{z}_1, \phi_1)\big] + \log\left[\frac{\prod_{t=2}^{T} Pr(\mathbf{z}_{t-1}|\mathbf{z}_t, \phi_t)}{\prod_{t=2}^{T} q(\mathbf{z}_{t-1}|\mathbf{z}_t, \mathbf{x})}\right] + \log\left[\frac{Pr(\mathbf{z}_T)}{q(\mathbf{z}_T|\mathbf{x})}\right]$$

$$\approx \log\big[Pr(\mathbf{x}|\mathbf{z}_1, \phi_1)\big] + \sum_{t=2}^{T} \log\left[\frac{Pr(\mathbf{z}_{t-1}|\mathbf{z}_t, \phi_t)}{q(\mathbf{z}_{t-1}|\mathbf{z}_t, \mathbf{x})}\right], \tag{18.24}$$

where all but two of the terms in the product of the ratios $q(\mathbf{z}_{t-1}|\mathbf{x})/q(\mathbf{z}_t|\mathbf{x})$ cancel out between lines two and three leaving only $q(\mathbf{z}_1|\mathbf{x})$ and $q(\mathbf{z}_T|\mathbf{x})$. The last term in the third line is approximately $\log[1] = 0$ since the result of the forward process $q(\mathbf{z}_T|\mathbf{x})$ is a standard normal distribution, and so is equal to the prior $Pr(\mathbf{z}_T)$.

The simplified ELBO is hence:

$$
\begin{aligned}
\text{ELBO}\big[\boldsymbol{\phi}_{1\ldots T}\big] & \hspace{6cm} (18.25) \\
&= \int q(\mathbf{z}_{1\ldots T}|\mathbf{x}) \log \left[\frac{Pr(\mathbf{x}, \mathbf{z}_{1\ldots T}|\boldsymbol{\phi}_{1\ldots T})}{q(\mathbf{z}_{1\ldots T}|\mathbf{x})} \right] d\mathbf{z}_{1\ldots T} \\
&\approx \int q(\mathbf{z}_{1\ldots T}|\mathbf{x}) \left(\log\big[Pr(\mathbf{x}|\mathbf{z}_1, \boldsymbol{\phi}_1)\big] + \sum_{t=2}^{T} \log \left[\frac{Pr(\mathbf{z}_{t-1}|\mathbf{z}_t, \boldsymbol{\phi}_t)}{q(\mathbf{z}_{t-1}|\mathbf{z}_t, \mathbf{x})} \right] \right) d\mathbf{z}_{1\ldots T} \\
&= \mathbb{E}_{q(\mathbf{z}_1|\mathbf{x})}\Big[\log\big[Pr(\mathbf{x}|\mathbf{z}_1, \boldsymbol{\phi}_1)\big]\Big] - \sum_{t=2}^{T} \mathbb{E}_{q(\mathbf{z}_t|\mathbf{x})}\Big[D_{KL}\Big[q(\mathbf{z}_{t-1}|\mathbf{z}_t, \mathbf{x})\big|\big|Pr(\mathbf{z}_{t-1}|\mathbf{z}_t, \boldsymbol{\phi}_t)\Big]\Big],
\end{aligned}
$$

Problem 18.7

Appendix C.5.1
KL divergence

where we have marginalized over the irrelevant variables in $q(\mathbf{z}_{1\ldots T}|\mathbf{x})$ between lines two and three and used the definition of KL divergence (see problem 18.7).

18.4.3 Analyzing the ELBO

The first probability term in the ELBO was defined in equation 18.16:

$$
Pr(\mathbf{x}|\mathbf{z}_1, \boldsymbol{\phi}_1) = \text{Norm}_{\mathbf{x}}\Big[\mathbf{f}_1[\mathbf{z}_1, \boldsymbol{\phi}_1], \sigma_1^2 \mathbf{I}\Big], \hspace{3cm} (18.26)
$$

and is equivalent to the reconstruction term in the VAE. The ELBO will be larger if the model prediction matches the observed data. As for the VAE, we will approximate the expectation over the log of this quantity using a Monte Carlo estimate (see equations 17.22–17.23), in which we estimate the expectation with a sample from $q(\mathbf{z}_1|\mathbf{x})$.

The KL divergence terms in the ELBO measure the distance between $Pr(\mathbf{z}_{t-1}|\mathbf{z}_t, \boldsymbol{\phi}_t)$ and $q(\mathbf{z}_{t-1}|\mathbf{z}_t, \mathbf{x})$, which were defined in equations 18.16 and 18.15, respectively:

$$
\begin{aligned}
Pr(\mathbf{z}_{t-1}|\mathbf{z}_t, \boldsymbol{\phi}_t) &= \text{Norm}_{\mathbf{z}_{t-1}}\Big[\mathbf{f}_t[\mathbf{z}_t, \boldsymbol{\phi}_t], \sigma_t^2 \mathbf{I}\Big] \hspace{3cm} (18.27) \\
q(\mathbf{z}_{t-1}|\mathbf{z}_t, \mathbf{x}) &= \text{Norm}_{\mathbf{z}_{t-1}}\left[\frac{(1-\alpha_{t-1})}{1-\alpha_t}\sqrt{1-\beta_t}\mathbf{z}_t + \frac{\sqrt{\alpha_{t-1}}\beta_t}{1-\alpha_t}\mathbf{x}, \frac{\beta_t(1-\alpha_{t-1})}{1-\alpha_t}\mathbf{I} \right].
\end{aligned}
$$

Appendix C.5.4
KL divergence
between normal
distributions

Problem 18.8

The KL divergence between two normal distributions has a closed-form expression. Moreover, many of the terms in this expression do not depend on $\boldsymbol{\phi}$ (see problem 18.8), and the expression simplifies to the squared difference between the means plus a constant C:

$$
\begin{aligned}
D_{KL}\Big[q(\mathbf{z}_{t-1}|\mathbf{z}_t, \mathbf{x})\big|\big|Pr(\mathbf{z}_{t-1}|\mathbf{z}_t, \boldsymbol{\phi}_t)\Big] &= \hspace{4cm} (18.28) \\
\frac{1}{2\sigma_t^2}\left\| \frac{(1-\alpha_{t-1})}{1-\alpha_t}\sqrt{1-\beta_t}\mathbf{z}_t + \frac{\sqrt{\alpha_{t-1}}\beta_t}{1-\alpha_t}\mathbf{x} - \mathbf{f}_t[\mathbf{z}_t, \boldsymbol{\phi}_t] \right\|^2 + C.
\end{aligned}
$$

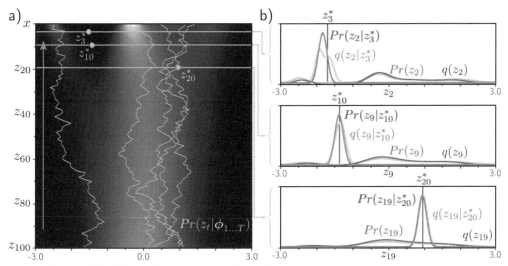

Figure 18.7 Fitted Model. a) Individual samples can be generated by sampling from the standard normal distribution $Pr(z_T)$ (bottom row) and then sampling z_{T-1} from $Pr(z_{T-1}|z_T) = \text{Norm}_{\mathbf{z}_{T-1}}[\mathbf{f}_T[z_T, \boldsymbol{\phi}_T], \sigma_T^2\mathbf{I}]$ and so on until we reach x (five paths shown). The estimated marginal densities (heatmap) are the aggregation of these samples and are similar to the true marginal densities (figure 18.4). b) The estimated distribution $Pr(z_{t-1}|z_t)$ (brown curve) is a reasonable approximation to the true posterior of the diffusion model $q(z_{t-1}|z_t)$ (cyan curve) from figure 18.5. The marginal distributions $Pr(z_t)$ and $q(z_t)$ of the estimated and true models (dark blue and gray curves, respectively) are also similar.

18.4.4 Diffusion loss function

To fit the model, we maximize the ELBO with respect to the parameters $\boldsymbol{\phi}_{1\ldots T}$. We recast this as a minimization by multiplying with minus one and approximating the expectations with samples to give the loss function:

$$
L[\boldsymbol{\phi}_{1\ldots T}] = \sum_{i=1}^{I}\Bigg(\overbrace{-\log\Big[\text{Norm}_{\mathbf{x}_i}\big[\mathbf{f}_1[\mathbf{z}_{i1}, \boldsymbol{\phi}_1], \sigma_1^2\mathbf{I}\big]\Big]}^{\text{reconstruction term}} \tag{18.29}
$$
$$
+ \sum_{t=2}^{T}\frac{1}{2\sigma_t^2}\Big\| \underbrace{\frac{1-\alpha_{t-1}}{1-\alpha_t}\sqrt{1-\beta_t}\,\mathbf{z}_{it} + \frac{\sqrt{\alpha_{t-1}}\beta_t}{1-\alpha_t}\mathbf{x}_i}_{\text{target, mean of } q(\mathbf{z}_{t-1}|\mathbf{z}_t, \mathbf{x})} - \underbrace{\mathbf{f}_t[\mathbf{z}_{it}, \boldsymbol{\phi}_t]}_{\text{predicted } \mathbf{z}_{t-1}} \Big\|^2 \Bigg),
$$

where $\mathbf{x}_i$ is the ith data point, and $\mathbf{z}_{it}$ is the associated latent variable at diffusion step t.

Figure 18.8 Fitted model results. Cyan and brown curves are original and estimated densities and correspond to the top rows of figures 18.4 and 18.7, respectively. Vertical bars are binned samples from the model, generated by sampling from $Pr(\mathbf{z}_T)$ and propagating back through the variables $\mathbf{z}_{T-1}, \mathbf{z}_{T-2}, \ldots$ as shown for the five paths in figure 18.7.

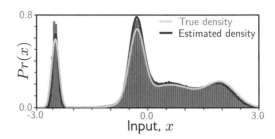

18.4.5 Training procedure

This loss function can be used to train a network for each diffusion time step. It minimizes the difference between the estimate $\mathbf{f}_t[\mathbf{z}_t, \boldsymbol{\phi}_t]$ of the hidden variable at the previous time step and the most likely value that it took given the ground truth de-noised data $\mathbf{x}$.

Figures 18.7 and 18.8 show the fitted reverse process for the simple 1D example. This model was trained by (i) taking a large dataset of examples $\mathbf{x}$ from the original density, (ii) using the diffusion kernel to predict many corresponding values for the latent variable $\mathbf{z}_t$ at each time t, and then (iii) training the models $\mathbf{f}_t[\mathbf{z}_t, \boldsymbol{\phi}_t]$ to minimize the loss function in equation 18.29. These models were nonparametric (i.e., lookup tables relating 1D input to 1D output), but more typically, they would be deep neural networks.

Notebook 18.2
1D diffusion
model

18.5 Reparameterization of loss function

Although the loss function in equation 18.29 can be used, diffusion models have been found to work better with a different parameterization; the loss function is modified so that the model aims to predict the noise that was mixed with the original data example to create the current variable. Section 18.5.1 discusses reparameterizing the target (first two terms in second line of equation 18.29), and section 18.5.2 discusses reparameterizing the network (last term in second line of equation 18.29).

18.5.1 Reparameterization of target

The original diffusion update was given by:

$$\mathbf{z}_t = \sqrt{\alpha_t} \cdot \mathbf{x} + \sqrt{1 - \alpha_t} \cdot \boldsymbol{\epsilon}. \tag{18.30}$$

It follows that the data term $\mathbf{x}$ in equation 18.28 can be expressed as the diffused image minus the noise that was added to it:

$$\mathbf{x} = \frac{1}{\sqrt{\alpha_t}} \cdot \mathbf{z}_t - \frac{\sqrt{1 - \alpha_t}}{\sqrt{\alpha_t}} \cdot \boldsymbol{\epsilon}. \tag{18.31}$$

Substituting this into the target terms from equation 18.29 gives:

$$\frac{(1-\alpha_{t-1})}{1-\alpha_t}\sqrt{1-\beta_t}\mathbf{z}_t + \frac{\sqrt{\alpha_{t-1}}\beta_t}{1-\alpha_t}\mathbf{x} \tag{18.32}$$

$$= \frac{(1-\alpha_{t-1})}{1-\alpha_t}\sqrt{1-\beta_t}\mathbf{z}_t + \frac{\sqrt{\alpha_{t-1}}\beta_t}{1-\alpha_t}\left(\frac{1}{\sqrt{\alpha_t}}\mathbf{z}_t - \frac{\sqrt{1-\alpha_t}}{\sqrt{\alpha_t}}\boldsymbol{\epsilon}\right)$$

$$= \frac{(1-\alpha_{t-1})}{1-\alpha_t}\sqrt{1-\beta_t}\mathbf{z}_t + \frac{\beta_t}{1-\alpha_t}\left(\frac{1}{\sqrt{1-\beta_t}}\mathbf{z}_t - \frac{\sqrt{1-\alpha_t}}{\sqrt{1-\beta_t}}\boldsymbol{\epsilon}\right),$$

where we have used the fact that $\sqrt{\alpha_t}/\sqrt{\alpha_{t-1}} = \sqrt{1-\beta_t}$ between the second and third lines. Simplifying further, we get:

Problem 18.9

$$\frac{(1-\alpha_{t-1})}{1-\alpha_t}\sqrt{1-\beta_t}\mathbf{z}_t + \frac{\sqrt{\alpha_{t-1}}\beta_t}{1-\alpha_t}\mathbf{x} \tag{18.33}$$

$$= \left(\frac{(1-\alpha_{t-1})\sqrt{1-\beta_t}}{1-\alpha_t} + \frac{\beta_t}{(1-\alpha_t)\sqrt{1-\beta_t}}\right)\mathbf{z}_t - \frac{\beta_t}{\sqrt{1-\alpha_t}\sqrt{1-\beta_t}}\boldsymbol{\epsilon}$$

$$= \left(\frac{(1-\alpha_{t-1})(1-\beta_t)}{(1-\alpha_t)\sqrt{1-\beta_t}} + \frac{\beta_t}{(1-\alpha_t)\sqrt{1-\beta_t}}\right)\mathbf{z}_t - \frac{\beta_t}{\sqrt{1-\alpha_t}\sqrt{1-\beta_t}}\boldsymbol{\epsilon}$$

$$= \frac{(1-\alpha_{t-1})(1-\beta_t)+\beta_t}{(1-\alpha_t)\sqrt{1-\beta_t}}\mathbf{z}_t - \frac{\beta_t}{\sqrt{1-\alpha_t}\sqrt{1-\beta_t}}\boldsymbol{\epsilon}$$

$$= \frac{1-\alpha_t}{(1-\alpha_t)\sqrt{1-\beta_t}}\mathbf{z}_t - \frac{\beta_t}{\sqrt{1-\alpha_t}\sqrt{1-\beta_t}}\boldsymbol{\epsilon}$$

$$= \frac{1}{\sqrt{1-\beta_t}}\mathbf{z}_t - \frac{\beta_t}{\sqrt{1-\alpha_t}\sqrt{1-\beta_t}}\boldsymbol{\epsilon},$$

where we have multiplied the numerator and denominator of the first term by $\sqrt{1-\beta_t}$ between lines two and three, multiplied out the terms, and simplified the numerator in the first term between lines three and four.

Substituting this back into the loss function (equation 18.29), we have:

Problem 18.10

$$L[\boldsymbol{\phi}_{1...T}] = \sum_{i=1}^{I} -\log\left[\text{Norm}_{\mathbf{x}_i}\left[\mathbf{f}_1[\mathbf{z}_{i1},\boldsymbol{\phi}_1],\sigma_1^2\mathbf{I}\right]\right] \tag{18.34}$$

$$+ \sum_{t=2}^{T}\frac{1}{2\sigma_t^2}\left\|\left(\frac{1}{\sqrt{1-\beta_t}}\mathbf{z}_{it} - \frac{\beta_t}{\sqrt{1-\alpha_t}\sqrt{1-\beta_t}}\boldsymbol{\epsilon}_{it}\right) - \mathbf{f}_t[\mathbf{z}_{it},\boldsymbol{\phi}_t]\right\|^2.$$

18.5.2   **Reparameterization of network**

Now we replace the model $\hat{\mathbf{z}}_{t-1} = \mathbf{f}_t[\mathbf{z}_t,\boldsymbol{\phi}_t]$ with a new model $\hat{\boldsymbol{\epsilon}} = \mathbf{g}_t[\mathbf{z}_t,\boldsymbol{\phi}_t]$, which predicts the noise $\boldsymbol{\epsilon}$ that was mixed with $\mathbf{x}$ to create $\mathbf{z}_t$:

$$\mathbf{f}_t[\mathbf{z}_t,\boldsymbol{\phi}_t] = \frac{1}{\sqrt{1-\beta_t}}\mathbf{z}_t - \frac{\beta_t}{\sqrt{1-\alpha_t}\sqrt{1-\beta_t}}\mathbf{g}_t[\mathbf{z}_t,\boldsymbol{\phi}_t]. \tag{18.35}$$

Substituting the new model into equation 18.34 produces the criterion:

$$L[\phi_{1...T}] = \tag{18.36}$$
$$\sum_{i=1}^{I} -\log\left[\text{Norm}_{\mathbf{x}_i}\left[\mathbf{f}_1[\mathbf{z}_{i1}, \phi_1], \sigma_1^2\mathbf{I}\right]\right] + \sum_{t=2}^{T} \frac{\beta_t^2}{(1-\alpha_t)(1-\beta_t)2\sigma_t^2}\left\|\mathbf{g}_t[\mathbf{z}_{it}, \phi_t] - \boldsymbol{\epsilon}_{it}\right\|^2.$$

The log normal can be written as a least squares loss plus a constant C_i (section 5.3.1):

$$L[\phi_{1...T}] = \sum_{i=1}^{I} \frac{1}{2\sigma_1^2}\left\|\mathbf{x}_i - \mathbf{f}_1[\mathbf{z}_{i1}, \phi_1]\right\|^2 + \sum_{t=2}^{T} \frac{\beta_t^2}{(1-\alpha_t)(1-\beta_t)2\sigma_t^2}\left\|\mathbf{g}_t[\mathbf{z}_{it}, \phi_t] - \boldsymbol{\epsilon}_{it}\right\|^2 + C_i.$$

Problem 18.11

Substituting in the definitions of $\mathbf{x}$ and $\mathbf{f}_1[\mathbf{z}_1, \phi_1]$ from equations 18.31 and 18.35, respectively, the first term simplifies to:

$$\frac{1}{2\sigma_1^2}\left\|\mathbf{x}_i - \mathbf{f}_1[\mathbf{z}_{i1}, \phi_1]\right\|^2 = \frac{1}{2\sigma_1^2}\left\|\frac{\beta_1}{\sqrt{1-\alpha_1}\sqrt{1-\beta_1}}\mathbf{g}_1[\mathbf{z}_{i1}, \phi_1] - \frac{\beta_1}{\sqrt{1-\alpha_1}\sqrt{1-\beta_1}}\boldsymbol{\epsilon}_{i1}\right\|^2. \tag{18.37}$$

Adding this back to the final loss function yields:

$$L[\phi_{1...T}] = \sum_{i=1}^{I}\sum_{t=1}^{T} \frac{\beta_t^2}{(1-\alpha_t)(1-\beta_t)2\sigma_t^2}\left\|\mathbf{g}_t[\mathbf{z}_{it}, \phi_t] - \boldsymbol{\epsilon}_{it}\right\|^2, \tag{18.38}$$

where we have disregarded the additive constants C_i.

In practice, the scaling factors (which might be different at each time step) are ignored, giving an even simpler formulation:

$$L[\phi_{1...T}] = \sum_{i=1}^{I}\sum_{t=1}^{T}\left\|\mathbf{g}_t[\mathbf{z}_{it}, \phi_t] - \boldsymbol{\epsilon}_{it}\right\|^2 \tag{18.39}$$
$$= \sum_{i=1}^{I}\sum_{t=1}^{T}\left\|\mathbf{g}_t\left[\sqrt{\alpha_t}\cdot\mathbf{x}_i + \sqrt{1-\alpha_t}\cdot\boldsymbol{\epsilon}_{it}, \phi_t\right] - \boldsymbol{\epsilon}_{it}\right\|^2,$$

where we have rewritten $\mathbf{z}_t$ using the diffusion kernel (equation 18.30) in the second line.

18.6   Implementation

Notebook 18.3
Reparameterized
model

This leads to straightforward algorithms for both training the model (algorithm 18.1) and sampling (algorithm 18.2). The training algorithm has the advantages that it is (i) simple to implement and (ii) naturally augments the dataset; we can reuse every original data point $\mathbf{x}_i$ as many times as we want at each time step with different noise instantiations $\boldsymbol{\epsilon}$. The sampling algorithm has the disadvantage that it requires serial processing of many neural networks $\mathbf{g}_t[\mathbf{z}_t, \phi_t]$ and is hence time-consuming.

Algorithm 18.1: Diffusion model training

Input: Training data $\mathbf{x}$
Output: Model parameters ϕ_t
repeat
    for $i \in \mathcal{B}$ **do**   // For every training example index in batch
        $t \sim \text{Uniform}[1, \ldots T]$ // Sample random timestep
        $\epsilon \sim \text{Norm}[\mathbf{0}, \mathbf{I}]$ // Sample noise
        $\ell_i = \left\| \mathbf{g}_t \left[\sqrt{\alpha_t}\mathbf{x}_i + \sqrt{1 - \alpha_t}\epsilon, \phi_t \right] - \epsilon \right\|^2$ // Compute individual loss
    Accumulate losses for batch and take gradient step
until converged

Algorithm 18.2: Sampling

Input: Model, $\mathbf{g}_t[\bullet, \phi_t]$
Output: Sample, $\mathbf{x}$
$\mathbf{z}_T \sim \text{Norm}_{\mathbf{z}}[\mathbf{0}, \mathbf{I}]$ // Sample last latent variable
for $t = T \ldots 2$ **do**
    $\hat{\mathbf{z}}_{t-1} = \frac{1}{\sqrt{1-\beta_t}}\mathbf{z}_t - \frac{\beta_t}{\sqrt{1-\alpha_t}\sqrt{1-\beta_t}}\mathbf{g}_t[\mathbf{z}_t, \phi_t]$ // Predict previous latent variable
    $\epsilon \sim \text{Norm}_\epsilon[\mathbf{0}, \mathbf{I}]$ // Draw new noise vector
    $\mathbf{z}_{t-1} = \hat{\mathbf{z}}_{t-1} + \sigma_t \epsilon$ // Add noise to previous latent variable
$\mathbf{x} = \frac{1}{\sqrt{1-\beta_1}}\mathbf{z}_1 - \frac{\beta_1}{\sqrt{1-\alpha_1}\sqrt{1-\beta_1}}\mathbf{g}_1[\mathbf{z}_1, \phi_1]$ // Generate sample from $\mathbf{z}_1$ without noise

---

18.6.1   Application to images

Diffusion models have been very successful in modeling image data. Here, we need to construct models that can take a noisy image and predict the noise that was added at each step. The obvious architectural choice for this image-to-image mapping is the U-Net (figure 11.10). However, there may be a very large number of diffusion steps, and training and storing multiple U-Nets is inefficient. The solution is to train a single U-Net that also takes a predetermined vector representing the time step as input (figure 18.9). In practice, this is resized to match the number of channels at each stage of the U-Net and used to offset and/or scale the representation at each spatial position.

A large number of time steps are needed as the conditional probabilities $q(\mathbf{z}_{t-1}|\mathbf{z}_t)$ become closer to normal when the hyperparameters β_t are close to zero, matching the form of the decoder distributions $Pr(\mathbf{z}_{t-1}|\mathbf{z}_t, \phi_t)$. However, this makes sampling slow. We might have to run the U-Net model through $T = 1000$ steps to generate good images.

18.6.2   Improving generation speed

The loss function (equation 18.39) requires the diffusion kernel to have the form $q(\mathbf{z}_t|\mathbf{x}) = \text{Norm}[\sqrt{\alpha_t}\mathbf{x}, \sqrt{1 - \alpha_t} \cdot \mathbf{I}]$. The same loss function will be valid for *any* forward process

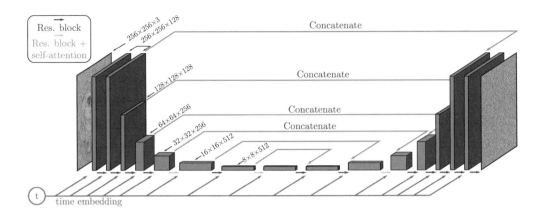

Figure 18.9 U-Net as used in diffusion models for images. The network aims to predict the noise that was added to the image. It consists of an encoder which reduces the scale and increases the number of channels and a decoder which increases the scale and reduces the number of channels. The encoder representations are concatenated to their partner in the decoder. Connections between adjacent representations consist of residual blocks, and periodic global self-attention in which every spatial position interacts with every other spatial position. A single network is used for all time steps, by passing a sinusoidal time embedding (figure 12.5) through a shallow neural network and adding the result to the channels at every spatial position at every stage of the U-Net.

with this relation, and there is a family of such compatible processes. These are all optimized by the same loss function but have different rules for the forward process and different corresponding rules for how to use the estimated noise $\mathbf{g}[\mathbf{z}_t, \boldsymbol{\phi}_t]$ to predict $\mathbf{z}_{t-1}$ from $\mathbf{z}_t$ in the reverse process (figure 18.10).

Among this family are *denoising diffusion implicit models*, which are no longer stochastic after the first step from $\mathbf{x}$ to $\mathbf{z}_1$, and *accelerated sampling* models, where the forward process is defined only on a sub-sequence of time steps. This allows a reverse process that skips time steps and hence makes sampling much more efficient; good samples can be created with 50 time steps when the forward process is no longer stochastic. This is much faster than before but still slower than most other generative models.

Notebook 18.4
Families of
diffusion models

18.6.3 Conditional generation

If the data has associated labels c, these can be exploited to control the generation. Sometimes this can improve generation results in GANs, and we might expect this to be the case in diffusion models as well; it's easier to denoise an image if you have some information about what that image contains. One approach to conditional synthesis in diffusion models is *classifier guidance*. This modifies the denoising update from $\mathbf{z}_t$ to $\mathbf{z}_{t-1}$ to take into account class information c. In practice, this means adding an extra

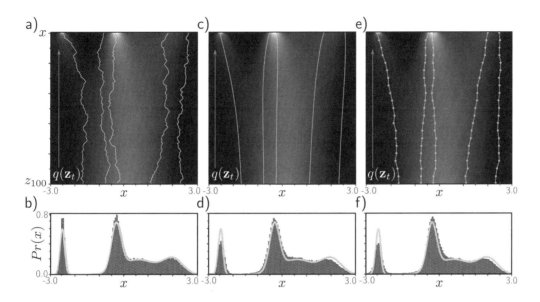

Figure 18.10 Different diffusion processes that are compatible with the same model. a) Five sampled trajectories of the reparameterized model superimposed on the ground truth marginal distributions. Top row represents $Pr(\mathbf{x})$ and subsequent rows represent $q(\mathbf{x}_t)$. b) Histogram of samples generated from reparameterized model plotted alongside ground truth density curve $Pr(\mathbf{x})$. The same trained model is compatible with a family of diffusion models (and corresponding updates in the opposite direction), including the denoising diffusion implicit (DDIM) model, which is deterministic and does not add noise at each step. c) Five trajectories from DDIM model. d) Histogram of samples from DDIM model. The same model is also compatible with accelerated diffusion models that skip inference steps for increased sampling speed. e) Five trajectories from accelerated model. f) Histogram of samples from accelerated model.

term into the final update step in algorithm 18.2 to yield:

$$\mathbf{z}_{t-1} = \hat{\mathbf{z}}_{t-1} + \sigma_t^2 \frac{\partial \log\left[Pr(c|\mathbf{z}_t)\right]}{\partial \mathbf{z}_t} + \sigma_t \boldsymbol{\epsilon}. \tag{18.40}$$

The new term depends on the gradient of a classifier $Pr(c|\mathbf{z}_t)$ that is based on the latent variable $\mathbf{z}_t$. This maps features from the downsampling half of the U-Net to the class c. Like the U-Net, it is usually shared across all time steps and takes time as an input. The update from $\mathbf{z}_t$ to $\mathbf{z}_{t-1}$ now makes the class c more likely.

Classifier-free guidance avoids learning a separate classifier $Pr(c|\mathbf{z}_t)$ but instead incorporates class information into the main model $\mathbf{g}_t[\mathbf{z}_t, \boldsymbol{\phi}_t, c]$. In practice, this usually takes the form of adding an embedding based on c to the layers of the U-Net in a similar way to how the time step is added (see figure 18.9). This model is jointly trained on conditional and unconditional objectives by randomly dropping the class information

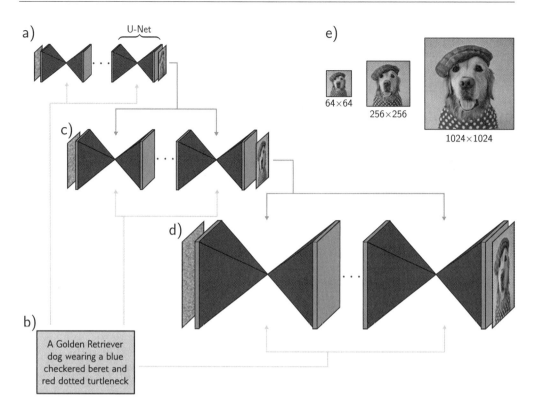

Figure 18.11 Cascaded conditional generation based on a text prompt. a) A diffusion model consisting of a series of U-Nets is used to generate a 64×64 image. b) This generation is conditioned on a sentence embedding computed by a language model. c) A higher resolution 256×256 image is generated and conditioned on the smaller image *and* the text encoding. d) This is repeated to create a 1024×1024 image. e) Final image sequence. Adapted from Saharia et al. (2022b).

Problem 18.12

during training. Hence, it can both generate unconditional or conditional data examples at test time or any weighted combination of the two. This brings a surprising advantage; if the conditioning information is over-weighted, the model tends to produce very high quality but slightly stereotypical examples. This is somewhat analogous to the use of truncation in GANs (figure 15.10).

18.6.4   Improving generation quality

As for other generative models, the highest quality results result from applying a combination of tricks and extensions to the basic model. First, it's been noted that it also helps to estimate the variances σ_t^2 of the reverse process as well as the mean (i.e., the widths of the brown normal distributions in figure 18.7). This particularly improves the results when sampling with fewer steps. Second, it's possible to modify the noise schedule in the forward process so that β_t varies at each step, and this can also improve results.

Third, to generate high-resolution images, a cascade of diffusion models is used. The first creates a low-resolution image (possibly guided by class information). The subsequent diffusion models generate progressively higher-resolution images. They condition on the lower-resolution image by resizing this and appending it to the layers of the constituent U-Net, as well as any other class information (figure 18.11).

Combining all of these techniques allows the generation of very high-quality images. Figure 18.12 shows examples of images generated from a model conditioned on the ImageNet class. It is particularly impressive that the same model can learn to generate such diverse classes. Figure 18.13 shows images generated from a model that is trained to condition on text captions encoded by a language model like BERT, which are inserted into the model in the same way as the time step (figures 18.9 and 18.11). This results in very realistic images that agree with the caption. Since the diffusion model is stochastic by nature, it's possible to generate multiple images that are conditioned on the same caption.

18.7   Summary

Diffusion models map the data examples through a series of latent variables by repeatedly blending the current representation with random noise. After sufficient steps, the representation becomes indistinguishable from white noise. Since these steps are small, the reverse denoising process at each step can be approximated with a normal distribution and predicted by a deep learning model. The loss function is based on the evidence lower bound (ELBO) and ultimately results in a simple least-squares formulation.

For image generation, each denoising step is implemented using a U-Net, so sampling is slow compared to other generative models. To improve generation speed, it's possible to change the diffusion model to a deterministic formulation, and here sampling with fewer steps works well. Several methods have been proposed to condition generation on class information, images, and text information. Combining these methods produces impressive text-to-image synthesis results.

Notes

Denoising diffusion models were introduced by Sohl-Dickstein et al. (2015), and early related work based on score-matching was carried out by Song & Ermon (2019). Ho et al. (2020) produced image samples that were competitive with GANs and kick-started a wave of interest in this area. Most of the exposition in this chapter, including the original formulation and the reparameterization, is derived from this paper. Dhariwal & Nichol (2021) improved the quality of these results and showed for the first time that images from diffusion models were quantitatively superior to GAN models in terms of Fréchet Inception Distance. At the time

Figure 18.12 Conditional generation using classifier guidance. Image samples conditioned on different ImageNet classes. The same model produces high quality samples of highly varied image classes. Adapted from Dhariwal & Nichol (2021).

Figure 18.13 Conditional generation using text prompts. Synthesized images from a cascaded generation framework, conditioned on a text prompt encoded by a large language model. The stochastic model can produce many different images compatible with the prompt. The model can count objects and incorporate text into images. Adapted from Saharia et al. (2022b).

of writing, the state-of-the-art results for conditional image synthesis have been achieved by Karras et al. (2022). Surveys of denoising diffusion models can be found in Croitoru et al. (2022), Cao et al. (2022), Luo (2022), and Yang et al. (2022).

Applications for images: Applications of diffusion models include text-to-image generation (Nichol et al., 2022; Ramesh et al., 2022; Saharia et al., 2022b), image-to-image tasks such as colorization, inpainting, uncropping and restoration (Saharia et al., 2022a), super-resolution (Saharia et al., 2022c), image editing (Hertz et al., 2022; Meng et al., 2021), removing adversarial perturbations (Nie et al., 2022), semantic segmentation (Baranchuk et al., 2022), and medical imaging (Song et al., 2021b; Chung & Ye, 2022; Chung et al., 2022; Peng et al., 2022; Xie & Li, 2022; Luo et al., 2022) where the diffusion model is sometimes used as a prior.

Different data types: Diffusion models have also been applied to video data (Ho et al., 2022b; Harvey et al., 2022; Yang et al., 2022; Höppe et al., 2022; Voleti et al., 2022) for generation, past and future frame prediction, and interpolation. They have been used for 3D shape generation (Zhou et al., 2021; Luo & Hu, 2021), and recently a technique has been introduced to generate 3D models using only a 2D text-to-image diffusion model (Poole et al., 2023). Austin et al. (2021) and Hoogeboom et al. (2021) investigated diffusion models for discrete data. Kong et al. (2021) and Chen et al. (2021d) applied diffusion models to audio data.

Alternatives to denoising: The diffusion models in this chapter mix noise with the data and build a model to gradually denoise the result. However, degrading the image using noise is not necessary. Rissanen et al. (2022) devised a method that progressively blurred the image and Bansal et al. (2022) showed that the same ideas work with a large family of degradations that do not have to be stochastic. These include masking, morphing, blurring, and pixelating.

Comparison to other generative models: Diffusion models synthesize higher quality images than other generative models and are simple to train. They can be thought of as a special case of a hierarchical VAE (Vahdat & Kautz, 2020; Sønderby et al., 2016b) where the encoder is fixed, and the latent space is the same size as the data. They are probabilistic, but in their basic form, they can only compute a lower bound on the likelihood of a data point. However, Kingma et al. (2021) show that this lower bound improves on the exact log-likelihoods for test data from normalizing flows and autoregressive models. The likelihood for diffusion models can be computed by converting to an ordinary differential equation (Song et al., 2021c) or by training a continuous normalizing flow model with a diffusion-based criterion (Lipman et al., 2022). The main disadvantages of diffusion models are that they are slow and that the latent space has no semantic interpretation.

Improving quality: Many techniques have been proposed to improve image quality. These include the reparameterization of the network described in section 18.5 and the equal weighting of the subsequent terms (Ho et al., 2020). Choi et al. (2022) subsequently investigated different weightings of terms in the loss function.

Kingma et al. (2021) improved the test log-likelihood of the model by learning the denoising weights β_t. Conversely, Nichol & Dhariwal (2021) improved performance by learning separate variances σ^2 of the denoising estimate at each time step in addition to the mean. Bao et al. (2022) show how to learn the variances *after* training the model.

Ho et al. (2022a) developed the cascaded method for producing very high-resolution images (figure 18.11). To prevent artifacts in lower-resolution images from being propagated to higher resolutions, they introduced *noise conditioning augmentation*; here, the lower-resolution conditioning image is degraded by adding noise at each training step. This reduces the reliance on the exact details of the lower-resolution image during training. It is also done during inference, where the best noise level is chosen by sweeping over different values.

Improving speed: One of the major drawbacks of diffusion models is that they take a long time to train and sample from. *Stable diffusion* (Rombach et al., 2022) projects the original data to a smaller latent space using a conventional autoencoder and then runs the diffusion process in this smaller space. This has the advantages of reducing the dimensionality of the training data for the diffusion process and allowing other data types (text, graphs, etc.) to be described by diffusion models. Vahdat et al. (2021) applied a similar approach.

Song et al. (2021a) showed that an entire family of diffusion processes is compatible with the training objective. Most of these processes are non-Markovian (i.e., the diffusion step does not only depend on the results of the previous step). One of these models is the denoising diffusion implicit model (DDIM), in which the updates are not stochastic (figure 18.10b). This model is amenable to taking larger steps (figure 18.10b) without inducing large errors. It effectively converts the model into an ordinary differential equation (ODE) in which the trajectories have low curvature and allows efficient numerical methods for solving ODEs to be applied.

Song et al. (2021c) propose converting the underlying stochastic differential equations into a *probability flow ODE* which has the same marginal distributions as the original process. Vahdat et al. (2021), Xiao et al. (2022b), and Karras et al. (2022) all exploit techniques for solving ODEs to speed up synthesis. Karras et al. (2022) identified the best-performing time discretization for sampling and evaluated different sampler schedules. The result of these and other improvements has been a significant drop in steps required during synthesis.

Sampling is slow because many small diffusion steps are required to ensure that the posterior distribution $q(\mathbf{z}_{t-1}|\mathbf{z}_t)$ is close to Gaussian (figure 18.5), so the Gaussian distribution in the decoder is appropriate. If we use a model that describes a more complex distribution at each denoising step, then we can use fewer diffusion steps in the first place. To this end, Xiao et al. (2022b) have investigated using conditional GAN models, and Gao et al. (2021) investigated using conditional energy-based models. Although these models cannot describe the original data distribution, they suffice to predict the (much simpler) reverse diffusion step.

Salimans & Ho (2022) distilled adjacent steps of the denoising process into a single step to speed up synthesis. Dockhorn et al. (2022) introduced momentum into the diffusion process. This makes the trajectories smoother and so more amenable to coarse sampling.

Conditional generation: Dhariwal & Nichol (2021) introduced classifier guidance, in which a classifier learns to identify the category of object being synthesized at each step, and this is used to bias the denoising update toward that class. This works well, but training a separate classifier is expensive. *Classifier-free guidance* (Ho & Salimans, 2022) concurrently trains conditional and unconditional denoising models by dropping the class information some proportion of the time in a process akin to dropout. This technique allows control of the relative contributions of the conditional and unconditional components. Over-weighting the conditional component causes the model to produce more typical and realistic samples.

The standard technique for conditioning on images is to append the (resized) image to the different layers of the U-Net. For example, this was used in the cascaded generation process for super-resolution (Ho et al., 2022a). Choi et al. (2021) provide a method for conditioning on images in an unconditional diffusion model by matching the latent variables with those of a conditioning image. The standard technique for conditioning on text is to linearly transform the text embedding to the same size as the U-Net layer and then add it to the representation in the same way that the time embedding is introduced (figure 18.9).

Existing diffusion models can also be fine-tuned to be conditioned on edge maps, joint positions, segmentation, depth maps, etc., using a neural network structure called a *control network* (Zhang & Agrawala, 2023).

Text-to-image: Before diffusion models, state-of-the-art text-to-image systems were based on transformers (e.g., Ramesh et al., 2021). GLIDE (Nichol et al., 2022) and Dall·E 2 (Ramesh et al., 2022) are both conditioned on embeddings from the CLIP model (Radford et al., 2021), which generates joint embeddings for text and image data. Imagen (Saharia et al., 2022b) showed that text embeddings from a large language model could produce even better results (see figure 18.13). The same authors introduced a benchmark (DrawBench) which is designed to evaluate the ability of a model to render colors, numbers of objects, spatial relations, and other characteristics. Feng et al. (2022) developed a Chinese text-to-image model.

Connections to other models: This chapter described diffusion models as hierarchical variational autoencoders because this approach connects most closely with the other parts of this book. However, diffusion models also have close connections with stochastic differential equations (consider the paths in figure 18.5) and with score matching (Song & Ermon, 2019, 2020). Song et al. (2021c) presented a framework based on stochastic differential equations that encompasses both the denoising and score matching interpretations. Diffusion models also have close connections to normalizing flows (Zhang & Chen, 2021). Yang et al. (2022) present an overview of the relationship between diffusion models and other generative approaches.

Problems

Problem 18.1 Show that if $\text{Var}[\mathbf{x}_{t-1}] = \mathbf{I}$ and we use the update:

$$\mathbf{x}_t = \sqrt{1 - \beta_t} \cdot \mathbf{x}_{t-1} + \sqrt{\beta_t} \cdot \boldsymbol{\epsilon}_t, \tag{18.41}$$

then $\text{Var}[\mathbf{x}_t] = \mathbf{I}$, so the variance stays the same.

Problem 18.2 Consider the variable:

$$z = a \cdot \epsilon_1 + b \cdot \epsilon_2, \tag{18.42}$$

where both ϵ_1 and ϵ_2 are drawn from independent standard normal distributions with mean zero and unit variance. Show that:

$$\begin{aligned} \mathbb{E}[z] &= 0 \\ \text{Var}[z] &= a^2 + b^2, \end{aligned} \tag{18.43}$$

so we could equivalently compute $z = \sqrt{a^2 + b^2} \cdot \epsilon$ where ϵ is also drawn from a standard normal distribution.

Problem 18.3 Continue the process in equation 18.5 to show that:

$$\mathbf{z}_3 = \sqrt{(1 - \beta_3)(1 - \beta_2)(1 - \beta_1)} \cdot \mathbf{x} + \sqrt{1 - (1 - \beta_3)(1 - \beta_2)(1 - \beta_1)} \cdot \boldsymbol{\epsilon}', \tag{18.44}$$

where $\boldsymbol{\epsilon}'$ is a draw from a standard normal distribution.

Problem 18.4[*] Prove the relation:

$$\text{Norm}_{\mathbf{v}}\left[\mathbf{A}\mathbf{w}, \mathbf{B}\right] \propto \text{Norm}_{\mathbf{w}}\left[(\mathbf{A}^T \mathbf{B}^{-1} \mathbf{A})^{-1} \mathbf{A}^T \mathbf{B}^{-1} \mathbf{v}, (\mathbf{A}^T \mathbf{B}^{-1} \mathbf{A})^{-1}\right]. \tag{18.45}$$

Problem 18.5[*] Prove the relation:

$$\text{Norm}_{\mathbf{x}}[\mathbf{a}, \mathbf{A}]\text{Norm}_{\mathbf{x}}[\mathbf{b}, \mathbf{B}] \;\; \propto \;\; \text{Norm}_{\mathbf{x}}\left[(\mathbf{A}^{-1} + \mathbf{B}^{-1})^{-1}(\mathbf{A}^{-1}\mathbf{a} + \mathbf{B}^{-1}\mathbf{b}), (\mathbf{A}^{-1} + \mathbf{B}^{-1})^{-1}\right].$$

$$(18.46)$$

Problem 18.6[*] Derive equation 18.15.

Problem 18.7[*] Derive the third line of equation 18.25 from the second line.

Problem 18.8[*] The KL-divergence between two normal distributions in D dimensions with means $\mathbf{a}$ and $\mathbf{b}$ and covariance matrices $\mathbf{A}$ and $\mathbf{B}$ is given by:

$$D_{KL}\left[\text{Norm}_{\mathbf{w}}[\mathbf{a}, \mathbf{A}]\big|\big|\text{Norm}_{\mathbf{w}}[\mathbf{b}, \mathbf{B}]\right] \;=\; \frac{1}{2}\left(\text{tr}\left[\mathbf{B}^{-1}\mathbf{A}\right] - d + (\mathbf{a} - \mathbf{b})^T\mathbf{B}^{-1}(\mathbf{a} - \mathbf{b}) + \log\left[\frac{|\mathbf{B}|}{|\mathbf{A}|}\right]\right).$$

$$(18.47)$$

Substitute the definitions from equation 18.27 into this expression and show that the only term that depends on the parameters ϕ is the first term from equation 18.28.

Problem 18.9[*] If $\alpha_t = \prod_{s=1}^{t} 1 - \beta_s$, then show that:

$$\sqrt{\frac{\alpha_t}{\alpha_{t-1}}} = \sqrt{1 - \beta_t}.$$

$$(18.48)$$

Problem 18.10[*] If $\alpha_t = \prod_{s=1}^{t} 1 - \beta_s$, then show that:

$$\frac{(1 - \alpha_{t-1})(1 - \beta_t) + \beta_t}{(1 - \alpha_t)\sqrt{1 - \beta_t}} = \frac{1}{\sqrt{1 - \beta_t}}.$$

$$(18.49)$$

Problem 18.11[*] Prove equation 18.37.

Problem 18.12 Classifier-free guidance allows us to create more stereotyped "canonical" images of a given class. When we described transformer decoders, generative adversarial networks, and the GLOW algorithm, we also discussed methods to reduce the amount of variation and produce more stereotyped outputs. What were these? Do you think it's inevitable that we should limit the output of generative models in this way?

Chapter 19

Reinforcement learning

Reinforcement learning (RL) is a sequential decision-making framework in which agents learn to perform actions in an environment with the goal of maximizing received rewards. For example, an RL algorithm might control the moves (actions) of a character (the agent) in a video game (the environment), aiming to maximize the score (the reward). In robotics, an RL algorithm might control the movements (actions) of a robot (the agent) in the world (the environment) to perform a task (earning a reward). In finance, an RL algorithm might control a virtual trader (the agent) who buys or sells assets (the actions) on a trading platform (the environment) to maximize profit (the reward).

Consider learning to play chess. Here, there is a reward of $+1$, -1, or 0 at the end of the game if the agent wins, loses, or draws and 0 at every other time step. This illustrates the challenges of RL. First, the reward is sparse; here, we must play an entire game to receive feedback. Second, the reward is temporally offset from the action that caused it; a decisive advantage might be gained thirty moves before victory. We must associate the reward with this critical action. This is termed the *temporal credit assignment problem*. Third, the environment is stochastic; the opponent doesn't always make the same move in the same situation, so it's hard to know if an action was truly good or just lucky. Finally, the agent must balance exploring the environment (e.g., trying new opening moves) with exploiting what it already knows (e.g., sticking to a previously successful opening). This is termed the *exploration-exploitation trade-off*.

Reinforcement learning is an overarching framework that does not necessarily require deep learning. However, in practice, state-of-the-art systems often use deep networks. They encode the environment (the video game display, robot sensors, financial time series, or chessboard) and map this directly or indirectly to the next action (figure 1.13).

19.1 Markov decision processes, returns, and policies

Reinforcement learning maps observations of an environment to actions, aiming to maximize a numerical quantity that is connected to the rewards received. In the most common case, we learn a *policy* that maximizes the expected *return* in a *Markov decision process*. This section explains these terms.

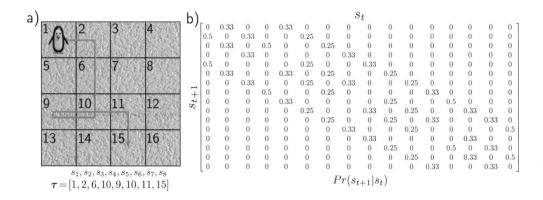

a)

b)

$$\tau = [1, 2, 6, 10, 9, 10, 11, 15]$$

Figure 19.1 Markov process. A Markov process consists of a set of states and transition probabilities $Pr(s_{t+1}|s_t)$ that define the probability of moving to state s_{t+1} given the current state is s_t. a) The penguin can visit 16 different positions (states) on the ice. b) The ice is slippery, so at each time, it has an equal probability of moving to any adjacent state. For example, in position 6, it has a 25% chance of moving to states 2, 5, 7, and 10. A trajectory $\tau = [s_1, s_2, s_3, \ldots]$ from this process consists of a sequence of states.

19.1.1 Markov process

A *Markov process* assumes that the world is always in one of a set of possible states. The word *Markov* implies that the probability of being in a state depends only on the previous state and not on the states before. The changes between states are captured by the *transition probabilities* $Pr(s_{t+1}|s_t)$ of moving to the next state s_{t+1} given the current state s_t, where t indexes the time step. Hence, a Markov process is an evolving system that produces a sequence $s_1, s_2, s_3 \ldots$ of states (figure 19.1).

19.1.2 Markov reward process

Problem 19.1

A *Markov reward process* extends the Markov process to include a distribution $Pr(r_{t+1}|s_t)$ over the possible rewards r_{t+1} received at the next time step, given that we are in state s_t. This produces a sequence $s_1, r_2, s_2, r_3, s_3, r_4 \ldots$ of states and the associated rewards (figure 19.2). The Markov reward process also includes a *discount factor* $\gamma \in (0, 1]$ that is used to compute the *return* G_t at time t:

$$G_t = \sum_{k=0}^{\infty} \gamma^k r_{t+k+1}. \tag{19.1}$$

The return is the sum of the cumulative discounted future rewards; it measures the future benefit of being on this trajectory. A discount factor of less than one makes rewards that are closer in time more valuable than rewards that are further away.

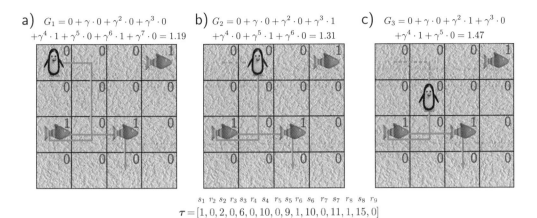

Figure 19.2 Markov reward process. This associates a distribution $Pr(r_{t+1}|s_t)$ of rewards r_{t+1} with each state s_t. a) Here, the rewards are deterministic; the penguin will receive a reward of $+1$ if it lands on a fish and 0 otherwise. The trajectory τ now consists of a sequence $s_1, r_2, s_2, r_3, s_3, r_4 \ldots$ of alternating states and rewards, terminating after eight steps. The return G_t of the sequence is the sum of discounted future rewards, here with discount factor $\gamma = 0.9$. b-c) As the penguin proceeds along the trajectory and gets closer to reaching the rewards, the return increases.

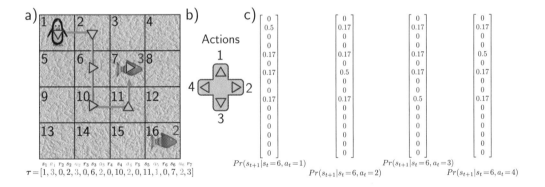

Figure 19.3 Markov decision process. a) The agent (penguin) can perform one of a set of actions in each state. The action influences both the probability of moving to the successor state and the probability of receiving rewards. b) Here, the four actions correspond to moving up, right, down, and left. c) For any state (here, state 6), the action changes the probability of moving to the next state. The penguin moves in the intended direction with 50% probability, but the ice is slippery, so it may slide to one of the other adjacent positions with equal probability. Accordingly, in panel (a), the action taken (gray arrows) doesn't always line up with the trajectory (orange line). Here, the action does not affect the reward, so $Pr(r_{t+1}|s_t, a_t) = Pr(r_{t+1}|s_t)$. The trajectory τ from an MDP consists of a sequence $s_1, a_1, r_2, s_2, a_2, r_3, s_3, a_3, r_4 \ldots$ of alternating states s_t, actions a_t, and rewards, r_{t+1}. Note that here the penguin receives the reward when it *leaves* a state with a fish (i.e., the reward is received for passing through the fish square, regardless of whether the penguin arrived there intentionally or not).

Figure 19.4 Partially observable Markov decision process (POMDP). In a POMDP, the agent does not have access to the entire state. Here, the penguin is in state three and can only see the region in the dashed box. This is indistinguishable from what it would see in state nine. In the first case, moving right leads to the hole in the ice (with -2 reward) and, in the latter, to the fish (with +3 reward).

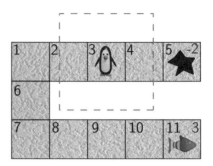

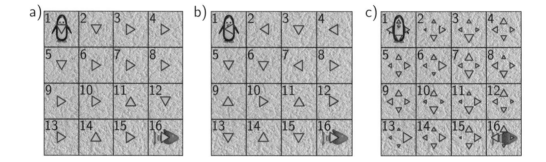

Figure 19.5 Policies. a) A deterministic policy always chooses the same action in each state (indicated by arrow). Some policies are better than others. This policy is not optimal but still generally steers the penguin from top-left to bottom-right where the reward lies. b) This policy is more random. c) A stochastic policy has a probability distribution over actions for each state (probability indicated by size of arrows). This has the advantage that the agent explores the states more thoroughly and can be necessary for optimal performance in partially observable Markov decision processes.

Figure 19.6 Reinforcement learning loop. The agent takes an action a_t at time t based on the state s_t, according to the policy $\pi[a_t|s_t]$. This triggers the generation of a new state s_{t+1} (via the state transition function) and a reward r_{t+1} (via the reward function). Both are passed back to the agent, which then chooses a new action.

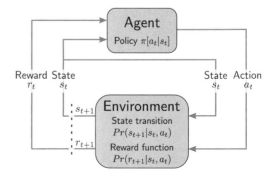

19.1.3 Markov decision process

A *Markov decision process* or *MDP* adds a set of possible *actions* at each time step. The action a_t changes the transition probabilities, which are now written as $Pr(s_{t+1}|s_t, a_t)$. The rewards can also depend on the action and are now written as $Pr(r_{t+1}|s_t, a_t)$. An MDP produces a sequence $s_1, a_1, r_2, s_2, a_2, r_3, s_3, a_3, r_4 \ldots$ of states, actions, and rewards (figure 19.3). The entity that performs the actions is known as the *agent*.

19.1.4 Partially observable Markov decision process

In a *partially observable Markov decision process* or *POMDP*, the state is not directly visible (figure 19.4). Instead, the agent receives an observation o_t drawn from $Pr(o_t|s_t)$. Hence, a POMDP generates a sequence $s_1, o_1, a_1, r_2, s_2, o_2, a_2, r_3, o_3, a_3, s_3, r_4, \ldots$ of states, observations, actions, and rewards. In general, each observation will be more compatible with some states than others but insufficient to identify the state uniquely.

19.1.5 Policy

The rules that determine the agent's action for each state are known as the *policy* (figure 19.5). This may be stochastic (the policy defines a distribution over actions for each state) or deterministic (the agent always takes the same action in a given state). A stochastic policy $\pi[a|s]$ returns a probability distribution over each possible action a for state s, from which a new action is sampled. A deterministic policy $\pi[a|s]$ returns one for the action a that is chosen for state s and zero otherwise. A *stationary* policy depends only on the current state. A *non-stationary* policy also depends on the time step.

The environment and the agent form a loop (figure 19.6). The agent receives the state s_t and reward r_t from the last time step. Based on this, it can modify the policy $\pi[a_t|s_t]$ if desired and choose the next action a_t. The environment then assigns the next state according to $Pr(s_{t+1}|s_t, a_t)$ and the reward according to $Pr(r_{t+1}|s_t, a_t)$.

Notebook 19.1
Markov decision
processes

19.2 Expected return

The previous section introduced the Markov decision process and the idea of an agent carrying out actions according to a policy. We want to choose a policy that maximizes the expected return. In this section, we make this idea mathematically precise. To do that, we assign a *value* to each state s_t and state-action pair $\{s_t, a_t\}$.

19.2.1 State and action values

The return G_t depends on the state s_t and the policy $\pi[a|s]$. From this state, the agent will pass through a sequence of states, taking actions and receiving rewards. This sequence differs every time the agent starts in the same place since, in general, the policy

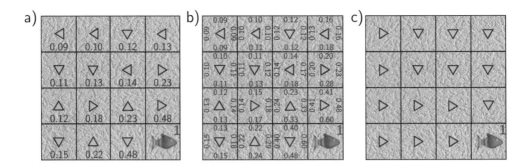

Figure 19.7 State and action values. a) The value $v[s_t|\pi]$ of a state s_t (number at each position) is the expected return for this state for a given policy π (gray arrows). It is the average sum of discounted rewards received over many trajectories started from this state. Here, states closer to the fish are more valuable. b) The value $q[s_t, a_t, \pi]$ of an action a_t in state s_t (four numbers at each position/state corresponding to four actions) is the expected return given that this particular action is taken in this state. In this case, it gets larger as we get closer to the fish and is larger for actions that head in the direction of the fish. c) If we know the action values at a state, then the policy can be modified so that it chooses the maximum of these values (red numbers in panel b).

$\pi[a_t|s_t]$, the state transitions $Pr(s_{t+1}|s_t, a_t)$, and the rewards issued $Pr(r_{t+1}|s_t, a_t)$ are all stochastic.

We can characterize how "good" a state is under a given policy π by considering the expected return $v[s_t|\pi]$. This is the return that would be received on average from sequences that start from this state and is termed the *state value* or *state-value function* (figure 19.7a):

Appendix C.2
Expectation

$$v[s_t|\pi] = \mathbb{E}\Big[G_t|s_t, \pi\Big]. \tag{19.2}$$

Informally, the state value tells us the *long-term* reward we can expect on average if we start in this state and follow the specified policy thereafter. It is highest for states where it's probable that subsequent transitions will bring large rewards soon (assuming the discount factor γ is less than one).

Similarly, the *action value* or *state-action value function* $q[s_t, a_t|\pi]$ is the expected return from executing action a_t in state s_t (figure 19.7b):

$$q[s_t, a_t|\pi] = \mathbb{E}\Big[G_t|s_t, a_t, \pi\Big]. \tag{19.3}$$

The action value tells us the long-term reward we can expect on average if we start in this state, take this action, and follow the specified policy thereafter. Through this quantity, reinforcement learning algorithms connect future rewards to current actions (i.e., resolve the temporal credit assignment problem).

19.2.2 Optimal policy

We want a policy that maximizes the expected return. For MDPs (but not POMDPs), there is always a deterministic, stationary policy that maximizes the value of every state. If we know this optimal policy, then we get the optimal state-value function $v^*[s_t]$:

$$v^*[s_t] = \max_\pi \left[\mathbb{E}\left[G_t | s_t, \pi \right] \right]. \tag{19.4}$$

Similarly, the optimal state-action value function is obtained under the optimal policy:

$$q^*[s_t, a_t] = \max_\pi \left[\mathbb{E}\left[G_t | s_t, a_t, \pi \right] \right]. \tag{19.5}$$

Turning this on its head, if we knew the optimal action-values $q^*[s_t, a_t]$, then we can derive the optimal policy by choosing the action a_t with the highest value (figure 19.7c):[1]

$$\pi[a_t | s_t] \leftarrow \operatorname*{argmax}_{a_t} \left[q^*[s_t, a_t] \right]. \tag{19.6}$$

Indeed, some reinforcement learning algorithms are based on alternately estimating the action values and the policy (see section 19.3).

19.2.3 Bellman equations

We may not know the state values $v[s_t]$ or action values $q[s_t, a_t]$ for any policy.[2] However, we know that they must be consistent with one another, and it's easy to write relations between these quantities. The state value $v[s_t]$ can be found by taking a weighted sum of the action values $q[s_t, a_t]$, where the weights depend on the probability under the policy $\pi[a_t | s_t]$ of taking that action (figure 19.8):

$$v[s_t] = \sum_{a_t} \pi[a_t | s_t] q[s_t, a_t]. \tag{19.7}$$

Similarly, the value of an action is the immediate reward $r_{t+1} = r[s_t, a_t]$ generated by taking the action, plus the value $v[s_{t+1}]$ of being in the subsequent state s_{t+1} discounted by γ (figure 19.9).[3] Since the assignment of s_{t+1} is not deterministic, we weight the values $v[s_{t+1}]$ according to the transition probabilities $Pr(s_{t+1} | s_t, a_t)$:

$$q[s_t, a_t] = r[s_t, a_t] + \gamma \cdot \sum_{s_{t+1}} Pr(s_{t+1} | s_t, a_t) v[s_{t+1}]. \tag{19.8}$$

Substituting equation 19.8 into equation 19.7 provides a relation between the state value at time t and $t + 1$:

---

[1] The notation $\pi[a_t | s_t] \leftarrow a$ in equations 19.6, 19.12, and 19.13 means set $\pi[a_t | s]$ to one for action a and $\pi[a_t | s]$ to zero for other actions.
[2] For simplicity, we will just write $v[s_t]$ and $q[s_t, a_t]$ instead of $v[s_t | \pi]$ and $q[s_t, a_t | \pi]$ from now on.
[3] We also assume from now on that the rewards are deterministic and can be written as $r[s_t, a_t]$.

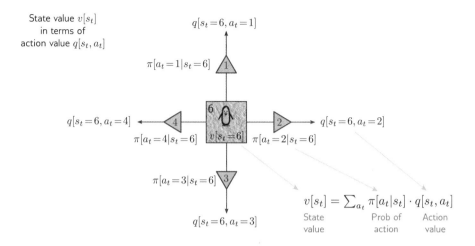

Figure 19.8 Relationship between state values and action values. The value of state six $v[s_t = 6]$ is a weighted sum of the action values $q[s_t = 6, a_t]$ at state six, where the weights are the policy probabilities $\pi[a_t | s_t = 6]$ of taking that action.

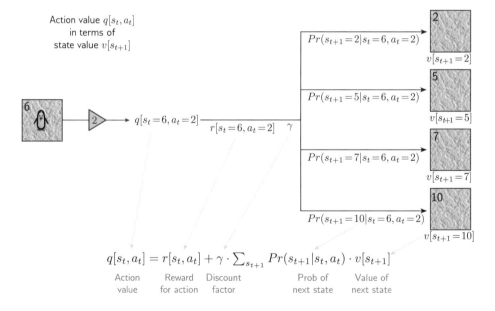

Figure 19.9 Relationship between action values and state values. The value $q[s_t = 6, a_t = 2]$ of taking action two in state six is the reward $r[s_t = 6, a_t = 2]$ from taking that action plus a weighted sum of the discounted values $v[s_{t+1}]$ of being in successor states, where the weights are the transition probabilities $Pr(s_{t+1} | s_t = 6, a_t = 2)$. The Bellman equations chain this relation with that of figure 19.8 to link the current and next (i) state values and (ii) action values.

$$v[s_t] = \sum_{a_t} \pi[a_t|s_t] \left(r[s_t, a_t] + \gamma \cdot \sum_{s_{t+1}} Pr(s_{t+1}|s_t, a_t) v[s_{t+1}] \right). \quad (19.9)$$

Similarly, substituting equation 19.7 into equation 19.8 provides a relation between the action value at time t and $t + 1$:

$$q[s_t, a_t] = r[s_t, a_t] + \gamma \cdot \sum_{s_{t+1}} Pr(s_{t+1}|s_t, a_t) \left(\sum_{a_{t+1}} \pi[a_{t+1}|s_{t+1}] q[s_{t+1}, a_{t+1}] \right). \quad (19.10)$$

The latter two relations are the *Bellman equations* and are the backbone of many RL methods. In short, they say that the state (action) values have to be self-consistent. Consequently, when we update an estimate of one state (action) value, this will have a ripple effect that causes modifications to all the others.

19.3 Tabular reinforcement learning

Tabular RL algorithms (i.e., those that don't rely on function approximation) are divided into *model-based* and *model-free* methods. *Model-based methods* use the MDP structure explicitly and find the best policy from the transition matrix $Pr(s_{t+1}|s_t, a_t)$ and reward structure $r[s, a]$. If these are known, this is a straightforward optimization problem that can be tackled using *dynamic programming*. If they are unknown, they must first be estimated from observed MDP trajectories.[4]

Conversely, *model-free* methods eschew a model of the MDP and fall into two classes:

1. *Value estimation* approaches estimate the optimal state-action value function and then assign the policy according to the action in each state with the greatest value.
2. *Policy estimation* approaches directly estimate the optimal policy using a gradient descent technique without the intermediate steps of estimating the model or values.

Within each family, *Monte Carlo* methods simulate many trajectories through the MDP for a given policy to gather information from which this policy can be improved. Sometimes it is not feasible or practical to simulate many trajectories before updating the policy. *Temporal difference (TD)* methods update the policy *while* the agent traverses the MDP.

We now briefly describe dynamic programming methods, Monte Carlo value estimation methods, and TD value estimation methods. Section 19.4 describes how deep networks have been used in TD value estimation methods. We return to policy estimation in section 19.5.

---

[4]In RL, a *trajectory* is an observed sequence of states, rewards, and actions. A *rollout* is a *simulated* trajectory. An *episode* is a trajectory that starts in an initial state and ends in a terminal state (e.g., a full game of chess starting from the standard opening position and ending in a win, lose, or draw.)

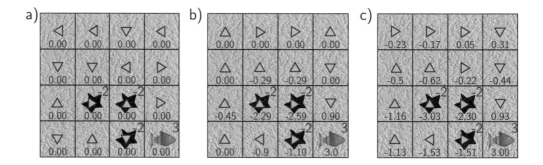

Figure 19.10 Dynamic programming. a) The state values are initialized to zero, and the policy (arrows) is chosen randomly. b) The state values are updated to be consistent with their neighbors (equation 19.11, shown after two iterations). The policy is updated to move the agent to states with the highest value (equation 19.12). c) After several iterations, the algorithm converges to the optimal policy, in which the penguin tries to avoid the holes and reach the fish.

19.3.1   Dynamic programming

Dynamic programming algorithms assume we have *perfect* knowledge of the transition and reward structure. In this respect, they are distinguished from most RL algorithms which observe the agent interacting with the environment to gather information about these quantities indirectly.

The state values $v[s]$ are initialized arbitrarily (usually to zero). The deterministic policy $\pi[a|s]$ is also initialized (e.g., by choosing a random action for each state). The algorithm then alternates between iteratively computing the state values for the current policy (*policy evaluation*) and improving that policy (*policy improvement*).

Policy evaluation: We sweep through the states s_t, updating their values:

$$v[s_t] \leftarrow \sum_{a_t} \pi[a_t|s_t] \left(r[s_t, a_t] + \gamma \cdot \sum_{s_{t+1}} Pr(s_{t+1}|s_t, a_t)v[s_{t+1}] \right), \qquad (19.11)$$

where s_{t+1} is the successor state and $Pr(s_{t+1}|s_t, a_t)$ is the state transition probability. Each update makes $v[s_t]$ consistent with the value at the successor state s_{t+1} using the Bellman equation for state values (equation 19.9). This is termed *bootstrapping*.

Policy improvement: To update the policy, we greedily choose the action that maximizes the value for each state:

$$\pi[a_t|s_t] \leftarrow \underset{a_t}{\mathrm{argmax}} \left[r[s_t, a_t] + \gamma \cdot \sum_{s_{t+1}} Pr(s_{t+1}|s_t, a_t)v[s_{t+1}] \right]. \qquad (19.12)$$

This is guaranteed to improve the policy according to the *policy improvement theorem*.

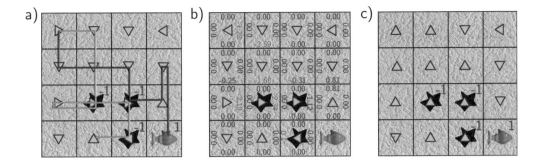

Figure 19.11 Monte Carlo methods. a) The policy (arrows) is initialized randomly. The MDP is repeatedly simulated, and the trajectories of these episodes are stored (orange and brown paths represent two trajectories). b) The action values are empirically estimated based on the observed returns averaged over these trajectories. In this case, the action values were all initially zero and have been updated where an action was observed. c) The policy can then be updated according to the action which received the best (or least bad) reward.

These two steps are iterated until the policy converges (figure 19.10).

There are many variations of this approach. In *policy iteration*, the policy evaluation step is iterated until convergence before policy improvement. The values can be updated either in place or synchronously in each sweep. In *value iteration*, the policy evaluation procedure sweeps through the values just once before policy improvement. *Asynchronous* dynamic programming algorithms don't have to systematically sweep through all the values at each step but can update a subset of the states in place in an arbitrary order.

Problems 19.2–19.3

Notebook 19.2
Dynamic
programming

19.3.2   Monte Carlo methods

Unlike dynamic programming algorithms, Monte Carlo methods don't assume knowledge of the MDP's transition probabilities and reward structure. Instead, they gain experience by repeatedly sampling trajectories from the MDP and observing the rewards. They alternate between computing the action values (based on this experience) and updating the policy (based on the action values).

To estimate the action values $q[s, a]$, a series of *episodes* are run. Each starts with a given state and action and thereafter follows the current policy, producing a series of actions, states, and returns (figure 19.11a). The action value for a given state-action pair under the current policy is estimated as the average of the empirical returns that follow after each time this pair is observed (figure 19.11b). Then the policy is updated by choosing the action with the maximum value at every state (figure 19.11c):

$$\pi[a|s] \leftarrow \underset{a}{\mathrm{argmax}}\Big[q[s, a]\Big]. \tag{19.13}$$

This is an *on-policy* method; the current best policy is used to guide the agent through the environment. This policy is based on the observed action values in every state, but of course, it's not possible to estimate the value of actions that haven't been used, and there is nothing to encourage the algorithm to explore these. One solution is to use *exploring starts*. Here, episodes with all possible state-action pairs are initiated, so every combination is observed at least once. However, this is impractical if the number of states is large or the starting point cannot be controlled. A different approach is to use an *epsilon greedy* policy, in which a random action is taken with probability ϵ, and the optimal action is allotted the remaining probability. The choice of ϵ trades off exploitation and exploration. Here, an on-policy method will seek the best policy from this epsilon-greedy family, which will *not* generally be the best overall policy.

Conversely, in *off-policy* methods, the optimal policy π (the *target policy*) is learned based on episodes generated by a different *behavior policy* π'. Typically, the target policy is deterministic, and the behavior policy is stochastic (e.g., an epsilon-greedy policy). Hence, the behavior policy can explore the environment, but the learned target policy remains efficient. Some off-policy methods explicitly use importance sampling (section 17.8.1) to estimate the action value under policy π using samples from π'. Others, such as Q-learning (described in the next section), estimate the values based on the greedy action, even though this is not necessarily what was chosen.

19.3.3 Temporal difference methods

Dynamic programming methods use a bootstrapping process to update the values to make them self-consistent under the current policy. Monte Carlo methods sampled the MDP to acquire information. Temporal difference (TD) methods combine both bootstrapping and sampling. However, unlike Monte Carlo methods, they update the values and policy *while* the agent traverses the states of the MDP instead of afterward.

SARSA (State-Action-Reward-State-Action) is an on-policy algorithm with update:

$$q[s_t, a_t] \leftarrow q[s_t, a_t] + \alpha\Big(r[s_t, a_t] + \gamma \cdot q[s_{t+1}, a_{t+1}] - q[s_t, a_t]\Big), \qquad (19.14)$$

where $\alpha \in \mathbb{R}^+$ is the learning rate. The bracketed term is called the *TD error* and measures the consistency between the estimated action value $q[s_t, a_t]$ and the estimate $r[s_t, a_t] + \gamma \cdot q[s_{t+1}, a_{t+1}]$ after taking a single step.

By contrast, *Q-Learning* is an off-policy algorithm with update (figure 19.12):

$$q[s_t, a_t] \leftarrow q[s_t, a_t] + \alpha\Big(r[s_t, a_t] + \gamma \cdot \max_a\big[q[s_{t+1}, a]\big] - q[s_t, a_t]\Big), \qquad (19.15)$$

where now the choice of action at each step is derived from a different behavior policy π'.

In both cases, the policy is updated by taking the maximum of the action values at each state (equation 19.13). It can be shown that these updates are contraction mappings (see equation 16.20); the action values will eventually converge, assuming that every state-action pair is visited an infinite number of times.

Problem 19.4

Notebook 19.3
Monte Carlo
methods

Notebook 19.4
Temporal difference
methods

Problem 19.5

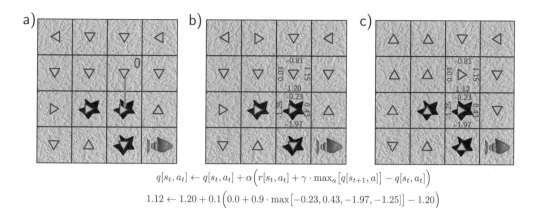

$$q[s_t, a_t] \leftarrow q[s_t, a_t] + \alpha\Big(r[s_t, a_t] + \gamma \cdot \max_a[q[s_{t+1}, a]] - q[s_t, a_t]\Big)$$

$$1.12 \leftarrow 1.20 + 0.1\Big(0.0 + 0.9 \cdot \max[-0.23, 0.43, -1.97, -1.25]] - 1.20\Big)$$

Figure 19.12 Q-learning. a) The agent starts in state s_t and takes action $a_t = 2$ according to the policy. It does not slip on the ice and moves downward, receiving reward $r[s_t, a_t] = 0$ for leaving the original state. b) The maximum action value at the new state is found (here 0.43). c) The action value for action 2 in the original state is updated to 1.12 based on the current estimate of the maximum action value at the subsequent state, the reward, discount factor $\gamma = 0.9$, and learning rate $\alpha = 0.1$. This changes the highest action value at the original state, so the policy changes.

19.4 Fitted Q-learning

The tabular Monte Carlo and TD algorithms described above repeatedly traverse the entire MDP and update the action values. However, this is only practical if the state-action space is small. Unfortunately, this is rarely the case; even for the constrained environment of a chessboard, there are more than 10^{40} possible legal states.

In *fitted Q-learning*, the discrete representation $q[s_t, a_t]$ of the action values is replaced by a machine learning model $q[\mathbf{s}_t, a_t, \boldsymbol{\phi}]$, where now the state is represented by a vector $\mathbf{s}_t$ rather than just an index. We then define a least squares loss based on the consistency of adjacent action values (similarly to in Q-learning, see equation 19.15):

$$L[\boldsymbol{\phi}] = \left(r[\mathbf{s}_t, a_t] + \gamma \cdot \max_a\Big[q[\mathbf{s}_{t+1}, a, \boldsymbol{\phi}]\Big] - q[\mathbf{s}_t, a_t, \boldsymbol{\phi}]\right)^2, \tag{19.16}$$

which in turn leads to the update:

$$\boldsymbol{\phi} \leftarrow \boldsymbol{\phi} + \alpha\left(r[\mathbf{s}_t, a_t] + \gamma \cdot \max_a\Big[q[\mathbf{s}_{t+1}, a, \boldsymbol{\phi}]\Big] - q[\mathbf{s}_t, a_t, \boldsymbol{\phi}]\right)\frac{\partial q[\mathbf{s}_t, a_t, \boldsymbol{\phi}]}{\partial \boldsymbol{\phi}}. \tag{19.17}$$

Fitted Q-learning differs from Q-Learning in that convergence is no longer guaranteed. A change to the parameters potentially modifies both the target $r[\mathbf{s}_t, a_t] + \gamma \cdot \max_{a_{t+1}}[q[\mathbf{s}_{t+1}, a_{t+1}, \boldsymbol{\phi}]]$ (the maximum value may change) and the prediction $q[\mathbf{s}_t, a_t, \boldsymbol{\phi}]$. This can be shown both theoretically and empirically to damage convergence.

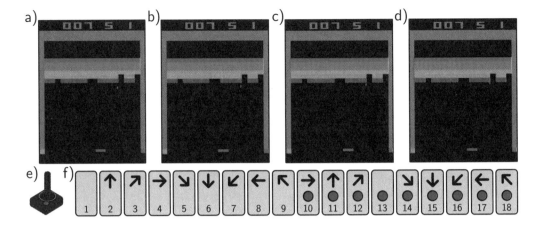

Figure 19.13 Atari Benchmark. The Atari benchmark consists of 49 Atari 2600 games, including Breakout (pictured), Pong, and various shoot-em-up, platform, and other types of games. a-d) Even for games with a single screen, the state is not fully observable from a single frame because the velocity of the objects is unknown. Consequently, it is usual to use several adjacent frames (here, four) to represent the state. e) The action simulates the user input via a joystick. f) There are eighteen actions corresponding to eight directions of movement or no movement, and for each of these nine cases, the button being pressed or not.

19.4.1   Deep Q-networks for playing ATARI games

Deep networks are ideally suited to making predictions from a high-dimensional state space, so they are a natural choice for the model in fitted Q-learning. In principle, they could take both state and action as input and predict the values, but in practice, the network takes only the state and simultaneously predicts the values for each action.

The *Deep Q-Network* was a breakthrough reinforcement learning architecture that exploited deep networks to learn to play ATARI 2600 games. The observed data comprises $220{\times}160$ images with 128 possible colors at each pixel (figure 19.13). This was reshaped to size $84{\times}84$, and only the brightness value was retained. Unfortunately, the full state is not observable from a single frame. For example, the velocity of game objects is unknown. To help resolve this problem, the network ingests the last four frames at each time step to form $\mathbf{s}_t$. It maps these frames through three convolutional layers followed by a fully connected layer to predict the value of every action (figure 19.14).

Several modifications were made to the standard training procedure. First, the rewards (which were driven by the score in the game) were clipped to -1 for a negative change and $+1$ for a positive change. This compensates for the wide variation in scores between different games and allows the same learning rate to be used. Second, the system exploited *experience replay*. Rather than update the network based on the tuple $<\mathbf{s}_t, a_t, r_{t+1}, \mathbf{s}_{t+1}>$ at the current step or with a batch of the last I tuples, all recent

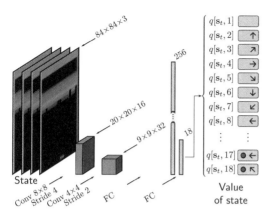

Figure 19.14 Deep Q-network architecture. The input $\mathbf{s}_t$ consists of four adjacent frames of the ATARI game. Each is resized to 84×84 and converted to grayscale. These frames are represented as four channels and processed by an 8×8 convolution with stride four, followed by a 4×4 convolution with stride 2, followed by two fully connected layers. The final output predicts the action value $q[\mathbf{s}_t, a_t]$ for each of the 18 actions in this state.

tuples were stored in a buffer. This buffer was sampled randomly to generate a batch at each step. This approach reuses data samples many times and reduces correlations between the samples in the batch that arise due to the similarity of adjacent frames.

Finally, the issue of convergence in fitted Q-Networks was tackled by fixing the target parameters to values ϕ^- and only updating them periodically. This gives the update:

$$\phi \leftarrow \phi + \alpha \left(r[\mathbf{s}_t, a_t] + \gamma \cdot \max_a \left[q[\mathbf{s}_{t+1}, a, \phi^-] \right] - q[\mathbf{s}_t, a_t, \phi] \right) \frac{\partial q[\mathbf{s}_t, a_t, \phi]}{\partial \phi}. \tag{19.18}$$

Now the network no longer chases a moving target and is less prone to oscillation.

Using these and other heuristics and with an ϵ-greedy policy, Deep Q-Networks performed at a level comparable to a professional game tester across a set of 49 games using the same network (trained separately for each game). It should be noted that the training process was data-intensive. It took around 38 full days of experience to learn each game. In some games, the algorithm exceeded human performance. On other games like "Montezuma's Revenge," it barely made any progress. This game features sparse rewards and multiple screens with quite different appearances.

19.4.2 Double Q-learning and double deep Q-networks

One potential flaw of Q-Learning is that the maximization over the actions in the update:

$$q[s_t, a_t] \leftarrow q[s_t, a_t] + \alpha \left(r[s_t, a_t] + \gamma \cdot \max_a \left[q[s_{t+1}, a] \right] - q[s_t, a_t] \right) \tag{19.19}$$

leads to a systematic bias in the estimated state values $q[s_t, a_t]$. Consider two actions that provide the same average reward, but one is stochastic and the other deterministic. The stochastic reward will exceed the average roughly half of the time and be chosen by the maximum operation, causing the corresponding action value $q[s_t, a_t]$ to be overestimated. A similar argument can be made about random inaccuracies in the output of the network $q[\mathbf{s}_t, a_t, \phi]$ or random initializations of the q-function.

The underlying problem is that the same network both selects the target (by the maximization operation) and updates the value. Double Q-Learning tackles this problem by training two models $q_1[s_t, a_t, \pi_1]$ and $q_2[s_t, a_t, \pi_2]$ simultaneously:

$$
\begin{aligned}
q_1[s_t, a_t] &\leftarrow q_1[s_t, a_t] + \alpha\left(r[s_t, a_t] + \gamma \cdot q_2\left[s_{t+1}, \underset{a}{\operatorname{argmax}}\left[q_1[s_{t+1}, a]\right]\right] - q_1[s_t, a_t]\right) \\
q_2[s_t, a_t] &\leftarrow q_2[s_t, a_t] + \alpha\left(r[s_t, a_t] + \gamma \cdot q_1\left[s_{t+1}, \underset{a}{\operatorname{argmax}}\left[q_2[s_{t+1}, a]\right]\right] - q_2[s_t, a_t]\right).
\end{aligned}
\tag{19.20}
$$

Now the choice of the target and the target itself are decoupled, which helps prevent these biases. In practice, new tuples $<s, a, r, s'>$ are randomly assigned to update one model or another. This is known as *double Q-learning*. *Double deep Q-networks* or *double DQNs* use deep networks $q[\mathbf{s}_t, a_t, \phi_1]$ and $q[\mathbf{s}_t, a_t, \phi_2]$ to estimate the action values, and the update becomes:

$$
\begin{aligned}
\phi_1 &\leftarrow \phi_1 + \alpha\left(r[\mathbf{s}_t, a_t] + \gamma \cdot q\left[\mathbf{s}_{t+1}, \underset{a}{\operatorname{argmax}}\left[q[\mathbf{s}_{t+1}, a, \phi_1]\right], \phi_2\right] - q[\mathbf{s}_t, a_t, \phi_1]\right)\frac{\partial q[\mathbf{s}_t, a_t, \phi_1]}{\partial \phi_1} \\
\phi_2 &\leftarrow \phi_2 + \alpha\left(r[\mathbf{s}_t, a_t] + \gamma \cdot q\left[\mathbf{s}_{t+1}, \underset{a}{\operatorname{argmax}}\left[q[\mathbf{s}_{t+1}, a, \phi_2]\right], \phi_1\right] - q[\mathbf{s}_t, a_t, \phi_2]\right)\frac{\partial q[\mathbf{s}_t, a_t, \phi_2]}{\partial \phi_2}.
\end{aligned}
\tag{19.21}
$$

19.5 Policy gradient methods

Q-learning estimates the action values first and then uses these to update the policy. Conversely, *policy-based methods* directly learn a stochastic policy $\pi[a_t|\mathbf{s}_t, \boldsymbol{\theta}]$. This is a function with trainable parameters $\boldsymbol{\theta}$ that maps a state $\mathbf{s}_t$ to a distribution $Pr(a_t|\mathbf{s}_t)$ over actions a_t from which we can sample. In MDPs, there is always an optimal deterministic policy. However, there are three reasons to use a stochastic policy:

1. A stochastic policy naturally helps with exploration of the space; we are not obliged to take the best action at each time step.

2. The loss changes smoothly as we modify a stochastic policy. This means we can use gradient descent methods even though the rewards are discrete. This is similar to using maximum likelihood in (discrete) classification problems. The loss changes smoothly as the model parameters change to make the true class more likely.

3. The MDP assumption is often incorrect; we usually don't have complete knowledge of the state. For example, consider an agent navigating in an environment where it can only observe nearby locations (e.g., figure 19.4). If two locations look identical, but the nearby reward structure is different, a stochastic policy allows the possibility of taking different actions until this ambiguity is resolved.

9.5.1 Derivation of gradient update

Consider a trajectory $\boldsymbol{\tau} = [\mathbf{s}_1, a_1, \mathbf{s}_2, a_2, \ldots, \mathbf{s}_T, a_T]$ through an MDP. The probability of this trajectory $Pr(\boldsymbol{\tau}|\boldsymbol{\theta})$ depends on both the state evolution function $Pr(\mathbf{s}_{t+1}|\mathbf{s}_t, a_t)$ and the current stochastic policy $\pi[a_t|\mathbf{s}_t, \boldsymbol{\theta}]$:

$$Pr(\boldsymbol{\tau}|\boldsymbol{\theta}) = Pr(\mathbf{s}_1) \prod_{t=1}^{T} \pi[a_t|\mathbf{s}_t, \boldsymbol{\theta}] Pr(\mathbf{s}_{t+1}|\mathbf{s}_t, a_t). \tag{19.22}$$

Policy gradient algorithms aim to maximize the expected return $r[\boldsymbol{\tau}]$ over many such trajectories:

$$\boldsymbol{\theta} = \underset{\boldsymbol{\theta}}{\operatorname{argmax}}\left[\mathbb{E}_{\boldsymbol{\tau}}\left[r[\boldsymbol{\tau}]\right]\right] = \underset{\boldsymbol{\theta}}{\operatorname{argmax}}\left[\int Pr(\boldsymbol{\tau}|\boldsymbol{\theta})r[\boldsymbol{\tau}]d\boldsymbol{\tau}\right], \tag{19.23}$$

where the return is the sum of all the rewards received along the trajectory.

To maximize this quantity, we use the gradient ascent update:

$$\begin{aligned} \boldsymbol{\theta} &\leftarrow \boldsymbol{\theta} + \alpha \cdot \frac{\partial}{\partial \boldsymbol{\theta}} \int Pr(\boldsymbol{\tau}|\boldsymbol{\theta})r[\boldsymbol{\tau}]d\boldsymbol{\tau} \\ &= \boldsymbol{\theta} + \alpha \cdot \int \frac{\partial Pr(\boldsymbol{\tau}|\boldsymbol{\theta})}{\partial \boldsymbol{\theta}} r[\boldsymbol{\tau}]d\boldsymbol{\tau}. \end{aligned} \tag{19.24}$$

where α is the learning rate.

We want to approximate this integral with a sum over empirically observed trajectories. These are drawn from the distribution $Pr(\boldsymbol{\tau}|\boldsymbol{\theta})$, so to make progress, we multiply and divide the integrand by this distribution:

$$\begin{aligned} \boldsymbol{\theta} &\leftarrow \boldsymbol{\theta} + \alpha \cdot \int \frac{\partial Pr(\boldsymbol{\tau}|\boldsymbol{\theta})}{\partial \boldsymbol{\theta}} r[\boldsymbol{\tau}]d\boldsymbol{\tau} \\ &= \boldsymbol{\theta} + \alpha \cdot \int Pr(\boldsymbol{\tau}|\boldsymbol{\theta})\frac{1}{Pr(\boldsymbol{\tau}|\boldsymbol{\theta})}\frac{\partial Pr(\boldsymbol{\tau}|\boldsymbol{\theta})}{\partial \boldsymbol{\theta}} r[\boldsymbol{\tau}]d\boldsymbol{\tau} \\ &\approx \boldsymbol{\theta} + \alpha \cdot \frac{1}{I}\sum_{i=1}^{I}\frac{1}{Pr(\boldsymbol{\tau}_i|\boldsymbol{\theta})}\frac{\partial Pr(\boldsymbol{\tau}_i|\boldsymbol{\theta})}{\partial \boldsymbol{\theta}} r[\boldsymbol{\tau}_i]. \end{aligned} \tag{19.25}$$

This equation has a simple interpretation (figure 19.15); the update changes the parameters $\boldsymbol{\theta}$ to increase the likelihood $Pr(\boldsymbol{\tau}_i|\boldsymbol{\theta})$ of an observed trajectory $\boldsymbol{\tau}_i$ in proportion to the reward $r[\boldsymbol{\tau}_i]$ from that trajectory. However, it also normalizes by the probability of observing that trajectory in the first place to compensate for the fact that some trajectories are observed more often than others. If a trajectory is already common and yields high rewards, then we don't need to change much. The biggest updates will come from trajectories that are uncommon but create large rewards.

We can simplify this expression using the *likelihood ratio identity:*

Figure 19.15 Policy gradients. Five episodes for the same policy (brighter indicates higher reward). Trajectories 1, 2, and 3 generate consistently high rewards, but similar trajectories already frequently occur with this policy, so there is no need to change. Conversely, trajectory 4 receives low rewards, so the policy should be modified to avoid producing similar trajectories. Trajectory 5 receives high rewards *and* is unusual. This will cause the largest change to the policy under equation 19.25.

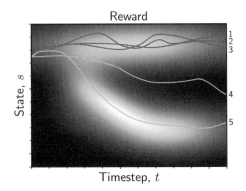

$$\frac{\partial \log[f[z]]}{\partial z} = \frac{1}{f[z]} \frac{\partial f[z]}{\partial z}, \tag{19.26}$$

which yields the update:

$$\boldsymbol{\theta} \leftarrow \boldsymbol{\theta} + \alpha \cdot \frac{1}{I} \sum_{i=1}^{I} \frac{\partial \log\big[Pr(\boldsymbol{\tau}_i|\boldsymbol{\theta})\big]}{\partial \boldsymbol{\theta}} r[\boldsymbol{\tau}_i]. \tag{19.27}$$

The log probability $\log[Pr(\boldsymbol{\tau}|\boldsymbol{\theta})]$ of a trajectory is given by:

$$
\begin{aligned}
\log[Pr(\boldsymbol{\tau}|\boldsymbol{\theta})] &= \log\Big[Pr(\mathbf{s}_1)\prod_{t=1}^{T}\pi[a_t|\mathbf{s}_t,\boldsymbol{\theta}]Pr(\mathbf{s}_{t+1}|\mathbf{s}_t,a_t)\Big] \tag{19.28}\\
&= \log\big[Pr(\mathbf{s}_1)\big] + \sum_{t=1}^{T}\log\big[\pi[a_t|\mathbf{s}_t,\boldsymbol{\theta}]\big] + \sum_{t=1}^{T}\log\big[Pr(\mathbf{s}_{t+1}|\mathbf{s}_t,a_t)\big],
\end{aligned}
$$

and noting that only the center term depends on $\boldsymbol{\theta}$, we can rewrite the update from equation 19.27 as:

$$\boldsymbol{\theta} \leftarrow \boldsymbol{\theta} + \alpha \cdot \frac{1}{I} \sum_{i=1}^{I}\sum_{t=1}^{T} \frac{\partial \log\big[\pi[a_{it}|\mathbf{s}_{it},\boldsymbol{\theta}]\big]}{\partial \boldsymbol{\theta}} r[\boldsymbol{\tau}_i], \tag{19.29}$$

where $\mathbf{s}_{it}$ is the state at time t in episode i, and a_{it} is the action taken at time t in episode i. Note that since the terms relating to the state evolution $Pr(\mathbf{s}_{t+1}|\mathbf{s}_t,a_t)$ disappear, this parameter update does not assume a Markov time evolution process.

We can further simplify this by noting that:

$$r[\boldsymbol{\tau}_i] = \sum_{t=1}^{T} r_{it} = \sum_{k=1}^{t-1} r_{ik} + \sum_{k=t}^{T} r_{ik}, \tag{19.30}$$

where r_{it} is the reward at time t in the ith episode. The first term (the rewards before time t) does not affect the update from time t, so we can write:

$$\boldsymbol{\theta} \;\leftarrow\; \boldsymbol{\theta} + \alpha \cdot \frac{1}{I} \sum_{i=1}^{I} \sum_{t=1}^{T} \frac{\partial \log\big[\pi[a_{it}|\mathbf{s}_{it}, \boldsymbol{\theta}]\big]}{\partial \boldsymbol{\theta}} \sum_{k=t}^{T} r_{ik}. \tag{19.31}$$

19.5.2 REINFORCE algorithm

REINFORCE is an early policy gradient algorithm that exploits this result and incorporates discounting. It is a Monte Carlo method that generates episodes $\boldsymbol{\tau}_i = [\mathbf{s}_{i1}, a_{i1}, r_{i2}, \mathbf{s}_{i2}, a_{i2}, r_{i3}, \ldots, r_{iT}]$ based on the current policy $\pi[a|\mathbf{s}, \boldsymbol{\theta}]$. For discrete actions, this policy could be determined by a neural network $\pi[\mathbf{s}|\boldsymbol{\theta}]$, which takes the current state $\mathbf{s}$ and returns one output for each possible action. These outputs are passed through a softmax function to create a distribution over actions, which is sampled at each time step.

For each episode i, we loop through each step t and calculate the empirical discounted return for the partial trajectory $\boldsymbol{\tau}_{it}$ that starts at time t:

$$r[\boldsymbol{\tau}_{it}] = \sum_{k=t+1}^{T} \gamma^{k-t-1} r_{ik}, \tag{19.32}$$

and then we update the parameters for each time step t in each trajectory:

$$\boldsymbol{\theta} \leftarrow \boldsymbol{\theta} + \alpha \cdot \gamma^{t} \frac{\partial \log\big[\pi_{a_{it}}[\mathbf{s}_{it}, \boldsymbol{\theta}]\big]}{\partial \boldsymbol{\theta}} r[\boldsymbol{\tau}_{it}] \qquad\qquad \forall\, i, t, \tag{19.33}$$

where $\pi_{a_t}[\mathbf{s}_t, \boldsymbol{\theta}]$ is the probability of a_t produced by the neural network given the current state $\mathbf{s}_t$ and parameters $\boldsymbol{\theta}$, and α is the learning rate. The extra term γ^t ensures that the rewards are discounted relative to the start of the sequence because we maximize the log probability of returns in the whole sequence (equation 19.23).

19.5.3 Baselines

Policy gradient methods have the drawback that they exhibit high variance; many episodes may be needed to get stable updates of the derivatives. One way to reduce this variance is to subtract the trajectory returns $r[\boldsymbol{\tau}]$ from a baseline b:

$$\boldsymbol{\theta} \leftarrow \boldsymbol{\theta} + \alpha \cdot \frac{1}{I} \sum_{i=1}^{I} \sum_{t=1}^{T} \frac{\partial \log\big[\pi_{a_{it}}[\mathbf{s}_{it}, \boldsymbol{\theta}]\big]}{\partial \boldsymbol{\theta}} \big(r[\boldsymbol{\tau}_{it}] - b\big). \tag{19.34}$$

As long as the baseline b doesn't depend on the actions:

Problem 19.6

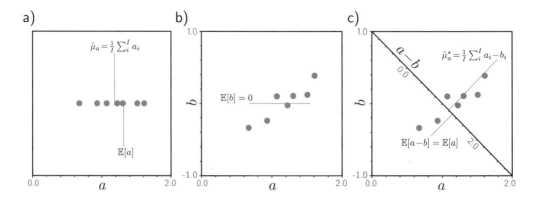

Figure 19.16 Decreasing variance of estimates using control variates. a) Consider trying to estimate $\mathbb{E}[a]$ from a small number of samples. The estimate (the mean of the samples) will vary based on the number of samples and the variance of those samples. b) Now consider observing another variable b that co-varies with a and has $\mathbb{E}[b] = 0$ and the same variance as a. c) The variance of the samples of $a - b$ is much less than that of a, but the expected value $\mathbb{E}[a - b] = \mathbb{E}[a]$, so we get an estimator with lower variance.

$$\mathbb{E}_{\boldsymbol{\tau}}\left[\sum_{t=1}^{T} \frac{\partial \log\left[\pi_{a_{it}}[\mathbf{s}_{it}, \boldsymbol{\theta}]\right]}{\partial \boldsymbol{\theta}} \cdot b\right] = 0, \qquad (19.35)$$

Notebook 19.5
Control variates

Problem 19.7

and the expected value will not change. However, if the baseline co-varies with irrelevant factors that add uncertainty, then subtracting it reduces the variance (figure 19.16). This is a special case of the method of *control variates* (see problem 19.7).

Problem 19.8

This raises the question of how we should choose b. We can find the value of b that minimizes the variance by writing an expression for the variance, taking the derivative with respect to b, setting the result to zero, and solving to yield:

$$b = \sum_{i} \frac{\sum_{t=1}^{T} \left(\partial \log\left[\pi_{a_{it}}[\mathbf{s}_{it}, \boldsymbol{\theta}]\right]/\partial \boldsymbol{\theta}\right)^2 r[\boldsymbol{\tau}_{it}]}{\sum_{t=1}^{T} \left(\partial \log\left[\pi_{a_{it}}[\mathbf{s}_{it}, \boldsymbol{\theta}]\right]/\partial \boldsymbol{\theta}\right)^2}. \qquad (19.36)$$

In practice, this is often approximated as:

$$b = \frac{1}{I} \sum_{i} r[\boldsymbol{\tau}_i]. \qquad (19.37)$$

Subtracting this baseline factors out variance that might occur when the returns $r[\boldsymbol{\tau}_i]$ from all trajectories are greater than is typical but only because they happen to pass through states with higher than average returns *whatever* actions are taken.

19.5.4 State-dependent baselines

A better option is to use a baseline $b[\mathbf{s}_{it}]$ that depends on the current state $\mathbf{s}_{it}$.

$$\boldsymbol{\theta} \leftarrow \boldsymbol{\theta} + \alpha \cdot \frac{1}{I} \sum_{i=1}^{I} \sum_{t=1}^{T} \frac{\partial \log\left[\pi_{a_{it}}[\mathbf{s}_{it}, \boldsymbol{\theta}]\right]}{\partial \boldsymbol{\theta}} \left(r[\boldsymbol{\tau}_{it}] - b[\mathbf{s}_{it}] \right). \tag{19.38}$$

Here, we are compensating for variance introduced by some states having greater overall returns than others, whichever actions we take.

A sensible choice is the expected future reward based on the current state, which is just the state value $v[\mathbf{s}]$. In this case, the difference between the empirically observed rewards and the baseline is known as the *advantage estimate*. Since we are in a Monte Carlo context, this can be parameterized by a neural network $b[\mathbf{s}] = v[\mathbf{s}, \boldsymbol{\phi}]$ with parameters $\boldsymbol{\phi}$, which we can fit to the observed returns using least squares loss:

$$L[\boldsymbol{\phi}] = \sum_{i=1}^{I} \sum_{t=1}^{T} \left(v[\mathbf{s}_{it}, \boldsymbol{\phi}] - \sum_{j=y}^{T} r_{ij} \right)^2. \tag{19.39}$$

19.6 Actor-critic methods

Actor-critic algorithms are temporal difference (TD) policy gradient algorithms. They can update the parameters of the policy network at each step. This contrasts with the Monte Carlo REINFORCE algorithm, which *must* wait for one or more episodes to complete before updating the parameters.

In the TD approach, we do not have access to the future rewards $r[\boldsymbol{\tau}_t] = \sum_{k=t}^{T} r_k$ along this trajectory. Actor-critic algorithms approximate the sum over all the future rewards with the observed current reward plus the discounted value of the next state:

$$r[\boldsymbol{\tau}_{it}] \approx r_{it} + \gamma \cdot v[\mathbf{s}_{i,t+1}, \boldsymbol{\phi}]. \tag{19.40}$$

Here the value $v[\mathbf{s}_{i,t+1}, \boldsymbol{\phi}]$ is estimated by a second neural network with parameters $\boldsymbol{\phi}$.

Substituting this into equation 19.38 gives the update:

$$\boldsymbol{\theta} \leftarrow \boldsymbol{\theta} + \alpha \cdot \frac{1}{I} \sum_{i=1}^{I} \sum_{t=1}^{T} \frac{\partial \log\left[Pr(a_{it}|\mathbf{s}_{it}, \boldsymbol{\theta})\right]}{\partial \boldsymbol{\theta}} \left(r_{it} + \gamma \cdot v[\mathbf{s}_{i,t+1}, \boldsymbol{\phi}] - v[\mathbf{s}_{i,t}, \boldsymbol{\phi}] \right). \tag{19.41}$$

Concurrently, we update the parameters $\boldsymbol{\phi}$ by bootstrapping using the loss function:

$$L[\boldsymbol{\phi}] = \sum_{i=1}^{I} \sum_{t=1}^{T} \left(r_{it} + \gamma \cdot v[\mathbf{s}_{i,t+1}, \boldsymbol{\phi}] - v[\mathbf{s}_{i,t}, \boldsymbol{\phi}] \right)^2. \tag{19.42}$$

The policy network $\pi[\mathbf{s}_t, \boldsymbol{\theta}]$ that predicts $Pr(a|\mathbf{s}_t)$ is termed the *actor*. The value network $v[\mathbf{s}_t, \boldsymbol{\phi}]$ is termed the *critic*. Often the same network represents both actor and

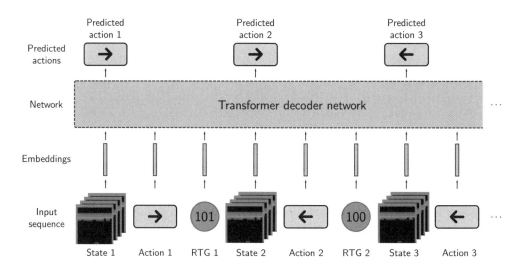

Figure 19.17 Decision transformer. The decision transformer treats offline reinforcement learning as a sequence prediction task. The input is a sequence of states, actions, and returns-to-go (remaining rewards in the episode), each of which is mapped to a fixed-size embedding. At each time step, the network predicts the next action. During testing, the returns-to-go are unknown; in practice, an initial estimate is made from which subsequent observed rewards are subtracted.

the critic, with two sets of outputs that predict the policy and the values, respectively. Note that although actor-critic methods can update the policy parameters at each step, this is rarely done in practice. The agent typically collects a batch of experience over many time steps before the policy is updated.

19.7 Offline reinforcement learning

Interaction with the environment is at the core of reinforcement learning. However, there are some scenarios where it is not practical to send a naïve agent into an environment to explore the effect of different actions. This may be because erratic behavior in the environment is dangerous (e.g., driving autonomous vehicles) or because data collection is time-consuming or expensive (e.g., making financial trades).

However, it *is* possible to gather historical data from human agents in both cases. *Offline RL* or *batch RL* aims to learn how to take actions that maximize rewards on future episodes by observing past sequences $\mathbf{s}_1, a_1, r_2, \mathbf{s}_2, a_2, r_3, \ldots$, without ever interacting with the environment. It is distinct from *imitation learning*, a related technique that (i) does not have access to the rewards and (ii) attempts to replicate the performance of a historical agent rather than improve it.

Although there are offline RL methods based on Q-Learning and policy gradients, this paradigm opens up new possibilities. In particular, we can treat this as a sequence learning problem, in which the goal is to predict the next action, given the history of states, rewards, and actions. The *decision transformer* exploits a transformer decoder framework (section 12.7) to make these predictions (figure 19.17).

However, the goal is to predict actions based on *future rewards*, and these are not captured in a standard $\mathbf{s}, a, r$ sequence. Hence, the decision transformer replaces the reward r_t with the *returns-to-go* $R_{t:T} = \sum_{t'=t}^{T} r_{t'}$ (i.e., the sum of the empirically observed future rewards). The remaining framework is very similar to a standard transformer decoder. The states, actions, and returns-to-go are converted to fixed-size embeddings via learned mappings. For Atari games, the state embedding might be converted via a convolutional network similar to that in figure 19.14. The embeddings for the actions and returns-to-go can be learned in the same way as word embeddings (figure 12.9). The transformer is trained with masked self-attention and position embeddings.

This formulation is natural during training but poses a quandary during inference because we don't know the returns-to-go. This can be resolved by using the desired total return at the first step and decrementing this as rewards are received. For example, in an Atari game, the desired total return would be the total score required to win.

Decision transformers can also be fine-tuned from online experience and hence learn over time. They have the advantage of dispensing with most of the reinforcement learning machinery and its associated instability and replacing this with standard supervised learning. Transformers can learn from enormous quantities of data and integrate information across large time contexts (making the temporal credit assignment problem more tractable). This represents an intriguing new direction for reinforcement learning.

19.8 Summary

Reinforcement learning is a sequential decision-making framework for Markov decision processes and similar systems. This chapter reviewed tabular approaches to RL, including dynamic programming (in which the environment model is known), Monte Carlo methods (in which multiple episodes are run and the action values and policy subsequently changed based on the rewards received), and temporal difference methods (in which these values are updated while the episode is ongoing).

Deep Q-Learning is a temporal difference method where deep neural networks are used to predict the action value for every state. It can train agents to perform Atari 2600 games at a level similar to humans. Policy gradient methods directly optimize the policy rather than assigning values to actions. They produce stochastic policies, which are important when the environment is partially observable. The updates are noisy, and many refinements have been introduced to reduce their variance.

Offline reinforcement learning is used when we cannot interact with the environment but must learn from historical data. The decision transformer leverages recent progress in deep learning to build a model of the state-action-reward sequence and predict the actions that will maximize the rewards.

Notes

Sutton & Barto (2018) cover tabular reinforcement learning methods in depth. Li (2017), Arulkumaran et al. (2017), François-Lavet et al. (2018), and Wang et al. (2022c) all provide overviews of deep reinforcement learning. Graesser & Keng (2019) is an excellent introductory resource that includes Python code.

Landmarks in deep reinforcement learning: Most landmark achievements of reinforcement learning have been in either video games or real-world games since these provide constrained environments with limited actions and fixed rules. Deep Q-Learning (Mnih et al., 2015) achieved human-level performance across a benchmark of ATARI games. AlphaGo (Silver et al., 2016) beat the world champion at Go. This game was previously considered very difficult for computers to play. Berner et al. (2019) built a system that beat the world champion team in the five vs. five-player game *Defense of the Ancients 2*, which requires cooperation across players. Ye et al. (2021) built a system that could beat humans on Atari games with limited data (in contrast to previous systems, which need much more experience than humans). More recently, the Cicero system demonstrated human-level performance in the game *Diplomacy* which requires natural language negotiations and coordination between players (FAIR, 2022).

RL has also been applied successfully to combinatorial optimization problems (see Mazyavkina et al., 2021). For example, Kool et al. (2019) learned a model that performed similarly to the best heuristics for the traveling salesman problem. Recently, AlphaTensor (Fawzi et al., 2022) treated matrix multiplication as a game and learned faster ways to multiply matrices using fewer multiplication operations. Since deep learning relies heavily on matrix multiplication, this is one of the first examples of self-improvement in AI.

Classical reinforcement learning methods: Very early contributions to the theory of MDPs were made by Thompson (1933) and Thompson (1935). The Bellman recursions were introduced by Bellman (1966). Howard (1960) introduced policy iteration. Sutton & Barto (2018) identify the work of Andreae (1969) as being the first to describe RL using the MDP formalism.

The modern era of reinforcement learning arguably originated in the Ph.D. theses of Sutton (1984) and Watkins (1989). Sutton (1988) introduced the term temporal difference learning. Watkins (1989) and Watkins & Dayan (1992) introduced Q-Learning and showed that it converges to a fixed point by Banach's theorem because the Bellman operator is a contraction mapping. Watkins (1989) made the first explicit connection between dynamic programming and reinforcement learning. SARSA was developed by Rummery & Niranjan (1994). Gordon (1995) introduced *fitted Q-learning* in which a machine learning model is used to predict the action value for each state-action pair. Riedmiller (2005) introduced *neural-fitted Q-learning*, which used a neural network to predict all the action values at once from a state. Early work on Monte Carlo methods was carried out by Singh & Sutton (1996), and the exploring starts algorithm was introduced by Sutton & Barto (1999). Note that this is an extremely cursory summary of more than fifty years of work. A much more thorough treatment can be found in Sutton & Barto (2018).

Deep Q-Networks: Deep Q-Learning was devised by Mnih et al. (2015) and is an intellectual descendent of neural-fitted Q-learning. It exploited the then-recent successes of convolutional networks to develop a fitted Q-Learning method that could achieve human-level performance on a benchmark of ATARI games. Deep Q-Learning suffers from the *deadly triad issue* (Sutton & Barto, 2018): training can be unstable in any scheme that incorporates (i) bootstrapping, (ii) off-policy learning, and (iii) function approximation. Much subsequent work has aimed to make training more stable. Mnih et al. (2015) introduced the experience replay buffer (Lin, 1992), which was subsequently improved by Schaul et al. (2016) to favor more important tuples and hence increase learning speed. This is termed *prioritized experience replay*.

The original Q-Learning paper concatenated four frames so the network could observe the velocities of objects and make the underlying process closer to fully observable. Hausknecht & Stone (2015) introduced *deep recurrent Q-learning*, which used a recurrent network architecture that only ingested a single frame at a time because it could "remember" the previous states. Van Hasselt (2010) identified the systematic overestimation of the state values due to the max operation and proposed double Q-Learning in which two models are trained simultaneously to remedy this. This was subsequently applied in the context of deep Q-learning (Van Hasselt et al., 2016), although its efficacy has since been questioned (Hessel et al., 2018). Wang et al. (2016) introduced *deep dueling networks* in which two heads of the same network predict (i) the state value and (ii) the *advantage* (relative value) of each action. The intuition here is that sometimes it is the state value that is important, and it doesn't matter much which action is taken, and decoupling these estimates improves stability.

Fortunato et al. (2018) introduced *noisy deep Q-Networks*, in which some weights in the Q-Network are multiplied by noise to add stochasticity to the predictions and encourage exploration. The network can learn to decrease the magnitudes of the noise over time as it converges to a sensible policy. Distributional DQN (Bellemare et al., 2017a; Dabney et al., 2018 following Morimura et al., 2010) aims to estimate more complete information about the distribution of returns than just the expectation. This potentially allows the network to mitigate against worst-case outcomes and can also improve performance, as predicting higher moments provides a richer training signal. *Rainbow* (Hessel et al., 2018) combined six improvements to the original deep Q-learning algorithm, including dueling networks, distributional DQN, and noisy DQN, to improve both the training speed and the final performance on the ATARI benchmark.

Policy gradients: Williams (1992) introduced the REINFORCE algorithm. The term "policy gradient method" dates to Sutton et al. (1999). Konda & Tsitsiklis (1999) introduced the actor-critic algorithm. Decreasing the variance by using different baselines is discussed in Greensmith et al. (2004) and Peters & Schaal (2008). It has since been argued that the value baseline primarily reduces the aggressiveness of the updates rather than their variance (Mei et al., 2022).

Policy gradients have been adapted to produce deterministic policies (Silver et al., 2014; Lillicrap et al., 2016; Fujimoto et al., 2018). The most direct approach is to maximize over the possible actions, but if the action space is continuous, this requires an optimization procedure at each step. The *deep deterministic policy gradient* algorithm (Lillicrap et al., 2016) moves the policy in the direction of the gradient of the action value (implying the use of an actor-critic method).

Modern policy gradients: We introduced policy gradients in terms of the parameter update. However, they can also be viewed as optimizing a surrogate loss based on importance sampling of the expected rewards, using trajectories from the current policy parameters. This view allows us to take multiple optimization steps validly. However, this can cause very large policy updates. Overstepping is a minor problem in supervised learning, as the trajectory can be corrected later. However, in RL, it affects future data collection and can be extremely destructive.

Several methods have been proposed to moderate these updates. *Natural policy gradients* (Kakade, 2001) are based on natural gradients (Amari, 1998), which modify the descent direction by the Fisher information matrix. This provides a better update which is less likely to get stuck in local plateaus. However, the Fisher matrix is impractical to compute in models with many parameters. In *trust-region policy optimization* or *TRPO* (Schulman et al., 2015), the surrogate objective is maximized subject to a constraint on the KL divergence between the old and new policies. Schulman et al. (2017) propose a simpler formulation in which this KL divergence appears as a regularization term. The regularization weight is adapted based on the distance between the KL divergence and a target indicating how much we want the policy to change. *Proximal policy optimization* or *PPO* (Schulman et al., 2017) is an even simpler approach in which the loss is clipped to ensure smaller updates.

Actor-critic: In the actor-critic algorithm (Konda & Tsitsiklis, 1999) described in section 19.6, the critic used a 1-step estimator. It's also possible to use k-step estimators (in which we observe k discounted rewards and approximate subsequent rewards with an estimate of the state value). As k increases, the variance of the estimate increases, but the bias decreases. *Generalized advantage estimation* (Schulman et al., 2016) weights together estimates from many steps and parameterizes the weighting by a single term that trades off the bias and the variance. Mnih et al. (2016) introduced *asynchronous actor-critic* or *A3C* in which multiple agents are run independently in parallel environments and update the same parameters. Both the policy and value function are updated every T time steps using a mix of k-step returns. Wang et al. (2017) introduced several methods designed to make asynchronous actor-critic more efficient. *Soft actor-critic* (Haarnoja et al., 2018b) adds an entropy term to the cost function, which encourages exploration and reduces overfitting as the policy is encouraged to be less confident.

Offline RL: In offline reinforcement learning, the policy is learned by observing the behavior of other agents, including the rewards they receive, *without* the ability to change the policy. It is related to imitation learning, where the goal is to copy the behavior of another agent without access to rewards (see Hussein et al., 2017). One approach is to treat offline RL in the same way as off-policy reinforcement learning. However, in practice, the distributional shift between the observed and applied policy manifests in overly optimistic estimates of the action value and poor performance (see Fujimoto et al., 2019; Kumar et al., 2019a; Agarwal et al., 2020). Conservative Q-learning (Kumar et al., 2020b) learns conservative, lower-bound estimates of the value function by regularizing the Q-values. The decision transformer (Chen et al., 2021c) is a simple approach to offline learning that takes advantage of the well-studied self-attention architecture. It can subsequently be fine-tuned with online training (Zheng et al., 2022).

Reinforcement learning and chatbots: Chatbots can be trained using a technique known as *reinforcement learning with human feedback* or *RLHF* (Christiano et al., 2018; Stiennon et al., 2020). For example, *InstructGPT* (the forerunner of ChatGPT, Ouyang et al., 2022) starts with a standard transformer decoder model. This is then fine-tuned based on prompt-response pairs where the response was written by human annotators. During this training step, the model is optimized to predict the next word in the ground truth response.

Unfortunately, such training data are expensive to produce in sufficient quantities to support high-quality performance. To resolve this problem, human annotators then indicate which of several model responses they prefer. These (much cheaper) data are used to train a *reward model*. This is a second transformer network that ingests the prompt and model response and returns a scalar indicating how good the response is. Finally, the fine-tuned chatbot model is further trained to produce high rewards using the reward model as supervision. Here, standard gradient descent cannot be used as it's not possible to compute derivatives through the sampling procedure in the chatbot output. Hence, the model is trained with proximal policy optimization (a policy gradient method where the derivatives are tractable) to generate higher rewards.

Other areas of RL: Reinforcement learning is an enormous area, which easily justifies its own book, and this literature review is extremely superficial. Other notable areas of RL that we have not discussed include *model-based RL*, in which the state transition probabilities and reward functions are modeled (see Moerland et al., 2023). This allows forward planning and has the advantage that the same model can be reused for different reward structures. *Hybrid methods* such as AlphaGo (Silver et al., 2016) and MuZero (Schrittwieser et al., 2020) have separate models for the dynamics of the states, the policy, and the value of future positions.

This chapter has only discussed simple methods for exploration, like the epsilon-greedy approach, noisy Q-learning, and adding an entropy term to penalize overconfident policies. *Intrinsic motivation* refers to methods that add rewards for exploration and thus imbue the agent with "curiosity" (see Barto, 2013; Aubret et al., 2019). *Hierarchical reinforcement learning* (see Pateria et al., 2021) refers to methods that break down the final objective into sub-tasks. *Multi-agent reinforcement learning* (see Zhang et al., 2021a) considers the case where multiple agents coexist in a shared environment. This may be in either a competitive or cooperative context.

Problems

Problem 19.1 Figure 19.18 shows a single trajectory through the example MDP. Calculate the return for each step in the trajectory given that the discount factor γ is 0.9.

Problem 19.2* Prove the policy improvement theorem. Consider changing from policy π to policy π', where for state s_t the new policy π' chooses the action that maximizes the expected return:

$$\pi'[a_t|s_t] = \underset{a_t}{\text{argmax}} \left[r[s_t, a_t] + \gamma \cdot \sum_{s_{t+1}} Pr(s_{t+1}|s_t, a_t) v[s_{t+1}|\pi] \right]. \tag{19.43}$$

and for all other states, the policies are the same. Show that the value $v[s_t|\pi]$ for the original policy must be less than or equal to $v[s_t|\pi'] = q[s_t, \pi'[a|s_t]|\pi]$ for the new policy:

$$
\begin{aligned}
v[s_t|\pi] &\leq q\left[s_t, \pi'[a_t|s_t]\Big|\pi\right] \\
&= \mathbb{E}_{\pi'}\left[r_{t+1} + \gamma \cdot v[s_{t+1}|\pi]\right].
\end{aligned}
\tag{19.44}
$$

Hint: Start by writing the term $v[s_{t+1}|\pi]$ in terms of the new policy.

Problem 19.3 Show that when the state values and policy are initialized as in figure 19.10a, they become those in figure 19.10b after two iterations of (i) policy evaluation (in which all states are updated based on their current values and then replace the previous ones) and (ii) policy improvement. The state transition allots half the probability to the direction the policy indicates and divides the remaining probability equally between the other valid actions. The reward function returns -2 irrespective of the action when the penguin leaves a hole. The reward function returns +3 regardless of the action when the penguin leaves the fish tile and the episode ends, so the fish tile has a value of +3.

Problem 19.4 The *Boltzmann policy* strikes a balance between exploration and exploitation by basing the action probabilities $\pi[a|s]$ on the current state-action reward function $q[s, a]$:

$$\pi[a|s] = \frac{\exp[q[s, a]/\tau]}{\sum_{a'} \exp[q[s, a']/\tau]}. \tag{19.45}$$

Explain how the temperature parameter τ can be varied to prioritize exploration or exploitation.

Problem 19.5* When the learning rate α is one, the Q-Learning update is given by:

$$\text{f}[q[s, a]] = r[s, a] + \gamma \cdot \max_a [q[s', a]]. \tag{19.46}$$

Show that this is a contraction mapping (equation 16.30) so that:

$$\left\| \text{f}[q_1[s, a]] - \text{f}[q_2[s, a]] \right\|_\infty < \left\| q_1[s, a] - q_2[s, a] \right\|_\infty \qquad \forall\, q_1, q_2. \tag{19.47}$$

where $||\bullet||_\infty$ represents the ℓ_∞ norm. It follows that a fixed point will exist by Banach's theorem and that the updates will eventually converge.

Appendix B.3.2
Vector norms

Figure 19.18 One trajectory through an MDP. The penguin receives a reward of $+1$ when it reaches the first fish tile, -2 when it falls in the hole, and $+1$ for reaching the second fish tile. The discount factor γ is 0.9.

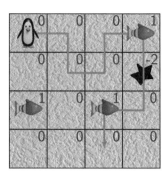

Problem 19.6 Show that:

$$\mathbb{E}_{\boldsymbol{\tau}}\left[\frac{\partial}{\partial\boldsymbol{\theta}}\log\big[Pr(\boldsymbol{\tau}|\boldsymbol{\theta})\big]b\right] = 0, \tag{19.48}$$

and so adding a baseline update doesn't change the expected policy gradient update.

Problem 19.7* Suppose that we want to estimate a quantity $\mathbb{E}[a]$ from samples $a_1, a_2 \ldots a_I$. Consider that we also have paired samples $b_1, b_2 \ldots b_I$ that are samples that co-vary with a where $\mathbb{E}[b] = \mu_b$. We define a new variable:

$$a' = a - c(b - \mu_b). \tag{19.49}$$

Show that $\text{Var}[a'] \leq \text{Var}[a]$ when the constant c is chosen judiciously. Find an expression for the optimal value of c.

Problem 19.8 The estimate of the gradient in equation 19.34 can be written as:

$$\mathbb{E}_{\boldsymbol{\tau}}\Big[g[\boldsymbol{\theta}](r[\boldsymbol{\tau}_t] - b)\Big], \tag{19.50}$$

where

$$g[\theta] = \sum_{t=1}^{T}\frac{\partial\log\big[Pr(a_t|\mathbf{s}_t, \boldsymbol{\theta})\big]]}{\partial\boldsymbol{\theta}}, \tag{19.51}$$

and

$$r[\boldsymbol{\tau}_t] = \sum_{k=t}^{T} r_k. \tag{19.52}$$

Show that the value of b that minimizes the variance of the gradient estimate is given by:

$$b = \frac{\mathbb{E}[g[\boldsymbol{\tau}]^2]r[\boldsymbol{\tau}]}{\mathbb{E}[g[\boldsymbol{\tau}]^2]}. \tag{19.53}$$

Chapter 20

Why does deep learning work?

This chapter differs from those that precede it. Instead of presenting established results, it poses questions about how and why deep learning works so well. These questions are rarely discussed in textbooks. However, it's important to realize that (despite the title of this book) understanding of deep learning is still limited.

We argue that it is surprising that deep networks are easy to train and also surprising that they generalize. Then we consider each of these topics in turn. We enumerate the factors that influence training success and discuss what is known about loss functions for deep networks. Then we consider the factors that influence generalization. We conclude with a discussion of whether networks need to be overparameterized and deep.

20.1 The case against deep learning

The MNIST-1D dataset (figure 8.1) has just forty input dimensions and ten output dimensions. With enough hidden units per layer, a two-layer fully connected network classifies 10000 MNIST-1D training data points perfectly and generalizes reasonably to unseen examples (figure 8.10a). Indeed, we now take it for granted that with sufficient hidden units, deep networks will classify almost any training set near-perfectly. We also take for granted that the fitted model will generalize to new data. However, it's not *at all* obvious either that the training process should succeed or that the resulting model should generalize. This section argues that both these phenomena are surprising.

20.1.1 Training

Performance of a two-layer fully connected network on 10000 MNIST-1D training examples is perfect once there are 43 hidden units per layer ($\sim$4000 parameters). However, finding the global minimum of an arbitrary non-convex function is NP-hard (Murty & Kabadi, 1987), and this is also true for certain neural network loss functions (Blum & Rivest, 1992). It's remarkable that the fitting algorithm doesn't get trapped in local minima or stuck near saddle points and that it can efficiently recruit spare model capacity to fit unexplained training data wherever they lie.

Perhaps this success is less surprising when there are far more parameters than training data. However, it's debatable whether this is generally the case. AlexNet had $\sim$60 million parameters and was trained with $\sim$1 million data points. However, to complicate matters, each training example was augmented with 2048 transformations. GPT-3 had 175 billion parameters and was trained with 300 billion tokens. There is not a clear-cut case that either model was overparameterized, and yet they were successfully trained.

In short, it's surprising that we can fit deep networks reliably and efficiently. Either the data, the models, the training algorithms, or some combination of all three must have some special properties that make this possible.

20.1.2 Generalization

If the efficient fitting of neural networks is startling, their generalization to new data is *dumbfounding*. First, it's not obvious *a priori* that typical datasets are sufficient to characterize the input/output mapping. The curse of dimensionality implies that the training dataset is tiny compared to the *possible* inputs; if each of the 40 inputs of the MNIST-1D data were quantized into 10 possible values, there would be 10^{40} possible inputs, which is a factor of 10^{35} more than the number of training examples.

Problem 20.1

Second, deep networks describe *very* complicated functions. A fully connected network for MNIST-1D with two hidden layers of width 400 can create mappings with up to 10^{42} linear regions. That's roughly 10^{37} regions per training example, so very few of these regions contain data at any stage during training; regardless, those regions that *do* encounter data points constrain the remaining regions to behave reasonably.

Third, generalization gets *better* with more parameters (figure 8.10). The model in the previous paragraph has 177,201 parameters. Assuming it can fit one training example per parameter, it has 167,201 spare degrees of freedom. This surfeit gives the model latitude to do *almost anything* between the training data, and yet it behaves sensibly.

20.1.3 The unreasonable effectiveness of deep learning

To summarize, it's neither obvious that we should be able to fit deep networks nor that they should generalize. *A priori*, deep learning shouldn't work. And yet it does. This chapter investigates why. Sections 20.2–20.3 describe what we know about fitting deep networks and their loss functions. Sections 20.4–20.6 examine generalization.

20.2 Factors that influence fitting performance

Figure 6.4 showed that loss functions for nonlinear models can have both local minima and saddle points. However, we can reliably fit deep networks to complex training sets. For example, figure 8.10 shows perfect training performance on MNIST-1D, MNIST, and CIFAR-100. This section considers factors that might resolve this contradiction.

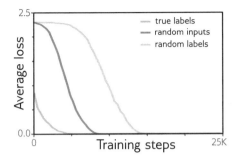

Figure 20.1 Fitting random data. Losses for AlexNet architecture trained on CIFAR-10 dataset with SGD. When the pixels are drawn from a Gaussian random distribution with the same mean and variance as the original data, the model can still be fit (albeit more slowly). When the labels are randomized, the model can still be fit (albeit even more slowly). Adapted from Zhang et al. (2017a).

20.2.1 Dataset

It's important to realize that we can't learn *any* function. Consider a completely random mapping from every possible 28×28 binary image to one of ten categories. Since there is no structure to this function, the only recourse is to memorize the 2^{784} assignments. However, it's easy to train a model on the MNIST dataset (figures 8.10 and 15.15), which contains 60,000 examples of 28×28 images labeled with one of ten categories. One explanation for this contradiction could be that it is easy to find global minima because the real-world functions that we approximate are relatively simple.[1]

This hypothesis was investigated by Zhang et al. (2017a), who trained AlexNet on the CIFAR-10 image classification dataset when (i) each image was replaced with Gaussian noise and (ii) the labels of the ten classes were randomly permuted (figure 20.1). These changes slowed down learning, but the network could still fit this finite dataset well. This suggests that the properties of the dataset aren't critical.

Notebook 20.1
Random data

Problem 20.2

20.2.2 Regularization

Another possible explanation for the ease with which models are trained is that some regularization methods like L2 regularization (weight decay) make the loss surface flatter and more convex. However, Zhang et al. (2017a) found that neither L2 regularization nor Dropout was required to fit random data. This does not eliminate implicit regularization due to the finite step size of the fitting algorithms (section 9.2). However, this effect increases with the learning rate (equation 9.9), and model-fitting does not get easier with larger learning rates.

20.2.3 Stochastic training algorithms

Chapter 6 argued that the SGD algorithm potentially allows the optimization trajectory to move between "valleys" during training. However, Keskar et al. (2017) show that several models (including fully connected and convolutional networks) can be fit to many

---

[1]In this chapter, we use the term "global minimum" loosely to mean any solution where all data are classified correctly. We have no way of knowing if there are solutions with a lower loss elsewhere.

Figure 20.2 MNIST-1D training. Four fully connected networks were fit to 4000 MNIST-1D examples with random labels using full batch gradient descent, He initialization, no momentum or regularization, and learning rate 0.0025. Models with 1,2,3,4 layers had 298, 100, 75, and 63 hidden units per layer and 15208, 15210, 15235, and 15139 parameters, respectively. All models train successfully, but deeper models require fewer epochs.

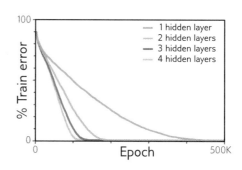

datasets (including CIFAR-100 and MNIST) almost perfectly with very large batches of 5000-6000 images. This eliminates most of the randomness but training still succeeds.

Notebook 20.2
Full batch
gradient descent

Problem 20.3

Figure 20.2 shows training results for four fully connected models fitted to 4000 MNIST-1D examples with randomized labels using full-batch (i.e., non-stochastic) gradient descent. There was no explicit regularization, and the learning rate was set to a small constant value of 0.0025 to minimize implicit regularization. Here, the true mapping from data to labels has no structure, the training is deterministic, and there is no regularization, and yet the training error *still* decreases to zero. This suggests that these loss functions may genuinely have no local minima.

20.2.4 Overparameterization

Overparameterization almost certainly *is* an important factor that contributes to ease of training. It implies that there is a large family of degenerate solutions, so there may always be a direction in which the parameters can be modified to decrease the loss. Sejnowski (2020) suggests that "... the degeneracy of solutions changes the nature of the problem from finding a needle in a haystack to a haystack of needles."

In practice, networks are frequently overparameterized by one or two orders of magnitude (figure 20.3). However, data augmentation makes it difficult to make precise statements. Augmentation may increase the data by several orders of magnitude, but these are manipulations of existing examples rather than independent new data points. Moreover, figure 8.10 shows that neural networks can sometimes fit the training data well when there are the same number or fewer parameters than data points. This is presumably due to redundancy in training examples from the same underlying function.

Several theoretical convergence results show that, *under certain circumstances*, SGD converges to a global minimum when the network is sufficiently overparameterized. For example, Du et al. (2019b) show that randomly initialized SGD converges to a global minimum for shallow fully connected ReLU networks with a least squares loss with enough hidden units. Similarly, Du et al. (2019a) consider deep, residual, and convolutional networks when the activation function is smooth and Lipschitz. Zou et al. (2020) analyzed the convergence of gradient descent on deep, fully connected networks using a hinge loss. Allen-Zhu et al. (2019) considered deep networks with ReLU functions.

If a neural network is sufficiently overparameterized so that it can memorize any

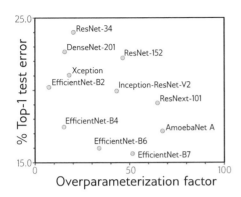

Figure 20.3 Overparameterization. ImageNet performance for convolutional nets as a function of overparameterization (in multiples of dataset size). Most models have 10–100 times more parameters than there were training examples. Models compared are ResNet (He et al., 2016a,b), DenseNet (Huang et al., 2017b), Xception (Chollet, 2017), EfficientNet (Tan & Le, 2019), Inception (Szegedy et al., 2017), ResNeXt (Xie et al., 2017), and AmoebaNet (Cubuk et al., 2019).

dataset of a fixed size, then all stationary points become global minima (Livni et al., 2014; Nguyen & Hein, 2017, 2018). Other results show that if the network is wide enough, local minima where the loss is higher than the global minimum are rare (see Choromanska et al., 2015; Pascanu et al., 2014; Pennington & Bahri, 2017). Kawaguchi et al. (2019) prove that as a network becomes deeper, wider, or both, the loss at local minima becomes closer to that at the global minimum for squared loss functions.

These theoretical results are intriguing but usually make unrealistic assumptions about the network structure. For example, Du et al. (2019a) show that residual networks converge to zero training loss when the width of the network D (i.e., the number of hidden units) is $\Omega[I^4K^2]$ where I is the amount of training data, and K is the depth of the network. Similarly, Nguyen & Hein (2017) assume that the network's width is larger than the dataset size, which is unrealistic in most practical scenarios. Overparameterization seems to be important, but theory cannot yet explain empirical fitting performance.

20.2.5   Activation functions

The activation function is also known to affect training difficulty. Networks where the activation only changes over a small part of the input range are harder to fit than ReLUs (which vary over half the input range) or Leaky ReLUs (which vary over the full range); For example, sigmoid and tanh nonlinearities (figure 3.13a) have shallow gradients in their tails; where the activation function is near-constant, the training gradient is near-zero, so there is no mechanism to improve the model.

20.2.6   Initialization

Another potential explanation is that Xavier/He initialization sets the parameters to values that are easy to optimize. Of course, for deeper networks, such initialization is necessary to avoid exploding and vanishing gradients, so in a trivial sense, initialization is critical to training success. However, for shallower networks, the initial variance of the weights is less important. Liu et al. (2023c) trained a 3-layer fully connected network with

Figure 20.4 Initialization and fitting. A three-layer fully connected network with 200 hidden units per layer was trained on 1000 MNIST examples with AdamW using one-hot targets and mean-squared error loss. It takes longer to fit networks when larger multiples of He initialization are used, but this doesn't change the outcome. This may simply reflect the extra distance that the weights must move. Adapted from Liu et al. (2023c).

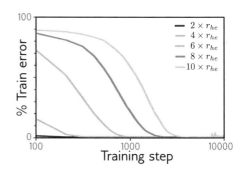

200 hidden units per layer on 1000 MNIST data points. They found that more iterations were required to fit the training data as the variance increased from that proposed by He (figure 20.4), but this did not ultimately impede fitting. Hence, initialization doesn't shed much light on why fitting neural networks is easy, although exploding/vanishing gradients do reveal initializations that make training difficult with finite precision arithmetic.

20.2.7   Network depth

Neural networks are harder to fit when the depth becomes very large due to exploding and vanishing gradients (figure 7.7) and shattered gradients (figure 11.3). However, these are (arguably) practical numerical issues. There is no definitive evidence that the underlying loss function is fundamentally more or less convex as the network depth increases. Figure 20.2 does show that for MNIST data with randomized labels and He initialization, deeper networks train in fewer iterations. However, this might be because either (i) the gradients in deeper networks are steeper or (ii) He initialization just starts wider, shallower networks further away from the optimal parameters.

Frankle & Carbin (2019) show that for small networks like VGG, you can get the same or better performance if you (i) train the network, (ii) prune the weights with the smallest magnitudes and (iii) retrain from the same initial weights. This does not work if the weights are randomly re-initialized. They concluded that the original over-parameterized network contains small trainable sub-networks, which are sufficient to provide the performance. They term this the *lottery ticket hypothesis* and denote the sub-networks as *winning tickets*. This suggests that the effective number of sub-networks may have a key role to play in fitting. This (perhaps) varies with the network depth for a fixed parameter count, but a precise characterization of this idea is lacking.

*Notebook 20.3
Lottery tickets*

20.3   Properties of loss functions

The previous section discussed factors that contribute to the ease with which neural networks can be trained. The number of parameters (degree of overparameterization) and the choice of activation function are both important. Surprisingly, the choice of dataset, the randomness of the fitting algorithm, and the use of regularization don't seem important. There is no definitive evidence that (for a fixed parameter count) the depth of the network matters (other than numerical problems due to exploding/vanishing/shattered gradients). This section tackles the same topic from a different angle by considering the empirical properties of loss functions. Most of this evidence comes from fully connected networks and CNNs; loss functions of transformer networks are less well understood.

20.3.1 Multiple global minima

We *expect* loss functions for deep networks to have a large family of equivalent global minima. In fully connected networks, the hidden units at each layer and their associated weights can be permuted without changing the output. In convolutional networks, permuting the channels and convolution kernels appropriately doesn't change the output. We can multiply the weight before any ReLU function and divide the weight after by a positive number without changing the output. Using BatchNorm induces another set of redundancies because the mean and variance of each hidden unit or channel are reset.

The above modifications all produce the same output for *every* input. However, the global minimum only depends on the output at the training data points. In overparameterized networks, there will also be families of solutions that behave identically at the data points but differently between them. All of these are also global minima.

20.3.2 Route to the minimum

Goodfellow et al. (2015b) considered a straight line between the initial parameters and the final values. They show that the loss function along this line usually decreases monotonically (except for a small bump near the start sometimes). This phenomenon is observed for several different types of networks and activation functions (figure 20.5a).

Of course, real optimization trajectories do not proceed in a straight line. However, Li et al. (2018b) find that they do lie in low-dimensional subspaces. They attribute this to the existence of large, nearly convex regions in the loss landscape that capture the trajectory early on and funnel it in a few important directions. Surprisingly, Li et al. (2018a) showed that networks still train well if optimization is *constrained* to lie in a random low-dimensional subspace (figure 20.6).

Li & Liang (2018) show that the relative change in the parameters during training decreases as network width increases; for larger widths, the parameters start at smaller values, change by a smaller proportion of those values, and converge in fewer steps.

20.3.3 Connections between minima

Goodfellow et al. (2015b) examined the loss function along a straight line between two minima that were found independently. They saw a pronounced increase in the loss between them (figure 20.5b); good minima are not generally linearly connected. However,

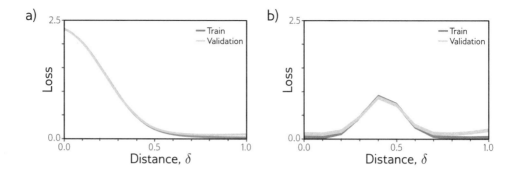

Figure 20.5 Linear slices through loss function. a) A two-layer fully connected ReLU network is trained on MNIST. The loss along a straight line starting at the initial parameters (δ=0) and finishing at the trained parameters (δ=1) descends monotonically. b) However, in this two-layer fully connected MaxOut network on MNIST, there is an increase in the loss along a straight line between one solution (δ=0) and another (δ=1). Adapted from Goodfellow et al. (2015b).

Figure 20.6 Subspace training. A fully connected network with two hidden layers, each with 200 units was trained on MNIST. Parameters were initialized using a standard method but then constrained to lie within a random subspace. Performance reaches 90% of the unconstrained level when this subspace is 750D (termed the *intrinsic dimension*), which is 0.4% of the original parameters. Adapted from Li et al. (2018a).

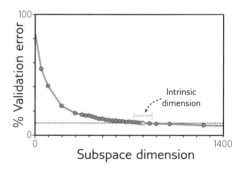

Frankle et al. (2020) showed that this increase vanishes if the networks are identically trained initially and later allowed to diverge by using different SGD noise and augmentation. This suggests that the solution is constrained early in training and that *some* families of minima are linearly connected.

Draxler et al. (2018) found minima with good (but different) performance on the CIFAR-10 dataset. They then showed that it is possible to construct paths from one to the other, where the loss function remains low along this path. They conclude that there is a single connected manifold of low loss (figure 20.7). This seems to be increasingly true as the width and depth of the network increase. Garipov et al. (2018) and Fort & Jastrzębski (2019) present other schemes for connecting minima.

20.3.4 Curvature of loss surface

Random Gaussian functions (in which points are jointly distributed with covariance given by a kernel function of their distance) have an interesting property: for points

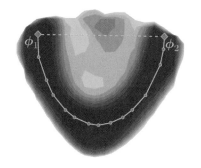

Figure 20.7 Connections between minima. A slice through the loss function of DenseNet on CIFAR-10. Parameters ϕ_1 and ϕ_2 are two independently discovered minima. Linear interpolation between these parameters reveals an energy barrier (dashed line). However, for sufficiently deep and wide networks, it is possible to find a curved path of low energy between two minima (cyan line). Adapted from Draxler et al. (2018).

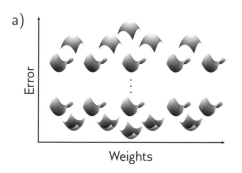

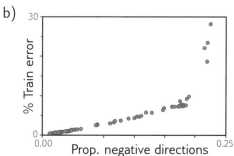

Figure 20.8 Critical points vs. loss. a) In random Gaussian functions, the number of directions in which the function curves down at points with zero gradient decreases with the height of the function, so minima all appear at lower function values. b) Dauphin et al. (2014) found critical points on a neural network loss surface (i.e., points with zero gradient). They showed that the proportion of negative eigenvalues (directions that point down) decreases with the loss. The implication is that all minima (points with zero gradient where no directions point down) have low losses. Adapted from Dauphin et al. (2014) and Bahri et al. (2020).

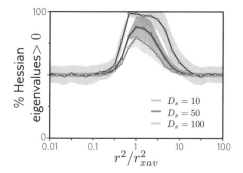

Figure 20.9 Goldilocks zone. The proportion of eigenvalues of the Hessian that are greater than zero (a measure of positive curvature/convexity) within a random subspace of dimension D_s in a two-layer fully connected network with ReLU functions applied to MNIST as a function of the squared radius r^2 of the parameters relative to Xavier initialization. There is a pronounced region of positive curvature known as the *Goldilocks zone*. Adapted from Fort & Scherlis (2019).

Figure 20.10 Batch size to learning rate ratio. Generalization of two models on the CIFAR-10 database depends on the ratio of batch size to the learning rate. As the batch size increases, generalization decreases. As the learning rate increases, generalization increases. Adapted from He et al. (2019).

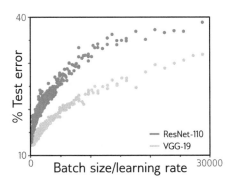

where the gradient is zero, the fraction of directions where the function curves down becomes smaller when these points occur at lower loss values (see Bahri et al., 2020). Dauphin et al. (2014) searched for saddle points in a neural network loss function and similarly found a correlation between the loss and the number of negative eigenvalues (figure 20.8). Baldi & Hornik (1989) analyzed the error surface of a shallow network and found that there were *no local minima* but only saddle points. These results suggest that there are few or no bad local minima.

Fort & Scherlis (2019) measured the curvature at random points on a neural network loss surface; they showed that the curvature of the surface is unusually positive when the ℓ_2 norm of the weights lies within a certain range (figure 20.9), which they term the *Goldilocks zone*. He and Xavier initialization fall within this range.

20.4 Factors that determine generalization

The last two sections considered factors that determine whether the network trains successfully and what is known about neural network loss functions. This section considers factors that determine how well the network generalizes. This complements the discussion of regularization (chapter 9), which explicitly aims to encourage generalization.

20.4.1 Training algorithms

Since deep networks are usually overparameterized, the details of the training process determine which of the degenerate family of minima the algorithm converges to. Some of these details reliably improve generalization.

LeCun et al. (2012) show that SGD generalizes better than full-batch gradient descent. It has been argued that SGD generalizes better than Adam (e.g., Wilson et al., 2017; Keskar & Socher, 2017), but more recent studies suggest that there is little difference when the hyperparameter search is done carefully (Choi et al., 2019). Keskar et al. (2017) show that deep nets generalize better with smaller batch-size when no other form of regularization is used. It is also well-known that larger learning rates tend to generalize better (e.g., figure 9.5). Jastrzębski et al. (2018), Goyal et al. (2018), and He

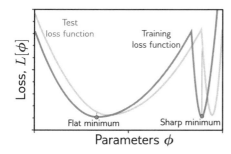

Figure 20.11 Flat vs. sharp minima. Flat minima are expected to generalize better. Small errors in estimating the parameters or in the alignment of the train and test loss functions are less problematic in flat regions. Adapted from Keskar et al. (2017).

et al. (2019) argue that the batch size/learning rate ratio is important. He et al. (2019) show a significant correlation between this ratio and the degree of generalization and prove a generalization bound for neural networks, which has a positive correlation with this ratio (figure 20.10).

These observations are aligned with the discovery that SGD implicitly adds regularization terms to the loss function (section 9.2), and their magnitude depends on the learning rate. The trajectory of the parameters is changed by this regularization, and they converge to a part of the loss function that generalizes well.

20.4.2   Flatness of minimum

There has been speculation dating at least to Hochreiter & Schmidhuber (1997a) that flat minima in the loss function generalize better than sharp minima (figure 20.11). Informally, if the minimum is flatter, then small errors in the estimated parameters are less important. This can also be motivated from various theoretical viewpoints. For example, minimum description length theory suggests models specified by fewer bits generalize better (Rissanen, 1983). For wide minima, the precision needed to store the weights is lower, so they should generalize better.

Flatness can be measured by (i) the size of the connected region around the minimum for which training loss is similar (Hochreiter & Schmidhuber, 1997a), (ii) the second-order curvature around the minimum (Chaudhari et al., 2019), or (iii) the maximum loss within a neighborhood of the minimum (Keskar et al., 2017). However, caution is required; estimated flatness can be affected by trivial reparameterizations of the network due to the non-negative homogeneity property of the ReLU function (Dinh et al., 2017).

Nonetheless, Keskar et al. (2017) varied the batch size and learning rate and showed that flatness correlates with generalization. Izmailov et al. (2018) average together weights from multiple points in a learning trajectory. This both results in flatter test and training surfaces at the minimum and improves generalization. Other regularization techniques can also be viewed through this lens. For example, averaging model outputs (ensembling) may also make the test loss surface flatter. Kleinberg et al. (2018) showed that large gradient variance during training helps avoid sharp regions. This may explain why reducing the batch size and adding noise helps generalization.

The above studies consider flatness for a single model and training set. However, sharpness is not a good criterion to predict generalization between datasets; when the labels in the CIFAR dataset are randomized (making generalization impossible), there is no commensurate decrease in the flatness of the minimum (Neyshabur et al., 2017).

20.4.3   Architecture

The inductive bias of a network is determined by its architecture, and judicious choices of model can drastically improve generalization. Chapter 10 introduced convolutional networks, which are designed to process data on regular grids; they implicitly assume that the input statistics are the same across the input, so they share parameters across position. Similarly, transformers are suited for modeling data that is invariant to permutations, and graph neural networks are suited to data represented on irregular graphs. Matching the architecture to the properties of the data improves generalization over generic, fully connected architectures (see figure 10.8).

20.4.4   Norm of weights

Section 20.3.4 reviewed the finding of Fort & Scherlis (2019) that the curvature of the loss surface is unusually positive when the ℓ_2 norm of the weights lies within a certain range. The same authors provided evidence that generalization is also good when the ℓ_2 weight norm falls within this Goldilocks zone (figure 20.12). This is perhaps unsurprising. The norm of the weights is (indirectly) related to the Lipschitz constant of the model. If this norm is too small, then the model will not be able to change fast enough to capture the variation in the underlying function. If the norm is too large, then the model will be unnecessarily variable between training points and will not interpolate smoothly.

This finding was used by Liu et al. (2023c) to explain the phenomenon of *grokking* (Power et al., 2022), in which a sudden improvement in generalization can occur many epochs after the training error is already zero (figure 20.13). It is proposed that grokking occurs when the norm of the weights is initially too large; the training data fits well, but the variation of the model between the data points is large. Over time, implicit or explicit regularization decreases the norm of the weights until they reach the Goldilocks zone, and generalization suddenly improves.

20.4.5   Overparameterization

Figure 8.10 showed that generalization performance tends to improve with the degree of overparameterization. When combined with the bias/variance trade-off curve, this results in double descent. The putative explanation for this improvement is that the network has more latitude to become smoother *between* the training data points when the model is overparameterized.

It follows that the norm of the weights can also be used to explain double descent. The norm of the weights increases when the number of parameters is similar to the number of data points (as the model contorts itself to fit these points exactly), causing

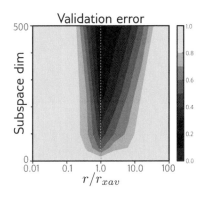

Figure 20.12 Generalization on hyperspheres. A fully connected network with two hidden layers, each with 200 units (198,450 parameters) was trained on the MNIST database. The parameters are initialized to a given ℓ_2 norm and then constrained to maintain this norm and to lie in a subspace (vertical direction). The network generalizes well in a small range around the radius r defined by Xavier initialization (cyan dotted line). Adapted from Fort & Scherlis (2019).

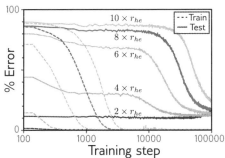

Figure 20.13 Grokking. When the parameters are initialized so that their ℓ_2 norm (radius) is considerably larger than is specified by He initialization, training takes longer (dashed lines), and generalization takes *much* longer (solid lines). The lag in generalization is attributed to the time taken for the norm of the weights to decrease back to the Goldilocks zone. Adapted from Liu et al. (2023c).

generalization to reduce. As the network becomes wider and the number of weights increases, the overall norm of these weights decreases; the weights are initialized with a variance that is inversely proportional to the width (i.e., with He or Glorot initialization), and the weights change very little from their original values.

20.4.6 Leaving the data manifold

Until this point, we have discussed how models generalize to new data that is drawn from the same distribution as the training data. This is a reasonable assumption for experimentation. However, systems deployed in the real world may encounter unexpected data due to noise, changes in the data statistics over time, or deliberate attacks. Of course, it is harder to make definite statements about this scenario, but D'Amour et al. (2020) show that the variability of identical models trained with different seeds on corrupted data can be enormous and unpredictable.

Goodfellow et al. (2015a) showed that deep learning models are susceptible to *adversarial attacks*. Consider perturbing an image that is correctly classified by the network as "dog" so that the probability of the correct class decreases as fast as possible until the class flips. If this image is now classified as an airplane, you might expect the perturbed image to look like a cross between a dog and an airplane. However, in practice, the perturbed image looks almost indistinguishable from the original dog image (figure 20.14).

Notebook 20.4
Adversarial attacks

Figure 20.14 Adversarial examples. In each case, the left image is correctly classified by AlexNet. By considering the gradients of the network output with respect to the input, it's possible to find a small perturbation (center, magnified by 10 for visibility) that, when added to the original image (right), causes the network to misclassify it as an ostrich. This is despite the fact that the original and perturbed images are almost indistinguishable to humans. Adapted from Szegedy et al. (2014).

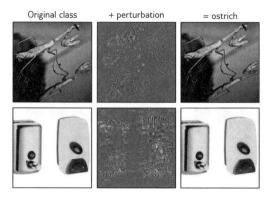
Original class   + perturbation   = ostrich

The conclusion is that there are positions that are close to but not on the data manifold that are misclassified. These are known as *adversarial examples*. Their existence is surprising; how can such a small change to the network input make such a drastic change to the output? The best current explanation is that adversarial examples aren't due to a lack of robustness to data from outside the training data manifold. Instead, they are exploiting a source of information that is in the training distribution but which has a small norm and is imperceptible to humans (Ilyas et al., 2019).

20.5   Do we need so many parameters?

Section 20.4 argued that models generalize better when over-parameterized. Indeed, there are almost no examples of state-of-the-art performance on complex datasets where the model has significantly fewer parameters than there were training data points.

However, section 20.2 reviewed evidence that training becomes easier as the number of parameters increases. Hence, it's not clear if some fundamental property of smaller models prevents them from performing as well or whether the training algorithms can't find good solutions for small models. *Pruning* and *distilling* are two methods for reducing the size of trained models. This section examines whether these methods can produce underparameterized models which retain the performance of overparameterized ones.

20.5.1   Pruning

Pruning trained models reduces their size and hence storage requirements (figure 20.15). The simplest approach is to remove individual weights. This can be done based on the second derivatives of the loss function (LeCun et al., 1990; Hassibi & Stork, 1993) or (more practically) based on the absolute value of the weight (Han et al., 2016, 2015). Other work prunes hidden units (Zhou et al., 2016a; Alvarez & Salzmann, 2016), channels in convolutional networks (Li et al., 2017a; Luo et al., 2017b; He et al., 2017; Liu et al., 2019a), or entire layers in residual nets (Huang & Wang, 2018). Often, the network is

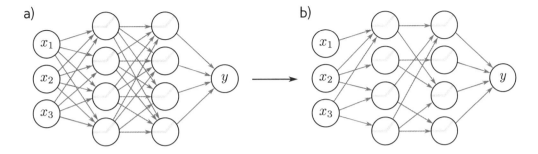

Figure 20.15 Pruning neural networks. The goal is to remove as many weights as possible without decreasing performance. This is often done just based on the magnitude of the weights. Typically, the network is fine-tuned after pruning. a) Example fully connected network. b) After pruning.

fine-tuned after pruning, and sometimes this process is repeated.

For example, Han et al. (2016) maintained good performance for the VGG network on ImageNet classification when 8% of the weights were retained. This significantly decreases the model size but isn't enough to show that overparameterization is not required; the VGG network has ∼100 times as many parameters as there are ImageNet training data (disregarding augmentation).

Pruning is a form of architecture search. In their work on lottery tickets (see section 20.2.7), Frankle & Carbin (2019) (i) trained a network, (ii) pruned the weights with the smallest magnitudes, and (iii) retrained the remaining network from the same initial weights. By iterating this procedure, they reduced the size of the VGG-19 network (originally 138 million parameters) by 98.5% on the CIFAR-10 database (60,000 examples) while maintaining good performance. For ResNet-50 (25.6 million parameters), they reduced the parameters by 80% without reducing the performance on ImageNet (1.28 million examples). These demonstrations are impressive but (disregarding data augmentation) these networks are still over-parameterized after pruning.

20.5.2 Knowledge distillation

The parameters can also be reduced by training a smaller network (the student) to replicate the performance of a larger one (the teacher). This is known as *knowledge distillation* and dates back to at least Buciluă et al. (2006). Hinton et al. (2015) showed that the pattern of information across the output classes is important and trained a smaller network to approximate the pre-softmax logits of the larger one (figure 20.16).

Zagoruyko & Komodakis (2017) further encouraged the spatial maps of the activations of the student network to be similar to the teacher network at various points. They use this *attention transfer* method to approximate the performance of a 34-layer residual network (∼63 million parameters) with an 18-layer residual network (∼11 million param-

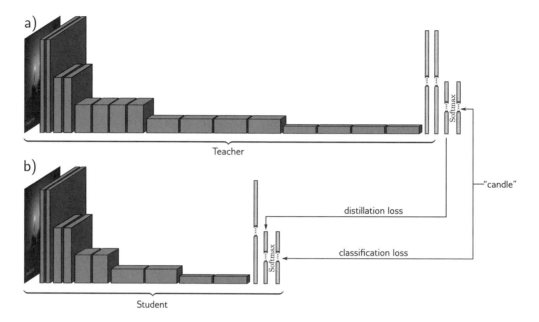

Figure 20.16 Knowledge distillation. a) A teacher network for image classification is trained as usual, using a multiclass cross-entropy classification loss. b) A smaller student network is trained with the same loss, plus also a distillation loss that encourages the pre-softmax activations to be the same as for the teacher.

eters) on the ImageNet classification task. However, this is still larger than the number of training examples (∼1 million images). Modern methods (e.g. Chen et al., 2021a) can improve on this result, but distillation has not yet provided convincing evidence that under-parameterized models can perform well.

20.5.3   Discussion

Current evidence suggests that overparameterization *is* needed for generalization — at least for the size and complexity of datasets that are currently used. There are no demonstrations of state-of-the-art performance on complex datasets where there are significantly fewer parameters than training examples. Attempts to reduce model size by pruning or distilling trained networks have not changed this picture.

Moreover, recent theory shows that there is a trade-off between the model's Lipschitz constant and overparameterization; Bubeck & Sellke (2021) proved that in D dimensions, *smooth* interpolation requires D times more parameters than mere interpolation. They argue that current models for large datasets (e.g., ImageNet) aren't overparameterized *enough*; increasing model capacity further may be key to improving performance.

20.6   Do networks have to be deep?

Chapter 3 discussed the universal approximation theorem. This states that shallow neural networks can approximate any function to arbitrary accuracy given enough hidden units. This raises the obvious question of whether networks *need* to be deep.

First, let's consider the evidence that depth *is* required. Historically, there has been a definite correlation between performance and depth. For example, performance on the ImageNet benchmark initially improved as a function of network depth until training became difficult. Subsequently, residual connections and batch normalization (chapter 11) allowed training of deeper networks with commensurate gains in performance. At the time of writing, almost all state-of-the-art applications, including image classification (e.g., the vision transformer), text generation (e.g., GPT3), and text-guided image synthesis (e.g., DALL·E-2), are based on deep networks with tens or hundreds of layers.

Despite this trend, there have been efforts to use shallower networks. Zagoruyko & Komodakis (2016) constructed shallower but wider residual neural networks and achieved similar performance to ResNet. More recently, Goyal et al. (2021) constructed a network that used parallel convolutional channels and achieved performance similar to deeper networks with only 12 layers. Furthermore, Veit et al. (2016) showed that it is predominantly shorter paths of 5–17 layers that drive performance in residual networks.

Nonetheless, the balance of evidence suggests that depth is critical; even the shallowest networks with good image classification performance require >10 layers. However, there is no definitive explanation for why. Three possible explanations are that (i) deep networks can represent more complex functions than shallow ones, (ii) deep networks are easier to train, and (iii) deep networks impose better inductive biases.

20.6.1   Complexity of modeled function

Chapter 4 showed that deep networks make functions with many more linear regions than shallow ones for the same parameter count. We also saw that "pathological" functions have been identified that require exponentially more hidden units to model with a shallow network than a deep one (e.g., Eldan & Shamir, 2016; Telgarsky, 2016). Indeed Liang & Srikant (2016) found quite general families of functions that are more efficiently modeled by deep networks. However, Nye & Saxe (2018) found that some of these functions cannot easily be fit by deep networks in practice. Moreover, there is little evidence that the real-world functions that we are approximating have these pathological properties.

20.6.2   Tractability of training

An alternative explanation is that shallow networks with a practical number of hidden units could support state-of-the-art performance, but it is just difficult to find a good solution that both fits the training data well and interpolates sensibly.

One way to show this is to distill successful deep networks into shallower (but wider) student models and see if performance can be maintained. Urban et al. (2017) distilled an ensemble of 16 convolutional networks for image classification on the CIFAR-10 dataset into student models of varying depths. They found that shallow networks could not replicate the performance of the deeper teacher and that the student performance increased as a function of depth for a constant parameter budget.

20.6.3 Inductive bias

Most current models rely on convolutional blocks or transformers. These networks share parameters for local regions of the input data, and often they gradually integrate this information across the whole input. These constraints mean that the functions that these networks can represent are not general. One explanation for the supremacy of deep networks, then, is that these constraints have a good inductive bias and that it is difficult to force shallow networks to obey these constraints.

Multi-layer convolutional architectures seem to be inherently helpful, even without training. Ulyanov et al. (2018) demonstrated that the structure of an untrained CNN can be used as a prior in low-level tasks such as denoising and super-resolution. Frankle et al. (2021) achieved good performance in image classification by initializing the kernels randomly, fixing their values, and just training the batch normalization offset and scaling factors. Zhang et al. (2017a) show that features from randomly initialized convolutional filters can support subsequent image classification using a kernel model.

Additional evidence that convolutional networks provide a useful inductive bias comes from Urban et al. (2017), who attempted to distill convolutional networks into shallower networks. They found that distilling into convolutional architectures systematically worked better than distilling into fully connected networks. This suggests that the convolutional architecture has some inherent advantages. Since the sequential local processing of convolutional networks cannot easily be replicated by shallower networks, this argues that depth is indeed important.

20.7 Summary

This chapter has made the case that the success of deep learning is surprising. We discussed the challenges of optimizing high-dimensional loss functions and argued that overparameterization and the choice of activation function are the two most important factors that make this tractable in deep networks. We saw that, during training, the parameters move through a low-dimensional subspace to one of a family of connected global minima and that local minima are not apparent.

Generalization of neural networks also improves with overparameterization, although other factors, such as the flatness of the minimum and the inductive bias of the architecture, are also important. It appears that both a large number of parameters and multiple network layers are required for good generalization, although we do not yet know why.

Many questions remain unanswered. We do not currently have any prescriptive theory that will allow us to predict the circumstances in which training and generalization will succeed or fail. We do not know the limits of learning in deep networks or whether much more efficient models are possible. We do not know if there are parameters that would generalize better within the same model. The study of deep learning is still driven by empirical demonstrations. These are undeniably impressive, but they are not yet matched by our understanding of deep learning mechanisms.

Problems

Problem 20.1 Consider the ImageNet image classification task in which the input images contain $224 \times 224 \times 3$ RGB values. Consider coarsely quantizing these inputs into ten bins per RGB value and training with $\sim 10^7$ training examples. How many possible inputs are there per training data point?

Problem 20.2 Consider figure 20.1. Why do you think that the algorithm fits the data faster when the pixels are randomized relative to when the labels are randomized?

Problem 20.3 Figure 20.2 shows a non-stochastic fitting process with a fixed learning rate successfully fitting random data. Does this imply that the loss function has no local minima? Does this imply that the function is convex? Justify your answer and give a counter-example if you think either statement is false.

Chapter 21

Deep learning and ethics

This chapter was written by Travis LaCroix and Simon J.D. Prince.

AI is poised to change society for better or worse. These technologies have enormous potential for social good (Taddeo & Floridi, 2018; Tomašev et al., 2020), including important roles in healthcare (Rajpurkar et al., 2022) and the fight against climate change (Rolnick et al., 2023). However, they also have the potential for misuse and unintended harm. This has led to the emergence of the field of *AI ethics*.

The modern era of deep learning started in 2012 with AlexNet, but sustained interest in AI ethics did not follow immediately. Indeed, a workshop on fairness in machine learning was rejected from NeurIPS 2013 for want of material. It wasn't until 2016 that AI Ethics had its "AlexNet" moment, with ProPublica's exposé on bias in the COMPAS recidivism-prediction model (Angwin et al., 2016) and Cathy O'Neil's book *Weapons of Math Destruction* (O'Neil, 2016). Interest has swelled ever since; submissions to the Conference on *Fairness, Accountability, and Transparency* (FAccT) have increased nearly ten-fold in the five years since its inception in 2018.

In parallel, many organizations have proposed policy recommendations for responsible AI. Jobin et al. (2019) found 84 documents containing AI ethics principles, with 88% released since 2016. This proliferation of non-legislative policy agreements, which depend on voluntary, non-binding cooperation, calls into question their efficacy (McNamara et al., 2018; Hagendorff, 2020; LaCroix & Mohseni, 2022). In short, AI Ethics is in its infancy, and ethical considerations are often reactive rather than proactive.

This chapter considers potential harms arising from the design and use of AI systems. These include algorithmic bias, lack of explainability, data privacy violations, militarization, fraud, and environmental concerns. The aim is not to provide advice on being more ethical. Instead, the goal is to express ideas and start conversations in key areas that have received attention in philosophy, political science, and the broader social sciences.

21.1 Value alignment

Problem 21.1

When we design AI systems, we wish to ensure that their "values" (objectives) are aligned with those of humanity. This is sometimes called the *value alignment problem* (Russell,

2019; Christian, 2020; Gabriel, 2020). This is challenging for three reasons. First, it's difficult to define our values completely and correctly. Second, it is hard to encode these values as objectives of an AI model, and third, it is hard to ensure that the model learns to carry out these objectives.

In a machine learning model, the loss function is a proxy for our true objectives, and a misalignment between the two is termed the *outer alignment problem* (Hubinger et al., 2019). To the extent that this proxy is inadequate, there will be "loopholes" that the system can exploit to minimize its loss function while failing to satisfy the intended objective. For example, consider training an RL agent to play chess. If the agent is rewarded for capturing pieces, this may result in many drawn games rather than the desired behavior (to win the game). In contrast, the *inner alignment problem* is to ensure that the behavior of an AI system does not diverge from the intended objectives even when the loss function is well specified. If the learning algorithm fails to find the global minimum or the training data are unrepresentative, training can converge to a solution that is misaligned with the true objective resulting in undesirable behavior (Goldberg, 1987; Mitchell et al., 1992; Lehman & Stanley, 2008).

Problem 21.2

Gabriel (2020) divides the value alignment problem into *technical* and *normative* components. The technical component concerns how we encode values into the models so that they reliably do what they should. Some concrete problems, such as avoiding reward hacking and safe exploration, may have purely technical solutions (Amodei et al., 2016). In contrast, the normative component concerns what the correct values are in the first place. There may be no single answer to this question, given the range of things that different cultures and societies value. It's important that the encoded values are representative of everyone and not just culturally dominant subsets of society.

Another way to think about value alignment is as a *structural* problem that arises when a human *principal* delegates tasks to an artificial *agent* (LaCroix, 2022). This is similar to the principal-agent problem in economics (Laffont & Martimort, 2002), which allows that there are competing incentives inherent in any relationship where one party is expected to act in another's best interests. In the AI context, such conflicts of interest can arise when either (i) the objectives are misspecified or (ii) there is an informational asymmetry between the principal and the agent (figure 21.1).

Many topics in AI ethics can be understood in terms of this structural view of value alignment. The following sections discuss problems of bias and fairness and artificial moral agency (both pertaining to specifying objectives) and transparency and explainability (both related to informational asymmetry).

21.1.1 Bias and fairness

From a purely scientific perspective, bias refers to statistical deviation from some norm. In AI, it can be pernicious when this deviation depends on *illegitimate* factors that impact an output. For example, gender is irrelevant to job performance, so it is illegitimate to use gender as a basis for hiring a candidate. Similarly, race is irrelevant to criminality, so it is illegitimate to use race as a feature for recidivism prediction.

Bias in AI models can be introduced in various ways (Fazelpour & Danks, 2021):

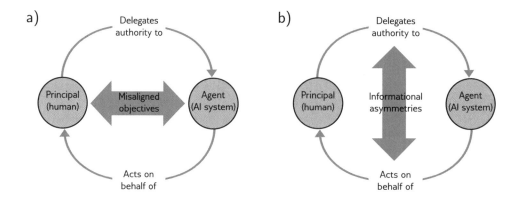

Figure 21.1 Structural description of the value alignment problem. a) Problems arise from a) misaligned objectives (e.g., bias) or b) informational asymmetries between a (human) principal and an (artificial) agent (e.g., lack of explainability). Adapted from LaCroix (2023).

- **Problem specification:** Choosing a model's goals requires a value judgment about what is important to us, which allows for the creation of biases (Fazelpour & Danks, 2021). Further biases may emerge if we fail to operationalize these choices successfully and the problem *specification* fails to capture our intended goals (Mitchell et al., 2021).

- **Data:** Algorithmic bias can result when the dataset is unrepresentative or incomplete (Danks & London, 2017). For example, the PULSE face super-resolution algorithm (Menon et al., 2020) was trained on a database of photos of predominantly white celebrities. When applied to a low-resolution portrait of Barack Obama, it generated a photo of a white man (Vincent, 2020).

  If the society in which training data are generated is structurally biased against marginalized communities, even complete and representative datasets will elicit biases (Mayson, 2018). For example, Black individuals in the US have been policed and jailed more frequently than white individuals. Hence, historical data used to train recidivism prediction models are already biased against Black communities.

- **Modeling and validation:** Choosing a mathematical definition to measure model fairness requires a value judgment. There exist distinct but equally-intuitive definitions that are logically inconsistent (Kleinberg et al., 2017; Chouldechova, 2017; Berk et al., 2017). This suggests the need to move from a purely mathematical conceptualization of fairness toward a more substantive evaluation of whether algorithms promote justice in practice (Green, 2022).

- **Deployment:** Deployed algorithms may interact with other algorithms, structures, or institutions in society to create complex feedback loops that entrench extant biases (O'Neil, 2016). For example, large language models like GPT3 (Brown et al., 2020) are trained on web data. However, when GPT3 outputs are published

Data collection	Pre-processing	Training	Post-processing
• Identify lack of examples or variates and collect	• Modify labels • Modify input data • Modify input/ output pairs	• Adversarial training • Regularize for fairness • Constrain to be fair	• Change thresholds • Trade-off accuracy for fairness

Figure 21.2 Bias mitigation. Methods have been proposed to compensate for bias at all stages of the training pipeline, from data collection to post-processing of already trained models. See Barocas et al. (2023) and Mehrabi et al. (2022).

online, the training data for future models is degraded. This may exacerbate biases and generate novel societal harm (Falbo & LaCroix, 2022).

Unfairness can be exacerbated by considerations of *intersectionality*; social categories can combine to create overlapping and interdependent systems of oppression. For example, the discrimination experienced by a queer woman of color is not merely the sum of the discrimination she might experience as queer, as gendered, or as racialized (Crenshaw, 1991). Within AI, Buolamwini & Gebru (2018) showed that face analysis algorithms trained primarily on lighter-skinned faces underperform for darker-skinned faces. However, they perform even worse on combinations of features such as skin color and gender than might be expected by considering those features independently.

Of course, steps can be taken to ensure that data are diverse, representative, and complete. But if the society in which the training data are generated is structurally biased against marginalized communities, even completely accurate datasets will elicit biases. In light of the potential for algorithmic bias and the lack of representation in training datasets described above, it is also necessary to consider how failure rates for the outputs of these systems are likely to exacerbate discrimination against already-marginalized communities (Buolamwini & Gebru, 2018; Raji & Buolamwini, 2019; Raji et al., 2022). The resulting models may codify and entrench systems of power and oppression, including capitalism and classism; sexism, misogyny, and patriarchy; colonialism and imperialism; racism and white supremacy; ableism; and cis- and heteronormativity. A perspective on bias that maintains sensitivity to power dynamics requires accounting for historical inequities and labor conditions encoded in data (Micelli et al., 2022).

To prevent this, we must actively ensure that our algorithms are fair. A naïve approach is *fairness through unawareness* which simply removes the *protected attributes* (e.g., race, gender) from the input features. Unfortunately, this is ineffective; the remaining features can still carry information about the protected attributes. More practical approaches first define a mathematical criterion for fairness. For example, the *separation* measure in binary classification requires that the prediction $\hat{y}$ is conditionally independent of the protected variable a (e.g., race) given the true label y. Then they intervene in various ways to minimize the deviation from this measure (figure 21.2).

A further complicating factor is that we cannot tell if an algorithm is unfair to a community or take steps to avoid this unless we can establish community membership. Most research on algorithmic bias and fairness has focused on ostensibly *observable* features

Notebook 21.1
Bias mitigation

that might be present in training data (e.g., gender). However, features of marginalized communities may be *unobservable*, making bias mitigation even more difficult. Examples include queerness (Tomasev et al., 2021), disability status, neurotype, class, and religion. A similar problem occurs when observable features have been excised from the training data to prevent models from exploiting them.

21.1.2   Artificial moral agency

Many decision spaces do not include actions that carry moral weight. For example, choosing the next chess move has no obvious moral consequence. However, elsewhere actions can carry moral weight. Examples include decision-making in autonomous vehicles (Awad et al., 2018; Evans et al., 2020), lethal autonomous weapons systems (Arkin, 2008a,b), and professional service robots for childcare, elderly care, and health care (Anderson & Anderson, 2008; Sharkey & Sharkey, 2012). As these systems become more autonomous, they may need to make moral decisions independent of human input.

This leads to the notion of *artificial moral agency*. An artificial moral agent is an autonomous AI system capable of making moral judgments. Moral agency can be categorized in terms of increasing complexity (Moor, 2006):

1. **Ethical impact agents** are agents whose actions have ethical impacts. Hence, almost any technology deployed in society might count as an ethical impact agent.

2. **Implicit ethical agents** are ethical impact agents that include some in-built safety features.

3. **Explicit ethical agents** can contextually follow general moral principles or rules of ethical conduct.

4. **Full ethical agents** are agents with beliefs, desires, intentions, free will, and consciousness of their actions.

The field of machine ethics seeks approaches to creating artificial moral agents. These approaches can be categorized as *top-down*, *bottom-up*, or *hybrid* (Allen et al., 2005). Top-down (theory-driven) methods directly implement and hierarchically arrange concrete rules based on some moral theory to guide ethical behavior. Asimov's "Three Laws of Robotics" are a trivial example of this approach.

In bottom-up (learning-driven) approaches, a model learns moral regularities from data without explicit programming (Wallach et al., 2008). For example, Noothigattu et al. (2018) designed a voting-based system for ethical decision-making that uses data collected from human preferences in moral dilemmas to learn social preferences; the system then summarizes and aggregates the results to render an "ethical" decision. Hybrid approaches combine top-down and bottom-up approaches.

Some researchers have questioned the very idea of artificial moral agency and argued that moral agency is unnecessary for ensuring safety (van Wynsberghe & Robbins, 2019). See Cervantes et al. (2019) for a recent survey of artificial moral agency and Tolmeijer et al. (2020) for a recent survey on technical approaches to artificial moral agency.

21.1.3 Transparency and opacity

A complex computational system is *transparent* if all of the details of its operation are known. A system is *explainable* if humans can understand how it makes decisions. In the absence of transparency or explainability, there is an asymmetry of information between the user and the AI system, which makes it hard to ensure value alignment.

Creel (2020) characterizes transparency at several levels of granularity. *Functional transparency* refers to knowledge of the algorithmic functioning of the system (i.e., the logical rules that map inputs to outputs). The methods in this book are described at this level of detail. *Structural transparency* entails knowing *how* a program executes the algorithm. This can be obscured when commands written in high-level programming languages are executed by machine code. Finally, *run transparency* requires understanding how a program was executed in a particular instance. For deep networks, this includes knowledge about the hardware, input data, training data, and interactions thereof. None of these can be ascertained by scrutinizing code.

Problem 21.4

For example, GPT3 is functionally transparent; its architecture is described in Brown et al. (2020). However, it does not exhibit structural transparency as we do not have access to the code, and it does not exhibit run transparency as we have no access to the learned parameters, hardware, or training data. The subsequent version GPT4 is not transparent at all. The details of how this commercial product works are unknown.

21.1.4 Explainability and interpretability

Even if a system is transparent, this does not imply that we can understand how a decision is made or what information this decision is based on. Deep networks may contain billions of parameters, so there is no way we can understand how they work based on examination alone. However, in some jurisdictions, the public may have a right to an explanation. Article 22 of the EU General Data Protection Regulation suggests all data subjects should have the right to "obtain an explanation of the decision reached" in cases where a decision is based solely on automated processes.[1]

These difficulties have led to the sub-field of explainable AI. One moderately successful area is producing local explanations. Although we can't explain the entire system, we can sometimes describe how a particular input was classified. For example, *Local interpretable model-agnostic explanations* or *LIME* (Ribeiro et al., 2016) samples the model output at nearby inputs and uses these samples to construct a simpler model (figure 21.3). This provides insight into the classification decision, even if the original model is neither transparent nor explainable.

Notebook 21.2
Explainability

It remains to be seen whether it is possible to build complex decision-making systems that are fully understandable to their users or even their creators. There is also an ongoing debate about what it means for a system to be explainable, understandable, or interpretable (Erasmus et al., 2021); there is currently no concrete definition of these concepts. See Molnar (2022) for more information.

---

[1]Whether Article 22 *actually* mandates such a right is debatable (see Wachter et al., 2017).

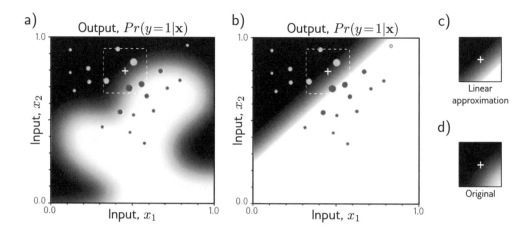

Figure 21.3 LIME. Output functions of deep networks are complex; in high dimensions, it's hard to know why a decision was made or how to modify the inputs to change it without access to the model. a) Consider trying to understand why $Pr(y = 1|\mathbf{x})$ is low at the white cross. LIME probes the network at nearby points to see if it identifies these as $Pr(y = 1|\mathbf{x}) < 0.5$ (cyan points) or $Pr(y = 1|\mathbf{x}) \geq 0.5$ (gray points). It weights these points by proximity to the point of interest (weight indicated by circle size). b) The weighted points are used to train a simpler model (here, logistic regression — a linear function passed through a sigmoid). c) Near the white cross, this approximation is close to d) the original function. Even though we did not have access to the original model, we can deduce from the parameters of this approximate model, that if we increase x_1 or decrease x_2, $Pr(y = 1|\mathbf{x})$ will increase, and the output class will change. Adapted from Prince (2022).

21.2 Intentional misuse

Problem 21.5

The problems in the previous section arise from poorly specified objectives and informational asymmetries. However, even when a system functions correctly, it can entail unethical behavior or be intentionally misused. This section highlights some specific ethical concerns arising from the misuse of AI systems.

21.2.1 Face recognition and analysis

Face recognition technologies have an especially high risk for misuse. Authoritarian states can use them to identify and silence protesters, thus risking democratic ideals of free speech and the right to protest. Smith & Miller (2022) argue that there is a mismatch between the values of liberal democracy (e.g., security, privacy, autonomy, and accountability) and the potential use cases for these technologies (e.g., border security, criminal investigation and policing, national security, and the commercialization of personal data). Thus, some researchers, activists, and policymakers have questioned whether this technology should exist (Barrett, 2020).

Moreover, these technologies often do not do what they purport to (Raji et al., 2022). For example, the New York Metropolitan Transportation Authority moved forward with and expanded its use of facial recognition despite a proof-of-concept trial reporting a 100% failure rate to detect faces within acceptable parameters (Berger, 2019). Similarly, facial analysis tools often oversell their abilities (Raji & Fried, 2020), dubiously claiming to be able to infer individuals' sexual orientation (Leuner, 2019), emotions (Stark & Hoey, 2021), hireability (Fetscherin et al., 2020), or criminality (Wu & Zhang, 2016). Stark & Hutson (2022) highlight that computer vision systems have created a resurgence in the "scientifically baseless, racist, and discredited pseudoscientific fields" of physiognomy and phrenology.

21.2.2 Militarization and political interference

Governments have a vested interest in funding AI research in the name of national security and state building. This risks an arms race between nation-states, which carries with it "high rates of investment, a lack of transparency, mutual suspicion and fear, and a perceived intent to deploy first" (Sisson et al., 2020).

Lethal autonomous weapons systems receive significant attention because they are easy to imagine, and indeed many such systems are under development (Heikkilä, 2022). However, AI also facilitates cyber-attacks and disinformation campaigns (i.e., inaccurate or misleading information that is shared with the intent to deceive). AI systems allow the creation of highly realistic fake content and facilitate the dissemination of information, often to targeted audiences (Akers et al., 2018) and at scale (Bontridder & Poullet, 2021).

Problem 21.6

Kosinski et al. (2013) suggest that sensitive variables, including sexual orientation, ethnicity, religious and political views, personality traits, intelligence, happiness, use of addictive substances, parental separation, age, and gender, can be predicted by "likes" on social media alone. From this information, personality traits like "openness" can be used for manipulative purposes (e.g., to change voting behavior).

21.2.3 Fraud

Unfortunately, AI is a useful tool for automating fraudulent activities (e.g., sending mass emails or text messages that trick people into revealing sensitive information or sending money). Generative AI can be used to deceive people into thinking they are interacting with a legitimate entity or generate fake documents that mislead or deceive people. Additionally, AI could increase the sophistication of cyber-attacks, such as by generating more convincing phishing emails or adapting to the defenses of targeted organizations.

This highlights the downside of calls for transparency in machine learning systems: the more open and transparent these systems are, the more vulnerable they may be to security risks or use by bad-faith actors. For example, generative language models, like ChatGPT, have been used to write software and emails that could be used for espionage,

Problem 21.7

ransomware, and other malware (Goodin, 2023).

The tendency to anthropomorphize computer behaviors and particularly the projection of meaning onto strings of symbols is termed the *ELIZA effect* (Hofstadter, 1995). This leads to a false sense of security when interacting with sophisticated chatbots, making people more susceptible to text-based fraud such as romance scams or business email compromise schemes (Abrahams, 2023). Véliz (2023) highlights how emoji use in some chatbots is inherently manipulative, exploiting instinctual responses to emotive images.

21.2.4 Data privacy

Problem 21.8

Modern deep learning methods rely on huge crowd-sourced datasets, which may contain sensitive or private information. Even when sensitive information is removed, auxiliary knowledge and redundant encodings can be used to de-anonymize datasets (Narayanan & Shmatikov, 2008). Indeed, this famously happened to the Governor of Massachusetts, William Weld, in 1997. After an insurance group released health records that had been stripped of obvious personal information like patient name and address, an aspiring graduate student was able to "de-anonymize" which records belonged to Governor Weld by cross-referencing with public voter rolls.

Hence, privacy-first design is important for ensuring the security of individuals' information, especially when applying deep learning techniques to high-risk areas such as healthcare and finance. Differential privacy and semantic security (homomorphic encryption or secure multi-party computation) methods can be used to ensure data security during model training (see Mireshghallah et al., 2020; Boulemtafes et al., 2020).

21.3 Other social, ethical, and professional issues

The previous section identified areas where AI can be deliberately misused. This section describes other potential side effects of the widespread adoption of AI.

21.3.1 Intellectual property

Intellectual property (IP) can be characterized as non-physical property that is the product of original thought (Moore & Himma, 2022). In practice, many AI models are trained on copyrighted material. Consequently, these models' deployment can pose legal and ethical risks and run afoul of intellectual property rights (Henderson et al., 2023).

Sometimes, these issues are explicit. When language models are prompted with excerpts of copyrighted material, their outputs may include copyrighted text verbatim, and similar issues apply in the context of image generation in diffusion models (Henderson et al., 2023; Carlini et al., 2022, 2023). Even if the training falls under "fair use," this may violate the moral rights of content creators in some cases (Weidinger et al., 2022).

More subtly, generative models (chapters 12, 14–18) raise novel questions regarding AI and intellectual property. Can the output of a machine learning model (e.g., art, music, code, text) be copyrighted or patented? Is it morally acceptable or legal to fine-tune a model on a particular artist's work to reproduce that artist's style? IP law is one area that highlights how existing legislation was not created with machine learning models in mind. Although governments and courts may set precedents in the near future, these questions are still open at the time of writing.

Problem 21.9

21.3.2   Automation bias and moral deskilling

As society relies more on AI systems, there is an increased risk of automation bias (i.e., expectations that the model outputs are correct because they are "objective"). This leads to the view that quantitative methods are better than qualitative ones. However, as we shall see in section 21.5, purportedly objective endeavors are rarely value-free.

The sociological concept of deskilling refers to the redundancy and devaluation of skills in light of automation (Braverman, 1974). For example, off-loading cognitive skills like memory onto technology may cause a decrease in our capacity to remember things. Analogously, the automation of AI in morally-loaded decision-making may lead to a decrease in our moral abilities (Vallor, 2015). For example, in the context of war, the automation of weapons systems may lead to the dehumanization of victims of war (Asaro, 2012; Heyns, 2017). Similarly, care robots in elderly-, child-, or healthcare settings may reduce our ability to care for one another (Vallor, 2011).

21.3.3   Environmental impact

Training deep networks requires significant computational power and hence consumes a large amount of energy. Strubell et al. (2019, 2020) estimate that training a transformer model with 213 million parameters emitted around 284 tonnes of CO_2.[2] Luccioni et al. (2022) have provided similar estimates for the emissions produced from training the BLOOM language model. Unfortunately, the increasing prevalence of closed, proprietary models means that we know nothing about their environmental impacts (Luccioni, 2023).

21.3.4   Employment and society

The history of technological innovation is a history of job displacement. In 2018, the McKinsey Global Institute estimated that AI may increase economic output by approximately US $13 trillion by 2030, primarily from the substitution of labor by automation (Bughin et al., 2018). Another study from the McKinsey Global Institute suggests that up to 30% of the global workforce (10-800 million people) could have their jobs displaced due to AI between 2016 and 2030 (Manyika et al., 2017; Manyika & Sneader, 2018).

---

[2]As a baseline, it is estimated that the average human is responsible for around 5 tonnes of CO_2 per year, with individuals from major oil-producing countries responsible for three times this amount. See https://ourworldindata.org/co2-emissions.

Problem 21.10

However, forecasting is inherently difficult, and although automation by AI may lead to short-term job losses, the concept of *technological unemployment* has been described as a "temporary phase of maladjustment" (Keynes, 2010). This is because gains in wealth can offset gains in productivity by creating increased demand for products and services. In addition, new technologies can create new types of jobs.

Even if automation doesn't lead to a net loss of overall employment in the long term, new social programs may be required in the short term. Therefore, regardless of whether one is optimistic (Brynjolfsson & McAfee, 2016; Danaher, 2019), neutral (Metcalf et al., 2016; Calo, 2018; Frey, 2019), or pessimistic (Frey & Osborne, 2017) about the possibility of unemployment in light of AI, it is clear that society will be changed significantly.

21.3.5   Concentration of power

As deep networks increase in size, there is a corresponding increase in the amount of data and computing power required to train these models. In this regard, smaller companies and start-ups may not be able to compete with large, established tech companies. This may give rise to a feedback loop whereby the power and wealth become increasingly concentrated in the hands of a small number of corporations. A recent study finds an increasing discrepancy between publications at major AI venues by large tech firms and "elite" universities versus mid- or lower-tier universities (Ahmed & Wahed, 2016). In many views, such a concentration of wealth and power is incompatible with just distributions in society (Rawls, 1971).

Problem 21.11

This has led to calls to democratize AI by making it possible for everyone to create such systems (Li, 2018; Knight, 2018; Kratsios, 2019; Riedl, 2020). Such a process requires making deep learning technologies more widely available and easier to use via open source and open science so that more people can benefit from them. This reduces barriers to entry and increases access to AI while cutting down costs, ensuring model accuracy, and increasing participation and inclusion (Ahmed et al., 2020).

21.4   Case study

We now describe a case study that speaks to many of the issues that we have discussed in this chapter. In 2018, the popular media reported on a controversial facial analysis model—dubbed "gaydar AI" (Wang & Kosinski, 2018)—with sensationalist headlines like *AI Can Tell If You're Gay: Artificial Intelligence Predicts Sexuality From One Photo with Startling Accuracy* (Ahmed, 2017); *A Frightening AI Can Determine Whether a Person Is Gay With 91 Percent Accuracy* (Matsakis, 2017); and *Artificial Intelligence System Can Tell If You're Gay* (Fernandez, 2017).

There are a number of problems with this work. First, the training dataset was highly biased and unrepresentative, being comprised mostly of Caucasian images. Second, modeling and validation are also questionable, given the fluidity of gender and sexuality. Third, the most obvious use case for such a model is the targeted discrimination and persecution of LGBTQ+ individuals in countries where queerness is criminalized. Fourth, with regard to transparency, explainability, and value alignment more generally, the "gaydar" model appears to pick up on spurious correlations due to patterns in grooming, presentation, and lifestyle rather than facial structure, as the authors claimed (Agüera y Arcas et al., 2018). Fifth, with regard to data privacy, questions arise regarding the ethics of scraping "public" photos and sexual orientation labels from a dating website. Finally, with regard to scientific communication, the researchers communicated their results in a way that was sure to generate headlines: even the title of the paper is an overstatement of the model's abilities: *Deep Neural Networks Can Detect Sexual Orientation from Faces.* (They cannot.)

It should also be apparent that a facial-analysis model for determining sexual orientation does *nothing* whatsoever to benefit the LGBTQ+ community. If it is to benefit society, the most important question is whether a particular study, experiment, model, application, or technology serves the interests of the community to which it pertains.

21.5   The value-free ideal of science

This chapter has enumerated a number of ways that the objectives of AI systems can unintentionally, or through misuse, diverge from the values of humanity. We now argue that scientists are not neutral actors; their values inevitably impinge on their work.

Perhaps this is surprising. There is a broad belief that science is—or ought to be—objective. This is codified by the *value-free ideal of science.* Many would argue that machine learning is objective because algorithms are just mathematics. However, analogous to algorithmic bias (section 21.1.1), there are four stages at which the values of AI practitioners can affect their work (Reiss & Sprenger, 2017):

1. The choice of research problem.
2. Gathering evidence related to a research problem.
3. Accepting a scientific hypothesis as an answer to a problem.
4. Applying the results of scientific research.

It is perhaps uncontroversial that values play a significant role in the first and last of these stages. The initial selection of research problems and the choice of subsequent applications are influenced by the interests of scientists, institutions, and funding agencies. However, the value-free ideal of science prescribes minimizing the influence of moral, personal, social, political, and cultural values on the intervening scientific process. This idea presupposes the *value-neutrality thesis*, which suggests that scientists can (at least in principle) attend to stages (2) and (3) without making these value judgments.

However, whether intentional or not, values are embedded in machine learning research. Most of these values would be classed as *epistemic* (e.g., performance, generalization, building on past work, efficiency, novelty). But deciding the set of values is itself a value-laden decision; few papers explicitly discuss societal need, and fewer still discuss potential negative impacts (Birhane et al., 2022b). Philosophers of science have questioned whether the value-free ideal of science is attainable or desirable. For example, Longino (1990, 1996) argues that these epistemic values are not *purely* epistemic. Kitcher (2011a,b) argues that scientists don't typically care about *truth* itself; instead, they pursue truths relevant to their goals and interests.

Machine learning depends on inductive inference and is hence prone to inductive risk. Models are only constrained at the training data points, and the curse of dimensionality means this is a tiny proportion of the input space; outputs can always be wrong, regardless of how much data we use to train the model. It follows that choosing to accept or reject a model prediction requires a value judgment: that the risks if we are wrong in acceptance are lower than the risks if we are wrong in rejection.

Hence, the use of inductive inference implies that machine learning models are deeply value-laden (Johnson, 2022). In fact, if they were not, they would have no application: it is precisely *because* they are value-laden that they are useful. Thus, accepting that algorithms are used for ranking, sorting, filtering, recommending, categorizing, labeling, predicting, etc., in the real world implies that these processes will have real-world effects. As machine learning systems become increasingly commercialized and applied, they become more entrenched in the things we care about.

These insights have implications for researchers who believe that algorithms are somehow more objective than human decision-makers (and, therefore, ought to replace human decision-makers in areas where we think objectivity matters).

21.6   Responsible AI research as a collective action problem

It is easy to defer responsibility. Students and professionals who read this chapter might think their work is so far removed from the real world or a small part of a larger machine that their actions could not make a difference. However, this is a mistake. Researchers often have a choice about the projects to which they devote their time, the companies or institutions for which they work, the knowledge they seek, the social and intellectual circles in which they interact, and the way they communicate.

Problem 21.12

Doing the right thing, whatever that may comprise, often takes the form of a social dilemma; the best outcomes depend upon cooperation, although it isn't necessarily in any individual's interest to cooperate: responsible AI research is a collective action problem.

21.6.1   Scientific communication

One positive step is to communicate responsibly. Misinformation spreads faster and persists more readily than the truth in many types of social networks (LaCroix et al., 2021; Ceylan et al., 2023). As such, it is important not to overstate machine learning systems' abilities (see case study above) and to avoid misleading anthropomorphism. It is also important to be aware of the potential for the misapplication of machine learning techniques. For example, pseudoscientific practices like phrenology and physiognomy have found a surprising resurgence in AI (Stark & Hutson, 2022).

21.6.2   Diversity and heterogeneity

A second positive step is to encourage diversity. When social groups are homogeneous (composed mainly of similar members) or homophilous (comprising members that tend to associate with similar others), the dominant group tends to have its conventions recapitulated and stabilized (O'Connor & Bruner, 2019). One way to mitigate systems of oppression is to ensure that diverse views are considered. This might be achieved through equity, diversity, inclusion, and accessibility initiatives (at an institutional level), participatory and community-based approaches to research (at the research level), and increased awareness of social, political, and moral issues (at an individual level).

The theory of *standpoint epistemology* (Harding, 1986) suggests that knowledge is socially situated (i.e., depends on one's social position in society). Homogeneity in tech circles can give rise to biased tech (Noble, 2018; Eubanks, 2018; Benjamin, 2019; Broussard, 2023). Lack of diversity implies that the perspectives of the individuals who create these technologies will seep into the datasets, algorithms, and code as the default perspective. Broussard (2023) argues that because much technology is developed by able-bodied, white, cisgender, American men, that technology is *optimized for* able-bodied, white, cisgender, American men, the perspective of whom is taken as the status quo. Ensuring technologies benefit historically marginalized communities requires researchers to understand the needs, wants, and perspectives of those communities (Birhane et al., 2022a). *Design justice* and participatory- and community-based approaches to AI research contend that the communities affected by technologies should be actively involved in their design (Constanza-Chock, 2020).

21.7   Ways forward

It is undeniable that AI will radically change society for better or worse. However, optimistic visions of a future Utopian society driven by AI should be met with caution and a healthy dose of critical reflection. Many of the touted benefits of AI are beneficial only in certain contexts and only to a subset of society. For example, Green (2019) highlights that one project developed using AI to enhance police accountability and alternatives to incarceration and another developed to increase security through predictive policing are both advertised as "AI for Social Good." Assigning this label is a value judgment that lacks any grounding principles; one community's good is another's harm.

When considering the potential for emerging technologies to benefit society, it is necessary to reflect on whether those benefits will be equally or equitably distributed. It is often assumed that the most technologically advanced solution is the best one—so-called *technochauvinism* (Broussard, 2018). However, many social issues arise from underlying social problems and do not warrant technological solutions.

Some common themes emerged throughout this chapter, and we would like to impress four key points upon the reader:

1. **Research in machine learning cannot avoid ethics.** Historically, researchers could focus on fundamental aspects of their work in a controlled laboratory set-

ting. However, this luxury is dwindling due to the vast economic incentives to commercialize AI and the degree to which academic work is funded by industry (see Abdalla & Abdalla, 2021); even theoretical studies may have social impacts, so researchers must engage with the social and ethical dimensions of their work.

2. **Even purely technical decisions can be value-laden.** There is still a widely-held view that AI is fundamentally just mathematics and, therefore, it is "objective," and ethics are irrelevant. This assumption is not true when we consider the creation of AI systems or their deployment.

3. **We should question the structures within which AI work takes place.** Much research on AI ethics focuses on specific situations rather than questioning the larger social structures within which AI will be deployed. For example, there is considerable interest in ensuring algorithmic fairness, but it may not always be possible to instantiate conceptions of fairness, justice, or equity within extant social and political structures. Therefore, technology is inherently political.

4. **Social and ethical problems don't necessarily require technical solutions.** Many potential ethical problems surrounding AI technologies are primarily social and structural, so technical innovation alone cannot solve these problems; if scientists are to effect positive change with new technology, they must take a political and moral position.

Problem 21.13

Where does this leave the average scientist? Perhaps with the following imperative: it is necessary to reflect upon the moral and social dimensions of one's work. This might require actively engaging those communities that are likely to be most affected by new technologies, thus cultivating relationships between researchers and communities and empowering those communities. Likewise, it might involve engagement with the literature beyond one's own discipline. For philosophical questions, the *Stanford Encyclopedia of Philosophy* is an invaluable resource. Interdisciplinary conferences are also useful in this regard. Leading work is published at both the Conference on Fairness, Accountability, and Transparency (FAccT) and the Conference on AI, Ethics, and Society (AIES).

21.8 Summary

This chapter considered the ethical implications of deep learning and AI. The value alignment problem is the task of ensuring that the objectives of AI systems are aligned with human objectives. Bias, explainability, artificial moral agency, and other topics can be viewed through this lens. AI can be intentionally misused, and this chapter detailed some ways this can happen. Progress in AI has further implications in areas as diverse as IP law and climate change.

Ethical AI is a collective action problem, and the chapter concludes with an appeal to scientists to consider the moral and ethical implications of their work. Every ethical issue is not within the control of every individual computer scientist. However, this does not imply that researchers have no responsibility whatsoever to consider—and mitigate where they can—the potential for misuse of the systems they create.

Problems

Problem 21.1 It was suggested that the most common specification of the value alignment problem for AI is "the problem of ensuring that the values of AI systems are aligned with the values of humanity." Discuss the ways in which this statement of the problem is underspecified.
Discussion Resource: LaCroix (2023).

Problem 21.2 Goodhart's law states that "when a measure becomes a target, it ceases to be a good measure." Consider how this law might be reformulated to apply to value alignment for artificial intelligence, given that the loss function is a mere proxy for our true objectives.

Problem 21.3 Suppose a university uses data from past students to build models for predicting "student success," where those models can support informed changes in policies and practices. Consider how biases might affect each of the four stages of the development and deployment of this model.
Discussion Resource: Fazelpour & Danks (2021).

Problem 21.4 We might think of functional transparency, structural transparency, and run transparency as orthogonal. Provide an example of how an increase in one form of transparency may not lead to a concomitant increase in another form of transparency.
Discussion Resource: Creel (2020).

Problem 21.5 If a computer scientist writes a research paper on AI or pushes code to a public repository, do you consider them responsible for future misuse of their work?

Problem 21.6 To what extent do you think the militarization of AI is inevitable?

Problem 21.7 In light of the possible misuse of AI highlighted in section 21.2, make arguments both for and against the open-source culture of research in deep learning.

Problem 21.8 Some have suggested that personal data is a source of power for those who own it. Discuss the ways personal data is valuable to companies that utilize deep learning and consider the claim that losses to privacy are experienced collectively rather than individually.
Discussion Resource: Véliz (2020).

Problem 21.9 What are the implications of generative AI for the creative industries? How do you think IP laws should be modified to cope with this new development?

Problem 21.10 A good forecast must (i) be specific enough to know when it is wrong, (ii) account for possible cognitive biases, and (iii) allow for rationally updating beliefs. Consider any claim in the recent media about future AI and discuss whether it satisfies these criteria.
Discussion Resource: Tetlock & Gardner (2016).

Problem 21.11 Some critics have argued that calls to democratize AI have focused too heavily on the *participatory* aspects of democracy, which can increase risks of errors in collective perception, reasoning, and agency, leading to morally-bad outcomes. Reflect on each of the following: *What* aspects of AI should be democratized? *Why* should AI be democratized? *How* should AI be democratized?
Discussion Resource: Himmelreich (2022).

Problem 21.12 In March 2023, the Future of Life Institute published a letter, "Pause Giant AI Experiments," in which they called on all AI labs to immediately pause for at least six months the training of AI systems more powerful than GPT-4. Discuss the motivations of the authors in writing this letter, the public reaction, and the implications of such a pause. Relate this episode to the view that AI ethics can be considered a collective action problem (section 21.6).
Discussion Resource: Gebru et al. (2023).

Problem 21.13 Discuss the merits of the four points in section 21.7. Do you agree with them?

Appendix A

Notation

This appendix details the notation used in this book. This mostly adheres to standard conventions in computer science, but deep learning is applicable to many different areas, so it is explained in full. In addition, there are several notational conventions that are unique to this book, including notation for functions and the systematic distinction between parameters and variables.

Scalars, vectors, matrices, and tensors

Scalars are denoted by either small or capital letters a, A, α. Column vectors (i.e., 1D arrays of numbers) are denoted by small bold letters $\mathbf{a}, \boldsymbol{\phi}$, and row vectors as the transpose of column vectors $\mathbf{a}^T, \boldsymbol{\phi}^T$. Matrices and tensors (i.e., 2D and ND arrays of numbers, respectively) are both represented by bold capital letters $\mathbf{B}, \boldsymbol{\Phi}$.

Variables and parameters

Variables (usually the inputs and outputs of functions or intermediate calculations) are always denoted by Roman letters $a, \mathbf{b}, \mathbf{C}$. Parameters (which are internal to functions or probability distributions) are always denoted by Greek letters $\alpha, \boldsymbol{\beta}, \boldsymbol{\Gamma}$. Generic, unspecified parameters are denoted by $\boldsymbol{\phi}$. This distinction is retained throughout the book except for the policy in reinforcement learning, which is denoted by π according to the usual convention.

Sets

Sets are denoted by curly brackets, so $\{0, 1, 2\}$ denotes the numbers 0, 1, and 2. The notation $\{0, 1, 2, \ldots\}$ denotes the set of non-negative integers. Sometimes, we want to specify a set of variables and $\{\mathbf{x}_i\}_{i=1}^I$ denotes the I variables $\mathbf{x}_1, \ldots \mathbf{x}_I$. When it's not necessary to specify how many items are in the set, this is shortened to $\{\mathbf{x}_i\}$. The notation $\{\mathbf{x}_i, \mathbf{y}_i\}_{i=1}^I$ denotes the set of I pairs $\mathbf{x}_i, \mathbf{y}_i$. The convention for naming sets is to use calligraphic letters. Notably, $\mathcal{B}_t$ is used to denote the set of indices in a batch at iteration t during training. The number of elements in a set $\mathcal{S}$ is denoted by $|\mathcal{S}|$.

The set $\mathbb{R}$ denotes the set of real numbers. The set $\mathbb{R}^+$ denotes the set of non-negative real numbers. The notation $\mathbb{R}^D$ denotes the set of D-dimensional vectors containing real numbers. The notation $\mathbb{R}^{D_1 \times D_2}$ denotes the set of matrices of dimension $D_1 \times D_2$. The notation $\mathbb{R}^{D_1 \times D_2 \times D_3}$ denotes the set of tensors of size $D_1 \times D_2 \times D_3$ and so on.

The notation $[a, b]$ denotes the real numbers from a to b, including a and b themselves. When the square brackets are replaced by round brackets, this means that the adjacent value is not included in the set. For example, the set $(-\pi, \pi]$ denotes the real numbers from $-\pi$ to π, but excluding $-\pi$.

Membership of sets is denoted by the symbol $\in$, so $x \in \mathbb{R}^+$ means that the variable x is a non-negative real number, and the notation $\boldsymbol{\Sigma} \in \mathbb{R}^{D \times D}$ denotes that $\boldsymbol{\Sigma}$ is a matrix of size $D \times D$. Sometimes, we want to work through each element of a set systematically, and the notation $\forall \{1, \ldots, K\}$ means "for all" the integers from 1 to K.

Functions

Functions are expressed as a name, followed by square brackets that contain the arguments of the function. For example, $\log[x]$ returns the logarithm of the variable x. When the function returns a vector, it is written in bold and starts with a small letter. For example, the function $\mathbf{y} = \mathbf{mlp}[\mathbf{x}, \boldsymbol{\phi}]$ returns a vector $\mathbf{y}$ and has vector arguments $\mathbf{x}$ and $\boldsymbol{\phi}$. When a function returns a matrix or tensor, it is written in bold and starts with a capital letter. For example, the function $\mathbf{Y} = \mathbf{Sa}[\mathbf{X}, \boldsymbol{\phi}]$ returns a matrix $\mathbf{Y}$ and has arguments $\mathbf{X}$ and $\boldsymbol{\phi}$. When we want to leave the arguments of a function deliberately ambiguous, we use the bullet symbol (e.g., $\mathbf{mlp}[\bullet, \boldsymbol{\phi}]$).

Minimizing and maximizing

Some special functions are used repeatedly throughout the text:

- The function $\min_x[\mathrm{f}[x]]$ returns the minimum value of the function $\mathrm{f}[x]$ over all possible values of the variable x. This notation is often used without specifying the details of how this minimum might be found.
- The function $\mathrm{argmin}_x[\mathrm{f}[x]]$ returns the value of x that minimizes $\mathrm{f}[x]$, so if $y = \mathrm{argmin}_x[\mathrm{f}[x]]$, then $\min_x[\mathrm{f}[x]] = \mathrm{f}[y]$.
- The functions $\max_x[\mathrm{f}[x]]$ and $\mathrm{argmax}_x[\mathrm{f}[x]]$ perform the equivalent operations for maximizing functions.

Probability distributions

Probability distributions should be written as $Pr(x = a)$, denoting that the random variable x takes the value of a. However, this notation is cumbersome. Hence, we usually simplify this and just write $Pr(x)$, where x denotes either the random variable or the value it takes according to the sense of the equation. The conditional probability of y given x is written as $Pr(y|x)$. The joint probability of y and x is written as $Pr(y, x)$. These two forms can be combined, so $Pr(\mathbf{y}|\mathbf{x}, \boldsymbol{\phi})$ denotes the probability of the variable $\mathbf{y}$, given that we know $\mathbf{x}$ and $\boldsymbol{\phi}$. Similarly, $Pr(\mathbf{y}, \mathbf{x}|\boldsymbol{\phi})$ denotes the probability of variables $\mathbf{y}$ and $\mathbf{x}$ given that we know $\boldsymbol{\phi}$. When we need two probability distributions over the same variable, we write $Pr(x)$ for the first distribution and $q(x)$ for the second. More information about probability distributions can be found in appendix C.

Asymptotic notation

Asymptotic notation is used to compare the amount of work done by different algorithms as the size D of the input increases. This can be done in various ways, but this book only uses *big-O* notation, which represents an upper bound on the growth of computation in an algorithm. A function $f[n]$ is $\mathcal{O}[g[n]]$ if there exists a constant $c > 0$ and integer n_0 such that $f[n] < c \cdot g[n]$ for all $n > n_0$.

This notation provides a bound on the worst-case running time of an algorithm. For example, when we say that inversion of a $D \times D$ matrix is $\mathcal{O}[D^3]$, we mean that the computation will increase no faster than some constant times D^3 once D is large enough. This gives us an idea of how feasible it is to invert matrices of different sizes. If $D = 10^3$, then it may take of the order of 10^9 operations to invert it.

Miscellaneous

A small dot in a mathematical equation is intended to improve ease of reading and has no real meaning (or just implies multiplication). For example, $\alpha \cdot f[x]$ is the same as $\alpha f[x]$ but is easier to read. To avoid ambiguity, dot products are written as $\mathbf{a}^T \mathbf{b}$ (see appendix B.3.4). A left arrow symbol $\leftarrow$ denotes assignment, so $x \leftarrow x + 2$ means that we are adding two to the current value of x.

Appendix B

Mathematics

This appendix reviews mathematical concepts that are used in the main text.

B.1 Functions

A *function* defines a mapping from a set $\mathcal{X}$ (e.g., the set of real numbers) to another set $\mathcal{Y}$. An *injection* is a one-to-one function where *every* element in the first set maps to a unique position in the second set (but there may be elements of the second set that are not mapped to). A *surjection* is a function where every element in the second set receives a mapping from the first (but there may be elements of the first set that are not mapped). A *bijection* or *bijective mapping* is a function that is both injective and surjective. It provides a one-to-one correspondence between all members of the two sets. A *diffeomorphism* is a special case of a bijection where both the forward and reverse mapping are differentiable.

B.1.1 Lipschitz constant

A function $f[z]$ is *Lipschitz continuous* if for all z_1, z_2:

$$||f[z_1] - f[z_2]|| \leq \beta ||z_1 - z_2||, \tag{B.1}$$

where β is known as the Lipschitz constant and determines the maximum gradient of the function (i.e., how fast the function can change) with respect to the distance metric. If the Lipschitz constant is less than one, the function is a contraction mapping, and we can use Banach's theorem to find the inverse for any point (see figure 16.9).

Composing two functions with Lipschitz constants β_1 and β_2 creates a new Lipschitz continuous function with a constant that is less than or equal to $\beta_1\beta_2$. Adding two functions with Lipschitz constants β_1 and β_2 creates a new Lipschitz continuous function with a constant that is less than or equal to $\beta_1 + \beta_2$. The Lipschitz constant of a linear transformation $\mathbf{f}[\mathbf{z}] = \mathbf{A}\mathbf{z} + \mathbf{b}$ with respect to a Euclidean distance measure is the maximum eigenvalue of $\mathbf{A}$.

B.1.2   Convexity

A function is *convex* if we can draw a straight line between any two points on the function, and this line always lies above the function. Similarly, a function is *concave* if a straight line between any two points always lies below the function. By definition, convex (concave) functions have at most one minimum (maximum).

A region of $\mathbb{R}^D$ is convex if we can draw a straight line between any two points on the boundary of the region without intersecting the boundary in another place. Gradient descent guarantees to find the global minimum of any function that is both convex and defined on a convex region.

B.1.3   Special functions

The following functions are used in the main text:

- The *exponential function* $y = \exp[x]$ (figure B.1a) maps a real variable $x \in \mathbb{R}$ to a non-negative number $y \in \mathcal{R}^+$ as $y = e^x$.
- The *logarithm* $x = \log[y]$ (figure B.1b) is the inverse of the exponential function and maps a non-negative number $y \in \mathcal{R}^+$ to a real variable $x \in \mathbb{R}$. Note that all logarithms in this book are natural (i.e., in base e).
- The *gamma function* $\Gamma[x]$ (figure B.1c) is defined as:

$$\Gamma[x] = \int_0^\infty t^{x-1} e^{-t} dt. \tag{B.2}$$

This extends the factorial function to continuous values so that $\Gamma[x] = (x-1)!$ for $x \in \{1, 2, \ldots\}$.

- The *Dirac delta function* $\delta[\mathbf{z}]$ has a total area of one, all of which is at position $\mathbf{z} = \mathbf{0}$. A dataset with N elements can be thought of as a probability distribution consisting of a sum of N delta functions centered at each data point $\mathbf{x}_i$ and scaled by $1/N$. The delta function is usually drawn as an arrow (e.g., figure 5.12). The delta function has the key property that:

$$\int \mathrm{f}[\mathbf{x}] \delta[\mathbf{x} - \mathbf{x}_0] d\mathbf{x} = \mathrm{f}[\mathbf{x}_0]. \tag{B.3}$$

B.1.4   Stirling's formula

Stirling's formula (figure B.2) approximates the factorial function (and hence the Gamma function) using the formula:

$$x! \approx \sqrt{2\pi x} \left(\frac{x}{e}\right)^x. \tag{B.4}$$

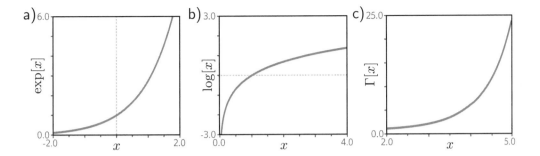

Figure B.1 Exponential, logarithm, and gamma functions. a) The exponential function maps a real number to a positive number. It is a convex function. b) The logarithm is the inverse of the exponential and maps a positive number to a real number. It is a concave function. c) The Gamma function is a continuous extension of the factorial function so that $\Gamma[x] = (x-1)!$ for $x \in \{1, 2, \ldots\}$.

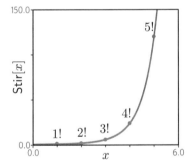

Figure B.2 Stirling's formula. The factorial function $x!$ can be approximated by Stirling's formula $\text{Stir}[x]$ which is defined for every real value.

B.2 Binomial coefficients

Binomial coefficients are written as $\binom{n}{k}$ and pronounced as "n choose k." They are positive integers that represent the number of ways of choosing an unordered subset of k items from a set of n items without replacement. Binomial coefficients can be computed using the simple formula:

$$\binom{n}{k} = \frac{n!}{k!(n-k)!}.$$

(B.5)

B.2.1 Autocorrelation

The autocorrelation $r[\tau]$ of a continuous function $f[z]$ is defined as:

$$r[\tau] = \int_{-\infty}^{\infty} f[t+\tau]f[t]dt,$$

(B.6)

where τ is the time lag. Sometimes, this is normalized by $r[0]$ so that the autocorrelation at time lag zero is one. The autocorrelation function is a measure of the correlation of the function with itself as a function of an offset (i.e., the time lag). If a function changes slowly and predictably, then the autocorrelation function will decrease slowly as the time lag increases from zero. If the function changes fast and unpredictably, then it will decrease quickly to zero.

B.3   Vector, matrices, and tensors

In machine learning, a vector $\mathbf{x} \in \mathbb{R}^D$ is a one-dimensional array of D numbers, which we will assume are organized in a column. Similarly, a matrix $\mathbf{Y} \in \mathbb{R}^{D_1 \times D_2}$ is a two-dimensional array of numbers with D_1 rows and D_2 columns. A tensor $\mathbf{z} \in \mathbb{R}^{D_1 \times D_2 \dots \times D_N}$ is an N-dimensional array of numbers. Confusingly, all three of these quantities are stored in objects known as "tensors" in deep learning APIs such as PyTorch and TensorFlow.

B.3.1   Transpose

The transpose $\mathbf{A}^T \in \mathbb{R}^{D_2 \times D_1}$ of a matrix $\mathbf{A} \in \mathbb{R}^{D_1 \times D_2}$ is formed by reflecting it around the principal diagonal so that the kth column becomes the kth row and vice-versa. If we take the transpose of a matrix product $\mathbf{AB}$, then we take the transpose of the original matrices but reverse the order so that

$$(\mathbf{AB})^T = \mathbf{B}^T \mathbf{A}^T. \tag{B.7}$$

The transpose of a column vector $\mathbf{a}$ is a row vector $\mathbf{a}^T$ and vice-versa.

B.3.2   Vector and matrix norms

For a vector $\mathbf{z}$, the ℓ_p norm is defined as:

$$||\mathbf{z}||_p = \left(\sum_{d=1}^{D} |z_d|^p \right)^{1/p}. \tag{B.8}$$

When $p = 2$, this returns the length of the vector, and this is known as the *Euclidean norm*. It is this case that is most commonly used in deep learning, and often the exponent p is omitted, and the Euclidean norm is just written as $||\mathbf{z}||$. When $p = \infty$, the operator returns the maximum absolute value in the vector.

Norms can be computed in a similar way for matrices. For example, the ℓ_2 norm of a matrix $\mathbf{Z}$ (known as the *Frobenius norm*) is calculated as:

$$||\mathbf{Z}||_F = \left(\sum_{i=1}^{I} \sum_{j=1}^{J} |z_{ij}|^2 \right)^{1/2}. \tag{B.9}$$

B.3.3 Product of matrices

The product $\mathbf{C} = \mathbf{AB}$ of two matrices $\mathbf{A} \in \mathbb{R}^{D_1 \times D_2}$ and $\mathbf{B} \in \mathbb{R}^{D_2 \times D_3}$ is a third matrix $\mathbf{C} \in \mathbb{R}^{D_1 \times D_3}$ where:

$$C_{ij} = \sum_{d=1}^{D_2} A_{id} B_{dj}. \tag{B.10}$$

B.3.4 Dot product of vectors

The dot product $\mathbf{a}^T\mathbf{b}$ of two vectors $\mathbf{a} \in \mathbb{R}^D$ and $\mathbf{b} \in \mathbb{R}^D$ is a scalar and is defined as:

$$\mathbf{a}^T\mathbf{b} = \mathbf{b}^T\mathbf{a} = \sum_{d=1}^{D} a_d b_d. \tag{B.11}$$

It can be shown that the dot product is proportional to the Euclidean norm of the first vector times the Euclidean norm of the second vector times the angle θ between them:

$$\mathbf{a}^T\mathbf{b} = ||\mathbf{a}|| \, ||\mathbf{b}|| \, \cos[\theta]. \tag{B.12}$$

B.3.5 Inverse

A square matrix $\mathbf{A}$ may or may not have an inverse $\mathbf{A}^{-1}$ such that $\mathbf{A}^{-1}\mathbf{A} = \mathbf{A}\mathbf{A}^{-1} = \mathbf{I}$. If a matrix does not have an inverse, it is called *singular*. If we take the inverse of a matrix product $\mathbf{AB}$ then we can equivalently take the inverse of each matrix individually and reverse the order of multiplication.

$$(\mathbf{AB})^{-1} = \mathbf{B}^{-1}\mathbf{A}^{-1}. \tag{B.13}$$

In general, it takes $\mathcal{O}[D^3]$ operations to invert a $D \times D$ matrix. However, inversion is more efficient for special types of matrices, including diagonal, orthogonal, and triangular matrices (see section B.4).

B.3.6 Subspaces

Consider a matrix $\mathbf{A} \in \mathbb{R}^{D_1 \times D_2}$. If the number of columns D_2 of the matrix is fewer than the number of rows D_1 (i.e., the matrix is "portrait"), the product $\mathbf{Ax}$ cannot reach all

Figure B.3 Eigenvalues. When the points $\{\mathbf{x}_i\}$ on the unit circle are transformed to points $\{\mathbf{x}'_i\}$ by a linear transformation $\mathbf{x}'_i = \mathbf{A}\mathbf{x}_i$, they are mapped to an ellipse. For example, the light blue point on the unit circle is mapped to the light blue point on the ellipse. The length of the major (longest) axis of the ellipse (long gray arrow) is the magnitude of the first eigenvalue of the matrix, and the length of the minor (shortest) axis of the ellipse (short gray arrow) is the magnitude of the second eigenvalue.

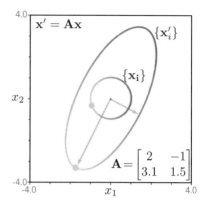

possible positions in the D_1-dimensional output space. This product consists of the D_2 columns of $\mathbf{A}$ weighted by the D_2 elements of $\mathbf{x}$ and can only reach the *linear subspace* that is spanned by these columns. This is known as the *column space* of the matrix. Conversely, for a landscape matrix $\mathbf{A}$, the part of the input space that maps to zero (i.e., those $\mathbf{x}$ where $\mathbf{A}\mathbf{x} = \mathbf{0}$) is termed the *nullspace* of the matrix.

B.3.7 Eigenspectrum

If we multiply the set of 2D points on a unit circle by a 2×2 matrix $\mathbf{A}$, they map to an ellipse (figure B.3). The radii of the major and minor axes of this ellipse (i.e., the longest and shortest directions) correspond to the magnitude of the *eigenvalues* λ_1 and λ_2 of the matrix. The eigenvalues also have a sign, which relates to whether the matrix reflects the inputs about the origin. The same idea applies in higher dimensions. A $D-$dimensional spheroid is mapped by a $D \times D$ matrix $\mathbf{A}$ to a D-dimensional ellipsoid. The radii of the D principal axes of this ellipsoid determine the magnitude of the eigenvalues.

The *spectral norm* of a square matrix is the largest absolute eigenvalue. It captures the largest possible change in magnitude when the matrix is applied to a vector of unit length. As such, it tells us about the Lipschitz constant of the transformation. The set of eigenvalues is sometimes called the *eigenspectrum* and tells us about the magnitude of the scaling applied by the matrix across all directions. This information can be summarized using the *determinant* and *trace* of the matrix.

B.3.8 Determinant and trace

Every square matrix $\mathbf{A}$ has a scalar associated with it called the determinant and denoted by $|\mathbf{A}|$ or $\det[\mathbf{A}]$, which is the product of the eigenvalues. It is hence related to the average scaling applied by the matrix for different inputs. Matrices with small absolute determinants tend to decrease the norm of vectors upon multiplication. Matrices with large absolute determinants tend to increase the norm. If a matrix is *singular*, the determinant will be zero, and there will be at least one direction in space that is mapped to the origin when the matrix is applied. Determinants of matrix expressions obey the following rules:

$$\begin{aligned}
|\mathbf{A}^T| &= |\mathbf{A}| \\
|\mathbf{AB}| &= |\mathbf{A}||\mathbf{B}| \\
|\mathbf{A}^{-1}| &= 1/|\mathbf{A}|.
\end{aligned} \tag{B.14}$$

The trace of a square matrix is the sum of the diagonal values (the matrix itself need not be diagonal) or the sum of the eigenvalues. Traces obey these rules:

$$\begin{aligned}
\text{trace}[\mathbf{A}^{\mathbf{T}}] &= \text{trace}[\mathbf{A}] \\
\text{trace}[\mathbf{AB}] &= \text{trace}[\mathbf{BA}] \\
\text{trace}[\mathbf{A} + \mathbf{B}] &= \text{trace}[\mathbf{A}] + \text{trace}[\mathbf{B}] \\
\text{trace}[\mathbf{ABC}] &= \text{trace}[\mathbf{BCA}] = \text{trace}[\mathbf{CAB}],
\end{aligned} \tag{B.15}$$

where in the last relation, the trace is invariant for cyclic permutations only, so in general, $\text{trace}[\mathbf{ABC}] \neq \text{trace}[\mathbf{BAC}]$.

B.4 Special types of matrix

Calculating the inverse of a square matrix $\mathbf{A} \in \mathbb{R}^{D \times D}$ has a complexity of $\mathcal{O}[D^3]$, as does the computation of the determinant. However, for some matrices with special properties, these computations can be more efficient.

B.4.1 Diagonal matrices

A *diagonal matrix* has zeros everywhere except on the principal diagonal. If these diagonal entries are all non-zero, the inverse is also a diagonal matrix, with each diagonal entry d_{ii} replaced by $1/d_{ii}$. The determinant is the product of the values on the diagonal. A special case of this is the *identity matrix*, which has ones on the diagonal. Consequently, its inverse is also the identity matrix, and its determinant is one.

B.4.2 Triangular matrices

A *lower triangular matrix* contains only non-zero values on the principal diagonal and the positions below this. An *upper* triangular matrix contains only non-zero values on the principal diagonal and the positions above this. In both cases, the matrix can be inverted in $\mathcal{O}[D^2]$ (see problem 16.4), and the determinant is just the product of the values on the diagonal.

B.4.3   Orthogonal matrices

Orthogonal matrices represent rotations and reflections around the origin, so in figure B.3, the circle would be mapped to another circle of unit radius but rotated and possibly reflected. Accordingly, the eigenvalues must all have magnitude one, and the determinant must be either one or minus one. The inverse of an orthogonal matrix is its transpose, so $\mathbf{A}^{-1} = \mathbf{A}^T$.

B.4.4   Permutation matrices

A permutation matrix has exactly one non-zero entry in each row and column, and all of these entries take the value one. It is a special case of an orthogonal matrix, so its inverse is its own transpose, and its determinant is always one. As the name suggests, it has the effect of permuting the entries of a vector. For example:

$$\begin{bmatrix} 0 & 1 & 0 \\ 0 & 0 & 1 \\ 1 & 0 & 0 \end{bmatrix} \begin{bmatrix} a \\ b \\ c \end{bmatrix} = \begin{bmatrix} b \\ c \\ a \end{bmatrix}. \tag{B.16}$$

B.4.5   Linear algebra

Linear algebra is the mathematics of linear functions, which have the form:

$$\mathrm{f}[z_1, z_2, \ldots z_D] = \phi_1 z_1 + \phi_2 z_2 + \ldots \phi_D z_D, \tag{B.17}$$

where $\phi_1, \ldots, \phi_D$ are parameters that define the function. We often add a constant term ϕ_0 to the right-hand side. This is technically an *affine* function but is commonly referred to as linear in machine learning. We adopt this convention throughout.

B.4.6   Linear equations in matrix form

Consider a collection of linear functions:

$$\begin{aligned} y_1 &= \phi_{10} + \phi_{11} z_1 + \phi_{12} z_2 + \phi_{13} z_3 \\ y_2 &= \phi_{20} + \phi_{21} z_1 + \phi_{22} z_2 + \phi_{23} z_3 \\ y_3 &= \phi_{30} + \phi_{31} z_1 + \phi_{32} z_2 + \phi_{33} z_3. \end{aligned} \tag{B.18}$$

These can be written in matrix form as:

$$\begin{bmatrix} y_1 \\ y_2 \\ y_3 \end{bmatrix} = \begin{bmatrix} \phi_{10} \\ \phi_{20} \\ \phi_{30} \end{bmatrix} + \begin{bmatrix} \phi_{11} & \phi_{12} & \phi_{13} \\ \phi_{21} & \phi_{22} & \phi_{23} \\ \phi_{31} & \phi_{32} & \phi_{33} \end{bmatrix} \begin{bmatrix} z_1 \\ z_2 \\ z_3 \end{bmatrix}, \tag{B.19}$$

or as $\mathbf{y} = \boldsymbol{\phi}_0 + \boldsymbol{\Phi} \mathbf{z}$ for short, where $y_i = \phi_{i0} + \sum_{j=1}^{3} \phi_{ij} z_j$.

B.5 Matrix calculus

Most readers of this book will be accustomed to the idea that if we have a function $y = f[x]$, we can compute the derivative $\partial y/\partial x$, and this represents how y changes when we make a small change in x. This idea extends to functions $y = f[\mathbf{x}]$ mapping a vector $\mathbf{x}$ to a scalar y, functions $\mathbf{y} = \mathbf{f}[\mathbf{x}]$ mapping a vector $\mathbf{x}$ to a vector $\mathbf{y}$, functions $\mathbf{y} = \mathbf{f}[\mathbf{X}]$ mapping a matrix $\mathbf{X}$ to a vector $\mathbf{y}$, and so on. The rules of *matrix calculus* help us compute derivatives of these quantities. The derivatives take the following forms:

- For a function $y = f[\mathbf{x}]$ where $y \in \mathbb{R}$ and $\mathbf{x} \in \mathbb{R}^D$, the derivative $\partial y/\partial \mathbf{x}$ is also a D-dimensional vector, where the ith element is computed as $\partial y/\partial x_i$.

- For a function $\mathbf{y} = \mathbf{f}[\mathbf{x}]$ where $\mathbf{y} \in \mathbb{R}^{D_y}$ and $\mathbf{x} \in \mathbb{R}^{D_x}$, the derivative $\partial \mathbf{y}/\partial \mathbf{x}$ is a $D_x \times D_y$ matrix where element (i, j) contains the derivative $\partial y_j/\partial x_i$. This is known as a *Jacobian* and is sometimes written as $\nabla_{\mathbf{x}} \mathbf{y}$ in other documents.

- For a function $\mathbf{y} = \mathbf{f}[\mathbf{X}]$ where $\mathbf{y} \in \mathbb{R}^{D_y}$ and $\mathbf{X} \in \mathbb{R}^{D_1 \times D_2}$, the derivative $\partial \mathbf{y}/\partial \mathbf{X}$ is a 3D tensor containing the derivatives $\partial y_i/\partial x_{jk}$.

Often these matrix and vector derivatives have superficially similar forms to the scalar case. For example, we have:

$$y = ax \quad \longrightarrow \quad \frac{\partial y}{\partial x} = a, \tag{B.20}$$

and

$$\mathbf{y} = \mathbf{A}\mathbf{x} \quad \longrightarrow \quad \frac{\partial \mathbf{y}}{\partial \mathbf{x}} = \mathbf{A}^T. \tag{B.21}$$

Appendix C

Probability

Probability is critical to deep learning. In supervised learning, deep networks implicitly rely on a probabilistic formulation of the loss function. In unsupervised learning, generative models aim to produce samples that are drawn from the same probability distribution as the training data. Reinforcement learning occurs within Markov decision processes, and these are defined in terms of probability distributions. This appendix provides a primer for probability as used in machine learning.

C.1 Random variables and probability distributions

A random variable x denotes a quantity that is uncertain. It may be *discrete* (take only certain values, for example integers) or *continuous* (take any value on a continuum, for example real numbers). If we observe several instances of a random variable x, it will take different values, and the relative propensity to take different values is described by a *probability distribution* $Pr(x)$.

For a discrete variable, this distribution associates a *probability* $Pr(x\!=\!k) \in [0, 1]$ with each potential outcome k, and the sum of these probabilities is one. For a continuous variable, there is a non-negative *probability density* $Pr(x\!=\!a) \geq 0$ associated with each value a in the domain of x, and the integral of this probability density function (PDF) over this domain must be one. This density can be greater than one for any point a. From here on, we assume that the random variables are continuous. The ideas are exactly the same for discrete distributions but with sums replacing integrals.

C.1.1 Joint probability

Consider the case where we have two random variables x and y. The *joint distribution* $Pr(x, y)$ tells us about the propensity that x and y take particular combinations of values (figure C.1a). Now there is a non-negative probability density $Pr(x\!=\!a, y\!=\!b)$ associated with each pair of values $x = a$ and $y = b$ and this must satisfy:

a)

$Pr(x,y)$

c) $Pr(y)$

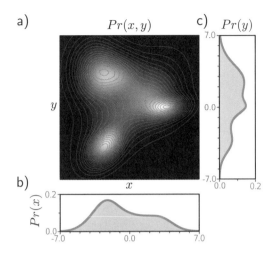

b)

Figure C.1 Joint and marginal distributions. a) The joint distribution $Pr(x,y)$ captures the propensity of variables x and y to take different combinations of values. Here, the probability density is represented by the color map, so brighter positions are more probable. For example, the combination $x=6, y=6$ is much less likely to be observed than the combination $x=5, y=0$. b) The marginal distribution $Pr(x)$ of variable x can be recovered by integrating over y. c) The marginal distribution $Pr(y)$ of variable y can be recovered by integrating over x.

$$\iint Pr(x,y) \cdot dxdy = 1. \tag{C.1}$$

This idea extends to more than two variables, so the joint density of x, y, and z is written as $Pr(x,y,z)$. Sometimes, we store multiple random variables in a vector $\mathbf{x}$, and we write their joint density as $Pr(\mathbf{x})$. Extending this, we can write the joint density of all of the variables in two vectors $\mathbf{x}$ and $\mathbf{y}$ as $Pr(\mathbf{x},\mathbf{y})$.

C.1.2 Marginalization

If we know the joint distribution $Pr(x,y)$ over two variables, we can recover the *marginal* distributions $Pr(x)$ and $Pr(y)$ by integrating over the other variable (figure C.1b-c):

$$\begin{aligned} \int Pr(x,y) \cdot dx &= Pr(y) \\ \int Pr(x,y) \cdot dy &= Pr(x). \end{aligned} \tag{C.2}$$

This process is called *marginalization* and has the interpretation that we are computing the distribution of one variable *regardless* of the value the other one took. The idea of marginalization extends to higher dimensions, so if we have a joint distribution $Pr(x,y,z)$, we can recover the joint distribution $Pr(x,z)$ by integrating over y.

C.1.3 Conditional probability and likelihood

The *conditional probability* $Pr(x|y)$ is the probability of variable x taking a certain value, assuming we know the value of y. The vertical line is read as the English word "given,"

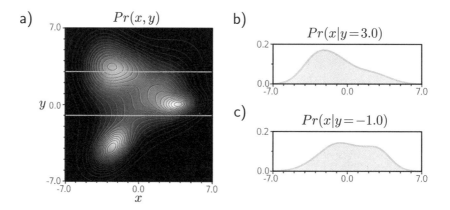

Figure C.2 Conditional distributions. a) Joint distribution $Pr(x, y)$ of variables x and y. b) The conditional probability $Pr(x|y = 3.0)$ of variable x, given that y takes the value 3.0, is found by taking the horizontal "slice" $Pr(x, y = 3.0)$ of the joint probability (top cyan line in panel a), and dividing this by the total area $Pr(y = 3.0)$ in that slice so that it forms a valid probability distribution that integrates to one. c) The joint probability $Pr(x, y = -1.0)$ is found similarly using the slice at $y = -1.0$.

so $Pr(x|y)$ is the probability of x given y. The conditional probability $Pr(x|y)$ can be found by taking a slice through the joint distribution $Pr(x, y)$ for a fixed y. This slice is then divided by the probability of that value y occurring (the total area under the slice) so that the conditional distribution sums to one (figure C.2):

$$Pr(x|y) = \frac{Pr(x, y)}{Pr(y)}. \tag{C.3}$$

Similarly,

$$Pr(y|x) = \frac{Pr(x, y)}{Pr(x)}. \tag{C.4}$$

When we consider the conditional probability $Pr(x|y)$ as a function of x, it must sum to one. When we consider the same quantity $Pr(x|y)$ as a function of y, it is termed the *likelihood* of x given y and does not have to sum to one.

C.1.4 Bayes' rule

From equations C.3 and C.4, we get two expressions for the joint probability $Pr(x, y)$:

$$Pr(x, y) = Pr(x|y)Pr(y) = Pr(y|x)Pr(x), \tag{C.5}$$

which we can rearrange to get:

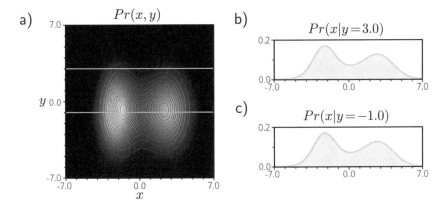

Figure C.3 Independence. a) When two variables x and y are independent, the joint distribution factors into the product of marginal distributions, so $Pr(x,y) = Pr(x)Pr(y)$. Independence implies that knowing the value of one variable tells us nothing about the other. b–c) Accordingly, all of the conditional distributions $Pr(x|y = \bullet)$ are the same and are equal to the marginal distribution $Pr(x)$.

$$Pr(x|y) = \frac{Pr(y|x)Pr(x)}{Pr(y)}. \tag{C.6}$$

This expression relates the conditional probability $Pr(x|y)$ of x given y to the conditional probability $Pr(y|x)$ of y given x and is known as *Bayes' rule*.

Each term in this Bayes' rule has a name. The term $Pr(y|x)$ is the *likelihood* of y given x, and the term $Pr(x)$ is the *prior probability* of x. The denominator $Pr(y)$ is known as the *evidence*, and the left-hand side $Pr(x|y)$ is termed the *posterior probability* of x given y. The equation maps from the prior $Pr(x)$ (what we know about x before observing y) to the posterior $Pr(x|y)$ (what we know about x after observing y).

C.1.5 Independence

If the value of the random variable y tells us nothing about x and vice-versa, we say that x and y are *independent*, and we can write $Pr(x|y) = Pr(x)$ and $Pr(y|x) = Pr(y)$. It follows that all of the conditional distributions $Pr(y|x = \bullet)$ are identical, as are the conditional distributions $Pr(x|y = \bullet)$.

Starting from the first expression for the joint probability in equation C.5, we see that the joint distribution becomes the product of the marginal distributions:

$$Pr(x,y) = Pr(x|y)Pr(y) = Pr(x)Pr(y) \tag{C.7}$$

when the variables are independent (figure C.3).

C.2 Expectation

Consider a function f[x] and a probability distribution $Pr(x)$ defined over x. The *expected value* of a function f[$\bullet$] of a random variable x with respect to the probability distribution $Pr(x)$ is defined as:

$$\mathbb{E}_x\big[f[x]\big] = \int f[x]Pr(x)dx. \tag{C.8}$$

As the name suggests, this is the expected or average value of f[x] after taking into account the probability of seeing different values of x. This idea generalizes to functions $\mathbf{f}[\bullet, \bullet]$ of more than one random variable:

$$\mathbb{E}_{x,y}\big[f[x,y]\big] = \iint f[x,y]Pr(x,y)dxdy. \tag{C.9}$$

An expectation is always taken with respect to a distribution over one or more variables. However, we don't usually make this explicit when the choice of distribution is obvious and write $\mathbb{E}[f[x]]$ instead of $\mathbb{E}_x[f[x]]$.

If we drew a large number I of samples $\{x_i\}_{i=1}^I$ from $Pr(x)$, calculated f[x_i] for each sample and took the average of these values, the result would approximate the expectation $\mathbb{E}[f[x]]$ of the function:

$$\mathbb{E}_x\big[f[x]\big] \approx \frac{1}{I}\sum_{i=1}^{I} f[x_i]. \tag{C.10}$$

C.2.1 Rules for manipulating expectations

There are four rules for manipulating expectations:

$$\begin{aligned}
\mathbb{E}\big[k\big] &= k \\
\mathbb{E}\big[k \cdot f[x]\big] &= k \cdot \mathbb{E}\big[f[x]\big] \\
\mathbb{E}\big[f[x] + g[x]\big] &= \mathbb{E}\big[f[x]\big] + \mathbb{E}\big[g[x]\big] \\
\mathbb{E}_{x,y}\big[f[x] \cdot g[y]\big] &= \mathbb{E}_x\big[f[x]\big] \cdot \mathbb{E}_y\big[g[y]\big] \qquad \text{if } x, y \text{ independent,}
\end{aligned} \tag{C.11}$$

where k is an arbitrary constant. These are proven below for the continuous case.

Rule 1: The expectation $\mathbb{E}[k]$ of a constant value k is just k.

$$\begin{aligned}
\mathbb{E}\big[k\big] &= \int k \cdot Pr(x)dx \\
&= k \cdot \int Pr(x)dx \\
&= k.
\end{aligned}$$

Rule 2: The expectation $\mathbb{E}[k \cdot f[x]]$ of a constant k times a function of the variable x is k times the expectation $\mathbb{E}[f[x]]$ of the function:

$$
\begin{aligned}
\mathbb{E}\big[k \cdot f[x]\big] &= \int k \cdot f[x] Pr(x) dx \\
&= k \cdot \int f[x] Pr(x) dx \\
&= k \cdot \mathbb{E}\big[f[x]\big].
\end{aligned}
$$

Rule 3: The expectation of a sum $\mathbb{E}[f[x] + g[x]]$ of terms is the sum $\mathbb{E}[f[x]] + \mathbb{E}[g[x]]$ of the expectations:

$$
\begin{aligned}
\mathbb{E}\big[f[x] + g[x]\big] &= \int (f[x] + g[x]) \cdot Pr(x) dx \\
&= \int \big(f[x] \cdot Pr(x) + g[x] \cdot Pr(x)\big) dx \\
&= \int f[x] \cdot Pr(x) dx + \int g[x] \cdot Pr(x) dx \\
&= \mathbb{E}\big[f[x]\big] + \mathbb{E}\big[g[x]\big].
\end{aligned}
$$

Rule 4: The expectation of a product $\mathbb{E}[f[x] \cdot g[y]]$ of terms is the product $\mathbb{E}[f[x]] \cdot \mathbb{E}[g[y]]$ if x and y are independent.

$$
\begin{aligned}
\mathbb{E}\big[f[x] \cdot g[y]\big] &= \iint f[x] \cdot g[y] Pr(x,y) dx dy \\
&= \iint f[x] \cdot g[y] Pr(x) Pr(y) dx dy \\
&= \int f[x] \cdot Pr(x) dx \int g[y] \cdot Pr(y) dy \\
&= \mathbb{E}\big[f[x]\big] \mathbb{E}\big[g[y]\big],
\end{aligned}
$$

where we used the definition of independence (equation C.7) between the first two lines.

The four rules generalize to the multivariate case:

$$
\begin{aligned}
\mathbb{E}\big[\mathbf{A}\big] &= \mathbf{A} \\
\mathbb{E}\big[\mathbf{A} \cdot \mathbf{f}[\mathbf{x}]\big] &= \mathbf{A}\mathbb{E}\big[\mathbf{f}[\mathbf{x}]\big] \\
\mathbb{E}\big[\mathbf{f}[\mathbf{x}] + \mathbf{g}[\mathbf{x}]\big] &= \mathbb{E}\big[\mathbf{f}[\mathbf{x}]\big] + \mathbb{E}\big[\mathbf{g}[\mathbf{x}]\big] \\
\mathbb{E}_{\mathbf{x},\mathbf{y}}\big[\mathbf{f}[\mathbf{x}]^{T}\mathbf{g}[\mathbf{y}]\big] &= \mathbb{E}_{\mathbf{x}}\big[\mathbf{f}[\mathbf{x}]\big]^{T}\mathbb{E}_{\mathbf{y}}\big[\mathbf{g}[\mathbf{y}]\big] \qquad \text{if } \mathbf{x}, \mathbf{y} \text{ independent}, \qquad \text{(C.12)}
\end{aligned}
$$

where now $\mathbf{A}$ is a constant matrix and $\mathbf{f}[\mathbf{x}]$ is a function of the vector $\mathbf{x}$ that returns a vector, and $\mathbf{g}[\mathbf{y}]$ is a function of the vector $\mathbf{y}$ that also returns a vector.

C.2.2   Mean, variance, and covariance

For some choices of function f[•], the expectation is given a special name. These quantities are often used to summarize the properties of complex distributions. For example, when f[x] = x, the resulting expectation $\mathbb{E}[x]$ is termed the *mean*, μ. It is a measure of the center of a distribution. Similarly, the expected squared deviation from the mean $\mathbb{E}[(x - \mu)^2]$ is termed the *variance*, σ^2. This is a measure of the spread of the distribution. The *standard deviation* σ is the positive square root of the variance. It also measures the spread of the distribution but has the merit that it is expressed in the same units as the variable x.

As the name suggests, the *covariance* $\mathbb{E}[(x - \mu_x)(y - \mu_y)]$ of two variables x and y measures the degree to which they co-vary. Here μ_x and μ_y represent the mean of the variables x and y, respectively. The covariance will be large when the variance of both variables is large and when the value of x tends to increase when the value of y increases.

If two variables are independent, then their covariance is zero. However, a covariance of zero does not imply independence. For example, consider a distribution $Pr(x, y)$ where the probability is uniformly distributed on a circle of radius one centered on the origin of the x, y plane. There is no tendency on average for x to increase when y increases or vice-versa. However, knowing the value of $x = 0$ tells us that y has an equal chance of taking the values ± 1, so the variables cannot be independent.

The covariances of multiple random variables stored in a column vector $\mathbf{x} \in \mathbb{R}^D$ can be represented by the $D \times D$ *covariance matrix* $\mathbb{E}[(\mathbf{x} - \boldsymbol{\mu}_x)(\mathbf{x} - \boldsymbol{\mu}_x)^T]$, where the vector $\boldsymbol{\mu}_x$ contains the means $\mathbb{E}[\mathbf{x}]$. The element at position (i, j) of this matrix represents the covariance between variables x_i and x_j.

C.2.3   Variance identity

The rules of expectation (appendix C.2.1) can be used to prove the following identity that allows us to write the variance in a different form:

$$\mathbb{E}\big[(x - \mu)^2\big] = \mathbb{E}\big[x^2\big] - \mathbb{E}\big[x\big]^2. \tag{C.13}$$

Proof:

$$
\begin{aligned}
\mathbb{E}\big[(x - \mu)^2\big] &= \mathbb{E}\big[x^2 - 2\mu x + \mu^2\big] \\
&= \mathbb{E}\big[x^2\big] - \mathbb{E}\big[2\mu x\big] + \mathbb{E}\big[\mu^2\big] \\
&= \mathbb{E}\big[x^2\big] - 2\mu \cdot \mathbb{E}\big[x\big] + \mu^2 \\
&= \mathbb{E}\big[x^2\big] - 2\mu^2 + \mu^2 \\
&= \mathbb{E}\big[x^2\big] - \mu^2 \\
&= \mathbb{E}\big[x^2\big] - \mathbb{E}\big[x\big]^2, \tag{C.14}
\end{aligned}
$$

where we have used rule 3 between lines 1 and 2, rules 1 and 2 between lines 2 and 3, and the definition $\mu = \mathbb{E}[x]$ in the remaining two lines.

C.2.4 Standardization

Setting the mean of a random variable to zero and the variance to one is known as *standardization*. This is achieved using the transformation:

$$z = \frac{x - \mu}{\sigma}, \tag{C.15}$$

where μ is the mean of x and σ is the standard deviation.

Proof: The mean of the new distribution over z is given by:

$$\begin{aligned} \mathbb{E}[z] &= \mathbb{E}\left[\frac{x - \mu}{\sigma}\right] \\ &= \frac{1}{\sigma}\mathbb{E}[x - \mu] \\ &= \frac{1}{\sigma}\left(\mathbb{E}[x] - \mathbb{E}[\mu]\right) \\ &= \frac{1}{\sigma}(\mu - \mu) = 0, \end{aligned} \tag{C.16}$$

where again, we have used the four rules for manipulating expectations. The variance of the new distribution is given by:

$$\begin{aligned} \mathbb{E}\left[(z - \mu_z)^2\right] &= \mathbb{E}\left[(z - \mathbb{E}[z])^2\right] \\ &= \mathbb{E}\left[z^2\right] \\ &= \mathbb{E}\left[\left(\frac{x - \mu}{\sigma}\right)^2\right] \\ &= \frac{1}{\sigma^2} \cdot \mathbb{E}[(x - \mu)^2] \\ &= \frac{1}{\sigma^2} \cdot \sigma^2 = 1. \end{aligned} \tag{C.17}$$

By a similar argument, we can take a standardized variable z with mean zero and unit variance and convert it to a variable x with mean μ and variance σ^2 using:

$$x = \mu + \sigma z. \tag{C.18}$$

In the multivariate case, we can standardize a variable $\mathbf{x}$ with mean $\boldsymbol{\mu}$ and covariance matrix $\boldsymbol{\Sigma}$ using:

$$\mathbf{z} = \boldsymbol{\Sigma}^{-1/2}(\mathbf{x} - \boldsymbol{\mu}). \tag{C.19}$$

The result will have a mean $\mathbb{E}[\mathbf{z}] = \mathbf{0}$ and an identity covariance matrix $\mathbb{E}[(\mathbf{z} - \mathbb{E}[\mathbf{z}])(\mathbf{z} - \mathbb{E}[\mathbf{z}])^T] = \mathbf{I}$. To reverse this process, we use:

$$\mathbf{x} = \boldsymbol{\mu} + \boldsymbol{\Sigma}^{1/2}\mathbf{z}. \tag{C.20}$$

C.3 Normal probability distribution

Probability distributions used in this book include the Bernoulli distribution (figure 5.6), categorical distribution (figure 5.9), Poisson distribution (figure 5.15), von Mises distribution (figure 5.13), and mixture of Gaussians (figures 5.14 and 17.1). However, the most common distribution in machine learning is the normal or Gaussian distribution.

C.3.1 Univariate normal distribution

A univariate normal distribution (figure 5.3) over scalar variable x has two parameters, the mean μ and the variance σ^2, and is defined as:

$$Pr(x) = \text{Norm}_x[\mu, \sigma^2] = \frac{1}{\sqrt{2\pi\sigma^2}} \exp\left[-\frac{(x-\mu)^2}{2\sigma^2}\right]. \tag{C.21}$$

Unsurprisingly, the mean $\mathbb{E}[x]$ of a normally distributed variable is given by the mean parameter μ and the variance $\mathbb{E}[(x - \mathbb{E}[x])^2]$ by the variance parameter σ^2. When the mean is zero and the variance is one, we refer to this as a *standard normal distribution*.

The shape of the normal distribution can be inferred from the following argument. The term $-(x-\mu)^2/2\sigma^2$ is a quadratic function that falls away from zero when $x = \mu$ at a rate that increases when σ becomes smaller. When we pass this through the exponential function (figure B.1), we get a bell-shaped curve, which has a value of one at $x = \mu$ and falls away to either side. Dividing by the constant $\sqrt{2\pi\sigma^2}$ ensures that the function integrates to one and is a valid distribution. It follows from this argument that the mean μ control the position of the center of the bell curve, and the square root σ of the variance (the standard deviation) controls the width of the bell curve.

C.3.2 Multivariate normal distribution

The multivariate normal distribution generalizes the normal distribution to describe the probability over a vector quantity $\mathbf{x}$ of length D. It is defined by a $D \times 1$ *mean vector* $\boldsymbol{\mu}$ and a symmetric positive definite $D \times D$ *covariance matrix* $\boldsymbol{\Sigma}$:

$$\text{Norm}_\mathbf{x}[\boldsymbol{\mu}, \boldsymbol{\Sigma}] = \frac{1}{(2\pi)^{D/2}|\boldsymbol{\Sigma}|^{1/2}} \exp\left[-\frac{(\mathbf{x} - \boldsymbol{\mu})^T\boldsymbol{\Sigma}^{-1}(\mathbf{x} - \boldsymbol{\mu})}{2}\right]. \tag{C.22}$$

The interpretation is similar to the univariate case. The quadratic term $-(\mathbf{x}-\boldsymbol{\mu})^T\boldsymbol{\Sigma}^{-1}(\mathbf{x}-\boldsymbol{\mu})/2$ returns a scalar that decreases as $\mathbf{x}$ grows further from the mean $\boldsymbol{\mu}$, at a rate that depends on the matrix $\boldsymbol{\Sigma}$. This is turned into a bell-curve shape by the exponential, and dividing by $(2\pi)^{D/2}|\boldsymbol{\Sigma}|^{1/2}$ ensures that the distribution integrates to one.

The covariance matrix can take spherical, diagonal, and full forms:

$$\boldsymbol{\Sigma}_{spher} = \begin{bmatrix} \sigma^2 & 0 \\ 0 & \sigma^2 \end{bmatrix} \quad \boldsymbol{\Sigma}_{diag} = \begin{bmatrix} \sigma_1^2 & 0 \\ 0 & \sigma_2^2 \end{bmatrix} \quad \boldsymbol{\Sigma}_{full} = \begin{bmatrix} \sigma_{11}^2 & \sigma_{12}^2 \\ \sigma_{21}^2 & \sigma_{22}^2 \end{bmatrix}. \tag{C.23}$$

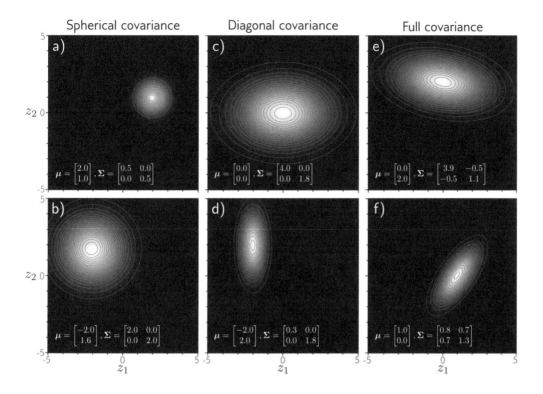

Figure C.4 Bivariate normal distribution. a–b) When the covariance matrix is a multiple of the diagonal matrix, the isocontours are circles, and we refer to this as spherical covariance. c–d) When the covariance is an arbitrary diagonal matrix, the isocontours are axis-aligned ellipses, and we refer to this as diagonal covariance e–f) When the covariance is an arbitrary symmetric positive definite matrix, the iso-contours are general ellipses, and we refer to this as full covariance.

In two dimensions (figure C.4), spherical covariances produce circular iso-density contours, and diagonal covariances produce ellipsoidal iso-contours that are aligned with the coordinate axes. Full covariances produce general ellipsoidal iso-density contours. When the covariance is spherical or diagonal, the individual variables are independent:

$$
\begin{aligned}
Pr(x_1, x_2) &= \frac{1}{2\pi\sqrt{|\boldsymbol{\Sigma}|}} \exp\left[-0.5 \begin{pmatrix} x_1 & x_2 \end{pmatrix} \boldsymbol{\Sigma}^{-1} \begin{pmatrix} x_1 \\ x_2 \end{pmatrix}\right] \\
&= \frac{1}{2\pi\sigma_1\sigma_2} \exp\left[-0.5 \begin{pmatrix} x_1 & x_2 \end{pmatrix} \begin{pmatrix} \sigma_1^{-2} & 0 \\ 0 & \sigma_2^{-2} \end{pmatrix} \begin{pmatrix} x_1 \\ x_2 \end{pmatrix}\right] \\
&= \frac{1}{\sqrt{2\pi\sigma_1^2}} \exp\left[-\frac{x_1^2}{2\sigma_1^2}\right] \cdot \frac{1}{\sqrt{2\pi\sigma_2^2}} \exp\left[-\frac{x_2^2}{2\sigma_2^2}\right] \\
&= Pr(x_1) \cdot Pr(x_2).
\end{aligned} \tag{C.24}
$$

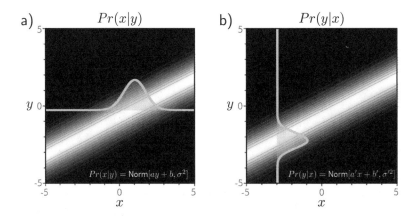

Figure C.5 Change of variables. a) The conditional distribution $Pr(x|y)$ is a normal distribution with constant variance and a mean that depends linearly on y. Cyan distribution shows one example for $y = -0.2$. b) This is proportional to the conditional probability $Pr(y|x)$, which is a normal distribution with constant variance and a mean that depends linearly on x. Cyan distribution shows one example for $x = -3$.

C.3.3   Product of two normal distributions

The product of two normal distributions is proportional to a third normal distribution according to the relation:

$$\text{Norm}_{\mathbf{x}}[\mathbf{a}, \mathbf{A}]\text{Norm}_{\mathbf{x}}[\mathbf{b}, \mathbf{B}] \;\propto\; \text{Norm}_{\mathbf{x}}\Big[(\mathbf{A}^{-1} + \mathbf{B}^{-1})^{-1}(\mathbf{A}^{-1}\mathbf{a} + \mathbf{B}^{-1}\mathbf{b}), (\mathbf{A}^{-1} + \mathbf{B}^{-1})^{-1}\Big].$$

This is easily proved by multiplying out the exponential terms and completing the square (see problem 18.5).

C.3.4   Change of variable

When the mean of a multivariate normal in $\mathbf{x}$ is a linear function $\mathbf{Ay} + \mathbf{b}$ of a second variable $\mathbf{y}$, this is proportional to another normal distribution in $\mathbf{y}$, where the mean is a linear function of $\mathbf{x}$:

$$\text{Norm}_{\mathbf{x}}\left[\mathbf{Ay} + \mathbf{b}, \boldsymbol{\Sigma}\right] \propto \text{Norm}_{\mathbf{y}}[(\mathbf{A}^T\boldsymbol{\Sigma}^{-1}\mathbf{A})^{-1}\mathbf{A}^T\boldsymbol{\Sigma}^{-1}(\mathbf{x} - \mathbf{b}), (\mathbf{A}^T\boldsymbol{\Sigma}^{-1}\mathbf{A})^{-1}]. \quad (C.25)$$

At first sight, this relation is rather opaque, but figure C.5 shows the case for scalar x and y, which is easy to understand. As for the previous relation, this can be proved by expanding the quadratic product in the exponential term and completing the square to make this a distribution in $\mathbf{y}$. (see problem 18.4).

C.4 Sampling

To sample from a univariate distribution $Pr(x)$, we first compute the cumulative distribution $F[x]$ (the integral of $Pr(x)$). Then we draw a sample z^* from a uniform distribution over the range $[0, 1]$ and evaluate this against the inverse of the cumulative distribution, so the sample x^* is created as:

$$x^* = F^{-1}[z^*]. \tag{C.26}$$

C.4.1 Sampling from normal distributions

The method above can be used to generate a sample x^* from a univariate standard normal distribution. A sample from a normal distribution with mean μ and variance σ^2 can then be created using equation C.18. Similarly, a sample $\mathbf{x}^*$ from a D-dimensional multivariate standard distribution can be created by independently sampling D univariate standard normal variables. A sample from a multivariate normal distribution with mean $\boldsymbol{\mu}$ and covariance $\boldsymbol{\Sigma}$ can be then created using equation C.20.

C.4.2 Ancestral sampling

When the joint distribution can be factored into a series of conditional probabilities, we can generate samples using *ancestral sampling*. The basic idea is to generate a sample from the root variable(s) and then sample from the subsequent conditional distributions based on this instantiation. This process is known as *ancestral sampling* and is easiest to understand with an example. Consider a joint distribution over three variables, $x, y,$ and z, where the distribution factors as:

$$Pr(x, y, z) = Pr(x)Pr(y|x)Pr(z|y). \tag{C.27}$$

To sample from this joint distribution, we first draw a sample x^* from $Pr(x)$. Then we draw a sample y^* from $Pr(y|x^*)$. Finally, we draw a sample z^* from $Pr(z|y^*)$.

C.5 Distances between probability distributions

Supervised learning can be framed in terms of minimizing the distance between the probability distribution implied by the model and the discrete probability distribution implied by the samples (section 5.7). Unsupervised learning can often be framed in terms of minimizing the distance between the probability distribution of real examples and the distribution of data from the model. In both cases, we need a measure of distance between two probability distributions. This section considers the properties of several different measures of distance between distributions (see also figure 15.8 for a discussion of the Wasserstein or earth mover's distance).

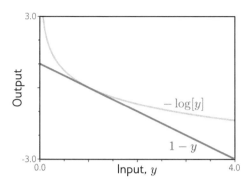

Figure C.6 Lower bound on negative logarithm. The function $1 - y$ is always less than the function $-\log[y]$. This relation is used to show that the Kullback-Leibler divergence is always greater than or equal to zero.

C.5.1   Kullback-Leibler divergence

The most common measure of distance between probability distributions $p(x)$ and $q(x)$ is the *Kullback-Leibler* or KL divergence and is defined as:

$$D_{KL}\big[p(x)||q(x)\big] = \int p(x) \log\left[\frac{p(x)}{q(x)}\right] dx. \tag{C.28}$$

This distance is always greater than or equal to zero, which is easily demonstrated by noting that $-\log[y] \geq 1 - y$ (figure C.6) so:

$$
\begin{aligned}
D_{KL}\Big[p(x)\big|\big|q(x)\Big] &= \int p(x) \log\left[\frac{p(x)}{q(x)}\right] dx \\
&= -\int p(x) \log\left[\frac{q(x)}{p(x)}\right] dx \\
&\geq \int p(x) \left(1 - \frac{q(x)}{p(x)}\right) dx \\
&= \int p(x) - q(x) dx \\
&= 1 - 1 = 0. \tag{C.29}
\end{aligned}
$$

The KL divergence is infinite if there are places where $q(x)$ is zero but $p(x)$ is non-zero. This can lead to problems when we are minimizing a function based on this distance.

C.5.2   Jensen-Shannon divergence

The KL divergence is not symmetric (i.e., $D_{KL}[p(x)||q(x)] \neq D_{KL}[q(x)||p(x)]$). The Jensen-Shannon divergence is a measure of distance that is symmetric by construction:

$$D_{JS}\Big[p(x)\big|\big|q(x)\Big] = \frac{1}{2}D_{KL}\left[p(x)\Big|\Big|\frac{p(x)+q(x)}{2}\right] + \frac{1}{2}D_{KL}\left[q(x)\Big|\Big|\frac{p(x)+q(x)}{2}\right]. \tag{C.30}$$

It is the mean divergence of $p(x)$ and $q(x)$ to the average of the two distributions.

C.5.3   Fréchet distance

The Fréchet distance D_{FR} between two distributions $p(x)$ and $q(x)$ is given by:

$$D_{Fr}\Big[p(x)||q(y)\Big] = \sqrt{\min_{\pi(x,y)}\left[\iint \pi(x,y)|x-y|^2 dxdy\right]}, \qquad \text{(C.31)}$$

where $\pi(x,y)$ represents the set of joint distributions that are compatible with the marginal distributions $p(x)$ and $q(y)$. The Fréchet distance can also be formulated as a measure of the maximum distance between the cumulative probability curves.

C.5.4   Distances between normal distributions

Often we want to compute the distance between two multivariate normal distributions with means $\boldsymbol{\mu}_1$ and $\boldsymbol{\mu}_2$ and covariances $\boldsymbol{\Sigma}_1$ and $\boldsymbol{\Sigma}_2$. In this case, various measures of distance can be written in closed form.

The KL divergence can be computed as:

$$D_{KL}\Big[\text{Norm}[\boldsymbol{\mu}_1,\boldsymbol{\Sigma}_1]\Big|\Big|\text{Norm}[\boldsymbol{\mu}_2,\boldsymbol{\Sigma}_2]\Big] = \qquad\qquad\qquad\qquad\qquad \text{(C.32)}$$
$$\frac{1}{2}\left(\log\left[\frac{|\boldsymbol{\Sigma}_2|}{|\boldsymbol{\Sigma}_1|}\right] - D + \text{tr}\left[\boldsymbol{\Sigma}_2^{-1}\boldsymbol{\Sigma}_1\right] + (\boldsymbol{\mu}_2-\boldsymbol{\mu}_1)\boldsymbol{\Sigma}_2^{-1}(\boldsymbol{\mu}_2-\boldsymbol{\mu}_1)\right).$$

where $tr[\bullet]$ is the trace of the matrix argument. The Fréchet/2-Wasserstein distance is given by:

$$D_{Fr/W_2}^2\Big[\text{Norm}[\boldsymbol{\mu}_1,\boldsymbol{\Sigma}_1]\Big|\Big|\text{Norm}[\boldsymbol{\mu}_2,\boldsymbol{\Sigma}_2]\Big] = |\boldsymbol{\mu}_1-\boldsymbol{\mu}_2|^2 + \text{tr}\left[\boldsymbol{\Sigma}_1+\boldsymbol{\Sigma}_2 - 2\left(\boldsymbol{\Sigma}_1\boldsymbol{\Sigma}_2\right)^{1/2}\right].$$
$$\text{(C.33)}$$

Bibliography

Abdal, R., Qin, Y., & Wonka, P. (2019). Image2StyleGAN: How to embed images into the StyleGAN latent space? *IEEE/CVF International Conference on Computer Vision*, 4432–4441. 301

Abdal, R., Qin, Y., & Wonka, P. (2020). Image2StyleGAN++: How to edit the embedded images? *IEEE/CVF Computer Vision & Pattern Recognition*, 8296–8305. 301

Abdal, R., Zhu, P., Mitra, N. J., & Wonka, P. (2021). StyleFlow: Attribute-conditioned exploration of StyleGAN-generated images using conditional continuous normalizing flows. *ACM Transactions on Graphics (ToG)*, *40*(3), 1–21. 300, 322

Abdalla, M., & Abdalla, M. (2021). The grey hoodie project: Big tobacco, big tech, and the threat on academic integrity. *AAAI/ACM Conference on AI, Ethics, and Society*, 287–297. 434

Abdel-Hamid, O., Mohamed, A.-r., Jiang, H., & Penn, G. (2012). Applying convolutional neural networks concepts to hybrid NN-HMM model for speech recognition. *IEEE International Conference on Acoustics, Speech and Signal Processing*, 4277–4280. 182

Abdelhamed, A., Brubaker, M. A., & Brown, M. S. (2019). Noise flow: Noise modeling with conditional normalizing flows. *IEEE/CVF International Conference on Computer Vision*, 3165–3173. 322

Abeßer, J., Mimilakis, S. I., Gräfe, R., Lukashevich, H., & Fraunhofer, I. (2017). Acoustic scene classification by combining autoencoder-based dimensionality reduction and convolutional neural networks. *Workshop on Detection and Classification of Acoustic Scenes and Events*, 7–11. 160

Abrahams, D. (2023). Let's talk about generative AI and fraud. *Forter Blog, March 27, 2023.* https://www.forter.com/blog/lets-talk-about-generative-ai-and-fraud/. 428

Abu-El-Haija, S., Perozzi, B., Kapoor, A., Alipourfard, N., Lerman, K., Harutyunyan, H., Ver Steeg, G., & Galstyan, A. (2019). MixHop: Higher-order graph convolutional architectures via sparsified neighborhood mixing. *International Conference on Machine Learning*, 21–29. 263

Adler, J., & Lunz, S. (2018). Banach Wasserstein GAN. *Neural Information Processing Systems*, *31*, 6755–6764. 299

Agarwal, R., Schuurmans, D., & Norouzi, M. (2020). An optimistic perspective on offline reinforcement learning. *International Conference on Machine Learning*, 104–114. 398

Aggarwal, C. C., Hinneburg, A., & Keim, D. A. (2001). On the surprising behavior of distance metrics in high dimensional space. *International Conference on Database Theory*, 420–434. 135

Agüera y Arcas, B., Todorov, A., & Mitchell, M. (2018). Do algorithms reveal sexual orientation or just expose our stereotypes? *Medium, Jan 11, 2018.* https://medium.com/@blaisea/do-algorithms-reveal-sexual-orientation-or-just-expose-our-stereotypes-d998fafdf477. 431

Ahmed, N., & Wahed, M. (2016). The de-democratization of AI: Deep learning and the compute divide in artificial intelligence research. *arXiv:1606.06565.* 430

Ahmed, S., Mula, R. S., & Dhavala, S. S. (2020). A framework for democratizing AI. *arXiv:2001.00818.* 430

Ahmed, T. (2017). AI can tell if you're gay: Artificial intelligence predicts sexuality from one photo with startling accuracy. *Newsweek, 8 Sept 2017.* https://www.newsweek.com/ai-can-tell-if-youre-gay-artificial-intelligence-predicts-sexuality-one-photo-661643. 430

Aiken, M., & Park, M. (2010). The efficacy of round-trip translation for MT evaluation. *Translation Journal, 14*(1). 160

Ainslie, J., Ontañón, S., Alberti, C., Cvicek, V., Fisher, Z., Pham, P., Ravula, A., Sanghai, S., Wang, Q., & Yang, L. (2020). ETC: Encoding long and structured inputs in transformers. *ACL Empirical Methods in Natural Language Processing*, 268–284. 237

Akers, J., Bansal, G., Cadamuro, G., Chen, C., Chen, Q., Lin, L., Mulcaire, P., Nandakumar, R., Rockett, M., Simko, L., Toman, J., Wu, T., Zeng, E., Zorn, B., & Roesner, F. (2018). Technology-enabled disinformation: Summary, lessons, and recommendations. *arXiv:1812.09383*. 427

Akuzawa, K., Iwasawa, Y., & Matsuo, Y. (2018). Expressive speech synthesis via modeling expressions with variational autoencoder. *INTERSPEECH*, 3067–3071. 343

Ali, A., Touvron, H., Caron, M., Bojanowski, P., Douze, M., Joulin, A., Laptev, I., Neverova, N., Synnaeve, G., Verbeek, J., et al. (2021). XCiT: Cross-covariance image transformers. *Neural Information Processing Systems, 34*, 20014–20027. 238

Allen, C., Smit, I., & Wallach, W. (2005). Artificial morality: Top-down, bottom-up, and hybrid approaches. *Ethics and Information Technology, 7*, 149–155. 424

Allen-Zhu, Z., Li, Y., & Song, Z. (2019). A convergence theory for deep learning via over-parameterization. *International Conference on Machine Learning, 97*, 242–252. 404

Alon, U., & Yahav, E. (2021). On the bottleneck of graph neural networks and its practical implications. *International Conference on Learning Representations*. 265

Alvarez, J. M., & Salzmann, M. (2016). Learning the number of neurons in deep networks. *Neural Information Processing Systems, 29*, 2262–2270. 414

Amari, S.-I. (1998). Natural gradient works efficiently in learning. *Neural Computation, 10*(2), 251–276. 397

Amodei, D., Olah, C., Steinhardt, J., Christiano, P., Schulman, J., & Mané, D. (2016). Concrete problems in AI safety. *arXiv:1606.06565*. 421

An, G. (1996). The effects of adding noise during backpropagation training on a generalization performance. *Neural Computation, 8*(3), 643–674. 158

An, J., Huang, S., Song, Y., Dou, D., Liu, W., & Luo, J. (2021). ArtFlow: Unbiased image style transfer via reversible neural flows. *IEEE/CVF Computer Vision & Pattern Recognition*, 862–871. 322

Anderson, M., & Anderson, S. L. (2008). Ethical healthcare agents. *Advanced Computational Intelligence Paradigms in Healthcare 3. Studies in Computational Intelligence*, vol. 107, 233–257. 424

Andreae, J. (1969). Learning machines: A unified view. *Encyclopaedia of Linguistics, Information and Control*, 261–270. 396

Angwin, J., Larson, J., Mattu, S., & Kirchner, L. (2016). Machine bias: There's software used across the country to predict future criminals. and it's biased against blacks. ProPublica, May 23, 2016. https://www.propublica.org/article/machine-bias-risk-assessments-in-criminal-sentencing. 420

Ardizzone, L., Kruse, J., Lüth, C., Bracher, N., Rother, C., & Köthe, U. (2020). Conditional invertible neural networks for diverse image-to-image translation. *DAGM German Conference on Pattern Recognition*, 373–387. 322

Arjovsky, M., & Bottou, L. (2017). Towards principled methods for training generative adversarial networks. *International Conference on Learning Representations*. 283, 299

Arjovsky, M., Chintala, S., & Bottou, L. (2017). Wasserstein generative adversarial networks. *International Conference on Machine Learning*, 214–223. 280, 299

Arkin, R. C. (2008a). Governing lethal behavior: Embedding ethics in a hybrid deliberative/reactive robot architecture—Part I: Motivation and philosophy. *ACM/IEEE International Conference on Human Robot Interaction*, 121–128. 424

Arkin, R. C. (2008b). Governing lethal behavior: Embedding ethics in a hybrid deliberative/reactive robot architecture—Part II: Formalization for ethical control. *Conference on Artificial General Intelligence*, 51–62. 424

Arnab, A., Dehghani, M., Heigold, G., Sun, C., Lučić, M., & Schmid, C. (2021). ViViT: A video vision transformer. *IEEE/CVF International Conference on Computer Vision*, 6836–6846. 238

Arora, R., Basu, A., Mianjy, P., & Mukherjee, A. (2016). Understanding deep neural networks with rectified linear units. *arXiv:1611.01491*. 52

Arora, S., Ge, R., Liang, Y., Ma, T., & Zhang, Y. (2017). Generalization and equilibrium in generative adversarial nets (GANs). *International Conference on Machine Learning*, 224–232. 300

Arora, S., Li, Z., & Lyu, K. (2018). Theoretical analysis of auto rate-tuning by batch normalization. *arXiv:1812.03981*. 204

Arora, S., & Zhang, Y. (2017). Do GANs actually learn the distribution? An empirical study. *arXiv:1706.08224*. 300

Arulkumaran, K., Deisenroth, M. P., Brundage, M., & Bharath, A. A. (2017). Deep reinforcement learning: A brief survey. *IEEE Signal Processing Magazine*, *34*(6), 26–38. 396

Asaro, P. (2012). On banning autonomous weapon systems: human rights, automation, and the dehumanization of lethal decision-making. *International Review of the Red Cross*, *94*(886), 687–709. 429

Atwood, J., & Towsley, D. (2016). Diffusion-convolutional neural networks. *Neural Information Processing Systems*, *29*, 1993–2001. 262

Aubret, A., Matignon, L., & Hassas, S. (2019). A survey on intrinsic motivation in reinforcement learning. *arXiv:1908.06976*. 398

Austin, J., Johnson, D. D., Ho, J., Tarlow, D., & van den Berg, R. (2021). Structured denoising diffusion models in discrete state-spaces. *Neural Information Processing Systems*, *34*, 17981–17993. 369

Awad, E., Dsouza, S., Kim, R., Schulz, J., Henrich, J., Shariff, A., Bonnefon, J.-F., & Rahwan, I. (2018). The moral machine experiment. *Nature*, *563*, 59–64. 424

Ba, J. L., Kiros, J. R., & Hinton, G. E. (2016). Layer normalization. *arXiv:1607.06450*. 203

Bachlechner, T., Majumder, B. P., Mao, H., Cottrell, G., & McAuley, J. (2021). ReZero is all you need: Fast convergence at large depth. *Uncertainty in Artificial Intelligence*, 1352–1361. 238

Bahdanau, D., Cho, K., & Bengio, Y. (2015). Neural machine translation by jointly learning to align and translate. *International Conference on Learning Representations*. 233, 235

Bahri, Y., Kadmon, J., Pennington, J., Schoenholz, S. S., Sohl-Dickstein, J., & Ganguli, S. (2020). Statistical mechanics of deep learning. *Annual Review of Condensed Matter Physics*, *11*, 501–528. 409, 410

Baldi, P., & Hornik, K. (1989). Neural networks and principal component analysis: Learning from examples without local minima. *Neural networks*, *2*(1), 53–58. 410

Balduzzi, D., Frean, M., Leary, L., Lewis, J., Ma, K. W.-D., & McWilliams, B. (2017). The shattered gradients problem: If ResNets are the answer, then what is the question? *International Conference on Machine Learning*, 342–350. 188, 202, 203, 205

Bansal, A., Borgnia, E., Chu, H.-M., Li, J. S., Kazemi, H., Huang, F., Goldblum, M., Geiping, J., & Goldstein, T. (2022). Cold diffusion: Inverting arbitrary image transforms without noise. *arXiv:2208.09392*. 369

Bao, F., Li, C., Zhu, J., & Zhang, B. (2022). Analytic-DPM: An analytic estimate of the optimal reverse variance in diffusion probabilistic models. *International Conference on Learning Representations*. 369

Baranchuk, D., Rubachev, I., Voynov, A., Khrulkov, V., & Babenko, A. (2022). Label-efficient semantic segmentation with diffusion models. *International Conference on Learning Representations*. 369

Barber, D., & Bishop, C. (1997). Ensemble learning for multi-layer networks. *Neural Information Processing Systems*, *10*, 395–401. 159

Barocas, S., Hardt, M., & Narayanan, A. (2023). *Fairness and Machine Learning: Limitations and Opportunities*. MIT Press. 423

Barratt, S., & Sharma, R. (2018). A note on the inception score. *Workshop on Theoretical Foundations and Applications of Deep Generative Models*. 274

Barrett, D. G. T., & Dherin, B. (2021). Implicit gradient regularization. *International Conference on Learning Representations*. 157

Barrett, L. (2020). Ban facial recognition technologies for children — and for everyone else. *Boston University Journal of Science and Technology Law*, *26*(2), 223–285. 427

Barron, J. T. (2019). A general and adaptive robust loss function. *IEEE/CVF Computer Vision & Pattern Recognition*, 4331–4339. 73

Bartlett, P. L., Foster, D. J., & Telgarsky, M. J. (2017). Spectrally-normalized margin bounds for neural networks. *Neural Information Processing Systems*, vol. 30, 6240–6249. 156

Bartlett, P. L., Harvey, N., Liaw, C., & Mehrabian, A. (2019). Nearly-tight VC-dimension and pseudodimension bounds for piecewise linear neural networks. *Journal of Machine Learning Research, 20*(1), 2285–2301. 134

Barto, A. G. (2013). Intrinsic motivation and reinforcement learning. *Intrinsically Motivated Learning in Natural and Artificial Systems,* 17–47. 398

Bau, D., Zhou, B., Khosla, A., Oliva, A., & Torralba, A. (2017). Network dissection: Quantifying interpretability of deep visual representations. *IEEE/CVF Computer Vision & Pattern Recognition,* 6541–6549. 184

Bau, D., Zhu, J.-Y., Wulff, J., Peebles, W., Strobelt, H., Zhou, B., & Torralba, A. (2019). Seeing what a GAN cannot generate. *IEEE/CVF International Conference on Computer Vision,* 4502–4511. 300

Baydin, A. G., Pearlmutter, B. A., Radul, A. A., & Siskind, J. M. (2018). Automatic differentiation in machine learning: A survey. *Journal of Marchine Learning Research, 18,* 1–43. 113

Bayer, M., Kaufhold, M.-A., & Reuter, C. (2022). A survey on data augmentation for text classification. *ACM Computing Surveys, 55*(7), 1–39. 160

Behrmann, J., Grathwohl, W., Chen, R. T., Duvenaud, D., & Jacobsen, J.-H. (2019). Invertible residual networks. *International Conference on Machine Learning,* 573–582. 318, 323

Belinkov, Y., & Bisk, Y. (2018). Synthetic and natural noise both break neural machine translation. *International Conference on Learning Representations.* 160

Belkin, M., Hsu, D., Ma, S., & Mandal, S. (2019). Reconciling modern machine-learning practice and the classical bias–variance trade-off. *Proceedings of the National Academy of Sciences, 116*(32), 15849–15854. 130, 134

Bellemare, M. G., Dabney, W., & Munos, R. (2017a). A distributional perspective on reinforcement learning. *International Conference on Machine Learning,* 449–458. 397

Bellemare, M. G., Danihelka, I., Dabney, W., Mohamed, S., Lakshminarayanan, B., Hoyer, S., & Munos, R. (2017b). The Cramer distance as a solution to biased Wasserstein gradients. *arXiv:1705.10743.* 299

Bellman, R. (1966). Dynamic programming. *Science, 153*(3731), 34–37. 396

Beltagy, I., Peters, M. E., & Cohan, A. (2020). Longformer: The long-document transformer. *arXiv:2004.05150.* 237

Bender, E. M., & Koller, A. (2020). Climbing towards NLU: On meaning, form, and understanding in the age of data. *Meeting of the Association for Computational Linguistics,* 5185–5198. 234

Bengio, Y., Ducharme, R., & Vincent, P. (2000). A neural probabilistic language model. *Neural Information Processing Systems, 13,* 932–938. 274

Benjamin, R. (2019). *Race After Technology: Abolitionist Tools for the New Jim Code.* Polity. 433

Berard, H., Gidel, G., Almahairi, A., Vincent, P., & Lacoste-Julien, S. (2019). A closer look at the optimization landscapes of generative adversarial networks. *arXiv:1906.04848.* 299

Berger, P. (2019). MTA's initial foray into facial recognition at high speed is a bust. April 07, 2019. https://www.wsj.com/articles/mtas-initial-foray-into-facial-recognition-at-high-speed-is-a-bust-11554642000. 427

Bergstra, J., & Bengio, Y. (2012). Random search for hyper-parameter optimization. *Journal of Machine Learning Research, 13*(10), 281–305. 136

Bergstra, J. S., Bardenet, R., Bengio, Y., & Kégl, B. (2011). Algorithms for hyper-parameter optimization. *Neural Information Processing Systems,* vol. 24, 2546–2554. 136

Berk, R., Heidari, H., Jabbari, S., Kearns, M., & Roth, A. (2017). Fairness in criminal justice risk assessments: the state of the art. *Sociological Methods & Research, 50*(1), 3–44. 422

Berner, C., Brockman, G., Chan, B., Cheung, V., Dębiak, P., Dennison, C., Farhi, D., Fischer, Q., Hashme, S., Hesse, C., et al. (2019). DOTA 2 with large scale deep reinforcement learning. *arXiv:1912.06680.* 396

Bertasius, G., Wang, H., & Torresani, L. (2021). Is space-time attention all you need for video understanding? *International Conference on Machine Learning,* 3, 813–824. 238

Beyer, K., Goldstein, J., Ramakrishnan, R., & Shaft, U. (1999). When is "nearest neighbor" meaningful? *International Conference on Database Theory,* 217–235. 135

Binns, R. (2018). Algorithmic accountability and public reason. *Philosophy & Technology, 31*(4), 543–556. 13

Birhane, A., Isaac, W., Prabhakaran, V., Diaz, M., Elish, M. C., Gabriel, I., & Mohamed, S. (2022a). Power to the people? Opportunities and challenges for participatory AI. *Equity and*

Access in Algorithms, Mechanisms, and Optimization. 433

Birhane, A., Kalluri, P., Card, D., Agnew, W., Dotan, R., & Bao, M. (2022b). The values encoded in machine learning research. *ACM Conference on Fairness, Accountability, and Transparency*, 173–184. 431

Bishop, C. (1995). Regularization and complexity control in feed-forward networks. *International Conference on Artificial Neural Networks*, 141–148. 157, 158

Bishop, C. M. (1994). Mixture density networks. *Aston University Technical Report.* 73

Bishop, C. M. (2006). *Pattern recognition and machine learning.* Springer. 15, 159

Bjorck, N., Gomes, C. P., Selman, B., & Weinberger, K. Q. (2018). Understanding batch normalization. *Neural Information Processing Systems*, *31*, 7705–7716. 204

Blum, A. L., & Rivest, R. L. (1992). Training a 3-node neural network is NP-complete. *Neural Networks*, *5*(1), 117–127. 401

Blundell, C., Cornebise, J., Kavukcuoglu, K., & Wierstra, D. (2015). Weight uncertainty in neural network. *International Conference on Machine Learning*, 1613–1622. 159

Bond-Taylor, S., Leach, A., Long, Y., & Willcocks, C. G. (2022). Deep generative modelling: A comparative review of VAEs, GANs, normalizing flows, energy-based and autoregressive models. *IEEE Transactions on Pattern Analysis & Machine Intelligence*, *44*(11), 7327–7347. 274

Bontridder, N., & Poullet, Y. (2021). The role of artificial intelligence in disinformation. *Data & Policy*, *3*, E32. 427

Borji, A. (2022). Pros and cons of GAN evaluation measures: New developments. *Computer Vision & Image Understanding*, *215*, 103329. 274

Bornschein, J., Shabanian, S., Fischer, A., & Bengio, Y. (2016). Bidirectional Helmholtz machines. *International Conference on Machine Learning*, 2511–2519. 346

Boscaini, D., Masci, J., Rodolà, E., & Bronstein, M. (2016). Learning shape correspondence with anisotropic convolutional neural networks. *Neural Information Processing Systems*, *29*, 3189–3197. 265

Bottou, L. (2012). Stochastic gradient descent tricks. *Neural Networks: Tricks of the Trade: Second Edition*, 421–436. 91

Bottou, L., Curtis, F. E., & Nocedal, J. (2018). Optimization methods for large-scale machine learning. *SIAM Review*, *60*(2), 223–311. 91

Bottou, L., Soulié, F. F., Blanchet, P., & Liénard, J.-S. (1990). Speaker-independent isolated digit recognition: Multilayer perceptrons vs. dynamic time warping. *Neural Networks*, *3*(4), 453–465. 181

Boulemtafes, A., Derhab, A., & Challal, Y. (2020). A review of privacy-preserving techniques for deep learning. *Neurocomputing*, *384*, 21–45. 428

Bousselham, W., Thibault, G., Pagano, L., Machireddy, A., Gray, J., Chang, Y. H., & Song, X. (2021). Efficient self-ensemble framework for semantic segmentation. *arXiv:2111.13280.* 162

Bowman, S. R., & Dahl, G. E. (2021). What will it take to fix benchmarking in natural language understanding? *ACL Human Language Technologies*, 4843–4855. 234

Bowman, S. R., Vilnis, L., Vinyals, O., Dai, A. M., Jozefowicz, R., & Bengio, S. (2015). Generating sentences from a continuous space. *ACL Conference on Computational Natural Language Learning*, 10–21. 343, 344, 345

Braverman, H. (1974). *Labor and monopoly capital: the degradation of work in the twentieth century.* Monthly Review Press. 429

Brock, A., Donahue, J., & Simonyan, K. (2019). Large scale GAN training for high fidelity natural image synthesis. *International Conference on Learning Representations.* 287, 299

Brock, A., Lim, T., Ritchie, J. M., & Weston, N. (2016). Neural photo editing with introspective adversarial networks. *International Conference on Learning Representations.* 345

Bromley, J., Guyon, I., LeCun, Y., Säckinger, E., & Shah, R. (1993). Signature verification using a "Siamese" time delay neural network. *Neural Information Processing Systems*, *6*, 737–744. 181

Bronstein, M. M., Bruna, J., Cohen, T., & Veličković, P. (2021). Geometric deep learning: Grids, groups, graphs, geodesics, and gauges. *arXiv:2104.13478.* 262

Broussard, M. (2018). *Artificial Unintelligence: How Computers Misunderstand the World.* The MIT Press. 433

Broussard, M. (2023). *More than a Glitch: Confronting Race, Gender, and Ability Bias in Tech.* The MIT Press. 433

Brown, T., Mann, B., Ryder, N., Subbiah, M., Kaplan, J. D., Dhariwal, P., Neelakantan, A., Shyam, P., Sastry, G., Askell, A., et al. (2020). Language models are few-shot learners. *Neural Information Processing Systems*, *33*, 1877–1901. 9, 159, 234, 237, 422, 425

Brügger, R., Baumgartner, C. F., & Konukoglu, E. (2019). A partially reversible U-Net for memory-efficient volumetric image segmentation. *International Conference on Medical Image Computing and Computer-Assisted Intervention*, 429–437. 322

Bruna, J., Zaremba, W., Szlam, A., & LeCun, Y. (2013). Spectral networks and locally connected networks on graphs. *International Conference on Learning Representations*. 262

Brynjolfsson, E., & McAfee, A. (2016). *The Second Machine Age: Work, Progress, and Prosperity in a Time of Brilliant Technologies*. W. W. Norton. 430

Bryson, A., Ho, Y.-C., & Siouris, G. (1979). Applied optimal control: Optimization, estimation, and control. *IEEE Transactions on Systems, Man & Cybernetics*, *9*, 366–367. 113

Bubeck, S., & Sellke, M. (2021). A universal law of robustness via isoperimetry. *Neural Information Processing Systems*, *34*, 28811–28822. 135, 416

Buciluǎ, C., Caruana, R., & Niculescu-Mizil, A. (2006). Model compression. *ACM SIGKDD International Conference on Knowledge Discovery and Data Mining*, 535–541. 415

Bughin, J., Seong, J., Manyika, J., Chui, M., & Joshi, R. (2018). *Notes from the AI Frontier: Modelling the Impact of AI on the World Economy*. McKinsey Global Institute, Sept 4, 2018. 429

Buolamwini, J., & Gebru, T. (2018). Gender shades: Intersectional accuracy disparities in commercial gender classification. *Proceedings of Machine Learning Research*, *81*. 423

Burda, Y., Grosse, R. B., & Salakhutdinov, R. (2016). Importance weighted autoencoders. *International Conference on Learning Representations*. 73, 346

Buschjäger, S., & Morik, K. (2021). There is no double-descent in random forests. *arXiv:2111.04409*. 134

Cai, T., Luo, S., Xu, K., He, D., Liu, T.-y., & Wang, L. (2021). GraphNorm: A principled approach to accelerating graph neural network training. *International Conference on Machine Learning*, 1204–1215. 265

Calimeri, F., Marzullo, A., Stamile, C., & Terracina, G. (2017). Biomedical data augmentation using adversarial neural networks. *International Conference on Artificial Neural Networks*, 626–634. 159

Calo, R. (2018). Artificial intelligence policy: A primer and roadmap. *University of Bologna Law Review*, *3*(2), 180–218. 430

Cao, H., Tan, C., Gao, Z., Chen, G., Heng, P.-A., & Li, S. Z. (2022). A survey on generative diffusion model. *arXiv:2209.02646*. 369

Cao, Z., Qin, T., Liu, T.-Y., Tsai, M.-F., & Li, H. (2007). Learning to rank: From pairwise approach to listwise approach. *International Conference on Machine Learning*, 129–136. 73

Carion, N., Massa, F., Synnaeve, G., Usunier, N., Kirillov, A., & Zagoruyko, S. (2020). End-to-end object detection with transformers. *European Conference on Computer Vision*, 213–229. 238

Carlini, N., Hayes, J., Nasr, M., Jagielski, M., Sehwag, V., Tramèr, F., Balle, B., Ippolito, D., & Wallace, E. (2023). Extracting training data from diffusion models. *arXiv:2301.13188*. 428

Carlini, N., Ippolito, D., Jagielski, M., Lee, K., Tramer, F., , & Zhang, C. (2022). Quantifying memorization across neural language models. *arXiv:2202.07646*. 428

Cauchy, A. (1847). Methode generale pour la resolution des systemes d'equations simultanees. *Comptes Rendus de l'Académie des Sciences*, *25*. 91

Cervantes, J.-A., López, S., Rodríguez, L.-F., Cervantes, S., Cervantes, F., & Ramos, F. (2019). Artificial moral agents: A survey of the current status. *Science and Engineering Ethics*, *26*, 501–532. 424

Ceylan, G., Anderson, I. A., & Wood, W. (2023). Sharing of misinformation is habitual, not just lazy or biased. *Proceedings of the National Academy of Sciences of the United States of America*, *120*(4). 432

Chami, I., Abu-El-Haija, S., Perozzi, B., Ré, C., & Murphy, K. (2020). Machine learning on graphs: A model and comprehensive taxonomy. *arXiv:2005.03675*. 261

Chang, B., Chen, M., Haber, E., & Chi, E. H. (2019a). AntisymmetricRNN: A dynamical system view on recurrent neural networks. *International Conference on Learning Representations*. 323

Chang, B., Meng, L., Haber, E., Ruthotto, L., Begert, D., & Holtham, E. (2018). Reversible architectures for arbitrarily deep residual neural networks. *AAAI Conference on Artificial Intelligence*, 2811–2818. 323

Chang, Y.-L., Liu, Z. Y., Lee, K.-Y., & Hsu, W. (2019b). Free-form video inpainting with 3D gated convolution and temporal Patch-GAN. *IEEE/CVF International Conference on Computer Vision*, 9066–9075. 181

Chaudhari, P., Choromanska, A., Soatto, S., LeCun, Y., Baldassi, C., Borgs, C., Chayes, J., Sagun, L., & Zecchina, R. (2019). Entropy-SGD: Biasing gradient descent into wide valleys. *Journal of Statistical Mechanics: Theory and Experiment*, 12, 124018. 158, 411

Chen, D., Mei, J.-P., Zhang, Y., Wang, C., Wang, Z., Feng, Y., & Chen, C. (2021a). Cross-layer distillation with semantic calibration. *AAAI Conference on Artificial Intelligence*, 7028–7036. 416

Chen, H., Wang, Y., Guo, T., Xu, C., Deng, Y., Liu, Z., Ma, S., Xu, C., Xu, C., & Gao, W. (2021b). Pre-trained image processing transformer. *IEEE/CVF Computer Vision & Pattern Recognition*, 12299–12310. 238

Chen, J., Ma, T., & Xiao, C. (2018a). FastGCN: Fast learning with graph convolutional networks via importance sampling. *International Conference on Learning Representations*. 264, 265

Chen, J., Zhu, J., & Song, L. (2018b). Stochastic training of graph convolutional networks with variance reduction. *International Conference on Machine Learning*, 941–949. 264

Chen, L., Lu, K., Rajeswaran, A., Lee, K., Grover, A., Laskin, M., Abbeel, P., Srinivas, A., & Mordatch, I. (2021c). Decision transformer: Reinforcement learning via sequence modeling. *Neural Information Processing Systems*, 34, 15084–15097. 398

Chen, L.-C., Papandreou, G., Kokkinos, I., Murphy, K., & Yuille, A. L. (2018c). DeepLab: Semantic image segmentation with deep convolutional nets, atrous convolution, and fully connected CRFs. *IEEE Transactions on Pattern Analysis & Machine Intelligence*, 40(4), 834—848. 181

Chen, M., Radford, A., Child, R., Wu, J., Jun, H., Luan, D., & Sutskever, I. (2020a). Generative pretraining from pixels. *International Conference on Machine Learning*, 1691–1703. 238

Chen, M., Wei, Z., Huang, Z., Ding, B., & Li, Y. (2020b). Simple and deep graph convolutional networks. *International Conference on Machine Learning*, 1725–1735. 266

Chen, N., Zhang, Y., Zen, H., Weiss, R. J., Norouzi, M., Dehak, N., & Chan, W. (2021d). WaveGrad 2: Iterative refinement for text-to-speech synthesis. *INTERSPEECH*, 3765–3769. 369

Chen, R. T., Behrmann, J., Duvenaud, D. K., & Jacobsen, J.-H. (2019). Residual flows for invertible generative modeling. *Neural Information Processing Systems*, 32, 9913–9923. 324

Chen, R. T., Li, X., Grosse, R. B., & Duvenaud, D. K. (2018d). Isolating sources of disentanglement in variational autoencoders. *Neural Information Processing Systems*, 31, 2615–2625. 343, 346

Chen, R. T., Rubanova, Y., Bettencourt, J., & Duvenaud, D. K. (2018e). Neural ordinary differential equations. *Neural Information Processing Systems*, 31, 6572–6583. 324

Chen, T., Fox, E., & Guestrin, C. (2014). Stochastic gradient Hamiltonian Monte Carlo. *International Conference on Machine Learning*, 1683–1691. 159

Chen, T., Kornblith, S., Norouzi, M., & Hinton, G. (2020c). A simple framework for contrastive learning of visual representations. *International Conference on Machine Learning*, 1597–1607. 159

Chen, T., Xu, B., Zhang, C., & Guestrin, C. (2016a). Training deep nets with sublinear memory cost. *arXiv:1604.06174*. 114

Chen, W., Liu, T.-Y., Lan, Y., Ma, Z.-M., & Li, H. (2009). Ranking measures and loss functions in learning to rank. *Neural Information Processing Systems*, 22, 315–323. 73

Chen, X., Duan, Y., Houthooft, R., Schulman, J., Sutskever, I., & Abbeel, P. (2016b). InfoGAN: Interpretable representation learning by information maximizing generative adversarial nets. *Neural Information Processing Systems*, 29, 2172–2180. 291, 301

Chen, X., Kingma, D. P., Salimans, T., Duan, Y., Dhariwal, P., Schulman, J., Sutskever, I., & Abbeel, P. (2017). Variational lossy autoencoder. *International Conference on Learning Representations*. 345

Chen, Y.-C., Li, L., Yu, L., El Kholy, A., Ahmed, F., Gan, Z., Cheng, Y., & Liu, J. (2020d). UNITER: Universal image-text representation learning. *European Conference on Computer Vision*, 104–120. 238

Chiang, W.-L., Liu, X., Si, S., Li, Y., Bengio, S., & Hsieh, C.-J. (2019). Cluster-GCN: An efficient algorithm for training deep and large graph convolutional networks. *ACM SIGKDD International Conference on Knowledge Discovery & Data Mining*, 257–266. 263, 264, 265

Child, R., Gray, S., Radford, A., & Sutskever, I. (2019). Generating long sequences with sparse transformers. *arXiv:1904.10509*. 237

Chintala, S., Denton, E., Arjovsky, M., & Matheiu, M. (2020). How to train a GAN? Tips and tricks to make GANs work. `https://github.com/soumith/ganhacks`. 299

Cho, K., van Merrienboer, B., Bahdanau, D., & Bengio, Y. (2014). On the properties of neural machine translation: Encoder-decoder approaches. *ACL Workshop on Syntax, Semantics and Structure in Statistical Translation*, 103–111. 233

Choi, D., Shallue, C. J., Nado, Z., Lee, J., Maddison, C. J., & Dahl, G. E. (2019). On empirical comparisons of optimizers for deep learning. *arXiv:1910.05446*. 94, 410

Choi, J., Kim, S., Jeong, Y., Gwon, Y., & Yoon, S. (2021). ILVR: Conditioning method for denoising diffusion probabilistic models. *IEEE/CVF International Conference on Computer Vision*, 14347–14356. 370

Choi, J., Lee, J., Shin, C., Kim, S., Kim, H., & Yoon, S. (2022). Perception prioritized training of diffusion models. *IEEE/CVF Computer Vision & Pattern Recognition*, 11472–11481. 369

Choi, Y., Choi, M., Kim, M., Ha, J.-W., Kim, S., & Choo, J. (2018). StarGAN: Unified generative adversarial networks for multi-domain image-to-image translation. *IEEE/CVF Computer Vision & Pattern Recognition*, 8789–8797. 301

Chollet, F. (2017). Xception: Deep learning with depthwise separable convolutions. *IEEE/CVF Computer Vision & Pattern Recognition*, 1251–1258. 405

Choromanska, A., Henaff, M., Mathieu, M., Arous, G. B., & LeCun, Y. (2015). The loss surfaces of multilayer networks. *International Conference on Artificial Intelligence and Statistics*. 405

Choromanski, K., Likhosherstov, V., Dohan, D., Song, X., Gane, A., Sarlos, T., Hawkins, P., Davis, J., Mohiuddin, A., Kaiser, L., et al. (2020). Rethinking attention with Performers. *International Conference on Learning Representations*. 236, 237

Chorowski, J., & Jaitly, N. (2017). Towards better decoding and language model integration in sequence to sequence models. *INTERSPEECH*, 523–527. 158

Chouldechova, A. (2017). Fair prediction with disparate impact: A study of bias in recidivism prediction instruments. *Big data*, 5(2), 153–163. 422

Chowdhery, A., Narang, S., Devlin, J., Bosma, M., Mishra, G., Roberts, A., Barham, P., Chung, H. W., Sutton, C., Gehrmann, S., et al. (2022). PaLM: Scaling language modeling with pathways. *arXiv:2204.02311*. 234

Christian, B. (2020). *The Alignment Problem: Machine Learning and Human Values*. W. W. Norton. 421

Christiano, P., Shlegeris, B., & Amodei, D. (2018). Supervising strong learners by amplifying weak experts. *arXiv:1810.08575*. 398

Chu, X., Tian, Z., Wang, Y., Zhang, B., Ren, H., Wei, X., Xia, H., & Shen, C. (2021). Twins: Revisiting the design of spatial attention in vision transformers. *Neural Information Processing Systems*, 34, 9355–9366. 238

Chung, H., Sim, B., & Ye, J. C. (2022). Come-closer-diffuse-faster: Accelerating conditional diffusion models for inverse problems through stochastic contraction. *IEEE/CVF Computer Vision & Pattern Recognition*, 12413–12422. 369

Chung, H., & Ye, J. C. (2022). Score-based diffusion models for accelerated MRI. *Medical Image Analysis*, 80, 102479. 369

Chung, J., Gulcehre, C., Cho, K., & Bengio, Y. (2014). Empirical evaluation of gated recurrent neural networks on sequence modeling. *Deep Learning and Representation Workshop*. 233

Chung, J., Kastner, K., Dinh, L., Goel, K., Courville, A. C., & Bengio, Y. (2015). A recurrent latent variable model for sequential data. *Neural Information Processing Systems*, 28, 2980–2988. 344, 345

Çiçek, Ö., Abdulkadir, A., Lienkamp, S. S., Brox, T., & Ronneberger, O. (2016). 3D U-Net: Learning dense volumetric segmentation from sparse annotation. *International Conference on Medical Image Computing and Computer-Assisted Intervention*, 424–432. 205

Clark, M. (2022). The engineer who claimed a Google AI is sentient has been fired. *The Verge*, July 22, 2022. `https://www.theverge.com/2022/7/22/23274958/google-ai-engineer-blake-lemoine-chatbot-lamda-2-sentience`. 234

Clevert, D.-A., Unterthiner, T., & Hochreiter, S. (2015). Fast and accurate deep network learning by exponential linear units (ELUs). *arXiv:1511.07289*. 38

Cohen, J. M., Kaur, S., Li, Y., Kolter, J. Z., & Talwalkar, A. (2021). Gradient descent on neural networks typically occurs at the edge of stability. *International Conference on Learning Representations.* 157

Cohen, N., Sharir, O., & Shashua, A. (2016). On the expressive power of deep learning: A tensor analysis. *PMLR Conference on Learning Theory*, 698–728. 53

Cohen, T., & Welling, M. (2016). Group equivariant convolutional networks. *International Conference on Machine Learning*, 2990–2999. 183

Collins, E., Bala, R., Price, B., & Susstrunk, S. (2020). Editing in style: Uncovering the local semantics of GANs. *IEEE/CVF Computer Vision & Pattern Recognition*, 5771–5780. 300

Conneau, A., Schwenk, H., Barrault, L., & Lecun, Y. (2017). Very deep convolutional networks for text classification. *Meeting of the Association for Computational Linguistics*, 1107–1116. 182

Constanza-Chock, S. (2020). *Design Justice: Community-Led Practices to Build the Worlds We Need.* Cambridge, MA: The MIT Press. 433

Cordonnier, J.-B., Loukas, A., & Jaggi, M. (2020). On the relationship between self-attention and convolutional layers. *International Conference on Learning Representations.* 236

Cordts, M., Omran, M., Ramos, S., Rehfeld, T., Enzweiler, M., Benenson, R., Franke, U., Roth, S., & Schiele, B. (2016). The Cityscapes dataset for semantic urban scene understanding. *IEEE/CVF Computer Vision & Pattern Recognition*, 1877–1901. 6, 153

Coulombe, C. (2018). Text data augmentation made simple by leveraging NLP cloud APIs. *arXiv:1812.04718.* 160

Creel, K. A. (2020). Transparency in complex computational systems. *Philosophy of Science*, *87*(4), 568–589. 425, 435

Crenshaw, K. (1991). Mapping the margins: Intersectionality, identity politics, and violence against women of color. *Stanford Law Review*, *43*(6), 1241–1299. 423

Creswell, A., & Bharath, A. A. (2018). Inverting the generator of a generative adversarial network. *IEEE Transactions on Neural Networks and Learning Systems*, *30*(7), 1967–1974. 301

Creswell, A., White, T., Dumoulin, V., Arulkumaran, K., Sengupta, B., & Bharath, A. A. (2018). Generative adversarial networks: An overview. *IEEE Signal Processing Magazine*, *35*(1), 53–65. 298

Cristianini, M., & Shawe-Taylor, J. (2000). *An Introduction to support vector machines.* CUP. 74

Croitoru, F.-A., Hondru, V., Ionescu, R. T., & Shah, M. (2022). Diffusion models in vision: A survey. *arXiv:2209.04747.* 369

Cubuk, E. D., Zoph, B., Mané, D., Vasudevan, V., & Le, Q. V. (2019). Autoaugment: Learning augmentation strategies from data. *IEEE/CVF Computer Vision & Pattern Recognition*, 113–123. 405

Cybenko, G. (1989). Approximation by superpositions of a sigmoidal function. *Mathematics of Control, Signals and Systems*, *2*(4), 303–314. 38

Dabney, W., Rowland, M., Bellemare, M., & Munos, R. (2018). Distributional reinforcement learning with quantile regression. *AAAI Conference on Artificial Intelligence.* 397

Dai, H., Dai, B., & Song, L. (2016). Discriminative embeddings of latent variable models for structured data. *International Conference on Machine Learning*, 2702–2711. 262

Dai, J., Qi, H., Xiong, Y., Li, Y., Zhang, G., Hu, H., & Wei, Y. (2017). Deformable convolutional networks. *IEEE/CVF International Conference on Computer Vision*, 764–773. 183

Daigavane, A., Balaraman, R., & Aggarwal, G. (2021). Understanding convolutions on graphs. Distill, `https://distill.pub/2021/understanding-gnns/`. 261

Danaher, J. (2019). *Automation and Utopia: Human Flourishing in a World without Work.* Harvard University Press. 430

Daniluk, M., Rocktäschel, T., Welbl, J., & Riedel, S. (2017). Frustratingly short attention spans in neural language modeling. *International Conference on Learning Representations.* 235

Danks, D., & London, A. J. (2017). Algorithmic bias in autonomous systems. *International Joint Conference on Artificial Intelligence*, 4691–4697. 422

Dao, D. (2021). *Awful AI.* Github. Retrieved January 17, 2023. `https://github.com/daviddao/awful-ai.` 14

Dar, Y., Muthukumar, V., & Baraniuk, R. G. (2021). A farewell to the bias-variance tradeoff? An overview of the theory of overparameterized machine learning. *arXiv:2109.02355.* 135

Das, H. P., Abbeel, P., & Spanos, C. J. (2019). Likelihood contribution based multi-scale architecture for generative flows. *arXiv:1908.01686.* 323

Dauphin, Y. N., Pascanu, R., Gülçehre, Ç., Cho, K., Ganguli, S., & Bengio, Y. (2014). Identifying and attacking the saddle point problem in high-dimensional non-convex optimization. *Neural Information Processing Systems,* vol. 27, 2933–2941. 409, 410

David, H. (2015). Why are there still so many jobs? The history and future of workplace automation. *Journal of Economic Perspectives, 29*(3), 3–30. 14

De, S., & Smith, S. (2020). Batch normalization biases residual blocks towards the identity function in deep networks. *Neural Information Processing Systems, 33,* 19964–19975. 205

De Cao, N., & Kipf, T. (2018). MolGAN: An implicit generative model for small molecular graphs. *ICML Workshop on Theoretical Foundations and Applications of Deep Generative Models.* 299

Dechter, R. (1986). Learning while searching in constraint-satisfaction-problems. *AAAI Conference on Artificial Intelligence,* 178—183. 52

Defferrard, M., Bresson, X., & Vandergheynst, P. (2016). Convolutional neural networks on graphs with fast localized spectral filtering. *Neural Information Processing Systems, 29,* 3837–3845. 262

Dehghani, M., Tay, Y., Gritsenko, A. A., Zhao, Z., Houlsby, N., Diaz, F., Metzler, D., & Vinyals, O. (2021). The benchmark lottery. *arXiv:2107.07002.* 234

Deisenroth, M. P., Faisal, A. A., & Ong, C. S. (2020). *Mathematics for machine learning.* Cambridge University Press. 15

Dempster, A. P., Laird, N. M., & Rubin, D. B. (1977). Maximum likelihood from incomplete data via the EM algorithm. *Journal of the Royal Statistical Society: Series B, 39*(1), 1–22. 346

Deng, J., Dong, W., Socher, R., Li, L.-J., Li, K., & Fei-Fei, L. (2009). ImageNet: A large-scale hierarchical image database. *IEEE Computer Vision & Pattern Recognition,* 248–255. 181, 272

Denton, E. L., Chintala, S., Fergus, R., et al. (2015). Deep generative image models using a Laplacian pyramid of adversarial networks. *Neural Information Processing Systems, 28,* 1486–1494. 300, 301

Devlin, J., Chang, M., Lee, K., & Toutanova, K. (2019). BERT: pre-training of deep bidirectional transformers for language understanding. *ACL Human Language Technologies,* 4171–4186. 159, 234

DeVries, T., & Taylor, G. W. (2017a). Dataset augmentation in feature space. *arXiv:1702.05538.* 158

DeVries, T., & Taylor, G. W. (2017b). Improved regularization of convolutional neural networks with Cutout. *arXiv:1708.04552.* 183

Dhariwal, P., & Nichol, A. (2021). Diffusion models beat GANs on image synthesis. *Neural Information Processing Systems, 34,* 8780–8794. 367, 368, 370

Ding, M., Xiao, B., Codella, N., Luo, P., Wang, J., & Yuan, L. (2022). DaViT: Dual attention vision transformers. *European Conference on Computer Vision,* 74–92. 238

Dinh, L., Krueger, D., & Bengio, Y. (2015). NICE: Non-linear independent components estimation. *International Conference on Learning Representations Workshop.* 323

Dinh, L., Pascanu, R., Bengio, S., & Bengio, Y. (2017). Sharp minima can generalize for deep nets. *International Conference on Machine Learning,* 1019–1028. 411

Dinh, L., Sohl-Dickstein, J., & Bengio, S. (2016). Density estimation using Real NVP. *International Conference on Learning Representations.* 322, 323

Dinh, L., Sohl-Dickstein, J., Larochelle, H., & Pascanu, R. (2019). A RAD approach to deep mixture models. *ICLR Workshop on Deep Generative Models for Highly Structured Data.* 323

Dockhorn, T., Vahdat, A., & Kreis, K. (2022). Score-based generative modeling with critically-damped Langevin diffusion. *International Conference on Learning Representations.* 370

Doersch, C., Gupta, A., & Efros, A. A. (2015). Unsupervised visual representation learning by context prediction. *IEEE International Conference on Computer Vision,* 1422–1430. 159

Domingos, P. (2000). A unified bias-variance decomposition. *International Conference on Machine Learning,* 231–238. 133

Domke, J. (2010). Statistical machine learning. https://people.cs.umass.edu/~domke/. 116

Donahue, C., Lipton, Z. C., Balsubramani, A., & McAuley, J. (2018a). Semantically decomposing the latent spaces of generative adversarial networks. *International Conference on Learning Representations.* 301

Donahue, C., McAuley, J., & Puckette, M. (2018b). Adversarial audio synthesis. *International Conference on Learning Representations.* 299, 301

Dong, X., Bao, J., Chen, D., Zhang, W., Yu, N., Yuan, L., Chen, D., & Guo, B. (2022). CSWin transformer: A general vision transformer backbone with cross-shaped windows. *IEEE/CVF Computer Vision & Pattern Recognition*, 12124–12134. 238

Dorta, G., Vicente, S., Agapito, L., Campbell, N. D., & Simpson, I. (2018). Structured uncertainty prediction networks. *IEEE/CVF Computer Vision & Pattern Recognition*, 5477–5485. 73, 340, 344

Dosovitskiy, A., Beyer, L., Kolesnikov, A., Weissenborn, D., Zhai, X., Unterthiner, T., Dehghani, M., Minderer, M., Heigold, G., Gelly, S., et al. (2021). An image is worth 16x16 words: Transformers for image recognition at scale. *International Conference on Learning Representations.* 234, 238

Dozat, T. (2016). Incorporating Nesterov momentum into Adam. *International Conference on Learning Representations — Workshop track.* 94

Draxler, F., Veschgini, K., Salmhofer, M., & Hamprecht, F. A. (2018). Essentially no barriers in neural network energy landscape. *International Conference on Machine Learning*, 1308–1317. 408, 409

Du, N., Huang, Y., Dai, A. M., Tong, S., Lepikhin, D., Xu, Y., Krikun, M., Zhou, Y., Yu, A. W., Firat, O., et al. (2022). GLaM: Efficient scaling of language models with mixture-of-experts. *International Conference on Machine Learning*, 5547–5569. 234

Du, S. S., Lee, J. D., Li, H., Wang, L., & Zhai, X. (2019a). Gradient descent finds global minima of deep neural networks. *International Conference on Machine Learning*, 1675–1685. 404, 405

Du, S. S., Zhai, X., Poczos, B., & Singh, A. (2019b). Gradient descent provably optimizes over-parameterized neural networks. *International Conference on Learning Representations.* 404

Duchi, J., Hazan, E., & Singer, Y. (2011). Adaptive subgradient methods for online learning and stochastic optimization. *Journal of Machine Learning Research*, *12*, 2121–2159. 93

Dufter, P., Schmitt, M., & Schütze, H. (2021). Position information in transformers: An overview. *Computational Linguistics*, 1–31. 236

Dumoulin, V., Belghazi, I., Poole, B., Mastropietro, O., Lamb, A., Arjovsky, M., & Courville, A. (2017). Adversarially learned inference. *International Conference on Learning Representations.* 301, 345

Dumoulin, V., & Visin, F. (2016). A guide to convolution arithmetic for deep learning. *arXiv:1603.07285.* 180

Dupont, E., Doucet, A., & Teh, Y. W. (2019). Augmented neural ODEs. *Neural Information Processing Systems*, *32*, 3134–3144. 324

Durkan, C., Bekasov, A., Murray, I., & Papamakarios, G. (2019a). Cubic-spline flows. *ICML Invertible Neural Networks and Normalizing Flows.* 323

Durkan, C., Bekasov, A., Murray, I., & Papamakarios, G. (2019b). Neural spline flows. *Neural Information Processing Systems*, *32*, 7509–7520. 323

Duvenaud, D. K., Maclaurin, D., Iparraguirre, J., Bombarell, R., Hirzel, T., Aspuru-Guzik, A., & Adams, R. P. (2015). Convolutional networks on graphs for learning molecular fingerprints. *Neural Information Processing Systems*, *28*, 2224–2232. 262

D'Amour, A., Heller, K., Moldovan, D., Adlam, B., Alipanahi, B., Beutel, A., Chen, C., Deaton, J., Eisenstein, J., Hoffman, M. D., et al. (2020). Underspecification presents challenges for credibility in modern machine learning. *Journal of Machine Learning Research*, 1–61. 413

Ebrahimi, J., Rao, A., Lowd, D., & Dou, D. (2018). HotFlip: White-box adversarial examples for text classification. *Meeting of the Association for Computational Linguistics*, 31–36. 160

El Asri, L., & Prince, J. D., Simon (2020). Tutorial #6: Neural natural language generation – decoding algorithms. https://www.borealisai.com/research-blogs/tutorial-6-neural-natural-language-generation-decoding-algorithms/. 235

Eldan, R., & Shamir, O. (2016). The power of depth for feedforward neural networks. *PMLR Conference on Learning Theory*, 907–940. 53, 417

Elfwing, S., Uchibe, E., & Doya, K. (2018). Sigmoid-weighted linear units for neural network function approximation in reinforcement learning. *Neural Networks*, *107*, 3–11. 38

Erasmus, A., Brunet, T. D. P., & Fisher, E. (2021). What is interpretability? *Philosophy & Technology*, *34*, 833–862. 425

Eren, L., Ince, T., & Kiranyaz, S. (2019). A generic intelligent bearing fault diagnosis system using compact adaptive 1D CNN classifier. *Journal of Signal Processing Systems*, *91*(2), 179–189. 182

Erhan, D., Bengio, Y., Courville, A., & Vincent, P. (2009). Visualizing higher-layer features of a deep network. *Technical Report, University of Montreal*, *1341*(3). 184

Errica, F., Podda, M., Bacciu, D., & Micheli, A. (2019). A fair comparison of graph neural networks for graph classification. *International Conference on Learning Representations*. 262

Eslami, S., Heess, N., Weber, T., Tassa, Y., Szepesvari, D., Hinton, G. E., et al. (2016). Attend, infer, repeat: Fast scene understanding with generative models. *Neural Information Processing Systems*, *29*, 3225–3233. 344

Eslami, S. A., Jimenez Rezende, D., Besse, F., Viola, F., Morcos, A. S., Garnelo, M., Ruderman, A., Rusu, A. A., Danihelka, I., Gregor, K., et al. (2018). Neural scene representation and rendering. *Science*, *360*(6394), 1204–1210. 344

Esling, P., Masuda, N., Bardet, A., Despres, R., et al. (2019). Universal audio synthesizer control with normalizing flows. *International Conference on Digital Audio Effects*. 322

Esser, P., Rombach, R., & Ommer, B. (2021). Taming transformers for high-resolution image synthesis. *IEEE/CVF Computer Vision & Pattern Recognition*, 12873–12883. 301

Esteves, C., Allen-Blanchette, C., Zhou, X., & Daniilidis, K. (2018). Polar transformer networks. *International Conference on Learning Representations*. 183

Etmann, C., Ke, R., & Schönlieb, C.-B. (2020). iunets: Fully invertible U-Nets with learnable up-and downsampling. *IEEE International Workshop on Machine Learning for Signal Processing*. 322

Eubanks, V. (2018). *Automating Inequality: How High-Tech Tools Profile, Police, and Punish the Poor*. New York: St. Martin's Press. 433

Evans, K., de Moura, N., Chauvier, S., Chatila, R., & Dogan, E. (2020). Ethical decision making in autonomous vehicles: the AV ethics project. *Science and Engineering Ethics*, *26*(6), 3285–3312. 424

FAIR (2022). Human-level play in the game of Diplomacy by combining language models with strategic reasoning. *Science*, *378*(6624), 1067–1074. 396

Falbo, A., & LaCroix, T. (2022). Est-ce que vous compute? Code-switching, cultural identity, and AI. *Feminist Philosophy Quarterly*, *8*(3/4). 423

Falk, T., Mai, D., Bensch, R., Çiçek, Ö., Abdulkadir, A., Marrakchi, Y., Böhm, A., Deubner, J., Jäckel, Z., Seiwald, K., et al. (2019). U-Net: Deep learning for cell counting, detection, and morphometry. *Nature Methods*, *16*(1), 67–70. 199

Falkner, S., Klein, A., & Hutter, F. (2018). BOHB: Robust and efficient hyperparameter optimization at scale. *International Conference on Machine Learning*, 1437–1446. 136

Fallah, N., Gu, H., Mohammad, K., Seyyedsalehi, S. A., Nourijelyani, K., & Eshraghian, M. R. (2009). Nonlinear Poisson regression using neural networks: A simulation study. *Neural Computing and Applications*, *18*(8), 939–943. 74

Fan, A., Lewis, M., & Dauphin, Y. N. (2018). Hierarchical neural story generation. *Meeting of the Association for Computational Linguistics*, 889–898. 235

Fan, H., Xiong, B., Mangalam, K., Li, Y., Yan, Z., Malik, J., & Feichtenhofer, C. (2021). Multiscale vision transformers. *IEEE/CVF International Conference on Computer Vision*, 6824–6835. 238

Fan, K., Li, B., Wang, J., Zhang, S., Chen, B., Ge, N., & Yan, Z. (2020). Neural zero-inflated quality estimation model for automatic speech recognition system. *Interspeech*, 606–610. 73

Fang, F., Yamagishi, J., Echizen, I., & Lorenzo-Trueba, J. (2018). High-quality nonparallel voice conversion based on cycle-consistent adversarial network. *International Conference on Acoustics, Speech and Signal Processing*, 5279–5283. 299

Fang, Y., Liao, B., Wang, X., Fang, J., Qi, J., Wu, R., Niu, J., & Liu, W. (2021). You only look at one sequence: Rethinking transformer in vision through object detection. *Neural Information Processing Systems*, *34*, 26183–26197. 238

Farnia, F., & Ozdaglar, A. (2020). Do GANs always have Nash equilibria? *International Conference on Machine Learning*, 3029–3039. 299

Fawzi, A., Balog, M., Huang, A., Hubert, T., Romera-Paredes, B., Barekatain, M., Novikov,

A., R Ruiz, F. J., Schrittwieser, J., Swirszcz, G., et al. (2022). Discovering faster matrix multiplication algorithms with reinforcement learning. *Nature, 610*(7930), 47–53. 396

Fazelpour, S., & Danks, D. (2021). Algorithmic bias: Senses, sources, solutions. *Philosophy Compass, 16.* 421, 422, 435

Fedus, W., Goodfellow, I., & Dai, A. M. (2018). MaskGAN: Better text generation via filling in the_. *International Conference on Learning Representations.* 299

Feng, S. Y., Gangal, V., Kang, D., Mitamura, T., & Hovy, E. (2020). GenAug: Data augmentation for finetuning text generators. *ACL Deep Learning Inside Out,* 29–42. 160

Feng, Z., Zhang, Z., Yu, X., Fang, Y., Li, L., Chen, X., Lu, Y., Liu, J., Yin, W., Feng, S., et al. (2022). ERNIE-ViLG 2.0: Improving text-to-image diffusion model with knowledge-enhanced mixture-of-denoising-experts. *arXiv:2210.15257.* 371

Fernandez, C. (2017). Can a computer tell if you're gay? Artificial intelligence system guesses your sexuality with 91% accuracy just by looking at a photo of your face. Daily Mail, 7 Sept, 2017. `https://www.dailymail.co.uk/sciencetech/article-4862676/Artificial-intelligence-tell-gay.html`. 430

Fernández-Madrigal, J.-A., & González, J. (2002). Multihierarchical graph search. *IEEE Transactions on Pattern Analysis and Machine Intelligence, 24*(1), 103–113. 242

Fetscherin, M., Tantleff-Dunn, S., & Klumb, A. (2020). Effects of facial features and styling elements on perceptions of competence, warmth, and hireability of male professionals. *The Journal of Social Psychology, 160*(3), 332–345. 427

Finlay, C., Jacobsen, J., Nurbekyan, L., & Oberman, A. M. (2020). How to train your neural ODE: The world of Jacobian and kinetic regularization. *International Conference on Machine Learning,* 3154–3164. 324

Fort, S., Hu, H., & Lakshminarayanan, B. (2019). Deep ensembles: A loss landscape perspective. *arXiv:1912.02757.* 158

Fort, S., & Jastrzębski, S. (2019). Large scale structure of neural network loss landscapes. *Neural Information Processing Systems,* vol. 32, 6706–6714. 408

Fort, S., & Scherlis, A. (2019). The Goldilocks zone: Towards better understanding of neural network loss landscapes. *AAAI Conference on Artificial Intelligence,* 3574–3581. 409, 410, 412, 413

Fortunato, M., Azar, M. G., Piot, B., Menick, J., Osband, I., Graves, A., Mnih, V., Munos, R., Hassabis, D., Pietquin, O., et al. (2018). Noisy networks for exploration. *International Conference on Learning Representations.* 397

François-Lavet, V., Henderson, P., Islam, R., Bellemare, M. G., Pineau, J., et al. (2018). An introduction to deep reinforcement learning. *Foundations and Trends in Machine Learning, 11*(3-4), 219–354. 396

Frankle, J., & Carbin, M. (2019). The lottery ticket hypothesis: Finding sparse, trainable neural networks. *International Conference on Learning Representations.* 406, 415

Frankle, J., Dziugaite, G. K., Roy, D. M., & Carbin, M. (2020). Linear mode connectivity and the lottery ticket hypothesis. *International Conference on Machine Learning,* 3259–3269. 158, 408

Frankle, J., Schwab, D. J., & Morcos, A. S. (2021). Training BatchNorm and only BatchNorm: On the expressive power of random features in CNNs. *International Conference on Learning Representations.* 418

Freund, Y., & Schapire, R. E. (1997). A decision-theoretic generalization of on-line learning and an application to boosting. *Journal of Computer and System Sciences, 55*(1), 119–139. 74

Frey, C. B. (2019). *The Technology Trap: Capital, Labour, and Power in the Age of Automation.* Princeton University Press. 430

Frey, C. B., & Osborne, M. A. (2017). The future of employment: How susceptible are jobs to computerisation? *Technological forecasting and social change, 114,* 254–280. 430

Friedman, J. H. (1997). On bias, variance, 0/1—loss, and the curse-of-dimensionality. *Data Mining and Knowledge Discovery, 1*(1), 55–77. 133

Fujimoto, S., Hoof, H., & Meger, D. (2018). Addressing function approximation error in actor-critic methods. *International Conference on Machine Learning,* 1587–1596. 397

Fujimoto, S., Meger, D., & Precup, D. (2019). Off-policy deep reinforcement learning without exploration. *International Conference on Machine Learning,* 2052–2062. 398

Fukushima, K. (1969). Visual feature extraction by a multilayered network of analog threshold elements. *IEEE Transactions on Systems Science and Cybernetics, 5*(4), 322–333. 37

Fukushima, K., & Miyake, S. (1982). Neocognitron: A self-organizing neural network model for a mechanism of visual pattern recognition. *Competition and Cooperation in Neural Nets*, 267–285. 180

Gabriel, I. (2020). Artificial intelligence, values, and alignment. *Minds and Machines, 30*, 411–437. 421

Gal, Y., & Ghahramani, Z. (2016). Dropout as a Bayesian approximation: Representing model uncertainty in deep learning. *International Conference on Machine Learning*, 1050—1059. 158

Gales, M. J. (1998). Maximum likelihood linear transformations for HMM-based speech recognition. *Computer Speech & Language, 12(2)*, 75–98. 160

Gales, M. J., Ragni, A., AlDamarki, H., & Gautier, C. (2009). Support vector machines for noise robust ASR. *2009 IEEE Workshop on Automatic Speech Recognition & Understanding*, 205–210. 160

Ganaie, M., Hu, M., Malik, A., Tanveer, M., & Suganthan, P. (2022). Ensemble deep learning: A review. *Engineering Applications of Artificial Intelligence, 115*. 158

Gao, H., & Ji, S. (2019). Graph U-Nets. *International Conference on Machine Learning*, 2083–2092. 265

Gao, R., Song, Y., Poole, B., Wu, Y. N., & Kingma, D. P. (2021). Learning energy-based models by diffusion recovery likelihood. *International Conference on Learning Representations*. 370

Garg, R., Bg, V. K., Carneiro, G., & Reid, I. (2016). Unsupervised CNN for single view depth estimation: Geometry to the rescue. *European Conference on Computer Vision*, 740–756. 205

Garipov, T., Izmailov, P., Podoprikhin, D., Vetrov, D., & Wilson, A. G. (2018). Loss surfaces, mode connectivity, and fast ensembling of DNNs. *Neural Information Processing Systems*, vol. 31, 8803—8812. 158, 408

Gastaldi, X. (2017a). Shake-shake regularization. *arXiv:1705.07485*. 203

Gastaldi, X. (2017b). Shake-shake regularization of 3-branch residual networks. 203

Gebru, T., Bender, E. M., McMillan-Major, A., & Mitchell, M. (2023). Statement from the listed authors of stochastic parrots on the "AI pause" letter. https://www.dair-institute. org/blog/letter-statement-March2023. 435

Gemici, M. C., Rezende, D., & Mohamed, S. (2016). Normalizing flows on Riemannian manifolds. *NIPS Workshop on Bayesian Deep Learning*. 324

Germain, M., Gregor, K., Murray, I., & Larochelle, H. (2015). MADE: Masked autoencoder for distribution estimation. *International Conference on Machine Learning*, 881–889. 323

Ghosh, A., Kulharia, V., Namboodiri, V. P., Torr, P. H., & Dokania, P. K. (2018). Multi-agent diverse generative adversarial networks. *IEEE/CVF Computer Vision & Pattern Recognition*, 8513–8521. 300

Gidaris, S., Singh, P., & Komodakis, N. (2018). Unsupervised representation learning by predicting image rotations. *International Conference on Learning Representations*. 159

Gilmer, J., Schoenholz, S. S., Riley, P. F., Vinyals, O., & Dahl, G. E. (2017). Neural message passing for quantum chemistry. *International Conference on Machine Learning*, 1263–1272. 262

Girdhar, R., Carreira, J., Doersch, C., & Zisserman, A. (2019). Video action transformer network. *IEEE/CVF Computer Vision & Pattern Recognition*, 244–253. 238

Girshick, R. (2015). Fast R-CNN. *IEEE International Conference on Computer Vision*, 1440–1448. 183

Girshick, R., Donahue, J., Darrell, T., & Malik, J. (2014). Rich feature hierarchies for accurate object detection and semantic segmentation. *IEEE Computer Vision & Pattern Recognition*, 580–587. 183

Glorot, X., & Bengio, Y. (2010). Understanding the difficulty of training deep feedforward neural networks. *International Conference on Artificial Intelligence and Statistics, 9*, 249–256. 113, 183

Glorot, X., Bordes, A., & Bengio, Y. (2011). Deep sparse rectifier neural networks. *International Conference on Artificial Intelligence and Statistics*, 315–323. 37, 38

Goh, G. (2017). Why momentum really works. Distill, http://distill.pub/2017/momentum. 92

Goldberg, D. E. (1987). Simple genetic algorithms and the minimal deceptive problem. *Genetic Algorithms and Simulated Annealing*, 74–88. Morgan Kaufmann. 421

Gomez, A. N., Ren, M., Urtasun, R., & Grosse, R. B. (2017). The reversible residual network: Backpropagation without storing activations. *Neural Information Processing Systems, 30*, 2214–2224. 114, 322, 323

Gómez-Bombarelli, R., Wei, J. N., Duvenaud, D., Hernández-Lobato, J. M., Sánchez-Lengeling, B., Sheberla, D., Aguilera-Iparraguirre, J., Hirzel, T. D., Adams, R. P., & Aspuru-Guzik, A. (2018). Automatic chemical design using a data-driven continuous representation of molecules. *ACS Central Science*, *4*(2), 268–276. 343, 344

Gong, S., Bahri, M., Bronstein, M. M., & Zafeiriou, S. (2020). Geometrically principled connections in graph neural networks. *IEEE/CVF Computer Vision & Pattern Recognition*, 11415–11424. 266

Goodfellow, I. (2016). Generative adversarial networks. *NIPS 2016 Tutorial*. 298

Goodfellow, I., Bengio, Y., & Courville, A. (2016). *Deep learning*. MIT Press. 15, 157

Goodfellow, I., Pouget-Abadie, J., Mirza, M., Xu, B., Warde-Farley, D., Ozair, S., Courville, A., & Bengio, Y. (2014). Generative adversarial networks. *Communications of the ACM*, *63*(11), 139–144. 273, 298, 300

Goodfellow, I. J., Shlens, J., & Szegedy, C. (2015a). Explaining and harnessing adversarial examples. *International Conference on Learning Representations*. 159, 413

Goodfellow, I. J., Vinyals, O., & Saxe, A. M. (2015b). Qualitatively characterizing neural network optimization problems. *International Conference on Learning Representations*. 407, 408

Goodin, D. (2023). ChatGPT is enabling script kiddies to write functional malware. ars Technica, June 1, 2023. https://arstechnica.com/information-technology/2023/01/chatgpt-is-enabling-script-kiddies-to-write-functional-malware/. 428

Gordon, G. J. (1995). Stable fitted reinforcement learning. *Neural Information Processing Systems*, *8*, 1052–1058. 396

Gori, M., Monfardini, G., & Scarselli, F. (2005). A new model for learning in graph domains. *IEEE International Joint Conference on Neural Networks*, 2005, 729–734. 262

Gouk, H., Frank, E., Pfahringer, B., & Cree, M. J. (2021). Regularisation of neural networks by enforcing Lipschitz continuity. *Machine Learning*, *110*(2), 393—416. 156

Goyal, A., Bochkovskiy, A., Deng, J., & Koltun, V. (2021). Non-deep networks. *arXiv:2110.07641*. 417

Goyal, P., Dollár, P., Girshick, R., Noordhuis, P., Wesolowski, L., Kyrola, A., Tulloch, A.,

Jia, Y., & He, K. (2018). Accurate, large minibatch SGD: Training ImageNet in 1 hour. *arXiv:1706.02677*. 92, 93, 237, 410

Graesser, L., & Keng, W. L. (2019). *Foundations of deep reinforcement learning*. Addison-Wesley Professional. 16, 396

Grathwohl, W., Chen, R. T., Bettencourt, J., Sutskever, I., & Duvenaud, D. (2019). Ffjord: Free-form continuous dynamics for scalable reversible generative models. *International Conference on Learning Representations*. 324

Grattarola, D., Zambon, D., Bianchi, F. M., & Alippi, C. (2022). Understanding pooling in graph neural networks. *IEEE Transactions on Neural Networks and Learning Systems*. 265

Green, B. (2019). "Good" isn't good enough. *NeurIPS Workshop on AI for Social Good*. 433

Green, B. (2022). Escaping the impossibility of fairness: From formal to substantive algorithmic fairness. *Philosophy & Technology*, *35*(90). 422

Greensmith, E., Bartlett, P. L., & Baxter, J. (2004). Variance reduction techniques for gradient estimates in reinforcement learning. *Journal of Machine Learning Research*, *5*(9), 1471–1530. 397

Gregor, K., Besse, F., Jimenez Rezende, D., Danihelka, I., & Wierstra, D. (2016). Towards conceptual compression. *Neural Information Processing Systems*, *29*, 3549–3557. 343, 344

Gregor, K., Papamakarios, G., Besse, F., Buesing, L., & Weber, T. (2019). Temporal difference variational auto-encoder. *International Conference on Learning Representations*. 344

Grennan, L., Kremer, A., Singla, A., & Zipparo, P. (2022). *Why businesses need explainable AI—and how to deliver it*. McKinsey, September 29, 2022. https://www.mckinsey.com/capabilities/quantumblack/our-insights/why-businesses-need-explainable-ai-and-how-to-deliver-it/. 13

Greydanus, S. (2020). Scaling down deep learning. *arXiv:2011.14439*. 119

Griewank, A., & Walther, A. (2008). *Evaluating derivatives: Principles and techniques of algorithmic differentiation*. SIAM. 113

Gu, J., Kwon, H., Wang, D., Ye, W., Li, M., Chen, Y.-H., Lai, L., Chandra, V., & Pan, D. Z. (2022). Multi-scale high-resolution vision transformer for semantic segmentation. *IEEE/CVF Computer Vision & Pattern Recognition*, 12094–12103. 238

Guan, S., Tai, Y., Ni, B., Zhu, F., Huang, F., & Yang, X. (2020). Collaborative learning for faster StyleGAN embedding. *arXiv:2007.01758.* 301

Gui, J., Sun, Z., Wen, Y., Tao, D., & Ye, J. (2021). A review on generative adversarial networks: Algorithms, theory, and applications. *IEEE Transactions on Knowledge and Data Engineering.* 299

Guimaraes, G. L., Sanchez-Lengeling, B., Outeiral, C., Farias, P. L. C., & Aspuru-Guzik, A. (2017). Objective-reinforced generative adversarial networks (ORGAN) for sequence generation models. *arXiv:1705.10843.* 299

Gulrajani, I., Kumar, K., Ahmed, F., Taiga, A. A., Visin, F., Vazquez, D., & Courville, A. (2016). PixelVAE: A latent variable model for natural images. *International Conference on Learning Representations.* 299, 343, 344, 345

Ha, D., Dai, A., & Le, Q. V. (2017). Hypernetworks. *International Conference on Learning Representations.* 235

Haarnoja, T., Hartikainen, K., Abbeel, P., & Levine, S. (2018a). Latent space policies for hierarchical reinforcement learning. *International Conference on Machine Learning*, 1851–1860. 322

Haarnoja, T., Zhou, A., Abbeel, P., & Levine, S. (2018b). Soft actor-critic: Off-policy maximum entropy deep reinforcement learning with a stochastic actor. *International Conference on Machine Learning*, 1861–1870. 398

Hagendorff, T. (2020). The ethics of AI ethics: An evaluation of guidelines. *Minds and Machines*, *30*(1), 99–120. 420

Hamilton, W., Ying, Z., & Leskovec, J. (2017a). Inductive representation learning on large graphs. *Neural Information Processing Systems*, *30*, 1024–1034. 262, 263, 264, 265, 267

Hamilton, W. L. (2020). Graph representation learning. *Synthesis Lectures on Artifical Intelligence and Machine Learning*, *14*(3), 1–159. 15, 261

Hamilton, W. L., Ying, R., & Leskovec, J. (2017b). Representation learning on graphs: Methods and applications. *IEEE Data Engineering Bulletin*, *40*(3), 52–74. 263

Han, S., Mao, H., & Dally, W. J. (2016). Deep compression: Compressing deep neural networks with pruning, trained quantization and Huffman coding. *International Conference on Learning Representations.* 414, 415

Han, S., Pool, J., Tran, J., & Dally, W. (2015). Learning both weights and connections for efficient neural network. *Neural Information Processing Systems*, vol. 28, 1135–1143. 414

Hannun, A. Y., Case, C., Casper, J., Catanzaro, B., Diamos, G., Elsen, E., Prenger, R., Satheesh, S., Sengupta, S., Coates, A., & Ng, A. Y. (2014). Deep speech: Scaling up end-to-end speech recognition. *arXiv:1412.5567.* 160

Hanson, S. J., & Pratt, L. Y. (1988). Comparing biases for minimal network construction with back-propagation. *Neural Information Processing Systems*, vol. 2, 177—185. 155

Harding, S. (1986). *The Science Question in Feminism.* Cornell University Press. 433

Härkönen, E., Hertzmann, A., Lehtinen, J., & Paris, S. (2020). GANSpace: Discovering interpretable GAN controls. *Neural Information Processing Systems*, *33*, 9841–9850. 300

Hartmann, K. G., Schirrmeister, R. T., & Ball, T. (2018). EEG-GAN: Generative adversarial networks for electroencephalograhic (EEG) brain signals. *arXiv:1806.01875.* 299

Harvey, W., Naderiparizi, S., Masrani, V., Weilbach, C., & Wood, F. (2022). Flexible diffusion modeling of long videos. *Neural Information Processing Systems*, *35.* 369

Hasanzadeh, A., Hajiramezanali, E., Boluki, S., Zhou, M., Duffield, N., Narayanan, K., & Qian, X. (2020). Bayesian graph neural networks with adaptive connection sampling. *International Conference on Machine Learning*, 4094–4104. 265

Hassibi, B., & Stork, D. G. (1993). Second order derivatives for network pruning: Optimal brain surgeon. *Neural Information Processing Systems*, vol. 6, 164–171. 414

Hausknecht, M., & Stone, P. (2015). Deep recurrent Q-learning for partially observable MDPs. *AAAI Fall Symposia*, 29–37. 397

Hayou, S., Clerico, E., He, B., Deligiannidis, G., Doucet, A., & Rousseau, J. (2021). Stable ResNet. *International Conference on Artificial Intelligence and Statistics*, 1324–1332. 205

He, F., Liu, T., & Tao, D. (2019). Control batch size and learning rate to generalize well: Theoretical and empirical evidence. *Neural Information Processing Systems*, *32*, 1143–1152. 92, 410, 411

He, J., Neubig, G., & Berg-Kirkpatrick, T. (2018). Unsupervised learning of syntactic structure with invertible neural projections. *ACL Empirical Methods in Natural Language Processing*, 1292–1302. 322

He, K., Zhang, X., Ren, S., & Sun, J. (2015). Delving deep into rectifiers: Surpassing human-level performance on ImageNet classification. *IEEE International Conference on Computer Vision*, 1026–1034. 38, 113, 183

He, K., Zhang, X., Ren, S., & Sun, J. (2016a). Deep residual learning for image recognition. *IEEE/CVF Computer Vision & Pattern Recognition*, 770–778. 188, 201, 323, 405

He, K., Zhang, X., Ren, S., & Sun, J. (2016b). Identity mappings in deep residual networks. *European Conference on Computer Vision*, 630–645. 202, 405

He, P., Liu, X., Gao, J., & Chen, W. (2021). DeBERTa: Decoding-enhanced BERT with disentangled attention. *International Conference on Learning Representations*. 236

He, X., Haffari, G., & Norouzi, M. (2020). Dynamic programming encoding for subword segmentation in neural machine translation. *Meeting of the Association for Computational Linguistics*, 3042–3051. 234

He, Y., Zhang, X., & Sun, J. (2017). Channel pruning for accelerating very deep neural networks. *IEEE/CVF International Conference on Computer Vision*, 1389–1397. 414

Heess, N., Wayne, G., Silver, D., Lillicrap, T., Erez, T., & Tassa, Y. (2015). Learning continuous control policies by stochastic value gradients. *Neural Information Processing Systems*, 28, 2944–2952. 344

Heikkilä, M. (2022). *Why business is booming for military AI startups*. MIT Technology Review, July 7 2022. https://www.technologyreview.com/2022/07/07/1055526/why-business-is-booming-for-military-ai-startups/. 13, 427

Henaff, M., Bruna, J., & LeCun, Y. (2015). Deep convolutional networks on graph-structured data. *arXiv:1506.05163*. 262

Henderson, P., Li, X., Jurafsky, D., Hashimoto, T., Lemley, M. A., & Liang, P. (2023). Foundation models and fair use. *arXiv:2303.15715*. 428

Hendrycks, D., & Gimpel, K. (2016). Gaussian error linear units (GELUs). *arXiv:1606.08415*. 38

Hermann, V. (2017). Wasserstein GAN and the Kantorovich-Rubinstein duality. https://vincentherrmann.github.io/blog/wasserstein/. 284, 299

Hernández, C. X., Wayment-Steele, H. K., Sultan, M. M., Husic, B. E., & Pande, V. S. (2018). Variational encoding of complex dynamics. *Physical Review E*, 97(6), 062412. 344

Hertz, A., Mokady, R., Tenenbaum, J., Aberman, K., Pritch, Y., & Cohen-Or, D. (2022). Prompt-to-prompt image editing with cross attention control. *arXiv:2208.01626*. 369

Hessel, M., Modayil, J., van Hasselt, H., Schaul, T., Ostrovski, G., Dabney, W., Horgan, D., Piot, B., Azar, M., & Silver, D. (2018). Rainbow: Combining improvements in deep reinforcement learning. *AAAI Conference on Artificial Intelligence*, 3215–3222. 397

Heusel, M., Ramsauer, H., Unterthiner, T., Nessler, B., & Hochreiter, S. (2017). GANs trained by a two time-scale update rule converge to a local Nash equilibrium. *Neural Information Processing Systems*, 30, 6626–6637. 274

Heyns, C. (2017). Autonomous weapons in armed conflict and the right to a dignified life: An African perspective. *South African Journal of Human Rights*, 33(1), 46–71. 429

Higgins, I., Matthey, L., Pal, A., Burgess, C., Glorot, X., Botvinick, M., Mohamed, S., & Lerchner, A. (2017). Beta-VAE: Learning basic visual concepts with a constrained variational framework. *International Conference on Learning Representations*. 345

Himmelreich, J. (2022). Against 'democratizing AI'. *AI & Society*. 435

Hindupur, A. (2022). The GAN zoo. GitHub Retrieved January 17, 2023. https://github.com/hindupuravinash/the-gan-zoo. 299

Hinton, G., Srivastava, N., & Swersky, K. (2012a). Neural networks for machine learning: Lecture 6a – Overview of mini-batch gradient descent. https://www.cs.toronto.edu/~tijmen/csc321/slides/lecture_slides_lec6.pdf. 93

Hinton, G., & van Camp, D. (1993). Keeping neural networks simple by minimising the description length of weights. *Computational learning theory*, 5–13. 159

Hinton, G., Vinyals, O., Dean, J., et al. (2015). Distilling the knowledge in a neural network. *arXiv:1503.02531*, 2(7). 415

Hinton, G. E., & Salakhutdinov, R. R. (2006). Reducing the dimensionality of data with neural networks. *Science*, 313(5786), 504–507. 344

Hinton, G. E., Srivastava, N., Krizhevsky, A., Sutskever, I., & Salakhutdinov, R. R.

(2012b). Improving neural networks by preventing co-adaptation of feature detectors. *arXiv:1207.0580*. 158

Ho, J., Chen, X., Srinivas, A., Duan, Y., & Abbeel, P. (2019). Flow++: Improving flow-based generative models with variational dequantization and architecture design. *International Conference on Machine Learning*, 2722–2730. 322, 323

Ho, J., Jain, A., & Abbeel, P. (2020). Denoising diffusion probabilistic models. *Neural Information Processing Systems*, 33, 6840–6851. 274, 367, 369

Ho, J., Saharia, C., Chan, W., Fleet, D. J., Norouzi, M., & Salimans, T. (2022a). Cascaded diffusion models for high fidelity image generation. *Journal of Machine Learning Research*, 23, 47–1. 369, 370

Ho, J., & Salimans, T. (2022). Classifier-free diffusion guidance. *NeurIPS Workshop on Deep Generative Models and Downstream Applications*. 370

Ho, J., Salimans, T., Gritsenko, A., Chan, W., Norouzi, M., & Fleet, D. J. (2022b). Video diffusion models. *International Conference on Learning Representations*. 369

Hochreiter, S., & Schmidhuber, J. (1997a). Flat minima. *Neural Computation*, 9(1), 1–42. 411

Hochreiter, S., & Schmidhuber, J. (1997b). Long short-term memory. *Neural Computation*, 9(8), 1735–1780. 233

Hoffer, E., Hubara, I., & Soudry, D. (2017). Train longer, generalize better: Closing the generalization gap in large batch training of neural networks. *Neural Information Processing Systems*, 30, 1731–1741. 203, 204

Hoffman, M. D., & Johnson, M. J. (2016). ELBO surgery: Yet another way to carve up the variational evidence lower bound. *NIPS Workshop in Advances in Approximate Bayesian Inference*, 2. 346

Hoffmann, J., Borgeaud, S., Mensch, A., Buchatskaya, E., Cai, T., Rutherford, E., Casas, D. d. L., Hendricks, L. A., Welbl, J., Clark, A., et al. (2023). Training compute-optimal large language models. *arXiv:2203.15556*. 234

Hofstadter, D. R. (1995). The ineradicable Eliza effect and its dangers (preface 4). *Fluid Concepts and Creative Analogies: Computer Models Of The Fundamental Mechanisms Of Thought*, 155–168. Basic Books. 428

Holland, C. A., Ebner, N. C., Lin, T., & Samanez-Larkin, G. R. (2019). Emotion identification across adulthood using the dynamic faces database of emotional expressions in younger, middle aged, and older adults. *Cognition and Emotion*, 33(2), 245–257. 9

Holtzman, A., Buys, J., Du, L., Forbes, M., & Choi, Y. (2020). The curious case of neural text degeneration. *International Conference on Learning Representations*. 235

Hoogeboom, E., Nielsen, D., Jaini, P., Forré, P., & Welling, M. (2021). Argmax flows and multinomial diffusion: Learning categorical distributions. *Neural Information Processing Systems*, 34, 12454–12465. 369

Hoogeboom, E., Peters, J., Van Den Berg, R., & Welling, M. (2019a). Integer discrete flows and lossless compression. *Neural Information Processing Systems*, 32, 12134–12144. 324

Hoogeboom, E., Van Den Berg, R., & Welling, M. (2019b). Emerging convolutions for generative normalizing flows. *International Conference on Machine Learning*, 2771–2780. 322

Höppe, T., Mehrjou, A., Bauer, S., Nielsen, D., & Dittadi, A. (2022). Diffusion models for video prediction and infilling. *ECCV Workshop on AI for Creative Video Editing and Understanding*. 369

Hornik, K. (1991). Approximation capabilities of multilayer feedforward networks. *Neural Networks*, 4(2), 251–257. 38

Howard, A., Sandler, M., Chu, G., Chen, L.-C., Chen, B., Tan, M., Wang, W., Zhu, Y., Pang, R., Vasudevan, V., et al. (2019). Searching for MobileNetV3. *IEEE/CVF International Conference on Computer Vision*, 1314–1324. 38

Howard, A. G., Zhu, M., Chen, B., Kalenichenko, D., Wang, W., Weyand, T., Andreetto, M., & Adam, H. (2017). MobileN ets: Efficient convolutional neural networks for mobile vision applications. *arXiv:1704.04861*. 181

Howard, R. A. (1960). *Dynamic programming and Narkov processes*. Wiley. 396

Hsu, C.-C., Hwang, H.-T., Wu, Y.-C., Tsao, Y., & Wang, H.-M. (2017a). Voice conversion from unaligned corpora using variational autoencoding Wasserstein generative adversarial networks. *INTERSPEECH*, 3364–3368. 345

Hsu, W.-N., Zhang, Y., & Glass, J. (2017b). Learning latent representations for speech generation and transformation. *INTERSPEECH*, 1273–1277. 343

Hu, H., Gu, J., Zhang, Z., Dai, J., & Wei, Y. (2018a). Relation networks for object detection. *IEEE/CVF Computer Vision & Pattern Recognition*, 3588–3597. 238

Hu, H., Zhang, Z., Xie, Z., & Lin, S. (2019). Local relation networks for image recognition. *IEEE/CVF International Conference on Computer Vision*, 3464–3473. 238

Hu, J., Shen, L., & Sun, G. (2018b). Squeeze-and-excitation networks. *IEEE/CVF Computer Vision & Pattern Recognition*, 7132–7141. 181, 235

Hu, W., Pang, J., Liu, X., Tian, D., Lin, C.-W., & Vetro, A. (2022). Graph signal processing for geometric data and beyond: Theory and applications. *IEEE Transactions on Multimedia*, 24, 3961–3977. 242

Hu, Z., Yang, Z., Liang, X., Salakhutdinov, R., & Xing, E. P. (2017). Toward controlled generation of text. *International Conference on Machine Learning*, 1587–1596. 343

Huang, C.-W., Krueger, D., Lacoste, A., & Courville, A. (2018a). Neural autoregressive flows. *International Conference on Machine Learning*, 2078–2087. 323, 324

Huang, G., Li, Y., Pleiss, G., Liu, Z., Hopcroft, J. E., & Weinberger, K. Q. (2017a). Snapshot ensembles: Train 1, get M for free. *International Conference on Learning Representations*. 158

Huang, G., Liu, Z., Van Der Maaten, L., & Weinberger, K. Q. (2017b). Densely connected convolutional networks. *IEEE/CVF Computer Vision & Pattern Recognition*, 4700–4708. 205, 405

Huang, G., Sun, Y., Liu, Z., Sedra, D., & Weinberger, K. Q. (2016). Deep networks with stochastic depth. *European Conference on Computer Vision*, 646–661. 202

Huang, W., Zhang, T., Rong, Y., & Huang, J. (2018b). Adaptive sampling towards fast graph representation learning. *Neural Information Processing Systems*, 31, 4563–4572. 264, 265

Huang, X., Li, Y., Poursaeed, O., Hopcroft, J., & Belongie, S. (2017c). Stacked generative adversarial networks. *IEEE/CVF Computer Vision & Pattern Recognition*, 5077–5086. 300

Huang, X. S., Perez, F., Ba, J., & Volkovs, M. (2020a). Improving transformer optimization through better initialization. *International Conference on Machine Learning*, 4475–4483. 114, 237

Huang, Y., Cheng, Y., Bapna, A., Firat, O., Chen, D., Chen, M., Lee, H., Ngiam, J., Le, Q. V., Wu, Y., et al. (2019). GPipe: Efficient training of giant neural networks using pipeline parallelism. *Neural Information Processing Systems*, 32, 103–112. 114

Huang, Z., Liang, D., Xu, P., & Xiang, B. (2020b). Improve transformer models with better relative position embeddings. *Empirical Methods in Natural Language Processing*. 236

Huang, Z., & Wang, N. (2018). Data-driven sparse structure selection for deep neural networks. *European Conference on Computer Vision*, 304–320. 414

Hubinger, E., van Merwijk, C., Mikulik, V., Skalse, J., & Garrabrant, S. (2019). Risks from learned optimization in advanced machine learning systems. *arXiv:1906.01820*. 421

Hussein, A., Gaber, M. M., Elyan, E., & Jayne, C. (2017). Imitation learning: A survey of learning methods. *ACM Computing Surveys*, 50(2), 1–35. 398

Huszár, F. (2019). Exponentially growing learning rate? Implications of scale invariance induced by batch normalization. `https://www.inference.vc/exponentially-growing-learning-rate-implications-of-scale-invariance-induced-by-BatchNorm/`. 204

Hutchinson, M. F. (1989). A stochastic estimator of the trace of the influence matrix for Laplacian smoothing splines. *Communications in Statistics-Simulation and Computation*, 18(3), 1059–1076. 324

Hutter, F., Hoos, H. H., & Leyton-Brown, K. (2011). Sequential model-based optimization for general algorithm configuration. *International Conference on Learning and Intelligent Optimization*, 507–523. 136

Iglovikov, V., & Shvets, A. (2018). TernausNet: U-Net with VGG11 encoder pretrained on ImageNet for image segmentation. *arXiv:1801.05746*. 205

Ilyas, A., Santurkar, S., Tsipras, D., Engstrom, L., Tran, B., & Madry, A. (2019). Adversarial examples are not bugs, they are features. *Neural Information Processing Systems*, 32, 125–136. 414

Inoue, H. (2018). Data augmentation by pairing samples for images classification. *arXiv:1801.02929*. 159

Inoue, T., Choudhury, S., De Magistris, G., & Dasgupta, S. (2018). Transfer learning from synthetic to real images using variational autoencoders for precise position detection. *IEEE International Conference on Image Processing*, 2725–2729. 344

Ioffe, S. (2017). Batch renormalization: Towards reducing minibatch dependence in batch-normalized models. *Neural Information Processing Systems*, *30*, 1945–1953. 203

Ioffe, S., & Szegedy, C. (2015). Batch normalization: Accelerating deep network training by reducing internal covariate shift. *International Conference on Machine Learning*, 448–456. 114, 203, 204

Ishida, T., Yamane, I., Sakai, T., Niu, G., & Sugiyama, M. (2020). Do we need zero training loss after achieving zero training error? *International Conference on Machine Learning*, 4604–4614. 134, 159

Isola, P., Zhu, J.-Y., Zhou, T., & Efros, A. A. (2017). Image-to-image translation with conditional adversarial networks. *IEEE/CVF Computer Vision & Pattern Recognition*, 1125–1134. 205, 293, 301

Izmailov, P., Podoprikhin, D., Garipov, T., Vetrov, D., & Wilson, A. G. (2018). Averaging weights leads to wider optima and better generalization. *Uncertainly in Artificial Intelligence*, 876–885. 158, 411

Jackson, P. T., Abarghouei, A. A., Bonner, S., Breckon, T. P., & Obara, B. (2019). Style augmentation: Data augmentation via style randomization. *IEEE Computer Vision and Pattern Recognition Workshops*, 10–11. 159

Jacobs, R. A., Jordan, M. I., Nowlan, S. J., & Hinton, G. E. (1991). Adaptive mixtures of local experts. *Neural Computation*, *3*(1), 79–87. 73

Jacobsen, J.-H., Smeulders, A., & Oyallon, E. (2018). i-RevNet: Deep invertible networks. *International Conference on Learning Representations*. 322, 323

Jaini, P., Kobyzev, I., Yu, Y., & Brubaker, M. A. (2020). Tails of Lipschitz triangular flows. *International Conference on Machine Learning*, 4673–4681. 324

Jaini, P., Selby, K. A., & Yu, Y. (2019). Sum-of-squares polynomial flow. *International Conference on Machine Learning*, 3009–3018. 323

Jaitly, N., & Hinton, G. E. (2013). Vocal tract length perturbation (VTLP) improves speech recognition. *ICML Workshop on Deep Learning for Audio, Speech and Language*. 160

Jarrett, K., Kavukcuoglu, K., Ranzato, M., & Le-Cun, Y. (2009). What is the best multi-stage architecture for object recognition? *IEEE International Conference on Computer Vision*, 2146–2153. 37

Jastrzębski, S., Arpit, D., Astrand, O., Kerg, G. B., Wang, H., Xiong, C., Socher, R., Cho, K., & Geras, K. J. (2021). Catastrophic fisher explosion: Early phase fisher matrix impacts generalization. *International Conference on Machine Learning*, 4772–4784. 157

Jastrzębski, S., Kenton, Z., Arpit, D., Ballas, N., Fischer, A., Bengio, Y., & Storkey, A. (2018). Three factors influencing minima in SGD. *arXiv:1711.04623*. 92, 410

Ji, S., Xu, W., Yang, M., & Yu, K. (2012). 3D convolutional neural networks for human action recognition. *IEEE Transactions on Pattern Analysis & Machine Intelligence*, *35*(1), 221–231. 182

Jia, X., De Brabandere, B., Tuytelaars, T., & Gool, L. V. (2016). Dynamic filter networks. *Neural Information Processing Systems*, *29*. 183

Jiang, Z., Zheng, Y., Tan, H., Tang, B., & Zhou, H. (2016). Variational deep embedding: An unsupervised and generative approach to clustering. *International Joint Conference on Artificial Intelligence*, 1965–1972. 344

Jin, C., Netrapalli, P., & Jordan, M. (2020). What is local optimality in nonconvex-nonconcave minimax optimization? *International Conference on Machine Learning*, 4880–4889. 299

Jin, L., Doshi-Velez, F., Miller, T., Schwartz, L., & Schuler, W. (2019). Unsupervised learning of PCFGs with normalizing flow. *Meeting of the Association for Computational Linguistics*, 2442–2452. 322

Jing, L., & Tian, Y. (2020). Self-supervised visual feature learning with deep neural networks: A survey. *IEEE Transactions on Pattern Analysis & Machine Intelligence*, *43*(11), 4037–4058. 159

Jobin, A., Ienca, M., & Vayena, E. (2019). The global landscape of AI ethics guidelines. *Nature Machine Intelligence*, *1*, 389–399. 420

Johnson, G. M. (2022). Are algorithms value-free? feminist theoretical virtues in machine learning. *198*. 432

Johnson, R., & Zhang, T. (2013). Accelerating stochastic gradient descent using predictive variance reduction. *Neural Information Processing Systems*, *26*, 315–323. 91

Jolicoeur-Martineau, A. (2019). The relativistic discriminator: A key element missing from standard GAN. *International Conference on Learning Representations.* 299

Jurafsky, D., & Martin, J. H. (2000). *Speech and Language Processing, 2nd Edition.* Pearson. 233

Kakade, S. M. (2001). A natural policy gradient. *Neural Information Processing Systems, 14,* 1531–1538. 397

Kanazawa, A., Sharma, A., & Jacobs, D. (2014). Locally scale-invariant convolutional neural networks. *Neural Information Processing Systems Workshop.* 183

Kanda, N., Takeda, R., & Obuchi, Y. (2013). Elastic spectral distortion for low resource speech recognition with deep neural networks. *IEEE Workshop on Automatic Speech Recognition and Understanding,* 309–314. 160

Kaneko, T., & Kameoka, H. (2017). Parallel-data-free voice conversion using cycle-consistent adversarial networks. *arXiv:1711.11293.* 299

Kang, G., Dong, X., Zheng, L., & Yang, Y. (2017). PatchShuffle regularization. *arXiv:1707.07103.* 159

Kanwar, G., Albergo, M. S., Boyda, D., Cranmer, K., Hackett, D. C., Racaniere, S., Rezende, D. J., & Shanahan, P. E. (2020). Equivariant flow-based sampling for lattice gauge theory. *Physical Review Letters, 125*(12), 121601. 322

Karras, T., Aila, T., Laine, S., & Lehtinen, J. (2018). Progressive growing of GANs for improved quality, stability, and variation. *International Conference on Learning Representations.* 286, 287, 299, 300, 319, 345

Karras, T., Aittala, M., Aila, T., & Laine, S. (2022). Elucidating the design space of diffusion-based generative models. *Neural Information Processing Systems.* 369, 370

Karras, T., Aittala, M., Hellsten, J., Laine, S., Lehtinen, J., & Aila, T. (2020a). Training generative adversarial networks with limited data. *Neural Information Processing Systems, 33,* 12104–12114. 300

Karras, T., Aittala, M., Laine, S., Härkönen, E., Hellsten, J., Lehtinen, J., & Aila, T. (2021). Alias-free generative adversarial networks. *Neural Information Processing Systems, 34,* 852–863. 300

Karras, T., Laine, S., & Aila, T. (2019). A style-based generator architecture for generative adversarial networks. *IEEE/CVF Computer Vision & Pattern Recognition,* 4401–4410. 299, 300

Karras, T., Laine, S., Aittala, M., Hellsten, J., Lehtinen, J., & Aila, T. (2020b). Analyzing and improving the image quality of Style-GAN. *IEEE/CVF Computer Vision & Pattern Recognition,* 8110–8119. 8, 300, 301

Katharopoulos, A., Vyas, A., Pappas, N., & Fleuret, F. (2020). Transformers are RNNs: Fast autoregressive transformers with linear attention. *International Conference on Machine Learning,* 5156–5165. 237

Kawaguchi, K., Huang, J., & Kaelbling, L. P. (2019). Effect of depth and width on local minima in deep learning. *Neural Computation, 31*(7), 1462–1498. 405

Ke, G., He, D., & Liu, T.-Y. (2021). Rethinking positional encoding in language pre-training. *International Conference on Learning Representations.* 236

Kearnes, S., McCloskey, K., Berndl, M., Pande, V., & Riley, P. (2016). Molecular graph convolutions: Moving beyond fingerprints. *Journal of computer-aided molecular design, 30*(8), 595–608. 264

Kendall, A., & Gal, Y. (2017). What uncertainties do we need in Bayesian deep learning for computer vision? *Neural Information Processing Systems, 30,* 5574–5584. 158

Keskar, N. S., Mudigere, D., Nocedal, J., Smelyanskiy, M., & Tang, P. T. P. (2017). On large-batch training for deep learning: Generalization gap and sharp minima. *International Conference on Learning Representations.* 158, 403, 410, 411

Keskar, N. S., & Socher, R. (2017). Improving generalization performance by switching from Adam to SGD. *arXiv:1712.07628.* 94, 410

Keynes, J. M. (2010). Economic possibilities for our grandchildren. *Essays in Persuasion,* 321–332. Palgrave Macmillan. 430

Khan, S., Naseer, M., Hayat, M., Zamir, S. W., Khan, F. S., & Shah, M. (2022). Transformers in vision: A survey. *ACM Computing Surveys, 54*(10), 200:1–200:41. 238

Killoran, N., Lee, L. J., Delong, A., Duvenaud, D., & Frey, B. J. (2017). Generating and designing DNA with deep generative models. *NIPS 2017 Workshop on Computational Biology.* 299

Kim, H., & Mnih, A. (2018). Disentangling by factorising. *International Conference on Machine Learning,* 2649–2658. 345, 346

Kim, I., Han, S., Baek, J.-w., Park, S.-J., Han, J.-J., & Shin, J. (2021). Quality-agnostic image recognition via invertible decoder. *IEEE/CVF Computer Vision & Pattern Recognition*, 12257–12266. 322

Kim, S., Lee, S.-g., Song, J., Kim, J., & Yoon, S. (2018). FloWaveNet: A generative flow for raw audio. *International Conference on Machine Learning*, 3370–3378. 322, 323

Kingma, D., Salimans, T., Poole, B., & Ho, J. (2021). Variational diffusion models. *Neural Information Processing Systems*, *34*, 21696–21707. 369

Kingma, D. P., & Ba, J. (2015). Adam: A method for stochastic optimization. *International Conference on Learning Representations*. 93, 237

Kingma, D. P., & Dhariwal, P. (2018). Glow: Generative flow with invertible 1x1 convolutions. *Neural Information Processing Systems*, *31*, 10236–10245. 319, 322, 323

Kingma, D. P., Salimans, T., Jozefowicz, R., Chen, X., Sutskever, I., & Welling, M. (2016). Improved variational inference with inverse autoregressive flow. *Neural Information Processing Systems*, *29*, 4736–4744. 323, 344

Kingma, D. P., Salimans, T., & Welling, M. (2015). Variational dropout and the local reparameterization trick. *Advances in neural information processing systems*, *28*, 2575–2583. 346

Kingma, D. P., & Welling, M. (2014). Auto-encoding variational Bayes. *International Conference on Learning Representations*. 273, 343

Kingma, D. P., Welling, M., et al. (2019). An introduction to variational autoencoders. *Foundations and Trends in Machine Learning*, *12*(4), 307–392. 343

Kipf, T. N., & Welling, M. (2016). Variational graph auto-encoders. *NIPS Bayesian Deep Learning Workshop*. 159, 344

Kipf, T. N., & Welling, M. (2017). Semi-supervised classification with graph convolutional networks. *International Conference on Learning Representations*. 262, 263, 264, 265

Kiranyaz, S., Avci, O., Abdeljaber, O., Ince, T., Gabbouj, M., & Inman, D. J. (2021). 1D convolutional neural networks and applications: A survey. *Mechanical Systems and Signal Processing*, *151*, 107398. 182

Kiranyaz, S., Ince, T., Hamila, R., & Gabbouj, M. (2015). Convolutional neural networks for patient-specific ECG classification. *International Conference of the IEEE Engineering in Medicine and Biology Society*, vol. 37, 2608–2611. 182

Kitaev, N., Kaiser, Ł., & Levskaya, A. (2020). Reformer: The efficient transformer. *International Conference on Learning Representations*. 237

Kitcher, P. (2011a). *The Ethical Project*. Harvard University Press. 432

Kitcher, P. (2011b). *Science in a Democratic Society*. Prometheus Books. 432

Klambauer, G., Unterthiner, T., Mayr, A., & Hochreiter, S. (2017). Self-normalizing neural networks. *Neural Information Processing Systems*, vol. 30, 972–981. 38, 113

Kleinberg, J., Mullainathan, S., & Raghavan, M. (2017). Inherent trade-offs in the fair determination of risk scores. *Innovations in Theoretical Computer Science Conference*, vol. 67, 1–23. 422

Kleinberg, R., Li, Y., & Yuan, Y. (2018). An alternative view: When does SGD escape local minima? *International Conference on Machine Learning*, 2703–2712. 411

Knight, W. (2018). One of the fathers of AI is worried about its future. *MIT Technology Review*, Nov 20, 2018. https://www.technologyreview.com/2018/11/17/66372/one-of-the-fathers-of-ai-is-worried-about-its-future/. 430

Kobyzev, I., Prince, S. J., & Brubaker, M. A. (2020). Normalizing flows: An introduction and review of current methods. *IEEE Transactions on Pattern Analysis & Machine Intelligence*, *43*(11), 3964–3979. xvi, 321, 324

Koenker, R., & Hallock, K. F. (2001). Quantile regression. *Journal of Economic Perspectives*, *15*(4), 143–156. 73

Köhler, J., Klein, L., & Noé, F. (2020). Equivariant flows: Exact likelihood generative learning for symmetric densities. *International Conference on Machine Learning*, 5361–5370. 322, 324

Koller, D., & Friedman, N. (2009). *Probabilistic graphical models: Principles and techniques*. MIT Press. 15

Kolomiyets, O., Bethard, S., & Moens, M.-F. (2011). Model-portability experiments for textual temporal analysis. *Meeting of the Association for Computational Linguistics*, 271–276. 160

Konda, V., & Tsitsiklis, J. (1999). Actor-critic algorithms. *Neural Information Processing Systems*, *12*, 1008–1014. 397

Kong, Z., Ping, W., Huang, J., Zhao, K., & Catanzaro, B. (2021). DiffWave: A versatile diffusion model for audio synthesis. *International Conference on Learning Representations.* 369

Kool, W., van Hoof, H., & Welling, M. (2019). Attention, learn to solve routing problems! *International Conference on Learning Representations.* 396

Kosinski, M., Stillwell, D., & Graepel, T. (2013). Private traits and attributes are predictable from digital records of human behavior. *Proceedings of the National Academy of Sciences of the United States of America, 110*(15), 5802–5805. 427

Kratsios, M. (2019). The national artificial intelligence research and development strategic plan: 2019 update. Tech. rep., Networking and Information Technology Research and Development. `https://www.nitrd.gov/pubs/National-AI-RD-Strategy-2019.pdf`. 430

Krizhevsky, A., & Hinton, G. (2009). Learning multiple layers of features from tiny images. *Technical Report, University of Toronto.* 188

Krizhevsky, A., Sutskever, I., & Hinton, G. E. (2012). ImageNet classification with deep convolutional neural networks. *Neural Information Processing Systems, 25*, 1097–1105. 52, 113, 159, 176, 181

Kruse, J., Detommaso, G., Köthe, U., & Scheichl, R. (2021). HINT: Hierarchical invertible neural transport for density estimation and Bayesian inference. *AAAI Conference on Artificial Intelligence*, 8191–8199. 323

Kudo, T. (2018). Subword regularization: Improving neural network translation models with multiple subword candidates. *Meeting of the Association for Computational Linguistics*, 66–75. 234

Kudo, T., & Richardson, J. (2018). SentencePiece: A simple and language independent subword tokenizer and detokenizer for neural text processing. *Empirical Methods in Natural Language Processing*, 66–71. 234

Kukačka, J., Golkov, V., & Cremers, D. (2017). Regularization for deep learning: A taxonomy. *arXiv:1710.10686.* 155

Kulikov, I., Miller, A. H., Cho, K., & Weston, J. (2018). Importance of search and evaluation strategies in neural dialogue modeling. *ACL International Conference on Natural Language Generation*, 76–87. 235

Kumar, A., Fu, J., Soh, M., Tucker, G., & Levine, S. (2019a). Stabilizing off-policy Q-learning via bootstrapping error reduction. *Neural Information Processing Systems, 32*, 11761–11771. 398

Kumar, A., Sattigeri, P., & Balakrishnan, A. (2018). Variational inference of disentangled latent concepts from unlabeled observations. *International Conference on Learning Representations.* 345

Kumar, A., Singh, S. S., Singh, K., & Biswas, B. (2020a). Link prediction techniques, applications, and performance: A survey. *Physica A: Statistical Mechanics and its Applications, 553*, 124289. 262

Kumar, A., Zhou, A., Tucker, G., & Levine, S. (2020b). Conservative Q-learning for offline reinforcement learning. *Neural Information Processing Systems, 33*, 1179–1191. 398

Kumar, M., Babaeizadeh, M., Erhan, D., Finn, C., Levine, S., Dinh, L., & Kingma, D. (2019b). VideoFlow: A flow-based generative model for video. *ICML Workshop on Invertible Neural Networks and Normalizing Flows.* 322

Kumar, M., Weissenborn, D., & Kalchbrenner, N. (2021). Colorization transformer. *International Conference on Learning Representations.* 238

Kurach, K., Lučić, M., Zhai, X., Michalski, M., & Gelly, S. (2019). A large-scale study on regularization and normalization in GANs. *International Conference on Machine Learning*, 3581–3590. 299

Kurenkov, A. (2020). *A Brief History of Neural Nets and Deep Learning.* `https://www.skynettoday.com/overviews/neural-net-history`. 37

Kynkäänniemi, T., Karras, T., Laine, S., Lehtinen, J., & Aila, T. (2019). Improved precision and recall metric for assessing generative models. *Neural Information Processing Systems, 32*, 3929–3938. 274

LaCroix, T. (2022). The linguistic blind spot of value-aligned agency, natural and artificial. *arXiv:2207.00868.* 421

LaCroix, T. (2023). *Artificial Intelligence and the Value-Alignment Problem: A Philosophical Introduction.* `https://value-alignment.github.io`. 422, 435

LaCroix, T., Geil, A., & O'Connor, C. (2021). The dynamics of retraction in epistemic networks. *Philosophy of Science, 88*(3), 415–438. 432

LaCroix, T., & Mohseni, A. (2022). The tragedy of the AI commons. *Synthese, 200*(289). 420

Laffont, J.-J., & Martimort, D. (2002). *The Theory of Incentives: The Principal-Agent Model.* Princeton University Press. 421

Lakshminarayanan, B., Pritzel, A., & Blundell, C. (2017). Simple and scalable predictive uncertainty estimation using deep ensembles. *Neural Information Processing Systems*, *30*, 6402–6413. 158

Lamb, A., Dumoulin, V., & Courville, A. (2016). Discriminative regularization for generative models. *arXiv:1602.03220*. 344

Lample, G., & Charton, F. (2020). Deep learning for symbolic mathematics. *International Conference on Learning Representations*. 234

Larsen, A. B. L., Sønderby, S. K., Larochelle, H., & Winther, O. (2016). Autoencoding beyond pixels using a learned similarity metric. *International Conference on Machine Learning*, 1558–1566. 344, 345

Lasseck, M. (2018). Acoustic bird detection with deep convolutional neural networks. *Detection and Classification of Acoustic Scenes and Events*, 143–147. 160

Lattimore, T., & Szepesvári, C. (2020). *Bandit algorithms*. Cambridge University Press. 136

Lawrence, S., Giles, C. L., Tsoi, A. C., & Back, A. D. (1997). Face recognition: A convolutional neural-network approach. *IEEE Transactions on Neural Networks*, *8*(1), 98–113. 181

LeCun, Y. (1985). Une procedure d'apprentissage pour reseau a seuil asymmetrique. *Proceedings of Cognitiva*, 599–604. 113

LeCun, Y., Bengio, Y., & Hinton, G. (2015). Deep learning. *Nature*, *521*(7553), 436–444. 52

LeCun, Y., Boser, B., Denker, J., Henderson, D., Howard, R., Hubbard, W., & Jackel, L. (1989a). Handwritten digit recognition with a back-propagation network. *Neural Information Processing Systems*, *2*, 396–404. 180, 181

LeCun, Y., Boser, B., Denker, J. S., Henderson, D., Howard, R. E., Hubbard, W., & Jackel, L. D. (1989b). Backpropagation applied to handwritten zip code recognition. *Neural Computation*, *1*(4), 541–551. 180

LeCun, Y., Bottou, L., Bengio, Y., & Haffner, P. (1998). Gradient-based learning applied to document recognition. *Proceedings of the IEEE*, *86*(11), 2278–2324. 159, 181

LeCun, Y., Chopra, S., Hadsell, R., Ranzato, M., & Huang, F. (2006). A tutorial on energy-based learning. *Predicting structured data*, *1*(0). 274

LeCun, Y., Denker, J. S., & Solla, S. A. (1990). Optimal brain damage. *Neural Information Processing Systems*, vol. 3, 598–605. 414

LeCun, Y. A., Bottou, L., Orr, G. B., & Müller, K.-R. (2012). Efficient backprop. *Neural Networks: Tricks of the trade*, 9–48. Springer. 113, 410

Ledig, C., Theis, L., Huszár, F., Caballero, J., Cunningham, A., Acosta, A., Aitken, A., Tejani, A., Totz, J., Wang, Z., et al. (2017). Photo-realistic single image super-resolution using a generative adversarial network. *IEEE/CVF Computer Vision & Pattern Recognition*, 4681–4690. 294, 301

Lee, J., Lee, I., & Kang, J. (2019). Self-attention graph pooling. *International Conference on Machine Learning*, 3734–3743. 265

Lee, J. B., Rossi, R. A., Kong, X., Kim, S., Koh, E., & Rao, A. (2018). Higher-order graph convolutional networks. *arXiv:1809.07697*. 263

Lehman, J., & Stanley, K. O. (2008). Exploiting open-endedness to solve problems through the search for novelty. *International Conference on Artificial Life*, 329–336. 421

Leuner, J. (2019). A replication study: Machine learning models are capable of predicting sexual orientation from facial images. *arXiv:1902.10739*. 427

Li, C., Chen, C., Carlson, D., & Carin, L. (2016a). Preconditioned stochastic gradient Langevin dynamics for deep neural networks. *AAAI Conference on Artificial Intelligence*, 1788–1794. 159

Li, C., Farkhoor, H., Liu, R., & Yosinski, J. (2018a). Measuring the intrinsic dimension of objective landscapes. *International Conference on Learning Representations*. 407, 408

Li, F.-F. (2018). How to make A.I. that's good for people. The New York Times, March 7, 2018. https://www.nytimes.com/2018/03/07/opinion/artificial-intelligence-human.html. 430

Li, G., Müller, M., Ghanem, B., & Koltun, V. (2021a). Training graph neural networks with 1000 layers. *International Conference on Machine Learning*, 6437–6449. 266, 322

Li, G., Müller, M., Qian, G., Perez, I. C. D., Abualshour, A., Thabet, A. K., & Ghanem, B. (2021b). DeepGCNs: Making GCNs go as deep as CNNs. *IEEE Transactions on Pattern Analysis and Machine Intelligence*. 266

Li, G., Xiong, C., Thabet, A., & Ghanem, B. (2020a). DeeperGCN: All you need to train deeper GCNs. *arXiv:2006.07739*. 266

Li, H., Kadav, A., Durdanovic, I., Samet, H., & Graf, H. P. (2017a). Pruning filters for efficient ConvNets. *International Conference on Learning Representations*. 414

Li, H., Xu, Z., Taylor, G., Studer, C., & Goldstein, T. (2018b). Visualizing the loss landscape of neural nets. *Neural Information Processing Systems*, 31, 6391–6401. 201, 202, 407

Li, L., Jamieson, K., DeSalvo, G., Rostamizadeh, A., & Talwalkar, A. (2017b). Hyperband: A novel bandit-based approach to hyperparameter optimization. *Journal of Machine Learning Research*, 18(1), 6765–6816. 136

Li, L. H., Yatskar, M., Yin, D., Hsieh, C.-J., & Chang, K.-W. (2019). VisualBERT: A simple and performant baseline for vision and language. *arXiv:1908.03557*. 238

Li, Q., Han, Z., & Wu, X.-M. (2018c). Deeper insights into graph convolutional networks for semi-supervised learning. *AAAI Conference on Artificial Intelligence*, 3438–3545. 265

Li, S., Zhao, Y., Varma, R., Salpekar, O., Noordhuis, P., Li, T., Paszke, A., Smith, J., Vaughan, B., Damania, P., & Chintala, S. (2020b). Pytorch distributed: Experiences on accelerating data parallel training. *International Conference on Very Large Databases*. 114

Li, W., Lin, Z., Zhou, K., Qi, L., Wang, Y., & Jia, J. (2022). MAT: Mask-aware transformer for large hole image inpainting. *IEEE/CVF Computer Vision & Pattern Recognition*, 10758–10768. 238

Li, Y. (2017). Deep reinforcement learning: An overview. *arXiv:1701.07274*. 396

Li, Y., Cohn, T., & Baldwin, T. (2017c). Robust training under linguistic adversity. *Meeting of the Association for Computational Linguistics*, 21–27. 160

Li, Y., & Liang, Y. (2018). Learning overparameterized neural networks via stochastic gradient descent on structured data. *Neural Information Processing Systems*, 31, 8168–8177. 407

Li, Y., Tarlow, D., Brockschmidt, M., & Zemel, R. (2016b). Gated graph sequence neural networks. *International Conference on Learning Representations*. 262

Li, Y., & Turner, R. E. (2016). Rényi divergence variational inference. *Neural Information Processing Systems*, 29, 1073–1081. 346

Li, Z., & Arora, S. (2019). An exponential learning rate schedule for deep learning. *International Conference on Learning Representations*. 204

Liang, D., Krishnan, R. G., Hoffman, M. D., & Jebara, T. (2018). Variational autoencoders for collaborative filtering. *World Wide Web Conference*, 689–698. 344

Liang, J., Zhang, K., Gu, S., Van Gool, L., & Timofte, R. (2021). Flow-based kernel prior with application to blind super-resolution. *IEEE/CVF Computer Vision & Pattern Recognition*, 10601–10610. 322

Liang, S., & Srikant, R. (2016). Why deep neural networks for function approximation? *International Conference on Learning Representations*. 53, 417

Lillicrap, T. P., Hunt, J. J., Pritzel, A., Heess, N., Erez, T., Tassa, Y., Silver, D., & Wierstra, D. (2016). Continuous control with deep reinforcement learning. *International Conference on Learning Representations*. 397

Lin, K., Li, D., He, X., Zhang, Z., & Sun, M.-T. (2017a). Adversarial ranking for language generation. *Neural Information Processing Systems*, 30, 3155–3165. 299

Lin, L.-J. (1992). Self-improving reactive agents based on reinforcement learning, planning and teaching. *Machine learning*, 8, 293–321. 396

Lin, M., Chen, Q., & Yan, S. (2014). Network in network. *International Conference on Learning Representations*. 181

Lin, T., Wang, Y., Liu, X., & Qiu, X. (2022). A survey of transformers. *AI Open*, 3, 111–132. 233

Lin, T.-Y., Dollár, P., Girshick, R., He, K., Hariharan, B., & Belongie, S. (2017b). Feature pyramid networks for object detection. *IEEE Computer Vision & Pattern Recognition*, 2117–2125. 184

Lin, T.-Y., Goyal, P., Girshick, R., He, K., & Dollár, P. (2017c). Focal loss for dense object detection. *IEEE/CVF International Conference on Computer Vision*, 2980–2988. 73

Lin, Z., Khetan, A., Fanti, G., & Oh, S. (2018). PacGAN: The power of two samples in generative adversarial networks. *Neural Information Processing Systems*, 31, 1505–1514. 300

Ling, H., Kreis, K., Li, D., Kim, S. W., Torralba, A., & Fidler, S. (2021). EditGAN: High-precision semantic image editing. *Neural Information Processing Systems*, 34, 16331–16345. 302

Lipman, Y., Chen, R. T., Ben-Hamu, H., Nickel, M., & Le, M. (2022). Flow matching for generative modeling. *arXiv:2210.02747*. 369

Lipton, Z. C., & Tripathi, S. (2017). Precise recovery of latent vectors from generative adversarial networks. *International Conference on Learning Representations.* 301

Liu, G., Reda, F. A., Shih, K. J., Wang, T.-C., Tao, A., & Catanzaro, B. (2018a). Image inpainting for irregular holes using partial convolutions. *European Conference on Computer Vision*, 85–100. 181

Liu, H., Simonyan, K., & Yang, Y. (2019a). DARTS: Differentiable architecture search. *International Conference on Learning Representations.* 414

Liu, L., Jiang, H., He, P., Chen, W., Liu, X., Gao, J., & Han, J. (2021a). On the variance of the adaptive learning rate and beyond. *International Conference on Learning Representations.* 93

Liu, L., Liu, X., Gao, J., Chen, W., & Han, J. (2020). Understanding the difficulty of training transformers. *Empirical Methods in Natural Language Processing*, 5747–5763. 237, 238

Liu, L., Luo, Y., Shen, X., Sun, M., & Li, B. (2019b). Beta-dropout: A unified dropout. *IEEE Access, 7*, 36140–36153. 158

Liu, P. J., Saleh, M., Pot, E., Goodrich, B., Sepassi, R., Kaiser, L., & Shazeer, N. (2018b). Generating Wikipedia by summarizing long sequences. *International Conference on Learning Representations.* 237

Liu, X., Zhang, F., Hou, Z., Mian, L., Wang, Z., Zhang, J., & Tang, J. (2023a). Self-supervised learning: Generative or contrastive. *IEEE Transactions on Knowledge and Data Engineering, 35*(1), 857–876. 159

Liu, Y., Qin, Z., Anwar, S., Ji, P., Kim, D., Caldwell, S., & Gedeon, T. (2021b). Invertible denoising network: A light solution for real noise removal. *IEEE/CVF Computer Vision & Pattern Recognition*, 13365–13374. 322

Liu, Y., Zhang, Y., Wang, Y., Hou, F., Yuan, J., Tian, J., Zhang, Y., Shi, Z., Fan, J., & He, Z. (2023b). A survey of visual transformers. *IEEE Transactions on Neural Networks and Learning Systems.* 238

Liu, Z., Hu, H., Lin, Y., Yao, Z., Xie, Z., Wei, Y., Ning, J., Cao, Y., Zhang, Z., Dong, L., Wei, F., & Guo, B. (2022). Swin transformer V2: Scaling up capacity and resolution. *IEEE/CVF Computer Vision & Pattern Recognition*, 12009–12019. 238

Liu, Z., Lin, Y., Cao, Y., Hu, H., Wei, Y., Zhang, Z., Lin, S., & Guo, B. (2021c). Swin transformer: Hierarchical vision transformer using shifted windows. *IEEE/CVF International Conference on Computer Vision*, 10012–10022. 231, 238

Liu, Z., Luo, P., Wang, X., & Tang, X. (2015). Deep learning face attributes in the wild. *IEEE International Conference on Computer Vision*, 3730–3738. 345

Liu, Z., Michaud, E. J., & Tegmark, M. (2023c). Omnigrok: Grokking beyond algorithmic data. *International Conference on Learning Representations.* 405, 406, 412, 413

Liu, Z., Sun, M., Zhou, T., Huang, G., & Darrell, T. (2019c). Rethinking the value of network pruning. *International Conference on Learning Representations.* 235

Livni, R., Shalev-Shwartz, S., & Shamir, O. (2014). On the computational efficiency of training neural networks. *Neural Information Processing Systems, 27*, 855–863. 405

Locatello, F., Weissenborn, D., Unterthiner, T., Mahendran, A., Heigold, G., Uszkoreit, J., Dosovitskiy, A., & Kipf, T. (2020). Object-centric learning with slot attention. *Neural Information Processing Systems, 33*, 11525–11538. 238

Long, J., Shelhamer, E., & Darrell, T. (2015). Fully convolutional networks for semantic segmentation. *IEEE/CVF Computer Vision & Pattern Recognition*, 3431–3440. 181

Longino, H. E. (1990). *Science as Social Knowledge: Values and Objectivity in Scientific Inquiry.* Princeton University Press. 432

Longino, H. E. (1996). Cognitive and non-cognitive values in science: Rethinking the dichotomy. *Feminism, Science, and the Philosophy of Science*, 39–58. 432

Loshchilov, I., & Hutter, F. (2019). Decoupled weight decay regularization. *International Conference on Learning Representations.* 94, 156

Louizos, C., Welling, M., & Kingma, D. P. (2018). Learning sparse neural networks through l_0 regularization. *International Conference on Learning Representations.* 156

Loukas, A. (2020). What graph neural networks cannot learn: Depth vs width. *International Conference on Learning Representations.* 262

Lu, J., Batra, D., Parikh, D., & Lee, S. (2019). ViLBERT: Pretraining task-agnostic visiolinguistic representations for vision-and-language tasks. *Neural Information Processing Systems, 32*, 13–23. 238

Lu, S.-P., Wang, R., Zhong, T., & Rosin, P. L. (2021). Large-capacity image steganography based on invertible neural networks. *IEEE/CVF Computer Vision & Pattern Recognition*, 10816–10825. 322

Lu, Z., Pu, H., Wang, F., Hu, Z., & Wang, L. (2017). The expressive power of neural networks: A view from the width. *Neural Information Processing Systems*, *30*, 6231–6239. 53

Lubana, E. S., Dick, R., & Tanaka, H. (2021). Beyond BatchNorm: Towards a unified understanding of normalization in deep learning. *Neural Information Processing Systems*, *34*, 4778–4791. 204

Lucas, J., Tucker, G., Grosse, R., & Norouzi, M. (2019a). Understanding posterior collapse in generative latent variable models. *ICLR Workshop on Deep Generative Models for Highly Structured Data*. 345

Lucas, J., Tucker, G., Grosse, R. B., & Norouzi, M. (2019b). Don't blame the ELBO! A linear VAE perspective on posterior collapse. *Neural Information Processing Systems*, *32*, 9403–9413. 345

Luccioni, A. S. (2023). The mounting human and environmental costs of generative AI. ars Technica, April 12, 2023.https://arstechnica.com/gadgets/2023/04/generative-ai-is-cool-but-lets-not-forget-its-human-and-environmental-costs. 429

Luccioni, A. S., Viguier, S., & Ligozat, A.-L. (2022). Estimating the carbon footprint of bloom, a 176b parameter language model. *arXiv:2211.02001*. 429

Lucic, M., Kurach, K., Michalski, M., Gelly, S., & Bousquet, O. (2018). Are GANs created equal? A large-scale study. *Neural Information Processing Systems*, *31*, 698–707. 299

Lücke, J., Forster, D., & Dai, Z. (2020). The evidence lower bound of variational autoencoders converges to a sum of three entropies. *arXiv:2010.14860*. 346

Luo, C. (2022). Understanding diffusion models: A unified perspective. *arXiv:2208.11970*. 369

Luo, G., Heide, M., & Uecker, M. (2022). MRI reconstruction via data driven Markov chain with joint uncertainty estimation. *arXiv:2202.01479*. 369

Luo, J., Xu, Y., Tang, C., & Lv, J. (2017a). Learning inverse mapping by autoencoder based generative adversarial nets. *Neural Information Processing Systems*, vol. 30, 207–216. 301

Luo, J.-H., Wu, J., & Lin, W. (2017b). ThiNet: A filter level pruning method for deep neural network compression. *IEEE/CVF International Conference on Computer Vision*, 5058–5066. 414

Luo, P., Wang, X., Shao, W., & Peng, Z. (2018). Towards understanding regularization in batch normalization. *International Conference on Learning Representations*. 205

Luo, S., & Hu, W. (2021). Diffusion probabilistic models for 3D point cloud generation. *IEEE/CVF Computer Vision & Pattern Recognition*, 2837–2845. 369

Luong, M.-T., Pham, H., & Manning, C. D. (2015). Effective approaches to attention-based neural machine translation. *Empirical Methods in Natural Language Processing*, 1412–1421. 235

Luther, K. (2020). Why BatchNorm causes exploding gradients. https://kyleluther.github.io/2020/02/18/BatchNorm-exploding-gradients.html. 203

Ma, Y., & Tang, J. (2021). *Deep learning on graphs*. Cambridge University Press. 261

Ma, Y.-A., Chen, T., & Fox, E. (2015). A complete recipe for stochastic gradient MCMC. *Neural Information Processing Systems*, *28*, 2917–2925. 159

Maaløe, L., Sønderby, C. K., Sønderby, S. K., & Winther, O. (2016). Auxiliary deep generative models. *International Conference on Machine Learning*, 1445–1453. 344, 345

Maas, A. L., Hannun, A. Y., & Ng, A. Y. (2013). Rectifier nonlinearities improve neural network acoustic models. *ICML Workshop on Deep Learning for Audio, Speech, and Language Processing*. 38

MacKay, D. J. (1995). Ensemble learning and evidence maximization. *Neural Information Processing Systems*, vol. 8, 4083–4090. 159

MacKay, M., Vicol, P., Ba, J., & Grosse, R. B. (2018). Reversible recurrent neural networks. *Neural Information Processing Systems*, *31*, 9043–9054. 322

Mackowiak, R., Ardizzone, L., Kothe, U., & Rother, C. (2021). Generative classifiers as a basis for trustworthy image classification. *IEEE/CVF Computer Vision & Pattern Recognition*, 2971–2981. 322

Madhawa, K., Ishiguro, K., Nakago, K., & Abe, M. (2019). GraphNVP: An invertible flow model for generating molecular graphs. *arXiv:1905.11600*. 322

Mahendran, A., & Vedaldi, A. (2015). Understanding deep image representations by inverting them. *IEEE/CVF Computer Vision & Pattern Recognition*, 5188–5196. 184

Makhzani, A., Shlens, J., Jaitly, N., Goodfellow, I., & Frey, B. (2015). Adversarial autoencoders. *arXiv:1511.05644*. 345

Mangalam, K., Fan, H., Li, Y., Wu, C.-Y., Xiong, B., Feichtenhofer, C., & Malik, J. (2022). Reversible vision transformers. *IEEE/CVF Computer Vision & Pattern Recognition*, 10830–10840. 322

Manning, C., & Schutze, H. (1999). *Foundations of statistical natural language processing*. MIT Press. 233

Manyika, J., Lund, S., Chui, M., Bughin, J., Woetzel, J., Batra, P., Ko, R., & Sanghvi, S. (2017). *Jobs Lost, Jobs Gained: Workforce Transitions in a Time of Automation*. McKinsey Global Institute. 429

Manyika, J., & Sneader, K. (2018). *AI, automation, and the future of work: Ten things to solve for*. McKinsey Global Institute. 429

Mao, Q., Lee, H.-Y., Tseng, H.-Y., Ma, S., & Yang, M.-H. (2019). Mode seeking generative adversarial networks for diverse image synthesis. *IEEE/CVF Computer Vision & Pattern Recognition*, 1429–1437. 300

Mao, X., Li, Q., Xie, H., Lau, R. Y., Wang, Z., & Paul Smolley, S. (2017). Least squares generative adversarial networks. *IEEE/CVF International Conference on Computer Vision*, 2794–2802. 299

Marchesi, M. (2017). Megapixel size image creation using generative adversarial networks. *arXiv:1706.00082*. 299

Martin, G. L. (1993). Centered-object integrated segmentation and recognition of overlapping handprinted characters. *Neural Computation*, 5(3), 419–429. 181

Masci, J., Boscaini, D., Bronstein, M., & Vandergheynst, P. (2015). Geodesic convolutional neural networks on Riemannian manifolds. *IEEE International Conference on Computer Vision Workshop*, 832–840. 265

Masrani, V., Le, T. A., & Wood, F. (2019). The thermodynamic variational objective. *Neural Information Processing Systems*, 32, 11521–11530. 346

Mathieu, E., Rainforth, T., Siddharth, N., & Teh, Y. W. (2019). Disentangling disentanglement in variational autoencoders. *International Conference on Machine Learning*, 4402–4412. 346

Matsakis, L. (2017). A frightening AI can determine whether a person is gay with 91 percent accuracy. Vice, Sept 8, 2017. https://www.vice.com/en/article/a33xb4/a-frightening-ai-can-determine-a-persons-sexuality-with-91-accuracy. 430

Maturana, D., & Scherer, S. (2015). VoxNet: A 3D convolutional neural network for real-time object recognition. *IEEE/RSJ International Conference on Intelligent Robots and Systems*, 922–928. 182

Mayson, S. G. (2018). Bias in bias out. *Yale Law Journal*, 128, 2122–2473. 422

Mazoure, B., Doan, T., Durand, A., Pineau, J., & Hjelm, R. D. (2020). Leveraging exploration in off-policy algorithms via normalizing flows. *Conference on Robot Learning*, 430–444. 322

Mazyavkina, N., Sviridov, S., Ivanov, S., & Burnaev, E. (2021). Reinforcement learning for combinatorial optimization: A survey. *Computers & Operations Research*, 134, 105400. 396

McCoy, R. T., Pavlick, E., & Linzen, T. (2019). Right for the wrong reasons: Diagnosing syntactic heuristics in natural language inference. *Meeting of the Association for Computational Linguistics*, 2428–3448. 234

McCulloch, W. S., & Pitts, W. (1943). A logical calculus of the ideas immanent in nervous activity. *The Bulletin of Mathematical Biophysics*, 5(4), 115–133. 37

McNamara, A., Smith, J., & Murphy-Hill, E. (2018). Does ACM's code of ethics change ethical decision making in software development? *ACM Joint Meeting on European Software Engineering Conference and Symposium on the Foundations of Software Engineering*, 729–733. 420

Mehrabi, N., Morstatter, F., Saxena, N., Lerman, K., & Galstyan, A. (2022). A survey on bias and fairness in machine learning. *ACM Computing Surveys*, 54(6), 1–35. 423

Mei, J., Chung, W., Thomas, V., Dai, B., Szepesvári, C., & Schuurmans, D. (2022). The role of baselines in policy gradient optimization. *Neural Information Processing Systems*, vol. 35, 17818–17830. 397

Meng, C., Song, Y., Song, J., Wu, J., Zhu, J.-Y., & Ermon, S. (2021). SDEdit: Image synthesis and editing with stochastic differential equations. *International Conference on Learning Representations*. 369

Menon, S., Damian, A., Hu, S., Ravi, N., & Rudin, C. (2020). PULSE: self-supervised photo upsampling via latent space exploration of generative models. *IEEE/CVF Computer Vision & Pattern Recognition*, 2434–2442. 422

Metcalf, J., Keller, E. F., & Boyd, D. (2016). Perspectives on big data, ethics, and society. *Council for Big Data, Ethics, and Society.* https://bdes.datasociety.net/council-output/perspectives-on-big-data-ethics-and-society/. 430

Metz, L., Poole, B., Pfau, D., & Sohl-Dickstein, J. (2017). Unrolled generative adversarial networks. *International Conference on Learning Representations.* 299

Mézard, M., & Mora, T. (2009). Constraint satisfaction problems and neural networks: A statistical physics perspective. *Journal of Physiology-Paris*, *103*(1-2), 107–113. 94

Micelli, M., Posada, J., & Yang, T. (2022). Studying up machine learning data: Why talk about bias when we mean power? *Proceedngs of ACM on Human-Computer Interaction*, *6.* 423

Milletari, F., Navab, N., & Ahmadi, S.-A. (2016). V-Net: Fully convolutional neural networks for volumetric medical image segmentation. *International Conference on 3D Vision*, 565–571. 205

Min, J., McCoy, R. T., Das, D., Pitler, E., & Linzen, T. (2020). Syntactic data augmentation increases robustness to inference heuristics. *Meeting of the Association for Computational Linguistics*, 2339–2352. 160

Minaee, S., Boykov, Y. Y., Porikli, F., Plaza, A. J., Kehtarnavaz, N., & Terzopoulos, D. (2021). Image segmentation using deep learning: A survey. *IEEE Transactions on Pattern Analysis & Machine Intelligence*, *44*(7), 3523–3542. 184

Minsky, M., & Papert, S. A. (1969). *Perceptrons: An introduction to computational geometry.* MIT Press. 37, 233

Mireshghallah, F., Taram, M., Vepakomma, P., Singh, A., Raskar, R., & Esmaeilzadeh, H. (2020). Privacy in deep learning: A survey. *arXiv:2004.12254.* 428

Mirza, M., & Osindero, S. (2014). Conditional generative adversarial nets. *arXiv:1411.1784.* 301

Mishkin, D., & Matas, J. (2016). All you need is a good init. *International Conference on Learning Representations.* 113

Mitchell, M., Forrest, S., & Holland, J. H. (1992). The royal road for genetic algorithms: Fitness landscapes and GA performance. *European Conference on Artificial Life.* 421

Mitchell, S., Potash, E., Barocas, S., D'Amour, A., & Lum, K. (2021). Algorithmic fairness: Choices, assumptions, and definitions. *Annual Review of Statistics and Its Application*, *8*, 141–163. 422

Miyato, T., Kataoka, T., Koyama, M., & Yoshida, Y. (2018). Spectral normalization for generative adversarial networks. *International Conference on Learning Representations.* 299

Miyato, T., & Koyama, M. (2018). cGANs with projection discriminator. *International Conference on Learning Representations.* 301

Mnih, V., Badia, A. P., Mirza, M., Graves, A., Lillicrap, T., Harley, T., Silver, D., & Kavukcuoglu, K. (2016). Asynchronous methods for deep reinforcement learning. *International Conference on Machine Learning*, 1928–1937. 398

Mnih, V., Kavukcuoglu, K., Silver, D., Rusu, A. A., Veness, J., Bellemare, M. G., Graves, A., Riedmiller, M., Fidjeland, A. K., Ostrovski, G., et al. (2015). Human-level control through deep reinforcement learning. *Nature*, *518*(7540), 529–533. 396

Moerland, T. M., Broekens, J., Plaat, A., Jonker, C. M., et al. (2023). Model-based reinforcement learning: A survey. *Foundations and Trends in Machine Learning*, *16*(1), 1–118. 398

Mogren, O. (2016). C-RNN-GAN: Continuous recurrent neural networks with adversarial training. *NIPS 2016 Constructive Machine Learning Workshop.* 299

Molnar, C. (2022). *Interpretable Machine Learning: A Guide for Making Black Box Models Explainable.* https://christophm.github.io/interpretable-ml-book. 425

Monti, F., Boscaini, D., Masci, J., Rodola, E., Svoboda, J., & Bronstein, M. M. (2017). Geometric deep learning on graphs and manifolds using mixture model CNNs. *IEEE/CVF Computer Vision & Pattern Recognition*, 5115–5124. 263, 265

Monti, F., Shchur, O., Bojchevski, A., Litany, O., Günnemann, S., & Bronstein, M. M. (2018). Dual-primal graph convolutional networks. *arXiv:1806.00770.* 264

Montúfar, G. (2017). Notes on the number of linear regions of deep neural networks. 52, 53

Montúfar, G. F., Pascanu, R., Cho, K., & Bengio, Y. (2014). On the number of linear regions of deep neural networks. *Neural Information Processing Systems*, 27, 2924–2932. 52, 53

Moor, J. (2006). The nature, importance, and difficulty of machine ethics. *Intelligence Systems*, 21(4), 18–21. 424

Moore, A., & Himma, K. (2022). Intellectual Property. *The Stanford Encyclopedia of Philosophy*. 428

Moreno-Torres, J. G., Raeder, T., Alaiz-Rodríguez, R., Chawla, N. V., & Herrera, F. (2012). A unifying view on dataset shift in classification. *Pattern Recognition*, 45(1), 521–530. 135

Morimura, T., Sugiyama, M., Kashima, H., Hachiya, H., & Tanaka, T. (2010). Nonparametric return distribution approximation for reinforcement learning. *International Conference on Machine Learning*, 799–806. 397

Müller, R., Kornblith, S., & Hinton, G. E. (2019a). When does label smoothing help? *Neural Information Processing Systems*, 32, 4696–4705. 158

Müller, T., McWilliams, B., Rousselle, F., Gross, M., & Novák, J. (2019b). Neural importance sampling. *ACM Transactions on Graphics (TOG)*, 38(5), 1–19. 322, 323

Mun, S., Shon, S., Kim, W., Han, D. K., & Ko, H. (2017). Deep neural network based learning and transferring mid-level audio features for acoustic scene classification. *IEEE International Conference on Acoustics, Speech and Signal Processing*, 796–800. 160

Murphy, K. P. (2022). *Probabilistic machine learning: An introduction.* MIT Press. 15

Murphy, K. P. (2023). *Probabilistic machine learning: Advanced topics.* MIT Press. 15

Murphy, R. L., Srinivasan, B., Rao, V., & Ribeiro, B. (2018). Janossy pooling: Learning deep permutation-invariant functions for variable-size inputs. *International Conference on Learning Representations.* 263

Murty, K. G., & Kabadi, S. N. (1987). Some NP-complete problems in quadratic and nonlinear programming. *Mathematical Programming*, 39(2), 117–129. 401

Mutlu, E. C., Oghaz, T., Rajabi, A., & Garibay, I. (2020). Review on learning and extracting graph features for link prediction. *Machine Learning and Knowledge Extraction*, 2(4), 672–704. 262

Nair, V., & Hinton, G. E. (2010). Rectified linear units improve restricted Boltzmann machines. *International Conference on Machine Learning*, 807–814. 37

Nakkiran, P., Kaplun, G., Bansal, Y., Yang, T., Barak, B., & Sutskever, I. (2021). Deep double descent: Where bigger models and more data hurt. *Journal of Statistical Mechanics: Theory and Experiment*, 2021(12), 124003. 130, 134

Narang, S., Chung, H. W., Tay, Y., Fedus, W., Fevry, T., Matena, M., Malkan, K., Fiedel, N., Shazeer, N., Lan, Z., et al. (2021). Do transformer modifications transfer across implementations and applications? *Empirical Methods in Natural Language Processing*, 5758–5773. 233

Narayanan, A., & Shmatikov, V. (2008). Robust de-anonymization of large sparse datasets. *IEEE Symposium on Security and Privacy*, 111–125. 428

Narayanan, D., Phanishayee, A., Shi, K., Chen, X., & Zaharia, M. (2021a). Memory-efficient pipeline-parallel DNN training. *International Conference on Machine Learning*, 7937–7947. 114

Narayanan, D., Shoeybi, M., Casper, J., LeGresley, P., Patwary, M., Korthikanti, V., Vainbrand, D., Kashinkunti, P., Bernauer, J., Catanzaro, B., et al. (2021b). Efficient large-scale language model training on GPU clusters using Megatron-LM. *International Conference for High Performance Computing, Networking, Storage and Analysis*, 1–15. 114

Nash, C., Menick, J., Dieleman, S., & Battaglia, P. W. (2021). Generating images with sparse representations. *International Conference on Machine Learning*, 7958–7968. 238, 274

Neal, R. M. (1995). *Bayesian learning for neural networks.* Springer. 159

Neimark, D., Bar, O., Zohar, M., & Asselmann, D. (2021). Video transformer network. *IEEE/CVF International Conference on Computer Vision*, 3163–3172. 238

Nesterov, Y. E. (1983). A method for solving the convex programming problem with convergence rate. *Doklady Akademii Nauk SSSR*, vol. 269, 543–547. 93

Newell, A., Yang, K., & Deng, J. (2016). Stacked hourglass networks for human pose estimation. *European Conference on Computer Vision*, 483–499. 200, 205

Neyshabur, B., Bhojanapalli, S., McAllester, D., & Srebro, N. (2017). Exploring generalization in deep learning. *Neural Information Processing Systems*, 30, 5947–5956. 134, 412

Neyshabur, B., Bhojanapalli, S., & Srebro, N. (2018). A PAC-Bayesian approach to spectrally-normalized margin bounds for neural networks. *International Conference on Learning Representations.* 156

Ng, N. H., Gabriel, R. A., McAuley, J., Elkan, C., & Lipton, Z. C. (2017). Predicting surgery duration with neural heteroscedastic regression. *PMLR Machine Learning for Healthcare Conference*, 100–111. 74

Nguyen, Q., & Hein, M. (2017). The loss surface of deep and wide neural networks. *International Conference on Machine Learning*, 2603–2612. 405

Nguyen, Q., & Hein, M. (2018). Optimization landscape and expressivity of deep CNNs. *International Conference on Machine Learning*, 3730–3739. 405

Nichol, A. Q., & Dhariwal, P. (2021). Improved denoising diffusion probabilistic models. *International Conference on Machine Learning*, 8162–8171. 369

Nichol, A. Q., Dhariwal, P., Ramesh, A., Shyam, P., Mishkin, P., McGrew, B., Sutskever, I., & Chen, M. (2022). GLIDE: towards photorealistic image generation and editing with text-guided diffusion models. *International Conference on Machine Learning*, 16784–16804. 369, 370

Nie, W., Guo, B., Huang, Y., Xiao, C., Vahdat, A., & Anandkumar, A. (2022). Diffusion models for adversarial purification. *International Conference on Machine Learning*, 16805–16827. 369

Nix, D. A., & Weigend, A. S. (1994). Estimating the mean and variance of the target probability distribution. *IEEE International Conference on Neural Networks*, 55–60. 73

Noble, S. (2018). *Algorithms of Oppression.* New York: NYU Press. 433

Noci, L., Roth, K., Bachmann, G., Nowozin, S., & Hofmann, T. (2021). Disentangling the roles of curation, data-augmentation and the prior in the cold posterior effect. *Neural Information Processing Systems*, *34*, 12738–12748. 159

Noé, F., Olsson, S., Köhler, J., & Wu, H. (2019). Boltzmann generators: Sampling equilibrium states of many-body systems with deep learning. *Science*, *365*(6457). 322

Noh, H., Hong, S., & Han, B. (2015). Learning deconvolution network for semantic segmentation. *IEEE International Conference on Computer Vision*, 1520–1528. 6, 179, 180, 184

Noothigattu, R., Gaikwad, S. N., Awad, E., Dsouza, S., Rahwan, I., Ravikumar, P., &

Procaccia, A. D. (2018). A voting-based system for ethical decision making. *AAAI Portuguese Conference on Artificial Intelligence*, 1587–1594. 424

Noroozi, M., & Favaro, P. (2016). Unsupervised learning of visual representations by solving jigsaw puzzles. *European Conference on Computer Vision*, 69–84. 159

Nowozin, S., Cseke, B., & Tomioka, R. (2016). f-GAN: Training generative neural samplers using variational divergence minimization. *Neural Information Processing Systems*, *29*, 271–279. 299

Nye, M., & Saxe, A. (2018). Are efficient deep representations learnable? *International Conference on Learning Representations (Workshop).* 417

O'Connor, C., & Bruner, J. (2019). Dynamics and diversity in epistemic communities. *Erkenntnis*, *84*, 101–119. 433

Odena, A. (2019). Open questions about generative adversarial networks. Distill, `https://distill.pub/2019/gan-open-problems`. 299

Odena, A., Dumoulin, V., & Olah, C. (2016). Deconvolution and checkerboard artifacts. Distill, `https://distill.pub/2016/deconv-checkerboard/`. 181

Odena, A., Olah, C., & Shlens, J. (2017). Conditional image synthesis with auxiliary classifier GANs. *International Conference on Machine Learning*, 2642–2651. 290, 301

O'Neil, C. (2016). *Weapons of Math Destruction.* Crown. 420, 422

Oono, K., & Suzuki, T. (2019). Graph neural networks exponentially lose expressive power for node classification. *International Conference on Learning Representations.* 265

Orhan, A. E., & Pitkow, X. (2017). Skip connections eliminate singularities. *International Conference on Learning Representations.* 202

Ouyang, L., Wu, J., Jiang, X., Almeida, D., Wainwright, C., Mishkin, P., Zhang, C., Agarwal, S., Slama, K., Ray, A., et al. (2022). Training language models to follow instructions with human feedback. *Neural Information Processing Systems*, *35*, 27730–27744. 398

Papamakarios, G., Nalisnick, E. T., Rezende, D. J., Mohamed, S., & Lakshminarayanan, B. (2021). Normalizing flows for probabilistic modeling and inference. *Journal of Machine Learning Research*, *22*(57), 1–64. 321

Papamakarios, G., Pavlakou, T., & Murray, I. (2017). Masked autoregressive flow for density estimation. *Neural Information Processing Systems*, *30*, 2338–2347. 323

Park, D., Hoshi, Y., & Kemp, C. C. (2018). A multimodal anomaly detector for robot-assisted feeding using an LSTM-based variational autoencoder. *IEEE Robotics and Automation Letters*, *3*(3), 1544–1551. 344

Park, D. S., Chan, W., Zhang, Y., Chiu, C.-C., Zoph, B., Cubuk, E. D., & Le, Q. V. (2019). SpecAugment: A simple data augmentation method for automatic speech recognition. *INTERSPEECH*. 160

Park, S., & Kwak, N. (2016). Analysis on the dropout effect in convolutional neural networks. *Asian Conference on Computer Vision*, 189–204. 183

Park, S.-W., Ko, J.-S., Huh, J.-H., & Kim, J.-C. (2021). Review on generative adversarial networks: Focusing on computer vision and its applications. *Electronics*, *10*(10), 1216. 299

Parker, D. B. (1985). *Learning-logic: Casting the cortex of the human brain in silicon*. Alfred P. Sloan School of Management, MIT. 113

Parmar, N., Ramachandran, P., Vaswani, A., Bello, I., Levskaya, A., & Shlens, J. (2019). Stand-alone self-attention in vision models. *Neural Information Processing Systems*, *32*, 68–80. 238

Parmar, N., Vaswani, A., Uszkoreit, J., Kaiser, L., Shazeer, N., Ku, A., & Tran, D. (2018). Image transformer. *International Conference on Machine Learning*, 4055–4064. 238

Pascanu, R., Dauphin, Y. N., Ganguli, S., & Bengio, Y. (2014). On the saddle point problem for non-convex optimization. *arXiv:1405.4604*. 405

Pascanu, R., Montúfar, G., & Bengio, Y. (2013). On the number of response regions of deep feed forward networks with piece-wise linear activations. *arXiv:1312.6098*. 53

Paschalidou, D., Katharopoulos, A., Geiger, A., & Fidler, S. (2021). Neural parts: Learning expressive 3D shape abstractions with invertible neural networks. *IEEE/CVF Computer Vision & Pattern Recognition*, 3204–3215. 322

Patashnik, O., Wu, Z., Shechtman, E., Cohen-Or, D., & Lischinski, D. (2021). StyleCLIP: Text-driven manipulation of StyleGAN imagery. *IEEE/CVF International Conference on Computer Vision*, 2085–2094. 300

Pateria, S., Subagdja, B., Tan, A.-h., & Quek, C. (2021). Hierarchical reinforcement learning: A comprehensive survey. *ACM Computing Surveys*, *54*(5), 1–35. 398

Pathak, D., Krahenbuhl, P., Donahue, J., Darrell, T., & Efros, A. A. (2016). Context encoders: Feature learning by inpainting. *IEEE/CVF Computer Vision & Pattern Recognition*, 2536–2544. 159

Patrick, M., Campbell, D., Asano, Y., Misra, I., Metze, F., Feichtenhofer, C., Vedaldi, A., & Henriques, J. F. (2021). Keeping your eye on the ball: Trajectory attention in video transformers. *Neural Information Processing Systems*, *34*, 12493–12506. 238

Peluchetti, S., & Favaro, S. (2020). Infinitely deep neural networks as diffusion processes. *International Conference on Artificial Intelligence and Statistics*, 1126–1136. 324

Peng, C., Guo, P., Zhou, S. K., Patel, V., & Chellappa, R. (2022). Towards performant and reliable undersampled MR reconstruction via diffusion model sampling. *Medical Image Computing and Computer Assisted Intervention*, *13436*, 623–633. 369

Pennington, J., & Bahri, Y. (2017). Geometry of neural network loss surfaces via random matrix theory. *International Conference on Machine Learning*, 2798–2806. 405

Perarnau, G., Van De Weijer, J., Raducanu, B., & Álvarez, J. M. (2016). Invertible conditional GANs for image editing. *NIPS 2016 Workshop on Adversarial Training*. 301

Pereyra, G., Tucker, G., Chorowski, J., Kaiser, ., & Hinton, G. (2017). Regularizing neural networks by penalizing confident output distributions. *International Conference on Learning Representations Workshop*. 158

Peters, J., & Schaal, S. (2008). Reinforcement learning of motor skills with policy gradients. *Neural Networks*, *21*(4), 682–697. 397

Peyré, G., Cuturi, M., et al. (2019). Computational optimal transport with applications to data science. *Foundations and Trends in Machine Learning*, *11*(5-6), 355–607. 299

Pezeshki, M., Mitra, A., Bengio, Y., & Lajoie, G. (2022). Multi-scale feature learning dynamics: Insights for double descent. *International Conference on Machine Learning*, 17669–17690. 134

Pham, T., Tran, T., Phung, D., & Venkatesh, S. (2017). Column networks for collective classification. *AAAI Conference on Artificial Intelligence*, 2485–2491. 263

Phuong, M., & Hutter, M. (2022). Formal algorithms for transformers. *Technical Report, DeepMind.* 233

Pieters, M., & Wiering, M. (2018). Comparing generative adversarial network techniques for image creation and modification. *arXiv:1803.09093.* 299

Pintea, S. L., Tömen, N., Goes, S. F., Loog, M., & van Gemert, J. C. (2021). Resolution learning in deep convolutional networks using scalespace theory. *IEEE Transactions on Image Processing, 30*, 8342–8353. 183

Poggio, T., Mhaskar, H., Rosasco, L., Miranda, B., & Liao, Q. (2017). Why and when can deep-but not shallow-networks avoid the curse of dimensionality: A review. *International Journal of Automation and Computing, 14*(5), 503–519. 53

Polyak, B. T. (1964). Some methods of speeding up the convergence of iteration methods. *USSR Computational Mathematics and Mathematical Physics, 4*(5), 1–17. 92

Poole, B., Jain, A., Barron, J. T., & Mildenhall, B. (2023). DreamFusion: Text-to-3D using 2D diffusion. *International Conference on Learning Representations.* 369

Power, A., Burda, Y., Edwards, H., Babuschkin, I., & Misra, V. (2022). Grokking: Generalization beyond overfitting on small algorithmic datasets. *arXiv:2201.02177.* 412

Prenger, R., Valle, R., & Catanzaro, B. (2019). Waveglow: A flow-based generative network for speech synthesis. *IEEE International Conference on Acoustics, Speech and Signal Processing*, 3617–3621. 322, 323

Prince, S. J. D. (2012). *Computer vision: Models, learning, and inference.* Cambridge University Press. 15, 159

Prince, S. J. D. (2021a). Transformers II: Extensions. https://www.borealisai.com/en/blog/tutorial-16-transformers-ii-extensions/. 236, 237

Prince, S. J. D. (2021b). Transformers III: Training. https://www.borealisai.com/en/blog/tutorial-17-transformers-iii-training/. 238

Prince, S. J. D. (2022). Explainability I: local post-hoc explanations. https://www.borealisai.com/research-blogs/explainability-i-local-post-hoc-explanations/. 426

Prokudin, S., Gehler, P., & Nowozin, S. (2018). Deep directional statistics: Pose estimation with uncertainty quantification. *European Conference on Computer Vision*, 534–551. 74

Provilkov, I., Emelianenko, D., & Voita, E. (2020). BPE-Dropout: Simple and effective subword regularization. *Meeting of the Association for Computational Linguistics*, 1882–1892. 234

Qi, G.-J. (2020). Loss-sensitive generative adversarial networks on Lipschitz densities. *International Journal of Computer Vision, 128*(5), 1118–1140. 299

Qi, J., Du, J., Siniscalchi, S. M., Ma, X., & Lee, C.-H. (2020). On mean absolute error for deep neural network based vector-to-vector regression. *IEEE Signal Processing Letters, 27*, 1485—1489. 73

Qin, Z., Yu, F., Liu, C., & Chen, X. (2018). How convolutional neural network see the world — A survey of convolutional neural network visualization methods. *arXiv:1804.11191.* 184

Qiu, S., Xu, B., Zhang, J., Wang, Y., Shen, X., De Melo, G., Long, C., & Li, X. (2020). EasyAug: An automatic textual data augmentation platform for classification tasks. *Companion Proceedings of the Web Conference 2020*, 249–252. 160

Radford, A., Kim, J. W., Hallacy, C., Ramesh, A., Goh, G., Agarwal, S., Sastry, G., Askell, A., Mishkin, P., Clark, J., et al. (2021). Learning transferable visual models from natural language supervision. *International Conference on Machine Learning*, 8748–8763. 238, 370

Radford, A., Metz, L., & Chintala, S. (2015). Unsupervised representation learning with deep convolutional generative adversarial networks. *International Conference on Learning Representations.* 280, 299

Radford, A., Wu, J., Child, R., Luan, D., Amodei, D., Sutskever, I., et al. (2019). Language models are unsupervised multitask learners. *OpenAI Blog, 1*(8), 9. 159, 234

Rae, J. W., Borgeaud, S., Cai, T., Millican, K., Hoffmann, J., Song, F., Aslanides, J., Henderson, S., Ring, R., Young, S., et al. (2021). Scaling language models: Methods, analysis & insights from training Gopher. *arXiv:2112.11446.* 234

Raffel, C., Shazeer, N., Roberts, A., Lee, K., Narang, S., Matena, M., Zhou, Y., Li, W., Liu, P. J., et al. (2020). Exploring the limits of transfer learning with a unified text-to-text transformer. *Journal of Machine Learning Research, 21*(140), 1–67. 236

Raji, I. D., & Buolamwini, J. (2019). Actionable auditing: Investigating the impact of publicly naming biased performance results of commercial AI products. *AAAI/ACM Conference on AI, Ethics, and Society*, 429–435. 423

Raji, I. D., & Fried, G. (2020). About face: A survey of facial recognition evaluation. *AAAI Workshop on AI Evaluation*. 427

Raji, I. D., Kumar, I. E., Horowitz, A., & Selbst, A. (2022). The fallacy of AI functionality. *ACM Conference on Fairness, Accountability, and Transparency*, 959–972. 423, 427

Rajpurkar, P., Chen, E., Banerjee, O., & Topol, E. J. (2022). AI in health and medicine. *Nature Medicine*, *28*(1), 31–38. 420

Rajpurkar, P., Zhang, J., Lopyrev, K., & Liang, P. (2016). SQuAD: 100,000+ questions for machine comprehension of text. *Empirical Methods in Natural Language Processing*, 2383–2392. 234

Ramachandran, P., Zoph, B., & Le, Q. V. (2017). Searching for activation functions. *arXiv:1710.05941*. 38

Ramesh, A., Dhariwal, P., Nichol, A., Chu, C., & Chen, M. (2022). Hierarchical text-conditional image generation with CLIP latents. *arXiv:2204.06125*. 10, 11, 238, 369, 370

Ramesh, A., Pavlov, M., Goh, G., Gray, S., Voss, C., Radford, A., Chen, M., & Sutskever, I. (2021). Zero-shot text-to-image generation. *International Conference on Machine Learning*, 8821–8831. 238, 370

Ramsauer, H., Schäfl, B., Lehner, J., Seidl, P., Widrich, M., Adler, T., Gruber, L., Holzleitner, M., Pavlović, M., Sandve, G. K., et al. (2021). Hopfield networks is all you need. *International Conference on Learning Representations*. 236

Ranganath, R., Tran, D., & Blei, D. (2016). Hierarchical variational models. *International Conference on Machine Learning*, 324–333. 345

Ravanbakhsh, S., Lanusse, F., Mandelbaum, R., Schneider, J., & Poczos, B. (2017). Enabling dark energy science with deep generative models of galaxy images. *AAAI Conference on Artificial Intelligence*, 1488–1494. 344

Rawat, W., & Wang, Z. (2017). Deep convolutional neural networks for image classification: A comprehensive review. *Neural Computation*, *29*(9), 2352–2449. 181

Rawls, J. (1971). *A Theory of Justice*. Belknap Press. 430

Razavi, A., Oord, A. v. d., Poole, B., & Vinyals, O. (2019a). Preventing posterior collapse with delta-VAEs. *International Conference on Learning Representations*. 345

Razavi, A., Van den Oord, A., & Vinyals, O. (2019b). Generating diverse high-fidelity images with VQ-VAE-2. *Neural Information Processing Systems*, *32*, 14837–14847. 344, 345

Recht, B., Re, C., Wright, S., & Niu, F. (2011). Hogwild!: A lock-free approach to parallelizing stochastic gradient descent. *Neural Information Processing Systems*, *24*, 693–701. 114

Reddi, S. J., Kale, S., & Kumar, S. (2018). On the convergence of Adam and beyond. *International Conference on Learning Representations*. 93

Redmon, J., Divvala, S., Girshick, R., & Farhadi, A. (2016). You only look once: Unified, real-time object detection. *IEEE/CVF Computer Vision & Pattern Recognition*, 779–788. 178, 184

Reed, S., Akata, Z., Yan, X., Logeswaran, L., Schiele, B., & Lee, H. (2016a). Generative adversarial text to image synthesis. *International Conference on Machine Learning*, 1060–1069. 301

Reed, S. E., Akata, Z., Mohan, S., Tenka, S., Schiele, B., & Lee, H. (2016b). Learning what and where to draw. *Neural Information Processing Systems*, *29*, 217–225. 301

Reiss, J., & Sprenger, J. (2017). Scientific Objectivity. *The Stanford Encyclopedia of Philosophy*. 431

Ren, S., He, K., Girshick, R., & Sun, J. (2015). Faster R-CNN: Towards real-time object detection with region proposal networks. *Neural Information Processing Systems*, *28*. 183

Rezende, D. J., & Mohamed, S. (2015). Variational inference with normalizing flows. *International Conference on Machine Learning*, 1530–1538. 273, 321, 322, 344

Rezende, D. J., Mohamed, S., & Wierstra, D. (2014). Stochastic backpropagation and approximate inference in deep generative models. *International Conference on Machine Learning*, 1278–1286. 346

Rezende, D. J., Racanière, S., Higgins, I., & Toth, P. (2019). Equivariant Hamiltonian flows. *arXiv:1909.13739*. 324

Rezende Jimenez, D., Eslami, S., Mohamed, S., Battaglia, P., Jaderberg, M., & Heess, N. (2016). Unsupervised learning of 3D structure from images. *Neural Information Processing Systems*, *29*, 4997–5005. 344

Riad, R., Teboul, O., Grangier, D., & Zeghidour, N. (2022). Learning strides in convolutional neural networks. *International Conference on Learning Representations*. 183

Ribeiro, M., Singh, S., & Guestrin, C. (2016). "Why should I trust you?": Explaining the predictions of any classifier. *Meeting of the Association for Computational Linguistics*, 97–101. 425

Ribeiro, M. T., Wu, T., Guestrin, C., & Singh, S. (2021). Beyond accuracy: Behavioral testing of NLP models with CheckList. 4824–4828. 234

Richardson, E., Alaluf, Y., Patashnik, O., Nitzan, Y., Azar, Y., Shapiro, S., & Cohen-Or, D. (2021). Encoding in style: A Style-GAN encoder for image-to-image translation. *IEEE/CVF Computer Vision & Pattern Recognition*, 2287–2296. 301

Riedl, M. (2020). AI democratization in the era of GPT-3. The Gradient, Sept 25, 2020. https://thegradient.pub/ai-democratization-in-the-era-of-gpt-3/. 430

Riedmiller, M. (2005). Neural fitted Q iteration — first experiences with a data efficient neural reinforcement learning method. *European Conference on Machine Learning*, 317–328. 396

Rippel, O., & Adams, R. P. (2013). High-dimensional probability estimation with deep density models. *arXiv:1302.5125*. 321

Rissanen, J. (1983). A universal prior for integers and estimation by minimum description length. *The Annals of Statistics*, *11*(2), 416–431. 411

Rissanen, S., Heinonen, M., & Solin, A. (2022). Generative modelling with inverse heat dissipation. *arXiv:2206.13397*. 369

Rives, A., Meier, J., Sercu, T., Goyal, S., Lin, Z., Liu, J., Guo, D., Ott, M., Zitnick, C. L., Ma, J., et al. (2021). Biological structure and function emerge from scaling unsupervised learning to 250 million protein sequences. *Proceedings of the National Academy of Sciences*, *118*(15). 234

Robbins, H., & Monro, S. (1951). A stochastic approximation method. *The Annals of Mathematical Statistics*, *22*(3), 400–407. 91

Rodrigues, F., & Pereira, F. C. (2020). Beyond expectation: Deep joint mean and quantile regression for spatiotemporal problems. *IEEE Transactions on Neural Networks and Learning Systems*, *31*(12), 5377–5389. 73

Roeder, G., Wu, Y., & Duvenaud, D. K. (2017). Sticking the landing: Simple, lower-variance gradient estimators for variational inference. *Neural Information Processing Systems*, *30*, 6925–6934. 346

Roich, D., Mokady, R., Bermano, A. H., & Cohen-Or, D. (2022). Pivotal tuning for latent-based editing of real images. *ACM Transactions on Graphics (TOG)*, *42*(1), 1–13. 300, 301

Rolfe, J. T. (2017). Discrete variational autoencoders. *International Conference on Learning Representations*. 344

Rolnick, D., Donti, P. L., Kaack, L. H., Kochanski, K., Lacoste, A., Sankaran, K., Ross, A. S., Milojevic-Dupont, N., Jaques, N., Waldman-Brown, A., Luccioni, A. S., Maharaj, T., Sherwin, E. D., Mukkavilli, S. K., Kording, K. P., Gomes, C. P., Ng, A. Y., Hassabis, D., Platt, J. C., Creutzig, F., Chayes, J. T., & Bengio, Y. (2023). Tackling climate change with machine learning. *ACM Computing Surveys*, *55*(2), 1–42. 420

Rombach, R., Blattmann, A., Lorenz, D., Esser, P., & Ommer, B. (2022). High-resolution image synthesis with latent diffusion models. *IEEE/CVF Computer Vision & Pattern Recognition*, 10684–10695. 370

Romero, D. W., Bruintjes, R.-J., Tomczak, J. M., Bekkers, E. J., Hoogendoorn, M., & van Gemert, J. C. (2021). FlexConv: Continuous kernel convolutions with differentiable kernel sizes. *International Conference on Learning Representations*. 183

Rong, Y., Huang, W., Xu, T., & Huang, J. (2020). DropEdge: Towards deep graph convolutional networks on node classification. *International Conference on Learning Representations*. 264

Ronneberger, O., Fischer, P., & Brox, T. (2015). U-Net: Convolutional networks for biomedical image segmentation. *International Conference on Medical Image Computing and Computer-Assisted Intervention*, 234–241. 184, 198, 205

Rosenblatt, F. (1958). The perceptron: A probabilistic model for information storage and organization in the brain. *Psychological review*, *65*(6), 386. 37

Rossi, E., Frasca, F., Chamberlain, B., Eynard, D., Bronstein, M., & Monti, F. (2020). SIGN: Scalable inception graph neural networks. *ICML Graph Representation Learning and Beyond Workshop*, *7*, 15. 263

Roy, A., Saffar, M., Vaswani, A., & Grangier, D. (2021). Efficient content-based sparse attention with routing transformers. *Transactions* of the *Association for Computational Linguistics*, *9*, 53–68. 237

Rozemberczki, B., Kiss, O., & Sarkar, R. (2020). Little ball of fur: A Python library for graph sampling. *ACM International Conference on Information & Knowledge Management*, 3133–3140. 264

Rubin, D. B., & Thayer, D. T. (1982). EM algorithms for ML factor analysis. *Psychometrika*, *47*(1), 69–76. 344

Ruder, S. (2016). An overview of gradient descent optimization algorithms. *arXiv:1609.04747*. 91

Rumelhart, D. E., Hinton, G. E., & Williams, R. J. (1985). Learning internal representations by error propagation. *Techical Report, La Jolla Institute for Cognitive Science, UCSD*. 113, 233, 344

Rumelhart, D. E., Hinton, G. E., & Williams, R. J. (1986). Learning representations by back-propagating errors. *Nature*, *323*(6088), 533–536. 113

Rummery, G. A., & Niranjan, M. (1994). *On-line Q-learning using connectionist systems*. Technical Report, University of Cambridge. 396

Russakovsky, O., Deng, J., Su, H., Krause, J., Satheesh, S., Ma, S., Huang, Z., Karpathy, A., Khosla, A., Bernstein, M., et al. (2015). ImageNet large scale visual recognition challenge. *International Journal of Computer Vision*, *115*(3), 211–252. 175, 181

Russell, S. (2019). *Human Compatible: Artificial Intelligence and the Problem of Control*. Viking. 420

Sabour, S., Frosst, N., & Hinton, G. E. (2017). Dynamic routing between capsules. *Neural Information Processing Systems*, *30*, 3856–3866. 235

Safran, I., & Shamir, O. (2017). Depth-width tradeoffs in approximating natural functions with neural networks. *International Conference on Machine Learning*, 2979–2987. 53

Saha, S., Singh, G., Sapienza, M., Torr, P. H., & Cuzzolin, F. (2016). Deep learning for detecting multiple space-time action tubes in videos. *British Machine Vision Conference*. 182

Saharia, C., Chan, W., Chang, H., Lee, C., Ho, J., Salimans, T., Fleet, D., & Norouzi, M. (2022a). Palette: Image-to-image diffusion models. *ACM SIGGRAPH*. 8, 369

Saharia, C., Chan, W., Saxena, S., Li, L., Whang, J., Denton, E., Ghasemipour, S. K. S., Ayan,

B. K., Mahdavi, S. S., Lopes, R. G., et al. (2022b). Photorealistic text-to-image diffusion models with deep language understanding. *arXiv:2205.11487*. 366, 368, 369, 371

Saharia, C., Ho, J., Chan, W., Salimans, T., Fleet, D. J., & Norouzi, M. (2022c). Image super-resolution via iterative refinement. *IEEE Transactions on Pattern Analysis & Machine Intelligence*, 1–14. 369

Sainath, T. N., Kingsbury, B., Mohamed, A.-r., Dahl, G. E., Saon, G., Soltau, H., Beran, T., Aravkin, A. Y., & Ramabhadran, B. (2013). Improvements to deep convolutional neural networks for LVCSR. *IEEE Workshop on Automatic Speech Recognition and Understanding*, 315–320. 182

Saito, Y., Takamichi, S., & Saruwatari, H. (2017). Statistical parametric speech synthesis incorporating generative adversarial networks. *IEEE/ACM Transactions on Audio, Speech, and Language Processing*, *26*(1), 84–96. 299, 301

Salamon, J., & Bello, J. P. (2017). Deep convolutional neural networks and data augmentation for environmental sound classification. *IEEE Signal Processing Letters*, *24*(3), 279–283. 160

Salimans, T., Goodfellow, I., Zaremba, W., Cheung, V., Radford, A., & Chen, X. (2016). Improved techniques for training GANs. *Neural Information Processing Systems*, *29*, 2226–2234. 274, 299, 300

Salimans, T., & Ho, J. (2022). Progressive distillation for fast sampling of diffusion models. *International Conference on Learning Representations*. 370

Salimans, T., Kingma, D., & Welling, M. (2015). Markov chain Monte Carlo and variational inference: Bridging the gap. *International Conference on Machine Learning*, 1218–1226. 345

Salimans, T., & Kingma, D. P. (2016). Weight normalization: A simple reparameterization to accelerate training of deep neural networks. *Neural Information Processing Systems*, *29*, 901–909. 204

Sanchez-Lengeling, B., Reif, E., Pearce, A., & Wiltschko, A. B. (2021). A gentle introduction to graph neural networks. Distill, `https://distill.pub/2021/gnn-intro/`. 261

Sankararaman, K. A., De, S., Xu, Z., Huang, W. R., & Goldstein, T. (2020). The impact of neural network overparameterization on gradient confusion and stochastic gradient descent. *International Conference on Machine Learning*, 8469–8479. 202

Santurkar, S., Tsipras, D., Ilyas, A., & Madry, A. (2018). How does batch normalization help optimization? *Neural Information Processing Systems*, *31*, 2488–2498. 204

Sauer, A., Schwarz, K., & Geiger, A. (2022). StyleGAN-XL: Scaling StyleGAN to large diverse datasets. *ACM SIGGRAPH*. 10

Scarselli, F., Gori, M., Tsoi, A. C., Hagenbuchner, M., & Monfardini, G. (2008). The graph neural network model. *IEEE Transactions on Neural Networks*, *20*(1), 61–80. 262

Schaul, T., Quan, J., Antonoglou, I., & Silver, D. (2016). Prioritized experience replay. *International Conference on Learning Representations*. 396

Scherer, D., Müller, A., & Behnke, S. (2010). Evaluation of pooling operations in convolutional architectures for object recognition. *International Conference on Artificial Neural Networks*, 92–101. 181

Schlag, I., Irie, K., & Schmidhuber, J. (2021). Linear transformers are secretly fast weight programmers. *International Conference on Machine Learning*, 9355–9366. 235

Schlichtkrull, M., Kipf, T. N., Bloem, P., Berg, R. v. d., Titov, I., & Welling, M. (2018). Modeling relational data with graph convolutional networks. *European Semantic Web Conference*, 593–607. 265

Schmidhuber, J. (2022). Annotated history of modern AI and deep learning. *arXiv:2212.11279*. 37

Schneider, S., Baevski, A., Collobert, R., & Auli, M. (2019). wav2vec: Unsupervised pre-training for speech recognition. *INTER-SPEECH*, 3465–3469. 159

Schrittwieser, J., Antonoglou, I., Hubert, T., Simonyan, K., Sifre, L., Schmitt, S., Guez, A., Lockhart, E., Hassabis, D., Graepel, T., et al. (2020). Mastering Atari, Go, chess and shogi by planning with a learned model. *Nature*, *588*(7839), 604–609. 398

Schroecker, Y., Vecerik, M., & Scholz, J. (2019). Generative predecessor models for sample-efficient imitation learning. *International Conference on Learning Representations*. 322

Schuhmann, C., Vencu, R., Beaumont, R., Kaczmarczyk, R., Mullis, C., Katta, A., Coombes, T., Jitsev, J., & Komatsuzaki, A. (2021). Laion-400m: Open dataset of clip-filtered 400 million image-text pairs. *NeurIPS Workshop on Data-centric AI*. 238

Schulman, J., Levine, S., Abbeel, P., Jordan, M., & Moritz, P. (2015). Trust region policy optimization. *International Conference on Machine Learning*, 1889–1897. 397

Schulman, J., Moritz, P., Levine, S., Jordan, M., & Abbeel, P. (2016). High-dimensional continuous control using generalized advantage estimation. *International Conference on Learning Representations*. 398

Schulman, J., Wolski, F., Dhariwal, P., Radford, A., & Klimov, O. (2017). Proximal policy optimization algorithms. *arXiv:1707.06347*. 397

Schuster, M., & Nakajima, K. (2012). Japanese and Korean voice search. *IEEE International Conference on Acoustics, Speech and Signal Processing*, 5149–5152. 234

Schwarz, J., Jayakumar, S., Pascanu, R., Latham, P., & Teh, Y. (2021). Powerpropagation: A sparsity inducing weight reparameterisation. *Neural Information Processing Systems*, *34*, 28889–28903. 156

Sejnowski, T. J. (2018). *The deep learning revolution*. MIT press. 37

Sejnowski, T. J. (2020). The unreasonable effectiveness of deep learning in artificial intelligence. *Proceedings of the National Academy of Sciences*, *117*(48), 30033–30038. 404

Selsam, D., Lamm, M., Bünz, B., Liang, P., de Moura, L., & Dill, D. L. (2019). Learning a SAT solver from single-bit supervision. *International Conference on Learning Representations*. 262

Selva, J., Johansen, A. S., Escalera, S., Nasrollahi, K., Moeslund, T. B., & Clapés, A. (2022). Video transformers: A survey. *arXiv:2201.05991*. 238

Sennrich, R., Haddow, B., & Birch, A. (2015). Neural machine translation of rare words with subword units. *Meeting of the Association for Computational Linguistics*. 234

Serra, T., Tjandraatmadja, C., & Ramalingam, S. (2018). Bounding and counting linear regions of deep neural networks. *International Conference on Machine Learning*, 4558–4566. 52

Shang, W., Sohn, K., Almeida, D., & Lee, H. (2016). Understanding and improving convolutional neural networks via concatenated rectified linear units. *International Conference on Machine Learning*, 2217–2225. 38

Sharif Razavian, A., Azizpour, H., Sullivan, J., & Carlsson, S. (2014). CNN features off-the-shelf: An astounding baseline for recognition. *IEEE*

Conference on Computer Vision and Pattern Recognition Workshop, 806–813. 159

Sharkey, A., & Sharkey, N. (2012). Granny and the robots: Ethical issues in robot care for the elderly. *Ethics and Information Technology, 14*(1), 27–40. 424

Shaw, P., Uszkoreit, J., & Vaswani, A. (2018). Self-attention with relative position representations. *ACL Human Language Technologies*, 464–468. 236

Shen, S., Yao, Z., Gholami, A., Mahoney, M., & Keutzer, K. (2020a). PowerNorm: Rethinking batch normalization in transformers. *International Conference on Machine Learning*, 8741–8751. 237

Shen, X., Tian, X., Liu, T., Xu, F., & Tao, D. (2017). Continuous dropout. *IEEE Transactions on Neural Networks and Learning Systems, 29*(9), 3926–3937. 158

Shen, Y., Gu, J., Tang, X., & Zhou, B. (2020b). Interpreting the latent space of GANs for semantic face editing. *IEEE/CVF Computer Vision & Pattern Recognition*, 9243–9252. 300

Shi, W., Caballero, J., Huszár, F., Totz, J., Aitken, A. P., Bishop, R., Rueckert, D., & Wang, Z. (2016). Real-time single image and video super-resolution using an efficient sub-pixel convolutional neural network. *IEEE/CVF Computer Vision & Pattern Recognition*, 1874–1883. 182

Shoeybi, M., Patwary, M., Puri, R., LeGresley, P., Casper, J., & Catanzaro, B. (2019). Megatron-LM: Training multi-billion parameter language models using model parallelism. *arXiv:1909.08053*. 114

Shorten, C., & Khoshgoftaar, T. M. (2019). A survey on image data augmentation for deep learning. *Journal of Big Data, 6*(1), 1–48. 159

Siddique, N., Paheding, S., Elkin, C. P., & Devabhaktuni, V. (2021). U-Net and its variants for medical image segmentation: A review of theory and applications. *IEEE Access*, 82031–82057. 205

Sifre, L., & Mallat, S. (2013). Rotation, scaling and deformation invariant scattering for texture discrimination. *IEEE/CVF Computer Vision & Pattern Recognition*, 1233–1240. 183

Silver, D., Huang, A., Maddison, C. J., Guez, A., Sifre, L., Van Den Driessche, G., Schrittwieser, J., Antonoglou, I., Panneershelvam, V., Lanctot, M., et al. (2016). Mastering the game of Go with deep neural networks and tree search. *Nature, 529*(7587), 484–489. 396, 398

Silver, D., Lever, G., Heess, N., Degris, T., Wierstra, D., & Riedmiller, M. (2014). Deterministic policy gradient algorithms. *International Conference on Machine Learning*, 387–395. 397

Simonovsky, M., & Komodakis, N. (2018). GraphVAE: Towards generation of small graphs using variational autoencoders. *International Conference on Artificial Neural Networks*, 412–422. 344

Simonyan, K., & Zisserman, A. (2014). Very deep convolutional networks for large-scale image recognition. *International Conference on Learning Representations*. 177, 181

Singh, S. P., & Sutton, R. S. (1996). Reinforcement learning with replacing eligibility traces. *Machine learning, 22*(1), 123–158. 396

Sinha, S., Zhao, Z., Goyal, A., Raffel, C., & Odena, A. (2020). Top-k training of GANs: Improving GAN performance by throwing away bad samples. *Neural Information Processing Systems, 33*, 14638–14649. 299

Sisson, M., Spindel, J., Scharre, P., & Kozyulin, V. (2020). The militarization of artificial intelligence. *United Nations Office for Disarmament Affairs*. 427

Sjöberg, J., & Ljung, L. (1995). Overtraining, regularization and searching for a minimum, with application to neural networks. *International Journal of Control, 62*(6), 1391–1407. 157

Smith, M., & Miller, S. (2022). The ethical application of biometric facial recognition technology. *AI & Society, 37*, 167–175. 426

Smith, S., Elsen, E., & De, S. (2020). On the generalization benefit of noise in stochastic gradient descent. *International Conference on Machine Learning*, 9058–9067. 157

Smith, S., Patwary, M., Norick, B., LeGresley, P., Rajbhandari, S., Casper, J., Liu, Z., Prabhumoye, S., Zerveas, G., Korthikanti, V., et al. (2022). Using DeepSpeed and Megatron to train Megatron-Turing NLG 530B, a large-scale generative language model. *arXiv:2201.11990*. 234

Smith, S. L., Dherin, B., Barrett, D. G. T., & De, S. (2021). On the origin of implicit regularization in stochastic gradient descent. *International Conference on Learning Representations*. 157

Smith, S. L., Kindermans, P., Ying, C., & Le, Q. V. (2018). Don't decay the learning rate, increase the batch size. *International Conference on Learning Representations*. 92

Snoek, J., Larochelle, H., & Adams, R. P. (2012). Practical Bayesian optimization of machine learning algorithms. *Neural Information Processing Systems*, vol. 25, 2951–2959. 136

Sohl-Dickstein, J., Weiss, E., Maheswaranathan, N., & Ganguli, S. (2015). Deep unsupervised learning using nonequilibrium thermodynamics. *International Conference on Machine Learning*, 2256–2265. 274, 367

Sohn, K., Lee, H., & Yan, X. (2015). Learning structured output representation using deep conditional generative models. *Neural Information Processing Systems*, 28, 3483–3491. 344

Sohoni, N. S., Aberger, C. R., Leszczynski, M., Zhang, J., & Ré, C. (2019). Low-memory neural network training: A technical report. *arXiv:1904.10631*. 114

Sønderby, C. K., Raiko, T., Maaløe, L., Sønderby, S. K., & Winther, O. (2016a). How to train deep variational autoencoders and probabilistic ladder networks. *arXiv:1602.02282*. 344

Sønderby, C. K., Raiko, T., Maaløe, L., Sønderby, S. K., & Winther, O. (2016b). Ladder variational autoencoders. *Neural Information Processing Systems*, 29, 738–3746. 369

Song, J., Meng, C., & Ermon, S. (2021a). Denoising diffusion implicit models. *International Conference on Learning Representations*. 370

Song, Y., & Ermon, S. (2019). Generative modeling by estimating gradients of the data distribution. *Neural Information Processing Systems*, 32, 11895–11907. 367, 371

Song, Y., & Ermon, S. (2020). Improved techniques for training score-based generative models. *Neural Information Processing Systems*, 33, 12438–12448. 371

Song, Y., Meng, C., & Ermon, S. (2019). MintNet: Building invertible neural networks with masked convolutions. *Neural Information Processing Systems*, 32, 11002–11012. 322

Song, Y., Shen, L., Xing, L., & Ermon, S. (2021b). Solving inverse problems in medical imaging with score-based generative models. *International Conference on Learning Representations*. 369

Song, Y., Sohl-Dickstein, J., Kingma, D. P., Kumar, A., Ermon, S., & Poole, B. (2021c). Score-based generative modeling through stochastic differential equations. *International Conference on Learning Representations*. 369, 370, 371

Springenberg, J. T., Dosovitskiy, A., Brox, T., & Riedmiller, M. (2015). Striving for simplicity: The all convolutional net. *International Conference on Learning Representations*. 182

Srivastava, A., Rastogi, A., Rao, A., Shoeb, A. A. M., Abid, A., Fisch, A., Brown, A. R., Santoro, A., Gupta, A., Garriga-Alonso, A., et al. (2022). Beyond the imitation game: Quantifying and extrapolating the capabilities of language models. *arXiv:2206.04615*. 234

Srivastava, A., Valkov, L., Russell, C., Gutmann, M. U., & Sutton, C. (2017). VEEGAN: Reducing mode collapse in GANs using implicit variational learning. *Neural Information Processing Systems*, 30, 3308–3318. 300

Srivastava, N., Hinton, G., Krizhevsky, A., Sutskever, I., & Salakhutdinov, R. (2014). Dropout: A simple way to prevent neural networks from overfitting. *Journal of Machine Learning Research*, 15(1), 1929–1958. 158

Srivastava, R. K., Greff, K., & Schmidhuber, J. (2015). Highway networks. *arXiv:1505.00387*. 202

Stark, L., & Hoey, J. (2021). The ethics of emotions in artificial intelligence systems. *ACM Conference on Fairness, Accountability, and Transparency*, 782–793. 427

Stark, L., & Hutson, J. (2022). Physiognomic artificial intelligence. *Fordham Intellectual Property, Media & Entertainment Law Journal*, XXXII(4), 922–978. 427, 432

Stiennon, N., Ouyang, L., Wu, J., Ziegler, D., Lowe, R., Voss, C., Radford, A., Amodei, D., & Christiano, P. F. (2020). Learning to summarize with human feedback. *Neural Information Processing Systems*, 33, 3008–3021. 398

Strubell, E., Ganesh, A., & McCallum, A. (2019). Energy and policy considerations for deep learning in NLP. *Meeting of the Association for Computational Linguistics*, 3645–3650. 429

Strubell, E., Ganesh, A., & McCallum, A. (2020). Energy and policy considerations for modern deep learning research. *Meeting of the Association for Computational Linguistics*, 13693–13696. 429

Su, H., Jampani, V., Sun, D., Gallo, O., Learned-Miller, E., & Kautz, J. (2019a). Pixel-adaptive convolutional neural networks. *IEEE/CVF Computer Vision & Pattern Recognition*, 11166–11175. 183

Su, J., Lu, Y., Pan, S., Wen, B., & Liu, Y. (2021). Roformer: Enhanced transformer with rotary position embedding. *arXiv:2104.09864*. 236

Su, W., Zhu, X., Cao, Y., Li, B., Lu, L., Wei, F., & Dai, J. (2019b). VL-BERT: Pre-training of generic visual-linguistic representations. *International Conference on Learning Representations.* 238

Sultan, M. M., Wayment-Steele, H. K., & Pande, V. S. (2018). Transferable neural networks for enhanced sampling of protein dynamics. *Journal of Chemical Theory and Computation, 14*(4), 1887–1894. 344

Summers, C., & Dinneen, M. J. (2019). Improved mixed-example data augmentation. *Winter Conference on Applications of Computer Vision,* 1262–1270. 159

Sun, C., Myers, A., Vondrick, C., Murphy, K., & Schmid, C. (2019). VideoBERT: A joint model for video and language representation learning. *IEEE/CVF International Conference on Computer Vision,* 7464–7473. 238

Sun, C., Shrivastava, A., Singh, S., & Gupta, A. (2017). Revisiting unreasonable effectiveness of data in deep learning era. *IEEE/CVF International Conference on Computer Vision,* 843–852. 238

Sun, R.-Y. (2020). Optimization for deep learning: An overview. *Journal of the Operations Research Society of China, 8*(2), 249–294. 91

Susmelj, I., Agustsson, E., & Timofte, R. (2017). ABC-GAN: Adaptive blur and control for improved training stability of generative adversarial networks. *ICML Workshop on Implicit Models.* 299

Sutskever, I., Martens, J., Dahl, G., & Hinton, G. (2013). On the importance of initialization and momentum in deep learning. *International Conference on Machine Learning,* 1139–1147. 93

Sutton, R. S. (1984). *Temporal credit assignment in reinforcement learning.* Ph.D., University of Massachusetts Amherst. 396

Sutton, R. S. (1988). Learning to predict by the methods of temporal differences. *Machine learning, 3*(1), 9–44. 396

Sutton, R. S., & Barto, A. G. (1999). *Reinforcement learning: An introduction.* MIT press. 396

Sutton, R. S., & Barto, A. G. (2018). *Reinforcement learning: An introduction, 2nd Edition.* MIT Press. 16, 396

Sutton, R. S., McAllester, D., Singh, S., & Mansour, Y. (1999). Policy gradient methods for reinforcement learning with function approximation. *Neural Information Processing Systems, 12,* 1057–1063. 397

Szegedy, C., Ioffe, S., Vanhoucke, V., & Alemi, A. A. (2017). Inception-v4, Inception-Resnet and the impact of residual connections on learning. *AAAI Conference on Artificial Intelligence,* 4278–4284. 181, 183, 405

Szegedy, C., Vanhoucke, V., Ioffe, S., Shlens, J., & Wojna, Z. (2016). Rethinking the Inception architecture for computer vision. *IEEE/CVF Computer Vision & Pattern Recognition,* 2818–2826. 155, 158, 274

Szegedy, C., Zaremba, W., Sutskever, I., Bruna, J., Erhan, D., Goodfellow, I., & Fergus, R. (2014). Intriguing properties of neural networks. *International Conference on Learning Representations.* 414

Szeliski, R. (2022). *Computer vision: Algorithms and applications, 2nd Edition.* Springer. 15

Tabak, E. G., & Turner, C. V. (2013). A family of nonparametric density estimation algorithms. *Communications on Pure and Applied Mathematics, 66*(2), 145–164. 321

Tabak, E. G., & Vanden-Eijnden, E. (2010). Density estimation by dual ascent of the log-likelihood. *Communications in Mathematical Sciences, 8*(1), 217–233. 321

Taddeo, M., & Floridi, L. (2018). How AI can be a force for good. *Science, 361*(6404), 751–752. 420

Tan, H., & Bansal, M. (2019). LXMERT: Learning cross-modality encoder representations from transformers. *Empirical Methods in Natural Language Processing,* 5099–5110. 238

Tan, M., & Le, Q. (2019). EfficientNet: Rethinking model scaling for convolutional neural networks. *International Conference on Machine Learning,* 6105–6114. 405

Tay, Y., Bahri, D., Metzler, D., Juan, D.-C., Zhao, Z., & Zheng, C. (2021). Synthesizer: Rethinking self-attention for transformer models. *International Conference on Machine Learning,* 10183–10192. 235

Tay, Y., Bahri, D., Yang, L., Metzler, D., & Juan, D.-C. (2020). Sparse Sinkhorn attention. *International Conference on Machine Learning,* 9438–9447. 237

Tay, Y., Dehghani, M., Bahri, D., & Metzler, D. (2023). Efficient transformers: A survey. *ACM Computing Surveys, 55*(6), 109:1–109:28. 237

Tegmark, M. (2018). *Life 3.0: Being human in the age of artificial intelligence.* Vintage. 14

Telgarsky, M. (2016). Benefits of depth in neural networks. *PMLR Conference on Learning Theory*, 1517–1539. 53, 417

Teru, K., Denis, E., & Hamilton, W. (2020). Inductive relation prediction by subgraph reasoning. *International Conference on Machine Learning*, 9448–9457. 265

Tetlock, P. E., & Gardner, D. (2016). *Superforecasting: The Art and Science of Prediction.* Toronto: Signal, McClelland & Stewart. 435

Tewari, A., Elgharib, M., Bharaj, G., Bernard, F., Seidel, H.-P., Pérez, P., Zollhofer, M., & Theobalt, C. (2020). StyleRig: Rigging StyleGAN for 3D control over portrait images. *IEEE/CVF Computer Vision & Pattern Recognition*, 6142–6151. 300

Teye, M., Azizpour, H., & Smith, K. (2018). Bayesian uncertainty estimation for batch normalized deep networks. *International Conference on Machine Learning*, 4907–4916. 204

Theis, L., Oord, A. v. d., & Bethge, M. (2016). A note on the evaluation of generative models. *International Conference on Learning Representations.* 322

Thompson, W. R. (1933). On the likelihood that one unknown probability exceeds another in view of the evidence of two samples. *Biometrika*, *25*(3-4), 285–294. 396

Thompson, W. R. (1935). On the theory of apportionment. *American Journal of Mathematics*, *57*(2), 450–456. 396

Thoppilan, R., De Freitas, D., Hall, J., Shazeer, N., Kulshreshtha, A., Cheng, H.-T., Jin, A., Bos, T., Baker, L., Du, Y., et al. (2022). LaMDA: Language models for dialog applications. *arXiv:2201.08239.* 234

Tipping, M. E., & Bishop, C. M. (1999). Probabilistic principal component analysis. *Journal of the Royal Statistical Society: Series B*, *61*(3), 611–622. 344

Tolmeijer, S., Kneer, M., Sarasua, C., Christen, M., & Bernstein, A. (2020). Implementations in machine ethics: A survey. *ACM Computing Surveys*, *53*(6), 1–38. 424

Tolstikhin, I., Bousquet, O., Gelly, S., & Schoelkopf, B. (2018). Wasserstein autoencoders. *International Conference on Learning Representations.* 345

Tomašev, N., Cornebise, J., Hutter, F., Mohamed, S., Picciariello, A., Connelly, B., Belgrave, D. C., Ezer, D., Haert, F. C. v. d., Mugisha, F., et al. (2020). AI for social good: Unlocking the opportunity for positive impact. *Nature Communications*, *11*(1), 2468. 420

Tomasev, N., McKee, K. R., Kay, J., & Mohamed, S. (2021). Fairness for unobserved characteristics: Insights from technological impacts on queer communities. *AAAI/ACM Conference on AI, Ethics, and Society*, 254–265. 424

Tomczak, J. M., & Welling, M. (2016). Improving variational auto-encoders using Householder flow. *NIPS Workshop on Bayesian Deep Learning.* 322

Tompson, J., Goroshin, R., Jain, A., LeCun, Y., & Bregler, C. (2015). Efficient object localization using convolutional networks. *IEEE/CVF Computer Vision & Pattern Recognition*, 648–656. 183

Torralba, A., Freeman, W., & Isola, P. (2024). *Foundations of Computer Vision.* MIT Press. 15

Touati, A., Satija, H., Romoff, J., Pineau, J., & Vincent, P. (2020). Randomized value functions via multiplicative normalizing flows. *Uncertainty in Artificial Intelligence*, 422–432. 322

Touvron, H., Cord, M., Douze, M., Massa, F., Sablayrolles, A., & Jégou, H. (2021). Training data-efficient image transformers & distillation through attention. *International Conference on Machine Learning*, 10347–10357. 238

Tran, D., Bourdev, L., Fergus, R., Torresani, L., & Paluri, M. (2015). Learning spatiotemporal features with 3D convolutional networks. *IEEE International Conference on Computer Vision*, 4489–4497. 182

Tran, D., Vafa, K., Agrawal, K., Dinh, L., & Poole, B. (2019). Discrete flows: Invertible generative models of discrete data. *Neural Information Processing Systems*, *32*, 14692–14701. 322, 324

Tran, D., Wang, H., Torresani, L., Ray, J., LeCun, Y., & Paluri, M. (2018). A closer look at spatiotemporal convolutions for action recognition. *IEEE/CVF Computer Vision & Pattern Recognition*, 6450–6459. 181

Tsitsulin, A., Palowitch, J., Perozzi, B., & Müller, E. (2020). Graph clustering with graph neural networks. *arXiv:2006.16904.* 262

Tzen, B., & Raginsky, M. (2019). Neural stochastic differential equations: Deep latent Gaussian models in the diffusion limit. *arXiv:1905.09883.* 324

Ulku, I., & Akagündüz, E. (2022). A survey on deep learning-based architectures for semantic segmentation on 2D images. *Applied Artificial Intelligence, 36*(1). 184

Ulyanov, D., Vedaldi, A., & Lempitsky, V. (2016). Instance normalization: The missing ingredient for fast stylization. *arXiv:1607.08022.* 203

Ulyanov, D., Vedaldi, A., & Lempitsky, V. (2018). Deep image prior. *IEEE/CVF Computer Vision & Pattern Recognition*, 9446–9454. 418

Urban, G., Geras, K. J., Kahou, S. E., Aslan, O., Wang, S., Caruana, R., Mohamed, A., Philipose, M., & Richardson, M. (2017). Do deep convolutional nets really need to be deep and convolutional? *International Conference on Learning Representations.* 417, 418

Vahdat, A., Andriyash, E., & Macready, W. (2018a). DVAE#: Discrete variational autoencoders with relaxed Boltzmann priors. *Neural Information Processing Systems, 31*, 1869–1878. 344

Vahdat, A., Andriyash, E., & Macready, W. (2020). Undirected graphical models as approximate posteriors. *International Conference on Machine Learning*, 9680–9689. 344

Vahdat, A., & Kautz, J. (2020). NVAE: A deep hierarchical variational autoencoder. *Neural Information Processing Systems, 33*, 19667–19679. 340, 345, 369

Vahdat, A., Kreis, K., & Kautz, J. (2021). Score-based generative modeling in latent space. *Neural Information Processing Systems, 34*, 11287–11302. 370

Vahdat, A., Macready, W., Bian, Z., Khoshaman, A., & Andriyash, E. (2018b). DVAE++: Discrete variational autoencoders with overlapping transformations. *International Conference on Machine Learning*, 5035–5044. 344

Vallor, S. (2011). Carebots and caregivers: Sustaining the ethical ideal of care in the 21st century. *Philosophy and Technology, 24*(3), 251–268. 429

Vallor, S. (2015). Moral deskilling and upskilling in a new machine age: Reflections on the ambiguous future of character. *Philosophy & Technology, 28*, 107–124. 429

Van den Oord, A., Dieleman, S., Zen, H., Simonyan, K., Vinyals, O., Graves, A., Kalchbrenner, N., Senior, A., & Kavukcuoglu, K. (2016a). WaveNet: A generative model for raw audio. *ISCA Speech Synthesis Workshop.* 323

Van den Oord, A., Kalchbrenner, N., Espeholt, L., Vinyals, O., Graves, A., et al. (2016b). Conditional image generation with PixelCNN decoders. *Neural Information Processing Systems, 29*, 4790–4798. 274

Van den Oord, A., Kalchbrenner, N., & Kavukcuoglu, K. (2016c). Pixel recurrent neural networks. *International Conference on Machine Learning*, 1747–1756. 233, 345

Van den Oord, A., Li, Y., Babuschkin, I., Simonyan, K., Vinyals, O., Kavukcuoglu, K., Driessche, G., Lockhart, E., Cobo, L., Stimberg, F., et al. (2018). Parallel WaveNet: Fast high-fidelity speech synthesis. *International Conference on Machine Learning*, 3918–3926. 323

Van Den Oord, A., Vinyals, O., et al. (2017). Neural discrete representation learning. *Neural Information Processing Systems, 30*, 6306–6315. 344, 345

Van Hasselt, H. (2010). Double Q-learning. *Neural Information Processing Systems, 23*, 2613–2621. 397

Van Hasselt, H., Guez, A., & Silver, D. (2016). Deep reinforcement learning with double Q-learning. *AAAI Conference on Artificial Intelligence*, 2094–2100. 397

Van Hoof, H., Chen, N., Karl, M., van der Smagt, P., & Peters, J. (2016). Stable reinforcement learning with autoencoders for tactile and visual data. *IEEE/RSJ International Conference on Intelligent Robots and Systems*, 3928–3934. IEEE. 344

van Wynsberghe, A., & Robbins, S. (2019). Critiquing the reasons for making artificial moral agents. *Science and Engineering Ethics, 25*, 719–735. 424

Vapnik, V. (1995). *The nature of statistical learning theory.* New York: Springer Verlag. 74

Vapnik, V. N., & Chervonenkis, A. Y. (1971). On the uniform convergence of relative frequencies of events to their probabilities. *Measures of Complexity*, 11–30. 134

Vardi, G., Yehudai, G., & Shamir, O. (2022). Width is less important than depth in ReLU neural networks. *PMRL Conference on Learning Theory*, 1–33. 53

Vaswani, A., Shazeer, N., Parmar, N., Uszkoreit, J., Jones, L., Gomez, A. N., Kaiser, Ł., & Polosukhin, I. (2017). Attention is all you need. *Neural Information Processing Systems, 30*, 5998–6008. 158, 233, 234, 235, 236, 237

Veit, A., Wilber, M. J., & Belongie, S. (2016). Residual networks behave like ensembles of relatively shallow networks. *Neural Information Processing Systems, 29*, 550–558. 202, 417

Veličković, P. (2023). Everything is connected: Graph neural networks. *Current Opinion in Structural Biology*, *79*, 102538. 261

Veličković, P., Cucurull, G., Casanova, A., Romero, A., Lio, P., & Bengio, Y. (2019). Graph attention networks. *International Conference on Learning Representations*. 234, 263, 265

Véliz, C. (2020). *Privacy is Power: Why and How You Should Take Back Control of Your Data*. Bantam Press. 435

Véliz, C. (2023). Chatbots shouldn't use emojis. *Nature*, *615*, 375. 428

Vijayakumar, A. K., Cogswell, M., Selvaraju, R. R., Sun, Q., Lee, S., Crandall, D., & Batra, D. (2016). Diverse beam search: Decoding diverse solutions from neural sequence models. *arXiv:1610.02424*. 235

Vincent, J. (2020). What a machine learning tool that turns Obama white can (and can't) tell us about AI bias / a striking image that only hints at a much bigger problem. The Verge, June 23, 2020. https://www.theverge.com/21298762/face-depixelizer-ai-machine-learning-tool-pulse-stylegan-obama-bias. 422

Vincent, P., Larochelle, H., Bengio, Y., & Manzagol, P.-A. (2008). Extracting and composing robust features with denoising autoencoders. *International Conference on Machine Learning*, 1096–1103. 344

Voita, E., Talbot, D., Moiseev, F., Sennrich, R., & Titov, I. (2019). Analyzing multi-head self-attention: Specialized heads do the heavy lifting, the rest can be pruned. *Meeting of the Association for Computational Linguistics*, 5797–5808. 235

Voleti, V., Jolicoeur-Martineau, A., & Pal, C. (2022). MCVD: Masked conditional video diffusion for prediction, generation, and interpolation. *Neural Information Processing Systems*, *35*. 369

Vondrick, C., Pirsiavash, H., & Torralba, A. (2016). Generating videos with scene dynamics. *Neural Information Processing Systems*, *29*, 613–621. 299

Wachter, S., Mittelstadt, B., & Floridi, L. (2017). Why a right to explanation of automated decision-making does not exist in the general data protection regulation. *International Data Privacy Law*, *7*(2), 76–99. 425

Waibel, A., Hanazawa, T., Hinton, G., Shikano, K., & Lang, K. J. (1989). Phoneme recognition using time-delay neural networks. *IEEE Transactions on Acoustics, Speech, and Signal Processing*, *37*(3), 328–339. 181

Wallach, W., Allen, C., & Smit, I. (2008). Machine morality: Bottom-up and top-down approaches for modeling human moral faculties. *AI & Society*, *22*(4), 565–582. 424

Wan, L., Zeiler, M., Zhang, S., Le Cun, Y., & Fergus, R. (2013). Regularization of neural networks using DropConnect. *International Conference on Machine Learning*, 1058–1066. 158

Wan, Z., Zhang, J., Chen, D., & Liao, J. (2021). High-fidelity pluralistic image completion with transformers. *IEEE/CVF International Conference on Computer Vision*, 4692–4701. 238

Wang, A., Pruksachatkun, Y., Nangia, N., Singh, A., Michael, J., Hill, F., Levy, O., & Bowman, S. (2019a). SuperGLUE: A stickier benchmark for general-purpose language understanding systems. *Neural Information Processing Systems*, *32*, 3261–3275. 234

Wang, A., Singh, A., Michael, J., Hill, F., Levy, O., & Bowman, S. R. (2019b). GLUE: A multitask benchmark and analysis platform for natural language understanding. *International Conference on Learning Representations*. 234

Wang, B., Shang, L., Lioma, C., Jiang, X., Yang, H., Liu, Q., & Simonsen, J. G. (2020a). On position embeddings in BERT. *International Conference on Learning Representations*. 236

Wang, C.-Y., Bochkovskiy, A., & Liao, H.-Y. M. (2022a). Yolov7: Trainable bag-of-freebies sets new state-of-the-art for real-time object detectors. *arXiv:2207.02696*. 184

Wang, P. Z., & Wang, W. Y. (2019). Riemannian normalizing flow on variational Wasserstein autoencoder for text modeling. *ACL Human Language Technologies*, 284–294. 324

Wang, S., Li, B. Z., Khabsa, M., Fang, H., & Ma, H. (2020b). Linformer: Self-attention with linear complexity. *arXiv:2006.04768*. 237

Wang, T., Liu, M., Zhu, J., Yakovenko, N., Tao, A., Kautz, J., & Catanzaro, B. (2018a). Video-to-video synthesis. *Neural Information Processing Systems*, vol. 31, 1152–1164. 299

Wang, T.-C., Liu, M.-Y., Zhu, J.-Y., Tao, A., Kautz, J., & Catanzaro, B. (2018b). High-resolution image synthesis and semantic manipulation with conditional GANs. *IEEE/CVF Computer Vision & Pattern Recognition*, 8798–8807. 300, 301

Wang, W., Xie, E., Li, X., Fan, D.-P., Song, K., Liang, D., Lu, T., Luo, P., & Shao, L.

(2021). Pyramid vision transformer: A versatile backbone for dense prediction without convolutions. *IEEE/CVF International Conference on Computer Vision*, 568–578. 238

Wang, W., Yao, L., Chen, L., Lin, B., Cai, D., He, X., & Liu, W. (2022b). Crossformer: A versatile vision transformer hinging on cross-scale attention. *International Conference on Learning Representations*. 238

Wang, X., Girshick, R., Gupta, A., & He, K. (2018c). Non-local neural networks. *IEEE/CVF Computer Vision & Pattern Recognition*, 7794–7803. 238

Wang, X., Wang, S., Liang, X., Zhao, D., Huang, J., Xu, X., Dai, B., & Miao, Q. (2022c). Deep reinforcement learning: A survey. *IEEE Transactions on Neural Networks and Learning Systems*. 396

Wang, Y., & Kosinski, M. (2018). Deep neural networks are more accurate than humans at detecting sexual orientation from facial images. *Journal of Personality and Social Psychology*, *114*(2), 246–257. 430

Wang, Y., Mohamed, A., Le, D., Liu, C., Xiao, A., Mahadeokar, J., Huang, H., Tjandra, A., Zhang, X., Zhang, F., et al. (2020c). Transformer-based acoustic modeling for hybrid speech recognition. *IEEE International Conference on Acoustics, Speech and Signal Processing*, 6874–6878. 234

Wang, Z., Bapst, V., Heess, N., Mnih, V., Munos, R., Kavukcuoglu, K., & de Freitas, N. (2017). Sample efficient actor-critic with experience replay. *International Conference on Learning Representations*. 398

Wang, Z., Schaul, T., Hessel, M., van Hasselt, H., Lanctot, M., & Freitas, N. (2016). Dueling network architectures for deep reinforcement learning. *International Conference on Machine Learning*, 1995–2003. 397

Ward, P. N., Smofsky, A., & Bose, A. J. (2019). Improving exploration in soft-actor-critic with normalizing flows policies. *ICML Workshop on Invertible Neural Networks and Normalizing Flows*. 322

Watkins, C. J., & Dayan, P. (1992). Q-learning. *Machine learning*, *8*(3-4), 279–292. 396

Watkins, C. J. C. H. (1989). *Learning from delayed rewards*. Ph.D., University of Cambridge. 396

Wehenkel, A., & Louppe, G. (2019). Unconstrained monotonic neural networks. *Neural Information Processing Systems*, *32*, 1543–1553. 323

Wei, J., Ren, X., Li, X., Huang, W., Liao, Y., Wang, Y., Lin, J., Jiang, X., Chen, X., & Liu, Q. (2019). NEZHA: Neural contextualized representation for Chinese language understanding. *arXiv:1909.00204*. 236

Wei, J., & Zou, K. (2019). EDA: Easy data augmentation techniques for boosting performance on text classification tasks. *ACL Empirical Methods in Natural Language Processing*, 6382–6388. 160

Weidinger, L., Uesato, J., Rauh, M., Griffin, C., Huang, P.-S., Mellor, J., Glaese, A., Cheng, M., Balle, B., Kasirzadeh, A., Biles, C., Brown, S., Kenton, Z., Hawkins, W., Stepleton, T., Birhane, A., Hendricks, L. A., Rimell, L., Isaac, W., Haas, J., Legassick, S., Irving, G., & Gabriel, I. (2022). Taxonomy of risks posed by language models. *ACM Conference on Fairness, Accountability, and Transparency*, 214–229. 428

Weisfeiler, B., & Leman, A. (1968). The reduction of a graph to canonical form and the algebra which appears therein. *NTI, Series*, *2*(9), 12–16. 264

Welling, M., & Teh, Y. W. (2011). Bayesian learning via stochastic gradient Langevin dynamics. *International Conference on Machine Learning*, 681–688. 159

Wen, Y.-H., Yang, Z., Fu, H., Gao, L., Sun, Y., & Liu, Y.-J. (2021). Autoregressive stylized motion synthesis with generative flow. *IEEE/CVF Computer Vision & Pattern Recognition*, 13612–13621. 322

Wenzel, F., Roth, K., Veeling, B. S., Świątkowski, J., Tran, L., Mandt, S., Snoek, J., Salimans, T., Jenatton, R., & Nowozin, S. (2020a). How good is the Bayes posterior in deep neural networks really? *International Conference on Machine Learning*, 10248–10259. 159

Wenzel, F., Snoek, J., Tran, D., & Jenatton, R. (2020b). Hyperparameter ensembles for robustness and uncertainty quantification. *Neural Information Processing Systems*, *33*, 6514–6527. 158

Werbos, P. (1974). Beyond regression: New tools for prediction and analysis in the behavioral sciences. *Ph.D. dissertation, Harvard University*. 113

White, T. (2016). Sampling generative networks. *arXiv:1609.04468*. 342, 344

Whitney, H. (1932). Congruent graphs and the connectivity of graphs. *Hassler Whitney Collected Papers*, 61–79. 264

Wightman, R., Touvron, H., & Jégou, H. (2021). ResNet strikes back: An improved training procedure in timm. *Neural Information Processing Systems Workshop.* 202

Williams, C. K., & Rasmussen, C. E. (2006). *Gaussian processes for machine learning.* MIT Press. 15

Williams, P. M. (1996). Using neural networks to model conditional multivariate densities. *Neural Computation, 8*(4), 843–854. 73

Williams, R. J. (1992). Simple statistical gradient-following algorithms for connectionist reinforcement learning. *Machine learning, 8*(3), 229–256. 397

Wilson, A. C., Roelofs, R., Stern, M., Srebro, N., & Recht, B. (2017). The marginal value of adaptive gradient methods in machine learning. *Neural Information Processing Systems, 30*, 4148–4158. 94, 410

Wirnsberger, P., Ballard, A. J., Papamakarios, G., Abercrombie, S., Racanière, S., Pritzel, A., Jimenez Rezende, D., & Blundell, C. (2020). Targeted free energy estimation via learned mappings. *The Journal of Chemical Physics, 153*(14), 144112. 322

Wolf, S. (2021). ProGAN: How NVIDIA generated images of unprecedented quality. https://towardsdatascience.com/progan-how-nvidia-generated-images-of-unprecedented-quality-51c98ec2cbd2. 286

Wolf, V., Lugmayr, A., Danelljan, M., Van Gool, L., & Timofte, R. (2021). DeFlow: Learning complex image degradations from unpaired data with conditional flows. *IEEE/CVF Computer Vision & Pattern Recognition*, 94–103. 322

Wolfe, C. R., Yang, J., Chowdhury, A., Dun, C., Bayer, A., Segarra, S., & Kyrillidis, A. (2021). GIST: Distributed training for large-scale graph convolutional networks. *NeurIPS Workshop on New Frontiers in Graph Learning.* 264

Wolpert, D. H. (1992). Stacked generalization. *Neural Networks, 5*(2), 241–259. 158

Wong, K. W., Contardo, G., & Ho, S. (2020). Gravitational-wave population inference with deep flow-based generative network. *Physical Review D, 101*(12), 123005. 322

Worrall, D. E., Garbin, S. J., Turmukhambetov, D., & Brostow, G. J. (2017). Harmonic networks: Deep translation and rotation equivariance. *IEEE/CVF Computer Vision & Pattern Recognition*, 5028–5037. 183

Wu, B., Xu, C., Dai, X., Wan, A., Zhang, P., Yan, Z., Tomizuka, M., Gonzalez, J., Keutzer, K., & Vajda, P. (2020a). Visual transformers: Token-based image representation and processing for computer vision. *arXiv:2006.03677.* 238

Wu, F., Fan, A., Baevski, A., Dauphin, Y. N., & Auli, M. (2019). Pay less attention with lightweight and dynamic convolutions. *International Conference on Learning Representations.* 235

Wu, H., & Gu, X. (2015). Max-pooling dropout for regularization of convolutional neural networks. *Neural Information Processing Systems*, vol. 18, 46–54. 183

Wu, J., Huang, Z., Thoma, J., Acharya, D., & Van Gool, L. (2018a). Wasserstein divergence for GANs. *European Conference on Computer Vision*, 653–668. 299

Wu, J., Zhang, C., Xue, T., Freeman, B., & Tenenbaum, J. (2016). Learning a probabilistic latent space of object shapes via 3D generative-adversarial modeling. *Neural Information Processing Systems, 29*, 82–90. 299

Wu, N., Green, B., Ben, X., & O'Banion, S. (2020b). Deep transformer models for time series forecasting: The influenza prevalence case. *arXiv:2001.08317.* 234

Wu, R., Yan, S., Shan, Y., Dang, Q., & Sun, G. (2015a). Deep image: Scaling up image recognition. *arXiv:1501.02876, 7*(8). 154

Wu, S., Sun, F., Zhang, W., Xie, X., & Cui, B. (2023). Graph neural networks in recommender systems: A survey. *ACM Computing Surveys, 55*(5), 97:1–97:37. 262

Wu, X., & Zhang, X. (2016). Automated inference on criminality using face images. *arXiv:1611.04135.* 427

Wu, Y., Burda, Y., Salakhutdinov, R., & Grosse, R. (2017). On the quantitative analysis of decoder-based generative models. *International Conference on Learning Representations.* 300

Wu, Y., & He, K. (2018). Group normalization. *European Conference on Computer Vision*, 3–19. 203, 204

Wu, Z., Lischinski, D., & Shechtman, E. (2021). Stylespace analysis: Disentangled controls for StyleGAN image generation. *IEEE/CVF Computer Vision & Pattern Recognition*, 12863–12872. 300

Wu, Z., Nagarajan, T., Kumar, A., Rennie, S., Davis, L. S., Grauman, K., & Feris, R. (2018b).

BlockDrop: Dynamic inference paths in residual networks. *IEEE/CVF Computer Vision & Pattern Recognition*, 8817–8826. 203

Wu, Z., Pan, S., Chen, F., Long, G., Zhang, C., & Philip, S. Y. (2020c). A comprehensive survey on graph neural networks. *IEEE Transactions on Neural Networks and Learning Systems*, 32(1), 4–24. 261

Wu, Z., Song, S., Khosla, A., Yu, F., Zhang, L., Tang, X., & Xiao, J. (2015b). 3D ShapeNets: A deep representation for volumetric shapes. *IEEE/CVF Computer Vision & Pattern Recognition*, 1912–1920. 182

Xia, F., Liu, T.-Y., Wang, J., Zhang, W., & Li, H. (2008). Listwise approach to learning to rank: theory and algorithm. *International Conference on Machine Learning*, 1192–1199. 73

Xia, W., Zhang, Y., Yang, Y., Xue, J.-H., Zhou, B., & Yang, M.-H. (2022). GAN inversion: A survey. *IEEE Transactions on Pattern Analysis and Machine Intelligence*, 1–17. 301

Xiao, L., Bahri, Y., Sohl-Dickstein, J., Schoenholz, S., & Pennington, J. (2018a). Dynamical isometry and a mean field theory of CNNs: How to train 10,000-layer vanilla convolutional neural networks. *International Conference on Machine Learning*, 5393–5402. 114, 183

Xiao, S., Wang, S., Dai, Y., & Guo, W. (2022a). Graph neural networks in node classification: Survey and evaluation. *Machine Vision and Applications*, 33(1), 1–19. 262

Xiao, T., Hong, J., & Ma, J. (2018b). DNA-GAN: Learning disentangled representations from multi-attribute images. *International Conference on Learning Representations*. 301

Xiao, Z., Kreis, K., & Vahdat, A. (2022b). Tackling the generative learning trilemma with denoising diffusion GANs. *International Conference on Learning Representations*. 370

Xie, E., Wang, W., Yu, Z., Anandkumar, A., Alvarez, J. M., & Luo, P. (2021). SegFormer: Simple and efficient design for semantic segmentation with transformers. *Neural Information Processing Systems*, 34, 12077–12090. 238

Xie, L., Wang, J., Wei, Z., Wang, M., & Tian, Q. (2016). DisturbLabel: Regularizing CNN on the loss layer. *IEEE/CVF Computer Vision & Pattern Recognition*, 4753–4762. 158

Xie, S., Girshick, R., Dollár, P., Tu, Z., & He, K. (2017). Aggregated residual transformations for deep neural networks. *IEEE/CVF Computer Vision & Pattern Recognition*, 1492–1500. 181, 202, 405

Xie, Y., & Li, Q. (2022). Measurement-conditioned denoising diffusion probabilistic model for under-sampled medical image reconstruction. *Medical Image Computing and Computer Assisted Intervention*, vol. 13436, 655–664. 369

Xing, E. P., Ho, Q., Dai, W., Kim, J. K., Wei, J., Lee, S., Zheng, X., Xie, P., Kumar, A., & Yu, Y. (2015). Petuum: A new platform for distributed machine learning on big data. *IEEE Transactions on Big Data*, 1(2), 49–67. 114

Xing, Y., Qian, Z., & Chen, Q. (2021). Invertible image signal processing. *IEEE/CVF Computer Vision & Pattern Recognition*, 6287–6296. 322

Xiong, R., Yang, Y., He, D., Zheng, K., Zheng, S., Xing, C., Zhang, H., Lan, Y., Wang, L., & Liu, T. (2020a). On layer normalization in the transformer architecture. *International Conference on Machine Learning*, 10524–10533. 237

Xiong, Z., Yuan, Y., Guo, N., & Wang, Q. (2020b). Variational context-deformable convnets for indoor scene parsing. *IEEE/CVF Computer Vision & Pattern Recognition*, 3992–4002. 183

Xu, B., Wang, N., Chen, T., & Li, M. (2015). Empirical evaluation of rectified activations in convolutional network. *arXiv:1505.00853*. 158, 160

Xu, K., Hu, W., Leskovec, J., & Jegelka, S. (2019). How powerful are graph neural networks? *International Conference on Learning Representations*. 264

Xu, K., Li, C., Tian, Y., Sonobe, T., Kawarabayashi, K.-i., & Jegelka, S. (2018). Representation learning on graphs with jumping knowledge networks. *International Conference on Machine Learning*, 5453–5462. 263, 265, 266

Xu, K., Zhang, M., Jegelka, S., & Kawaguchi, K. (2021a). Optimization of graph neural networks: Implicit acceleration by skip connections and more depth. *International Conference on Machine Learning*, 11592–11602. 266

Xu, P., Cheung, J. C. K., & Cao, Y. (2020). On variational learning of controllable representations for text without supervision. *International Conference on Machine Learning*, 10534–10543. 343, 345

Xu, P., Kumar, D., Yang, W., Zi, W., Tang, K., Huang, C., Cheung, J. C. K., Prince, S. J. D., & Cao, Y. (2021b). Optimizing deeper transformers on small datasets. *Meeting of the Association for Computational Linguistics*. 114, 234, 238

Yamada, Y., Iwamura, M., Akiba, T., & Kise, K. (2019). Shakedrop regularization for deep residual learning. *IEEE Access, 7*, 186126–186136. 202, 203

Yamada, Y., Iwamura, M., & Kise, K. (2016). Deep pyramidal residual networks with separated stochastic depth. *arXiv:1612.01230.* 202

Yan, X., Yang, J., Sohn, K., & Lee, H. (2016). Attribute2Image: Conditional image generation from visual attributes. *European Conference on Computer Vision*, 776–791. 301

Yang, F., Yang, H., Fu, J., Lu, H., & Guo, B. (2020a). Learning texture transformer network for image super-resolution. *IEEE/CVF Computer Vision & Pattern Recognition*, 5791–5800. 238

Yang, G., Pennington, J., Rao, V., Sohl-Dickstein, J., & Schoenholz, S. S. (2019). A mean field theory of batch normalization. *International Conference on Learning Representations.* 203

Yang, K., Goldman, S., Jin, W., Lu, A. X., Barzilay, R., Jaakkola, T., & Uhler, C. (2021). Mol2Image: Improved conditional flow models for molecule to image synthesis. *IEEE/CVF Computer Vision & Pattern Recognition*, 6688–6698. 322

Yang, Q., Zhang, Y., Dai, W., & Pan, S. J. (2020b). *Transfer learning.* Cambridge University Press. 159

Yang, R., Srivastava, P., & Mandt, S. (2022). Diffusion probabilistic modeling for video generation. *arXiv:2203.09481.* 369, 371

Yao, W., Zeng, Z., Lian, C., & Tang, H. (2018). Pixel-wise regression using U-Net and its application on pansharpening. *Neurocomputing, 312*, 364–371. 205

Ye, H., & Young, S. (2004). High quality voice morphing. *IEEE International Conference on Acoustics, Speech, and Signal Processing*, 1–9. 160

Ye, L., Rochan, M., Liu, Z., & Wang, Y. (2019). Cross-modal self-attention network for referring image segmentation. *IEEE/CVF Computer Vision & Pattern Recognition*, 10502–10511. 238

Ye, W., Liu, S., Kurutach, T., Abbeel, P., & Gao, Y. (2021). Mastering Atari games with limited data. *Neural Information Processing Systems, 34*, 25476–25488. 396

Ying, R., He, R., Chen, K., Eksombatchai, P., Hamilton, W. L., & Leskovec, J. (2018a). Graph convolutional neural networks for web-scale recommender systems. *ACM SIGKDD International Conference on Knowledge Discovery & Data Mining*, 974–983. 264, 265

Ying, Z., You, J., Morris, C., Ren, X., Hamilton, W., & Leskovec, J. (2018b). Hierarchical graph representation learning with differentiable pooling. *Neural Information Processing Systems, 31*, 4805–4815. 265

Yoshida, Y., & Miyato, T. (2017). Spectral norm regularization for improving the generalizability of deep learning. *arXiv:1705.10941.* 156

You, Y., Chen, T., Wang, Z., & Shen, Y. (2020). When does self-supervision help graph convolutional networks? *International Conference on Machine Learning*, 10871–10880. 159

Yu, F., & Koltun, V. (2015). Multi-scale context aggregation by dilated convolutions. *International Conference on Learning Representations.* 181

Yu, J., Lin, Z., Yang, J., Shen, X., Lu, X., & Huang, T. S. (2019). Free-form image inpainting with gated convolution. *IEEE/CVF International Conference on Computer Vision*, 4471–4480. 181

Yu, J., Zheng, Y., Wang, X., Li, W., Wu, Y., Zhao, R., & Wu, L. (2021). FastFlow: Unsupervised anomaly detection and localization via 2D normalizing flows. *arXiv:2111.07677.* 322

Yu, J. J., Derpanis, K. G., & Brubaker, M. A. (2020). Wavelet flow: Fast training of high resolution normalizing flows. *Neural Information Processing Systems, 33*, 6184–6196. 322

Yu, L., Zhang, W., Wang, J., & Yu, Y. (2017). SeqGAN: Sequence generative adversarial nets with policy gradient. *AAAI Conference on Artificial Intelligence*, 2852–2858. 299

Yun, S., Han, D., Oh, S. J., Chun, S., Choe, J., & Yoo, Y. (2019). CutMix: Regularization strategy to train strong classifiers with localizable features. *IEEE/CVF International Conference on Computer Vision*, 6023–6032. 160

Zagoruyko, S., & Komodakis, N. (2016). Wide residual networks. *British Machine Vision Conference.* 202, 417

Zagoruyko, S., & Komodakis, N. (2017). Paying more attention to attention: Improving the performance of convolutional neural networks via attention transfer. *International Conference on Learning Representations.* 415

Zaheer, M., Kottur, S., Ravanbakhsh, S., Poczos, B., Salakhutdinov, R. R., & Smola, A. J. (2017). Deep sets. *Neural Information Processing Systems, 30*, 3391–3401. 263

Zaheer, M., Reddi, S., Sachan, D., Kale, S., & Kumar, S. (2018). Adaptive methods for nonconvex optimization. *Neural Information Processing Systems, 31*, 9815–9825. 93

Zaslavsky, T. (1975). *Facing up to arrangements: Face-count formulas for partitions of space by hyperplanes: Face-count formulas for partitions of space by hyperplanes.* Memoirs of the American Mathematical Society. 38, 40

Zeiler, M. D. (2012). ADADELTA: An adaptive learning rate method. *arXiv:1212.5701.* 93

Zeiler, M. D., & Fergus, R. (2014). Visualizing and understanding convolutional networks. *European Conference on Computer Vision*, 818–833. 181, 184

Zeiler, M. D., Taylor, G. W., & Fergus, R. (2011). Adaptive deconvolutional networks for mid and high level feature learning. *IEEE International Conference on Computer Vision*, 2018–2025. 181

Zeng, H., Zhou, H., Srivastava, A., Kannan, R., & Prasanna, V. (2020). GraphSAINT: Graph sampling based inductive learning method. *International Conference on Learning Representations.* 264

Zeng, Y., Fu, J., Chao, H., & Guo, B. (2019). Learning pyramid-context encoder network for high-quality image inpainting. *IEEE/CVF Computer Vision & Pattern Recognition*, 1486–1494. 205

Zhai, S., Talbott, W., Srivastava, N., Huang, C., Goh, H., Zhang, R., & Susskind, J. (2021). An attention free transformer. 235

Zhang, A., Lipton, Z. C., Li, M., & Smola, A. J. (2023). *Dive into deep learning.* Cambridge University Press. 15

Zhang, C., Bengio, S., Hardt, M., Recht, B., & Vinyals, O. (2017a). Understanding deep learning requires rethinking generalization. *International Conference on Learning Representations.* 156, 403, 418

Zhang, C., Ouyang, X., & Patras, P. (2017b). ZipNet-GAN: Inferring fine-grained mobile traffic patterns via a generative adversarial neural network. *International Conference on emerging Networking EXperiments and Technologies*, 363–375. 299

Zhang, H., Cisse, M., Dauphin, Y. N., & Lopez-Paz, D. (2017c). mixup: Beyond empirical risk minimization. *International Conference on Learning Representations.* 160

Zhang, H., Dauphin, Y. N., & Ma, T. (2019a). Fixup initialization: Residual learning without normalization. *International Conference on Learning Representations.* 114, 205

Zhang, H., Goodfellow, I., Metaxas, D., & Odena, A. (2019b). Self-attention generative adversarial networks. *International Conference on Machine Learning*, 7354–7363. 299

Zhang, H., Hsieh, C.-J., & Akella, V. (2016a). Hogwild++: A new mechanism for decentralized asynchronous stochastic gradient descent. *IEEE International Conference on Data Mining*, 629–638. 114

Zhang, H., Xu, T., Li, H., Zhang, S., Wang, X., Huang, X., & Metaxas, D. N. (2017d). StackGAN: Text to photo-realistic image synthesis with stacked generative adversarial networks. *IEEE/CVF International Conference on Computer Vision*, 5907–5915. 300, 301

Zhang, J., & Meng, L. (2019). GResNet: Graph residual network for reviving deep gnns from suspended animation. *arXiv:1909.05729.* 263

Zhang, J., Shi, X., Xie, J., Ma, H., King, I., & Yeung, D.-Y. (2018a). GaAN: Gated attention networks for learning on large and spatiotemporal graphs. *Uncertainty in Artificial Intelligence*, 339–349. 263

Zhang, J., Zhang, H., Xia, C., & Sun, L. (2020). Graph-Bert: Only attention is needed for learning graph representations. *arXiv:2001.05140.* 263

Zhang, K., Yang, Z., & Başar, T. (2021a). Multi-agent reinforcement learning: A selective overview of theories and algorithms. *Handbook of Reinforcement Learning and Control*, 321–384. 398

Zhang, L., & Agrawala, M. (2023). Adding conditional control to text-to-image diffusion models. *arXiv:2302.05543.* 370

Zhang, M., & Chen, Y. (2018). Link prediction based on graph neural networks. *Neural Information Processing Systems, 31*, 5171–5181. 262

Zhang, M., Cui, Z., Neumann, M., & Chen, Y. (2018b). An end-to-end deep learning architecture for graph classification. *AAAI Conference on Artificial Intelligence*, 4438–4445. 262, 265

Zhang, Q., & Chen, Y. (2021). Diffusion normalizing flow. *Neural Information Processing Systems, 34*, 16280–16291. 371

Zhang, R. (2019). Making convolutional networks shift-invariant again. *International Conference on Machine Learning*, 7324–7334. 182, 183

Zhang, R., Isola, P., & Efros, A. A. (2016b). Colorful image colorization. *European Conference on Computer Vision*, 649–666. 159

Zhang, S., Tong, H., Xu, J., & Maciejewski, R. (2019c). Graph convolutional networks: A comprehensive review. *Computational Social Networks*, *6*(1), 1–23. 262

Zhang, S., Zhang, C., Kang, N., & Li, Z. (2021b). iVPF: Numerical invertible volume preserving flow for efficient lossless compression. *IEEE/CVF Computer Vision & Pattern Recognition*, 620–629. 322

Zhang, X., Zhao, J., & LeCun, Y. (2015). Character-level convolutional networks for text classification. *Neural Information Processing Systems*, *28*, 649–657. 182

Zhao, H., Jia, J., & Koltun, V. (2020a). Exploring self-attention for image recognition. *IEEE/CVF Computer Vision & Pattern Recognition*, 10076–10085. 238

Zhao, J., Mathieu, M., & LeCun, Y. (2017a). Energy-based generative adversarial network. *International Conference on Learning Representations*. 299

Zhao, L., & Akoglu, L. (2020). PairNorm: Tackling oversmoothing in GNNs. *International Conference on Learning Representations*. 265

Zhao, L., Mo, Q., Lin, S., Wang, Z., Zuo, Z., Chen, H., Xing, W., & Lu, D. (2020b). UCTGAN: Diverse image inpainting based on unsupervised cross-space translation. *IEEE/CVF Computer Vision & Pattern Recognition*, 5741–5750. 238

Zhao, S., Song, J., & Ermon, S. (2017b). InfoVAE: Balancing learning and inference in variational autoencoders. *AAAI Conference on Artificial Intelligence*, 5885–5892. 345

Zhao, S., Song, J., & Ermon, S. (2017c). Towards deeper understanding of variational autoencoding models. *arXiv:1702.08658*. 345

Zheng, C., Cham, T.-J., & Cai, J. (2021). TFill: Image completion via a transformer-based architecture. *arXiv:2104.00845*. 238

Zheng, G., Yang, Y., & Carbonell, J. (2017). Convolutional normalizing flows. *arXiv:1711.02255*. 322

Zheng, Q., Zhang, A., & Grover, A. (2022). Online decision transformer. *International Conference on Machine Learning*, *162*, 27042–27059. 398

Zhong, Z., Zheng, L., Kang, G., Li, S., & Yang, Y. (2020). Random erasing data augmentation. *AAAI Conference on Artificial Intelligence*, 13001–13008. 159

Zhou, C., Ma, X., Wang, D., & Neubig, G. (2019). Density matching for bilingual word embedding. *ACL Human Language Technologies*, 1588–1598. 322

Zhou, H., Alvarez, J. M., & Porikli, F. (2016a). Less is more: Towards compact CNNs. *European Conference on Computer Vision*, 662–677. 414

Zhou, J., Cui, G., Hu, S., Zhang, Z., Yang, C., Liu, Z., Wang, L., Li, C., & Sun, M. (2020a). Graph neural networks: A review of methods and applications. *AI Open*, *1*, 57–81. 261

Zhou, K., Huang, X., Li, Y., Zha, D., Chen, R., & Hu, X. (2020b). Towards deeper graph neural networks with differentiable group normalization. *Neural Information Processing Systems*, *33*, 4917–4928. 265

Zhou, L., Du, Y., & Wu, J. (2021). 3D shape generation and completion through point-voxel diffusion. *IEEE/CVF International Conference on Computer Vision*, 5826–5835. 369

Zhou, T., Krahenbuhl, P., Aubry, M., Huang, Q., & Efros, A. A. (2016b). Learning dense correspondence via 3D-guided cycle consistency. *IEEE/CVF Computer Vision & Pattern Recognition*, 117–126. 301

Zhou, Y.-T., & Chellappa, R. (1988). Computation of optical flow using a neural network. *IEEE International Conference on Neural Networks*, 71–78. 181

Zhou, Z., & Li, X. (2017). Graph convolution: A high-order and adaptive approach. *arXiv:1706.09916*. 263

Zhou, Z., Rahman Siddiquee, M. M., Tajbakhsh, N., & Liang, J. (2018). UNet++: A nested U-Net architecture for medical image segmentation. *Deep Learning in Medical Image Analysis Workshop*, 3–11. 205

Zhu, C., Ni, R., Xu, Z., Kong, K., Huang, W. R., & Goldstein, T. (2021). GradInit: Learning to initialize neural networks for stable and efficient training. *Neural Information Processing Systems*, *34*, 16410–16422. 113

Zhu, J., Krähenbühl, P., Shechtman, E., & Efros, A. A. (2016). Generative visual manipulation on the natural image manifold. *European Conference on Computer Vision*, 597–613. 301

Zhu, J., Shen, Y., Zhao, D., & Zhou, B. (2020a). In-domain GAN inversion for real image editing. *European Conference on Computer Vision*, 592–608. 301

Zhu, J.-Y., Park, T., Isola, P., & Efros, A. A. (2017). Unpaired image-to-image translation using cycle-consistent adversarial networks. *IEEE/CVF International Conference on Computer Vision*, 2223–2232. 296, 301

Zhu, X., Su, W., Lu, L., Li, B., Wang, X., & Dai, J. (2020b). Deformable DETR: Deformable transformers for end-to-end object detection. *International Conference on Learning Representations*. 238

Zhuang, F., Qi, Z., Duan, K., Xi, D., Zhu, Y., Zhu, H., Xiong, H., & He, Q. (2020). A comprehensive survey on transfer learning. *Proceedings of the IEEE*, *109*(1), 43–76. 159

Ziegler, Z., & Rush, A. (2019). Latent normalizing flows for discrete sequences. *International Conference on Machine Learning*, 7673–7682. 322, 323

Zong, B., Song, Q., Min, M. R., Cheng, W., Lumezanu, C., Cho, D., & Chen, H. (2018). Deep autoencoding Gaussian mixture model for unsupervised anomaly detection. *International Conference on Learning Representations*. 344

Zou, D., Cao, Y., Zhou, D., & Gu, Q. (2020). Gradient descent optimizes over-parameterized deep ReLU networks. *Machine Learning*, *109*, 467–492. 404

Zou, D., Hu, Z., Wang, Y., Jiang, S., Sun, Y., & Gu, Q. (2019). Layer-dependent importance sampling for training deep and large graph convolutional networks. *Neural Information Processing Systems*, *32*, 11247–11256. 264

Zou, H., & Hastie, T. (2005). Regularization and variable selection via the elastic net. *Journal of the Royal Statistical Society: Series B*, *67*(2), 301–320. 156

Zou, Z., Chen, K., Shi, Z., Guo, Y., & Ye, J. (2023). Object detection in 20 years: A survey. *Proceedings of the IEEE*. 184

Index